Limited Classical

Reprint Library

INTRODUCTION
TO THE NEW TESTAMENT

INTRODUCTION

TO THE

NEW TESTAMENT

BY

THEODOR ZAHN
PROFESSOR OF NEW TESTAMENT EXEGESIS, ERLANGEN UNIVERSITY

TRANSLATED FROM THE THIRD GERMAN EDITION

BY

JOHN MOORE TROUT, WILLIAM ARNOT MATHER, LOUIS
HODOUS, EDWARD STRONG WORCESTER, WILLIAM
HOYT WORRELL, AND ROWLAND BACKUS DODGE
FELLOWS AND SCHOLARS OF HARTFORD THEOLOGICAL SEMINARY

UNDER THE DIRECTION AND SUPERVISION OF

MELANCTHON WILLIAMS JACOBUS
HOSMER PROFESSOR OF NEW TESTAMENT CRITICISM AND EXEGESIS
AND DEAN OF THE FACULTY

ASSISTED BY

CHARLES SNOW THAYER
DIRECTOR OF THE CASE MEMORIAL LIBRARY

IN THREE VOLUMES
VOL. II.

Klock & Klock Christian Publishers
2527 Girard Ave. N.   Minneapolis, Minnesota   55411

Reprinted by
Kregel Publications
1953

Printed by Klock & Klock in the U.S.A.
1977 Reprint

CONTENTS

———◆———

v

CONTENTS

ABBREVIATIONS FOR REVIEW TITLES

PEF . . .	Palestine Exploration Fund.
RB . . .	Revue Biblique.
REJ . . .	Revue des Études Juives.
RKZ . . .	Reformirte Kirchenzeitung.
SBAW . .	Sitzungsberichte der Berliner Akademie der Wissenschaften.
SWAW . .	Sitzungsberichte der Wiener Akademie der Wissenschaften.
ThJb . . .	Theologische Jahrbücher.
ThLb . . .	Theologisches Litteraturblatt.
ThLz . . .	Theologische Literaturzeitung.
TQ, TThQ, or ThQSc	(Tübingen) Theologische Quartalschrift.
ThR . . .	Theologische Rundschau.
ThStKr . .	Theologische Studien und Kritiken.
ThTij or ThTjd	Theologische Tijdschrift.
TU . . .	Texte und Untersuchungen.
TZfTh . .	Tübinger Zeitschrift für Theologie.
WZfKM . .	Wiener Zeitschrift für Kunde des Morgenlandes.
ZfÄgSp or ZfÄ	Zeitschrift für Ägyptische Sprache und Altertumskunde.
ZfA . . .	Zeitschrift für Assyriologie und Verwandte Gebiete.
ZfATW . .	Zeitschrift für Alttestamentliche Wissenschaft.
ZDMG . .	Zeitschrift der deutschen Morgenländischen Gesellschaft.
ZDPV . .	Zeitschrift des deutschen Palästina-Vereins.
ZfHTh . .	Zeitschrift für Historische Theologie.
ZfKG . .	Zeitschrift für Kirchengeschichte.
ZfKTh . .	Zeitschrift für Katholische Theologie.
ZfKW or ZfKWuKL	Zeitschrift für Kirkliche Wissenschaft und Kirchliches Leben.
ZfLTh . .	Zeitschrift für lutherische Theologie.
ZfNTW . .	Zeitschrift für Neutestamentliche Wissenschaft.
ZfThuK . .	Zeitschrift für Theologie und Kirche.
ZfWTh . .	Zeitschrift für Wissenschaftliche Theologie.

INTRODUCTION TO THE NEW TESTAMENT.

———•———

VII.

THE LAST THREE EPISTLES OF PAUL.

§ 33. THE FACTS PRESUPPOSED IN THE SECOND EPISTLE TO TIMOTHY.

It seems best to consider the Second Epistle first, because it records more tangible facts than do either 1 Tim. or Titus, and because it is natural to attempt to establish an historical connection between this letter, which was written in prison, and the four letters which have just been investigated.

When it was written Paul had been for some time in chains (i. 8, 16, ii. 9) and in Rome (i. 17). The primary cause of this imprisonment was his fulfilment of his apostolic calling (i. 12). His situation, however, is essentially different from that which obtained when Ephesians, Colossians, and Philemon, and even Philippians, were written. When he comforts himself and his friend regarding his present captivity by remarking that the word of God is not bound, but can and must continue its course (ii. 9), he does not refer at all to his own preaching activity as if it were practically unhindered by his captivity; for this remark stands at the close of an exhortation to Timothy, not only to continue to preach the gospel unweariedly as Paul had done, but also to make provision for the further propagation of this preaching through other trustworthy teachers (ii. 1–8). It is primarily because Paul himself is unable longer to preach, and because he will never be able to resume his preaching, that Timothy is urged to carry on the work with even greater zeal than heretofore (iv. 1–8). The other notices regarding Paul's condition at the time also indicate that when 2 Tim. was written, preaching activity on his part was practically impossible. He is bound with chains like a criminal (ii. 9). A certain Onesiphorus from Asia Minor, who went to Rome to visit the imprisoned apostle and to alleviate his condition, had difficulty in reaching him. It required great devotion on Onesiphorus' part even to ascertain Paul's whereabouts, and unflinching courage, when he had found him, to visit him repeatedly, and to minister to his wants (n. 1). For some time at least intercourse between Paul and the other Christians in Rome must have been broken off. Probably one result of Onesiphorus' self-sacrifice in seeking him, and placing his personal services or his means at the apostle's disposal, was the restoration of communication between Paul and his friends by letter and by personal intercourse (n. 1). Luke is with him constantly (iv. 11). He had been able some time before to send Tychicus to Ephesus (iv. 12). He is able to convey the greetings of certain Roman Christians, and formally to extend those of all the Christians in the place where he was (iv. 21, n. 2). Paul seems to have no doubt as to his ability to receive the visit and to accept the services of Timothy and Mark, if they reach Rome in time (iv. 9, 11, 21). The isolation, therefore, in which Onesiphorus had found Paul was relieved, but his personal condition, however, remained essentially the same. It was such that his friends near and far were tempted to break off and to deny their relations with him. Demas, who in Col. iv. 14, Philem. 24, is mentioned with the faithful Luke as a fellow-labourer of Paul's in Rome, has now through love of the world deserted the apostle and gone to Thessalonica (iv. 10). Even Timothy needs to be earnestly exhorted not to be ashamed through cowardice of the testimony of the gospel or even of the imprisoned apostle, but, following his teacher's example with strength and love, to endure the sufferings which the preaching of the gospel and his relation to the apostle might bring upon him (i. 8, cf. i. 7, 12, ii. 3, 12, iii. 10–12, iv. 5). Inasmuch as Onesiphorus, who meanwhile had died, is evidently held up to Timothy as a model in this regard (i. 16–18, n. 1), mention of the conduct of certain persons in the province of Asia, with which Timothy was familiar (i. 15), can only be designed as a terrible warning. Paul charged, naturally not all the Christians in Asia, but all of the group known to Timothy, as that of Phygelus and Hermogenes, with having turned away from him and having refused to have anything to do with him. From the context it is clear that here, as in the preceding exhortation to Timothy, and the praise of Onesiphorus which follows, the reference is to relations with the apostle, who at the time was in close confinement and serious danger. But we would have to know what Timothy knew (οἶδας, i. 15), in order to state what occasion Phygelus, Hermogenes, and their friends had for either acknowledging or denying their relationship with Paul; and in order to say whether their unworthy conduct was due, as in Timothy's case, to lack of courage, or, as in Demas' case, to love of the world and desire to escape suffering, or whether their renunciation of Paul was the outcome of differences of opinion of a more serious character and of long standing (n. 3). However, from what has been said this much is certain, namely, that Paul had been for some time in prison, which at first had cut him off

from all communication with the outside world, and finally
was considered so dangerous that all his friends not absolutely trustworthy deemed it advisable to sever their
connections with him lest they should become involved in
his fate. This condition had apparently existed for several
months, since it had not only worked this effect upon the
feelings of Christians as far away as Asia, but the apostle
in Rome had also been informed of the same, possibly by
Onesiphorus.

Difference of condition greater than that between the one
described in Philippians and that which meets us in 2 Tim.
can scarcely be imagined. In the former letter the state
and progress of Paul's trial gave new courage to all the
Christians gathered about the imprisoned apostle to proclaim their faith ; and even those who had little kindly feeling toward him were making abundant use of the favour
shown the gospel through the trial of its foremost preacher
(vol. i. 542 f.). In 2 Tim. nearly all of Paul's friends
are withdrawing in fear. Even a person like Timothy,
whom Paul praises so highly in Phil. ii. 20, is tempted in
a cowardly manner to desert the apostle, and in so doing to
forsake his calling. Just as striking is the contrast between
Philippians and 2 Tim. as to Paul's judgment concerning
his present situation and his forecast of the future. Then
he thought it certain that the trial which so far had proceeded favourably to him would soon end in his acquittal.
Now he is just as certain that his present imprisonment
can only terminate with his martyrdom. Using the same
figure that he had then used to describe the violent death
which he thought he was destined to meet after a period
of liberty and of new and varied labours (Phil. ii. 17 ;
vol. i. 456), he now writes (iv. 6): "I am now being
poured out as a drink-offering." He is no longer in the
midst of a heated and restless conflict (Phil. i. 27, 30,
iii. 12–14); he *has* ended this conflict and *has* run his
course (iv. 7, cf. Acts xx. 24). All that remains now is

for him to receive the victor's crown, which is ready in the hands of the righteous judge to be placed upon his head in the day of judgment (iv. 8). He seems to expect that the decisive day will or may possibly be postponed for several months. If upon the reception of this letter Timothy sets out at once upon the long journey to Rome and reaches his destination before the beginning of winter (iv. 9, 21), probably he will find the apostle still alive, and the latter may be able for some time yet to make use of the articles which Timothy is instructed to bring (iv. 13). Any permanent change, however, in his present condition seems to be out of the range of possibility. For the brief span of earthly life that remains he relies also upon the protection of his Lord ; the only deliverance, however, from the evil of this world which he expects at the hands of Christ is a translation into His kingdom above (iv. 18).

It is on account of the near approach of his martyr-dom that Paul exhorts Timothy so earnestly to be unre-mitting in his efforts to preach the gospel (iv. 1–5 and iv. 6–8). Exercising all the powers that he has, Timothy is to fill the place of the departing apostle. Mindful of the future, when Paul will be no longer alive, Timothy is to bear in mind his own calling (ii. 17, iii. 1–9, iv. 3), and to see to it that in his own time and afterwards there shall not be lacking other faithful representatives of the doctrine which he has received from his teacher, also men to take his own place when he is gone (ii. 2). In view of the fact that, during the hasty journey to Rome upon which presumably he would set out as soon as possible after receiving the letter, Timothy could not very well have acted upon the exhortations to be found in 2 Tim. i. 6–iv. 5, which form the main contents of the letter, it is clear that Paul was by no means certain that Timothy would find him still alive. It may have been his desire to cheer this discouraged disciple that kept Paul from mentioning expressly the possibility of his demise before his arrival. But the letter which he writes is of the character of a last testament. In case of his death before Timothy's arrival, this "beloved child" (i. 2) of his is not to be left without a solemn, affecting, written statement of the last will of his spiritual father. It is this peculiarity of the letter and the imminence of the apostle's death which leads him more than once to reflect upon his own past and that of his disciple. Just as Paul regards his own Christian piety as an inheritance from his Pharisaic forefathers, so does he consider Timothy's faith to be an inheritance from his Jewish mother and grandmother (n. 4). Timothy is reminded of the fact that, from his earliest youth, long before he came into contact with Paul and the gospel, he had been introduced to the knowledge of the Holy Scriptures by his pious mother (iii. 15). He is reminded also of his conversion, his instruction by Paul, and his confession made before the assembled congregation at the time of his baptism (ii. 2, cf. 1 Tim. vi. 12), also of his dedication to missionary service by the laying on of the apostle's hands (n. 5), and of the long series of years during which he had shared Paul's labours and sufferings (iii. 10), special mention being made of the persecutions which Paul had endured at the time of Timothy's conversion in Lystra, Timothy's native city, and shortly before at Iconium, and Antioch in Pisidia (iii. 11, cf. Acts xiii. 50, xiv. 5, 19). In this retrospect is to be included not only passages like i. 15–18, where it is expressly stated that the contents were known to Timothy, but also such a passage as iv. 16 f. That this latter passage is not to be taken as a statement of a new fact is clear from the lack of concrete and definite expressions, the somewhat figurative character of the language, and the rhetorical quality of the style, which is strikingly unlike that of the short notices and business directions that precede (iv. 9–15) and follow (iv. 19–22). The only related passage is iv. 18. Just before concluding the letter with a statement of the only thing which in existing circumstances he could hope for from the Lord, Paul himself recalls and reminds Timothy of an earlier occasion when he had been in similar danger. In his first defence no one had stood by him, but all those who might have given him aid left him. Paul does not consider this conduct praiseworthy, nevertheless he does not threaten his enemy with divine judgment, as in the verse just preceding (iv. 14). On the other hand, speaking in a tone strikingly different from that which characterises other remarks apparently similar (i. 15, iv. 10), he attributes this desertion to weakness, and prays God to forgive his friends. This incident is mentioned primarily in order to exalt the faithfulness of the Lord in contrast to the untrustworthiness of men (cf. ii. 13). The Lord alone stood by him then and strengthened him, and he was delivered out of the mouth of the lion. Because of the use of this figurative language it is not to be assumed that some definite person is referred to who might be compared to a lion, as the emperor Nero or the *præfectus prætorii*, who represented the latter as judge, or Satan (n. 6). It means rather that at that time, by reason of the help which the Lord supplied him in his defence before the court, Paul was delivered out of extreme danger. This proves that by πρώτη ἀπολογία cannot be meant the first stage of a legal proceeding still in progress when this letter was written. If after such an ἀπολογία Paul continued in prison under charges, particularly in the severe imprisonment and the hopeless condition in which he was at the time of 2 Tim. and had been for some months preceding, then the words καὶ ἐρύσθην ἐκ στόματος λέοντος are meaningless. No matter how successfully, with the Lord's help, he had defended himself in a first hearing, and no matter how strong the expectation of an acquittal aroused by it in himself and others may have been, if, now, he were languishing in a dungeon with the definite expectation of being executed as a

criminal, he had not been delivered out of the mouth of a
lion, but only painfully disillusioned.   Hence the first
ἀπολογία must refer to a defence which Paul had made at
an earlier trial, which by reason of his successful defence
had ended in his acquittal and actual release.   Consequently it could not have been his defence before Festus
and Agrippa (Acts xxv. 1–xxvi. 31), nor a defence before
the imperial court at Rome, which left him under arrest
and increased his hardships, as these are described in
2 Tim. and in no other of the captivity letters.

The same conclusion follows, if possible with even
greater certainty, from a consideration of the purpose of
his deliverance stated in iv. 17.   In standing by him and
strengthening him in that trial which ended in his deliverance from extreme danger, the Lord designed, so the
apostle thinks, that the proclamation of the gospel should
be carried to its completion, so that all peoples should
hear it.   At the time of this defence this purpose had
by no means been accomplished, either by Paul or by
other missionaries.   That, however, it would necessarily
be accomplished, Paul and every other Christian, on the
strength of the promise of Jesus, fully believed.   The
only question was by whom.   If Paul succumbed in the
trial, and was devoured by the lion, then it must be
accomplished by others after his death.   But in order
that it might be accomplished by Paul—by him and not
by someone else, as shown by the strong emphasis upon
the δι' ἐμοῦ—the Lord had stood by him, and enabled him
successfully to defend himself; and in order that this
purpose might be actually accomplished, he had been saved
out of the lion's jaws.   It is very evident that nothing
which followed upon his deliverance from the fanaticism
of the Jews, through his appeal to Cæsar (Acts xxv. 11),
is in any degree commensurate with the divine purpose
here indicated.   As a result of that deliverance he had
been sent a prisoner to Rome ; and it is possible that his

skilful defence before Festus and Agrippa, and the report
of it which Festus made (Acts xxv. 26, xxvi. 31), contributed much to his comparative freedom in Rome, and
his unhindered preaching of the gospel for two years.
But through that preaching no nation heard the gospel
which had not heard it before. To the mixed populace of
Rome, which Paul looks upon as an ἔθνος ʻΡωμαίων (vol. i.
373, n. 3), the gospel had already been brought at the time
when Romans was written. This is even more true if, some
time subsequent to the writing of Philippians, in consequence of his powerful defence before the imperial court,
Paul was permitted to resume the work in Rome which
he had carried on during the two years prior to the writing
of Philippians, and which had been broken off. Unless he
did more than obtain through his labours " some fruit "
in Rome (Rom. i. 13 ; vol. i. 373, n. 3), where a Christian
Church had long existed, and where numerous independent missionaries were at work (Col. iv. 11 ; Phil. i. 14–18 ;
vol. i. 441, 543), he could not claim to have completed
the Christian preaching. Rome was not the end of the
world, nor the goal of the missionary plans which had been
in Paul's mind for so many years. On the other hand, he
could not, at the time when 2 Tim. was written, have
thought that the great purpose which the Lord had in
view when He stood by him in the first defence, namely,
the spreading of the gospel to all peoples by Paul, was
yet to be fulfilled. For now all that he expects from the
Lord is a blessed death (iv. 18). He has just said
(iv. 7), and everywhere the tone of the letter implies,
that his course is ended. Since, now, a pious man could
not ascribe to the Lord a purpose which neither had been
realised in the past nor in his judgment could be realised
in the future, it follows that the purpose for which Christ
had so powerfully sustained him in the earlier trial had
been accomplished. Subsequent to the successful issue of
his trial and his acquittal, Paul had resumed his mission-

ary work, and had preached the gospel in regions where heretofore it had not been preached, either by himself or by other missionaries.

A similar conclusion follows from iv. 7. When Philippians was written, Paul was full of energy and of the thought of progress, not only as regards his own moral and religious life (Phil. iii. 12–14), but also with reference to his work ; and one reason why he believed he would be acquitted in the trial then in progress, and begin his course anew, was his knowledge that the cause of the gospel demanded a continuance of his life and his further labours (vol. i. 541, 545). Now his course is ended. Just as his statements in Philippians were not due to any specially joyous mood, so it is impossible to explain those in 2 Tim. as due to a discouraged and gloomy state of mind. Indeed, the whole tone of 2 Tim. gives an opposite impression. While Paul does write with deep feeling, it is a feeling which uplifts him, and is designed to enhearten with him the discouraged Timothy. The great difference between the two letters in their outlook upon the past and future is due, not to feeling, but to fact. Now, from Rom. xv. 15–29 we know that at the beginning of the year 58 Paul felt that his work in the regions about the eastern part of the Mediterranean was done, and it was under the influence of this feeling that he entertained the purpose and hope of carrying out a plan which he had had in mind for some years, namely, of continuing his work west of the Adriatic. Rome was to be only a stopping point on the way ; the goal which he had primarily in mind was Spain (Rom. xv. 24, 28). How could Paul say that he had finished his course if he had remained continuously in Rome, where he is now about to be executed ! If Paul wrote both Rom. xv. and 2 Tim. iv., then from 2 Tim. iv. 7 it may be certainly concluded that Paul regained his liberty as he expected when he wrote Philippians, and visited, among other places, Spain.

The language in which Paul describes the purpose
which the Lord had in standing by him in his earlier trial,
which purpose, as we have seen, had actually been accomplished in the interval between his trials (iv. 17), seems
somewhat exaggerated. It is to be judged, however, in
comparison with Paul's language elsewhere, and by that
of his contemporaries. It was considered that the gospel
had been preached to a people or a country when it had
been received in a number of places, and Churches had
been organised (n. 7). Thus, for example, in the year 58
Paul felt that there was no further room for missionary
work (at least for missionary work of the kind that he was
specially commissioned to do, namely, the laying of the
foundations) in all the region from Jerusalem to Illyricum
(Rom. xv. 19, 23). There is no consideration of the regions
lying inland from the civilised countries along the coast,
nor of barbarians outside of the Roman empire, it evidently being taken for granted that the work of preaching
the gospel in these vast regions, as yet very little known,
should fall to the Churches that had been organised in the
more civilised provinces. It is also to be borne in mind
that, as is indicated by the letters to the Churches in the
province of Asia, Paul regarded as his own the work done
from centres where he laboured by helpers associated with
him, considering the Churches thus organised as under
his jurisdiction (vol. i. 449, n. 3). This throws light
upon the statement in 2 Tim. iv. 10, that Titus at that
time had gone to Dalmatia, and a certain Crescens to
Gaul (n. 8). There is no indication that they, like Demas,
had deserted the apostle and sought safety for themselves;
or that, like Tychicus, they had been sent by the apostle
upon some special errand (iv. 10a, 12). In either case
it would be a question why they went to these particular countries, with which, so far as we know, Paul,
up to this time, had never had anything to do. The
probability is that Titus, who had long been associated

with Paul (Gal. ii. 3), who, as his commissioner, had
executed difficult offices in Corinth (2 Cor. vii.–ix. ; vol. i.
308 ff., 329 f.), and who, as we shall see, not very long
before 2 Tim. was written had completed some missionary
work in Crete that had been begun by others, had gone
as a missionary and as Paul's representative and helper to
Dalmatia.   It is also probable that the unknown Crescens
went for a similar purpose to Gaul.   If, by this means,
beginnings of Church organisations had been made westward, north-westward, and north-eastward from Rome, in
Spain by Paul himself, in Gaul by Crescens, in Dalmatia
by Titus, then, in reality, the missionary map had been
very much changed since Paul's first defence.   Mention is
made of these facts in a purely incidental way, without
any intention on the writer's part of giving his readers
information.   Consequently to us they lack in clearness.
To attempt from such incidental hints to estimate what
actual events lie behind the sonorous words of 2 Tim.
iv. 17 would be presumptuous.   The omission, for example, of any reference to preaching in the province of
Africa is less strange than the failure to mention Alexandria and Egypt in Rom. xv. 19, 23, although, as a
matter of fact, we know that Paul never visited these
places (vol. i. 377, n. 11).   We know enough, possibly,
to render 2 Tim. iv. 7, 17 intelligible, but by no means
enough to test the passage by actual history.

By "apology" in 2 Tim. iv. 16 (cf. Phil. i. 7, 16) is to
be understood not a single hearing nor a single speech of
defence made at this hearing, as distinct from subsequent
hearings and speeches in the course of the same trial, but
an entire legal defence made at an earlier trial, now ended,
and to be distinguished from the trial in which Paul was
involved at the time when 2 Tim. was written.   What
Paul says in this letter about the conduct of his friends
at the time of his first defence does not contradict what
is said in Philippians.   The joyful and courageous state

of mind which at that time had taken possession of those
about Paul (Phil. i. 12–18 ; vol. i. 542) was only the
result of a favourable turn which, contrary to expectation,
his trial had recently taken because of his successful self-
defence. When the trial began and Paul was deprived of
the liberty which he had enjoyed for two years, the mood
of the Christians in Rome must have been very different.
From Philippians we learn something of the apprehensive
reports which reached the Philippian Christians from Rome.
Furthermore, it would have defeated the purpose of Philippians had Paul, instead of emphasising the favourable
aspects of his trial, and the hope of release, which conditions at the time justified him in entertaining, complained
that, at the decisive moment, which now fortunately was
past, no one of his friends had had the courage to take
sides with him before the court, either as a witness for
him or as his advocate. This weakness he forgave at
the time, as he confesses in 2 Tim. iv. 16. On the other
hand, there is no indication that any of his friends had
contributed aught to the successful progress of his trial
(Phil. i. 12 f.). He and he alone seems at that time to have
represented his own cause and that of the gospel before
the court (Phil. i. 7, 16) ; while, for the final decision of
the court, which he still awaits, and in the further hearings necessary to this end, he depends only upon the
petitions of his fellow-Christians and the fact that the
Holy Spirit will put the right words into his mouth (Phil.
i. 19 ; vol. i. 544). This is in perfect keeping with the
retrospect in 2 Tim. iv. 16 f. Considering the trial as a
whole, Paul can say, "The Lord alone stood by me, and
strengthened me ; and so I was delivered out of the lion's
mouth." If 2 Tim. is genuine, it follows that the imprisonment in which Paul found himself at the time when
it was written was not a continuance of that during which
Ephesians, Colossians, and Philemon, and, somewhat later,
Philippians were written, so that the expectation so

strongly expressed in Philippians must have been realised
and that after the ensuing acquittal by the imperial court,
he had used his regained freedom, among other things,
to resume his missionary labour, and in carrying out his
original plan to preach the gospel in the West.

During this interval Paul was also in the East, as he
expected to be when he wrote Philippians (Phil. i. 25 f.,
ii. 24). If it be clear both from the connection and tone
of iv. 9–13 and iv. 19–21 that the facts here mentioned
were not already familiar to Timothy, but that the communications and reports were quite as new to him as
were the accompanying instructions, then special importance attaches to the notice that Paul had left Trophimus
behind in Miletus sick (n. 9). This man, who was an
Ephesian, had accompanied Paul upon the journey from
Macedonia through Miletus to Jerusalem, which ended
with the apostle's arrest, and had reached Jerusalem
with him (Acts xx. 4, 15–38, xxi. 29); so that on this
journey he could not have been left behind at Miletus
sick. Even if, on this point, the account in Acts, which
in other respects is credible enough, be considered entirely
untrustworthy, it is quite impossible to understand how,
five years later, Paul could communicate this as a piece of
news to Timothy, who, together with Trophimus, had accompanied the apostle on this journey, and had since
resided with him in Rome (Col. i. 1 ; Philem. 1 ; 1 Phil. i. 1,
ii. 19–23). We therefore assume that, after he was set at
liberty from his Roman imprisonment, and not very long
before 2 Tim. was written, Paul must have been with Trophimus at Miletus. From the close connection between this
communication and the statement that Erastus remained in
Corinth, it is necessary also to assume that on this same
journey Paul touched at Corinth, being accompanied as far
as this point by Erastus, who, as we learn from Rom. xvi.
23, was treasurer of the city of Corinth, and, from Acts
xix. 22, a temporary helper of the apostle. That the present

notice does not have reference to the journey of Erastus
from Ephesus to Corinth about Easter 57, mentioned in
Acts, and to the departure of Paul from Corinth for
Jerusalem about Easter 58, is clear from the close connection between this notice and the news about Trophimus.
It is also shown by the fact that Erastus was accompanied
by Timothy on that journey to Corinth, and that Timothy
accompanied Paul on his return from Corinth to Macedonia
and thence to Jerusalem, so that if Erastus, who is not
mentioned in Acts xx. 4, failed on this occasion to accompany Paul and Timothy and the representatives of the
contributing Churches, but remained behind in Corinth,
Timothy must have known it at the time.   Of course it
was perfectly possible for Paul to remind Timothy of this
fact at some later time, if there was any clear reason for
it, or if he wanted to use it for some practical purpose.
But merely to state a fact with which Timothy was perfectly familiar, five years after the event in question took
place, would be senseless.   For the same reasons the
sending of Tychicus from Rome to Ephesus, iv. 12, is not
to be identified with the sending of the same person to
the province of Asia, of which we learn in Eph. vi. 21 ;
Col. iv. 7 ; for, in the latter case, Timothy was with
Paul at the time (Col. i. 1 ; Philem. 1).   The reference must therefore be to a later journey of Tychicus.
Similarly the sojourn of Paul in Troas, presupposed in
iv. 13, must have been of very recent date, and cannot
be identified with the visit the account of which is given
in Acts xx. 6–12.   On the latter occasion Paul was
accompanied by Timothy, of which there is no hint in
2 Tim. iv. 13.   Moreover, the nature of the errand with
which Timothy is here charged argues against the assumption that at least five years had elapsed since Paul was in
Troas.   Timothy is to bring with him from Troas, at
which point he will touch on his journey to Rome, a
cloak, certain books and leaves of parchment, which the

apostle had left there in the hands of one Carpus. From the exact enumeration of the articles, the special mention of the parchments, which probably contained written notes (*GK*, ii. 938 f.), it is to be inferred that the things in question were especially needed by the apostle. Evidently he needed the warm cloak for the coming winter (iv. 21), and how is it conceivable that he would allow himself to be any longer than necessary without books and notes which were important enough to be taken with him on his journeys and to be sent for from Rome to Asia. That Paul should have left them for more than five years in the hands of Carpus without making any effort to get them, is inconceivable. Paul's intercourse with the Churches in Asia, during his two years' imprisonment in Cæsarea, which was nearer than Rome, was at least as frequent as it was during his Roman imprisonment. Tychicus was sent from Rome to visit most of the Churches in the province of Asia (vol. i. 481), so was probably in Troas, afterward returning to Rome. Sometime before this Onesiphorus had journeyed from Asia Minor, perhaps from Iconium, to Rome. His way thither would have led him through Troas and Philippi, a route which was taken by Timothy soon afterwards, according to Paul's presupposition, and some fifty years later by Ignatius. Other friends of Paul's, *e.g.* Epaphras (Col. i. 7, iv. 12), may have travelled by the same route. During the course of these five years or more he must have had abundant opportunity to get back the things that had been left behind in Troas. Consequently, the only natural supposition is that Paul had been in Troas not long before 2 Tim. was written, and had left these things there. This conclusion is confirmed by a consideration of what follows in iv. 14 f. Since the remark about the smith Alexander ends with a warning to Timothy against him, and since, as soon as possible after receiving the letter, Timothy is to set out upon a journey to Rome, Alexander could not have been in the place

where Timothy was, and which he was about to leave.
Neither could he have been in Rome, for in that case Paul
could have warned Timothy against him much more
effectively after the latter's arrival. He is to be sought,
consequently, in one of the places at which Timothy is to
touch on his way to Rome ; and since Troas has just been
mentioned as one place at which Timothy is to stop and
perform an errand for Paul, the natural supposition is that
Alexander was to be found there. This explains the
sequence of thought. The errand which Timothy is to
perform in Troas makes Paul think of his own last
residence there, and recalls the opposition he had encountered from Alexander. It is natural to suppose that
this hostility had compelled him to leave Troas in haste,
and so had caused him to leave his things behind.
There follows very naturally the exhortation to Timothy
to beware of this hostile person, a warning which is
emphasised by the statement that Alexander had resisted
the preaching of Paul and his helpers to the utmost, consequently was not so much a personal enemy of Paul's as
a sworn foe of the apostolic doctrine (n. 3). Therefore,
Timothy also is to beware of him. From the contrast
between " me " and " thou also " we infer that Timothy
had not shared with Paul this hostility of Alexander in
Troas, and so was not with Paul in Troas at the time.
Consequently, whether he had heard of the matter before
or learned of it now for the first time from Paul's letter,
so far as he was concerned personally he had had no
occasion to encounter Alexander's enmity. We conclude,
therefore, that, after being released from his long imprisonment, Paul had gone to Troas, Miletus, and Corinth,
in each case unaccompanied by Timothy.

But that Paul did not see Timothy at all on this
journey is altogether unlikely. When Phil. ii. 19 was
written, Paul was planning to send him to Philippi. From
1 Tim. i. 3 (cf. 2 Tim. i. 18) we learn that subsequent to

this visit he remained continuously in Ephesus, and from
1 Tim. iii. 14, iv. 13, that Paul was intending to visit him
there (§ 34). In the meantime Paul had been in Troas and
Miletus (2 Tim. iv. 13, 20). Very extraordinary circumstances, therefore, must be assumed in order to maintain
that Paul was prevented on this occasion, as he had been
on a previous occasion (Acts xx. 16), from visiting Ephesus,
or that Timothy, in case he left Ephesus in the meantime
against Paul's wishes, or in case Paul was prevented from
coming to Ephesus, was unable to arrange a meeting with
him somewhere else. It is also to be noticed that in connection with the longing expressed in 2 Tim. i. 4 to see
Timothy again, Paul mentions his sorrowful recollection of
Timothy's tears. The only natural inference is that not
long before Timothy had taken tearful leave of Paul; a scene
which will not be forgotten until, as Paul hopes, he shall
greet Timothy again in Rome. Where this painful separation took place we do not know, only, as has been shown,
it could not have been in Troas, or Miletus, or Corinth.

Furthermore, where Timothy was at the time 2 Tim.
was written we can only conjecture. If on his journey to
Rome he was to pass through Troas (2 Tim. iv. 13–15),
he must have been somewhere in Asia Minor, but hardly
at Ephesus (n. 10). Nothing is said in 2 Tim. about the
oversight of the Church, such as Timothy is represented
as exercising at Ephesus in 1 Tim. Moreover, if Timothy
had been at Ephesus, Paul could not have failed to mention
in 2 Tim. iv. 12 that Tychicus, whom he had sent to Ephesus,
would see him, particularly if Tychicus brought 2 Tim.
(cf. Col. iv. 8 ; Eph. vi. 22 ; Phil. ii. 19, 25 ; 1 Cor. iv. 17).
If, however, as is more probable, Tychicus left Paul after
2 Tim. was despatched, it is difficult to understand why
Paul did not inform Timothy of Tychicus' coming, provided that Paul expected Tychicus to meet Timothy in
Ephesus. Furthermore, the report that Trophimus had
been left behind in Miletus (iv. 20), and the manner in

which Paul speaks of the events that had taken place in Troas (iv. 13–15), are most naturally explained, if at the time when these things happened and subsequently Timothy was living at some distance from the coast cities. If Onesiphorus' home was Iconium (n. 1), the greeting sent to him (iv. 19) would indicate that at the time Timothy was at or near Iconium, possibly at his home in Lystra. In order to convey such a greeting, Paul could not have urged Timothy to take so long a journey as that from Ephesus to Iconium.

Quite different is the case with reference to the greeting to Prisca and Aquila (iv. 19). Since coming into contact with Paul, this couple had already changed their place of residence twice in the interest of his missionary work and of the Churches. They had gone from Corinth to live in Ephesus, and thence back to Rome, whence they had originally come to Corinth (vol. i. 389 f.). If they were now in the East again, it is at least likely that they had returned to Ephesus, where earlier they had spent at least three years. Journeying from Iconium or Lystra by way of Troas to Rome, Timothy would touch at Ephesus, and so could convey the greeting which Paul sent to Prisca and Aquila.

The investigation of the trustworthiness of all these statements, and the endeavour to bring them into an historical connection with one another and with other known facts, must be deferred until the facts to be found only in 1 Tim. and Titus have been stated.

1. (Pp. 2, 3, 19.) Cf. Acts xi. 25 with 2 Tim. i. 17 ; in the latter, however, the stronger expression σπουδαίως ἐζήτησεν points to even greater difficulties which had to be overcome before the well-nigh lost apostle could be found. The ἀναψύχειν, i. 16 (cf. Ign. *Eph.* ii. 1, where it occurs along with the Pauline ἀναπαύειν, 1 Cor. xvi. 18 ; 2 Cor. vii. 13 ; Philem. 7, 20 ; cf. Ign. *Trall.* xii. 1 ; *Magn.* xv. ; *Smyrn.* ix. 2, xii. 1) can of itself indicate bodily as well as spiritual refreshing. The aim of such a long journey, however, can only have been to ascertain Paul's outward condition, and to ameliorate it as far as possible (cf. Phil. ii. 25, 30, iv. 10–20 ; Acts xxiv. 23, xxvii. 3). This certainly involved gifts to the jailers to make sure that they would give him friendly

treatment and all reasonable liberty. Paul would not have suffered him to bribe the judge even if it had been possible (Acts xxiv. 26). But even a Christian like Ignatius, who so passionately longed for martyrdom, does not conceal the fact that the soldiers who were conducting him were induced to treat him well by gifts and entertainment, *ad Rom.* v. 1; cf. *Mart. Polyc.* vii. 2; *Passio Perpetuæ*, chap. iii. 16 (ed. Robinson, 64. 15, 84. 22 ff.) ; *Acta Pionii*, xi. 3 f. (*Acta mart. selecta*, ed. Gebhardt p. 104 f.) ; Lucian, *Peregrin.* 12 ; *Const. apost.* v. 1. We do not know whether Onesiphorus was commissioned by some Church to do this or not ; equally uncertain is it whether it was on this journey or earlier that he found occasion to do a service to someone in Ephesus, such as he had just done to Paul (i. 18). All that we know of his home is that it was somewhere in Asia Minor, i. 15–18, iv. 19. The Acts of Paul (*Acta Theclæ*, i.–vii., xxiii., xxvi., xlii.), represents Onesiphorus as a citizen of Iconium, in whose house Paul found quarters and preached to the Church. The author of this work certainly could not have gathered this from 2 Tim., nor even have conjectured it from this source, and it is true that elsewhere he combines independent traditions with statements from the N.T. (*GK*, i. 788, ii. 892–910 ; *Forsch.* v. 97, A. 1). The Jew Onesiphorus, the host of Peter and Andrew in Ancyra, or in the land of the barbarians, is a worthless imitation of this representation (*Suppl. cod. apocr.*, ed. Bonnet, ii. 9 ; *Acta apost. apocr.*, ed. Lipsius et Bonnet, ii. part 1. 123 ff.). Since Paul sends greeting, not to Onesiphorus, but only to his family (iv. 19), and in praying that the Lord will reward his devotion speaks of his family first (i. 16), and mentions him only in connection with the judgment day (i. 18), it follows that Onesiphorus had died since his arrival in Rome, and that Timothy already knew of it. Certain minuscules (Tischendorf, 2 Tim. iv. 19) have borrowed from the *Acta Theclæ*, chap. ii., the names Lectra, the wife of Onesimus, and Simmias and Zeno, his sons. Amphilochius of Iconium (in Ficker, *Amphilochiana*, i. 56 f. cf. S. 111–135) mentions the house of Onesiphorus at Iconium as an example of the fact that the Apostles often used a heathen house as a church.

2. (P. 2.) Of the four names in 2 Tim. iv. 21, Linus is the only one upon which history throws any light. Considering the great rarity of this Greek mythological name (Herodot. ii. 79) as a proper name for persons (*C. I. Gr.* No. 8518, p. 261, line 53 ; *I. Gr. Sic. et It.* No. 2276), we can hardly doubt that here, as Irenæus directly asserted, the same Roman Christian is meant who, according to ancient tradition, became, after Peter (and Paul), the first bishop of Rome (Iren. iii. 3. 3 ; Eus. iii. 2, v. 6 ; pseudo-Tert. *c. Marc.* iii. 277 ; Epiph. *Hær.* xxvii. 6 ; *Lib. pontif.*, ed. Duchesne, i. 3, 53, 121, where is found also a discussion about a sarcophagus found in the seventeenth century, having, as alleged, the inscription *Linus* ; cf. V. Schultze, *Arch. Stud.* 235–239 ; Erbes, *ZfKG*, vii. 20). His name does not occur in the remains which are left us of the older *Acts of Paul* and those of *Peter*. However, a Latin recasting of the closing part of the Gnostic *Acts of Peter* was ascribed to him, also of the last part of the Catholic *Acts of Paul*, though less definitely (*Acta Petri*, etc., ed. Lipsius, pp. 1–44 ; cf. *GK*, ii. 833 ff., 872). Among the mythical characters in *Const. ap.* vii. 46 occurs Λίνος ὁ Κλαυδίας, who is declared to have been ordained by Paul as the first bishop of Rome. He is thus represented as the son (or husband) of the Claudia whose name comes after his in 2 Tim. iv. 21. These meagre statements have been

enlarged upon by English investigators. The Claudia mentioned here is, they hold, identical with the one who, according to Martial, *Epigr.* iv. 13, married a certain Pudens (85–90 A.D.), and she in turn with the Claudia Rufina from Britain in *Epigr.* xi. 53, who is then made out to be a daughter of the British king Cogidumnus (Tac. *Agric.* xiv.) or [Titus] Claudius Cogidubnus (*C. I. L.* vii. No. 11). For a refutation of these assumptions, which even chronologically considered are impossible, see Lightfoot, *St. Clement,* i. 76–79. As a matter of course there were countless Claudiæ in Rome at the time of 2 Tim., cf. *e.g. C. I. L.* vi. 15335–15664 ; also under Claudius, Nos. 14858–15334. Among these occur some that are joined with the names of others of the earliest Christians in Rome, or with their derivatives (vol. i. 419 f.) ; No. 14913 *Claudia Olympias* (according to which also the name in a Greek inscription from the neighbourhood of Rome, *I. Gr. Sic. et It.* No. 1914, should be amended Κλαυδία 'Ολυμπιά[δι]), No. 14940 *Ti. Claudius Olympus* (cf. Rom. xvi. 15), No. 14918 *Claudius Ampliatus* (cf. Rom. xvi. 8), No. 15564 *Claudia Sp. F. Priscilla* (Rom. xvi. 3), No. 15066 *Ti. Cl. Ti. Lib.* " Pudens et Cl(audia) Quintilla filio dulcissimo et sibi " (*i.e.* a combination of two names from 2 Tim. iv. 21). Later legends tell of a Roman senator Pudens who had two daughters, Praxedis and Pudentiana, and two sons, Timothy and Novatus ; but this gives a very slight basis for historical conjectures, cf. Baronius, *Annales Eccles.* ad annum 44, n. 61 ; *Acta SS.,* Mai, iv. 296 ff. ; Tillemont, *Mém.* i. 172, ii. 314, 658 ff. ; Lipsius, *Apokr. Apostelgesch.* ii. 1. 207, 418 ff., ii. 2. 399. It must be said, however, that the cognomen Pudens occurs among the higher classes from Martial's time down (*Epigr.* iv. 13 ; Klein, *Fasti cons.* for the years 165, 166 ; Tert. *Scap.* iv. ; *C. I. G.* No. 4241, cf. 5142).

3. (Pp. 3, 17.) Tradition has nothing to say about Phygelus (i. 15), but Hermogenes and Demas (iv. 10) are mentioned in the *Acta Theclæ,* cc. i. iv. xi.–xiv., which represents them even as early as Paul's first visit to Iconium (chap. i., cf. Acts xiii. 51) as false friends of Paul, who love money and a luxurious life, and, at the same time, develop the false doctrine hinted at in 2 Tim. ii. 18, though there attributed to others. In the *Acta Theclæ,* chap. i., Alexander's epithet ὁ χαλκεύς (2 Tim. iv. 14) is transferred to Hermogenes ; cf. *GK,* i. 789, ii. 901, 903. It is uncertain whether this combination of Demas and Hermogenes has been carried over into Leucius' *Acts of John,* cf. the writer's *Acta Jo.* p. lxii ; Epiph. *Hær.* li. 6. The name Alexander is so common that the designation of an Alexander as ὁ χαλκεύς is much less striking than the ὁ ἰατρός in Col. iv. 14. It is very possible that he is identical with the Alexander in 1 Tim. i. 20 whom Paul had delivered over to Satan with a view to his chastisement and improvement (cf. 1 Cor. v. 5). Hymenæus, who is joined with him in this connection (1 Tim. i. 20), is mentioned again in 2 Tim. ii. 17, along with a certain Philetus, as the champion of a heresy. According to this, Hymenæus, Philetus, Phygelus, Hermogenes, and the Alexander in 1 Tim. i. 20 must have belonged for a time to the Christian Church, at least in name. But it also agrees best with the tone of 2 Tim. iv. 14 f. if we take the man there mentioned to be within the Church. At all events, τοῖς ἡμετέροις λόγοις refers not to some chance saying of Paul, but to the teaching which Paul jointly with others has proclaimed or defended in the presence of this Alexander ; cf. iii. 8. In itself, ἡμετέροις might very well include Timothy ; but the whole drift of

iv. 13–15 forces us to conclude that Timothy had not shared in the experiences of Paul there reported. The Antiochian reading ἀνθέστηκεν may have arisen through a misunderstanding, it being assumed that the reference is to resistance which Alexander is now making to Paul, possibly as prosecutor, or witness for the prosecution ; but this does not agree with the fact that Alexander was in Asia at the time, probably in Troas. There is not a hint that he was ever in Rome and opposed Paul in his trial there. If he was an opponent of Christian doctrine as Paul preached it, his identity with the Alexander in 1 Tim. i. 20 is exceedingly probable. On the other hand, there is nothing to support the conjecture that he is identical with the Alexander in Ephesus, Acts xix. 33. This man was a Jew, and seems to have had the purpose of repelling the charge that he and his compatriots were enemies of the heathen cult like Paul, whose race his accusers must have emphasised (Acts xvi. 20) ; or perhaps his aim was rather to defend Paul and the Christian teaching against the charge of ἀθεότης, which would imply that he was also a Christian.

4. (P. 6.) In the light of Acts xvi. 1, it is perfectly natural that in 2 Tim. i. 5 only Timothy's mother and grandmother are mentioned, and not his Gentile father. The parallelism between Paul (i. 3) and Timothy (i. 5) runs throughout the whole section i. 3–14 (ἐπαισχύνεσθαι, i. 8 and 12 ; παραθήκη, i. 12 and 14, and purely formal δι᾽ ἣν αἰτίαν, i. 6 and 12); and this of itself makes it probable that it is not the Christian faith of the two women that is here praised. Since Timothy was chosen by Paul to be his assistant on Paul's second visit to Lystra, Timothy's home (Acts xvi. 1 ; vol. i. 209, n. 2), and since he owed his conversion to Paul himself (1 Tim. i. 2 ; 2 Tim. i. 2, ii. 1, iii. 14), he must have been converted during Paul's first visit (Acts xiv. 6–23 ; Gal. iv. 13). He was no neophyte (1 Tim. iii. 6, v. 22) when Paul chose him as his helper in the mission work, and to this end had him circumcised and ordained ; he was already an approved member of the Church (Acts xvi. 2). Therefore Lois and Eunice could not have become believers earlier than he. All that we can gather about the women from Acts xvi. 1 is that Eunice was still living at the time of Paul's second visit, and was a Christian. She was converted, therefore, at the same time as her son. The πρῶτον, then, in i. 5— if Acts here deserves credence—cannot mean that the women received the Christian faith earlier than Timothy. Nor, on the other hand, can it mean that "such faith did not exist in the family of Timothy until with these two women, and these alone, it came to dwell there" (Hofmann, vi. 226), for Lois did not belong to the family of his Gentile father at all. But what measure of faith these Jewesses possessed before their conversion to Christianity, they, like Paul, had inherited from their forefathers. The alleged contrast to Paul does not agree with the context, and must have been expressed by a reference to the heathen character of his father and his paternal ancestors. What his father and forefathers were for Paul (Acts xxiii. 6 ; Gal. i. 14 ; vol. i. 68, n. 15), Timothy's mother and grandmother were to him. Timothy's faith forms the contrast to πρῶτον, which here, as so often, is not appreciably different from πρότερον, and expresses priority to the action of the main statement (Matt. v. 24, vii. 5, viii. 21, xii. 29, xvii. 10 ; 2 Thess. ii. 3). Paul might also have written προενῴκησεν. Paul could speak of the instruction in the O.T. imparted to Timothy at home, i.e. by his mother, and perhaps also his grandmother, before their conversion, as a preparation for

his calling as preacher of the gospel (iii. 15); he could characterise his own Christian piety as the normal continuation of the Pharisaic piety of his earlier years, and of his Pharisaic ancestors (i. 3; Acts xxiii. 1, 6, xxvi. 5–7); and with just as good reason he could speak in praise of the sincere piety of these Jewesses, even though perhaps Lois died without hearing the gospel. Only in case he had opposed the revelation of Christ when it came to him (cf. Gal. i. 16; Phil. iii. 7; Acts xxvi. 19), and ignoring it had held fast to his Pharisaism, would his inherited piety have become hypocrisy—worship vitiated by an unclean and evil conscience. In a like case Paul would have passed the same judgment upon the pre-Christian piety of Lois and Eunice.

5. (P. 6.) As the sense of ii. 2 is to be explained and completed from 1 Tim. vi. 12 (cf. the writer's essay on the *Apostol. Symbolum*, S. 39 ff.), so 2 Tim. i. 6 should be viewed in the light of 1 Tim. iv. 14. Probably it was prophetic voices (διὰ προφητείας; cf. 1 Tim. i. 18, κατὰ τὰς προαγούσας ἐπὶ σὲ προφητείας) which suggested the choice of Timothy as assistant of Paul and Silvanus, and his consecration to this work with prayer and the laying on of hands (cf. Acts xiii. 2 f.). The laying on of hands by the presbyters (1 Tim. iv. 14) and by Paul (2 Tim. i. 6) are not mutually exclusive, especially since the former is mentioned merely as an accompanying circumstance of his endowment with special grace, the latter as the efficient cause of this endowment. The Churches in the neighbourhood of Timothy's home, according to Acts xiv. 23, had been furnished with a body of presbyters soon after their founding; see, further, § 37.

6. (P. 7.) The earlier Greek Fathers (Eus. *H. E.* ii. 22; the real Euthalius, Zacagni, p. 533; Chrysost. xi. 190, 658, 722; Theodore, Swete, ii. 230 f.; cf. i. 117, 205 f., and Theodoret) understood 2 Tim. iv. 16 f. on the whole correctly, though they referred the lion too definitely to Nero. The proverbial and figurative character of the expression (Ps. xxii. 21; cf. 1 Macc. ii. 60; Ps. vii. 3, xxxv. 17; Midrash Beresh. r. par. 64 at end), which we find so used in Amos iii. 12, would have been no hindrance to writing τοῦ λέοντος (Judg. xiv. 9; 1 Sam. xvii. 37; Dan. vi. 21) even if the intention were to liken a definite individual to a lion; but, apart from the prophetic announcement in Acts xxvii. 24, there is no hint in the N.T. of a single person upon whose decision Paul's fate in Rome depended. On the other hand, this expression and the fixed usage of ῥύεσθαι (2 Tim. iii. 11, iv. 18; 2 Cor. i. 10; 2 Thess. iii. 2; Rom. vii. 24, xv. 31; 2 Pet. ii. 7) does not admit of interpretation as an inner protection from inclination to sin or unbelief. Even when deliverance from temptations is meant (2 Pet. ii. 9; Matt. vi. 13), it is actual rescue from definite situations in real life; and the devil too, when he is likened to a lion instead of a serpent (2 Cor. xi. 3), is represented as the persecutor who seeks the death of believers (1 Pet. v. 8). His terrifying roar is simply a prelude to opening his jaws and devouring the prey. The expression ἐνεδυνάμωσεν cannot justify the giving of this spiritual meaning to ἐρύσατο; this can be seen even from 1 Macc. ii. 61 (οὐκ ἀσθενήσουσιν = σωθήσονται; cf. ii. 60) and still better from a passage similarly misinterpreted, Phil. i. 19 (vol. i. 545); it follows also from the simple consideration that rescue from the danger of condemnation and execution depends essentially upon how skilfully and energetically a man is defended or defends himself. Spitta at one time (*ThStKr.* 1878, S. 582 ff.)

returned to the correct interpretation of the passage. But later (*Urchristentum*, i. 43 ff. ; cf. also Hesse, *Entstehung der Hirtenbriefe*, 29 ff.) he proposed again his earlier view, according to which ver. 17, in contrast with ver. 16, refers to all the divine assistance and deliverance experienced by Paul since his call to apostleship. In the sentence connected by δέ with ver. 16, ὁ κύριός μοι παρέστη plainly forms an antithesis to οὐδείς μοι παραγένετο ; consequently, since no other time or occasion is mentioned, the force of the ἐν τῇ πρώτῃ μου ἀπολογίᾳ is continued. Even apart from this, the bare aorists in ver. 17 without a πάντοτε, πολλάκις, ἀεί ποτε (cf. ἐκ πάντων, iii. 11 ; ἐν τούτοις πᾶσιν, Rom. viii. 37), cannot possibly sum up all instances of the kind, especially after two single instances have been adduced, vv. 14, 16, in the same form. Besides, it is by no means in every case that rescue from great danger is conditioned upon being strengthened by the Lord or is brought about by this means, but only when the deliverance of the person in danger depends upon his presence of mind and his courageous words and deeds, as, *e.g.* in a legal trial. Nor can the correct interpretation be disturbed by the fact that the purpose clause in iv. 17 comes after the second verb, and not at the end after the third verb. It could even come after παρέστη without any essential change in the meaning. It stands where it does because the statement about the Lord's purpose naturally follows the completed account of His action. But the deliverance which was the final result of this support and strengthening by the Lord, Paul did not describe as the immediate act of the Lord, and for the simple reason that he was speaking, not of a miraculous deliverance, as, *e.g.* those in Acts xvi. 26, xxviii. 5, nor even of a strange combination of circumstances, but rather of the very natural result of his happy defence at the trial. As he stood at the bar, deprived of all human assistance, he could plainly trace the assistance of the Lord, the strengthening through Him, the supply of the appropriate means on the part of the Spirit (Phil. i. 19). At this point, then, naturally comes the reflection over the aim which the Lord had in this act of His. Since πληροφορεῖν is a synonym of πληροῦν, only more emphatic (cf. 2 Tim. iv. 5 with Acts xii. 25), what is said of Christian preaching in the eastern half of the Roman Empire in Rom. xv. 19, 23 is simply repeated here in a stronger expression with reference to Christian preaching in general ; every limitation of this preaching, as, *e.g.* to that in Rome, is excluded by the added καὶ ἀκούσωσιν πάντα τὰ ἔθνη. To refer this expression to the *corona populi*, who, it is held, attended the trial and heard Paul's defence (Wieseler, Huther, *et al.*), is particularly out of place ; for not only was the public excluded, as a rule, from criminal trials before the imperial court (Mommsen, *R. Staatsrecht*,[3] ii. 965), but also and especially was the circle of the ἔθνη, to whom the preaching is here said to have been brought, widened even less by a legal defence than by Paul's missionary preaching for two years in Rome (see above, p. 8). Paul writes δι᾽ ἐμοῦ (cf. 2 Cor. i. 19 ; Rom. xv. 18; 1 Cor. iii. 5) and not ὑπ᾽ ἐμοῦ, which would have been hardly possible in connection with ἀκούσωσιν. But the former phrase, as well as the latter, makes it clear that Paul is speaking of a result to be effected through his personal activity, and cannot justify Hofmann's exegesis (vi. 301), according to which the Lord merely takes care that the nerve of the further propagation of the gospel shall not be cut by a weak defence of this gospel, or even a denial of it, on Paul's part.

7. (P. 11.) With regard to the tendency to idealise the results of missionary work, cf. *Skizzen*, 76–82, and vol. i. 415 f., n. 19 on Rom. xv. 19 f. Here belongs the use of " Macedonia " and " Achaia," as if they were Christian lands, 2 Cor. ix. 2 (viii. 1, 4); Rom. xv. 26 ; further, Acts viii. 14 ; also the exaggerated expressions Rom. x. 18 ; Col. i. 6.

8. (P. 11.) The reading Γαλατίαν, iv. 10 (Γαλλίαν, אC, Epiph. *Hær.* li. 11 ; cf. Eus. *H. E.* iii. 4. 8, ἐπὶ τὰς Γαλλίας), is by far the best attested ; but even aside from this, it should be retained because the commentators have from the first understood by it European Gaul, and that, too, though at the time when our oldest Greek MSS. were written, the Greeks, following Roman precedent, regularly called the land ἡ Γαλλία, αἱ Γαλλίαι ; cf. Theodorus, ii. 227, " Galatiam dixit quas nunc nominamus Gallias," and also Lightfoot on this point, *Galatians*, pp. 3, 31. The older Greeks regularly used until well down in Christian times Γαλάται, Γαλατία for Gaul and its inhabitants, along with the still older names, Κέλται, Κελτοί, Κελτική ; so that on occasion the Asiatic Galatians and their 'and had to be more closely defined as οἱ ἐν 'Ασίᾳ Γαλάται (Plut. *Mor.* p. 258), ἡ κατὰ τὴν 'Ασίαν Γαλατία (Dioscor. *Mat. Med.* iii. 56,'62), Γαλλογραικοί, Γαλλογραικία (Strabo, pp. 130, 566). Epictetus is cited as the oldest witness for the Latinised form Γάλλοι ; but he is really no witness at all, for he understands by this word, *Diss.* ii. 20. 17, the castrated priests of the Phrygian Cybele. Even Plutarch uses only Γαλάται, Γαλατία (along with Κελτοί, Κελτική), and generally leaves to his readers to decide from the context whether they are to be found in Western Europe (*Camillus*, cc. xv.–xviii. ; *Cæsar*, cc. xiv.–xxv. ; *Pompeius*, chap. xlviii.) or in Asia Minor (*Lucullus*, chap. xxviii.; *Marius*, chap. xxxi. ; *Pompeius*, cc. xxxi. xxxiii. ; *Moralia*, pp. 257–259). The oldest Greek witness for Γάλλοι, in the sense of the European Celts, would be the physician Dioscorides in the time of Nero (*de Mat. Med.* ii. 101, iii. 33, 75, 108, 117, 122, iv. 16, 42, 69, 71 ; nowhere else), if all the statements about barbarian names for medicinal herbs were not under suspicion of being later interpolations (Sprengel, tom. i. p. xvi). He would also be the oldest witness for Γαλλία (*de Mat. Med.* ii. 92, ἀπὸ Γαλλίας καὶ Τυρρηνίας), if only we did not read two lines farther down ἀπὸ Γαλατίας τῆς πρὸς ταῖς "Αλπεσιν as a designation of the same land or a part of it ; cf. iii. 25 ; and, *per contra*, ἐν τῇ κατὰ τὴν 'Ασίαν Γαλατίᾳ, iii. 56, 62. It was very easy for later scribes to change ΓΑΛΑΤΙΑ, which had become strange to them in this sense, into ΓΑΛΛΙΑ. So also, apparently, we should restore in the text of Jos. *Ant.* xviii. 7. 2, *Bell.* ii. 7. 3 the older Γαλατία, which Josephus uses commonly elsewhere (see Niese's apparatus, *ad loc.*, and index under Γαλάται, Γαλατία). On the other hand, we actually find in the *Acts of Paul*, about 170 A.D. (ed. Lipsius, p. 104. 3, in the Lat. text *Galilœa* ; as to the confounding here of Luke and Crescens, see *GK*, ii. 888), in the letter of the Lyonese, 177 A.D. (Eus. *H. E.* v. 1. 49), and in Theoph. *ad Autol.* ii. 32, αἱ (καλούμεναι, Theoph.) Γαλλίαι. Galen (*de Antid.* i. 14 ; Kühn, xiv. 80) is led by a quotation from Nero's time, in which Gaul was called ἡ Γαλατεία, to speak of the fluctuation in usage between Γάλλοι, Γαλάται, Κέλται, but without once thinking of the Galatians in Asia Minor. Appian's standpoint is the same, *Prooem.* iii. and *Iber.* i. Herodian seems to be the first who distinguished consciously between ἡ Γαλλία (iii. 7. 1)=Gaul and ἡ Γαλατία (iii. 2. 6, 3. 1)=Galatia in

Asia Minor. This usage is too late to be taken into account in connection with 2 Tim. iv. 10. Lexically considered, it may be here either Gaul or Galatia. But its position next to Dalmatia, which has its parallel in the famous *Monumentum Ancyrarum* (*Res gestæ D. Augusti*, ed.² Mommsen, p. xxxv, 124, ἐξ Ἰσπανίας καὶ Γαλατίας καὶ παρὰ Δαλματῶν ; cf. pp. 98, 103), leaves no doubt that Gaul is meant. The circumstance that Galatia was nearer to Timothy than Gaul, is counterbalanced by the fact that to Paul, writing from Rome, Gaul was nearer. Indeed, this very nearness of Crescens to Timothy could hardly have been left unexpressed, especially if Timothy were then staying in Lystra or Iconium (above, p. 19, n. 1), *i.e.* in the province of Galatia. The lack of ancient tradition concerning Crescens as missionary to Gaul, and also concerning Titus as missionary to Dalmatia, is certainly to be regretted, but cannot be used as a basis for any historical conclusions. It was not until long afterward that the founding of the Church in Vienna was ascribed to Crescens, and, still later, that of the Church in Mayence (Tillemont, *Mém.* i. 615). It corresponds to the fluctuating usage of the time that Paul should write Δαλματία here, and, *per contra*, τὸ Ἰλλυρικόν in Rom. xv. 19 (Marquardt, *R. Staatsverw.*² i. 299) ; and, in particular, this variation proves that the statements in 2 Tim. iv. relating to missions and geography are independent of Rom. xv.

9. (P. 14.) Hug's suggestion (*Einl.*³ ii. 418), adopted by many since his time, that we should take the ἀπέλιπον in iv. 20, in distinction from that in iv. 13, as third person plural, is inadmissible, since in that case the subject could not be divined. Erastus alone—mentioned just before—cannot be the subject. Nor can we find in iv. 19 one or more persons who can be joined with Erastus to make up the subject of ἀπέλιπον ; for it was not the household of Onesiphorus, but only Onesiphorus himself, who had lately made a journey (i. 16–18, above, p. 2). Equally inadmissible is the proposal of Baronius (ad annum, 59, n. 1), supported also by Knoke (*Prakt. theol. Kommentar zu den Pastoralbr.* i. 116), to change Μιλήτῳ (*al.* μηλιτω, μηλητω, μηλωτω) into Μελίτῃ, and thus to understand Malta as referred to (Acts xxviii. 1–10). For, in the first place, Trophimus (Acts xxi. 29) is not mentioned in Acts xxvii. 2, where the author's plain intention is to indicate Paul's companions on the journey to Rome. In the second place, such a communication would have been unintelligible to Timothy unless 2 Tim. were written in the very first part of the first Roman imprisonment, before Timothy arrived for the first time in Rome, and before Eph., Col., and Philem. were written. But in view of what has been said above (p. 1 f.) this is impossible. Even Baronius felt constrained to refute the view that a Miletus in Crete, now Milato or Milata, is meant, and that, therefore, we are to think of Acts xxvii. 7–13. The arguments which hold against the preceding view are equally applicable here ; but aside from these, this Miletus is situated on the north shore of the island, whereas Paul, on his journey to Rome, sailed along the south shore. Wieseler's opinion (*Chronol.* 467), that while Paul exchanged at Myra the Adramyttian ship for an Alexandrian vessel sailing to Italy direct (Acts xxvii. 5 f.), Trophimus may have continued his journey on the former ship as far as Miletus, where illness detained him ; and that this is the meaning of the words in 2 Tim. iv. 20 needs no refutation.

10. (P. 18.) From the mere mention of Ephesus by name in 2 Tim. i.

18, iv. 12, we cannot conclude that Timothy was then living elsewhere.
Paul, when he was himself in Rome, wrote ἐν Ῥώμῃ, 2 Tim. i. 17, and when
in Ephesus, ἐν Ἐφέσῳ, 1 Cor. xv. 32, xvi. 8, instead of ὧδε or ἐν ταύτῃ τῇ
πόλει ; and in like manner, when writing to Timothy in Ephesus, he used
not ἐκεῖ, but ἐν Ἐφέσῳ, 1 Tim. i. 3 (cf. iii. 14 f.) ; and when he had occasion
to speak of Corinth to the Corinthians he used εἰς Κόρινθον (2 Cor. i. 23).
Nevertheless, Theodorus, ii. 190, is plainly right when he remarks with reference to 2 Tim. iv. 12 : "dixisset utique 'ad te,' si Ephesi adhuc Timotheus
moraretur, quando et hanc ad eum scribebat epistolam."

§ 34. THE FACTS ATTESTED BY THE FIRST EPISTLE TO TIMOTHY.

Unlike the shorter letter to Timothy, which on this
account was placed after the longer one of the collection,
and in which are found numerous notices concerning
Paul's personal situation, 1 Tim. has very few such notices.
It is, however, clear that when 1 Tim. was written
Paul was at liberty, and somewhere in the eastern part of
the empire. He mentions a journey to Macedonia, which
had been made recently, as will be shown below (i. 3),
and expresses the hope of coming shortly to Ephesus,
where Timothy was at the time (iii. 14, iv. 13). Although
the sentence with which the letter begins is left uncompleted (i. 3 ff.), and although the construction at the
beginning is somewhat loose, its general meaning is clear
(n. 1). Some time before, Paul had asked Timothy to
remain a while longer in Ephesus, where Timothy was at
the time the request was made. These instructions had
been given by Paul to his disciple just as the apostle was
setting out on a journey to Macedonia, or after it had
been begun. The latter is more likely, since there were
better ways in which to express the former thought than
that which he here uses (ἐκπορεύεσθαι, Acts xxv. 4 ; Mark
x. 46 ; ἐξέρχεσθαι, 2 Cor. ii. 13 ; Phil. iv. 15 ; cf. Acts
xx. 1, xxi. 5). Since Paul does not say that he had left
Timothy behind in Ephesus (cf. Tit. i. 5 ; 2 Tim. iv. 13,
20), he could not have been in Ephesus at the time, nor

have set out on his journey to Macedonia from that
point, but, when this instruction was sent to Timothy,
must have been journeying to Macedonia from the West.
Assuming — as the language seems to require — that
Timothy was in Ephesus when he received the instruction,
also that the apostle's directions take for granted an
opposite intention or inclination on Timothy's part, the
most natural supposition is that, in a letter written from
Ephesus, Timothy had expressed to the apostle his desire
to join him on this journey, which was to take him,
among other places, into Macedonia, or to set out to
meet him there.   But from some point on his route Paul
had written to Timothy to remain in Ephesus.   It is
probable that in this reply he expressed the intention of
himself coming to Ephesus; for in iii. 14, iv. 13 he
speaks of his coming as if it had already been announced.
That Timothy did not refuse to obey this advice of the
apostle's, and that when 1 Tim. was written he was still
in Ephesus, is proved not only by the absence of all
evidence to the contrary, but, more positively, by the way
in which the exhortations and instructions, which constitute the main contents of 1 Tim., are all connected
with this injunction that Timothy remain at his post.
When he began to write he evidently intended merely to
remind Timothy of the purpose for which he had been
instructed to remain where he was; but this he afterwards
enlarges into an independent statement (i. 3–8), the
detailed character of which is accounted for by the fact
that he here reminds Timothy of the tasks to the zealous
performance of which this letter is meant to urge him.
In accordance with Paul's earlier request, and the purpose
which Paul had then set before him as most pressing,
Timothy is to continue his work in Ephesus until the
apostle himself comes.

It is, however, because the prospect of his coming to
Ephesus is only a hope, and because he is not sure how

long this coming may be deferred, that Paul writes this
letter to Timothy. In case he is compelled to remain
away longer, the instructions in the letter will serve to
assist Timothy in the right performance of his duties in
the Church (iii. 14 f., iv. 13). In view of the urgent
character of the exhortations (i. 18, iv. 11, 14–16, vi. 3,
11, 20), and the solemn manner in which he is reminded
of his duties (v. 21, vi. 3–16), it is to be inferred
that Timothy was endeavouring to escape from the
duty enjoined upon him. From iv. 12 we gather that
he had urged his youth as an excuse for a certain lack
of energy which the apostle thought he showed in the
discharge of his office. Besides, there were constant
physical disorders which made him anxious about his
health, and had led him to abstain from wine and from the
use of hearty foods (v. 23, iv. 8). More noteworthy is the
fact that Timothy should be warned by the citation of
terrible examples of the apathy of the religious and moral
life (i. 19 ; cf. iv. 16, vi. 12), against the love of money
(vi. 11 ; cf. vi. 5–10), and against having anything to do
with useless and unfruitful theoretical discussions and
investigations, which it was his duty to forbid other
teachers to carry on (iv. 7, vi. 20 ; cf. i. 4, vi. 4).

The work which Timothy has to do in and about
Ephesus is very different from his vocation in 2 Tim.
Where Timothy may have been at the time of 2 Tim.,
whether in Iconium, or Ephesus, or Rome, or on his
way thither, the one thing which he is to keep in
mind is that the proclamation of the gospel is his
distinctive and essential mission, as it is that of the
apostle (2 Tim. i. 8, iv. 5 ; cf. i. 10, ii. 8). With this
function was, of course, associated—in Timothy's case, as
in the case of Paul himself and of all apostles and
evangelists who happened to be for a time in localities
where there were Christian Churches (vol. i. 507 f.)—a
teaching function which ministered to the faith and life

of the members of the Church, and, generally speaking, an
administrative activity in the Church's affairs (2 Tim. ii. 2,
14–21, 24–26, iii. 16 f., iv. 2–4). But the fact is not to
be denied, that in 1 Tim. this oversight of the Church by
Timothy is the only function spoken of, and that no mention
is made anywhere of his missionary calling. Not only do
we miss the word "evangelist," which is used in 2 Tim.
iv. 5 as a comprehensive description of Timothy's calling,
but even the word εὐαγγέλιον occurs only once in 1 Tim.,
and then with reference not to Timothy's calling, but to
the ministry of Paul (i. 11 ; cf. ii. 7). This explains why,
in 2 Tim., Timothy's vocation is treated as a life-calling,
whereas the task to which he is exhorted in 1 Tim. is
limited to the time he shall be in Ephesus until Paul's
arrival (1 Tim. iii. 14 f., iv. 13). From the time when
Paul made him his helper in the prosecution of missionary
work he had been an evangelist (2 Tim. i. 6). In manifold ways on his journeys with Paul he had proved
himself such (2 Tim. iii. 10 f.). This work and service of
an evangelist he is to continue to the end, even after
the apostle's work on earth is finished (2 Tim. iv. 1–8).
Of course, there is to be recognised a connection between
the special task of which Timothy is reminded in the first
letter and his consecration as a helper in missionary work,
including the prophetic gifts which he then received,
particularly that of pastoral teaching (1 Tim. iv. 14 ;
cf. i. 18). But even leaving out of account the noticeable
difference of language between 1 Tim. iv. 14 and 2 Tim.
i. 6 (above, p. 23, n. 5), the marked distinction between
the two offices cannot be explained by simply assuming
that the special and temporary office which Timothy was
to perform in Ephesus grew out of his life-calling as an
evangelist and missionary, like similar temporary commissions performed earlier (1 Cor. iv. 17 ; Phil. ii. 19–23).

What in detail these duties were which Paul instructed Timothy to perform in the Church, will be

discussed in connection with the question of the genuine·
ness of the Epistle (§ 37).   Here we are concerned with
the character of these duties only as this throws light
upon the question, at what time in Paul's life this letter
could have been written.   The description of these duties
given in the middle of the letter, where Paul states its
purpose, namely, that in case he is compelled to remain
away longer than he anticipates, Timothy may know how
persons ought to conduct themselves in the house of
God, is very general (iii. 15, n. 2).   From this passage
we gather that Timothy's position in one portion of the
Church was similar to that of the head of a household.
The principal reason why Paul thought it necessary for
Timothy to remain longer in Ephesus is stated in i. 3 f.
and emphasised again from a different point of view in
vi. 3–5, and is this, namely, the necessity of warning
certain persons not to teach in a manner which to the
apostle seems perverse, and, to put it mildly, not profitable
to the Church.   He is also to warn them against occupying themselves with profitless speculations instead of with
sound Christian doctrine, evidently because their activity
as teachers was prompted by such speculations (n. 3).
He was also charged to a certain extent with the cure of
souls ; since his other instructions were such that their
carrying out would for the most part involve personal
intercourse with the people of his charge (e.g. v. 1–7,
vi. 1–2, 17).   On the other hand, it is self-evident
that Timothy was authorised and bound to publicly
exhort, advise, and reprove persons who assumed the rôle
of teachers, the young widows, slaves, the rich, and elders.)
In one case he is expressly enjoined to do so (v. 20), and
throughout the letter, where teaching as well as exhortation and injunction is spoken of (iv. 6, 11, 16, vi. 3), the
reference is to public teaching in the Church.   But this
does not by any means place Timothy on the same
footing with the member of the Church possessing special

gifts for teaching and speaking, or with officials in the Church who exercised this office (v. 17). The fact that Timothy is to forbid false teachers to teach in their own way, presupposes that he exerted a determining influence over all that was taught in the public gatherings of the Church, and so over its entire worship. This is presupposed in the *textus receptus* of ii. 1, where, although it is not said in so many words that Timothy has charge of the matter, Paul enjoins that prayers of various kinds be offered for all men, particularly for rulers. The very fact that this is said in a letter directed to Timothy makes Timothy responsible for the observance of this rule in all public worship. Neither the offering of prayer nor teaching is official, but every male member of the Church is privileged to exercise both functions. Only Timothy is to see to it that both are exercised in a correct manner (n. 4). Since Paul does not define Timothy's duties in this letter, but simply reminds him of them, details are for the most part only indirectly and incidentally given. In iii. 1–13 are set forth the qualifications which must be had by a bishop or deacon ; iii. 1 brings before us the situation where one desires the office of bishop ; iii. 10 speaks of the examination which must precede entrance into the office ; from all which it is to be inferred that the rules here laid down are those to be observed in connection with the induction of these officials into office. Since, however, these rules are given in a letter to Timothy, who neither is nor will become a bishop or a deacon, it follows that Timothy's influence was paramount with reference to these officials, and that he was to observe these rules in inducting them into office. Of Timothy's part in the appointment and consecration of Church officials, which was certainly one of importance and responsibility, we learn only incidentally from the warning that he is not to lay hands on anyone in consecration hastily or lightly (v. 22), which does not exclude the co-operation of others, any more than the laying on of Paul's hands excluded those of the presbytery (iv. 14 ; 2 Tim. i. 6). Quite as incidentally we learn from v. 19–21 that among other functions Timothy was to act as judge over the presbyters, and to see to it, on the other hand, that those presbyters who filled their office worthily received the honour due them (v. 17 f.). Further, he was to have oversight over the Church's care of widows, the reception of them into the fellowship, and the registering of those among them who were active in the service of the Church and deserving of special honour (v. 3–16). In short, there was no branch of Church life over which his authority did not extend ; he is not, however, one of the ἐπίσκοποι or πρεσβύτεροι, but he is over them.

It is to be noted also that Timothy's office was not limited to the local Church. Paul had asked him to continue in Ephesus, merely because he had expressed a desire to join Paul on his journey (i. 3, above, p. 27 f.). The request does not imply that Timothy was not to leave the limits of the city, and that Paul's instructions were to be carried out only in this one Church. We saw in connection with ii. 1–15 (cf. also n. 4) that Timothy was to put into operation in a number of Churches Paul's principles with reference to public prayer. This is still clearer in the instructions regarding the appointment of bishops and deacons (iii. 1–13 ; cf. v. 22). Even if it be assumed that the time which these instructions were meant to cover (iii. 15, iv. 13), i.e. the time before his own arrival in Ephesus, might be extended over two or three years, as Paul thought it might, they are altogether superfluous if intended to apply only to the local Ephesian Church. In so brief a time within one Church there could not possibly have been more than one or two occasions when the apostle's regulations would have applied. It is quite possible, and the shorter the period the more probable it becomes, that during this interval there was no occasion in this Church—which had

been organised some time—for the appointment of new
bishops and deacons, and that no ordinations took place.
Consequently it must have been a large group of Churches,
the direction and oversight of which were committed to
Timothy, in residence at Ephesus, and among them probably such as were in process of formation and therefore in
need of ecclesiastical organisation (n. 5). Without any
question, these were the Churches of the province of Asia
(1 Cor. xvi. 19), of which Ephesus was the centre. That
Paul felt himself responsible, as the founder of the Church
in Ephesus, for the development of all the other Churches
in the province, and for the oversight of the same, is
abundantly proved by the first three letters of his imprisonment, while from Col. i. 7 it is clear that even at
this time he regarded Timothy, who had been his helper
in the planting of Christianity in the province of Asia,
as sharing his relation to this large group of Churches
(vol. i. 449 f., n. 3).

The position which Timothy occupied in Ephesus, as it
is described in 1 Tim., cannot without doing the greatest
violence to history be called that of a bishop (n. 6); for
the office of bishop existed also where the one bishop,
superior to the presbytery, represented the highest expression of the common Church life. The office was for life,
and confined to the local Church. This was particularly
the case in Asia Minor, where, although as early as the time
of Revelation and the letters of Ignatius, bishoprics were
numerous and closely adjacent, the office always retained
its local character. (On the other hand, Timothy's position
at the head of the Churches of Asia was due to the
position which he occupied as Paul's helper in missionary
work. It was his part in the apostolic calling, as this
calling involved the oversight of existing Churches.
Timothy was acting as a temporary representative of Paul
in his apostolic capacity at Ephesus, as he had done
earlier in Corinth, and in Thessalonica and Philippi

(1 Cor. iv. 17 ; 1 Thess. iii. 2 f. ; Phil. ii. 19–23). His
relation was not closer to one Church than to the other
Churches of the province; its rise and disappearance did
not affect at all the organisation of the local congregations.)

Compared with 2 Tim., 1 Tim. contains few personal
notices (n. 7). But the few that it does contain give the
impression of genuineness. They show at least that Paul
did not write the letter prior to his five years' imprisonment
in Cæsarea and Rome. Since, however, Paul is at liberty,
the letter and the events immediately preceding fall in
the interval between the first and a second Roman imprisonment, of which we learn in 2 Tim. The journey
spoken of in i. 3 cannot, as Hug (*Einl.*³ ii. 377) assumes,
be identified with that of Acts xx. 1 ; for at that time
Timothy had not been, as is assumed in 1 Tim. i. 3, for a
considerable time in Ephesus, nor could Paul at that time
have requested him to continue there, for Timothy had
just returned to Ephesus from a journey to Macedonia
and Corinth, and soon afterward accompanied Paul on
this journey to Macedonia and Greece (2 Cor. i. 1, 8,
vii. 5 ; vol. i. 316, n. 3). He was also with him on the
return journey from Greece, through Macedonia, to Troas,
Miletus, and Jerusalem (Acts xx. 3 ff.). Even assuming
that Timothy remained in Ephesus some time after Paul
left, following later to Macedonia, or that he left the
party, say at Troas (Acts xx. 5), and went to Ephesus to
execute some commissions for the apostle, while Paul and
the other members of the party did not stop at Ephesus
(Acts xx. 16 f.), neither προσμεῖναι (i. 3), nor Paul's
intention to come shortly to Ephesus (iii. 14), nor the
tasks referred to in 1 Tim., agree with the representation
of this journey which we have in Acts. For this reason it
has been suggested that the letter, and the events presupposed by it as immediately preceding, belong in the period
of Paul's labours in Ephesus, which covered approximately

three years, more definitely, near the end of his stay there (n. 8). Then the journey referred to in 1 Tim. i. 3 would be the journey of Paul from Ephesus to Corinth not mentioned in Acts, but attested by 2 Cor. (vol. ·i. 263, 271 f.), and from this passage we should have to assume that on that occasion Paul went to Corinth by way of Macedonia. But the assumption which this involves, namely, that after having himself been for some time in Ephesus, Paul *left Timothy behind*, charged with the tasks mentioned in 1 Tim. i. 3 f., has against it, as has been shown (above, p. 271), the language of the passage. Besides, there is nothing to indicate that the prospective arrival of Paul in the place where Timothy remains (iii. 14, iv. 13), is a return of Paul to his place of residence after a temporary absence. It is also difficult to understand why Paul should have written Timothy a letter like 1 Tim., if in his capacity as Paul's helper he was simply to carry on the work which he had seen the apostle do for some time past, when Paul had already had ample opportunity, and the most urgent occasion just before setting out on his journey, to give Timothy instructions for the time during which he was to be absent. During this time Paul would have had no occasion to write Timothy except in answer to questions about individual cases that presented difficulty, of which, however, there is no suggestion. The instructions of the letter would be quite without point unless Paul assumed that Timothy would have to remain at his post in Ephesus alone for at least several months. Adding to this the time that had elapsed since the supposed departure of Paul to Macedonia and Corinth, the interruption of Paul's work in Ephesus caused by this journey is drawn out to a length which renders the silence of Acts with reference to it not only very strange, but its representation of Paul's work in Ephesus positively erroneous (xix. 8–10, xx. 18, 31). Moreover, the letter assumes the existence in the province of Asia of a considerable group of Churches, some of which at least had been in existence for some time. Since a newly baptized person is not to be made a bishop (i. 6), there must have been in Ephesus and vicinity a number of men who had been for some years members of the Church. But even as late as the third year after the beginning of missionary work in Ephesus there were no persons tested by a long period of Christian experience, but only neophytes. This would be even more true of the other cities of the province. Furthermore, at the time when this letter was written there were in these cities persons who had fallen away again from the faith (i. 19 f., v. 15), and Timothy is informed anew that Paul has given these persons over to Satan (i. 20); hence it could not have happened while Timothy was in Ephesus, nor could Paul have been there at the time when this was done. Finally, it is hard to see how, in a Church so recently organised as that in Ephesus, and until very recently under the personal oversight of the apostle, the unprofitable teachers, whom Timothy is especially instructed to oppose, could have secured such a footing; or if, in spite of his influence, they had acquired so much power, how in the circumstances Paul could have left Ephesus. Then the assumption has against it the close connection between 1 Tim. and 2 Tim., which certainly could not have been written before 63. The relation of 1 Tim. to Titus is closer, and, as will be shown, this letter could not have been written before the same year. Between the three letters there is an affinity of language, a similarity of thought, and a likeness of errors combated, which prevents our referring any of them to a period much earlier than the others. Certainly this assumption cannot be maintained on the ground of Timothy's youthful age, suggested by the statement that he is not to let anyone despise him on account of his youth (iv. 12), and by his apparent disposition to excuse himself from his duties on

this ground (above, p. 29).   Paul speaks of Timothy's
youth (2 Tim. ii. 22) in the very latest of his letters;
and in any case, Timothy, who became Paul's helper in
missionary work in the year 52, was not in the year 64
necessarily more than thirty-five or forty years of age,
and so still a *juvenis*, who on account of his immaturity
might be regarded by himself and others as unsuited for
the office in the Church described above.   His task was
really no easy one, especially if there were older men in
the Churches, whether occupying official positions or not
(v. 1, 19).

1. (P. 27.)   Otto, *Geschichtl. Verh. der Pastoralbr.* S. 48, followed by
Kölling, *Erster Br. an Tim.* i. 207–221, translated 1 Tim. i. 3 : "Just as (in
accordance with the fact that) I exhorted thee in Ephesus (*i.e.* while I was
staying there), to hold out (to stand fast), so do thou, when setting out on the
journey to Macedonia, command certain persons not to cleave to strange
teachers, nor to give heed to endless fables and genealogies." The grain of
truth in the elaborate discussions of these theologians is that in Paul's
writings καθώς does not have just the same meaning as simple ὡς, ὥσπερ,
so that, as has been admitted by others, in this respect passages like Gal. i. 9
are not altogether comparable.   Paul points to the earlier request and
exhortation which he had addressed to Timothy (cf. against Kölling, 211, with
regard to παρακαλεῖν, Matt. viii. 34 ; Mark v. 17 ; Luke viii. 41 ; Acts
xxviii. 14 ; 2 Cor. viii. 6) as the standard for what he has now to say to
Timothy, and for what Timothy has now to do.   For this very reason he
reproduces not only this former request itself, but also its aim and real
intention (ἵνα παραγγείλῃς—ἐν πίστει) ; and the more detailed he makes this
reproduction, the more natural it seems that with his tendency to anacolutha
he should leave unexpressed the new request, which was to be expected
grammatically, but which would have been of essentially similar content and
of quite the same sense.   The προσμένειν here (in distinction from the cases
where it occurs in connection with a dative governed by the πρός, Matt.
xv. 32 ; Acts xi. 23 ; 1 Tim. v. 5) is used absolutely = "to remain steadfastly,
beyond the measure hitherto attained, still longer to persevere at one's post"
(Acts xviii. 18 ; Herodot. viii. 4).   But this cannot in any way prevent us
from connecting ἐν Ἐφέσῳ with it as the designation of the place where
Timothy shall longer remain.   The case is the same with the essentially
synonymous ἐπιμένειν, which likewise occurs, sometimes with the dative
(Rom. vi. 1 ; 1 Tim. iv. 16), sometimes without such completion of the idea,
but with the most various determinations of the place (Acts xv. 34, xxi. 4,
αὐτοῦ ; 1 Cor. xvi. 8, ἐν Ἐφέσῳ ; 1 Cor. xvi. 7 ; Gal. i. 18, πρός τινα ; Acts
xxviii. 14, παρ' αὐτοῖς), the time (Acts x. 48, xxi. 10, xxviii. 12), or even the
action in which one perseveres (Acts xii. 16 ; John viii. 7).   The position of
the words as imperatively demands that we connect ἐν Ἐφέσῳ with προσμένειν,

as it forbids our connecting it with παρεκάλεσα. Moreover, it is an arbitrary assumption to claim that πορευόμενος must have stood before παρεκάλεσα, if the author's purpose had been to couple it with that verb as an attendant circumstance. In consideration of passages like Acts xix. 9, it would be more natural to ask if Paul's journey to Macedonia or departure thither, though in form it is mentioned as the attendant circumstance of παρεκάλεσα, did not in fact directly follow this exhortation. The position of these words, like the whole sentence structure, is unquestionably careless. It is only as an afterthought that Paul characterises the situation at that time by re-marking that he was then on a journey to Macedonia, when he requested Timothy, against the latter's inclinations, to prolong his stay and his labour in Ephesus.

2. (P. 31.)   The present γράφω, on the one hand (cf. *per contra*, Rom. xv. 15 ; 1 Cor. ix. 15 ; Gal. vi. 11 ; Philem. 19, 21 ; vol. i. 472, n. 4, 345, n. 5), and ταῦτα, on the other, forbid referring iii. 14 f. exclusively either to what precedes or to what follows. The instructions of i. 3–iii. 13 are followed in iv. 6–vi. 21 by others essentially similar. Here, as in 1 Cor. iv. 14, Paul stops in the middle of his letter to make a remark bearing upon the essential content of the whole Epistle. In both cases the remark is occasioned by what has just been said here, because the preceding instructions may have given the impression that Timothy must keep the post assigned him inter-minably, and that Paul had given up all thought of visiting him and releasing him. The σέ after δεῖ is abundantly attested (also Ephrem arm. 259 ?) ; and even if it is a gloss, it is a correct one. Elsewhere, ἀναστρέ-φεσθαι, ἀναστροφή may not differ essentially from περιπατεῖν, πολιτεύεσθαι (2 Cor. i. 12 ; Eph. ii. 3, iv. 22 ; 1 Tim. iv. 12) ; but the connection with ἐν οἴκῳ θεοῦ here suggests the idea of a manager or overseer engaged about the house, and moving hither and thither (cf. Heb. iii. 2–6 ; Zech. iii. 7 ; Ezek. xxii. 29 f. ; and for οἰκονομίαν θεοῦ, cf. n. 3) ; for the member of the family as such (the private Church member) does not move about the house, but dwells, sits therein.

3. (P. 31.)   The prohibition μηδὲ προσέχειν, i. 4, cannot apply to Timothy, for in that case we must have had μηδὲ προσέχῃς continuing the construction of ἵνα παραγγείλῃς. No further proof is needed. Nor does it refer to the Church members as hearers, but rather, like μὴ ἑτεροδιδασκαλεῖν, to the false teachers, as appears for the following reasons : (1) the very connection of the words compels us to take both warnings as addressed to the same per-sons, since there is no new dative object opposed to τισίν. (2) οἰκονομίαν θεοῦ, ver. 4, for which οἰκοδομήν and οἰκοδομίαν are ancient emendations intended to make an easier reading, indicates the exercise of the calling of an οἰκονόμος θεοῦ (cf. Tit. i. 7 ; 1 Cor. iv. 1, ix. 17 ; 1 Pet. iv. 10 ; Eph. iii. 2 ; Col. i. 25 ; vol. i. 471, n. 1 ; Ign. *Eph.* vi. 1) ; but this calling is exercised not by the hearing, but by the teaching member of the Church. (3) In Tit. i. 14 the same thing is said of mischievous teachers, and in 1 Tim. vi. 3, προσέχεται, which is most certainly the correct reading (א*, Latini omnes, Ephrem arm. ? Theod. Mops. ?), has the same subject as ἑτεροδιδασκαλεῖ.

4. (Pp. 32, 33.)   In 1 Tim. ii. 1 we should read παρακάλει with the Westerns (DG, Hil., Ambrosiaster ?), with whom the Sahidic also agrees. It was natural for the copyists, whose task it was to prepare a text adapted for the

edification of the Church, to make the apostle himself address this exhortation to the Church directly. Besides, a glance at ii. 8 (v. 14), where the verb
indeed is not the same as παρακάλει, ii. 1, but has the same force and general
meaning, would mislead them into writing παρακαλῶ. After the somewhat
digressive remarks of i. 19–20, Paul in ii. 1 directs the thought back to i. 12
by means of παρακάλει οὖν, and then goes on to describe more in detail the
commission given to Timothy, there expressed only in general terms. The
teaching within the Church, with its practical application, consonant with
the gospel, but by no means identical with it,—for this is what is meant by
ἡ παραγγελία, i. 5, 18,—is recommended to his faithful care and diligent exercise. The instructions for guarding against false teachers, which have been
given even earlier (i. 3 f.), do not belong properly to this commission. The
positive development of its details begins rather in ii. 1. The exhortation
here is not to assiduous prayer in general, whether in the closet or in the
family circle, or in public worship (1 Thess. v. 17 ; Col. iv. 2 ; Eph. vi. 18 ;
Phil. iv. 6 ; Rom. xii. 12), but simply to prayer in the congregation assembled
for worship, as is perfectly evident. For (1) the passive expression, "Exhort
therefore that above all prayers, etc., be offered for all men, for kings," etc.,
shows that the regulation under discussion is a public one. (2) In a list of
things for which Christians should pray in private as well as in public, we
should certainly expect to see mention of their own spiritual and bodily
welfare, and of the good of their fellow-believers. Here, however, we find
merely directions to pray for all men, the vast majority of whom were still
unconverted ; and for rulers, who at that time were still heathen ; together
with elaborate reasons for such prayer. This can be explained only on the
supposition that the prayer referred to was public. (3) In ii. 8 men are
spoken of as those who offer this prayer, as if this were self-evident ; consequently a kind of prayer must be referred to from which women were
excluded, *i.e.* praying aloud before the assembled congregation. For the
silent prayer of the individual is plainly a right and a duty of the women
just as much as of the men, and Paul had not the least intention of excluding
the women even from praying aloud in family worship (1 Cor. xi. 5, cf. vii. 5).
It is only in public worship that they are to be silent (1 Cor. xiv. 34–36), *i.e.*
neither leading in prayer nor teaching. The very same thing is enjoined
here, ii. 11 f., in words which clearly recall 1 Cor. xiv. 35 ; and from this it
follows again that in this whole context the reference is exclusively to Church
worship. The man who raises his hands in prayer before the congregation,
and is selected to voice their prayer, must see to it that the hands which he
thus stretches forth to God before the eyes of all are pure from all unclean,
dishonourable, and violent deeds (Isa. i. 15 ; Jas. iv. 8 ; Clem. 1 *Cor.* xxix. 1 ;
Jos. *Bell.* v. 9. 4 [Niese, 380, 403] ; Horace, *Sat.* i. 4. 68 ; and on ὅσιος, Tit. i. 8 ;
Heb. vii. 26 ; Luke i. 75 ; *GK*, i. 102 f.), and that his heart is free from anger
at the persecutions inflicted by the heathen, and from questionings as to the
rightfulness of the civil order, a disposition which would choke sincere prayer
for all men and for the heathen rulers. The force of προσεύχεσθαι in ii. 8
grammatically cannot extend into ii. 9, since γυναῖκας has a predicate of its
own, κοσμεῖν ἑαυτάς. It does continue the sense logically, but only to this
extent, that ii. 9–12*a* still treats of the congregation assembled for prayer.
The women are not here asked to pray in like manner as the men ; else why

the diversity in the two commands, or why at all the separation of those praying into men and women? Such a misunderstanding of the passage has led to the insertion of a spurious καί before γυναῖκας. Simple ὡσαύτως does not justify ascribing to the women the same function as to the men, indeed, not even a similar one. It merely places (otherwise than in iii. 8, 11) the commands to the women, which follow on the same plane, with those to the men. " In like manner also I desire that the women," etc. Since this whole passage treats only of prayer before the assembled congregation, ἐν παντὶ τόπῳ cannot include all the various places where a Christian can pray, as, e.g. the closet, the family living-room, and the meeting-place of the congregation. Rather, as in 1 Cor. i. 2, 1 Thess. i. 8 (cf. 2 Cor. ii. 14), it means all the places where there are Christian congregations, and where Christian meetings for prayer are held. Paul will have these instructions carried out everywhere, in all congregations (cf. 1 Cor. iv. 17, vii. 17, xi. 16, xiv. 33, 36). But why should Paul speak thus universally when requesting Timothy to look after this matter in the part of the Church entrusted to his care? The only possible explanation is that this part of the Church embraced a number of places and local Churches.

5. (P. 34.) As an illustration, we may take, aside from Tit. i. 5, what Clement of Alexandria (*Quis dives*, xlii.) says of the apostle John : ἐπειδὴ γὰρ τοῦ τυράννου τελευτήσαντος ἀπὸ τῆς Πάτμου τῆς νήσου μετῆλθεν ἐπὶ τὴν Ἔφεσον, ἀπῄει παρακαλούμενος καὶ ἐπὶ τὰ πλησιόχωρα τῶν ἐθνῶν, ὅπου μὲν ἐπισκόπους καταστήσων, ὅπου δὲ ὅλας ἐκκλησίας ἁρμόσων, ὅπου δὲ κλήρῳ ἕνα γέ τινα κληρώσων τῶν ὑπὸ τοῦ πνεύματος σημαινομένων.

6. (P. 34.) The notion that Timothy was the first bishop of Ephesus was firmly established even as early as the time of Eusebius (*H. E.* iii. 4. 6). According to the worthless *Acta Timothei* (ed. Usener, 1877 ; cf. *GGA*, 1878, S. 97–114 ; Lipsius, *Apokr. Apostelgesch.* ii. 2. 373 ff. ; Ergänzungsheft, 86), which was written probably about 400–500 A.D. under the name of the very venerable bishop Polycrates of Ephesus, Paul had consecrated Timothy as bishop during Nero's reign on the occasion of a visit to Ephesus which they made in company. Then, under Nerva, Timothy suffers a martyr's death during a heathen festival, and while John is an exile on the island of Patmos ; and it is not until after this that John suffers the bishops of Asia to transfer the See of Ephesus to him. In *Const. ap.* vii. 46 nothing is said about the apostle John being a bishop, as is in accordance with the method there pursued ; but Paul consecrates Timothy as bishop of Ephesus, and (later) the apostle John consecrates another John to that office. The Johannine legends have altogether ignored Timothy's labours in Ephesus, and even those of Paul. It is a later hand that has inserted in the prolix narrative of Prochorus the section about Paul, and about Timothy's episcopate in Ephesus before John's arrival in that city ; cf. the writer's *Acta Jo.* 166 f., xxxix. With better discrimination the ancient commentators Ephrem, Theodorus, and Theodoret recognised in their prologues the exceptional character of Timothy's position, e.g. Theodorus, ii. 67 : "S. ap. Paulus beatum Timotheum Ephesi reliquit (*per contra*, above, p. 27), scilicet ut omnem peragrans Asiam universas quae illo (=illic) sunt ecclesias gubernaret." The contents of the letter, however, seemed to him useful for every bishop of his time (p. 68). The *Vita Polycarpi*, chap. ii., a work ascribed to Pionius, states, as if on good authority, that a

certain Stratæas, the first (according to *Const. ap.* vii. 46 the second) bishop of Smyrna, was a brother of Timothy ; cf. *GGA*, 1882, S. 300.   In 356 A.D. the emperor Constantine had what were supposed to be the bones of Timothy brought from Ephesus to Constantinople, and deposited in the Church of the Apostles (Jerome, *Chron.*, ed. Schoene, ii. 195).   Nevertheless Ephesus continued to be known as the city of John and of Timothy (Acts of the "Robber Synod" of 449 A.D., ed. Hoffmann, p. 81. 45).

7. (P. 35.)   The Alexander in i. 20 may be identical with the one in 2 Tim. iv. 14, and hence to be found in Troas (above, p. 16 f.), in which case Hymenæus also must be somewhere in Asia at least (i. 20, cf. 2 Tim. ii. 17) ; but it does not follow from this that Paul had been lately in Troas, or indeed in Asia at all, for Paul could carry out the παραδιδόναι τῷ σατανᾷ even when absent in the body (1 Cor. v. 3–5).   We should need to assume, however, that Paul, if it was on the basis of reports that he had passed such a sentence, communicated the same in writing to the persons concerned or to the Church to which they belonged.   This, then, must have been the cause of Alexander's hostility to him when they met later in Troas (2 Tim. iv. 14 ; above, p. 21, n. 3).   In any case the association of the names Alexander and Hymenæus, which is lacking in 2 Tim. iv. 14 and is replaced by another combination in 2 Tim. ii. 17, is unfavourable to the supposition that one of the letters was forged in imitation of the other, or that both were written by the same pseudo-Paul.   One of the marks of individuality, which are not borrowed from the earlier letters of Paul at any rate, is found in v. 23. General truths, such as are elsewhere to be found (Rom. xiii. 14, xiv. 21 ; Eph. v. 18), could have suggested sentences like those in iii. 8, iv. 4, 8, but not this medical advice.   Paul may have obtained this from Luke, who in that case would agree with another physician of his time, Dioscorides (*de Mat. Med.* v. 11), as to the usefulness of wine, especially for the stomach.   The lack of personal greetings, in which respect this letter is like those directed to the Churches of Achaia (2 Cor. xiii. 12) and of Asia (Eph. vi. 23), may perhaps be explained on the ground that Paul presupposes that Timothy will communicate the contents of this letter to all the Churches under his charge. He had difficulties to contend with, his authority needed strengthening (iv. 12) ; so, when occasion required, he could exhibit this letter and read it publicly.   Indeed, discussions such as those in ii. 1–iii. 13 are put in such objective form that they seem originally intended for wide circulation.   The closing greeting, vi. 21, would point to the same thing were the reading ἡ χάρις μεθ' ὑμῶν to be retained.   Yet not only is μετὰ σοῦ likewise excellently attested, but even the texts without any benediction are worthy of attention in spite of the slight external evidence in their favour.   Still more suspicious is the close of 2 Tim. (iv. 22), where after πνεύματός σου we find the following variants : (1) nothing at all (?) ; (2) ἡ χ. μεθ' ὑμῶν ; (3) ἡ χ. μεθ' ἡμῶν ; (4) ἡ χ. μετὰ σοῦ ; (5) ἔρρωσο ἐν εἰρήνῃ.

8. (P. 36.)   Wieseler especially, *Chron.* 311 ff., sought to establish this hypothesis, following similar discussions by Mosheim and Schrader (Wieseler, 295 ff.).

.§ 35. THE FACTS PRESUPPOSED IN THE EPISTLE TO TITUS.

From the first sentence which follows the elaborate and solemn greeting of the letter, " For this cause left I thee in Crete, that thou shouldest set in order the things that were wanting, and appoint elders in every city, as I gave thee charge," we infer, first, that not long previous to this Paul and Titus had been together on the island ; secondly, that Paul had not been able at that time to effect such organisation of the Church as he had had in mind, the establishment of which was the chief purpose for which he had instructed Titus to remain there,—a task to which Titus was to devote himself for a considerable time (iii. 12). Whether Paul himself actually began the correction of the condition indicated by τὰ λείποντα, we do not know. At any rate, he here speaks of the appointment of elders in such a way as to imply that when he left Crete the Christians there were quite without Church organisation. The very resemblance between what follows (i. 6–9) concerning the qualifications for the office of headship in the Church, and similar instructions in 1 Tim., only serves to emphasise the different circumstances presupposed in the two cases. Nothing is here said of elders already appointed (1 Tim. v. 17–21), of a house of God over which the representative of the apostle is to exercise oversight (1 Tim. iii. 15), nor of Cretan Churches (cf. 1 Cor. xvi. 19) ; mention is made only of persons who had believed (iii. 8, 14, οἱ ἡμέτεροι ; cf. Iren. v. 28. 4). Now, when we remember that in Thessalonica there were constituted officers of the Church (1 Thess. v. 12) after only three weeks of preaching (vol. i. 212, n. 5), and recall how promptly in other places the pioneer missionary preaching was followed by the appointment of elders (Acts xiv. 23), it is clear that Paul's stay in Crete must have been very short, so that he had probably just been able to proclaim the gospel for the first time in some of the cities, leaving Titus to organise the Christians in these places into Churches.

If it had been Titus who some time prior to Paul's coming had brought the gospel to Crete, and if it had been to Titus' work that the Christians in Crete owed their conversion, we should expect that to be referred to rather than Paul's own missionary preaching. We consequently infer that when Paul and Titus came to the island there were already Christians there, who may have received their faith through Christians who had come thither from Corinth or Athens. Since Paul himself was hindered by duties elsewhere from remaining for any length of time, he commissioned Titus in his stead to organise thoroughly the yet unarranged affairs of the Christians in Crete. It is taken for granted that, either because of its geographical position or the source from which Christianity was received, Paul reckoned Crete within his apostolic jurisdiction, although politically Crete was connected with Cyrene, not with Achaia. So he had done with the Churches of inland Asia, which, without personal co-operation on his part, had been organised through influences emanating from Ephesus (vol. i. 449, n. 3). Paul had been long enough in Crete to form a definite conception of local conditions, and of the special dangers which threatened to hinder the vigorous development of Church life there. Tit. i. 10–16 does not read like an echo of reports which Titus had sent to Paul, but like instructions to Titus based upon personal observa-tion. Paul states his own impressions by quoting a verse from the Cretan poet Epimenides, in which the Cretan character is unfavourably judged, and expressly affirms that Epimenides' testimony is true (n. 1). Here, as in Ephesus (above, p. 31 f.), he considers the chief hindrance to the vigorous growth and good order of the life of the Church to be certain persons who persist in teaching doctrine which is unprofitable, unsound, and positively harmful.   The worst of these persons he represents to be those of Jewish origin (i. 10 f., 14–16, iii. 9, n. 1). They resist sound doctrine (i. 9), are especially unruly (i. 10, 16), and by their teaching and disputation disturb the Christian households (i. 11, iii. 9).   Some of them persist in maintaining their own views even to the point of creating schisms in the Church (iii. 10, cf. 1 Cor. xi. 19 ; vol. i. 284 f.).   Those who go as far as this, Titus, after repeated warnings, is to leave to themselves and to the judgment of their own conscience ; to the others he is to set forth strongly and sharply the wrongfulness of their action, and to silence them (i. 11, 13, ii. 15).   The manner in which Paul speaks of these persons is very severe, and shows that he is greatly exasperated by them. From the character of the greeting which, at the close, iii. 15, he asks Titus to convey—"Salute them that love us in faith (or in faithfulness)"—it is to be inferred that Paul himself had met with opposition among the Cretan Christians, and that by no means all of them had given him a kindly reception, or recognised his apostolic rights (cf. 3 John 9–10, 15).   The fact that he here writes ἡμᾶς, thereby including Titus with himself, is fully explained by the assumption that Paul had not been in Crete except in company with Titus, who therefore had shared the vicissitudes of Paul's reception.   The expression is even more natural if Titus continued to encounter the hostility of certain Christians after the apostle's departure.   We are led to the same conclusion by ii. 8, where, reversing the order, Paul includes himself with Titus.   Here Titus is represented as a teacher both of the younger and older members of the Church.   In this capacity he is to be himself an example of good conduct ; in fulfilling his office he is to be incorruptible and dignified, and what he teaches is to be above all criticism.   To this description of Titus' chief work is added the remark, "That he

that is of the contrary part may be ashamed, having no
evil thing to say of us."   Now, since non-Christians would
have only the rarest opportunity to hear Titus' preaching,
it is manifest that no reference is here had to the opinions
of those outside the Christian circle, unlike ii. 5, 10,
where the language is very different, and where reference
is had to conduct that could be observed.   Rather must
these persons be the obstinate teachers (i. 9), who have
no love for Paul and Titus (iii. 15), whose method of
teaching, mercenary, unsound, and condemned as it is by
their own consciences (i. 11, 13, 15, iii. 11), is quite the
opposite of that enjoined upon Titus.   These teachers
were inclined to speak evil of Paul and Titus, and actually indulged in such talk.   It is mainly because of this
attitude of theirs toward Titus that Paul adds to his
injunction that Titus speak, exhort, and reprove with all
authority, the remark, "Let no man despise thee," *i.e.*
assume a contemptuous attitude toward him, as if he had
said nothing, and had administered no reproof (ii. 15).

The letter presupposes that the apostle had before him
a written communication from Titus, in which the latter
had informed him of the difficulties with which he had to
contend in carrying out the instructions which had been
given him, expressing at least doubt as to the possibility
of carrying out the most important of them.   Only on the
assumption that Paul is writing in reply to expressions
of this kind on Titus' part can the strongly emphasised
τούτου χάριν, with which he begins, be explained (i. 5).
This, and this primarily, was the purpose for which Paul
had left Titus there.   He is consequently not fulfilling
his obligation if he is merely endeavouring to help the
Christians there in his capacity as a teacher, and fails at
the same time, on account of existing difficulties, to do
anything appreciable in the way of organising the
Churches.   Just as definite a contrast is presupposed by
the ἐγώ in the relative sentence, as by the τούτου χάριν,

otherwise it is quite without point (cf. vol. i. 526, in connection with Phil. i. 3 ; cf. also similar sentences elsewhere without ἐγώ, 1 Tim. i. 3 ; 1 Thess. iv. 11 ; 1 Cor. xvi. 1, xi. 2, vii. 17). In opposition to what is said by those persons who create difficulties for Titus, either by denying his commission and capacity for organising the Church, or by giving him advice concerning the same contrary to instructions left him by the apostle, Paul lays emphasis upon the fact that *he, the apostle*, has given Titus instructions with reference to this matter which Titus is to carry out. The attentive reader observes a connection between this ἐγώ and the equally significant ἐγώ in i. 3. It is this contrast, just coming to light in i. 5, and expressed in various ways throughout the letter, which explains why in the greeting of this letter Paul speaks of his calling with a detail and an emphasis not observable in 1 Tim. i. 1 ; 2 Tim. i. 1, and comparable only to Rom. i. 1–7. To be sure, he is no lord over other Christians and their faith (2 Cor. i. 24), but, like all Christians, a servant of God (cf. Rom. i. 1 ; vol. i. 352); indeed, without the faith which all the elect of God have (i. 1), and the faith which he has in common with Titus (i. 4), he would be nothing. But at the same time he is an apostle of Jesus Christ (i. 1), and so personally and in special measure, by divine commission, he is entrusted with the preaching of that eternal life which has been promised of old, but has now become manifest through the word of the gospel (i. 2 f.). The same is to be said with reference to the commission given to Titus by Paul, and is to be borne in mind by the Christians among whom Titus is to carry out this commission.

The letter is concluded by a benediction upon all the Christians in Titus' vicinity, which benediction is preceded by a personal greeting to Paul's friends in Crete, the expectation being disclosed much more clearly than in either 1 Tim. or 2 Tim. (above, p. 42, n. 7 end) that Titus will communicate the contents of the letter to the Christians there.

Titus' position (n. 2) is practically the same as that of Timothy in Ephesus, with the difference already noted, that the problem in Crete was the primary organisation of the Church, whereas in Asia a group of Churches that had been already organised was placed under Timothy's care, and only in exceptional cases, such as the organisation of a new Church, was he called upon to appoint officers (above, p. 34). This difference explains why Titus' office was even more temporary than Timothy's. Titus had gone to Crete with Paul only a short time before, and he is to leave again, without any promise on Paul's part to come back, and without the appointment of his successor. Paul does intend, however, to send to Crete a certain Artemas, of whom we have no other mention, or Tychicus, mentioned so often as the companion and messenger of Paul (Acts xx. 4 ; Eph. vi. 21 ; Col. iv. 7 ; 2 Tim. iv. 12). As soon as one or the other of these men arrives Titus is to hasten at once to Paul, going to Nicopolis, where Paul plans to spend the winter (iii. 12, n. 3). This is the apostle's intention. At the same time, from the fact that he does not set a definite date when Titus is to arrive in Nicopolis, apparently intending to summon him through Artemas or Tychicus when he is ready, we infer that at the time of his writing Paul did not know just when he himself would reach Nicopolis.

Possibly he intended to utilise the time of his sojourn there in extending his work, in verification of certain earlier statements of his about the extension of his missionary work in this direction (Rom. xv. 19 ; vol. i. 415 f.). It is also natural to suppose that the journey of Titus to Dalmatia (2 Tim. iv. 10) was made soon after a sojourn of Paul and Titus in the neighbouring province of Epirus. Still, all that can positively be inferred from Tit. iii. 12 is that Paul intended to remain in

Nicopolis until the end of winter, and at the opening of navigation in March following to set out at once from this point upon a sea journey (cf. 1 Cor. xvi. 6). The choice of Nicopolis as a point of departure shows that this journey was to be in a westward direction, and that its ultimate destination was Italy. In regard to a certain Zenas, a lawyer, and Apollos, who is so well known as to need no further designation, Paul makes request that Titus, with the help of the Cretan Christians, furnish all they need for a journey and set them on their way (iii. 13 f., n. 4). If Paul had meant, as Chrysostom thought he did (xi. 729), that Titus was to send these men to him, he would certainly have said so. That they were with Titus prior to the arrival of this letter is unlikely, because in outlining Titus' duties the presence of so distinguished a teacher as Apollos could not have been so entirely overlooked had he been on the island with Titus at the time. Nor is it clear why Paul should have requested the Christians in Crete to set Zenas and Apollos on their way, if they neither came from him nor were going to him, or to a place he had designated. In the last case the place would be named. Whence they came and their destination Titus would learn from the men themselves; all that we know is that they did not arrive after the letter reached its destination. The only natural assumption is the one pointed out by Theodorus (ii. 256), namely, that Zenas and Apollos were the bearers of the letter, and that the first stage of their journey took them from the place where Paul was to Crete, whence, replenished and set forward by Titus, they were to continue their journey to some destination unknown to us.

From what is here said of Apollos, we infer that Paul already knew him personally, an acquaintanceship formed during the latter part of the apostle's three years' work in Ephesus. To the earlier part of this period belongs the Corinthian work of Apollos, whom

Paul had not then come to know (Acts xviii. 24–xix. 1)
In the spring of 57 Apollos was in Ephesus with Paul,
and had been there for some time, being for the present unwilling to leave (1 Cor. xvi. 12). A journey of
Apollos to Corinth is here certainly spoken of; and it is
possible that some weeks after 1 Cor. was written, about
the time that Paul left Ephesus to go to Macedonia (Acts
xx. 1; 2 Cor. i. 8, ii. 12 f.), Apollos also left and set out
upon a journey to Corinth, which could have been made
by way of Crete. In this case, however, Paul must have
written Titus during the months that he was in Macedonia. But this is clearly impossible, since at this time
Paul was planning to spend the winter, not in Nicopolis,
but in Corinth (1 Cor. xvi. 6), and in the following spring
it was his purpose to journey, not from Nicopolis westward, but from Corinth to Jerusalem. Both projects were
carried out practically as he had planned. Furthermore,
during the period following the composition of 1 Cor.,
Titus was not in Crete, but in accordance with Paul's
instructions journeyed from Ephesus to Corinth, whence
he went to meet Paul who was journeying slowly by way
of Troas through Macedonia on his way to Corinth, joining him in Macedonia (2 Cor. ii. 12 f., vii. 5–16; vol. i.
326 f.). Nor is there any more opportunity for the residence of Paul in Crete, presupposed in Tit. i. 3, during
the months immediately following the events described in
1 Cor. xvi. 1–9, than there is for the activity of Titus
there, which followed Paul's sojourn. Neither can room
be made for the Cretan sojourn in the three months spent
in Greece after Paul's departure from Ephesus (Acts
xx. 3); for these were the closing months of the winter,
the end of which he intended to await in Corinth (1 Cor.
xvi. 6). In these circumstances he could not have written
Titus that he intended to spend the winter in Nicopolis;
and although, as we learn from Rom. xv. 25–32, his mind
was turning toward the West at that time, he did not

plan to journey directly thither with the coming of spring, but held to his original purpose of first visiting Jerusalem. From Acts xx. 3–xxi. 17 we know that this plan was actually carried out. In order, therefore, to find a place in Paul's career for Titus, and the facts upon which it is based prior to his long imprisonment, one must go back beyond the middle of the period of work in Ephesus, and assume that Paul stopped in Crete on the occasion of his flying journey from Ephesus to Corinth, about which Acts is silent, left Titus there, and wrote Titus some time after his return to Ephesus. If in addition to the assumption that Paul made this journey, which Acts does not mention, by way of Macedonia, — an assumption made in the supposed interest of 1 Tim. (above, p. 35 f.),—it be assumed that the apostle also touched in Crete, the journey becomes such an important part of the apostle's life-history that the silence of Acts is almost unintelligible. Furthermore, it leaves quite unexplained Paul's intention to spend the ensuing winter in Nicopolis ; for at that time the important work in Ephesus, covering as it did the whole province of Asia,—a work which, when 1 Cor. xvi. 8–11 was written, was nowhere near completion,—could have been scarcely more than begun. But it is altogether unlikely that long before actually leaving Ephesus Paul should have formed the definite plan of spending a winter or part of a winter in Nicopolis, making his way thence farther westward. On the other hand, it is very improbable that the plans of which his mind was so full at the time of his correspondence with the Corinthians, and which were carried out at the beginning of 58, should have suddenly displaced the entirely different plans of which we learn in Titus. The collection, with which the journey to Jerusalem was intimately connected, was a matter of long standing, having been carried on for a considerable period before Paul left Ephesus (2 Cor. viii. 10, ix. 2 ; vol. i. 318 f.). Finally, it is to be

noticed that the resemblance between 1 Tim. and Titus is so
great that they must be classed together, both as regards
language and thought, just as Ephesians and Colossians.
If Paul wrote them at all, he must have written them
within a short time of each other. The proof that Paul
could not have written 1 Tim. until after he was liberated
from his first Roman imprisonment (above, p. 35 f.) is
valid also for Titus, and *vice versa*. If the latter was
written in the interval between the first and second
Roman imprisonments, then his short residence in Crete
belongs in the same interval. On the journey from
Cæsarea to Rome, Paul did not touch at Crete (Acts xxvii.
7–15), and Titus was not with him at that time (Acts
xxvii. 2). Furthermore, the manner in which Paul speaks
in Tit. i. 3 of his residence in Crete and of Titus' commission, precludes the possibility of the intervention of the
two years spent in Rome, and of several months preceding
and following these two years, between the sojourn of Paul
and Titus in Crete and this Epistle.

The letter gives us, therefore, two more stations of
that journey in the eastern part of the empire which Paul
made in the interval between Philippians and 2 Tim.,
namely, Crete and, at least prospectively, Nicopolis.

1. (P. 44.)   Concerning Jews in Crete, cf. 1 Macc. xv. 23 (Gortyna);
Acts ii. 11; Philo, *Leg. ad Cai.* xxxvi.; Jos. *Ant.* xvii. 12. 1; *Bell.* ii. 7. 1; *Vita,*
76 (his last wife an " aristocratic " Jewess from Crete); Socr. *H. E.* vii. 38
(concerning a pseudo-Moses, who led the Jews astray, καθ' ἑκάστην τῆς νήσου
πόλιν). Moreover, the legend that the Jews came originally from Crete, and
that their name is derived from Mount Ida there (Tac. *Hist.* v. 2), would
hardly have arisen if there had not been a considerable number of Jews on
the island. Homer, *Iliad*, ii. 649, followed by many poets, calls Crete ἑκατόμ-
πολις ; and even though perhaps it may have become comparatively depopu-
lated since the Roman occupation, its cities were not few (Strabo, p. 476 ;
Ptol. iii. 17). In the second century we hear of bishops in Gortyna and in
Knossus (Eus. *H. E.* iv. 23. 5, 7).   According to Jerome (vii. 706, cf. Socr.
H. E. iii. 16), the verse quoted in Tit. i. 12 is to be found in a book entitled
Περὶ Χρησμῶν, by Epimenides, a contemporary of Solon.   In calling this poet,
then, a prophet of the Cretans, Paul shows a knowledge of the tradition con-
cerning him (Plato, *Leg.* p. 642 ; Plut. *Solon,* xii. ; Diog. Laert. i. 10. 109–115).
Theodoret thought mistakenly that Paul was citing from Callimachus, who

was a native of Cyrene, not Crete, and who in his "Hymn to Zeus," ver. 8, appropriated only the first half of Epimenides' hexameter, namely, the charge of untruthfulness, a trait of the Cretans which had become proverbial (cf. Wettstein's *Sammlungen, ad loc.*). Theodoret was misled by Chrysostom, who, while he names the right author Epimenides, quotes the words which in Callimachus follow ψεῦσται, ver. 8 f., as if they came from Epimenides (xi. 744). Theodore is the first Father from whom we are able to ascertain clearly what is only hinted at in Chrysostom and Jerome, namely, that the heathen opponents of Christianity (Porphyry? Julian?) inferred from this passage that Paul agreed with the poet in his defence of the eternal deity of Zeus against the lies of the Cretans, who thought that Zeus' grave was on their island. Consequently these heathen writers, too, must have been thinking not of Epimenides, but of Callimachus, who did actually appropriate part of the older poet's verse with this very end in view. And some of the Christian apologists and commentators have followed them.

2. (P. 48.) Titus is called bishop of Crete by Eus. *H. E.* iii. 4. 6; Ambrosiaster, p. 313, in his Prologue; *Const. ap.* vii. 46. More guarded and more nearly correct are Ephrem, 269; Theodorus, ii. 233, cf. p. 122; Theodoret, 698. With regard to mistaken identifications of Titus with Titius Justus and with Silvanus, see vol. i. 208, 266. Beside the statements in Gal. ii. 1–3; 2 Cor. ii. 13, vii. 6–14, viii. 6, 16, 23, xii. 18; 2 Tim. iv. 10, we have no reliable testimony concerning Titus, except perhaps the assertion of *Acta Theclæ*, cc. ii. iii., that he was staying with Onesiphorus in Iconium when Paul came thither for the first time. Possibly the Zeno mentioned there and called the son of Onesiphorus may be the Zenas of Tit. iii. 13. Concerning later fabulous tales, which are referred to a *Vita Titi* written by Zenas, cf. Lipsius, *Apokr. Apostelgesch.* ii. part 2, 401 ff.; also the passages of the *Vita Titi* published by M. R. James in *JThS.* vi. 549 ff. (July 1905) are without historical value.

3. (P. 48.) Of the numerous cities which were named Nicopolis in commemoration of a victory, some must be excluded in a consideration of Tit. iii. 12 on account of their location, some on account of their late origin. (1) The Nicopolis in Armenia (Strabo, 555; Ptolem. viii. 17. 40) is ruled out on this ground, as also (2) the one in Egypt, near Alexandria (Jos. *Bell.* iv. 11. 5); (3) Emmaus in Palestine, not called Nicopolis until the third century; (4) the one founded by Trajan on the Danube, which still retains the name; and (5) another in the Hæmus (Ptolem. iii. 11. 11, cf. Forbiger, iii. 750, A. 66, S. 753; Mommsen, *Röm. Gesch.* v. 282, who, however, identifies No. 4 with No. 5; *C. I. L.* iii. p. 141). (6) Likewise the Nicopolis on the Nestus (Ptolem. iii. 11. 13) which was founded by Trajan (Forbiger, Pauly, *RE*, v. 637, under No. 2; Mommsen, *op. cit.* 281). This must have been the city meant by those writers who remarked, in commenting on Tit. iii. 12, that it lay in Thrace (Cramer, *Cat.* vii. 99). (7) A city of this name in Bithynia (Plin. *H. N.* v. 32. 150; Steph. Byz. *sub verbo*) offers no point of connection for any probable conjectures. (8) Similarly, the Nicopolis in the north-east corner of Cilicia (Strabo, 675; Ptolem. v. 8. 7) is not to be thought of; for no reason can be conceived which could have induced Paul to spend the winter in this out of the way mountain town rather than in a large community like Antioch; or, if rest were his aim, in his native city, Tarsus, or in some place from which he would have

abundant opportunities to continue his journey in the spring. The only one remaining is (9) the Nicopolis founded by Augustus at the outlet of the Ambracian Gulf as a memorial of the victory at Actium, by far the most important and famous city of this name, and a generation later the chief scene of Epictetus' labours as a teacher. Tacitus, *Ann.* ii. 53 (for the year 18), calls it *urbem Achaiæ*; on the contrary, Epictetus, *Diss.* iii. 4. 1, speaks of an ἐπίτροπος Ἠπείρου residing in Nicopolis and governing the land from thence ; cf. *C. I. G.* No. 1813*b* (add. p. 983) ; *C. I. L.* iii. No. 536 (?) ; about the year 150, Ptolemy, iii. 14. 1, 15. 1, distinguishes Epirus, in which Nicopolis is situated (xiv. 5), from Achaia as a separate province. Our information as to these changing conditions is not very clear (Mommsen, *op. cit.* 234; Marquardt[2], i. 331). Jerome (Vall. vii. 686, 738) considered it self-evident that this Nicopolis was meant ; and even those who called it *Nicopolis Macedoniæ* (see Tischendorf's apparatus on the subscription) could hardly have had another in mind ; for no other of the cities mentioned above was in Macedonia proper, not even No. 6. Jerome, 686, assumed mistakenly, with many Greeks and Syrians, that the letter was written from Nicopolis. Wieseler, *Chron.* 353, sought to prove, on the ground that Nicopolis belonged to Achaia, that Tit. iii. 12 is simply a more definite statement of the purpose expressed in 1 Cor. xvi. 6. But this is impossible, since 1 Cor. is addressed solely to the local Church at Corinth, and not, like 2 Cor., to all the Christians of Achaia. And even in 2 Cor. πρὸς ὑμᾶς would mean "to" or "in Corinth."

4. (P. 49.) In itself, νομικός, iii. 13, cf. Luke vii. 30, x. 25 = νομοδιδάσκαλος, Luke v. 17 ; Acts v. 34 = γραμματεύς, Luke v. 21, vi. 7 ; 1 Cor. i. 20, could denote a rabbi (cf. Ambrosiaster, p. 317, "quia Zenas hujus professionis fuerat in synagoga, sic illum appellat "). But since the Jewish scribe who became a Christian by that very act separated himself from the rabbinic body, and since the retention of rabbinic methods and ways of thinking was anything but a recommendation in Paul's eyes (1 Tim. i. 7), Zenas is here characterised not as *legis* (*Mosaicæ*) *doctor*, but as *juris peritus.* The word denotes not an office, but usually the practical lawyer, through whose assistance, *e.g.* a will is made (Epict. *Diss.* ii. 13. 6–8 ; *Berl. äg. Urk.* No. 326, νομικὸς Ῥωμαϊκός, No. 361, col. iii. 2, 15), or a lawsuit carried on (Artemid. *Oneirocr.* iv. 80, cf. iv. 33, νομικοὶ νομικὰ ἢ ἰατροὶ ἰατρικὰ . . . λέγουσιν). Plutarch (*Sulla,* 36) applies this name to the renowned jurist Mucius Scaevola. προπέμπειν means here, as elsewhere in the N.T., to speed the departing traveller on his way, whether he is just setting forth on his journey or is passing through the place. Occasionally this consisted simply in accompanying him a short distance (Acts xx. 38, xxi. 5) ; as a rule, however, and here also, if we may judge from what follows, it includes equipping him with all things needful for the journey, cf. 3 John 6 (Rom. xv. 24 ; 1 Cor. xvi. 6, 11), and is almost synonymous with ἐφοδιάζειν, Jos. *Bell.* ii. 7. 1 ; *Ant.* xx. 2. 5. For an illustration, cf. *Acta Petri cum Simone,* ed. Lipsius, 48. 1–18.

§ 36. THE END OF PAUL'S LIFE.

If we were certain that Paul was put to death at the end of the Roman imprisonment in which we find him

when he wrote Ephesians, Colossians, Philemon, and Philippians, it would be necessary to reject as forgeries the three
letters which have been inappropriately called the Pastoral
Epistles (n. 1).   This belief, which has long been one of
the principal grounds of objection to the genuineness of
these Epistles, and which has been a source of insufferable
violence done to the Epistles by those defending their
genuineness, either wholly or in part, does not rest upon
the foundation even of ancient, to say nothing of trustworthy tradition.   It is simply an hypothesis, which has
strong historical evidence against it, and nothing in its
favour (n. 2).   An expectation of early release so definite
as that expressed by Paul in Phil. i. 19, 25, ii. 24, is not
likely to have failed of fulfilment, since this expectation
is based not upon desires, conjectures, and inferences,
which, judging from Acts xxv. 18, 25, xxvi. 31 f., xxviii.
15, 18, pointed in that direction from the first (cf. Philem.
22), but primarily upon the actual course of the trial,
which after protracted delay had been actually begun.
Moreover, it was not Paul's personal opinion alone, but
the judgment of all who followed the course of his trial,
even of non-Christians, that it would shortly terminate
in his release (vol. i. 540 ff.).   For this reason we are
not justified in comparing the repeated οἶδα of Philippians
with the οἶδα which Paul used at Miletus shortly before he
was arrested in Jerusalem (Acts xx. 25, 38) to declare his
expectation that the elders and the Church in Ephesus
would see his face no more (n. 3).   It is to be observed,
first of all, that we do not have here, as in Phil. i. 19, 25,
ii. 24, Paul's own language, but at most only a saying of
the apostle's as Luke, his companion, remembered it.
But, leaving that out of account, the later "I know," in
which is expressed the hope of reunion with the Philippian Christians and the Christians in the East generally,
would quite annul the "I know" spoken five years before,
when reunion with the Christians in Ephesus seemed quite

impossible.   Then it must be remembered that in the
prophetic utterances on the basis of which Paul made this
statement, — being careful to note that it is only his
personal conviction (xx. 25),—nothing is said of his death,
but only of chains and persecution (Acts xx. 23, xxi. 11),
and that Paul simply explains that he is ready, if necessary, even to die in Jerusalem, expressly stating, however,
that he *does not know* what awaits him there (Acts xx.
22, 24, xxi. 13, cf. Rom. xv. 31).   The expression of
this indefinite feeling of Paul's, accompanied by the
acknowledgment that all is uncertainty, that possibly his
life might end where on three different occasions later it
was actually threatened (xxi. 31, xxiii. 12–15, xxv. 3),
refers only to Jerusalem and Palestine.   According to
Acts, he was desirous of seeing Rome, and it did become
later the scene of the labours for which he was rescued
from all dangers (xix. 21, xxiii. 11, xxv. 10–12, xxvii.
24, xxviii. 5, 15, 30, 31); so that, in view of the connection in Acts, it is hardly likely that the author intended
the passage in the 20th chapter of Acts (xx. 25) to be a
prophecy of Paul's martyrdom in Rome.   By a more
careful consideration of the text, the meaning of the expression seems to be only that the personal intercourse,
often broken off, but always taken up again, which had
existed between Paul and the Eastern Churches up to the
present time had at last reached its end, since Paul, in
case he should not lose his life in Jerusalem, purposed
now to go to the West.   But even assuming that when
he left Miletus Paul was confident that he would never see
the elders of Ephesus again, this is no reason for assuming
that he never did.   Paul never claimed to be able to predict the future, and insisted particularly that statements
of his with reference to his future plans should not be
considered irrevocable (2 Cor. i. 15–17 ; vol. i. 344, n. 2).

It is, of course, possible that Paul was deceived in his
expectation of an early release, so confidently expressed

in Philippians; but this is not at all likely, because of the
facts upon which this expectation was based.   Events entirely unforeseen must suddenly have given an unfavourable turn to the trial, which, when Philippians was written,
was as good as ended.   The Sanhedrin in Jerusalem, which
for nearly three years (from the hearing before Festus in
the latter part of the summer of 60 A.D. to the writing
of Philippians, which did not take place until after the
spring of 63) had made no effort to renew the charges
against Paul before the imperial court (n. 4), are not
likely to have done so after so long an interval, particularly since under Albinus (62–64), Festus' successor
in the procuratorship, there were things enough in Jerusalem to keep them occupied (cf. Schürer, i. 583 [Eng.
trans. I. ii. 188]).   Moreover, after their experiences in
Palestine (Acts xxiv.–xxvi.), the Sanhedrin could have
entertained very little hope of accomplishing anything
against Paul in Rome.   The assumption that before the
trial was entirely ended, the favourable outcome of which
in the near future Paul expected when he was writing
Philippians, the persecution of the Roman Christians
under Nero broke out, and that Paul was one of the
victims of the same, is improbable on chronological
grounds.   If Paul reached Rome in March or April of the
year 61 (Part XI. vol. iii.), and if in the spring of the
year 63 the trial began, which, according to Philippians,
gave rise at once to confident expectations of a successful
outcome, it is impossible to understand what could have
protracted it until the summer, or rather the autumn, of
the following year 64.   Such, however, must have been
the case if Paul was one of those Christians who, according
to Tacitus' account (*Ann.* xv. 44), were executed for the
burning of Rome, since Nero did not accuse the Christians
until he had availed himself of every other means of avert-
ing from himself the suspicion of having burned the city.
This accusation was probably not made before October 64

(n. 5). It is thus easily understood why those who feel that Paul's execution must be associated with the whole-sale execution of Christians which took place in the latter part of the summer or in the autumn of the year 64, are inclined to date Paul's arrival in Rome in the spring of 62, and the composition of Philippians at the beginning of the summer of 64 (see *per contra*, Part XI. vol. iii.).

But the particular presupposition which is the main reason for a change of date, namely, that Paul was exe-cuted shortly after the writing of Philippians, and that he was one of a number of Christians to suffer martyrdom, and hence must have been put to death in the year 64, gets no certain support in ancient tradition. The only thing that can be directly inferred from Acts xxviii. 30 f. is that the author knew what it was that terminated the situa-tion which is there briefly described, and which he says lasted for two whole years. Why does he fail to state what this was? Whether we assume that Acts xxviii. 30 f. is the conclusion of the work as Luke planned it, or whether he intended to complete the work in a third book, in either case—in the former case even more than in the latter—his silence about the event marking the close of the two years is inexplicable, if the trial which ended with the apostle's execution occurred at this time. Neither the book nor the whole work could have had a more fitting close than the account of the martyrdom of the apostle upon whose history the attention of the reader has been kept constantly fixed from the thirteenth chapter ; and certainly a writer who was able in three lines to convey to the reader an idea of the great work which Paul did during two years in the capital of the empire, was able just as briefly and just as skilfully to tell of the glorious ending of this work, and of the apostle's career. The author could not leave the reader to guess this end, because after all the deliverances and consolations through which Paul had been brought to Rome (Acts xxi. 31–35,

xxiii.10–30, xxv. 3, xxvii. 24, 42–44, xxviii. 5, 15), and after
the opinions expressed by the highest officials concerning
the charges made by the Jews (Acts xxv. 2–8, 18–20, 26 f.,
xxvi. 31 f., xxviii. 18), the death-sentence of Paul would
be the last thing that the reader would expect.   The only
plausible inference to be drawn from the sudden breaking
off of the narrative in Acts xxviii. 30 f. is that these two
years were followed by another period in Paul's life history and missionary work of such considerable length
that it could not be treated in Luke's second book without
making this disproportionately long compared with the
first.

Now, even assuming that the Epistles to Timothy and
Titus are spurious, they furnish important evidence that
Paul's life continued beyond the two years in Rome and
beyond the time when Philippians was written; for, as has
been shown, they presuppose that after his acquittal by the
imperial court at Rome, and after his liberation from his
imprisonment in Rome, which had lasted until then, Paul
visited his eastern Churches in Macedonia and Crete,
Miletus and Troas, probably also in Corinth and Ephesus;
and, on the other hand, engaged in missionary work in
regions lying westward from Rome, probably in Spain.
If all this were told in the letters, or even clearly stated as
information, we might assume that it was forged, either
with a view to enlarging the history of Paul's life or
supplying the Epistles with a historic background.   But,
as a matter of fact, the most of these events and those of
greatest importance are simply taken for granted, as we
should expect them to be in genuine Epistles.   What we
are compelled to infer from incidental hints, and that
rather vaguely, e.g. the fact that he was in prison when
2 Tim. was written, and how he came to be there; the
missionary work carried on after he was set free from his
first imprisonment in regions hitherto unvisited by him;
what took him to Crete; why he planned to go to Nico-

polis,—all this and much more must have been known to the readers, whose knowledge of the situation the author took for granted. If this author were Paul himself, then these letters are standards by which every other account of this period, inside the Canon and out of it, is to be judged, and any additional evidence is superfluous. If the author was a pseudo-Paul belonging to the period between the years 70 and 140,—the latest possible date for the composition of the letters,—the tradition of which he made use must have existed in such clear outlines and have been so generally known, that it required only the slightest reference and the most casual connections to recall to the readers' minds the course of events and induce them to accept this forgery, which was based thus upon recognised historical facts.

Evidence of the existence of such a tradition regarding the closing years of Paul's life, covering the period after the close of Acts, but independent of the Pastoral Epistles, is furnished by the letter sent by the Roman Church to the Church in Corinth of which Clement of Rome is commonly regarded as the author (n. 6). Since Clement's letter was written certainly not later than the year 96, and expressly mentions the apostles Paul and Peter as heroes and sufferers of the then living generation, it is evident that Clement and the Roman Church were not wholly dependent for their knowledge concerning the close of the apostle's life upon written sources, which so far as we know were not yet in existence, but made use of trustworthy oral traditions. An officer in the Roman Church in the year 96, who would certainly have been a man of years, would have been a younger contemporary of Paul's, and could recall the time when the apostle's death took place. It is quite possible, as Irenæus testifies (iii. 3. 3), that Clement had had personal intercourse with Paul and Peter. Certainly he possessed independent information about Paul's history, as is evidenced by his statement

that Paul was bound with chains seven times (n. 6).   His
other somewhat rhetorical statements in praise of the two
apostles seem to take for granted acquaintance with the
events in question on the part even of his younger readers.
However, although not acquainted with the events, we of
to-day may recognise the following points :—(1) Peter and
Paul died in Rome as martyrs.   (2) Paul had preached
the gospel in the most western portion of the then known
world, *i.e.* in Spain.   (3) As regards the order of events,
Peter's martyrdom seems to have preceded that of Paul ;
for, otherwise, the name of Paul would be mentioned first,
since he is praised more at length, and with more high-
sounding phrases, than is Peter, and seems to have been
regarded by the author as the more important personality,
either in general or in this particular regard.   As the text
stands, however, Paul's name is inserted between that of
Peter, of whom Clement says little, and the mention of
a large number of Christian martyrs, men and women,
whose sufferings are summarily referred to, without names
(chap. vi.).   Even if we did not know independently that
Paul had not been in Spain prior to his imprisonment in
Cæsarea and Rome, of which account is given in Acts, so
that this journey, if it took place at all, must have followed
his release from this imprisonment, and his martyrdom, if
suffered in consequence of a judicial sentence, must have
followed a second arrest after the Spanish journey,—in
any case we should infer from the order of Clement's
sentences that Paul's Spanish journey took place at the
very end of his life, and that he was arrested and brought
before the authorities subsequent to the Spanish journey.
Clement's general statement that these events happened
within the memory of the generation living at the time
when the letter was written (96 A.D.), agrees with the other
traditions which place them in the reign of Nero ; and this
agreement is still further confirmed by the fact that from
earliest times the impression could not be avoided that

the sufferings of Christian men and women in Rome, the
story of which Clement relates immediately after the account of the martyrdom of the two apostles, were the same
as those described by Tacitus (*Ann.* xv. 44), and hinted at
by Suetonius (*Nero*, xvi). The most that can be inferred
from Clement's statements is that the martyrdom of Peter
and of Paul, and the persecutions of the year 64, belong
to the same period, and that is all that is affirmed by the
earlier traditions (n. 8). Almost without exception, in
this earlier tradition, the name of Peter precedes that of
Paul, as in Clement, which would indicate that Peter's
death preceded that of Paul; thus contradicting the view
which arose after the middle of the fourth century, that
the two apostles suffered martyrdom on the same day of
the same year, the 29th of June. It can be shown that
this story grew out of a Roman festival commemorative
of the removal of the remains, or what were supposed to
be the remains, of the two apostles to the Appian Way in
the year 258 (n. 9); so that it can be left out of account
in any attempt to determine the real date of the apostles'
death. The only thing which can be definitely concluded
from the establishment of this festival in or near the year
258, is that up to the middle of the third century the
Roman Church had no definite tradition regarding the
exact date of the apostles' martyrdom (n. 8).

On the other hand, the memory of Paul's journey to
Spain lingered long (n. 7). In the Muratorian Canon
Paul's journey to Spain is put on exactly the same footing
as the martyrdom, the circumstance that these two facts
are not mentioned in Acts being adduced as proof that
Luke confined his narrative in Acts to what he himself
had experienced (n. 7). Although the fragmentist may be
dependent, here as elsewhere, upon apocryphal accounts,
he takes for granted that in the year 200 these two facts
were commonly accepted in the circle to which he belonged,
i.e. in the Roman Church, or a Church closely associated

with the same.   The *Acts of Peter*, which were certainly
not written in Rome, and which embody Gnostic tendencies,
are some thirty or forty years older.   According to these
legends, Paul, who had remained until then a prisoner in
Rome, journeyed to Spain to preach the gospel there in
consequence of a vision.   During his absence in Spain,
which did not cover a period of more than a year (ed.
Lipsius, p. 46. 3), Peter came from Jerusalem to Rome,
and after successful contests with Simon Magus was crucified head downwards.   Although in this account Peter's
departure from Jerusalem is set twelve years after the
beginning of the apostolic preaching (p. 49. 22), Nero is
declared to be the emperor in whose reign Peter worked
and died in Rome (pp. 100. 15, 102. 2, 103. 2).   Likewise
the martyrdom of Paul, which took place later than that
of Peter, and which is referred to occasionally in these
legends, is dated still in the reign of Nero (p. 46. 8).
The testimony of the *Acts of Paul*, which show a catholic
tendency, and are evidently of later date than Leucius'
Acts of Peter and *John*, is not so clear, and at this point
the newly found Coptic fragments, which have been
recently published, do not furnish any more light (n. 10).

That as time went on the tradition concerning Paul's
liberation from his first protracted imprisonment, the
resumption of his missionary work, and another arrest
shortly before his execution, should gradually die out, is
not to be wondered at.   There was no connected account
of these events which was regarded as trustworthy.   In
the West, confusion was caused especially by the Roman
legend about the simultaneous martyrdom of Paul and
Peter.   This legend certainly made it difficult to find a
place for so important a period of Paul's career subsequent
to the time when Philippians was written as was required
by the tradition of the first and second centuries.   The
testimony of this earlier tradition is, however, quite
independent of that which we have in the Epistles to

Timothy and Titus.   The latter tell us of extended journeys
which Paul made in the East (Crete, Macedonia, Miletus,
Ephesus (?), Corinth (?), Nicopolis), after he was freed from
his first imprisonment.   There is only one passage which
would indicate any considerable extension of Paul's missionary work at this time, namely, 2 Tim. iv. 17 ; and
from this passage it must be inferred that Paul pressed
westward from Rome in order to do missionary work.
On the other hand, in the tradition traced from Clement
to the Muratorian Canon nothing is said of a tour among
the Churches in the East after Paul was released from his
imprisonment, while the fact that after being set at liberty
Paul preached in Spain—a fact which we learn from 2 Tim.
iv. 16 f. only after careful interpretation and correct inference—is clearly stated.   Taken together, these two entirely
independent witnesses furnish a trustworthy historical
picture.   Such a relation subsisting between documents
which at latest must have been written at the beginning
of the second century, and a tradition first vouched for by
a witness living at the end of the first century, proves that
both rest upon yet older foundations, namely, upon an
account of the close of Paul's life which was circulated
in the decades immediately following his death.   To
suppose that this account was drawn from Rom. xv.
24, 28, rather than from fact, is unreasonable on several
grounds.   (1) No one could help but recognise that the
hopes which Paul there expresses remained in large part
unfulfilled.   At that time Paul hoped in the following
summer to journey from Palestine to Italy, and after a
short stay in Rome to visit Spain.   Instead, he reached
Rome in the spring of the year 61 a prisoner, and remained
there for years ; so that no one would have felt tempted
by Rom. xv. 24, 28 to invent the story of his subsequent
visit to Spain.   Only let it be remarked in passing that if
the chapter in which this passage is found was appended
to Romans in the interval between Paul's death and

the time of Marcion (vol. i. 379 f.), the passage is strong proof that Paul did actually go to Spain. For, while it is perfectly natural for Paul himself to talk of plans and hopes which were never carried out nor realised, it is inconceivable that statements of this kind should be put into his mouth after his life had ended, without his having gone to Spain. (2) There is not the slightest suggestion in Rom. xv. which would occasion the invention of the later journeys in the East presupposed in the "Pastoral Epistles." If these journeys were invented on the strength of Phil. i. 25 f., ii. 24, Philem. 22, we should find mentioned in the "Pastoral Epistles" Philippi and Colossæ, not Crete, Miletus, and Nicopolis. (3) It is inconceivable that Clement and the other younger contemporaries of Paul, especially Romans of their generation, should have formed their conception of the last events in the apostle's life from a very arbitrary interpretation of one or more passages in Paul's Epistles, rather than from their own recollection of the events. In view of all this we are led to conclude that Paul was set at liberty by the imperial court, as he so confidently expected when he wrote Philippians, and not long after this letter was written visited the East again and preached the gospel in Spain, before he was arrested a second time in Rome and put to death. Regarding the order of these events we can do no more than make conjectures. The consideration suggested (vol. i. 547 f.) in favour of the view that Paul visited the Churches in the East in the summer of 63 shortly after he was released, preaching in Spain later, must give way before the stronger reasons which make the reverse order seem probable. The statements of 2 Tim. iv. 13, 20 would seem to be in the highest degree unnatural, if between the events there mentioned, namely, the sojourn of Paul in Miletus (Corinth ?) and Troas and the writing of 2 Tim., there intervened not only the winter in Nicopolis (Tit. iii. 12), a second arrest in Rome, and the journey of Onesiphorus to Rome (2 Tim. i. 16), but also missionary work in Spain, which must have occupied at least several months. Assuming, as we must from Phil. ii. 19–23 (vol. i. 547 f.), that when his trial was completed Paul did not leave Rome at once, but awaited the return of Timothy, whom he did not send to Philippi until his case was decided, at the very earliest he could not have gone to Spain until the autumn of the year 63. Possibly he did not reach his destination until the spring of the year 64. In neither case could the winter which he planned to spend in Nicopolis at the close of his extended journeys in the East (Tit. iii. 12) have been the winter of 63–64, hardly that of 64–65; for in the latter case it would be necessary to compress the missionary work in Spain and the tour of the Eastern Churches all into a single year, from autumn 64 to autumn 65, if indeed it be not necessary to crowd both these extended journeys, which lay in opposite directions and required much time for the fulfilment of their objects, into the summer of 64. If for this reason the winter spent in Nicopolis could not have been prior to 65–66, then the winter 66–67 is the earliest winter at the beginning of which the imprisoned Paul could have hoped to have Timothy with him in Rome (2 Tim. iv. 21). If events happened as Paul expected they would when he wrote his last letter, he was still alive at the beginning of the winter of 66–67, but suffered martyrdom not very long afterward. In accordance with the results of the preceding investigations, the following is suggested as the probable order in which the events following the imprisonment recorded in Acts took place. If Timothy returned to Rome from Philippi in the autumn of 63, Paul set out upon his journey to Spain either immediately or at latest in the spring of 64. If the statement of the *Acts of Peter*, that his work in Spain covered a year, be accepted, he left there at the earliest in the autumn of 64, or possibly in the spring of 65, in order to carry out the other part of his plan—the promised visiting of his Eastern Churches. Whether he stopped in Rome, where in the autumn of 64 the Christians there suffered such severe persecution (above, p. 57 f.), or passed by Rome on his way to the East, going possibly to Apollonia and thence to Philippi by the Via Egnatia, no one knows. Nor can it be determined with any degree of probability in what order he reached the various points visited upon this last journey (Corinth (?), Crete, Macedonia, Troas, Ephesus (?), Miletus).

Since Timothy had been for some time in Ephesus when Paul made this journey in the summer of 65 (above, p. 57 f.), he apparently did not accompany him to Spain, but during this time was engaged in carrying out Paul's commission in Ephesus. The winter of 65–66, or the end of it, Paul and Titus seem to have spent in Nicopolis. When Paul started in the spring of 66 from Nicopolis for Italy, Titus may have set out from the same point on his preaching tour in the neighbouring district of Dalmatia. Paul's second arrest after his return to Rome, the journey of Onesiphorus to Rome, and the writing of 2 Tim., belong in the summer of 66. Paul was beheaded on the Ostian Way not before the end of the year 66, but at the latest before the death of Nero (June 9th, 68).

1. (P. 55.) According to Heydenreich, *Pastoralbr.* i. 7 (*anno* 1826), the name " Pastoral Epistles " has been applied to the letters to Timothy and Titus "from the remotest times." But the present writer cannot find the name in either Bengel, J. D. Michaelis, Semler, Schleiermacher (1807), or Planck (*Bemerkungen über den 1 Tim. gegen Schleiermacher*, 1808) ; on the contrary, it appears first in P. Anton, *Exeget. Abh. der Pastoralbriefe S. Pauli*, 2 Teile, Halle, 1753, 1755, then in Wegscheider, *Der 1 Tim.* 1810, S. vi ; Eichhorn, *Einl.* iii. 315 (1812). In a measure it is appropriate for 1 Tim. and Tit., but not at all for 2 Tim. In the ancient Church, passages like 1 Tim. iii. 1–7 and Tit. i. 5–9 were read on the occasion of the choice and ordination of bishops and elders (*Polycarpi vita*, by Pionius, xxii. ; cf. the Jacobite liturgy in the *Revue de l'Orient chrétien*, i. 2 [1896], p. 10). Bengel, in the *Gnomon*, on 1 Tim. i. 2 still follows the isagogics of the ancient Church (*GK*, ii. 75 ff.), and groups together rather the four letters which Paul addressed to individuals.

2. (P. 55.) In reference to the last events of Paul's life, cf. especially

HOFMANN, *NT*, v. 3–17; SPITTA, *Zur Gesch. u. Liter. des Urchristentums*, i. 1-108 ; STEINMETZ, *Die zweite röm. Gefangenschaft des Ap. Paulus*, 1897 ; also the remarks of RANKE, *Weltgesch.* iii. 1. 191 f. ; ERBES, *Die Todestage der Apostel Paulus und Petrus*, 1899 (*Texte u. Unters.*, N. Folge, iv. 1), treats the Biblical accounts and those of the early Church in a manner so defective, high-handed, and superficial, that the present writer must here forego a refutation of his position.

3. (P. 55.) Acts xx. 25, 38 was turned to account by Baur long ago as an argument against a release from the first Roman imprisonment (*Pastoralbriefe*, 92 ff.). The emphasis here is not upon the contrast between what Paul does not know (xx. 22) and what he really knows, but between the vague suggestions of prophetic utterances (xx. 23) and what Paul himself (ἐγώ must not be overlooked) knows. He knows what his future relation to the Ephesians will be ; he does not know what will befall him in Jerusalem. The former, then, must be independent of the latter, and οὐκέτι ὄψεσθε κτλ. holds good even if he loses neither freedom nor life in Jerusalem. Besides, this phrase does not mean that none of the elders of Ephesus will ever see him again ; Paul makes this statement not of them, but of all the Christians of those regions among whom he had gone about during the last years. Now the prediction that none of these many Christians would ever see him again before his death would certainly not be put in the apostle's mouth *ex eventu* ; for Christians from Asia, *e.g.* Tychicus, Epaphras, and Onesiphorus, did actually see Paul when a prisoner in Rome. Then οὐκέτι has not the same meaning as οὐ πάλιν, but implies that an end has now come to the personal intercourse which Paul has kept up for years, though not uninterruptedly, with the Christians of Ephesus and with the Churches of the province of Asia. At the same time nothing at all is said as to how long a time the negative shall retain its force, and the possibility is in no wise excluded that a time will come again when Paul will resume personal intercourse with the Churches of Asia. Cf. John xvi. 10 and xvi. 19. All that is said is that what has existed so long now terminates. It is a parting for a long time, but not necessarily for ever.

4. (P. 57.) According to Acts xxviii. 21, the Sanhedrin had done nothing to secure the co-operation of the Jews in Rome in its prosecution of Paul up to his arrival in that city. These Jews were ready enough at other times to lend a hand in affairs of this kind, cf. Jos. *Ant.* xvii. 11. 1 ; *Bell.* ii. 6. 1 ; *Vita*, 3 ; Philo, *Leg. ad Cai.* xxiii.

5. (P. 58.) The conflagration began in the night of July 18 - 19, was extinguished six days later (July 24), but then broke out afresh and burned several days longer (Tac. *Ann.* xv. 38–41 ; Suet. *Nero*, xxxviii. ; Eus. *Chron.*, *anno Abr.* 2079, *incendia multa*). Then followed, according to Tacitus' description, several things which must have taken time before the Christians were attacked (Tac. *Ann.* xv. 44), *e.g.* care for the homeless, beginning of the rebuilding, religious expiatory rites (cc. xlii.–xliv. mid-year, cf. chap. xlv. "*interea*," chap. xlvi. "*per idem tempus*," chap. xlvii. "*fine anni*"). All this, however, falls within the year 64.

6. (P. 60.) After recounting a number of Biblical examples of righteous men who had to suffer from the jealousy of the unrighteous, Clement writes, chap. **v. 1** : ἀλλ' ἵνα τῶν ἀρχαίων ὑποδειγμάτων παυσώμεθα, ἔλθωμεν ἐπὶ τοὺς

ἔγγιστα γενομένους ἀθλητάς· λάβωμεν τῆς γενεᾶς ἡμῶν τὰ γενναῖα ὑποδείγματα·
2. διὰ ζῆλον καὶ φθόνον οἱ μέγιστοι καὶ δικαιότατοι στῦλοι ἐδιώχθησαν καὶ ἕως
θανάτου ἤθλησαν. 3. λάβωμεν πρὸ ὀφθαλμῶν ἡμῶν τοὺς ἀγαθοὺς ἀποστόλους.
4. Πέτρον, ὃς διὰ ζῆλον ἄδικον οὐχ ἕνα οὐδὲ δύο ἀλλὰ πλείονας ὑπήνεγκεν
πόνους, καὶ οὕτω μαρτυρήσας ἐπορεύθη εἰς τὸν ὀφειλόμενον τόπον τῆς δόξης.
5. διὰ ζῆλον καὶ ἔριν Παῦλος ὑπομονῆς βραβεῖον ἔδειξεν. 6. ἑπτάκις δεσμὰ
φορέσας, φυγαδευθείς, λιθασθείς, κῆρυξ γενόμενος ἔν τε τῇ ἀνατολῇ καὶ ἐν τῇ
δύσει, τὸ γενναῖον τῆς πίστεως αὐτοῦ κλέος ἔλαβεν. 7. δικαιοσύνην διδάξας
ὅλον τὸν κόσμον καὶ ἐπὶ τὸ τέρμα τῆς δύσεως ἐλθὼν καὶ μαρτυρήσας ἐπὶ τῶν
ἡγουμένων, οὕτως ἀπηλλάγη τοῦ κόσμου · καὶ εἰς τὸν ἅγιον τόπον ἐπορεύθη,
ὑπομονῆς γενόμενος μέγιστος ὑπογραμμός. With regard to this, we may
remark : (1) The text here given, which, aside from slight changes of
punctuation, follows Gebhardt-Harnack (cf. Lightfoot, *Clement*, ii. 25, and
Spitta, *Urchrist.* i. 51, 57), is confirmed in all essentials by the Latin translation since discovered, though it cannot be decided from the *ostendit* of the
Latin translation whether we should read ἔδειξεν (Cod. C), or ὑπέδειξεν, or
possibly ἐπέδειξεν (cf. Clem. Alex. in Cramer's *Cat.* vii. 426, and Euthalius,
ed. Zacagni, 522, ἐπιδείξασθαι, in a similar connection). (2) Since in phrases
like λαμβάνειν, ἔχειν, τιθέναι πρὸ ὀφθαλμῶν (Polyb. ii. 35. 8 ; Epict. *Diss.* i.
16. 27, iv. 10. 31 ; Iren. iii. 3. 3), and in all similar expressions (ἐν χερσίν,
πρὸ ποδῶν), the Greeks are not accustomed to append a possessive genitive of
the personal pronoun, it is exceedingly improbable that Clement intended
the ἡμῶν of § 3 to be taken with ὀφθαλμῶν. Rather, he calls Peter and Paul
"our good apostles"—the apostles of the Romans and likewise of the
Corinthians, whom he is addressing (chap. xlvii. 3 f. ; Dion. Corinth., quoted
in Eus. *H. E.* ii. 25. 8 ; Iren. iii. 1. 1, 3. 2, 3 ; *GK*, i. 806, A. 4). And he
gives ἡμῶν an emphatic position before τοὺς . . . ἀποστόλους (cf. *per contra*,
chap. xliv. 1, οἱ ἀπόστολοι ἡμῶν), because he wishes to single them out as
the apostles who stood in closest relation to the Romans (and Corinthians).
They are οἱ ἔγγιστα γενόμενοι ἀθληταί in the first place with regard to time
(τῆς γενεᾶς ἡμῶν), and also with regard to the place where they received the
victor's prize for their patience, namely, Rome. Likewise the ἐν ἡμῖν in
chap. vi. 1 (cf. lv. 2) is meaningless, unless we are to understand Rome as
the place where the Christian martyrs who followed Peter and Paul were
put to death. If Clement is here bidding the readers picture to themselves
the whole body of apostles, it is incomprehensible why he should say
nothing of the execution of James the son of Zebedee (Acts xii. 2), of John's
exile, and of other sufferings of the apostles about which tradition gives us
less certain knowledge, or at least why he should not indicate by a comprehensive καὶ οἱ λοιποὶ ἀπόστολοι that these are meant. The construction
and interpretation given above of ἡμῶν τοὺς ἀποστόλους, and that alone,
explains this silence. He is speaking only of the two apostles of whom, at
the outset, he bade the readers think as "*our* good apostles." (3) That
Clement possessed information about Peter and Paul not derived from books
is clear from his own historical position (above, p. 60), and is also confirmed
by the ἑπτάκις δεσμὰ φορέσας. It is hard to see why this number should
point to the existence of a comprehensive written account from which it was
taken (so Spitta, *Urchrist.* i. 51). Paul found occasion once, while writing,
to express the repetition of similar experiences in numbers (2 Cor. xi. 24 f.) ;

but there is no reason why he may not have done the very same thing in oral narratives, and his friends likewise. At any rate, the statement is not drawn from sources preserved to us. Adding the five scourgings by the Jews (2 Cor. xi. 24) to the two imprisonments in Cæsarea and Rome does not give seven imprisonments, as Zeller, *ThJb*, 1848, S. 530, thought (cf. also Hilgenfeld, *Clem. Ep.* ed. 2, p. 90). With just as good reason the thrice repeated beating with rods (2 Cor. xi. 25) could be transformed into three imprisonments to help along such addition. In 1900, without any idea that Mommsen (*ZfNTW*, 1901, S. 84, A. 1) would really work it out, the present writer published the suggestion, that the seven imprisonments of Clement were to be explained as due to the addition of πεντάκις and τρίς, at the same time assuming a confusion of seven and eight. Blass, *NKZ*, 1895, S. 721, claims that these seven imprisonments are to be found in Acts, namely, (1) in Philippi (Acts xvi. 23) ; (2) in Jerusalem ; (3) in Cæsarea under Felix ; (4) under Festus ; (5) on the voyage ; (6) in Rome ; and in addition to these (7) the second Roman imprisonment, from which 2 Tim. dates. But this cannot be even artificially done. Nos. 2–6 represent only a single period in which Paul bore chains continuously, except for very brief interruptions (Acts xxii. 30, and perhaps xxvii. 42–44), which Acts touches upon only lightly, or leaves altogether to conjecture. There is no basis either in the text of Acts or in the nature of the case for distinguishing Nos. 3, 4, 5. Nor is it correct to hold that Clement presupposed on the part of the Corinthians an acquaintance with these facts, which in its turn would imply that Acts was the common source of the knowledge then extant in Rome and Corinth. In this case Clement would have contented himself with a general statement about Paul's imprisonments, as he has done in all the other particulars. The fact that he writes ἑπτάκις and not πολλάκις proves independent knowledge of Paul's life history. According to 2 Cor. xi. 23 (ἐν φυλακαῖς ὑπερβαλλόντως), Paul had suffered, even before his arrest in Jerusalem, several imprisonments of no trifling kind beside that in Philippi. If Clement regarded the confinement beginning in Jerusalem and ending in Rome as a single imprisonment, and if he knew of a second Roman imprisonment ending with death, there are still five left which Paul may have had in mind in 2 Cor. xi. 23. Of these we know only the one in Philippi (Acts xvi.). (4) The word μαρτυρεῖν in Clement does not by itself mean "to die a martyr's death," as it does not infrequently after the middle of the second century (*Mart. Polyc.* xix. 1, cf. Lightfoot, *op. cit.* 26), but rather "to bear witness." This is proved by the added phrase, ἐπὶ τῶν ἡγουμένων, § 7, which, since it designates no particular persons as the rulers at that time, cannot be intended to indicate the date, like ἐπὶ Κύρου βασιλέως, ἐπὶ Πεισιστράτου ἄρχοντος, or like ἐπὶ Ποντίου Πιλάτου (παθόντα or σταυρωθέντα) in the Apostles' Creed. Its meaning is rather *coram magistratibus* which does not suit the act of execution, but is appropriate enough in describing a spoken testimony and confession (cf. 1 Tim. vi. 13). As far as this expression itself goes, it might include each and every confession which Paul had ever witnessed before any magistrates, whether in Philippi, Jerusalem, Cæsarea, or Rome (so Hofmann, v. 71 ; Spitta, i. 57). The context, however, makes it plain that Clement here has in mind the last confession of both apostles, the confession which resulted immediately in their execution.

Even earlier, in § 2, ἕως θανάτου does not mean "as long as they lived," in which case it would stand before ἐδιώχθησαν, but characterises the death of the apostles as the culmination of sufferings undeserved but patiently endured, *i.e.* as martyrdom (cf. Phil. ii. 8). Paul's death is the theme of the very first sentence which treats of him (§ 5), and forms the closing thought in both of the sentences co-ordinated with this, §§ 6, 7. Further, in § 4 we have two parts : First, a summary reference to Peter's sufferings; second, an account of his entrance into glory. These parts are separated by οὕτως, which implies that the former is the presupposition of the latter. μαρτυρήσας, then, since it follows οὕτως, is so closely connected with the statement about Peter's death that it is best to translate : "And so (at the end of a life of such suffering and because of it) did he, bearing witness, proceed to the well-deserved place of glory." In the corresponding statement about Paul, indeed, while οὕτως, as before, brings to an end the description of his life, and indicates this life experience as the presupposition of his death, μαρτυρήσας precedes this adverb instead of following it. The "testimony before the rulers" seems therefore to be viewed as an incident in the course of his life, not as a circumstance connected with his death. But (1) it is the very last incident in his life story. And (2) οὕτως necessarily refers in particular to that event in Paul's previous life last mentioned : "So (*i.e.* not, therefore, without having first borne witness before the rulers) was he released from the world." (3) The meaning of μαρτυρήσας must be the same in § 7 as in § 4. While (4) ἡγούμενοι is used of all persons who have a share in the government (Acts vii. 10 ; Clem. 1 *Cor.* xxxii. 2, xxxvii. 2 ; in lxi. 1 the emperor himself is included, though in xxxvii. 3 he is mentioned separately), even within the community of the Church (Acts xv. 22 ; Heb. xiii. 7, 17, 24 ; Clem. 1 *Cor.* i. 3) ; where, however, as here, there is no definite specification, local or otherwise, οἱ ἡγούμενοι can refer only to the supreme authority in Rome (Clem. 1 *Cor.* lxi. 1 ; *Altertümer von Pergamum*, viii. 2. 347, Inscription No. 356, and the inscription cited there from the *Bull. de Cor. héllén.* ix. 75). At the same time, if Clement had known of a personal meeting between Paul and Nero on the occasion of Paul's second legal defence, he certainly would not have failed, when speaking of the magistrates with whom Paul as the accused had to do, to mention the emperor (cf. xxxvii. 3, li. 5, lv. 1 ; Mark xiii. 9 ; 1 Tim. ii. 2 ; 1 Pet. ii. 14, 17, but particularly Acts xxvii. 24). With reference to chap. vi., cf. the commentaries of Lightfoot and Harnack, and above, p. 60. It is true that ·ούτοις τοῖς ἀνδράσι . . . συνηθροίσθη πολὺ πλῆθος ἐκλεκτῶν means not only that these many, like the apostles, have died as martyrs or entered into blessedness, but also that this great multitude have joined themselves to the apostles—have gathered about them (cf. 1 Kings xi. 24 ; 1 Macc. i. 55). This could be said all the more aptly of the victims of the Neronian persecution, if one of the two apostles, namely, Peter, was actually a victim of this persecution (§ 39) ; but even if this were not the case, it would be appropriate in a comprehensive retrospect like this if the death of Peter and of Paul only fell somewhere within the time of Nero. Just as for the German nation the years 1813–1815, with their triumphs, heroes, and victims, form the one epoch of the War of Liberation, although a period of peace divides this war into two unequal parts, so to the Christians of the year ?6 the martyrdoms of 64–67 meant a single group of struggles and sufferings, upon which a peace of thirty years had ensued. (5) Anyone who divides the then known world or the Roman world empire into East and West, as Clement does here, must necessarily assign Italy and Rome to the West; for the Adriatic and Ionian Seas formed the natural boundary between the two parts of the empire, and were actually regarded as the boundary (*Monumentum Ancyr.* v. 31, cf. Mommsen, *Res gestæ Augusti*[2], p. 118; Treaty of Brundisium between Antony and Octavian, 40 ˙ B.C., in which Scondra [Scutari] was established as the boundary, Appian, *Bell. civ.* v. 64; Plut. *Antonius,* xxx.). Clement could have said, then, simply with reference to Paul's preaching in Rome, that he had preached in the West as well as in the East (v. 6; cf. Ign. *Rom.* ii. 2; pseudo-Clement, *ad Jac.* i.; Jul. Afric. *Chron.*; Routh, *Rel.*[2] v. 264. 7), and perhaps also, considering the rhetorical character of the passage, that Paul had taught the whole world righteousness (v. 7). But when Clement goes even beyond this last expression, and adds, plainly in order to define it more closely, καὶ ἐπὶ τὸ τέρμα τῆς δύσεως ἐλθών, he evidently means that Paul carried his preaching beyond Rome, where Clement is writing, to the very limit of the western half of the then known world, or, in other words, to the westernmost boundary of the lands bordering the Mediterranean, *i.e.* to Spain. The boundary of the West is the Atlantic Ocean, cf. Appian, *Bell. civ.* v. 64, τὰ δὲ ἐς δύσιν τὸν Καίσαρα (ἔχειν) μέχρι ὠκεανοῦ. The situation of Gades is described by Vell. *Paterc.* i. 2, as *in ultimo Hispaniæ tractu, in extremo nostri orbis termino*; by Philostr. *vita Apoll.* v. 4, as κατὰ τὸ τῆς Εὐρώπης τέρμα. Cf. Strabo, pp. 67, 106, 137, 169, 170; Appian, *prœm.* iii.; *Hispan.* i.; Eus. *v. Const.* i. 8. 2–4; Credner, *Gesch. d. Kan.* 53; Gams, *Kirchengesch. Spaniens,* i. 11–16; Lightfoot, *Clement,* ii. 30. Paul had come from the East, and so from this standpoint Clement could not possibly have called Rome the (as respects the East) limit of the West (so Hilgenfeld, *Apost. Väter,* 109); for τέρμα denotes, not the point or line where something begins, but the point or line where something ends; cf. Polyb. xl. epil. 14, παραγεγονότες ἐπὶ τὸ τέρμα ὅλης τῆς πραγματείας = τὸ τέλος, opp. to ἀρχή; Epiph. *Hær.* xxix. 8, ἦλθεν ἐπὶ τὸ τέρμα τῆς βίβλου, or in a geographical connection, Herod. vii. 54, ἐπὶ τέρμασι τοῖσι ἐκείνης (*sc.* τῆς Εὐρώπης), in contrast to the Hellespont, the crossing of which marked Xerxes' first entrance into Europe. Besides, on Malta and in Puteoli, Paul was already in the West before he came to Rome. It is equally impossible for τὸ τέρμα to mean the goal of Paul's life, or of the course set before him, so that τῆς δύσεως would merely signify that this goal was in the West, *i.e.* in Rome (essentially this view is held by Baur, *Pastoralbr.* 63; *Paulus,* i. 264; Hilgenfeld, *Einl.* 349; Otto, *Gesch. Verh. der Pastoralbr.* 167). Since it was unavoidable that every unbiassed reader would take the genitive with τὸ τέρμα as the designation of the territory of which it was the boundary, Clement must have expressed such a thought in other language, possibly by καὶ ἐν τῇ δύσει ἐπὶ τὸ τέρμα τοῦ βίου (τοῦ δρόμου) ἐλθών. Further, to take τῆς δύσεως attributively (= τὸ ἐν τῇ δύσει) would force upon us the absurd idea of a western, in contradistinction to an eastern, end of Paul's life. Nor can it avail here to recall to mind the circus with its double *meta*; for Clement must have said that the world is a circus, and that the second *meta,* the goal of the race, lies in the western part of this circus, if he wished to be understood. There is no better ground for the claim, which Lipsius seems to have made up to the very end of his life (*Apokr. Apostelgesch.* ii. 1. 13 : alsc Hesse, *Hirtenbriefe*, 247), that "the boundary of the West" must denote the same place as that in which Paul "bore witness before the rulers," and in which he "was released from the world." In reaching the limit of the West, Paul did not necessarily reach at the same time the end of his life also. He may quite well have turned back, and, so far as this phrase is concerned, may have died in Jerusalem. The participles δίδάξας, ἐλθών, μαρτυρήσας, just like the participles in § 6, describe what Paul did or suffered before his death, without placing the individual acts in any more definite relation to one another.

7. (P. 62.) Can. Mur. line 37, "sicuti et semote (-ta) passionem (-ne) Petri evidenter declarat, sed et profectionem (-ne) Pauli ab urbe ad Spaniam proficiscentis"; cf. *GK*, ii. 6, 56 f., 141 ; Spitta, *Urchrist.* i. 60–64. Concerning the Gnostic *Acts of Peter* (ed. Lipsius, pp. 45–103), cf. *GK*, ii. 832–855. The approximate date of its composition can be determined only on the presupposition—which is hardly to be contested, however—that it is very intimately connected with the *Acts of John*, and was written, if not by the same author, then at least by one of similar views, and at the same time a fellow-worker ; such a view is supported both by the similarity of their content and by the general consensus of tradition ; cf. *GK*, ii. 839 ff., 858, 860 ; James, *Anecd. apocr.* ii. (*Texts and Studies*, vol. v. Cambridge, 1897) pp. xxiv f., 151 f. The new fragments of the *Acts of John*, published partly in the book just cited, pp. 1–25, and partly by Bonnet (together with the earlier known passages in *Acta Apost. apocr.*, ed. Lipsius et Bonnet, ii. part 1, pp. 151–216), show, as in spite of many objections the present writer still maintains, that the alleged author "Leucius" was a Valentinian, who, however, considered it advisable to speak the language of his school openly in only a few passages. The date of composition, then, is probably as determined by the present writer, *circa* 160–170 A.D. (cf. *GK*, ii. 864 ; *NKZ*, 1899, S. 210–218). With regard to the probable dependence of the Can. Mur. upon the *Acts of Peter* and of *John*, see *GK*, ii. 36–38, 844, 862 f. According to the *Acts of Peter*, Paul's release from his first imprisonment was not the result of a judicial decision, but the jailer, *Quartus*, who had become a Christian, "permansit (read permisit) Paulo ut ubi vellet iret ab urbe" (Lipsius, 45. 6). Paul received the direction to go to Spain through a vision after having fasted three days ("jejunans triduo," 45. 8 ; cf. 63. 11, and Can. Mur. line 10). As soon as the Roman Christians besought Paul not to forget them and not to stay away long ("ut annum plus non abesset," p. 46. 3), there came the voice from heaven with regard to Paul : "inter manus Neronis . . . sub oculis vestris consummabitur," p. 46. 8. Many accompanied him to the place of embarkation, and two youths sailed with him to Spain (p. 48. 8, 17). Reference is made to this journey also in a later passage (51. 26, "Paulus profectus est in Spaniam," cf. 45. 10, "qui in Spania sunt"; 45. 12, "ut proficisceretur ab urbe"; cf. Can. Mur. l. 38); there is also an allusion to his return to Rome after Peter's death (p. 100. 13). It should be added that at about the time of Paul's journey to Spain, Timothy and Barnabas set forth from Rome for Philippi on a commission from Paul (p. 49. 9), which is clearly an elaboration of Phil. ii. 19. Concerning the *Acts of Paul*, see below, n. 10. This ancient tradition is confirmed also by the words ἐλθόντος

εἰς τὴν Ῥώμην τοῦ ἁγίου Παύλου ἀπὸ τῶν Σπανιῶν (pp. 118. 3, 120. 12), at the beginning of the combined *Acts of Peter* and *Paul*, according to which both apostles die as martyrs on June 29th of the same year (Lipsius, 176. 5). This work has not only lost track of the original significance of the festival on that day, but proceeds to invent tales on the basis of a misinterpretation of the inscription, "ad catacumbas," which the bishop Damasus caused to be put upon the common tomb of the two apostles (p. 174, see below, n. 9). It could not, therefore, have been written earlier than 400 A.D. Origen (quoted in Eus. *H. E.* iii. 1) describes Paul's missionary activity in the apostle's own words, Rom. xv. 19 ; but naturally it does not follow from this that he knew nothing of the journey to Spain, or that he gave no credence to the story. We might conclude with as much reason that Origen intended by this use of Rom. xv. 19 to give the lie to the statements in the N.T. about Paul's preaching in Rome. Whether or not Origen refers to the Spanish journey in *Hom.* xiii. *in Gen.* (Delarue, ii. 95), as Spitta, i. 84, thinks, is not quite clear. Of the later writers who speak definitely of the journey to Spain may be mentioned : Cyril of Jerusalem (*Cat.* xvii. 26, probably in dependence upon Clement's letter, with which he was acquainted; cf. *Cat.* xviii. 9; Spitta, i. 55); Epiphanius (*Hær.* xxvii. 6) ; Ephrem Syr. (*Expos. ev. concord.* 286, " Paulus ab urbe Jerusalem usque ad Hispaniam [prædicavit]) ; Chrysostom, who had read the *Acts of Paul* several times and placed confidence in it (*GK*, ii. 886) (*de laud. Pauli hom.* vii. ; *act. ap. hom.* lv. ; 2 *Tim. hom.* x. ; *epist. Hebr.* hypoth., Montfaucon, ii. 516, ix. 414, xi. 724, xii. 2) ; Theodoret *in Phil.* i. 25 and 2 *Tim.* iv. 17. The *Acta Xanthippæ et Polyxenæ* (*Apocr. anecd.*, ed. James, 1893, i. 58–85), which, at the very outset, is clearly dependent upon the Gnostic *Acts of Peter* (Lipsius, 45. 10), makes Paul go from Rome to Spain and stay there several months at least, while Peter journeys from the East to Rome to thwart Simon Magus (James, *op. cit.* 75. 6). The groundlessness of the opinion that the tradition of the Spanish journey and of the second Roman imprisonment has arisen from Rom. xv. 24, 28, can be seen from the fact that important defenders of the view that Paul was twice imprisoned in Rome do not mention Spain at all, but merely speak in general of a resumption of missionary preaching in the interval between the two imprisonments ; so Eus. *H. E.* ii. 22. 2 (see below, n. 8), the real Euthalius, *circa* 350, who reckoned the interval at ten years (Zacagni, 532), and Theodore (Swete, i. 116 f., 205 f., ii. 191, 231). Jerome also, who in the main follows Eus. *H. E.* ii. 22, only hints indefinitely at Spain in the words " in occidentis partibus" (*Vir. Ill.* v. ; cf. the Prologue in Thomasius, ed. Vezzosi, i. 382 f.). In his commentary on Isa. viii. 23, ix. 1 (Vall. iv. 130), Jerome is not giving his own view, but is reporting in direct discourse the view of the Nazarenes, who saw a fulfilment of that prediction in Paul's extended preaching activity ("in terminos gentium et viam universi maris Christi evangelium splenduit"). If Jerome reports them correctly, these Jewish Christians, removed from the world as they were, certainly knew that Paul travelled as far as Spain. Jerome gives this as a matter of personal knowledge in his comment on Isa. xi. (p. 164, "ad Italiam quoque et, ut ipse scribit, ad Hispanias alienigenarum portatus est navibus). The " ut ipse scribit " can refer only to Rom. xv. 24, 28, not to 2 Tim. iv. 17. Jerome says the same thing again, *tract. de ps.* lxxxiii. (*Anecd. Maredsol.* iii. 2. 80) after giving a free rendering of Rom. xv. 19–21 : "deinde dicit, quod de urbe Roma ierit (al. iturus sit) ad Hispaniam." In his careless fashion he mistakes the expression of the purpose for an attestation of its execution. But this is occasioned and in a measure excused by the contrast to the *Ecclesiasticæ historiæ* (p. 163), in which we are told of the journeys of other apostles to Persia, India, and Ethiopia. The tradition about the Spanish journey finds its starting-point in Paul's own words. Concerning *c. Helvid.* iv., see Spitta, i. 92. But Jerome (*Vir. Ill.* i., v.), by accepting the Roman tradition of the simultaneous martyrdom of the two apostles on June 29th of the same year (below, n. 9), helped to spread an error which, by its contradiction of the older tradition, must have had a confusing effect ; since it necessarily led to a lengthening of Peter's stay in Rome in a way quite unhistorical (§ 39, n. 5), or to a shortening of the last part of Paul's life in a manner equally disregardful of the facts. Particularly those who, like Sulpicius Severus (*Chron.* ii. 28, 29), connected the alleged simultaneous martyrdom of the two apostles with the burning of Rome in 64, could hardly withstand this temptation. Furthermore, the Roman Church had a political interest in the matter ; for in the year 416 Innocent I. (*Epist.* xxv. 2) denied that any beside priests ordained by Peter or his successors had founded Churches in Italy, Gaul, Spain, or Africa, or in Sicily and the other islands of the West ; and he formally challenged those who claimed that another apostle had founded the Church in any one of these provinces to prove this by written records. It is plain that Innocent knew of such claims. The Spanish Church could not take up his challenge ; its literature begins with the Biblical poems of Juvencus, 330 A.D. No more than the Churches of Gaul and Africa did it possess a tradition concerning its origin based on documents. Since Rome had spoken and Spain had made no reply, Gelasius in 495 could state as a fact that Paul had never carried out his purpose of going to Spain, using this statement in defence of changes in the papal policy (*Ep.* xxx. 11, ed. Thiel, i. 444 ; cf. the opinion of the same Gelasius as to the time when the two apostles died, below, n. 9). Consequently it is almost a matter of surprise that not only Spaniards, like Isidorus (*de Ortu et Obitu Patrum*, chap. lxix., ed. Arevalus, v. 181), but also Gregory of Rome (*Moral.* xxxi. 103), ventured to speak again of Paul's journey to Spain as an historical fact.

8. (P. 62.) DIONYSIUS of Corinth, in his letter to the Romans and the bishop then in office, Soter (about 166–174 A.D. ; Eus. *H. E.* ii. 25. 8 ; cf. iv. 23. 9–12) writes in terms not exactly elegant : ταῦτα καὶ ὑμεῖς διὰ τῆς τοσαύτης νουθεσίας τὴν ἀπὸ Πέτρου καὶ Παύλου φυτείαν γενηθεῖσαν Ῥωμαίων τε καὶ Κορινθίων συνεκεράσατε· καὶ γὰρ ἄμφω καὶ εἰς τὴν ἡμετέραν Κόρινθον φυτεύσαντες ἡμᾶς ὁμοίως ἐδίδαξαν, ὁμοίως δὲ καὶ εἰς τὴν Ἰταλίαν ὁμόσε διδάξαντες ἐμαρτύρησαν κατὰ τὸν αὐτὸν καιρόν. The present writer translates the last sentence : " For both of them, planting (or founding a Church) also in our city of Corinth, taught us (Corinthians) in like fashion (in a similar manner, in mutual agreement and harmony) ; and in like fashion (in the same harmonious manner) they taught also in Italy in the same place, and suffered a martyr's death at the same time." The words φυτεία, φυτεύειν refer to 1 Cor. iii. 6 ff. ; cf. *Acta Petri*, ed. Lipsius, 88. 19. The better known fact, and the one generally admitted, seems to be that Peter and Paul were the founders of the Roman Church. His emphatic claim that the same two apostles founded the Church in Corinth is perhaps based only on 1 Cor. i. 12, iii. 22. The repeated ὁμοίως

must naturally have the same meaning in both sentences. Therefore ὁμόσε certainly cannot mean "labouring together, working hand in hand," a possible translation in other connections. This thought would presuppose, indeed, that they laboured at the same time, but that has been expressed already by ὁμοίως. We must take it rather in its original local sense as a reinforcement of εἰς τὴν Ἰταλίαν, and, so far as Italy is an extended territory containing various places, as a closer definition of it. εἰς τὴν Ῥώμην might be substituted for it. With regard to the thrice repeated use of a phrase of direction to indicate place in which, cf. Mark i. 39, xiii. 10, xiv. 9 ; Acts xxiii. 11 ; 2 Cor. x. 16. Whether both apostles preached at the same time is not the question in regard to Rome any more than in regard to Corinth. Besides, only a very heedless reader could find in the words of Dionysius any reference to a journey of the two apostles to Rome in company ; cf. Spitta i. 82. It is their deaths which are said to have occurred at about the same time, nothing more. IRENÆUS regards the time when Peter and Paul were engaged in preaching the gospel at Rome, and in founding and building up the Church there, as a continuous period, which serves him as a time for dating the Gospel of Matthew. In speaking of the writing of Mark, he also makes a combined reference to the death of the two apostles (iii. 1. 1, 3. 2, 3). If he assumed a long interval between these two deaths, both statements would be impossible. No more can be inferred from it, however, than from a remark about the time when Hegel (1818–1831) and Schleiermacher (1810–1834) were teaching in Berlin, followed by another, in which reference is made to the time "after the death of the two great teachers." The statement in a work about Peter and Paul, falsely attributed to Symeon Metaphrastes (Acta SS. Jun. v. 411 ff. ; cf. Lipsius, Ap. AG. ii. 1. 8–11 ; 217–227), deserves attention. The unknown author appeals to many ancient writings, correctly, e.g. (414), to Justin and Irenæus with reference to the statue of Simon Magus in Rome ; to Eusebius not quite precisely (422), since the citation comes through Euthalius, who is not mentioned ; incorrectly (423) to Caius, Zephyrinus, and Dionysius. He writes, p. 423c : λέγουσι δέ τινες προλαβεῖν μὲν τὸν Πέτρον ἐνιαυτὸν ἕνα καὶ τὸ μακάριον ἐκεῖνο καὶ δεσποτικὸν δέξασθαι πάθος, τὴν ψυχὴν τῶν προβάτων προθέμενον, ἀκολουθῆσαι δὲ τούτῳ τὸν μέγαν ἀπόστολον Παῦλον, ὡς Ἰουστῖνος καὶ Εἰρηναῖός φησιν, ἐφ᾽ ὅλοις ἔτεσι πέντε τὰς συνάξεις καὶ τὰς ἀντιθέσεις πρὸ τῆς εἰς Χριστὸν ἀναλύσεως καθ᾽ ἑαυτοὺς ποιουμένους, καίγε τούτοις ἐγὼ μᾶλλον πείθομαι. If we understand aright these words, which are misinterpreted by Erbes (64) in such incredible fashion, Irenæus is adduced, along with Justin, as a witness not only for the fact that Paul suffered martyrdom in Rome one year later than Peter, which reminds us of the one year between Paul's first and second Roman imprisonments in the Acts of Peter (above, p. 73, line 12 from end), but also for the further fact that the period during which Peter and Paul laboured at laying foundations in Rome (Irenæus' assumption, as we have seen above) lasted full five years in all. If Paul came to Rome in the spring of 61, he must have been executed in the spring of 66, and Peter a year earlier, i.e. in the spring of 65. This calculation is not far astray from the probable dates, especially if we may take the one year as a round number for a year and several months. TERTULLIAN is the first writer of repute who expressly assigns Peter's crucifixion and Paul's beheading to the time of Nero, who, according to

Apol. v., was the first persecutor of the Christians (*Scorp.* xv.; cf. *Marc* iv. 5; *Præscr.* xxxvi.; *Apol.* xxi., *discipuli* without mention of names; moreover, *Bapt.* iv., Peter baptizing in the Tiber; *Præscr.* xxxii., Clement ordained by Peter). Tertullian hints in *Scorp.* xv. that he derived these facts from writings, the trustworthiness of which is by no means universally recognised. The words "quæ ubicumque jam legero pati disco" cannot relate to the *instrumenta imperii* and the *vitæ Cæsarum*, to which he has previously referred the heretics who doubt the duty of martyrdom (Prodicus, Valentinus; cf. Heracleon, as quoted in Clem. *Strom.* iv. 71); for such details about the martyrdom of Peter and Paul are to be found not in these writings, but in the *Acts of Peter and Paul*, in distinction from the absolutely trustworthy canonical *Acta* which he has previously cited. Concerning Caius, see the following note. HIPPOLYTUS, who was acquainted with the *Acts of Paul* (*Comm. in Dan.* iii. 29; cf. Niceph. *H. E.* ii. 25; *GK*, ii. 880; Bonwetsch, *Stud. zu d. Komment. des Hipp.* 1897, S. 27), touches upon the last part of the apostles' life but once, and then only to say that Simon Magus in Rome opposed "the apostles," *i.e.* Paul and Peter (*Refut.* vi. 20). ORIGEN (quoted in Eus. *H. E.* iii. 1) knows that Peter was crucified head downwards in Rome, and that Paul likewise suffered martyrdom in Rome under Nero. The author of the work *de Rebaptismate*, written in Cyprian's name, had read in a book, which he entitles *Prædicatio Pauli*—probably the *Acts of Paul*—of a meeting of Paul and Peter in Rome (Cypr. *Opp.*, ed. Vindob. Append. 90; *GK*, ii. 881 ff.; but also *ThLb*, 1899, col. 316). Lactantius, *Inst.* iv. 21 (*GK*, ii. 884) probably draws from the same book his account of the preaching in Rome, and of the execution of both apostles by Nero. With regard to the latter event, he speaks more precisely in *de Mort. Persec.* ii.; "cumque jam Nero imperaret, Petrus Romam advenit. . . . (Nero) Petrum cruci affixit et Paulum interfecit." Peter, bishop of Alexandria, says the same thing, and emphasises the fact that both apostles died in the same city, without, however, expressing himself more definitely as to the time (*Epist. Canon.* chap. ix.; Routh, *Rel. S.*[2] iv. 34). EUSEBIUS, who, in *H. E.* ii. 25. 5, iii. 21. 1, 31. 1, puts Paul before Peter, nevertheless follows the usual order at other times when he is speaking of their martyrdom or their tombs in Rome: *Demonstr. Evang.* iii. 5. 65; *Theoph. Syr.* iv. 7 (see following n.); v. 31 (not correctly translated by Lee, p. 315; the proper rendering is: "Moreover, Simon Peter was crucified in Rome head downwards [κατὰ κεφαλῆς], and Paul was put to death, and John was consigned to an island"). Cf. also the translation by Gressmann, S. 241, 25. After he has followed Paul's history up to the end of Acts, he continues (*H. E.* ii. 22. 2): τότε μὲν οὖν ἀπολογησάμενον αὖθις ἐπὶ τὴν τοῦ κηρύγματος διακονίαν λόγος ἔχει στείλασθαι τὸν ἀπόστολον, δεύτερον δ' ἐπιβάντα τῇ αὐτῇ πόλει τῷ κατ' αὐτὸν τελειωθῆναι μαρτυρίῳ. On the occasion of this second Roman imprisonment he wrote 2 Tim., which confirms this tradition by its reference to the first defence, as a result of which he was rescued from the clutches of Nero, etc. In his *Church History*, Eusebius refrains from making any more definite chronological statement, except to say that Paul's death, as well as Peter's, falls in Nero's reign; and Theodore went too far when he claimed (Swete, i. 115)—plainly relying upon the arrangement of the material in Eus. *H. E.* ii. 25, 26—that Paul was executed at the time when the Jewish

War broke out.   In his *Chronicum*, also, Eusebius shows that he has no more exact tradition at his command.   According to the Armenian version (Schoene, ii. 156), he remarks under *anno Abrah.* 2083 (67 A.D.) : " Nero super omnia delicta primus *persecutiones* in Christianos excitavit, *sub quo* Petrus et Paulus apostoli Romæ martyrium passi sunt." Jerome in his rearrangement of this work under *anno Abrah.* 2084 (68 A.D.), instead of the italicised words, writes *persecutionem . . . in qua*, and in *Vir. Ill.* i. and v., puts the death of both apostles in the fourteenth year of Nero, which in the *Chronicum* coincides with *anno Abrah.* 2084 ; but this must have been through a misunderstanding, or a forcing of Eusebius' very carefully chosen expression.   The same must have been the case with the real Euthalius earlier, about 350 A.D., when, appealing to Eusebius' *Chronicum* (Zacagni, 529), he places the death of Paul in the thirteenth year of Nero (p. 532), *anno Abrah.* 2083.   Perhaps also it was in this way that Epiph. *Hær.* xxvii. 6 came to make the statement that both apostles died in the twelfth year of Nero.   Eusebius himself knows no more than what he says, namely, that Peter and Paul died under Nero, and does not intend that 67 shall be regarded as the year in which both apostles died, as is proved also by his remark at the year preceding (*anno Abrah.* 2082 = 66 A.D.), that Linus succeeded Peter as bishop of Rome.   It was only his way of looking at the history, according to which the slaying of the Christians was the climax of Nero's crimes (Eus. *H. E.* ii. 25. 2–5), that caused him in his *Chronicum* to place the persecution of the Christians at the end of that emperor's reign.   And even so, by speaking of *persecutiones* in the plural, he also acknowledges that what he has in mind is not a single event confined to a definite year.   He puts the burning of Rome under *anno Abrah.* 2079 = 63 A.D. (Jerome, *anno Abrah.* 2080 = 64 A.D,) and mentions Paul's death incidentally under *anno Abrah.* 2083 = 67 A.D.   But since he could not make out a definite year for Paul's death, either from tradition or by an artificial computation of the bishops' terms of office, which perhaps served in Peter's case, he contented himself with jotting down under the heading, " Nero the Persecutor of the Christians," that Paul, as well as Peter, suffered martyrdom under this emperor.

§9. (P. 62.)   The earliest information concerning 29th June as " Peter and Paul's Day " is found in the Roman *Depositio martyrum* of the year 336 (*Lib. Pontificalis*, ed. Duchesne, i. 11) ; " iii. Kal. Jul. Petri in Catacumbas et Pauli Ostense Tusco et Basso cons." (258 A.D.).   Alongside of this confused statement of the calendar should be placed rightly the statement, in itself also but slightly illumining, of the so-called *Martyrol. Hieron.* (ed. Duchesne et de Rossi, *Acta SS. Nov.* tom. ii. part 1, p. [84] : " iii. Kal. Jul. Romæ Via Aurelia, Natale sanctorum apostolorum Petri et Pauli, Petri in Vaticano, Pauli vero in via Ostensi, utrumque in Catacumbas, passi sub Nerone, Basso et Tusco consulibus." This clearly distinguishes three places at which the 29th of June was celebrated as *Natale*,—the commemoration-day of Peter and Paul, as martyrs (cf. the *Depos. Mart.* : " xviii. Kal. Octob. Cypriani Africæ, Romæ *celebratur* in Callisti ").   The three places are the Vatican Basilica, as specially connected with Peter, the St. Paul's Church on the road to Ostia, as connected with Paul, and the cemetery, called *ad Catacumbas* by the Church of St. Sebastian, on the Via Appia in memory of both apostles.   A hymn bearing the name of Ambrosium (cf. Dreves, *Ambros. als Vater des Kirchengesangs*, S.

139, No. 15. 7) gives evidence that the processions on 29th of June visited all three places. The year 258, indicated by the consuls named in the *Depositio* and in the *Martyrol. Hieron.* is, of course, not the time of the apostles' death, or of their first interment, but, just as in both of the instances, in which the *Depositio* designates a definite year by naming the consuls (xiv Kal. Jun. und x Kal. Oct.), denotes the time of a later transference of the bones of the martyrs. Consequently we may regard it as certain that in the year 258 and, indeed, on the 29th of June of this year, the bones of both apostles were placed *ad Catacumbas*, and that this has been the reason for the celebration of that particular day. For the month in the date given cannot be separated from the year. The former comes first, and the year, separated from it, forms the end of the statement. This is the simple and necessary result of the fact that the *Depositio* and the *Martyrol. Hieron.* are festival calendars for all years. Through a metrical inscription of the Pope Damasus (366–384) we know that the alleged or actual remains of the apostle rested for a long time *ad Catacumbas* (*Damasi Epigr.* 26, ed. Ihm, p. 31 ; cf. *Liber Pontif.*, ed. Duchesne, pp. 84, 85, 212). This inscription and the buildings erected there by Damasus, as well as the continued celebration of the 29th of June *ad Catacumbas*, at a time when the bones of Peter had long rested in the Vatican, and those of Paul on the road to Ostia, prove that their temporary common interment *ad Catacumbas* had left a deep impression. This interment cannot have been for a short period, and the question arises, When did it end ? As evident fables are to be rejected, the statements of *Liber Pontifi.* (pp. 66, 67, 150) that Pope Cornelius (251–253 A.D.) transferred the bodies of the two apostles from *ad Catacumbas* to their final resting places on the Via Ostia and in the Vatican ; and the traditions in the Syriac *Acts of Sharbil* (Cureton, *Anc. Docum.* 61 f.) that this occurred under Pope Fabian (236–250 A.D.) are untrustworthy ; for, according to the reliable date of the *Depositio*, the interment *ad Catacumbas* did not take place until 258, under Pope Sixtus II. Just as worthless is the statement of a letter of the Areopagite, translated into Syriac and other languages, about the discovery of the head of Paul during the papacy of Sixtus (Xystus), but according to a Latin version during that of Fabellius (!), Pitra, *Analecta*, iv. 245, 267, 270, cf. Salomo Bassor. trans. by Schönfelder, p. 79). Depending solely on a misunderstanding of the inscription of Damasus (cf. V. Schultze, *Archäol. Stud.* S. 242 ff. ; Lightfoot, *S. Clement*, ii. 50), the author of the Catholic *Acts of Peter and Paul* makes the fantastic statement that the bodies of the apostles were interred on the Via Appia immediately after their death, but provisionally only for a year and seven months, while a worthier burial place was being built (*Acta apost. apocr.*, ed. Lipsius et Bonnet, i. 174, more accurately in the accompanying Latin text, cf. also the second Greek recension, p. 221, where one year and six months are given). More reliable seems the account of the ancient Itineraries, that the remains rested for forty years *ad Catacumbas* (de Rossi, *Roma Sot.* i. 180). Since forty is a round number, one might always add a few years more to 298 (258 and 40), and find here the tradition that at the beginning of the fourth century the bodies were removed, one to the Vatican, and the other to the Via Ostiensis. This at all events is pretty near the historical truth. On the other hand, the opinion of Erbes is not tenable (*Die Todestage der Apostel.* 118, von de Wall, *Roma Sacra,*

S. 85 *et al*), namely, that at the time of the *Depositio* of 336, and also of the chronographer of 354, who introduced the *Depositio* into his collected work, the remains of Peter still rested *ad Catacumbas*, while the bones of Paul had already been transferred to the Ostian road. This view depends solely on the uncorrected text of the *Depositio*, which at all events does not state this clearly. Moreover, it has against it not only the later text, according to which Constantine the Great had the bones of Peter interred in St. Peter's at the Vatican, and those of Paul in St. Paul's on the Via Ostiensis (*Liber Pontif.* pp. 78, 79, 176, 178, 193–195 ; de Rossi, *Inscr. Christ.* ii. 20, 21, 345 f.), but most of all the testimony of Eusebius († *circa* 340). Besides the less clear statements of his *Church History* (ii. 25. 5, iii. 31. 1), what Eusebius has to say in his *Theoph.* written about 330–340, and preserved only in Syriac, should not always be overlooked (cf. Lightfoot, *Dict. of Christ. Biog.* ii. 333 ; Gressmann, *TU*, N. F. viii. 3 ; also *Theoph. Griechische Christliche Schriftsteller*, Eusebius, 2te Hälfte, 3te Bd., ed. Gressmann, p. xx*). In iv. 7 of this work Eusebius relates of Peter (inaccurately translated by Lee in the English trans. p. 221, more correctly by Gressmann, S. 175*) : "His memory among the Romans up to the present time is greater than that of those who lived earlier ; so that he was honoured also with a magnificent mausoleum outside the city, and countless multitudes from all over the Roman Empire hasten to it as to a great sanctuary and temple of God." (Cf. Jerome, *Vir. Ill.* i : "Sepultus Romæ in Vaticano juxta viam triumphalem, totius orbis veneratione celebratur "). After some remarks about the writings of John and about his grave, Eusebius continues : "So in like manner the writings of the apostle Paul also are made known throughout the world and enlighten the souls of men ; moreover, the martyr-character of his death, and the mausoleum over him, are extraordinarily and splendidly praised in the city of Rome until this day." From this it is evident (1) that about 330–340 Peter and Paul were no longer resting together, *i.e. ad Catacumbas*, but each had his own particular memorial church in separate places. (2) Eusebius, who of course knew of the *Basilica Petri* at the Vatican, built by Constantine, can have meant nothing else than this by the memorial church which he so pompously described. He certainly could not have referred to the unpretentious tombs of both apostles on the Via Appia. Moreover, St. Peter's at the Vatican stood "outside the city." (3) Constantius, while he was ruling in the West (351–361), may have added so much to the adornment of St. Peter's, built by his father, that he could pass for the finisher of the edifice ; it was, however, not at that date that the remains of Peter were interred in the Vatican basilica, but before the writing of the *Theoph.*, in fact, according to the description of Eusebius, considerably earlier, therefore certainly before 330. Accordingly, the text of the *Depositio* is badly mutilated, and is to be corrected by other traditions ; an *et Pauli* has fallen out after *Petri*, and similarly, by an ocular error—a mistake more easily explainable—a *Petri in Vaticano* has fallen out before *et Pauli*, and, further, an *in via* before *Ostense*. Moreover, even after such a restoration of the text, this statement of the calendar gives evidence of a misunderstanding of the tradition which it contains. It is quite impossible for the reader to see which of the facts stated concerns the date "June 29 . . . under the consuls Tuscus and Bassus," while the author himself seems no longer to have known it. At least the

chronographer of 354, who inserted the calendar of martyrs in his compilation, takes the 29th of June (naturally not of the year 258, but of the year
55) as the common date of the death of Peter and Paul, both in the catalogue
of Roman bishops—the so-called *Catalogus Liberianus*—and in the *Fasti
Consul.* (Mommsen, *Chron. minora*, i. 57, 73). While the chronologists give
varying dates for the year of the apostles' death (Jerome, *Vir. Ill.* i. v., cf.
above, p. 78, gave the year 68), yet since the middle of the fourth century
at the latest there prevailed in Rome the tradition that both apostles died at
the same time, *i.e.* on the 29th of June in the same year. In the so-called
Decretum Gelasii (*Epist. pontif.*, ed. Thiel. i. 455), the opinion that Peter and
Paul died at different times is condemned as heretical twaddle (*sicut hæretici
garriunt*). It is not impossible, though not demonstrable, that this part of the
Decretum, as also others (*GK*, ii. 259–267), had been already discussed at a
Roman Synod under Damasus. Once the 29th of June had become in the
West the memorial day for both apostles, the older tradition, according to
which Peter died a considerable time before Paul, could maintain itself only
in a modest form by allowing that both indeed died on the 29th of June, but
that Paul died a year later than Peter (here following ancient tradition,
above, pp. 73, 76). So Prudentius (*Peristeph.* xii. 3–6, 11–24), and even in the
sixth century, Gregory of Tours (*Glor. Mart.* i. 29), and the Roman deacon,
Aratus, at the end of his metrical version of Acts (Migne, lxviii. 246).
Augustine assumes a rather critical attitude toward the Roman tradition in his
sermons on " Peter and Paul's day " (*Serm.* ccxcv.–ccxcix. ccclxxxi.), *e.g. Serm.*
ccxcv. (ed. Bass. vii. 1197 : "quamquam diversis diebus paterentur, unum
erant. Præcessit Petrus, secutus est Paulus "), and *Serm.* ccclxxxi. (vii. 1508 :
"Petri et Pauli apostolorum dies, in quo triumphalem coronam devicto
diabolo meruerunt, *quantum fides Romana testatur*, hodiernus est . . . Sicut
traditione patrum cognitum memoria retinetur, non uno die passi sunt per
cœli spatia decurrente. Natalitio ergo Petri passus est Paulus ac per hoc ita
singuli dies dati sunt duobus, ut nunc unus celebretur ambobus "). Cf. also
the pseudo-Augustinian *Serm.* ccv. (Bass. xvi. 1209), and another given by
Lipsius, *Ap. AG.* ii. part 1, 240. The celebration of the 29th of June
arose from an event in the local church history of Rome, and for a long
time also was confined to Rome. The true Euthalius, who belongs to the
period before 390 (*NKZ*, 1904, S. 388 f.) knows of the celebration as one
peculiar to Rome (Zacagni, *Monum. coll.* i. 522), and does not say, like the
author of the *Martyrium*, falsely ascribed to him (Zac. 536), that Paul suffered
martyrdom on the 29th of June, but simply that the Romans celebrate his
memory and his martyrdom annually on that day. Outside of Rome this
" Peter and Paul's Day " was not widely observed. The *Calendar of Martyrs*,
preserved in Syriac in a MS. of 412 (ed. Wright, p. 1 ; *Acta SS. Nov.* ii. p.
lii.), puts the martyrdom of both apostles on the 28th of December ; but
this has no more significance than the assignment of the death of Stephen,
the first martyr, to the 26th of December, and of James and John, the sons
of Zebedee, to the 27th in the same calendar. In fact, there was no tradition
concerning either the day or the year of the death of the two apostles. Also
in Rome during the third century there existed no such tradition ; otherwise
how could the interment of the remains of both apostles *ad Catacumbas* on
the 29th of June 258 have become the only memorial day of the great

martyred apostles of Rome! The question where the alleged or actual bones of the apostles rested before the 29th of June 258, is of less significance for our knowledge concerning the end of Paul's life than for our criticism about Peter in Rome (§ 39). It receives the same answer whether we start from what was believed forty years before, or from what happened sixty to seventy years afterward. Since the interment beside the Via Appia was a late and temporary expedient, it seems almost self-evident that when, perhaps sixty years after their lodgment there, the apostles' remains were again removed, it was that they might be buried, not at random, but in the places already hallowed by their memory, *i.e.* that they were brought back to the very places whence they were taken in 258. The final interment of Paul on the Via Ostiensis, and of Peter in the Vatican, attests the fact that it was believed that they were buried there originally. But we are led to the same conclusion by what the Roman Caius under the bishop Zephyrinus (199–217 A.D., *i.e.* about forty to fifty years before the *Depositio* by the Via Appia) certifies in his dialogue with the Montanist Proclus (Eus. *H. E.* ii. 25. 7) : ἐγὼ γὰρ τὰ τρόπαια τῶν ἀποστόλων ἔχω δεῖξαι· ἐὰν γὰρ θελήσῃς ἀπελθεῖν ἐπὶ τὸν Βατικανὸν ἢ ἐπὶ τὴν ὁδὸν τὴν Ὠστίαν, εὑρήσεις τὰ τρόπαια τῶν ταύτην ἱδρυσαμένων τὴν ἐκκλησίαν. In contrast to 'the authority of the apostles and their followers, to whose labours and graves in the province of Asia the Montanist had appealed (Eus. *H. E.* iii. 31. 4, cf. v. 24. 1–6, iii. 31. 3), the Roman names the authority of his Church, its apostles and their graves, which could still be pointed out. Eusebius, without hesitation, took τρόπαια to mean the graves and monuments of the apostles (*H. E.* ii. 25. 5 f., iii. 31. 1) ; the later writers for the most part understood by it the places where they were executed (Hofmann, v. 10, vii. 1. 205 ; Lipsius, *Ap. AG.* ii. part 1. 21 ; Erbes, 68 ff.). Taken by itself, the word has neither of these meanings, but denotes a token commemorating some victory won, set up on the spot where the enemy was turned to flight—originally a bundle of captured weapons hung up on a tree or a pole (Pauly, *RE*, vi. 2165 f.). The memory, however, of the martyrs and other illustrious dead always clung about their graves. It was not the place where Polycarp was burned, but where he was buried, that was considered sacred (*Mart. Polyc.* xvii. xviii. ; cf. the letter of Polycrates quoted in Eus. *H. E.* v. 24. 4, and Pionius, *Vita Polycarpi*, chap. xx., concerning the grave of Thraseas of Eumeneia at Smyrna). In particular cases it may have been actually true, or at least so preserved in people's memory, that the place of death and that of burial coincided altogether or nearly so. John expires in the grave which he himself has ordered to be dug (*Acta Joannis*, ed. Zahn, 250). In Jerusalem, in Hegesippus' time, there was pointed out, near what was once the temple, a pillar which marked the spot where James was said to have been slain and buried (Eus. *H. E.* ii. 23. 18 ; see vol. i. 108, n. 4). This may have been so also in the case of Peter and Paul. The Gnostic *Acts of Peter* (ed. Lipsius, 100. 8) show the greatest indifference as to his burial, putting this sentiment in the mouth of Peter himself, and contain no statements at all about the place of his crucifixion and interment (pp. 90, 100). The same is true with reference to Paul in the ancient *Acts of Paul* (pp. 112–117). Both writings lack every trace of Roman local tradition, and certainly arose in the East (*GK*, ii. 841, 890). But from all analogies it would seem clear that the tradition in Rome during the second century about the death of Peter and Paul and their graves must have been connected with certain definite spots, even if this fact were not also attested by Caius about 210 and, indirectly, by the two later transferences of the remains. Previously, Erbes (*ZfKG*, vii. 33) assumed that suddenly in 258, perhaps as the result of a pretended revelation, the remains were found in some corner or other where up to that time they had lain neglected and hidden. He has now himself given up this view (1899, S. 132), and claims that Paul lay buried on the Via Appia from the very first, and that Peter's bones were likewise to be found there after about 200. But on this supposition the separation of the remains of the two apostles, who were so intimately connected in the tradition, and their removal from the Via Appia, where they had been honoured so long, to their separate tombs on the Via Ostiensis and in the Vatican, seems an act arbitrary in the extreme. The tradition that Peter was executed in the one place and Paul in the other, would not be a sufficient motive for such an act. The writer at least knows of no case in which the body of a martyr was subsequently removed from his grave to the place where he was executed. Rather those who separated the remains of Peter and Paul and buried them in places wide apart—and this was accomplished before Constantine's death in 337—must have believed that they were restoring the original conditions. The interment *ad Catacumbas*, which must have arisen out of the necessities of the times, was from the first intended to be only a temporary entombment. In view of all this, we are probably to understand by the τρόπαια of Caius, as Eusebius did, the tokens marking the places where the two apostles were buried. Nevertheless, as in the case of James, these may very well have been regarded as marking at the same time the places of execution. That they were actually so regarded is attested by the later tradition, according to which both apostles were buried near to where they died; cf. with reference to Peter, Linus, *Martyr. Petri*, x. ed., Lipsius, 11. 16; the Catholic *Acts* of both apostles, 168. 8, 172. 13, 177. 1, 212. 12, 216. 15, 221. 6; cf. with reference to Paul the *Mart. Pauli*, likewise ascribed to Linus, 38. 21, 41. 10 (outside a gate of the city); the Catholic *Acts* of both apostles, 170. 3, 177. 1, 213. 6, 214. 8, 221. 8; cf. with reference to both, *Lib. pontif.* under Cornelius (Duchesne, i. 150). The tokens to which Caius refers need not have been monuments erected by Christians in the apostles' honour; such tokens could be any objects whatever which were supposed to date from the time of the events in question, *e.g.* a pillar, as that which marked the spot where James was killed and buried (Eus. ii. 23. 18), or a tree, as the myrtle on the grave of Thraseas at Smyrna (Pionius, *Vita Polyc.* xx.), or the vine which grew on the spot where the blood of the martyr Philip fell to the earth (*Acta apocr.*, ed. Tischendorf, 92, 94), or the plane-tree under which Simon Magus was supposed to have taught while in Rome (*Hippol. refut.* vi. 20). As a matter of fact we read in one of the recensions of the Catholic *Acts of Peter and Paul* (Lipsius, 214. 9), that Paul was executed near a cembra (stone-pine) or pine, and in both recensions that Peter was buried under a terebinth on the Vatican (pp. 172. 13, 216. 15). The expressions ὑπὸ τὴν τερέβινθον and (214. 9) πλησίον τοῦ δένδρου τοῦ στροβίλου refer in each case to a well-known tree which can be seen at a distance. It is not impossible that this terebinth was the ancient oak on the Vatican, of which Pliny, *H. N.* xvi. 44. 237, gives an account; cf. Erbes, *ZfKG*, vii. 12 A. 2. Concerning the genus pine, cf. Erbes, 1899, S. 92.

10. (P. 63.) The recovery and publication of the Coptic Fragments of the *Acts of Paul* (*Acta Pauli* aus der Heidelberger Koptischen Papyrus Hs. Nr. 1 Herausgeg. von C. Schmidt, Uebersetzung, Untersuchungen und Koptischer Text, 1904) has given us much new information, corrected old mistakes, and happily confirmed certain conjectures, though it has thrown no new light on the presentation of the close of Paul's life which this legend contains. These Fragments have removed every doubt as to the fact that the *Martyrdom of Paul*, which has come down to us in the original Greek and in several translations as an independent writing (Lipsius, pp. 104–117; Schmidt, S. 85–90) formed the concluding portion of the entire work. But we know now, no more than formerly, what immediately preceded this conclusion, though this is the point of especial interest. The wholly arbitrary way in which that elder in the province of Asia, who around 170 to 190 wrote the *Acts of Paul*, made use of the material of Acts and the Pauline Epistles for his fabrication, renders uncertain every conjecture concerning the progress and content of his narrative where the text is in doubt. The *Martyrdom* which closes with the execution of the apostle begins with his arrival in Rome; for it begins with the statement that Luke, who had come thither from Gaul, and Titus from Dalmatia were awaiting him, and the meeting with these friends had rejoiced and enheartened him. From this it would seem to be out of the question that this should have been preceded by an account of any intercourse between Paul and the Roman Christians and of other important events following his arrival in the city. On the contrary, his expectant friends were in all probability the first ones whom he greeted. The only thing that could have preceded it is an account of his journey to Rome. At first Paul finds himself at liberty in the city, and only after a lapse of some time is arrested together with many other Christians. There is not the slightest intimation of a contemporaneous presence of Peter in Rome. Especially of any meeting of Paul and Peter, concerning which old authors always have something to say on the authority of the *Acts of Paul* (above, p. 77), not only is there no intimation, but there is really no room in this connection for stating it. The inference is consequently to be drawn that the *Acts of Paul* are here narrating a second arrival of Paul in Rome, having recorded in a previous passage an earlier presence and imprisonment of the apostle in the city. As the statement that Paul hired a barn and carried on there a successful ministry of preaching (Lipsius, p. 104, 4 ff.), calls to mind Acts xxviii. 16, 30, so the statement regarding Titus and Luke suggests 2 Tim. iv. 10 f. The friends, who at the time of an imprisonment of the apostle had gone to Gaul and Dalmatia (Luke instead of Crescens), had returned from these journeys to Rome before the arrival of Paul, whose liberty of action was in no wise impaired. An earnest consideration is due the conjecture of M. R. James (*JThSt*—January 1905, p. 244 ff.), who is the best informed scholar of the Christian apocryphal literature—that the *Acts of Paul* did not interpolate its fabrications at all into the gaps of Luke's Acts of the Apostles, but appended them to the canonical Acts.

§ 37. THE GENUINENESS OF THE EPISTLES TO TIMOTHY AND TITUS.

The confident denial of the genuineness of these letters —which has been made now for several generations more positively than in the case of any other Pauline Epistles (n. 1)—has no support from tradition. The fact that Marcion did not include them in his collection does not prove that he was unacquainted with them; on the contrary, according to tradition, he knew and rejected them, stating his reasons for so doing (*GK*, i. 834). Traces of their circulation in the Church before Marcion's time are clearer than those which can be found for Romans and 2 Cor. A strong argument in favour of their genuineness is the large number of personal references which they contain,—references that can be explained neither as derived from other probable sources nor as growing out of the idea under the influence of which the letters might have been forged. This is especially true in the case of 2 Tim., least so in the case of 1 Tim.; although, comparing the letters as a whole with those which in the second century and later were attributed to Paul and the other apostles, all three of them furnish proof of their own genuineness (n. 2). What was said above (p. 60 f.) in connection with the discussion concerning the historical value of the letters, even if spurious, about the way in which facts presupposed are handled in all three letters, especially in 2 Tim., also goes to prove their genuineness (n. 3). Historical facts which a forger finds it necessary or advantageous to invent he is wont to state clearly and expressly for the benefit of his reader, who, of course, cannot know these facts beforehand. Furthermore, these facts are generally borrowed from older sources which are genuine or supposed to be genuine, which in this case would have been the other Pauline Epistles and Acts. Now the whole group of facts presupposed in these letters

carry us beyond the period dealt with in Acts and veri-
fied by references in the earlier Epistles of Paul. Moreover, these facts, which are new to us, are everywhere
incidentally referred to in a manner intelligible only to
readers already familiar with the actual situation. The
majority of the persons introduced in these letters are
not mentioned anywhere else in the N.T., nor in the post-
apostolic literature not dependent upon these Epistles;
as, for example, Hymenæus, 1 Tim. i. 20, 2 Tim. ii. 17;
Philetus, 2 Tim. ii. 17; Phygelus and Hermogenes, 2 Tim.
i. 15; Lois and Eunice, 2 Tim. i. 5; Onesiphorus and his
house, 2 Tim. i. 16, iv. 19; Crescens, Carpus, Eubulus,
Pudens, Linus, Claudia, 2 Tim. iv. 10, 13, 21; Artemas
and Zenas, Tit. iii. 12 f.; Alexander, 1 Tim. i. 20, 2 Tim.
iv. 14. Even if the last named person could be identified
with the Alexander mentioned in Acts xix. 33 (against this
identification cf. above, p. 21, n. 3), this latter passage does
not account for the reference in the Epistles to Timothy;
for the Alexander in Acts is described simply as a Jew,
without any indication of the relation which he sustained to Paul and Christianity; whereas in 1 and 2 Tim.
he is represented as a Christian, hostile to Paul and his
doctrine, fallen from the faith, put under the ban by the
apostle, and not an ἀργυροκόπος, as we should expect if the
passage were dependent upon Acts (Acts xix. 24), but a
χαλκεύς (2 Tim. iv. 14). These sixteen new names are by
no means mere names, the introduction of which can be
explained by the necessity which the writer felt of giving
his forgery the appearance of a genuine letter by putting
in personal notices, a necessity, let it be said, which other
writers who forged Apostolic Epistles in the second century seem hardly to have experienced (n. 2). They represent real persons. Even though this may not be said of
the Roman Christians, who in 2 Tim. iv. 21 send greetings, the fact that no one of their names is taken from
Rom. xvi. does argue in favour of their historicity. The

difficulty of gaining definite ideas from the statements about Onesiphorus (above, p. 20, n. 1), Lois and Eunice (p. 22, n. 4), Crescens (above, p. 11 f.), Hymenæus and Philetus, Phygelus and Hermogenes, Alexander (above, p. 21, n. 3), Zenas (above, p. 54, n. 4), Carpus and the articles which Paul left with him (above, p. 16), is that which is natural in connection with such notices found in genuine letters belonging to the remote past. On the other hand, what is said is of such a character that it is difficult to believe it to be invented. This is true also of statements about the persons mentioned elsewhere in the N.T. A pseudo-Paul might have taken the name Demas (2 Tim. iv. 10) from Col. iv. 14; Philem. 24; but what could have influenced him to set the conduct of Demas in such sharp and unfavourable contrast to that of Luke when he is mentioned in Colossians and Philemon along with Luke as one of Paul's honoured helpers? What led him to associate Demas with Thessalonica? The forger might have been influenced by Eph. vi. 21 to speak of the sending of Tychicus to Ephesus (2 Tim. iv. 12), *i.e.* if the Epistle was already provided with the false title πρὸς Ἐφεσίους. But even if no account be taken of the fact that the whole of 2 Tim. introduces us to a period in Paul's life considerably later than the composition of Ephesians, it would have been very much more natural for him to speak of the sending of Tychicus to Colossæ, and almost inevitably there would have been some trace of the influence of Eph. vi. 21 f. or Col. iv. 7 f. ; but no such influence is discernible ; indeed, in Tit. iii. 12 we find Tychicus on his way to Crete with an unknown person named Artemas. To be sure, Apollos (Tit. iii. 13) was a distinguished name ; but there is not the slightest hint which would remind the reader of the well-known and thoroughly individual character of this person as he appears in 1 Cor. and Acts, while here, too, he appears in company with a person otherwise unknown, on a journey to Crete. From Acts xx.

4, 15, xxi. 29, one might learn that Trophimus had once been at Miletus with Paul; but in order to invent the further statement that Paul had left him there sick (2 Tim. iv. 20), it would be necessary directly to contradict what is there said about him. That Erastus' home was Corinth might be inferred from Rom. xvi. 23 (cf. xvi. 1); but any-one writing in dependence upon Rom. xvi. would not be likely to represent him as a traveller stopping in Corinth instead of continuing his journey beyond that point (2 Tim. iv. 20). These various statements are not derived from earlier writings which have come down to us, nor are they due to the influence of ideas which we can detect in the Epistles. Both Timothy (1 Thess. iii. 2; 1 Cor. iv. 17, xvi. 10; Phil. ii. 19–23) and Titus (2 Cor. vii. 6–15, viii. 6, xii. 18) had occasionally performed functions as the apostle's representatives in the Churches organised by Paul. Therefore it was not unnatural to conceive of them as having been temporarily at work in the same way in Churches other than those mentioned in the earlier Epistles, and to give literary currency to his wishes with reference to the organisation of Church life in the form of letters from Paul to them. But it is inconceivable that a pseudo-Paul, who with this purpose in view wrote these letters on the basis of the earlier Epistles, should have presented to the readers such a very unfavourable picture of Timothy, whom the real Paul praises so often and so highly (e.g. Phil. ii. 20–22). All the legendary tales of the ancient Church were lauda-tory in spirit, and all the unfavourable judgments which became current in the second century concerning persons mentioned with honour or praise are either due to ten-dencies opposed to the N.T. tradition and the tradition of the early Church, e.g. in Marcion and the pseudo-Clemen-tines, or are to be regarded as historical testimony of a kind that could not be invented, and of value because supple-menting our imperfect knowledge of these times and

personalities, *e.g.* the unfavourable stories about Nicolaus
Now there can be no idea of any intention on the author's
part to present Timothy in an unfavourable light, since by
the very act of addressing to him two letters of Paul he
accords him special honour, and in spite of all the defects
of his character which we discern in the Epistles, represents him as being tenderly beloved by the apostle.   Consequently this picture of Timothy and the letters in which
it is found must be considered genuine.   It is hard to
understand how anyone can feel this critical argument
weakened by the sentimental consideration that, if the
Epistles to Timothy are accepted as genuine, the image of
a saint is destroyed.

At this point the question arises as to the purpose of
the alleged forgery, which must be satisfactorily answered
before anyone acquiesces in the judgment that the letters
are spurious.   The principal motives of the forger have
been found in what is said in 1 Tim. and Titus concerning
the *regulation of the life of the Church* and in all three
letters in opposition to certain *doctrinal errors.*

With reference to the first point, it is to be remarked
at the outset that the pastoral office described above (pp.
29 ff., 43 f.), which Titus temporarily occupied in Crete
and Timothy in the province of Asia over large groups of
Churches, is quite without parallel in the organised Church
life of the post-apostolic age.   It grew out of the unique and
general relation of the apostolate to the establishment and
oversight of the Churches, a function which these helpers
of Paul exercised under his commission and as his temporary representatives.   Now if, following the misleading
precedent of interpretation in the ancient Church (above,
p. 41, n. 6, and p. 53, n. 2), and influenced by certain imperfect modern analogies, anyone is inclined to consider
their position, that of a bishop, he ought at least to regard
Timothy not as a bishop of Ephesus, but as a bishop of
Asia, and Titus as a bishop of Crete ; and then perhaps it

will be recalled that while there were bishops of Ephesus, Smyrna, and Laodicea in the province of Asia, and bishops of Gortyna and Knossus in Crete, there were never any bishops of Asia and of Crete. The local Churches of the post-apostolic and early catholic age were autonomous corporations; the monarchical episcopate was the highest office in this local Church, and lasted for life. And so it remained up to a time prior to which the "Pastoral Epistles" must certainly have been written, when it became customary to look upon bishops as successors to the apostles, and more and more to regard as peculiarly theirs certain Church functions. Although the personal distinction of individual bishops like Ignatius and Polycarp, or the historical dignity of the Churches over which they presided, may have given them the moral right to reprove and to advise Churches other than their own, in the second century no bishop of Ephesus, or even of Rome, could have exercised in any Church save his own so much authority over the organisation, and so determinative an influence in regulating the details, of the Church life as that which Timothy and Titus were instructed to exercise over all the Churches scattered through wide regions; and, as a matter of fact, no bishop ever did assume such authority and influence. Therefore it is inconceivable that between 70 and 170 a pseudo-Paul should have written 1 Tim. and Titus, in which the whole Church life of entire districts is represented as being under the determining influence of a form of personal government which in his time was not even in existence, and of the working of which, in the apostolic age, there is hardly the least suggestion in the rest of the N.T.

Furthermore, with regard to offices in local Churches, there is not to be found anywhere in the Epistles an enumeration of the officials and a description of their functions, such as might give the impression that a definite number and order of officers is recommended or

introduced, over against another system then in vogue
On the contrary, a fixed order is presupposed, and the
qualifications are mentioned necessary for the election and
installation of officers in the Church, also the qualities
which these officers must show in performing their functions. Consequently it is impossible to derive from the
letters a definite answer to the question as to the number
of officers in the Church, for this is always presupposed.
If we had only 1 Tim. we might infer from iii. 1–13 that
the officers of the Church were simply one ἐπίσκοπος and
a number of διάκονοι. The error of this conception we
should immediately discover, however, from the fact that
in both apostolic and post-apostolic times, whenever these
two titles are used comprehensively to denote the officers
of the local Church, several ἐπίσκοποι as well as several
διάκονοι are mentioned (n. 4). A form of government in
which all the official service in the local Church was
performed by one bishop and a number of deacons never
existed. Moreover, in a different connection but in the
same letter (v. 17–22), we learn of Church officials called
πρεσβύτεροι. That there were several of these officers in
every Church we would naturally assume, even if special
mention were not made of those elders who devoted
themselves to teaching (v. 17), and of the individual
elder against whom a charge may be preferred (v. 19),
and if we did not read in iv. 14 of the πρεσβυτέριον of
Timothy's home Church as a corporation acting as a unit.
Evidently the name is derived from the office, for there
could not be πρεσβύτεροι in the clear sense here intended,
namely, "ruling elders," without a presbytery, any more
than there could be senators without a senate (n. 5).
Being members of the body which administered the
affairs of the Church, the individual elders were officers
in the Church. From the connection in which 1 Tim.
v. 22 stands, there can be no doubt that when persons
became members of the presbytery hands were laid upon

them, and they were set apart to this position and work by the prayer of the Church, just as were other members of the Church who were appointed to perform special service and to occupy a special position in the Church. Consequently the only difference between them and the ἐπίσκοπος in iii. 1–7 is a difference of name; for the care of the Church which the latter is to exercise is described as προΐστασθαι, προστῆναι (iii. 4 f.), as is also the office of the elders (v. 17). The fact that the latter are not mentioned in the apparently complete list of the officers of the Church in iii. 1–13, can be explained only if the same persons were sometimes called πρεσβύτεροι, sometimes ἐπίσκοποι. The fact that in one place Paul calls them πρεσβύτεροι is explained by the circumstance that in the preceding context he has been exhorting Timothy to proper conduct in relation to the older members of the Church (n. 6). From among the πρεσβύτεραι (v. 2) special mention is made of the widows (v. 3–16); from the class πρεσβύτεροι, in the wider sense (v. 2), the προεστῶτες πρεσβύτεροι are distinguished (v. 17–19); so that he is thinking of their official position only as that which gives them a place of honour and determines the treatment they are to receive. On the other hand, where the special point under discussion is their office proper and the qualifications necessary in order to its assumption, they are very properly called ἐπίσκοποι and their office ἐπισκοπή (iii. 1 f.). That this was really the relation subsisting between elders and bishops is positively proved by Tit. i. 5–9; for no exegetical device can obscure the fact that in this Epistle the identity of ἐπίσκοπος and πρεσβύτερος is taken for granted (n. 7). Titus is to appoint elders in every city in Crete, *i.e.* to provide the local Church with a presbytery. When, now, we find that the statement of qualifications necessary in order to the appointment of an *elder* is confirmed by a statement as to the requirements which are to be made of a *bishop*, it follows, not only that the elder was a bishop, but

also that there was no official with the title ἐπίσκοπος who
stood at the head of the presbytery.   It is the same sort
of Church organisation which, according to Acts, existed
in the Churches of Asia Minor in Paul's lifetime ; according to the *Epistle of Clement*, in Rome and Corinth at
the close of the first century ; and, according to the
Epistle of Polycarp, in Philippi as late as the beginning
of the second century (n. 8).   Now, however, from Revelation, the *Epistles of Ignatius*, and the tradition concerning
the disciples of John, we learn that by the close of the
first century the monarchical episcopate had been generally introduced and firmly established in the Churches
of Asia Minor, which was the destination of 1 Tim., and
that after the middle of the second century this form of
government became more and more common in the
Churches of Europe.   How could a pseudo-Paul, writing
in the year 100 or 160 with a view to exerting some
influence upon the system of Church organisation in his
time, ignore so completely the Church life which he
observed about him, and present Paul and his helpers so
entirely in the dress and language of 50–70 in all that
affected the essential forms of Church organisation ?
The aim on the forger's part in this way to avoid all tell-
tale anachronisms would directly contradict his other
purpose, namely, in Paul's name to influence the Church
of his own time ; while everyone acquainted with ancient
literature particularly the literature of the ancient Church,
knows that a forger or fabricator of those times could not
possibly have avoided anachronisms.

No objection can be raised on the ground that in these
letters alone Paul discusses specifically the arrangement
of offices in the Church and the duties of chief officers and
deacons, whereas in the other letters he limits himself to
indefinite hints and incidental references (1 Thess. v. 12 ;
1 Cor. xii. 28, xvi. 15 f. ; Rom. xii. 7 f., xvi. 1 ; Gal. vi. 6 ;
Eph. iv. 11 ; Col. iv. 17 ; Phil. i. 1) ; for the reason that

there are no other Epistles of Paul in which the external
conditions are the same as in Titus and 1 Tim. Even in
2 Tim. nothing is said about bishops, deacons, elders, and
widows, nor about Timothy's pastoral relation, he being
represented simply as an evangelist, and as a sharer of
the apostle's preaching and teaching office (above, pp.
5 f., 29 f.). It cannot, therefore, be claimed that an interest in the official organisation of the Church, such as
Paul himself did not feel, is a peculiarity of the author
of the Pastoral Epistles. Effort to supply the Churches
which had just come into existence in Crete with officers
by the apostle's express command (Tit. i. 5) may not
be in accordance with certain fancies of constructive
historians, but agrees perfectly with Acts (Acts xiv. 23;
cf. n. 7), and with the *Epistle of Clement* (chaps. xlii. 4–
xliii. 1, xliv. 1–3), the earliest sources which we have that
deal with the development of the organisation of the
Gentile Christian Churches, as well as with the fact that
a few weeks, or at most a few months, after it came into
existence, the Church in Thessalonica had officers charged
with arduous duties (1 Thess. v. 12). According to the
most probable interpretation of 1 Tim. iii. 11, female
διάκονοι are mentioned; but this does not take us beyond
Paul's own time (Rom. xvi. 1). The obscurity to us of
the instructions with regard to widows (1 Tim. v. 3–16),
particularly their relation to the deaconesses, is due solely
to the meagreness of the reports that have come down
to us. Two points are of critical importance—(1) The
explicitness and exactness which in very marked degree
distinguish these instructions from those concerning
bishops and deacons (*e.g.* v. 9), show that the distinction given to certain widows in the Church is an
arrangement not nearly so old nor so well established
as the episcopate (office of presbyter) and diaconate.
(2) No traces are found here of that development of
this arrangement, testified to by Ignatius, by virtue of

which unmarried women were reckoned among the widows (n. 9).

It would necessarily be a cause of suspicion if the conception of the spiritual office that appears in these letters were different, not only from Paul's, but also from that of the N.T. generally. Such would be the case if a higher kind of morality were demanded of the "clergy" than of ordinary Christians, *e.g.* if they were forbidden to marry a second time. This ancient interpretation of Tit. i. 6, 1 Tim. iii. 2, 12 is proved to be false by the fact that the μιᾶς γυναικὸς ἀνήρ is simply one of the duties and virtues—the first mentioned—that become every Christian. A writer with any other idea must have regarded the remarriage of widowers as an exceedingly heinous sin. But that our author did so regard it is impossible to believe; since the re-marriage of widows, which has always been regarded as more objectionable than that of widowers, is not only declared allowable, in accordance with 1 Cor. vii. 39, but in the case of the younger widows it is even commended (1 Tim. v. 14); while in general the writer seems to look with favour upon the married life (1 Tim. ii. 15, iv. 3). The main question that Paul asks with reference to overseers and deacons seeking installation, and with reference to widows claiming special honour from the Church, is whether their married life has been, and is, pure, untainted by unlawful sexual intercourse (n. 10). Only when the rule is so interpreted is it possible to see the connection between it and the other requirements that follow and are directly connected with it, especially the requirement that before being installed as an officer in the Church a man must have proved himself efficient in managing his own house-hold and in bringing up his own children (Tit. i. 6; 1 Tim. iii. 4 f., 12; cf. v. 7, 10, 14).

While these personal qualifications, without which no one may assume any office in the Church, are very carefully enumerated, positively and negatively, the functions of the different officers are nowhere named, it being constantly assumed that they are known. Hence it could have been no part of the author's purpose to broaden the scope of their offices, to increase their authority, or to introduce any change whatever in the relation between the Church and its officers. The difference in this respect between these letters and the Epistles of Ignatius, and even those of Clement and Polycarp, is very marked. Any member of the Church may offer prayer in the public gatherings (above, 40, n. 4). Teaching is not limited to an office. This is evident as well from the whole impression of the letters as from the teaching done by Titus and Timothy, who held no office in the local Church, but are engaged in teaching as representatives of Paul and sharers of his apostolic vocation, which included not only missionary effort among those who did not yet believe, but also the instruction and guidance of existing Churches. From the fact that women are forbidden to teach publicly in the congregation (1 Tim. ii. 12, above, p. 40 f.), while they are permitted, especially the older women, to teach other women by word and good example (Tit. ii. 3), it is to be inferred that every man had the right to engage in teaching. Only on this presupposition is it possible to understand what is said in 1 Tim. i. 3–7, vi. 3–5 about ἑτεροδιδασκαλοῦντες, and in 2 Tim. iii. 6–9, Tit. i. 10–14 about persons of a worse character. They are not blamed for teaching without having the proper authority to do so. Consequently they are not official teachers who have made improper use of their office and are to be deposed, but simply members of the Church who, believing themselves to possess unusual insight and special ability to teach, have put themselves forward as teachers in the Churches and homes in a perverse or even injurious manner, whose activity Timothy is to forbid and Titus strenuously to oppose. The same conditions are here presupposed that we observe in Jas. iii. 1 ; Rom. xii. 7 ; 1 Cor. xii.–xiv. ; Col. iii. 16.   There is nothing said in 2 Tim. ii. 2 which would imply that teaching was an official function.   It is true that among the elders officially appointed those who engage in the arduous work of speaking and teaching are especially mentioned, and with special warmth commended to the support of the Church (1 Tim. v. 17 f. ; cf. Gal. vi. 6 ; 1 Cor. ix. 6–14).   Because of the large number of teachers who do harm, special care is also to be exercised in choosing persons who are to be at the head of the Church ; they are to hold the true Christian doctrine, and must be able with sound doctrine to exhort the members of the Church and to controvert those who oppose it (Tit. i. 9).   In this sense ability to teach is mentioned as one of the necessary qualifications of the head of a Church (διδακτικός, 1 Tim. iii. 2 ; cf. 2 Tim. ii. 24).   But it is to be observed that in the latter passages nothing is said about public addresses before the congregations, and from the one first quoted it is clear that an elder .(i.e. a bishop) could exercise his office satisfactorily without teaching at all.   That frequently the head of the Church should be also a teacher is certainly no innovation of the post-apostolic age (vol. i. 465, with reference to Eph. iv. 11) ; it is rather the natural presupposition of the later development, when the heads of the Churches came to be also regularly its teachers (Clement, 2 *Cor.* xvii. 3–5 ; Just. *Apol.* i. 67).

In addition to this quiet work of the teacher, an important rôle was still played in the life of the Church by prophecy.   In the passages where Paul makes predictions concerning the future of the Church, he depends not upon written prophecies, nor upon some special revelation made to himself, but upon the prophetic spirit present in the Church and expressed in the utterances of individual prophets (1 Tim. iv. 1 ; cf. 2 Tim. iii. 1 ; below, p. 110).   Prophecy within the Church must have been the

determinative influence in the selection of Timothy to
assist the apostle in preaching and in his endowment
with the necessary qualifications for the office (1 Tim.
i. 18, iv. 14 ; above, p. 23, n. 5).   In 1 Tim. iv. 14 this
endowment is directly attributed to prophecy, the laying
on of the hands of the presbytery being mentioned as a
concurring circumstance, while in 2 Tim. i. 6 the laying
on of the hands of the apostle himself is declared to be
the means by which Timothy became possessed of the
charisma, the use of which is the same as the exercise of
his calling.   The fact that in one instance the laying on
of the apostle's hands is mentioned, in the other, of the
hands of the presbytery, is due to the different point of
view from which Timothy's work in the Church is conceived in the two letters.   Where Timothy is thought of
as overseer and director of the life of the Church in the
province of Asia, he is reminded of the fact that the
officers of the Church to which he originally belonged had
a part in calling him to service in the Church.   But where
he is thought of as an evangelist, having part in the
apostle's preaching vocation, emphasis is given to the
laying on of the apostle's hands.   Between endowment
by prophecy and endowment by the laying on of hands
there is no more contradiction than between the fact that
in one instance Paul, in the other the presbytery, laid
hands upon Timothy.   The author did not find the two
contradictory ; why should we ?   We have the same representation in Acts xiii. 2–4 (cf. Clement, 1 *Cor.* xlii. 4,
above, p. 41, n. 5).   It would be extremely arbitrary to
declare the passages in a book which attribute to the Holy
Spirit the installation of officers in the Church, or the
appointment and commissioning of missionaries (Acts xx.
28, xiii. 4 ; cf. Ignatius, *Philad.* address), to be in contradiction to other passages in the same book which speak
of the choice of officials by the Church (Acts vi. 5), or of
the installation of such by missionaries engaged in organ-

ising Churches (Acts xiv. 23). Neither can it be argued
that in 1 Tim. iv. 14, v. 22, 2 Tim. i. 6 the ordination was
regarded as a sort of sacrament with magic effect, because
the laying on of hands is used as an abbreviated technical
expression without mention of the petition and the con-
secrating prayer, which probably were always accompanied
by the laying on of hands, symbolising the bestowment
of the desired gifts, since in other passages the abbreviated expression (Acts viii. 17–19, ix. 17, xix. 6 ; cf. Mark
vi. 5, viii. 23, 25 ; Luke xiii.13 ; Heb. vi. 2) is found as
well as the longer one (Acts vi. 6, xiii. 3 ; cf. xxviii. 8).
From cases of this kind it can no more be inferred that
magic powers were attributed to the laying on of hands,
quite apart from prayer and faith, than it can be inferred
from cases where only prayer is mentioned, without the
laying on of hands (Acts i. 24 ; in cases of healing, Jas.
v. 14 ; Acts ix. 40), that the latter was omitted.

Evidence of the late date of these Epistles and one of
the main motives for their composition have been found
in what is said in them about *false teachers* and *false
doctrines* (n. 11). If one is to avoid making the spuri-
ousness of the Epistles—which is the point to be proved—
the presupposition of the argument, it is necessary at the
outset to distinguish between what Paul says about certain
phenomena existing at that time, and phenomena which
he expects to appear in the future ; also between persons
who have forsaken the faith and have separated themselves from the Church, or who have been expelled, and
others who are still within the Church, but either teach
in a manner positively harmful or countenance such
teaching. In the nature of the case there are various
points of connection between these groups, in particular
the prophecy of future degeneracy is suggested by existing
phenomena ; but this does not justify us in treating these
distinctions as if they were merely negligible differences
in the form of the presentation. The persons, the oppos-

ing of whose harmful activity is Timothy's chief business
in Ephesus (1 Tim. i. 3, n. 12, and above, p. 39, n. 3),
are members of the Church, subject to its confession and
discipline; for Timothy is not directed to warn the
Churches under his care against them, but is to command
them to refrain from teaching. What Paul says in describing their work as teachers is manifestly designed
not only to open Timothy's eyes and convince him of the
peril to which the Church is exposed through them, but
to furnish him with the truths by the presentation of
which he is to influence them to leave off their harmful
activity. These persons are not yet αἱρετικοί, i.e. they
have not yet separated themselves from the worship and
fellowship of the Church; persons of this character are to
be left to their fate (Tit. iii. 10; cf. 1 Cor. xi. 19). Only
in case of persistence in their work, in spite of the reprimand of Timothy or Titus, is it expected that they will continue outside the organised Church what they are forbidden
to carry on within the same. This conclusion, namely,
that until now these persons had remained in the Church,
follows not only from the fact that Timothy is to command them to cease teaching, but also from the fact that
individuals belonging to this party who had gone farther
than the rest had been subjected to Church discipline by
Paul (1 Tim. i. 20; cf., however, 1 Cor. v. 12). From Tit.
i. 9 it appears, further, that the opposition to sound doctrine by these persons was made within the sphere of the
same Church life as that affected by the teaching and
exhortation of the teaching bishop. For Titus to have
sharply controverted and stopped the mouths (Tit. i. 11,
13) of these persons would merely have exposed him to
ridicule had they been non-Christians. Moreover, the purpose of this interference on Timothy's part, namely, that
the persons in question might become sound in the faith,
very clearly takes it for granted that they in some degree
possess the faith and have confessed it publicly (cf. Tit.

i. 16). They are described as unbelievers (Tit. i. 15),
if not, indeed, as worse than unbelievers (1 Tim. v. 8),
because they do not hold the true doctrine taught by
Jesus and His Church, and, following the unhealthy tendencies of their minds, set forth things both foolish and
worthless (1 Tim. vi. 3 f. ; cf. Col. ii. 19 ; above, pp. 31 f.,
39, n. 3).

The function of teaching had not yet come to be
associated with a churchly office (above, p. 97); still
there were διδάσκαλοι, persons who made teaching in the
Church their chief business (Eph. iv. 11 ; 1 Cor. xii. 28 f.;
Rom. xii. 7 ; Acts xiii. 1 ; *Didache* xiii. 15 ; cf. 2 Tim.
ii. 2, iv. 2). Besides the apostles, upon whom there de-
volved, in addition to preaching the gospel to unbelievers,
the duty of teaching within the Church (1 Cor. ii. 6–iii. 3,
iv. 17 ; Col. i. 28 ; 1 Tim. ii. 7 ; 2 Tim. i. 11 ; Acts ii.
42), and Paul's helpers, who had part in this work (above,
pp. 31 f., 46), such teachers were to be found both among
the officers of the Church and outside of this circle (above,
p. 97). But if these ἑτεροδιδασκαλοῦντες had been elders
or bishops there would certainly be some trace of it, either
in the passages which discuss the ἑτεροδιδασκαλεῖν, or in
those dealing with the officers of the Church. Consequently
these are to be sought among the "laity." On the other
hand, the teaching in question is not the deliverance of a
single discourse (1 Cor. xiv. 26), but teaching work regularly
practised, as is evidenced by the word ἑτεροδιδασκαλεῖν
(n. 12). From 1 Tim. vi. 3–10 it is clear that these
persons made a profession of teaching in the technical
sense, for which they took compensation, realising considerable profit (n. 13). It is not simply their incidental
purpose of profiting from their work, nor their overween-
ing sense of superior knowledge of the Scriptures and of
Christianity (1 Tim. vi. 4, 20, i. 7), that Paul condemns,
but he twice describes their commercial method of teaching as ἑτεροδιδασκαλεῖν, which would imply, not that they

set forth a false doctrine differing from Christian doctrine and the gospel of Paul, but that they worked like false teachers, played the rôle of false teachers,—in other words, used abnormal and wrong methods (n. 12). This error would not, of course, be serious if it were only some defect of delivery, without reference to what they taught. That, however, their presentation of the fundamental truths of Christianity was not regarded by Paul as false and deceptive, is evident. Such an error, above all, would not be left unmentioned. Paul himself would surely have indicated the character of its contents, and have directly condemned it; still more would this have been done by a pseudo-Paul, who in Paul's name was endeavouring to check the spread of these false doctrines. These teachers are charged, rather, with paying attention to matters that give rise to disputations and do not promote the exercise of his calling on the part of a steward of God (1 Tim. i. 4, above, p. 39, n. 3), whereas they should hold fast the sound words and teachings revealed by Jesus Himself, and the pious doctrine which has since existed in the Church (1 Tim. vi. 4). They are accused of an unwholesome disposition to engage in disputes and strife of words (vi. 4), disputes just as profitless and worthless (Tit. iii. 9) as are the subjects to which they are fond of paying attention. To be sure, they do discuss the law,—and only the Mosaic law can be meant,—claiming to be its correct interpreters, on the ground of their fundamental acquaintance with it (1 Tim. i. 7). For this reason the discussions which usually followed in the wake of their teaching are called strifes about the law (Tit. iii. 9). But they make no attempt to set forth the moral purpose of law (1 Tim. i. 5), or to unfold its typical and prophetic significance, which, according to 1 Tim. i. 8 (cf. 2 Tim. iii. 15 f.), they would be entirely right in doing; but they prefer rather to discuss unauthenticated fables and endless genealogies (1 Tim. i. 4; Tit. iii. 9), with Jewish (Tit. i. 14),

profane, and old wives' fables (1 Tim. iv. 7). To attempt
to identify these μῦθοι and γενεαλογίαι with the fantastic
speculations of the second century, particularly with the
gradations of æons of the Gentile-Christian gnosis, as has
been done, is much less natural than to suppose that men
like Irenæus and Tertullian in their contest with the
Valentinians used phrases of Paul's in describing his
system (n. 14). Even if it were not expressly stated in
Tit. i. 10 that the chief persons to be opposed were
teachers of Jewish origin, and in Tit. i. 14 that these
persons occupied themselves with 'Ιουδαϊκοὶ μῦθοι, and in
Tit. iii. 9 that they occasioned νομικαὶ μάχαι, all this, which
is formally expressed in these passages would be clear
from their claim to be νομοδιδάσκαλοι (1 Tim. i. 7),—a
designation elsewhere given to the rabbis (Luke v. 17 ;
Acts v. 34 ; cf. Rom. ii. 17–23). Although some of these
ἑτεροδιδάσκαλοι may have been Gentiles by birth, who
either had become Jewish proselytes before their conversion
to Christianity, or had become acquainted with Judaism
after they became members of the Church, there can be
no doubt that the whole movement represented by the
" false teachers" had its roots in Judaism, more specifically
in rabbinic Judaism. Consequently the fables and genealogies which they were so fond of discussing can be no
other than those discussed by Jewish scribes. These
legendary traditions and endless genealogies were, in all
probability, based upon the text of the Pentateuch, or,
since νόμος, from which νομοδιδάσκαλος is derived, signifies
the entire O.T. (1 Cor. xiv. 21 ; John x. 34), upon the
text of the O.T. generally (n. 15). Even if the Pastoral
Epistles are spurious, every word here used proves that
they have nothing to do with the gradations of æons and
syzygies of the gnostic systems. In contrast to the
language of the ecclesiastical opponents of these teachings,
who regarded them as blasphemous obscurations of the
one true God, and shunned their authors as creators of

idols (Iren. i. 15. 6), all that is here said against the genealogies is that they are endless (1 Tim. i. 4) and foolish,
as are also the disputations about them (2 Tim. ii. 23),
and the wranglings about the law with which these disputations are connected in Tit. iii. 9.   The fables, of
which, according to 1 Tim. i. 4, the genealogies seem to
have been a part, are not only described as Jewish (Tit.
i. 14), which of itself would be nothing against them, but
are also called βέβηλοι καὶ γραώδεις (1 Tim. iv. 7).   The
latter is certainly an opprobrious term, but at the same
time is proof positive that the errors here under discussion are not destructive in character ; the former term,
which is employed to describe all the teachings of the
ἑτεροδιδάσκαλοι (1 Tim. vi. 20 ; 2 Tim. ii. 16), when used
of things, is simply the opposite of ἱερός.   While the
orthodox teacher derives his truth from the ἱερὰ γράμματα
(2 Tim. iii. 15), which accordingly has to do only with
things relating to the religious life and to salvation, and
so is holy, these teachers handle profane subjects and set
forth doctrines which, while they may have their starting-
point in the Holy Scriptures, really lie quite outside the
sacred sphere within which the orthodox teacher moves.
Both teachers and doctrines are spoken of with a great
deal of contempt.   The knowledge of which they boast
cannot properly be called such (1 Tim. vi. 20).   In reality
they know nothing of the things about which they speak,
and do not understand the scope of their own claims
(1 Tim. i. 7, vi. 4).   The very questions which they and
their hearers discuss prove their lack of common sense and
want of real culture (2 Tim. ii. 23).   Their teaching is
described as vain words (1 Tim. i. 6, ματαιολογία ; Tit.
i. 10, ματαιολόγοι ; cf. Tit. iii. 9, μάταιοι), words without
meaning (1 Tim. vi. 20 ; 2 Tim. ii. 16, κενοφωνίαι), and both
directly and by contrast as worthless (Tit. iii. 9, ἀνωφελεῖς ;
cf. ὠφέλιμος, Tit. iii. 8 ; 1 Tim. iv. 8 ; 2 Tim. iii. 16).   It
is called worthless because it contributes nothing to the

intelligent fulfilment of the Christian teacher's office, giving rise only to fruitless investigations and strifes about words (1 Tim. i. 4, vi. 4 ; 2 Tim. ii. 14, 23). Moreover, Paul's helpers are exhorted not to permit themselves to become involved in these useless and profane teachings, investigations, and disputations (1 Tim. iv. 7, vi. 20 ; 2 Tim. ii. 16 ; Tit. iii. 9). The very language in which these warnings are expressed, and the suggestions of the warning not to make their teaching a means of profit (1 Tim. vi. 5–11 ; cf. 2 Tim. ii. 4) as do these teachers, together with the exhortations rather to be zealous in the presentation of the real truth (1 Tim. i. 18, iv. 6, vi. 2, 20 ; 2 Tim. ii. 1–15, iii. 14–iv. 5 ; Tit. ii. 1, iii. 1–8), prove that these warnings to Timothy and Titus are very seriously intended. In the mouth of a pseudo-Paul, whose purpose was in the name of the apostle to combat the known errorists of the second century, such language would be proof of the utmost stupidity, as it would be in the case of Paul himself, if he were dealing with teachers who denied any of the fundamentals of the faith of the Church.

The same conclusion follows if we look at these phenomena from a side other than that indicated by their designation as μῦθοι and γενεαλογίαι. It stands to reason that persons who called themselves teachers of the law handled the legal contents of the Torah, and from 1 Tim. i. 8–11 it is clear that, contrary to the spirit of the gospel, they considered certain requirements of the Mosaic law binding upon Christians. But if, after the manner of the Galatian Judaisers, they had made the observance of the Mosaic law, or even only of essential parts of it, a condition of salvation, thereby denying the gospel of Paul, neither Paul nor a pseudo-Paul could have passed it by, nor have spoken in the above manner of their absurd and profitless teaching. Nothing is said of circumcision, the Sabbath, or similar legal requirements. But from Tit. i. 14–16 we learn that they developed out of the law and on the basis of it all sorts of regulations concerning things "clean and unclean," and from the description in this passage of these regulations as commandments of men (cf. Col. ii. 22 ; vol. i. 465), we infer that they prescribed ascetic rules with reference to foods and the whole manner of living which went beyond the obligations of the Mosaic law. This conclusion is confirmed by the manner in which this warning against profane and old wives' fables is coupled with the exhortation to prepare for a life of piety upon earth and for the glory of the life to come, not by bodily asceticism, but by a discipline of the inner self (1 Tim. iv. 7–10); since Timothy is repeatedly warned himself not to follow the false tendencies of these persons, possibly we are to infer from 1 Tim. v. 23 (cf. Rom. xiv. 21) that they forbade the use of wine. While from what has been said these teachers seem not to have been of any great importance, at the same time Paul does not conceal either from himself or from his disciples the harm which they are doing in the Church, and the danger in which they themselves are involved. Being quarrelsome and dogmatic, it is difficult to correct them; they are insubordinate and disobedient (Tit. i. 10, 16); puffed up by their imaginary knowledge, they resist the representatives of genuine Christianity (Tit. i. 9; 2 Tim. ii. 25). In Crete, particularly, Paul seems to have had unfortunate experiences with these persons (above, p. 45). And indeed Timothy also is instructed not to enter into discussion with them, but simply to command them to desist from their work (1 Tim. i. 3, cf. iv. 11). However, in one passage, where evidently the same or similar persons are referred to (2 Tim. ii. 14–16, 24), Timothy is exhorted not to act unkindly in dealing with them, always bearing in mind the possibility of their conversion to true knowledge (2 Tim. ii. 25 f.). Titus, on the other hand, is emphatically told to silence them, and to reprimand them sharply and authoritatively

(i. 11, 13, cf. ii. 15), and then if they withdraw from the
Church, to whose discipline they will not submit, after
exhorting them once again, or at most twice, he is to
leave them to their fate (iii. 10).   Consequently the whole
tendency of the movement must have been away from the
Church.   In proportion as they were prevented from
teaching publicly in the assemblies of the Church, they
must have made an effort to introduce their ideas into
homes ; though it is to be observed that this feature of
their work is mentioned in Tit. i. 11 and not in 1 Tim.
Concerning 2 Tim. iii. 6, see below, p. 114 f.

Not only were these persons injurious to the Churches,
but they themselves were in great danger.   Paul considers
their condition diseased (1 Tim. vi. 4 ; Tit. i. 13), as proved
chiefly by his regular designation of the true doctrine,
which they do not hold, and which on that account is to
be preached with all the greater zeal as sound (n. 16).
Their spiritual life therefore is in peril, and, unless they are
converted, they must remain the prey of Satan (2 Tim.
ii. 25 f.).   The harmful effects of their departure from the
real truth and their capricious meddling with questions
entirely secondary, morally unfruitful, and without religious value, are already apparent in their moral life.
While prescribing all sorts of ascetic rules for themselves
and others, they are the victims of covetousness, and
really deny the God whom they profess to know (1 Tim.
vi. 3–10 ; Tit. i. 13–16).   Here again it is apparent that
they did not teach an immoral doctrine of God, as did
the " Gnostics " according to the unanimous testimony of
the Church of the time, but accepted, formally at least,
the God of the common Christian faith.

The question now arises as to the relation between these
ἑτεροδιδάσκαλοι and those who are described as having fallen
from the faith and as being outside the Church.   According
to 1 Tim. vi. 21, some of those who belonged apparently to
the party or the movement represented by the ἑτεροδιδάσ-

καλοι had missed the mark with regard to the faith, and so
had gone astray, from which it is to be inferred incidentally
that this was by no means true of them all. From the
context of 1 Tim. vi. 3–10 it appears that those who had
erred from the faith in consequence of their love of money
belonged to the ἑτεροδιδάσκαλοι. A certain connection
seems to exist also between the ἑτεροδιδάσκαλοι described
in 1 Tim. i. 3–7 and the two men mentioned in i. 20 ;
for while the former have disregarded the great underlying
principle of every commandment, namely, love, which presupposes a pure heart, a good conscience, and an unfeigned
faith (cf. also Tit. i. 15), the class of whom Alexander and
Hymenæus are mentioned as terrible examples have completely abandoned οι " thrown overboard" (Hofmann) a
good conscience, in consequence of which their faith has
suffered shipwreck. They had reached the point where
they reviled that which was holy to the Christians, and
Alexander at least, if he be the same as the Alexander
spoken of in 2 Tim. iv. 14 (above, p. 21, n. 3), had
gone so far as openly to oppose the apostolic preaching.
If Paul had given them over to Satan for correction,
he had not done so without communicating with the
Church to which they belonged, and so not without
their excommunication from the same. The blasphemous
doctrines which they confessed may have been as
various as the conduct by which they showed that
they had renounced obedience to their own conscience.
That the two cases were not entirely alike is evident from
2 Tim. ii. 17, where Hymenæus' name is not coupled with
that of Alexander, but with that of a certain Philetus, it
being declared that the two had proclaimed the doctrine
that the resurrection was past already, and had secured
some following. Here again things are said in the preceding context which seem to connect these persons with
the ἑτεροδιδάσκαλοι (ii. 14–16α) ; although both the language and the contents of the passage render impossible

the assumption (cf. Hofmann, vi. 257) that Hymenæus and
Philetus are mentioned as examples of this group, so that
everything is true of the latter which is said of the former.
This identification is impossible, because in all the passages
which have been considered (1 Tim. i. 3–20, vi. 10, 21),
those who had openly fallen from the faith are distinguished from the ἑτεροδιδάσκαλοι, and the latter are never
accused of godlessness, blasphemy, and destructive errors.
Besides, if this were the case, it would not be enough for
the apostle to say that Timothy, in view of the anticipated
progress of this godless teaching, is to proclaim the word
of truth fearlessly and urgently, and not to occupy his
attention with strifes about words and the unspiritual
scholasticism of these teachers—poor weapons, indeed,
against such serious errors! From the analogy of the
other passages, we conclude that the relation between the
ἑτεροδιδάσκαλοι and those who had openly fallen from the
faith of the Church, some of whom, like Alexander,
Hymenæus, and Philetus, had already been excommuni-
cated, was genetic. Not a few of these apostates must
have come from the ἑτεροδιδάσκαλοι, and served to illustrate the harmful character of this method of teaching,
which overlooked and diverted attention from the fundamentals of Christianity. It does not necessarily follow
that Alexander, Hymenæus, and Philetus were Jews by
birth, for this was not uniformly the case with the ἑτεροδιδάσκαλοι (above, pp. 44, 103). Connection with Judaism
is, however, proved from extra-Biblical traditions. According to these traditions, the doctrine in question, which, of
course, never consisted solely of the bald contention that
the resurrection is already past, existed in a twofold form.
According to the one form of the doctrine, a man experienced a resurrection in his children. According to the
other, the resurrection in which the Church believed meant
the rise of the new man from the old in conversion and
baptism (n. 17). As the authors and earliest representa-

tives of the latter view, which seems to have been suggested by conceptions of Paul's (Eph. ii. 5 f., iv. 23 ; Col. ii. 12 f., iii. 1, 10), are mentioned the Antiochian proselyte Nicolaüs (Acts vi. 5), who seems eventually to have gained a following in the Churches of Asia Minor (Rev. ii. 6, 15), and the Samaritan Menander, a follower of Simon Magus, who was half-Jewish, had been circumcised, and lived in Antioch (Just. *Apol.* i. 26). The former view, which was suggested by Jewish expressions, such as " to awaken seed or children," according to an early legend was disseminated by disloyal followers of Paul in the apostle's lifetime. The cruder forms of the doctrine are probably the earliest, and nothing is more natural than to suppose that it was taught first by teachers of pure Jewish blood, and that the doctrine was given its more refined and spiritual form by half-Jews like Nicolaüs and Menander, whence it passed in this form into the various systems of the Gentile Christian gnosis.

That Paul expected these abnormal phenomena which existed in the Church of his time to affect the future, is evidenced not only by the way in which he expresses his expectation that the doctrine of Hymenæus and Philetus will spread like a gangrene, attacking other members of the Church, and that those who hold it will become more and more godless (2 Tim. ii. 16–18, cf. iii. 13), but also by the manner in which, on the basis of prophecy, he predicts new facts, which, while they may and do have their prelude in the present, really belong to a future, indeed, to the final age. The τὸ δὲ πνεῦμα ῥητῶς λέγει ὅτι κτλ. in 1 Tim. iv. 1 is not quoted as scripture (Heb. iii. 7), neither is the tense used historical (Acts i. 16), from which it may be concluded, first of all, that Paul is referring to prophetic utterances which at the time this letter was written were still current in the Churches (cf. Acts xx. 23, xxi. 4, 12, xiii. 2, xvi. 6). We know how highly Paul prized such prophecies, and what definite expectations he based upon them (1 Thess. v. 19 f. ; 2 Thess. ii. 2 ; vol. i. 226 f.). He uses the indirect form of discourse, evidently because he wants to state in a few words what the prophets had said in numerous discourses. Still the ῥητῶς indicates that he intends to reproduce the special prophecy which he has in mind, just as explicitly and definitely as is possible in the case of predictions made at various times often only suggested, and, so far as we know, never written down. In this connection it is, of course, to be remembered that the fruitful source of all Christian prophecy was the prophetic testimony of Jesus Himself (Rev. xix. 10), and there is much here that reminds one of many recorded sayings of Jesus (Matt. vii. 15–23, xxiv. 4 f., 11 f., 24 ; *GK*, ii. 545 ff.). But what the Spirit said to the Churches at that time goes far beyond these sayings. At a later time, which does not necessarily mean the final age, but simply the future as distinguished from the present (cf. Acts xx. 29), many shall depart from the faith, because they give heed to seductive spirits and the teachings of dæmons, who in hypocritical guise speak lies. Even though the correct meaning of the separate words and their proper connection be subject to doubt and debate, it is at least clear that not only the apostasy of numerous members of the Church, but also the appearance of the false teachers through whom this is to be brought about, is referred to the future ; for if the reference were to definite phenomena, which were known either because the prophecies in question had been heard before, or because the readers of the letter had learned of the facts through their own experience, or by having been previously informed of them, the articles could not possibly be omitted in describing these phenomena. Consequently it can be neither the ἑτεροδιδάσκαλοι nor the false teachers and blasphemers of 1 Tim. i. 20, 2 Tim. ii. 17 f. that are here referred to. Furthermore, the terms used to describe these teachers who are to appear in the future are not intended simply to express horror at the sinister and seductive power of these men (cf. 2 Cor. xi. 14 ; 2 Thess. ii. 11 ; 1 John iv. 1–3, 6 ; 2 John 7), but are chosen in view of the character of their teaching (cf. Ign. *Smyrn.* ii.). By forbidding believers to marry on the ground that it is impure, and by forbidding the use of certain foods on the ground that they are evil and not intended by God for use by pious men or by others, they act as if they were bodiless spirits endeavouring to realise in themselves and those whom they seek to win a type of spirituality contrary to nature.   Although they may declare it necessary for Christians to be like angels (Luke xx. 36 ; Col. ii. 18 ; vol. i. 466, 469), the prophetic spirit pronounces them deceptive spirits and lying dæmons.   If it be regarded as certain that these teachers and the doctrines attributed to them belong to the future, it follows that it must have been conditions in the Churches under Timothy's care which influenced Paul or a pseudo-Paul to recall this prophecy, and to urge Timothy to preach truths that would counteract these false doctrines which were to appear in the future (1 Tim. iv. 4–6).   From the fact that in the very next verse we have statements which apply to the ἑτεροδιδάσκαλοι (iv. 7 f.), it is clear beyond question that it was the ascetic rules of these teachers, derived from the Mosaic law (above, p. 105), that occasioned the exhortation.   The ἑτεροδιδάσκαλοι did not forbid marriage nor declare that certain forms of food in customary use were of themselves objectionable and not fit to be used by Christians ; this was to be done in the future by the deceiving spirits ; but these commandments of men with reference to the disciplining of the body (Tit. i. 14 f. ; 1 Tim. iv. 8) prepared the way for false doctrines which deny the fundamental laws of life established at the creation.

In 2 Tim. iv. 3, without appeal to a definite prophecy, Paul speaks of a future time when men generally, including thus at least numerous Christians, will not bear sound doctrine, *i.e.* will find it too strict or too monotonous, and in their wanton desire for what is new and interesting will provide for themselves teachers after their own liking, finally closing their ears entirely to the truth and giving heed to fables. In view of this prospect, Timothy is to devote himself the more earnestly to preaching before the evil time comes (2 Tim. iv. 2–5); he is to see to it that there are others besides himself and after him who shall propagate sound doctrine (2 Tim. ii. 2). While it is not here stated in so many words that the beginnings of this very unsound development of ecclesiastical taste, so to speak, existed already in the present, it must have been the case; for otherwise the ἑτεροδιδάσκαλοι in Ephesus and Crete would not have met with approval. In 2 Tim. iv. 4 the word translated fables has the article prefixed, so that it designates the whole class of unauthenticated fables, including thus the rabbinic tales of which the ἑτεροδιδάσκαλοι made so much (1 Tim. i. 4; Tit. i. 14, iii. 9); while the recurrence here of the word "sound doctrine" proves that Paul had in mind their unsound methods and the morbid taste of numerous members of the Church who gave heed to them. Nevertheless Paul's words are still prophetic, because he speaks of a future time when this perverted taste, now to be observed in isolated cases, shall become general in the Church, resulting in the increased number and more perverse character of these teachers.

There is a third passage (2 Tim. iii. 1–5) written in the prophetic spirit relating less directly to harmful teachers and doctrines. In the last days, reads the passage, shall come evil times. The future tense makes it impossible to assume that the reference is to the present Christian era, treated as the final age (Heb. i. 1; 1 Pet. i. 20; Jas. v. 3; 1 Cor. x. 11; Acts ii. 17). It can mean only the future which still lies before the persons for whom

the letter was intended—the time approaching, the end
of the age (2 Pet. iii. 3). The thing that will make these
times so evil and so hard for Christians to bear will be a
widespread moral degeneracy. The prediction is made
with reference to men in general. But from the statement at the end of the passage that in these times men
will love pleasure more than God, and that while retaining outwardly a form of godliness they will deny its
power, it is clear that the persons referred to are members
of the Church, showing that it is a general moral decline
of Christianity that is here predicted, or rather that a
prophecy to this effect is recalled to Timothy's mind (cf.
Matt. xxiv. 12, 38, 48 f., xxv. 5 ; Luke xviii. 8 ; 2 Thess.
ii. 3 ; vol. i. 240). Clearly this would not happen did
there not exist in the present foreshadowings and examples of such sham Christianity, which it is necessary
for Timothy as a teacher rightly to judge and handle.
Similarly, the sudden transition from the description of
evil times to come and of the general character of the
generation then living to the exhortation, "From these
persons turn away," has its justification in the fact that
he goes on to speak of persons now living who belong to
the class of sham Christians just described (2 Tim. iii. 6–9).
But these living sham Christians are described as teachers
whose conduct bears a certain resemblance to that of the
true teacher, just as the Egyptian sorcerers did to Moses,
but who in reality, like those sorcerers, are opposed to
the truth represented by the servant of God.

Inasmuch as 2 Tim., unlike 1 Tim. and Titus, was not
written with a definite group of Churches in view among
which Paul's helper was to work, neither iii. 6–9 nor
iv. 3 (cf. ii. 14–16α, 23) can be interpreted as referring
exclusively to the ἑτεροδιδάσκαλοι in Ephesus and Cret
That, however, Paul had these and persons of a similar
character in view there is no reason to doubt. Like the
ἑτεροδιδάσκαλοι (Tit. i. 11), the persons described in 2 Tim.

teach from house to house, and neglect the moral aspects
of Christian truth (1 Tim. i. 5), persuading sinful women
to become their disciples instead of exhorting them to
repentance, and gratifying their idle curiosity by telling
them all sorts of fables and Biblical curiosities. These
persons in Tit. i. 10 are condemned in practically the
same terms as in 2 Tim. iii. 5 ; τετυφωμένοι, 2 Tim. iii. 4,
is to be found also in 1 Tim. vi. 4 ; the expression ἄνθρωποι
κατεφθαρμένοι τὸν νοῦν, 2 Tim. iii. 8, is almost exactly the
same as that which is found in 1 Tim. vi. 5. The fact
that Paul himself enters the realm of Jewish mythology
in quoting the names of Jannes and Jambres only serves to
strengthen the impression that he has principally in mind
false teachers who were for the most part Jewish. This
impression is not at all weakened by the fact that he assures
Timothy for his encouragement that these sham Christian
teachers will not be able to accomplish more, since their
folly will soon become manifest to all Christians (iii. 9) ; for
the contrary remark in 2 Tim. ii. 16 applies not to the
ἑτεροδιδάσκαλοι, but to the false doctrine of Hymenæus ;
and wherever the former are mentioned they are spoken of
slightingly, and described as foolish persons who, without
much ceremony, are to be forbidden to carry on their
work. Although individuals of evil character, both
Christians and teachers, will wax worse and worse
(2 Tim. iii. 13), the sham Christian teachers described in
2 Tim. iii. 6–9, who in their essential characteristics represent the same class as the ἑτεροδιδάσκαλοι in Ephesus
and Crete, have no future, no matter how much harm
they may do in the present. On the other hand, the
false doctrine mentioned in 2 Tim. ii. 17 f. was to have a
future, while the false doctrine predicted by the prophetic
spirit in 1 Tim. iv. 1–3 belonged wholly to the future.
All this is in agreement with history only if these Epistles
were written in the apostolic age. Nothing resembling
the ἑτεροδιδάσκαλοι is to be found in the post-apostolic age.

Cerinthus is out of the question, for his Judaism is only a
learned myth (vol. i. 515, n. 4). The Naassenes, who,
to be sure, according to Hippolytus' description, adopted
Jewish elements in their syncretistic system (n. 11), were
anything but Jewish teachers of the law. From the
letters of Ignatius we learn that in the year 110 wandering teachers of Jewish origin, with reference to whom
Ignatius uses several phrases to be found in the Pastoral
Epistles, were seeking entrance into the Churches of Asia
Minor (vol. i. 497, and below, n. 14). These, however,
were real false teachers ; they taught that the essentials of the Mosaic law were binding upon all Christians,
as for example the law concerning the Sabbath. They
denied the reality of Christ's humanity, especially the
reality of His death and resurrection, and of the resurrection of Christians from the dead, none of which were tenets
of the ἑτεροδιδάσκαλοι (cf. Zahn, *Ignatius*, pp. 356–399).
Neither does the picture of the Judaisers opposed in the
Epistle of Barnabas, nor the Ebionism that appears in
the pseudo-Clementine literature, show features resembling
the ἑτεροδιδάσκαλοι of the Pastoral Epistles. On the other
hand, as has been pointed out, the manner in which they
make a business of teaching allies these teachers with
the Petrine party in Corinth (vol. i. 288 f.), while their
neglect of the essentials of Christianity and their emphasis
upon ascetic rules based upon the Mosaic law connect
them with the Jewish Christian teachers in Colossæ
(vol. i. 462). But in the Pastoral Epistles we have no
appeal on the part of the ἑτεροδιδάσκαλοι to the authority
of another apostle or of the mother Church ; nor is anything said about philosophy and philosophical speculations
concerning nature, while the Epistles to the Corinthians
and the Colossians are silent about rabbinic myths, investigations and disputations about genealogies, and specific
legal requirements of the O.T. Furthermore, if the earlier
Epistles of Paul really reflect conditions in the Church

at the time when they were written, the rise and spread
in various directions, such as Ephesus and Crete—and,
judging from the hints of 2 Tim., even more widely—of
a form of a pious sounding doctrine assuming to be Christian, but really representing the worst sort of rabbinism—
of sufficient importance to be opposed as seriously and energetically as it is in these Epistles—is a new phenomenon,
to which Paul bears witness only in his last letters.   For
a pseudo-Paul in the post-apostolic age—when Christians
of Jewish birth had become more and more exceptions in
the Gentile Christian Church—to have invented a description of and then vigorously to have opposed the
ἑτεροδιδάσκαλοι, who did not exist in his own age and who
were without parallel in the earlier Epistles of Paul, would
have been to expose himself to ridicule without apparent
purpose or meaning.   As has been shown above (p. 107 f.,
and n. 17), the real heresy, which, according to 2 Tim.
ii. 18, existed at the time, is represented by ancient
accounts, the trustworthiness of which at this point cannot be questioned, as having existed in a twofold form
even in the apostolic age.   So far as we are able to trace
its development, it originated in Jewish and semi-Jewish
circles in Palestine (n. 17).   The fact that this is not
directly stated proves that what we have here is not the
attempt of some later writer artificially to put himself
and his readers back in the apostolic age; while the fact
that it is assumed in 2 Tim. ii. 17 that this development
will take place, and the fact that we are able to form an
idea of its character only from the context, prove that the
author did not live at a time when Gentile Christian
Gnostics of different schools were actually proclaiming this
or a similar doctrine.   The fact that this prophecy was
fulfilled, and that this doctrine did develop and spread, is
no proof that it was not Paul who gave utterance to the
same.   The same is true with reference to the prophecy
concerning a future false teaching in 1 Tim. iv. 1–3 and

the related passages, 2 Tim. iii. 1–5, iv. 3 f., unless it be assumed as self-evident that Christian prophecy which began with Jesus and was developed in His Church never developed anything but phantasies. Marcion forbade the members of his Church to marry, and degraded the God of creation and His work. Ideas of this kind were developed further by Encratism and Manichæism. That, however, a pseudo-Paul, who had lived through the experience of Marcion's activity, writing in the name of Paul and of the prophets of the early Christian Church, would have used only the language of 1 Tim. iv. 1–3 in opposing him, it is impossible to believe. Neither can we suppose that he would have found in certain doctrines of Jewish Christian teachers of the law (above, pp. 102 f., 105 f.) the antetype of Marcion's anti-Jewish teaching, nor is it any more likely that in another passage he would have finally betrayed himself by the use of Marcion's antitheses (n. 18).

A comparison of the statements in these Epistles about various kinds of false doctrine, and of those portions of the same that deal with the organisation and officers of the Church with conditions actually existing in the Church, especially the Church of Asia Minor, at the beginning and during the course of the second century, proves just as clearly as does the external evidence that they must have been written at latest before the year 100. But they could not have been written during the first two decades after Paul's death, because of the character of the references to persons, facts, and conditions in Paul's lifetime and his own personal history, and because of the impossibility on this assumption of discovering a plausible motive for their forgery (above, p. 88 ff.). Consequently the claim that they are post-Pauline, and contain matter which is un-Pauline, is to be treated with the greatest suspicion. Passing by altogether or with the briefest mention what is manifestly foolish (n. 19), we must admit that

it is really a cause for suspicion if in 1 Tim. v. 18 we have
cited as Scripture a gospel-saying to be found in exactly
the same form in Luke x. 7, and with slight differences in
Matt. x. 10, inasmuch as elsewhere Paul quotes the sayings
of Jesus only from the oral tradition, and in 1 Cor. ix. 14
reproduces this same command of Jesus, but in a free
rendering.   Especially is this suspicion justified in view
of the fact that considerable time elapsed after the death
of Paul before the Gospels came to be quoted as Scripture.
But, assuming that a pseudo-Paul wanted to support the
Mosaic regulation, which required a somewhat bold interpretation in order to render it applicable to the teachers
(1 Cor. ix. 9), by adding a saying of Jesus' which referred
directly to Christian teachers and had greater authority,
it would have been quite out of keeping with the custom
of the second century for him to have quoted it without
saying that it was a word of the Lord, and so smuggling
it in, as it were, obscurely as a word of Scripture.   It is
very much more likely that the ἡ γραφὴ λέγει refers only
to the passage from the law, and that the other is a
proverb of which Jesus Himself made use.   There are
other sentences of Paul's which seem to be proverbs,
although we have no means of proving that they are
such (1 Cor. v. 6 ; Gal. v. 9 ; 2 Thess. iii. 10).   In 1 Cor.
xv. 32 f. only the scholar would recognise the verse from
an Attic comedian which follows a quotation from Isa.
(xxii. 13), with only two words intervening (vol. i. 71,
n. 19).   Without question we do find in these letters,
and only in these letters, the unmistakable traces of a
fixed baptismal formula (n. 20); but this is a cause for
suspicion only if we know certainly that such a formula
did not originate until after Paul's death.   But this is
precisely what we do not know.   It is also to be admitted
that Paul does speak in these Epistles more frequently and
more definitely than in the earlier letters, of orthodox teaching which was to be handed down from teacher to disciple,

of a confession to be made publicly before the Church, of a form of words which the disciple when he teaches is to use as a summary of Christian truth, and of the truth embraced in this doctrine as the norm of speech and conduct for all (2 Tim. i. 13, ii. 2, 8, 14, iii. 10, 14; 1 Tim. i. 10, iv. 6, vi. 1, 3; Tit. i. 9, ii. 1, 10). That this point of view was not altogether foreign to Paul is evident from Rom. vi. 17, xvi. 17; 1 Cor. iv. 17, xv. 1-3; Col. ii. 6 f.; Eph. iv. 20 f. That in the course of time this way of looking at things should be confirmed, and that it should come more and more to view in face of the growing tendency about him to teach perversely for gain and even to teach false doctrines, is perfectly conceivable, as is also his anxiety, in view of his approaching death, that there shall be faithful and able witnesses of the truth proclaimed by him among the Gentiles. Similarly can we understand the manner in which, in view of the perils that exist and still threaten, he comforts himself by recalling that immovableness which through her divine origin belongs to the Church as the pillar of the truth (1 Tim. iii. 15; 2 Tim. ii. 19). That the idea of the unity of the Church was not foreign to Paul nor a late development of his thought, has been shown in the discussion of Ephesians (vol. i. 503 f.). The fact that the form of Christianity and the teaching here dealt with are unhealthy, explains why orthodox teaching is so often spoken of in these Epistles as sound (above, p. 107, and n. 16). In proportion as the ἑτεροδιδάσκαλοι subordinated the moral aspects of Christianity to their rabbinic fancies and ascetic hobbies, it was natural that this side of Christianity should come strongly to view, and that its opposition to all immorality should be emphasised (1 Tim. i. 10, vi. 1; Tit. ii. 1-4), and that the whole doctrine of the Church based upon the gospel and faith in the same (cf. 1 Tim. i. 11-16; Tit. iii. 3-7) should be described as a single commandment (ἡ ἐντολή, 1 Tim. vi. 14; ἡ παραγγελία, 1 Tim. v. 18, cf. iv. 11). To call this un-Pauline is to forget that Paul speaks of a law of Christ and of God which Christians are to fulfil (Gal. vi. 2; 1 Cor. ix. 21; cf. Rom. viii. 4), and also calls the gospel itself, which excludes all boasting, a law of faith (Rom. iii. 27, 31), and speaks of faith and of its manifestation in the life as obedience (Rom. i. 5, vi. 16, xvi. 26). Nowhere in these Epistles do we find sentences that sound so " un-Pauline " as 1 Cor. vii. 19, and which can be so readily mistaken as a fusion of genuine Pauline teaching with its opposite, as Gal. v. 6. Here full emphasis is laid upon the doctrine of redemption and of justification not by works but by grace (Tit. ii. 11–14, iii. 4–7; 1 Tim. i. 12–16, ii. 4–7; 2 Tim. i. 9), while in addition we have the bold statement (1 Tim. i. 9) that for the just man, and consequently for the sinner who has been made righteous by the mercy of the Saviour (1 Tim. i. 13–16), there is no law.

With regard to that last refuge of so-called criticism, namely, the linguistic character of the letters, it is to be remarked at the outset that a pseudo-Paul, by repeating and imitating Pauline expressions, would be sure to make mistakes and so betray himself. The opposite is what we really find. Even the greetings, which would be most apt to be handled in this way, are thoroughly original, showing dependence neither upon earlier letters nor upon the common model (n. 21). Here also is to be observed the peculiarity of Paul's style, by which he repeats within short range a characteristic word once used or a related word (vol. i. 516, n. 7), without prejudice to the fact that for one not a Greek he has command of an unusually large number of words and expressions (n. 21), which would tend rather to increase with time than to diminish. It is also to be observed that 1 Tim. and Titus were written within a short time of each other and for like reasons, and that 2 Tim. also is considerably closer to these letters both in time and purpose than it is to any of the Epistles that we have investigated. Consequently the fact that these

three letters have certain expressions in common which
either are not found in the earlier Pauline Epistles at
all, or occur only rarely, is no proof that they are
spurious, but only goes to confirm the conclusion arrived
at from the investigation of their contents, that they all
belong to the same period in Paul's life, and that the
last.   If it be admitted that the linguistic phenomena
of the letters controvert altogether the efforts of numerous
" apologists " to find a place for 1 Tim. and Titus in the
earlier period of Paul's life, then the " critics " in their
turn ought not to deny that 2 Tim. is different from the
other two not only in content, but also linguistically.
Such difference is very difficult to understand if all three
are the work of a forger, but very easy to explain if they
were written by Paul under the conditions which the letters
themselves disclose.

1. (P. 85.)   SCHLEIERMACHER was the first to deny positively the genuineness of 1 Tim. (*Über den sogen. ersten Brief des Paulos an den Timotheos.
Kritisches Sendschr. an Gass*, 1807 ; *Werke zur Theol.* ii. 221–320), at the same
time admitting the genuineness of 2 Tim. and of Tit.   BAUR (*Die sogenann-
ten Pastoralbr. des Ap. Pl.* 1835) pronounced them all spurious.   With many,
who in other respects have not followed the critical paths which Baur struck
out, this opinion has gained the weight of a dogma.   A summary of the
works in which this view is taken is given by HOLTZMANN (*Die Pastoralbriefe,
krit. u. exeg. behandelt*, 1880).   At the outset the " critics " (*e.g.* v. Soden, *HK²*,
iii. 1. 196) always make the assertion that " there is no place in Paul's life for
the situations presupposed " in these letters, the worth of which assertion can
be judged in the light of p. 54 ff.   Not a few have made the attempt to
find a genuine kernel in the letters, while at the same time rejecting the
whole mass of enveloping material; in recent times, LEMME (*Das echte
Ermahnungsschreiben des Paulus an Tim.* 1882) and HESSE (*Entstehung der
ntl. Hirtenbriefe*, 1889).   The former made the attempt with 2 Tim., the latter
with all three letters, the conclusion of the investigation being that a genuine
letter to Titus lies at the basis of our Tit., and that at least the fragment
of a genuine letter to Timothy is retained at the close of 2 Tim.   In like
fashion KRENKEL (*Beiträge* [1890], 395–468) thinks that he is able to distinguish parts of three genuine letters, namely (1) a letter dating from the time
of Acts xx. 1 f., probably addressed to Titus while he was staying in Crete
(=Tit. iii. 12 ; 2 Tim. iv. 20 ; Tit. iii. 13) ; (2) one dating from the imprisonment in Cæsarea, probably to Timothy (=2 Tim. iv. 9–18) ; and (3) one
written during the imprisonment in Rome to an assistant staying in Ephesus
(=2 Tim. iv. 19, i. 16, 17, 18*b*, iv. 21).   Hypotheses of this kind, in which a

a rule only their inventors believe, could establish a claim to serious con
sideration only if developed with an unusual degree of ingenuity and care
But this we fail to find when, *e.g.* we read that according to 2 Tim. ii. 14–
iv. 5, Timothy, instead of hastening to Rome, as he is commanded to do in the
genuine part (iv. 9, 21), is to labour officially in a circle of Churches as a
resident successor of the apostles there (Lemme, 37) ; or that Paul maintained a thoroughly negative attitude toward the religion of the O.T. (including that of Abraham, David, and Elijah ?), accepting only its scriptures (55) ;
or when Krenkel, 421, seeks to support the essential historicity of the facts
presupposed in Tit. by the assumption that Titus at the time of Acts xx. 1–3
went to Crete, possibly from Athens, while Paul turned aside to Corinth
(cf. *per contra*, Tit. i. 5, ἀπέλιπόν σε ἐν Κρήτῃ) ; or when the same critic (422)
discovers in Acts xxvii. 7 f. that Paul landed in Crete, but met no Christians
there ; or when, further on (444), he explains the difference between 2 Tim.
iv. 18 and Philem. 22—a sentence which, he alleges, was written shortly
before—as due to a change of mood for which there was no real motive.

2. (Pp. 85, 86.) The *Epistle to the Laodiceans* (*GK*, ii. 584) and the *Third
Epistle of Paul to the Corinthians* contain the name of no person belonging
to the time when they purport to have been written except that of Paul ; the
Epistle of Peter to James (*Clementina*, ed. Lagarde, p. 3) none except those of
Peter and James. It is only in the apocryphal *Epistle of the Corinthians to
Paul* (ed. Vetter, p. 52) that certain other names are to be found, namely,
Stephanas, from 1 Cor. i. 16, xvi. 15–17, as bishop of Corinth, and among the
members of the presbytery associated with him, in addition to two unknown
persons, a Theophilus (Luke i. 3 ; Acts i. 1) and a Eubulus (2 Tim. iv. 21).
Further, in association with the Simon of Acts viii., a Cleobios, an unfaithful
disciple of the apostles, repeatedly mentioned in the literature of the second
century, sometimes in connection with Simon, sometimes not (*GK*, ii. 596,
n. 3) ; finally a Theonas, perhaps the Theodas who was known in the second
century as a disciple of Paul (Vetter, p. 53, A. 1; *Forsch.* iii. 125). Only in
the last of the four forged letters mentioned are to be found hints of definite
historical situations (vv. 2, 8) ; yet even here we have not independent
fiction, but a component part of a larger narrative fiction, the old *Acts of
Paul*. Moreover, this letter is composed on the basis of 1 Cor. vii. 1 quite as
mechanically as Paul's reply based on 1 Cor. v. 9, and the *Epistle to the
Laodiceans* based on Col. iv. 16. Suffice it merely to mention later and more
wretched inventions, such as a letter of John preserved by Prochorus (*Acta
Jo.* p. 63 ; cf. *GK*, i. 217, A. 2), and the correspondence between Seneca and
Paul, which are even poorer in quality.

3. (P. 85.) Ranke (*Weltgesch.* iii. 1. 191) : "The widespread doubt as to
the genuineness of the Epistles to Timothy is due to the fact that we possess
no reliable information whatever concerning that epoch. Various circumstances are mentioned which we are unable to place in relation to others
about which we possess knowledge. But they are details of a minor character, and who would be likely to have invented them ?"

4. (P. 91.) Phil. i. 1 of the single Church, σὺν ἐπισκόποις καὶ διακόνοις.
Just so Clem. 1 *Cor.* xlii. 4 ; Herm. *Sim.* ix. 26. 2, 27. 2 ; cf. *Vis.* iii. 5. 1 ;
Didache, chap. xv., cf. *Forsch.* iii. 302–310. The single προεστώς over against
the plurality of διάκονοι in Just. *Apol.* i. 65, 67, can prove nothing to the

contrary; for the διάκονος is here viewed as the leader of the worship, and
such leading can hardly be performed by more than one at a time.

5. (P. 91.) Just as the πρεσβύτεροι τοῦ λαοῦ in Jerusalem (Matt. xxi.
23; Acts iv. 8) form the πρεσβυτέριον (Acts xxii. 5) or γερουσία (Acts v. 21),
i.e. the great Sanhedrin, in the same way the πρεσβύτεροι τῆς ἐκκλησίας
(Acts xx. 17; Jas. v. 14) everywhere make up a πρεσβυτέριον (Ign. *Eph.* ii. 2,
iv. 1; in all twelve times). The name πρεσβύτερος among Jews and early
Christians was not, any more than "senator" among the Romans, an official
title, or more precisely, the designation of an official, but denoted membership in the senate which had the rule over the congregation. But for
that very reason the πρεσβύτερος was assured of a share in the government of the congregation (κυβέρνησις, 1 Cor. xii. 28; ποιμένες, Eph. iv. 11;
ποιμαίνειν, 1 Pet. v. 2 f.; Acts xx. 28; 1 Cor. ix. 7; προΐστασθαι, 1 Thess. v. 12;
Rom. xii. 8; 1 Tim. v. 17; Herm. *Vis.* ii. 4. 3; ἡγεῖσθαι, Acts xv. 22; Heb.
xiii. 7, 17, 24; Clem. 1 *Cor.* i. 3, perhaps also lxiii. 1; προηγεῖσθαι, Clem.
1 *Cor.* ii. 6; Herm. *Vis.* ii. 2. 6, iii. 9. 7), and an official character was lent to
his actions in so far as he performed any functions whatever in his capacity
as πρεσβύτερος.   E. Kühl (*Die Gemeindeordnung in den Pastoralbr.* 1885)
treated this subject with especial reference to Hatch's hypotheses. Cf. also
Zöckler, *Bibl. u. kirchenhistor. Studien* (1893), ii., "Diakonen und Evangelisten,"
where ample notice is taken of the more recent literature; see especially
S. 33–37, 63–71.

6. (P. 92.) One reason for the choice of the word ἐπίσκοπος instead of
πρεσβύτερος (1 Tim. iii. 2) may be found in the *locus communis* immediately
preceding (iii. 1). The reading ἀνθρώπινος (instead of πιστός) ὁ λόγος, which
was the only prevalent reading in the West until Jerome's time, seems to the
present writer so incapable of invention, and the change in uniformity with
i. 15, iv. 9, 2 Tim. ii. 11, Tit. iii. 8, so comprehensible, that in spite of its
incomplete attestation (Greek only in D*) he is compelled to conclude that it
was the original reading. It was probably a proverb of rather broad significance and non-Christian origin (cf. Rom. vi. 19). Moreover, the use of the
singular τὸν ἐπίσκοπον, which of itself is not peculiar (1 Cor. vii. 32–35, xiv.
2–4; 2 Cor. xii. 12, τοῦ ἀποστόλου; cf. also the change of number in 1 Tim.
v. 1, 2 and v. 3–5), was particularly natural after the saying in iii. 1, in which
the individual who desires an office is mentioned. In like manner the
transition from τοὺς πρεσβυτέρους (Tit. i. 5) to τὸν ἐπίσκοπον (i. 7) is occasioned by the intervening εἴ τις (i. 6).

7. (Pp. 92, 94.) Baur (*Pastoralbriefe*, 80 f.), who admits that πρεσβύτερος
and ἐπίσκοπος refer to the same office, argues that Tit. i. 5 means that in each
of several cities a presbyter was to be appointed, who was called ἐπίσκοπος
in relation to the individual Church, but πρεσβύτερος in relation to his
colleagues in the other Churches. But herein are two claims that contradict
the history. Churches with a single bishop which did not at the same time
have a number of presbyters are as thoroughly unknown in the whole
extent of the early Church (n. 4) as is a college of presbyters composed
of the overseers of the various local congregations. But aside from this,
the difficulty with this view is not so much that the two elements of the
command, namely, "to appoint a man as ἐπίσκοπος of each single church,"
and "thereby to make him member of the general presbytery of Crete," are

not clearly expressed; they are rather not expressed at all. The construction necessitates such an interpretation here just as little as in Acts xiv. 23
(cf. *per contra* Matt. xxvii. 15, κατὰ δὲ ἑορτὴν . . . ἕνα). It would be possible
with Hofmann to take πρεσβυτέρους as a second predicate accusative, supplying the first accusative or direct object from i. 6; but considering the
common occurrence of combinations like καθιστάναι τύραννον (Herodot. v. 92
at the beginning; βασιλεῖς, Dan. ii. 21; κριτάς, 2 Chron. xix. 5, everywhere
without a double accusative), and in view of the analogy of χειροτονεῖν (Acts
xiv. 23; Ign. *Smyrn.* xi. 2), such an interpretation is not very probable. Cf.
Clem. 1 *Cor.* liv. 2, οἱ καθεσταμένοι πρεσβύτεροι. The early commentators
without exception recognised the identity of presbyter and bishop in Phil.
i. 1; Tit. i. 7; 1 Tim. iii. 1–7 (Ambrosiaster on these passages; Jerome, Vall.
vii. 694 f.; Theod. Mops. i. 199, ii. 118–126, 168 f., 239). The Syrians
(Ephrem, *Comm. in Pauli Epist.* 249, 269, and the Peshito) go so far as to
translate ἐπίσκοπος and ἐπισκοπή in Tit. i. 7, 1 Tim. iii. 1 f. by *presbyter* and
presbyteratus.

8. (P. 93.) Acts xiv. 23, xx. 17, 28 (which latter passage, Acts xx., treats
only of the elders of Ephesus, and not, as Irenæus (iii. 14. 2) and Baur (83)
interpreted it, of the bishops and presbyters of the western part of Asia
Minor, where also the πρεσβύτεροι of the local Church, as Luke calls them,
are called by Paul ἐπίσκοποι in view of their official work among the flock
entrusted to them). Further, cf. 1 Pet. v. 1–4 (πρεσβύτεροι—ποιμαίνειν [in
addition to this ἐπισκοπεῖν, according to the majority of the witnesses]—
ποίμνιον—ἀρχιποίμην = ii. 25, ποιμένα καὶ ἐπίσκοπον). For Rome and Corinth,
Clem. 1 *Cor.* 42. 4 (the first converts appointed by the apostles everywhere
in town and country as ἐπίσκοποι καὶ διάκονοι), xlii. 5 (foretold in Isa. lx.
17), 40 (foreshadowed by priests and Levites, cf. xliii.), xliv. 1, 4 (ἐπισκοπή,
the office of the foremost men); xliv. 3–6, xlvii. 6, liv. 2, lvii. 1 (the super-
intendents appointed by the apostles in Corinth, *i.e.* the ἐπίσκοποι, yet
πρεσβύτεροι for all that). Concerning the concurrent testimony of Hermas,
cf. the writer's *Hirt des Hermas*, 98 ff.; with reference to Philippi, his
Ignatius, 297–301, 535; concerning the *Didache, Forsch.* iii. 302–310. As for
the testimony of Acts, suspicions of its trustworthiness cannot influence our
judgment in this matter; for the incidental and incomplete character of
the statements on the subject excludes the possibility that the author was
endeavouring to ɔrace a definite official organisation of his time back to an
apostolic foundation.

9. (P. 95.) With reference to widows, cf. the writer's *Ignatius*, S.
333–337, 580–585; Uhlhorn, *Die christl. Liebestätigkeit*, i. 159 ff.

10. (P. 95.) The interpretation and practical application of Tit. i. 6,
1 Tim. iii. 2, 12, according to which the clergy, in distinction from the
laity, are forbidden to marry a second time, is of early date, and was known
to Tertullian, *de Exhort. cast.* vii.; *Monog.* xii., who combated it with no little
skill. The content of the prohibition, however, he understood in the same
sense, and his object was simply to extend its application to all Christians.
The Catholic interpretation and praxis are attested by Origen, *Hom.* xvii. *in
Luc.; in Matt. hom.* xiv. 22 (Delar. iii. 645, 953); Hippol. *Refut.* ix. 12; the
so-called *Apostolical Constitutions*, xvi. 3 (Funk, *Doctr. XII. apost.* p. 60),
according to the most likely interpretation; *Ambrosiaster*, ed. Bened. pp.

294, 295. Jerome, while rejecting what he terms Tertullian's exaggeration likewise accepts this view (Vall. vii. 696 f.), as also Chrysostom (xi. 598 f., 605, 738), although both were acquainted with the correct exegesis, which before this had been supported by Ephrem, p. 249, and with especial positiveness by Theodorus (ii. 99–106). Among moderns, cf. particularly Hofmann on Tit. i. 6. Schleiermacher, who (191) recognised the correct interpretation of Tit. i. 6, would not admit that it held for the similar words in 1 Tim. iii. 2, since, as he claimed, such a meaning is impossible in v. 9, at least, and a uniform interpretation is required throughout the same letter. If it is sufficiently established that Tit. i. 6 should be taken as a prohibition of all sexual intercourse out of wedlock, then the same interpretation holds also in 1 Tim. iii. 2, 12. But these sentences are related to 1 Tim. v. 9 exactly as the two halves of 1 Cor. vii. 2 to each other ; for the meaning of this latter passage is not only that men and women should as a rule be married, but also that each one, whether man or woman, should confine sexual intercourse to the consort; cf. 1 Thess. iv. 3 ; Eph. v. 22, 28, 33. The implied contrast is never a recognised and regulated bigamy, polygamy, or polyandry, but always sexual intercourse that is out of wedlock and adulterous. Not infrequently expressions are used for such intercourse which the ill-informed might understand as denoting a formal marriage relation (1 Cor. v. 1 ; John iv. 18, vol. i. p. 296, n. 4). The impossibility of referring the prohibition to a second marriage is, however, still more clear in 1 Tim. v. 9 than in the other passages, since this sentence stands in the closest proximity to the command that the younger widows should marry again (v. 14).

11. (Pp. 99, 116.) Baur says (*Pastoralbriefe*, 10) : " In a word, we have before us in the heretics of the Pastoral Epistles the Gnostics of the second century, particularly the Marcionites " (see below, n. 18). Hilgenfeld (*Einl.* 748, 752), while agreeing with Baur in essentials, distinguishes, however, a double heresy, the Gentile Christian Gnosis, including that of Marcion, and a Jewish legalistic tendency, both of which, he holds, are opposed in 1 Tim. i. 3–11 as well as in Tit. i. 14, iii. 9. Mangold (*Die Irrlehrer des Pastoralbr.* 1856), partly in dependence upon Ritschl, who holds the false teachers of Tit. to be Therapeutæ, *i.e.* degenerate Essenes, and partly following Credner, though he most warmly opposes that writer's division of the false teachers in the Pastoral Epistles into four classes, undertakes to show that in all three Epistles, Essenism is attacked. In Tit. he thinks this party, who are seeking to force their teaching upon the Church, is still altogether outside of Christianity ; in 2 Tim., which was written earlier than 1 Tim., they are attempting a "fusion of their dogmas with Christian ideas," to the support of which they are attempting to win over individual Christians (28) ; lastly, in 1 Tim. they are making a menacing assault upon the whole Church of Ephesus. Lightfoot (*Bibl. Essays*, 1893, pp. 408, 411–418, this part written as early as 1865) attempted to prove that the attack here is aimed against the party of the Naassenes described by Hippolytus, *Refut.* v. 6–11, or a party very closely related to this sect. Careful exegesis, in which regard Hofmann has rendered the greatest services here also, excludes all these and similar interpretations. Hort's discussion (*Judaistic Christianity*, 1894, pp. 130–146), which exegetically closely follows B. Weiss, is the best thus far.

12. (Pp. 100, 101, 102.) Ἑτεροδιδασκαλεῖν, formed from a word ἑτεροδιδάσ-

καλος (Eus. *H. E.* iii. 32. 8), which may have been already in use at that time or only made up for the occasion,—it makes no difference which,—belongs to that numerous class of verbs derived from compound nouns or adjectives which "denote the existence in a state or the customary exercise of an activity" (Blass-Kühner, i. 2. 337; cf. S. 260). Examples in Paul's writings are ἀγαθοεργεῖν, ἑτεροζυγεῖν, ξενοδοχεῖν, οἰκοδεσποτεῖν, τεκνογονεῖν, τεκνο-τροφεῖν. There was no such verb as διδασκαλέω, which one MS. of Clem. *Hom.* ii. 15 gives, any more than ἐργέω, γονέω, δοχέω. Furthermore, the analogy of νομοδιδάσκαλος (1 Tim. i. 7), καλοδιδάσκαλος (Tit. ii. 3), ψευδοδιδάσκαλος (2 Pet. ii. 1), κακοδιδάσκαλος (κακοδιδασκαλεῖν, Clem. 2 *Cor.* x. 5; Sextus Emp. *c. Rhet.* xlii., even with *acc. pers.*), γεροντοδιδάσκαλος (Plato, *Euthyd.* 272), γραμματοδιδάσκαλος (Plut. *Alcib.* vii.), δουλοδιδάσκαλος (title of a comedy by Pherecrates), ἱεροδιδάσκαλος (Dion. Halic. ii. 73), παιδοδιδάσκαλος, πορνοδιδάσ-καλος, χοροδιδάσκαλος κτλ., proves beyond doubt that ἑτεροδιδάσκαλος is a teacher of the kind denoted by ἑτερο-, and certainly not, as Otto, 45; Kölling, i. 254 ff.; Hesse, 77, 125, tried to make out, "one who has another teacher." The word ἑτεροδέσποτος, which, according to Kölling, 261, decides the matter, is not pertinent, since διδάσκαλος is a very common substantive, while δέσποτος, on the contrary, is no word at all. The rule which is given to justify this remarkable interpretation (Kölling, 254) is contradicted by the whole great class of so-called attributive compounds (Blass-Kühner, i. 2. 312 f.), *e.g.* καλλιέλαιος, Rom. xi. 24; καλλίχθυς, κακόδουλος, κακόμαντις, γλυκύμηλον, παμβασιλεύς, παμμήτωρ, ἀρχιερεύς, πρωτόμαρτυς, to which also the word ἑτεροδιδάσκαλος belongs. Of the two chief meanings of ἕτερος (illustrated also in compounds, *e.g.* ἑτερόφθαλμος, one-eyed; ἑτερόγλωσσος, speaking another tongue), naturally only the second is in place here. As in ἑτερόδοξος, ἑτεροδοξέω, ἑτεροδοξία (Ign. *Magn.* viii. 1; *Smyrn.* vi. 2; Jos. *Bell.* ii. 8. 5), it may retain its primary significance of simple difference or divergence, whether from the standpoint of the speaker or from that of the person or thing spoken of; but quite commonly also may denote more specifically divergence from what is correct. A "teacher of a different kind," a "teacher with divergent views" (Hofmann), is an abnormal, perverse teacher (cf. ἕτερον εὐαγγέλιον, Gal. i. 6; 2 Cor. xi. 4). To exercise the functions, to perform the part, of such a teacher is ἑτεροδιδασκαλεῖν. To be sure, such activity cannot very well be carried on without ἑτέρως διδάσκειν, and often implies also ἕτερα or ἀλλότρια διδάσκειν. But the ecclesiastical use of the word in the sense of "to propound a false doctrine" (Ign. *ad Pol.* iii. 1; Eus. *H. E.* vii. 17. 4; cf. κακοδιδασκαλία, Ign. *Philad.* ii. 1; Hippol. *Refut.* ix. 8) was an inexact applica-tion of an expression perhaps coined by Paul himself. Although we are not justified in referring every word in Tit. i. 10–16, iii. 9, or even iii. 9–11, to the same phenomenon which is characterised in 1 Tim. i. 3–11, vi. 3–10, but should rather assume that various sorts of people were to be found among the "many" in Tit. i. 10, yet the repetition of the same or similar expressions admits of no doubt that in Tit. also Paul had in mind primarily ἑτεροδιδασκαλοῦντες of the same kind as were then busy in Ephesus and its vicinity. And other sentences as well, 1 Tim. iv. 7, vi. 20, 2 Tim. ii. 14, 16a, 23, are through their similar terminology connected with these passages.

13. (P. 101.) According to well-known classical usage, ἐπαγγέλλεσθαι, 1 Tim. vi. 21, also points to the plying of the business of teaching as a pro-

fession; so likewise αἰσχροῦ κέρδους χάριν, Tit. i. 11. The rule that the preacher of the gospel should also draw his support from this labour, which Paul had recognised as a principle in 1 Cor. ix. 6–14 (cf. Matt. x. 10; Luke x. 7), had been applied by the Petrine party to themselves, although they were not so much missionaries as teachers within existing Churches (vol. i. 290). Paul himself extends it to the presbyters, especially those who devote themselves to the calling of teachers, 1 Tim. v. 18; hence he could not oppose on principle the custom of these ἑτεροδιδασκαλοῦντες of receiving remuneration, but, just as in 2 Cor. ii. 17, in opposition to the Petrine party, limited himself to reproving the sordid mind, the base greed of gain, with which they made use of their acknowledged right.

14. (Pp. 103, 116.) In comparison with the procedure of many modern critics, it seems pardonable that the ancient Catholic writers against heresy should have been fond of regarding without sharp discrimination the most various sayings in these and other Pauline Epistles as predictions of the false doctrines of their own times. Cf. Tert. *Præscr.* vi., "providerat jam tunc spiritus sanctus," etc., referring to Gal. i. 8; Irenæus in the title of his great work, ἔλεγχος καὶ ἀνατροπὴ τῆς ψευδωνύμου γνώσεως, following 1 Tim. vi. 20 (cf. Iren. ii. 14. 7). 1 Tim. i. 4 and the related passages were especially favourite citations in connection with the Valentinian doctrine of æons, though they were taken not so much as specific predictions of this doctrine as general statements which could be applied to it (Iren. i. procem. 1; Tert. *c. Val.* iii.; *Præscr.* iii. xxxiii.). On the other hand, Ign. *Mgn.* viii. uses language which suggests 1 Tim. i. 4, Tit. i. 14, iii. 9 of the Judaistic teachers of his time, without, however, mentioning γενεαλογίαι. The ancient commentators uniformly maintain the Jewish character of the "false teachers in the Pastoral Epistles," suggest rabbinic fables, and are too much inclined to view these teachers as men of like opinions with the Judaists in Gal.; Ambrosiaster, pp. 269, 314, 316; Jerome, Vall. vii. 710 f., 734 ff.; Pelagius (Jerome, Vall. xi.), pp. 405, 431 f., 434; Ephrem, pp. 244, 251, 271, 275; Theodorus, ii. 70–74; Chrysost. xi. 551, 556, who, however, p. 552, refers incidentally also to Greek legends about the gods; Theodoret, p. 639, who yet cannot let the opportunity slip, p. 673, in commenting on 1 Tim. vi. 20, of bringing in also the Gnostics who sprang from Simon.

15. (P. 103.) Even in the N.T. we have examples of such rabbinic traditions, in part of a genealogical nature : Matt. i. 5, Rahab, the mother of Boaz; 2 Tim. iii. 8, the names of the Egyptian magicians; Heb. xi. 37, the sawing asunder of Isaiah. All that the Jews called haggadah (agadah) belongs here. "Haggadoth" can be translated by "legends," hence in Greek by μῦθοι. But see Schürer, ii. 339, A 26 [Eng. trans. II. i. 339], who here accepts Bacher's conclusions. What an important part of these "haggadoth" were the genealogies, the forefathers' wives, whom the O.T. leaves nameless, or their sons and daughters, who are not enumerated with any completeness, is shown by the Book of Jubilees (*e.g.* iv. 8; cf. Dillmann in Ewald's *Bibl. Jahrb.* iii. 79 f., 87; Rönsch, *Buch der Jubil.* 485–489). Ancient history, even among the Greeks, consisted of myths and genealogies (Polyb. ix. 1. 4, 2. 1; Diod. Sic. iv. 1, cited by Hort, p. 135); and this was all the more true in the case of the Jew, who had Genesis to build upon. Not a little of such history had found its way even to Hellenistic Jews like Philo and Justin

Martyr's Trypho ; cf. Goldfahn (*Just. M. und die Agada*; Siegfried, *Philo*, 146). Philo calls the whole content of the Pentateuchal narrative which lies between the creation of the world and the giving of the law τὸ γενεαλογικόν (*de vita Mos.* ii. 8 ; elsewhere, however, he calls it τὸ ἱστορικόν, *de præm. et pœn.* 1). Theodorus, ii. 72, cites, as a proof of the confusion of Jewish genealogies, the difference between the lists of Jesus' ancestors in Matt. and in Luke. Jerome (Vall. vii. 735 f.) tells of a Jewish Christian in Rome who perplexed the simple by the display of his genealogical wisdom with regard to Matt. i. and Luke iii. This was probably the proselyte Isaac, perhaps identical with the Christian exegete known as "Ambrosiaster" (cf. *ThLb*, 1899, No. 27 ; *ZKom. Gal.* 22 f. ; *NKZ*, 1905, S. 419–427). It is not at all impossible that even in Paul's time Jewish Christians had set on foot endless discussions about Christ's lineage, a matter which Paul also considered important (2 Tim. ii. 8 ; Rom. i. 3).

16. (Pp. 107, 120.) 1 Tim. i. 10, vi. 3 ; Tit. i. 9, ii. 1 ; 2 Tim. i. 13, iv. 3 ; cf. Tit. ii. 8, λόγος ὑγιής ; Tit. i. 13, ii. 2, ὑγιαίνειν (ἐν) τῇ πίστει. It is hardly necessary to recall that ὑγιαίνων, ὑγιής means simply "healthy" (*sanus*), and not also "wholesome" (*saluber*).

17. (Pp. 109, 117.) According to *Acta Theclæ*, xiv., Demas and Hermogenes (2 Tim. i. 15, iv. 10), who are here substituted for Hymenæus and Philetus (above, p. 21 ; *GK*, i. 789, ii. 901 f.), say of Paul : καὶ ἡμεῖς σε διδάξομεν ἣν λέγει οὗτος ἀνάστασιν γίνεσθαι (*al.* γενέσθαι), ὅτι ἤδη γέγονεν, ἐφ' οἷς ἔχομεν τέκνοις [καὶ ἀνιστάμεθα θεὸν ἐπεγνωκότες ἀληθῆ]. The words in brackets, which are essentially confirmed by the Coptic translation (Schmidt, S. 35. 24), but are wanting in two Lat. VSS. and one Syr. VS., and which were also lacking in the copy which Ambrosiaster read (Ambros. *Opera*, ii. App. p. 308 on 2 Tim. ii. 18), as shown by the construction, are a later addition. In addition to Ambrosiaster, only the first explanation is ascribed to the persons mentioned in 2 Tim. ii. 17 ; Epiph. *Hær.* xl. 8 ; Pelagius (Jerome, Vall. xi. 425 in connection with another allegorical interpretation modelled after Ezk. xxxvii.) ; Theodorus, ii. 209 ; Theodoret, p. 685. The second explanation, a hint of which Ephrem (p. 261) gives in connection with the same passage ("resurrectio . . . non corporum sed animarum," cf. a Coptic fragment of the *Acts of Paul*, ed. Schmidt, p. 73. 15), is ascribed by Hippolytus (*de resurr. ad Mammæam*, Syriac in Pitra, *Anal.* iv. 61, German in *Hippolyts klein. Schriften*, ed. Achelis, S. 251) to Nicolaüs, from whom he thinks Hymenæus and Philetus and other Gnostics received it ; a resurrection through conversion and baptism. Hippolytus ascribes similar opinions to the Naassenes (*Refut.* v. 8, p. 158). According to Irenæus, i. 23. 5, Menander also taught a resurrection through baptism which makes one immortal ; cf. the hint in Just. *Apol.* i. 26 ; Iren. ii. 31. 2 of the Simonians and Carpocratians : "esse autem resurrectionem a mortuis agnitionem ejus, quæ ab eis dicitur, veritatis." This is given more at length in Tert. *Resurr.* xix. In *Præscr.* iii. the same writer, after citing 2 Tim. ii. 17, adds : "id de se Valentiniani asseverant." Justin wrote against this doctrine of a merely spiritual resurrection (ed. Otto, ii. 211–249, especially p. 243 ; cf. *ZfKG*, viii. 1–37). The antiquity of this spiritual explanation of the Christian doctrine of the resurrection is attested by its dissemination in the most various circles before 150, as well as by the σαρκὸς ἀνάστασιν in the Apostles' Creed ; cf. the writer's *Das apostolische*

Symbolum, 96–100. How much older may be the first mentioned interpretation of the doctrine quoted in 2 Tim. ii. 18 ?

18. (P. 118.) Baur (*Pastoralbr.* 26 f.) was the first to find in 1 Tim. vi. 20 a play upon the title of Marcion's famous *Antitheses*. He also (15–18) understood the word νομοδιδάσκαλοι, 1 Tim. i. 7, of the Marcionites, hostile as they were to the Mosaic law, and took 1 Tim. i. 8 not as a concession, but rather as directed against them. Moreover, he found in the contests about the law, Tit. iii. 9, from which Titus is to refrain, the battles between the Marcionites and their opponents concerning the worth of the law, in which battles even the author himself had taken part. Not even the much abused Church Fathers ever contrived anything like this. Where Irenæus (ii. 14. 7) applies 1 Tim. vi. 20 to Gnostics, he leaves out the words καὶ ἀντιθέσεις ; if he had applied it to Marcion, he would have exchanged γνῶσις for some other word, for that did not characterise Marcion in the least. Concerning Marcion's work, *The Antitheses*, see *GK*, i. 596 f. It is plain that the νομο-διδάσκαλοι, if they are meant in this passage too, did not, like Marcion, bring out *contrarietates* between the law and the gospel, but sought in rabbinical fashion to force their own way to knowledge, and to lead others thither through the mutually contradictory decisions of the "wise." They cultivated the Halakah as well as the Haggadah ; cf. Hort (*op. cit.* 140 ff.) ; Weber, *Jüd. Theol.* § 24.

19. (P. 118.) Baur (126), Hilgenf. (*Einl.* 764, cf. Holtzmann, *Pastoralbr.* 269) thought that they could infer from the plural βασιλεῖς, 1 Tim. ii. 2,—which occurs in a similar connection also in Polyc. *Phil.* xii. 3 (cf. *per contra*, 1 Pet. ii. 13, 17), and has led to a similar conclusion with respect to that letter,—that 1 Tim. was not written until the time of Antoninus, or not until after 137. In reply, it should first be remarked that a joint rule of two Augusti occurred for the first time in 161, and that, on the contrary, co-regencies, as that, *e.g.* in which Marcus Aurelius shared after 147, occurred repeatedly after the time of Augustus (Mommsen, *R. Staatsrecht²*, ii. 1089 ff., 1109 ff. ; Wieseler, *Beiträge zur Würdigung der Evv.* 186–196). Justin in the time of Antoninus Pius could speak of βασιλεῖς with reference to the co-regency of Marcus Aurelius (*Apol.* i. 14, 17), although there was only one αὐτοκράτωρ (*Apol.* i. 1, ii. 2) ; and this could have been done just as well under Augustus or Vespasian with reference to the co-regency of Tiberius or of Titus. Further, it is arbitrary to take the anarthrous βασιλεῖς ("such as are kings") as referring exclusively to the man or men who possessed supreme power in Rome at the time ; for in N.T. times, in addition to the emperor, there was more than one bearer of the title of king who had significance for the Christians ; cf. the closing sentence of Strabo's *Geography*, xvii. 25. We can see from the N.T. what a part kings like Herod Agrippa I. and II. and Aretas IV. played in the history of the apostles (Acts xii. 1–22, xxv. 13–26, 32 ; 2 Cor. xi. 32). The extensive kingdom of Pontus, in which Christian Churches existed (1 Pet. i. 1), continued until 63 A.D., and a queen dowager, Tryphæna, a Thracian by birth, but belonging to the royal house of Pontus by marriage, is connected in ancient tradition with the earliest history of the Christians of Asia Minor (*GK*, ii. 906). Are we to suppose that the Christians were not permitted to pray for these kings, or that they did not reckon these among the βασιλεῖς and βασιλεύοντες (Matt. x. 18, xvii. 25 ;

Mark xiii. 9 ; Luke xxi. 12, xxii. 25 ; Acts ix. 15; Rev. i. 5 ; 1 Tim. vi. 15),
or that all the books in which we read such things were written later than
137 ? But the plural can just as well be understood as denoting a class (cf.
Matt. ii. 20). In the same sense Tatian (*Oratio ad Græc.* iii. 10) writes of
βασιλεῖς and οἱ βασιλεῖς, without losing sight of the fact that only one was
ὁ βασιλεύς (chap. iv.), Epictetus, probably under Trajan, speaks of καταφρονεῖν
τῶν βασιλέων (*Diss.* i. 29. 9), although for the most part he represents the
one emperor as ὁ τύραννος, and Galenus in addressing the one emperor says
ὑμῶν τῶν βασιλέων (ed. Kühn, xiv. 659). As this apostolic precept then
came to be applied in the changeful course of the political history, the
actual result was that the Christians even in apostolic times as well as later
prayed for the successive Roman emperors and other possessors of princely
power on earth, though Paul himself need not have reflected particularly
upon the co-existence and succession of power involved in βασιλεῖς. Cf. for
this co-existence Clem. 1 *Cor.* lxi. 1, according to which the Roman Church
prayed for a plurality of rulers to whom God had intrusted royal authority,
and for the succession (Tert. *Apol.* xxx., " precantes sumus semper pro omnibus
imperatoribus"), which is followed, chap. xxxi., by the quotation from 1 Tim.
ii. 2., Lightfoot cites still other examples, Lightf. *Ign. Pol.* i. 576.

20. (P. 119.) Traces of a baptismal creed, 1 Tim. vi. 12–16 ; 2 Tim.
ii. 2–8, iv. 1 ; cf. the writer's *Das apostol. Symbolum*, 38–44 ; Haussleiter, *Zur
Vorgeschichte des ap. Glaubensbekenntnisses*, 32–39. If in 1 Tim. iii. 16 we read
ὁμολογοῦμεν ὡς, according to Cod. D, this verb (cf. vi. 12) might seem to point
to a formulated confession, and it seems to the present writer certain that
the clauses so introduced were not constructed by Paul off hand. However,
the poetic strain in these words suggests more naturally a psalm than a
baptismal confession.

21. (P. 121.) While the *Epistle to the Laodiceans* (*GK*, ii. 584) constructs
its greeting from Gal. i. 1 and Phil. i. 2, and hence uses also the solemn
Pauline form of the greeting proper (χάρις ὑμῖν καὶ εἰρήνη κτλ.), we find the
latter neither in 1 Tim. nor in 2 Tim., though in a measure at least it is
retained in Tit. i. 4 (according to the better MSS.). On the contrary, in
1 Tim. i. 2, 2 Tim. i. 2, ἔλεος, which is never used by Paul at this point in
his letters (cf., however, Gal. vi. 16 ; 2 John 3), is placed between χάρις and
εἰρήνη ; and, moreover, at this place in all three letters we find employed a
mass of thoughts and words, some of which are not used by Paul at all, and
others not in greetings. It is altogether incomprehensible that a forger
should have taken the beginning and end of Rom. as his model in forming
such a salutation as Holtzmann (116) claims with reference to Tit. i. 1–4.
The diction is treated extensively enough by Holtzmann (*Pastoralbr.* 84–118),
Kölling (i. 17–206); briefly and well by Hofmann (vi. 57 f., 211 f., 320),
Lightfoot, *Bibl. Essays* (401 f.) ; cf. all the remarks above upon the diction of
Eph. and Col. (366 ff.). With the fundamentally wrong opinion of Schleiermacher (77), who calls Paul a writer " whose vocabulary is, as is well known,
so very limited," cf. the opinion of E. Curtius, vol. i. 70, n. 18. In the
first place, we find a correspondence to the usage of Paul of which examples
were given, vol. i. 516, in those words used several times either in 1 Tim.
and Tit. alone or in 2 Tim. only which do not occur elsewhere in Paul, or at
least not with the same signification. Here naturally we need not take into

account, even aside from the fact that they occur but once, ordinary designations of persons and things of which Paul has not had occasion to speak else
where, as μάμμη, 2 Tim. i. 5; βιβλία, μεμβράνα, φελόνης, χαλκεύς, 2 Tim.
iv. 13 f.; στόμαχος, 1 Tim. v. 23.   (a) Among the words used more than
once those peculiar to 2 Tim. are : κακοπαθεῖν and συγκακοπαθεῖν, i. 8, ii. 3, 9,
iv. 5 (cf. Jas. v. 10, 13); προκόπτειν, ii. 16, iii. 9, 13 (cf., however, Gal. i. 14);
ἐπαισχύνεσθαι, ἀνεπαίσχυντος, i. 8, 12, 16, ii. 15 (Rom. i. 16 is the only
other passage where it is used similarly) ; σωρεύω, ἐπισωρεύω, iii. 6, iv. 3 ;
εὔχρηστος, ii. 21, iv. 11 (Philem. 11).   (b) 1 Tim. and Tit. have in common,
to begin with, certain expressions in the greeting : γνήσιον τέκνον ἐν πίστει
and γνήσιον τέκνον κατὰ κοινὴν πίστιν respectively (cf. Phil. ii. 20, 22, γνησίως
. . . τέκνον), ἐλπίς, κατ᾽ ἐπιταγὴν (τοῦ σωτῆρος ἡμῶν) θεοῦ. The latter expression occurs in just the same form in Rom. xvi. 26 (cf. 1 Cor. vii. 6 ;
2 Cor. viii. 8 ; Tit. ii. 15), a passage the Pauline authorship of which has
been denied without good grounds (vol. i. 386 f.), and in which are still
other resemblances to Tit. i. 2 f., namely, χρόνοι αἰώνιοι (this also in 2 Tim.
i. 9), φανεροῦν, κήρυγμα ; these recur also in 1 Tim. iii. 16, though only in
part (μυστήριον . . . ἐφανερώθη . . . ἐκηρύχθη ἐν τοῖς ἔθνεσιν). Furthermore,
peculiar to 1 Tim. and Tit. are a multitude of attributes of the bishops and
deacons who are to be appointed (Tit. i. 6–9 ; 1 Tim. iii. 1–13, and in related
passages): ἀνέγκλητος, Tit. i. 6, 7 ; 1 Tim. iii. 10, for which, however, the
very common word in Paul, ἀνεπίληπτος, is substituted in 1 Tim. iii. 2, v. 7,
vi. 14 ; further, μιᾶς γυναικὸς ἀνήρ (cf. also 1 Tim. v. 9, and above, p. 125) ;
τέκνα ἔχων κτλ., μὴ πάροινος, μὴ πλήκτης, φιλόξενος, νηφάλιος, 1 Tim. iii. 2, 11 ;
Tit. ii. 2 ; αἰσχροκερδής, 1 Tim. iii. 8 ; Tit. i. 7 ; σεμνός, σεμνότης, 1 Tim.
ii. 2, iii. 4, viii. 11 ; Tit. ii. 2, 7 (but also in Phil. iv. 8) ; σώφρων, σωφρόνως,
σωφρονίζειν, 1 Tim. iii. 2 ; Tit. i. 8, ii. 2, 4, 5, 12 ; only once in 2 Tim. i. 7,
σωφρονισμός. εὐσέβεια occurs nine times in 1 Tim. and Tit. (1 Tim. ii. 2,
iii. 16, iv. 7, 8, vi. 3, 5, 6, 11 ; Tit. i. 1), in addition to εὐσεβεῖν, 1 Tim. v. 4 ;
εὐσεβῶς, Tit. ii. 12, as over against a single εὐσέβεια and εὐσεβῶς in 2 Tim.
iii. 5, 12. Certain terms applied to the perverse teachers are lacking in
2 Tim.: ἑτεροδιδασκαλεῖν, 1 Tim. i. 3, vi. 3 (cf. καλοδιδάσκαλος, Tit. ii. 3);
μῦθοι καὶ γενεαλογίαι, 1 Tim. i. 4 ; Tit. i. 14, iii. 9 (only μῦθοι alone in 2 Tim.
iv. 4) ; προσέχειν, 1 Tim. i. 4, iii. 8, iv. 1, 13, vi. 3 (middle voice). In addition
to ἔργον ἀγαθόν, which is a common expression from the time of the older letters
on (Rom. xiii. 3 ; 2 Cor. ix. 8 ; Eph. ii. 10 ; Phil. i. 6 ; Col. i. 10 ; 2 Thess.
ii. 17), and which is to be found in all three letters (especially in the connection πρὸς or εἰς πᾶν ἔργον ἀγαθόν, Tit. i. 16, iii. 1 ; 2 Tim. ii. 21, iii. 17) ;
ἐν παντὶ ἔργῳ ἀγαθῷ, 1 Tim. v. 10 ; Col. i. 10 (cf. also 1 Tim. ii. 10 ; 2 Tim.
iv. 18), we read καλὸν ἔργον (sing. and plur.) only in Tit. ii. 7, 14, iii. 8, 14 ;
1 Tim. iii. 1, v. 10, 25, vi. 18, never in 2 Tim. Just as Eph., written at the
same period as Col., is, for this very reason, and because of the similarity of
the subjects treated, most closely related in vocabulary to that Epistle, so, in
like manner and for the same reasons, 1 Tim. is more closely related to Tit.
than to any other Epistle of Paul, including 2 Tim.   (c) But it is also
apparent that 2 Tim. has a certain similarity of diction, sometimes to 1 Tim.
sometimes to Tit., and again to both letters. Here belongs, in the first place,
what was remarked above under (b) concerning εὐσεβεῖν, σώφρων, πρὸς πᾶν
ἔργον ἀγαθόν. καλὸν ἔργον is not used in 2 Tim., indeed, but it is nevertheless

worthy of note that καλός, which Paul used only sixteen times in all his other Epistles, occurs twenty-four times in these three small letters, and that, while it is used elsewhere by Paul only predicatively (Gal. iv. 8; 1 Cor. v. 6; Rom. vii. 16, cf. 1 Tim. i. 8, ii. 3, iv. 4) or substantively (Rom. vii. 18, 21; 2 Cor. xiii. 7), it occurs here twenty-one times as attribute, and that, too, also in 2 Tim. i. 14, ii. 3 (κ. στρατιώτης, cf. 1 Tim. i. 18), iv. 7 (κ. ἀγών, cf. 1 Tim. vi. 12). There should be mentioned, further, παρατίθεσθαι, παραθήκη, 1 Tim. i. 18, vi. 20; 2 Tim. i. 12, 14, ii. 2 (different in 1 Cor. x. 27); πιστὸς ὁ λόγος, with or without further addition, 1 Tim. i. 15 (concerning iii. 1 see above, p. 124, n. 6), iv. 9; 2 Tim. ii. 11; Tit. iii. 8; διαμαρτύρομαι ἐνώπιον κτλ., 1 Tim. v. 21; 2 Tim. ii. 14, iv. 1 (cf. 1 Thess. iv. 6, also for the enforcing of a command). While διδαχή elsewhere (Rom. vi. 17, xvi. 17; 1 Cor. xiv. 6, 26; so also Tit. i. 9) denotes the subject-matter of the teaching given or the particular didactic discourse, it is used in 2 Tim. iv. 2 of the teaching function. On the other hand, διδασκαλία, which occurs in our letters fifteen times, in all the rest only four times, denotes not only, as in Rom. xii. 7, xv. 4, the teaching function or the act of instructing (1 Tim. iv. 13, 16, v. 17; 2 Tim. iii. 10, 16; Tit. ii. 7), but also, as in Col. ii. 22, Eph. iv. 14 (?), the content of the teaching given : Tit. ii. 1, 10; 1 Tim. i. 10, iv. 1, 6, vi. 1, 3, perhaps also Tit. i. 9; 2 Tim. iv. 3. Concerning "sound teaching" see above, p. 129, n. 16. To be mentioned also are βέβηλοι κενοφωνίαι, 1 Tim. vi. 20; 2 Tim. ii. 16; λογομαχία, -εῖν, 1 Tim. vi. 4; 2 Tim. ii. 14; ἀστοχεῖν, 1 Tim. i. 6, vi. 21; 2 Tim. ii. 18; τυφοῦσθαι, 1 Tim. iii. 6, vi. 4; 2 Tim. iii. 4; ἄνθρωποι κατεφθαρμένοι τὸν νοῦν, 2 Tim. iii. 8, cf. 1 Tim. vi. 5; εἰς ἐπίγνωσιν ἀληθείας (ἐλθεῖν), 1 Tim. ii. 4; 2 Tim. ii. 25, iii. 7, cf. Tit. i. 1; 1 Tim. iv. 3, where it should be remarked concerning ἐπίγνωσις in general that it is not until the Epistles of the imprisonment that it occurs with any frequency, namely, eight times in Eph., Col., Philem., Phil., elsewhere only in Rom. (three times). A development in diction seems unmistakable, and that, too, with reference to matters of belief. Paul represents Christ elsewhere also as σωτήρ (Eph. v. 23; Phil. iii. 20), and speaks not only of a saving work on the part of God (1 Cor. i. 21, cf. 2 Tim. i. 9), but also of such a work on the part of Christ (Rom. v. 9, cf. 1 Tim. i. 15); nevertheless it is felt to be a different usage when now we find "our Saviour" as a regular designation, sometimes of Christ (Tit. i. 4, iii. 6; 2 Tim. i. 10), sometimes of God (1 Tim. i. 1, ii. 3, iv. 10; Tit. i. 3, ii. 10, iii. 4), and once even "our great God and Saviour Christ Jesus" (Tit. ii. 13). A usage which has its analogy, perhaps, in 2 Thess. ii. 8, but which is new notwithstanding, is that here the future appearing of Christ, of which Paul has spoken elsewhere, indeed, by no means infrequently, is called regularly ἡ ἐπιφάνεια, Tit. ii. 13; 1 Tim. vi. 14; 2 Tim. iv. 1, 8. The same is also used of the first appearance of Christ, 2 Tim. i. 10, cf. Tit. ii. 11, iii. 4. If the context in which this occurs twice should possibly point to the wording of an original form of the baptismal confession, the word ἐπιφάνεια could suggest to us the name and original meaning of the very ancient festival of Epiphany.

VIII.

THE EPISTLES OF PETER AND JUDE, AND THE EPISTLE TO THE HEBREWS.

§ 38. THE READERS AND THE AUTHOR OF THE FIRST EPISTLE OF PETER — THE INTERNAL EVIDENCE.

ACCORDING to 1 Pet. i. 1, this Epistle is addressed to Christians in Pontus, Galatia, Cappadocia, Asia, and Bithynia. When it is observed that not a single one of the old geographical names is here mentioned which is not also the name of a Roman province, and when the fact is recalled that the province of Galatia included Lycaonia and those parts of Phrygia and Pisidia which did not belong to the province of Asia (vol. i. 174 f., 183 f. n. 3), it becomes clear that the letter is intended for the whole of Asia Minor, with the exception of Cilicia (n. 1). Inasmuch as there were Christian Churches in Cilicia at a very early date (Acts xv. 23, 41 ; cf. Gal. i. 21 ; Acts ix. 30, xi. 25), we must assume that they are not here overlooked ; but being more closely allied to the group of Churches centring in Syrian Antioch, are intentionally excluded from the group of Churches on the other side of the Taurus, all of which had a similar origin.

It is perfectly evident that the letter has to do with the Christian Churches in the provinces mentioned, and not with individual Christians of a particular sort resident there, in addition to whom there may have been other Christians or Christian Churches in the same region. This

is conclusively proved by the parting benediction in v.
14 ; for here the readers are spoken of as all the Christians
—naturally all the Christians in the provinces mentioned
in i. 1.   Cared for by their own presbyters, they are the
flocks of Christ, the Chief Shepherd (v. 1–4), in Asia
Minor.   They are spoken of only in contrast either to
their heathen neighbours (ii. 12, 15, iii. 1, 13–17, iv.
3 f., 12 f.), the whole Church upon earth (v. 9), or a single
local Church outside of Asia Minor (v. 13).

This decides at once the question regarding the previous
history of the readers and their national and ecclesiastical
character ; for, from Acts (xiii. 14–xiv. 25, xvi. 1–10, xviii.
19–xx. 38) and from Galatians, Colossians, Ephesians, and
Philemon, we know through whose efforts mainly the
Churches in the provinces of Galatia and Asia were founded
(1 Cor. xvi. 1, 19), and what their character was from the
beginning.   According to the testimony of his own letters
and of Acts, Paul was the missionary who, in the sense of
Rom. xv. 20, 1 Cor. iii. 10, 2 Cor. x. 15, laid the foundations of Christianity in all this region.   In the cities to
which he did not bring the gospel himself, it was preached
by the friends and helpers who followed up his personal
labours and acted as his representatives ; and although
these Churches were only thus indirectly founded by himself, Paul reckoned them among the Churches committed
to his special care.   This view is presupposed in his letters
to the Churches in the province of Asia which remained
personally unacquainted with him (Ephesians, Colossians,
also Philemon, cf. vol. i. p. 449, n. 3, 460), and in such
expressions as are found in Rom. xv. 16–23, xvi. 4, 16 ;
2 Cor. xi. 28 ; 2 Tim. iv. 17 (cf. above, p. 11).   The supposition that Paul found in Ephesus or Iconium Christian
Churches already organised or even individual Christians,
or that Epaphras discovered such in Colossæ or in Laodicea,
is contrary to the evidence of all existing sources of information.   As regards the province of Asia and its capital

city, Ephesus, this is contradicted by the testimony of
Acts xviii. 19, xix. 8, and also xix. 1–7. It was just
because there was no Christian Church in Ephesus before
Paul's arrival, not even of the most elementary kind, that
it was possible there, as in Alexandria (Acts xviii. 24 f.),
for single confessors of Jesus to remain without Christian
baptism and without any relation to the development of
the Church (vol. i. p. 262).

It is just as certain also that the Churches in the provinces of Asia and Galatia founded by Paul and his helpers
were all Gentile Christian in character, notwithstanding
the fact that they were always organised in connection
with synagogues already existing, and in spite of the reception into their membership of numerous Jews. This is
almost as strongly expressed in Acts (Acts xv. 3, 12, 19,
xxi. 19), which records facts that might lead one to suppose that the Churches were partly Jewish, partly Gentile
Christian in character, as by Paul himself (Gal. iv. 8 ;
Eph. ii. 11–iii. 13). On the other hand, Paul does not
deny that there were native Jews in the membership of
these Gentile Christian Churches (vol. i. p. 192, n. 6).
Regarding the founding of the Churches in Cappadocia,
Pontus, and Bithynia, regions which Paul did not visit
personally, we have no information. But it is probable
that in these provinces, which, viewed from the direction
of Jerusalem and Antioch, were only the *Hinterland* of
the provinces of Galatia and Asia, the gospel was preached
somewhat later, but under practically the same conditions, except that the proportion of Jews in the population
was less, and consequently there were fewer of them in
the membership of the Churches organised there than in
Galatia and Asia.

In view of the clear facts in the case, it is one of the
most striking proofs of the lack of historical insight in
the handling of the N.T. writings, that from the time
of Origen on the view could gain ground in the Greek

Church that 1 Peter was directed to the Jewish Christians scattered in the provinces named (n. 2). It is even more strange that this view should find stubborn defenders to-day, though modified to the extent of holding that the letter was addressed by Peter to Jewish Christian Churches existing in Asia Minor before Paul began his missionary labours in that region (n. 3). Nothing could be further from the truth than to claim that the only argument against the assumption of the existence of such Jewish Christian Churches in Asia Minor before Paul's labours began is the silence of Acts. As already indicated, we have to do here with the very explicit testimony both of Acts and of Paul's letters. If Jewish Christian Churches existed in Galatia and Asia, especially in the larger cities where there were numerous Jews, *e.g.* Pisidian Antioch and Iconium, Ephesus and the cities on the Lycus, before the gospel was preached in these places by Paul, Barnabas, Epaphras, and other co-labourers of theirs unknown to us, then the whole representation in Acts is not only incomplete, but positively false. In all these districts Paul finds only Jews and Gentiles who had never heard the gospel until they heard it from him, and who were constrained by his preaching to take a stand with reference to it. Even if the agreement in Gal. ii. 6–10 be still falsely interpreted to mean that Paul was compelled to give up all missionary work among persons of Jewish birth (cf. *per contra*, vol. i. p. 265 f.), it is nevertheless impossible to explain the fact that repeatedly Paul begins his preaching in the syna-gogue,—indeed, in Ephesus he confined his work to the synagogue for the whole of three months (Acts xix. 8),—and, on the other hand, fails even to greet the Jewish Christian Churches in the same places, and makes no use of the foundation which in them was already laid. And who were the missionaries who established Churches all the way to the coast of the Black Sea before the Christians in Antioch gained courage to send Paul and Barnabas out

into the world ? (Acts xiii. 2). If, in view of 1 Pet. i. 12,
it be suggested that this was done by persons from Cappa
docia, Pontus, Asia, Phrygia, and Pamphylia (Acts ii. 9 f.),
who heard the preaching at Pentecost, it must be remembered that these hearers were not pilgrims to the feast,
who, after the feast, returned to the lands of their birth,
but Jews from abroad residing in Jerusalem (Acts ii. 5, vi. 9,
vol. i. 61), who became members of the Church in Jerusalem. It is true that after the death of Stephen many of
these Christians did attempt successfully to spread their
faith outside of Palestine (Acts xi. 19 f.). The gospel, however, was not carried beyond Antioch and Cyprus by their
efforts, but, according to all existing accounts, by Paul and
Barnabas. Moreover, what is to be done with Paul's own
testimony ? It was "the Churches of Galatia" (Gal. i. 2 ;
1 Cor. xvi. 1), not individual Christians in Galatia, who
received the gospel from Paul, working sometimes in conjunction with Barnabas, sometimes with Silvanus (Gal.
i. 8, iv. 13 ; vol. i. p. 179), in quite the same way that the
Church in Corinth received the gospel (Gal. i. 9 ; cf.
1 Cor. xv. 1-3). Under the figure of the mother (Gal.
iv. 19) is expressed, if possible, even more strongly
than by the figure of the father (1 Cor. iv. 15), the
fact that all the Churches in this province owed their
origin to Paul. Where, then, are the Jewish Christian
Churches, governed by their own presbyters (1 Pet. v.
1-4), which are supposed to have existed in the province before Paul's coming ? Similarly in Colossæ and
Laodicea, Epaphras brought the gospel not to individual
Christians of a particular class or race, but to the
Churches (Col. i. 1, 7, iv. 13, 16). Furthermore, when
Paul mentions Epænetus (Rom. xvi. 5), he speaks of
him not as a first-fruit of his personal labours in Asia,
but as the first convert of this province ; and from the
connection in which he is spoken of, he must have become
acquainted with the gospel in the house of Aquila, who

came to Ephesus for the first time along with Paul (vol i. 417, n. 21).

The terms that are here used to characterise the Christian readers and Churches have been misunderstood from very early times, because of their relation to Israel and to Jewish conditions. This association is true of παρεπίδημοι (i. 1) and πάροικοι, which is joined with it (ii. 11 ; παροικία, i. 17), only to the extent that the combination occurs twice in the LXX (n. 4). In themselves the words are quite secular in character, as is abundantly evidenced by their use in literature and inscriptions. The first expression means the stranger who comes from a foreign land, and remains only temporarily in a given place of residence. In distinction from ἐπιδημεῖν (Acts ii. 10), it emphasises more definitely the merely temporary character of the residence. Πάροικος, on the other hand, which is practically synonymous with μέτοικος, more commonly used by the older writers, means the resident, that is to say, the stranger, who, as distinguished from the citizen, lives by the tolerance and under the protection of the State. It may also mean the tenant, as distinguished from the property holder and his family. With these words is joined as practically synonymous ξένος (Eph. ii. 19; Heb. xi. 13). J. D. Michaelis (*Einl.* 1445 ff.) thought that the words were used to describe persons who before their conversion were Jewish proselytes. That this is not the case, and that no comparison is implied between the readers and such proselytes as regards their relation to Christianity, is evident from the simple fact that in the two passages in the LXX (Gen. xxiii. 4 ; Ps. xxxix. 13, n. 4) where παρεπίδημος occurs—in both instances joined with πάροικος, as in 1 Pet. ii. 11—the reference is not to strangers living in Israel, but to the patriarchs living in strange countries, without fixed abode or permanent possessions, and to pious Israelites whose whole life was conceived after the pattern of the life of their ancestors.

It will be seen that even in the O.T. these two synonymous ideas are used to denote, on the one hand, the relation of the pious to God, and, on the other hand, their relation to earthly rights, possessions, and abode. In conscious imitation of this O.T. usage, as evidenced by Heb. xi. 13–16, xiii. 14, there grew up the view, already discussed (vol. i. p. 81 f.), which comes to light in all the N.T. writings, that Christians, being citizens of a heavenly commonwealth, are strangers, residing only temporarily in this world, or residents without rights of citizenship, remaining here only by the sufferance of the possessors and rulers of this world. While the Jews of the diaspora made every effort either to become citizens with full rights in Gentile communities, or to secure legal recognition as a separate community (n. 4), Christians, even when they possessed landed property and rights of citizenship, regarded themselves, nevertheless, as πάροικοι καὶ παρεπίδημοι, thereby bearing witness that they possessed and sought a fatherland not to be found upon this earth (Heb. xi. 14–16). That these words are used in quite the same sense in 1 Peter is shown by ii. 11, where these particular characteristics of the readers are mentioned as a motive for a distinctive Christian manner of life, as distinguished from that led by the heathen. It is even more clearly demonstrated by i. 17, where manifestly the whole earthly life of Christians is described as the time of their παροικία (cf. iv. 2; Gen. xlvii. 9). This also proves that the expressions are not at all meant to imply that the readers are persons living far from their earthly home, e.g. Jews dwelling outside of Palestine; for then it would follow that they needed only to return to Palestine, in order to be exempt from all the moral obligations spoken of in i. 17, ii. 11. Furthermore, in i. 1 f., the language shows that the readers are strangers and sojourners in the world, not by reason of the external circumstarces of their life, but because they have been chosen by God, i.e.

in accordance with His own original provision, and through
conversion and baptism (i. 1 f.). These words describe
readers simply as Christians, and the names of the
provinces that follow in the genitive might have been
added directly, just as it is possible to say αἱ ἐκκλησίαι τῆς
'Ιουδαίας (Gal. i. 22), in the sense of αἱ οὖσαι ἐν τῇ 'Ιουδαίᾳ
(1 Thess. ii. 14). This connection is not interfered with
by the intervening διασπορᾶς, which is used without the
article, and so cannot possibly further describe the readers
as those elect strangers, i.e. Christians, who belong to the
Jewish diaspora of Pontus, Galatia, etc. (n. 5). Rather
does it serve to emphasise the thought expressed by
παρεπίδημοι by adding the thought of Jas. i. 1, that as
Christians the readers live scattered abroad like the
Israelites after they were driven from the Holy Land.
As indicated above (vol. i. 93, 100, n. 12), this idea grew up
originally out of very concrete conditions ; and so here Peter
probably has in mind the actual conditions of his readers.
It is, of course, possible in itself to conceive of all the
Christians as dwelling together in one place like the
Mormons on the Great Salt Lake, instead of scattered
abroad in little groups over the wide world like oases in
the desert or islands in the sea (Theoph. *ad Autol.* ii. 14).
But at the beginning of a letter intended for a large
number of Churches scattered over the whole of Asia
Minor it was very natural to recall their actual condition,
and this thought is very properly followed by the
enumeration of all the provinces where these Churches
were. But notwithstanding this fact, διασπορᾶς, like the
preceding παρεπίδημοι, is used to describe the religious
condition of the readers. For it will be observed, the
thing contrasted with their present scattered condition
is not the return of them all to an earthly home, but their
gathering into the kingdom of Christ (Matt. xxiv. 31 ;
Didache x.), when the Chief Shepherd shall appear
(1 Pet. v. 4). Still, the fact that up to this time these

small Churches had always existed scattered abroad over the wide world, outnumbered a hundred or even a thousand times by the heathen who surrounded them, must have intensified the feeling that as Christians they were only strangers and sojourners in the world, as it would also tend to make them constantly mindful of the inheritance laid up for them in heaven (i. 4).

In this manner the greeting opens the way for the main thoughts of the Epistle. But it contains nothing which can obscure the fact, firmly established by historical evidence, that the letter was directed to the Gentile Christian Churches in Asia Minor founded by Paul and his helpers. This is confirmed in the further course of the letter itself, particularly by the manner in which characteristics of Israel are applied to the readers. Thus in ii. 5, 9, in accordance with Ex. xix. 5 f., Isa. xliii. 20, they are called a royal priesthood, a chosen race, a holy people, God's peculiar people. In ii. 10, by a free application of the words with which Hosea (ii. 1–3, 25) prophesies the restoration of Israel to the rank of God's people, it is said of the readers that they who once were no people have become a people of God, that they who once were not the objects of the divine mercy have now experienced this mercy (ii. 5–10). Nor is the fact concealed that they have obtained all this mercy and dignity because by faith they have followed the call of the gospel by which they have been summoned out of darkness into His marvellous light (ii. 9, cf. i. 12, 15, 22–25, ii. 2, 7). In contrast to them stand not the unbelieving majority of the Jewish people, but all who have heard the gospel and not accepted it. They are not called *the* true people of God, or *the* spiritual Israel, in contrast to the Jewish people who have become unworthy of this name. On the contrary, the definite article is consistently avoided (cf. the opposite usage in Jas. i. 1 ; Gal. vi. 16 ; Phil. iii. 3), *i.e.* without the implication of any such contrast these exalted titles are applied

to them in just the same way in which James, Paul, and
John speak of the rise of a people of God from among the
Gentiles in Acts xv. 14 ; Gal. iii. 7, 29, iv. 28 ; Eph. ii.
11–22 ; Rev. v. 9 f. They are not sons of Abraham and
daughters of Sarah (which simply expresses the same
thought with reference to women) by reason of birth,
but have become such through their conversion and the
character of their subsequent life (iii. 6). That the readers
are Gentiles, is proved most decisively by the way in which
the words of Hosea, referred to above, are used. Paul,
who understood the words as a prophecy of the ultimate
pardon of Israel, to be fulfilled at the last day (Rom. ix.
25, xi. 26–31),—frequently overlooked by the interpreters
without any apparent necessity,—quotes the substance of
the passage accurately. Peter, who only uses the language
of the prophet to clothe his own thoughts, modifies the
passage essentially to suit his purpose, using, in order to
describe the readers before their conversion, the words
οἱ πότε οὐ λαός instead of οὐ λαὸς τοῦ θεοῦ (Hos. ii. 1, 25 ;
cf. i. 9, οὐ λαός μου). Unlike the degenerate Israel, they
were not deprived of the rank of the people of God after
having once had it, but before their conversion were not
yet a people at all. It was not until after they had
received the gospel that the readers, who belonged to the
most diverse races, Greeks and Barbarians, Phrygians, Celts,
Scythians, became united into one people, in fact into a holy
people of God (Col. iii. 11 ; Acts xiv. 11, xvii. 26). Having
become such in consequence of the divine call, the obligations devolving upon the people of God in the O.T. passed
over to them (i. 15 f.). But the contrast to the holy life,
which they must now lead as Christians, is their former
life in heathen immorality. This is indicated most clearly
in iv. 2–4, where participation in immoral idol worship
is mentioned last in the list of the vices to which they
were addicted before their conversion. Moreover, there
are unequivocal references to this same practice in i. 14, 18.

While it is true that hostility to Christ (Acts iii. 17 ; 1 Tim. i. 13) and the legalistic bias of the Jews, which made them so unfriendly to the gospel (Rom. x. 3), may be described as accompanied by ἄγνοια, it will be observed that neither of these attitudes is referred to in i. 14, but rather the sinful lusts in which the readers lived in the time of their ignorance (cf. ii. 11, 24, iv. 1–4). This can mean only that ignorance of God and His will which characterised the Gentile in distinction from the Jew (1 Thess. iv. 5 ; 2 Thess. i. 8 ; Gal. iv. 9 ; 1 Tim. ii. 4 ; 1 Pet. ii. 15 ; Acts xvii. 23, 30). Judged by the Christian standard, there were evil traditions even among the Jews (Matt. xv. 2, xvi. 6), with which it was necessary for Jews to break in order to become Christians (Gal. i. 13 f. ; Phil. iii. 7 ff.). But, in contrast to these, no Christian in ancient times was so foolish as to call the sinful life of heathenism (iv. 3), even when led by Jews, a vain manner of life handed down from their fathers (i. 18, more explicitly described in Eph. iv. 17 f.). The use of such an expression cannot be justified by assuming that a contemptuous judgment of the Jewish cultus and the Pharisaic manner of life is here expressed ; for of such a judgment there is not the slightest suggestion throughout the entire letter. In contrast to the holy life which they are now required to live, stand rather the lusts of the flesh (i. 14, ii. 11). Furthermore, the clear comparison of the redemption of the readers with that of Israel from Egypt, implying as it does a comparison of their former walk with the life of Israel while they were in heathen bondage, indicates that they have come from heathenism and not out of a life under the Mosaic law. Only by exegesis of the worst sort can it be made to appear from ii. 25 that such language could be used exclusively of Jews who had always been members of the household of God (n. 6). To the unbiassed judgment all the passages in the letter bearing upon the question as to the character of the readers only confirm what is certainly

known from history concerning the origin and character
of the Christian Churches in Asia Minor.   From this
point of view alone is the expressed purpose of the letter
intelligible.

It is Peter's intention to encourage his readers, and to
confirm them by bearing witness to the fact that it is the
true grace of God into which they have been brought by their
conversion, and in which they have since stood (v. 12).
The oppressed condition in which they were at the time is,
of course, an additional reason why he writes to them.   But
nothing is anywhere said which would imply that the
readers were in danger even under the stress of persecution
of doubting the truth of their faith.   Apart from this, the
significant thing for them is the fact that it is Peter who
bears witness to the genuineness of their state of grace.
Inasmuch as there is no trustworthy tradition and not the
slightest hint in the letter itself that Peter had had direct
personal relations with these Christians, had ever been
among them, or was personally known to individuals among
them (n. 7), it could have been only his ecclesiastical
position, known throughout the entire Christian world,
and the character of the Churches in Asia Minor, equally
well known, that gives his letter the significance which he
indicates at the close.   To them as *Gentile Christians* it is
an encouragement, and tends to strengthen their faith, that
the foremost amongst the apostles, the most distinguished
apostle of the circumcision (Gal. ii. 7), bears such testimony
to their Christian character.   It is with this in view that he
praises the word of the gospel which was preached to them,
describing it as the means of a second birth, and as the
living word of God, having the promise of eternal continuance (i. 23–25).   This explains also why he declares
that the missionaries who brought this word to them
preached the gospel in the spirit sent from heaven (i. 12),
and finally his assurance that even the O.T. prophets,
or rather the spirit of Christ dwelling in them, which,

reaching out beyond the clear knowledge of the prophets themselves, made predictions concerning the grace that was to reach even to the readers,—a preliminary revelation, the recording of which by the prophets was not so much for their own benefit as for that of the readers (i. 10–12).

If in this passage Peter had in mind only the contrast between the ancient prophets and Christians of the present (cf. Matt. xiii. 17 ; Heb. i. 1, xi. 40), it is impossible to understand why he continued to address the readers, distinguishing them from himself instead of identifying them with himself and with all Christians by the use of "we" and "us." The contrast here cannot be, as in i. 3–4a and 4b–9, that between the apostle and other eye-witnesses of the gospel history on the one hand, and Christians converted later through the gospel on the other (see below); since in the prophets there is no hint of any kind concerning this temporal distinction within the Church. On the contrary, Peter has in mind words like Isa. ii. 1–4, xlii. 1–12 (Matt. xii. 18–21), Isa. xlix. 6 (Acts xiii. 47), and here expresses thoughts concerning the relation of O.T. prophecy to the preaching of the gospel among the Gentiles such as are found in Rom. i. 2, xv. 4–13, xvi. 26 ; Eph. iii. 5–12.

In introducing himself, the author uses the name given him by Jesus, and the official title received from Him (i. 1). He does not, however, use the original Aramaic form of the name, Kepha, but the Greek translation which was current among Gentile Christians (n. 8). He does not say much about himself, but what he does say is significant. When in v. 1, in addressing the πρεσβύτεροι, and pointing out his own relation to them, he calls himself συμπρεσ-βύτερος, this cannot mean that he like them is an old man ; for although the contrast between πρεσβύτεροι and νεώτεροι (v. 1, 5) does suggest difference of age, the character of the exhortations addressed to both show that the πρεσβύτεροι are here viewed in their capacity as heads of the Churches, to whom obedience is due and who have the power to demand and to compel the same authoritatively, and for their own ends (cf. Tit. i. 7 ; 1 Tim. iii. 3, 8), but who, if they are true shepherds, ought not so to do.   In this calling Peter is their companion, only with the self-evident distinction that their exercise of the same is limited to the local Church, while that of Peter, being an apostle (i. 1), extends over the entire Church (v. 9).   Attention is called to this distinctive position by the statement which the author here makes, that he was a witness, *i.e.* an eye-witness, of the sufferings of Christ (n. 9).   Here are only two strokes of the pen ; but by the one we have sharply outlined the figure of the disciple, who, with a few others, had been an eye-witness of the struggle in Gethsemane, and had seen Jesus bound and taken from one judge to another (Mark xiv. 33, 37, 47, 54 ; Luke xxii. 61 ; John xviii. 10–27) ; the other pictures the apostle, to whom especially Jesus had given the command to feed his sheep (John xxi. 15–17) and strengthen his brethren (Luke xxii. 32).   Furthermore, no one but an eye-witness of the events recorded in the gospel history (Luke i. 2) could well describe the attitude and relation to Christ of persons in Asia Minor, converted after Jesus' death, not only as that of faith without sight, but also as that of love for one whom they had never seen (i. 8).   In the Epistles of Paul, of whose language we are so often reminded by 1 Peter, we seek in vain for similar expressions, even where it would have been most natural for one who could speak in this way to have done so (*e.g.* Gal. iii. 1 ; Eph. i. 13).   This note is struck by only one other of the original apostles (John i. 14, xix. 35, xx. 29 ; 1 John i. 1–4, iv. 14).   Finally, no one could speak of the resurrection of the Lord as the means of his regeneration (i. 3), except one who through the conviction of Jesus' resurrection had been roused from the doubt into which he had been cast by the death of Jesus, to a new life of

hope and faith. Peter does not speak in this way con
cerning the readers, the instrument of whose regeneration
is rather the living word of God (i. 23), but where he
specially speaks of himself and those like himself, and
before he passes to his address to the readers (i. 4b, n. 10).

As has already been remarked, the writer of the letter
had no share in the conversion of the readers, and there
is nothing to indicate that there had been direct personal
relations between himself and them. This impression is
strengthened, especially by what is said in v. 12–14.
Peter sends special greeting neither to an individual nor
to a particular class among the readers, which is all the
more striking when compared with the very different
manner in which Paul writes to Churches not founded by
himself (Rom. xvi. 3–16; Col. iv. 15–17; vol. i. 387 f.).
The only greetings which he sends are those from the
local Church where he was, and from Mark, whom he
calls his son, to all the readers. The latter is only a
figurative way of saying that Mark, with whose family
Peter had long been intimate (Acts xii. 12), had become
a believer through Peter's influence (cf. 1 Tim. i. 1 ; 2 Tim.
i. 1 ; Tit. i. 4 ; Philem. 10). In the same way, the Church
in Babylon is not spoken of in a prosaic manner, but is
personified, and in order to bring out its spiritual relationship to the readers, who are the elect of God (i. 1), is
called fellow-elect (2 John 1, 13, n. 11).

While this greeting does not necessitate at all the
assumption of intimate relations between the Church in
" Babylon " and the Churches in Asia Minor (cf. Rom. xvi.
16b; Phil. iv. 22 ; Gal. i. 2), such relations are presupposed by the greeting from Mark. Now, since Mark did
not accompany Paul on any of his three missionary journeys
through Asia Minor,—having separated himself from the
apostle at the beginning of the first journey, and not
joining him again for a long time (Acts xiii. 13, xv. 38),—
but in the year 62 or 63 did intend to make a journey

from Rome to Asia Minor (Col. iv. 10), this letter could
not have been written until after Mark had carried out
this intention, and so had come into personal contact with
all, or some of the Churches of Asia Minor, or with individual members of them. On the other hand, Silvanus,
who accompanied Paul on his second missionary journey,
had become acquainted with many of the Churches in Asia
Minor, and had helped in the building up, possibly also in
the founding, of many of them (Acts xv. 40, xvi. 5 ; cf. Gal.
iv. 13, vol. i. p.178 f.). For this reason Peter could describe
Silvanus, through whom he addressed the readers in this
letter, as a faithful, trustworthy brother, with the evident
expectation that they would agree with him (v. 12). But
what does he mean when he says—and the order of the
words indicates a certain emphasis—" By Silvanus, the
faithful brother, as I account him, I have written to
you briefly"? So far as the words themselves are con-
cerned (n. 12), the expression $\gamma\rho\acute{a}\phi\epsilon\iota\nu$ $\delta\iota\acute{a}$ $\tau\iota\nu o\varsigma$ might
refer to the person who delivered the letter. But, in
the first place, it strikes one as strange to find the bearer
of the letter specifically mentioned, whereas in the other
N.T. Epistles either the identity of the bearer is not
disclosed at all, or is left to be inferred from indirect
statements (Rom. xvi. 1 ; 1 Cor. xvi. 17 ; 2 Cor. viii.
16–24 ; Eph. vi. 21 ; Col. iv. 7). Furthermore, it is
impossible to explain why Silvanus should be mentioned
with so much emphasis in this passage as the bearer of
the letter, and why the concurrence of the readers in the
praise bestowed upon him should be expressly asked. If
this is the meaning, the remark is in all respects without
point; for if Silvanus delivered the letter as it was
addressed, then the readers, when the letter was in their
hands, no longer needed to be told that Peter had believed
him possessed of the modest amount of trustworthiness
requisite for this task before he sent him. If, contrary to
all expectations, Silvanus failed to deliver the letter, then

the written testimony at the end of the letter, of the
writer's confidence in Silvanus, which the latter was on
the point of basely betraying, would be of value neither to
the persons addressed, who in that case would not receive
the letter, nor to Peter himself.   It scarcely needs to be
remarked that the statement is even more meaningless
if Silvanus is here thought of as the amanuensis to whom
Peter dictated his message ; since Peter could not express
his deliberate opinion as to the trustworthiness requisite
for this task—and anything less than trustworthiness
would imply a degree of deceit on the part of the
amanuensis entirely incredible—without implying his
suspicion as to the person in question ; and if he had
any suspicion he could satisfy himself by reading the
letter through, while in a matter of this sort the readers
could not have an opinion of any kind.   The only alterna-
tive that remains is the most natural one, namely, that
Silvanus' part in the composition was so important and
so large that its performance required a considerable
degree of trustworthiness.   It is not Silvanus' letter,
written merely at Peter's direction ; for from beginning
to end Peter is the one who speaks in the letter, without
even formally mentioning Silvanus as a joint author, as
Paul sometimes does (1 Thess. i. 1 ; 2 Thess. i. 1).   In
fact, to have done so would have tended to defeat the
expressed purpose of the letter, namely, to be a testimony
of the apostle of the circumcision to Gentile Christians
(above, p. 145 f.).   It purports to be a letter of Peter's ; and
such it is, except that Peter left its composition to Silvanus,
because he regarded him as better fitted than himself,
indeed as better fitted than anyone else, to express in an
intelligible and effective manner the thoughts and feelings
which Peter entertained toward the Gentile Christians of
Asia Minor.   Just as Peter believed that in the performance of this duty Silvanus would have the best
interests of the readers in view, and would write with

appreciation of their needs, so he hopes that the readers, who have come to know Silvanus in part through his labours among them as a missionary preacher, will believe that he has faithfully reproduced Peter's sentiments, and that he would not have written what he did in Peter's name if he had known that this was not Peter's mind. So, instead of making the distance between himself and the readers seem greater by speaking to them through another, Peter by this means introduces himself to them in the most effective way possible.   All that we know of Silvanus from other sources, his prominent place among the officers and prophets of the mother Church, the duty which he performed in Antioch as their ambassador (Acts xv. 22–40), the favourable testimony to his character which we gather from Paul's Epistles (2 Cor. i. 19 ; cf. 1 and 2 Thess.), as well as the trustworthiness to which Peter bears testimony here, tends to justify the assumption that he would prove himself worthy of the confidence placed in him in the entrusting to him of the composition of this letter.   We have no *a priori* means of determining how comprehensive the conferences between Peter and Silvanus, which necessarily preceded the writing of such a letter, may have been.

1. (P. 134.) The omission from 1 Pet. i. 1 of the two small districts of Lycia and Pamphylia, of whose Church history in early time we know practically nothing (Acts xiv. 25), will scarcely be accounted strange, especially in view of the fact that, prior to 74 A.D., they were not permanently organised into an independent province (Marquardt, *R. Staatsverw.*[2] i. 375 f.). On the other hand, it is peculiar that Pontus and Bithynia, which had been united in one province since 65 B.C. (Marquardt, 351), are separated as far as possible in this list. It is possible that this entire province is designated by the name "Bithynia" (cf. Tac. *Ann.* i. 74, xvi. 18), and that Pontus stands for Pontus Polemoniacus, which was a principality until 63 A.D. (Marquardt, 360). If 1 Pet. was written in 63 (§ 39), account need not yet necessarily be taken of the union of this land with Galatia, which is also placed in the year 63. In any case, the order of the names is peculiar : starting from the north coast (Pontus), we go inland to Galatia, then eastward (Cappadocia), then westward (Asia), and, finally, in a northerly direction until we reach the shore of the Black Sea again.   Bengel's remark, "Quinque provincias nominat eo ordine, quo occurrebant scribenti ex oriente" (cf. v. 13), which has been

accepted by Wetstein (ii. 698) and Niebuhr, following Bunsen (*Anal. antenic.*
i. 134), does not explain the order nor even the name with which the list
begins, since the person in Babylon facing or journeying toward Asia Minor
was nearer Cappadocia than Pontus.   The differing order in the free reproduction of Origen (see n. 2) has no more significance than the omission of
Asia in א, of Bithynia in B.   Pontus is mentioned elsewhere in the N.T.
only in Acts ii. 9, xviii. 2; in both cases as the home of Jews (cf. Philo, *ad
Cai.* xxxvi.).   Is it perhaps possible that Aquila and Priscilla, who were living
in Asia Minor sometime after 1 Pet. was written (2 Tim. iv. 19), laboured on
behalf of the gospel in their native Pontus?   In these regions also it is
natural to seek the Scythian Christians to whom reference is made in Col.
iii. 11, who may have come hither in consequence of the commerce between
the northern and southern shores of the Black Sea.   Here, too, may have
been found slaves who had wandered far from their homes.   In 112, Pliny
had to deal with persons (*Ep.* xcvi. *ad Traj.*) who claimed that they had
abandoned the Christian faith twenty years before.   They may have become
Christians many years earlier.   The fact that, according to the testimony
of Pliny, Christianity was widely spread in this region, is evidence that it
was brought hither not very much later than it was preached in the province
of Asia.   For in the second century we have evidence of the existence of
the episcopates of Sinope (Epiph. *Hær.* xlii. 1) and Amastris (Eus. *H. E.*
iv. 23. 6, v. 23. 2).

2. (P. 137.)   Origen, quoted by Eus. iii. 1. 2, Πέτρος δὲ ἐν Πόντῳ κ. Γαλ.
κ. Βιθ., Καππαδ. τε καὶ Ἀσίᾳ κεκηρυχέναι τοῖς ἐκ διασποράς (*al.* ἐν διασπορᾷ)
Ἰουδαίοις ἔοικεν.   Thus, indirectly, we have characterised the readers of the
letter, whose title is here made use of.   More directly and definitely by Eus.
himself, iii. 4. 2, τοῖς ἐξ Ἑβραίων οὖσιν ἐν διασπορᾷ Πόντου—Βιθυνίας γράφει.
Cf. the prologue in Zacagni (*Mon. coll.* 492), Cramer (*Cat.* viii. 41),
Matthæi (*Epist. cath.* 44).   Just as Eusebius (*op. cit.*) implies a contrast between Peter's work and the missionary labours of Paul among the Gentiles,
so Didymus (Migne, 39, 1755; cf. the scholion in Matthæi, p. 196) treats it
as an extension of his preaching among the Jews beyond the boundary of
Palestine.   In the West, at least at a later time, a more correct view prevailed, as is proved by the title of the letter (*ad gentes*), which, in spite of
the original text, the person who translated Didymus into Latin, a contemporary of Cassiodorus (cf. *Forsch.* iii. 11, 135), made the old Alexandrian
employ in his comment on 1 Pet. ii. 9 f.

3. (P. 137.)   The view briefly described on p. 136 f. has been maintained
mainly by B. Weiss (*Der petrin. Lehrbegriff*, 99 ff.) since 1855, and by many
later writers.   It is defended at great length by Kühl in the revision of
Huther's *Kommentar über die Briefe Petri und Judae*, 5te Aufl. 1887, 6te Aufl.
1897.

4. (Pp. 139, 140.)   In Gen. xxiii. 4 בֵּז וְתוֹשָׁב, LXX πάροικος καὶ παρεπίδημος, we
find Abraham among the children of Heth, and distinguished from the
"people of the land," who owned the ground.   There is a retrospective
reference to this position of the patriarchs also in Ps. xxxix. 13 (xxxviii. 12;
cf. Gen. xlvii. 9; 1 Chron. xxix. 15).   Here belong also Lev. xxv. 23, where
the same combination of words (but LXX reads προσήλυτοι καὶ πάροικοι) is
used to designate the Israelites in their own land in contrast to God, the

real possessor of the land, and the passages where πάροικος = גֵּר, used of Israel in Egypt, or of Moses among the Midianites (Gen. xv. 13 ; Ex. ii. 22, xviii. 3 ; Deut. xxiii. 8). Where גֵּר means the non-Israelite resident in Israel, LXX seldom (Deut. xiv. 21) renders it by πάροικος, which more often corresponds to תּוֹשָׁב (frequently with μισθωτός, Ex. xii. 45 ; Lev. xxii. 10, xxv. 6, 40), but often by προσήλυτος (Ex. xx. 10 ; Lev. xxv. 35, 47), and even by the Aramaic γειώρας (Ex. xii. 19 ; Isa. xiv. 1 ; cf. Just. Dial. cxxii., address), from which was derived the opprobrious term giaur, used in the Islamic period. It has yet to be proved that πάροικος was ever used in Christian or in post-Biblical Jewish literature in the sense of proselyte. Cf. further, vol. i. 82, and Lightfoot (St. Clement, ii. 5 f.). The difference between the Christian and Jewish points of view is very clearly indicated by the Jewish inscriptions in Hierapolis (Altertümer von Hierapolis, by Humann, etc., 1898, S. 138, No. 212, τῇ κατοικίᾳ τῶν ἐν Ἱεραπόλει κατοικούντων Ἰουδαίων). Here they formed a separate community (ὁ λάος τῶν Ἰουδαίων, S. 96, No. 69, 4–6), with their own city hall and archives (No. 69, 7, No. 212, 6 ; cf. S. 174, No. 342). Cf. also Jos. Ant. xvi. 6, 7. It also deserves notice that the only parallel in the N.T. Epistles to the designation of the readers, entirely without the article, is to be found in 2 John 1 (ἐκλεκτῇ κυρίᾳ). This is not to be explained by assuming that there were other Christians to whom the same name might be applied, since in that case it would be sufficient to say τοῖς οὖσιν ἐν Πόντῳ (cf. Phil. i. 1), even if τοῖς ἐκλεκτοῖς had preceded. The real explanation is that the omission of the article serves here, as in 2 John 1, to emphasise more strongly the qualities mentioned, and to make more easily recognisable the figurative meaning of phrases used (cf. Jas. i. 18, ἀπαρχήν τινα). Where the readers are called Christians in a literal sense, the article is not wanting, v. 14.

5. (P. 141.) It is taken for granted as certain that ἐκλεκτός in i. 1 is used in an attributive sense, as is always the case where the word stands in an attributive relation to another idea (1 Pet. ii. 4, 6, 9 ; 1 Tim. v. 21 ; Ex. xiv. 7, xxx. 23 ; 2 Sam. viii. 8) ; and, on the other hand, that παρεπίδημοι is used substantively, as in ii. 11 and in the LXX, where it is used as a translation of a substantive (n. 4). Furthermore, it is assumed that ver. 2 is not dependent upon ἐκλεκτοῖς alone, but upon the whole phrase, ἐκλ. . . . διασπορᾶς, for otherwise (τοῖς) ἐκλ. would need immediately to precede κατὰ πρόγνωσιν. Consequently it is not simply change of residence that makes the readers παρεπίδημοι διασπορᾶς, but the Divine election and separation ; and this election, in turn, together with the position of the readers in the world and their attitude toward God, corresponding to a Divine purpose, is due to the sanctifying work of the Spirit, and has for its purpose a constant obedience (cf. i. 14, 22) and a continuously needful purification through the blood of Christ (cf. 1 John i. 7). Since, besides the Christians here addressed, there were very many others to whom the ἐκλεκτοὶ παρεπίδημοι applied equally well, it is perfectly evident that if the purpose here were to distinguish these Christians from others, ἐκλεκτοὶ παρεπίδημοι would have to be followed by τοῖς ἐν τῇ διασπορᾷ, especially in view of the fact that it is without the article (cf. Jas. i. 1 ; vol. i. p. 79 f., n. 6), or by τοῖς ἐκ τῆς διασπορᾶς, if the word be used in its concrete sense ("Jews scattered among the heathen"). In this case the connection of ver. 2 would be rendered at least very difficult, since what

is said in this verse has no connection with the alleged membership of the readers in the Jewish diaspora, but relates solely to their Christian character. That the insertion of a simple local name, such as Πόντου κτλ., does not preclude modification by clauses that follow, is proved by 1 Cor. i. 2; 1 Thess. i. 1. Consequently διασπορᾶς, like so many similar genitives in the N.T. (Jas. i. 25, ἐπιλησμονῆς; 1 Pet. i. 14, ὑπακοῆς; Luke xviii. 6, τῆς ἀδικίας), is purely attributive = διεσπαρμένοις, and like ἐκλεκτοῖς παρεπιδήμοις, applicable to all Christians.

6. (P. 144.) Kühl claims that ἐπιστρέφεσθαι, in ii. 25 (which would apply also to the intransitive active, the sense of which is not essentially different), means in this passage, according to the predominant usage of the N.T., " to turn one's self again to that which one has formerly been." This meaning does not suit in those passages where the word is used of the conversion of the Gentiles (1 Thess. i. 9; Acts xi. 21, xiv. 15, xv. 19, xxvi. 18, 20; ἐπιστροφὴ τῶν ἐθνῶν, Acts xv. 3), which proves that this cannot possibly be the meaning of a word which is used alike of the conversion of Jews (Acts iii. 19, ix. 35; 2 Cor. iii. 16) and of the conversion of sinners generally (Jas. v. 16 f.; Mark iv. 12; Luke i. 16 f., xxii. 32). Nor is this meaning possible in passages like Matt. ix. 22; Mark v. 30, viii. 33 (cf. Matt. xvi. 23); Acts ix. 40, xvi. 18; Rev. i. 12; nor in Gal. iv. 9, where πάλιν would then be superfluous. The only passages remaining where ὑποστρέφειν (cf. the variant readings in Luke ii. 20; 2 Pet. ii. 21) and ἀνακάμπτειν (Luke x. 6 = Matt. x. 13) are used in practically the same sense are Mark xiii. 16; Matt. x. 13, xii. 44; Luke viii. 55, xvii. 4; Acts xv. 36; but here there is no reference to conversion. The attempt to give the word this meaning is not any more successful if " bishop " be taken as referring to God, not to Christ, as is done by Kühl and Weiss, without any good reason (cf. per contra, v. 4). Then it has also to be assumed that God was the Shepherd and Bishop of the souls of alleged Jewish Christians in Asia Minor before they fell into a heathen manner of life (iv. 2–4), from which manner of life it is assumed they have now returned again to their God. In proof of this fantastic representation of the personal history of all the Christians in Asia Minor, —quite as unknown to Peter as to ourselves,—it is claimed that in speaking of their wanderings (πλανώμενοι, not πλανώμενα), Peter compares them to sheep, which implies that they have always belonged to the flock of God, i.e. the people of Israel. But suppose that Peter not only compared them with sheep who had gone astray, but called them that in so many words, are we to assume that the sheep in Matt. xxv. 32 or John x. 16 are only Jews? In order to escape these interpreters, Peter ought to have called his readers swine or dogs (Matt. vii. 16, xv. 26). Possibly not even this would have sufficed, since in Phil. iii. 2 Jewish Christians are called dogs!

7. (P. 145.) The sole source of the tradition that Peter laboured in Pontus and other provinces of Asia Minor is 1 Pet. i. 1. This is proved by the language of Origen (above, p. 152, n. 2), who refers to this work as only probable. Cf. what Origen says with the more definite but very brief remarks in Epiph. Hær. xxvii. 6; Ephrem, Expos. ev. conc. 286. With regard to the other Syrians who refer to such work on Peter's part, see § 39, n. 3. In a later recension of the Acts of Andrew (ed. Bonnet, 1895, pp. 9, 14, not included in the collected edition of the elide Acta apocr., ed. Lipsius et Bonnet).

there is to be found a confirmation of an alleged journey of Peter and Andrew to Sinope: καθὼς αὐτὸς Πέτρος ἐν τῇ καθολικῇ αὐτοῦ ἐπιστολῇ γράφει διεληλυθέναι Πόντον καὶ Γαλατίαν; cf. Epiph. *Mon.*, ed. Dressel, p. 45. So this story is not even a legend, to say nothing of a primitive legend (as affirmed by Lipsius, *Die apokryph. Apostelges.* ii. 1. 4), but is simply the fabrication of exegesis.

8. (P. 146.) John is the only one of the evangelists who preserves the original Κηφᾶς (John i. 42); but the fact that he adds immediately a translation, and from this point on throughout the book—indeed, before this point —uses only Πέτρος (i. 40), shows that the readers were as unfamiliar with Κηφᾶς as they were with Μεσσίας (for Χριστός) or ῥαββί (for διδάσκαλος); cf. i. 38, 41. That this was true even more widely, is proved by the entire avoidance of Κηφᾶς in the Synoptics and in Acts even where the names of the disciples are given (Mark iii. 16; Luke vi. 14; especially peculiar is its omission in Matt. xvi. 16–18, where the Aramaic Βαριωνᾶ is used). Paul's constant use of Κεφᾶς in 1 Cor. (i. 12, iii. 22, ix. 5, xv. 5) is explained by the fact that he has in mind the followers of Cephas from Palestine, of whose language we learn in 1 Cor. xvi. 22; vol. i. 288 ff. In Galatians the tradition wavers, and is also rendered uncertain by the fact that the versions give no sure support for the correct reading, inasmuch as the Syriac versions use *Kepha* everywhere, and the Latin as well as the Greek texts of the West almost without exception offer *Petrus.* If, as the present writer believes to be the case, Πέτρος is to be read in Gal. ii. 7, 8 (but in i. 18, ii. 9, 11, 14 Κηφᾶς, *ZKom. Gal.* 68) the very remarkable change in ii. 9 to the Aramaic form of the name, after the Greek form had been used twice in ii. 7–8, is very naturally explained by the fact that thereby, just as by the use of στῦλοι, Paul desires to give the form of speech used by the Judaistic teachers who had come to Galatia from Palestine. He then retains in ii. 11, 14 the form of the name used by these teachers, since he wishes to place in its proper light an incident which had been misrepresented by them in a hostile spirit. This motive also suits i. 18. Cf. in addition also § 41, n. 9. The fact that a number of ancient writers discover in several N.T. passages a Cephas distinct from Peter deserves mention only as a matter of curiosity: see Clemens Al. in Eus. *H. E.* i. 12. 2. (Cephas is here held to be one of the seventy disciples; cf. *Forsch.* iii. 68, and above, vol. i. 267 f.); *Apost. Const.* chap. i. (*Doctr. XII. Apost.*, ed. Funk, p. 50); *Chron. pasch.*, ed. Bonn, i. 421. Cf. Jerome *in Gal.* ii. (Vall. vii. 408).

9. (P. 147.) Modern usage ("to give testimony, witness for Christ," and similar expressions) very easily obscures the meaning of biblical expressions which sound the same. Christ Himself would not be the faithful and true witness (Rev. i. 5, iii. 14) had not His revelation in the world of the truth of salvation been based upon His own immediate knowledge (John iii. 11, 32, v. 31, viii. 14, xviii. 37; 1 Tim. vi. 13). Seeing and testifying are inseparable (Rev. i. 2; John i. 34; 1 John i. 2, iv. 14). The disciples of Jesus could not be His witnesses unless with their own eyes they had seen Him who lived on earth and died and rose again, and unless they had perceived through all their senses His entire manifestation of Himself (John xv. 27, xxi. 24; Acts i. 8, 21 f., ii. 32, iii. 15, v. 32, x. 39, 41; 1 John i. 1–3; 2 Pet. i. 16–18); nor could Paul, had he not seen and heard Him at least once (Acts xxii. 15,

xxvi. 16 ; 1 Cor. ix. 1, xv. 8, 15 ; and, on the other hand, cf. the distinction made in Acts xiii. 31 f.). With reference to Stephen, cf. Acts xxii. 20 with vii. 55. That Peter means in this strict sense to designate himself a witness of the sufferings, and so of the life of Jesus, is proved by the clause which follows, ὁ καὶ τῆς μελλούσης ἀποκαλύπτεσθαι δόξης κοινωνός, which does not mean participation purely in thought or in speech, but in fact and in person. Although the suffering of Christians born later than the time of Christ may be called fellow-suffering with Him (Rom. viii. 17 ; 2 Tim. ii. 11 f.; 2 Cor. i. 5), that does not of itself make anyone a witness of the sufferings of Christ. And even if it did, in the whole of 1 Pet. no trace is to be found of personal suffering on the part of Peter. If the participation in the glory of Christ for which Peter hopes, of which, according to Mark ix. 3–12, 2 Pet. i. 16–18, Luke xxiv. 34, John xxi. 2–23, 1 Cor. xv. 5, Acts x. 40 f., he already had a foretaste, is to be construed as in correlated contrast to the statement that he was a witness of His sufferings, then this last statement must imply also that Peter was an eye-witness of the Passion of Jesus.

10. (P. 148.) That δι' ἀναστάσεως κτλ., i. 3, is to be taken with ζῶσαν instead of with ἀναγεννήσας (thus Bengel, Hofmann), is extremely improbable. (1) ζῶν used attributively without the article cannot well be modified by an adverbial clause (cf. i. 23, ii. 4 f.; John vii. 38 ; Acts vii. 38 ; Rom. xii. 1); (2) it would require, not διά with the genitive, but διά with the accusative (John vi. 57 ; Rom. viii. 10), or ἐξ ἀναστάσεως (John iii. 5 ; Rom. i. 4 ; 2 Cor. xiii. 4). Of course, the interchange between " we " and " you," which may be compared to the similar interchange in Eph. i. 3, 13, Gal. iii. 23–iv. 7, is not to be understood as implying an absolute contrast applicable without exception to every single sentence. That would imply, for example, that Peter and men like him had already ceased to believe without seeing (i. 8) ; or that their inheritance was no longer preserved in heaven, but had been already received by them on earth ; or that the readers had not been born again unto a living hope ; or that the resurrection of Christ had no significance for their regeneration (cf. *per contra*, 1 Pet. iii. 21). It will be noticed, however, that where Peter describes the Christian state from the point of view of himself, he expresses himself in accordance with his own experience, just as in speaking of the Christian state of the readers he emphasises what is peculiar about their relation to the blessings of redemption in distinction from his own. That in i. 3, 4 he transfers himself vividly in imagination to the moment when he and his fellow-disciples were begotten again to a life of hope through the self-witness of the Risen Christ, is very clearly shown by the τετηρημένην ... εἰς ὑμᾶς ; since, if he merely intended to say here without reference to any specific point of time that all Christians would have to wait until the parousia in order to receive the inheritance which is laid up for them in heaven, it would have been necessary to use the expression τηρουμένην ὑμῖν, or rather ἡμῖν. But Peter is speaking from the point of view of the resurrection of Jesus. He and his fellow-disciples did not then immediately enter upon the possession of their inheritance (cf. Acts i. 6), but were quickened to a lively hope of the same, while the inheritance itself was deposited in heaven with Christ who had been raised to heaven (cf. Col. i. 12, iii. 2), where the inheritance had since been preserved. This took place, however, with a view to those who were to be called later, among whom the readers belonged. In order that

these might be called and converted, the first disciples had to be content with expectation and hope of the inheritance which was not to be received until afterward.

11. (P. 148.) The interpretation of ἡ ἐν Βαβυλῶνι συνεκλεκτή to mean Peter's wife, advanced, e.g. by Mill (Nov. Test. p. 718), and Bengel in his Gnomon, is not found, to the writer's knowledge, in any ancient author. It is true that Clemens Al. (Forsch. iii. 92, 102) understood by ἐκλεκτή κυρία, 2 John 1, "quandam Babyloniam Electam nomine," a real woman named "Eklekte," although this does not prevent him from interpreting the phrase allegorically with reference to the Church. The fact that he places her in Babylon can hardly be explained otherwise than by assuming that he identifies this Eklekte, or her sister mentioned in 2 John 13, whose name likewise must have been Eklekte (if, indeed, τῆς ἐκλεκτῆς is not to be taken only as an appositive to σοῦ), with the Syneklekte of 1 Pet. v. 13. But of the opinion that she was the wife of Peter, of whom Clement relates stories elsewhere derived from apocryphal sources (Strom. vii. 63 = Eus. H. E. iii. 30. 2 ; GK, ii. 828), the present writer finds no trace either in Clement or in any ancient writer. The Commentary of Didymus ends with 1 Pet. iv. An orator by the name of Chrysostom (Montfaucon, i. 821) is able to justify the contention that Peter had a wife only on the ground that mention is made in the Gospels of his mother-in-law. As a matter of fact, the opinion common in the early Church, that, according to Matt. xix. 27, Peter forsook even his wife (Orig. tom. xv. 21 in Matth. vol. iii. 683), and the consequent rejection of the interpretation of 1 Cor. ix. 5 to mean the wives of the apostles,—a view held by Clemens Al. Strom. iii. 53 (Jerome, c. Jovin. i. 26),—prevented the interpretation of 1 Pet. v. 13 to mean Peter's wife. The first trace of this interpretation which the present writer finds is that in the somewhat confused account of Barhebræus concerning various opinions on 1 Pet. v. 13 and Acts xii. 12 f. (ed. Klamroth, pp. 15, 29). On the other hand, the interpretation of the word to mean the Church of the place in question is represented by the insertion of ἐκκλησία before συνεκλεκτή in ℵ, several cursives, Pesh. ("The elect Church"), Vulg. (Ecclesia quæ est in B. conelecta), Jerome (Vall. vi. 757), Cramer (Cat. viii. 82). That this is the correct interpretation is proved (1) by the fact that otherwise the relationship to Peter of the person sending greetings would have to be expressed, whereas the use of συν- to express the relation of the one sending greetings to those to whom the greetings are sent is entirely intelligible and sufficiently anticipated by i. 1 and ii. 9 ; (2) by the fact that a greeting from the wife of Peter to the whole Church of Asia Minor would presuppose a peculiar ecclesiastical importance on her part, which is all the more improbable because of the fact that Peter had had no direct relations with the readers ; (3) by the fact that there is no plausible way in which to explain the mention of the place where this woman was residing, which at that time could not have been the place of Peter's residence.

12. (P. 149.) Ignatius, Philad. xi. 2 ; Smyrn. xii. 1, γράφω ὑμῖν διὰ Βούρρου, is, taken alone, quite as ambiguous as 1 Pet. v. 12. But from the analogy of Ignat. Rom. x. 1, γράφω ὑμῖν δι' Ἐφεσίων, which manifestly describes the Ephesian Christians, among them Crocus (cf. Ign. Eph. ii. 1), who is mentioned immediately in the same passage, as the forwarders and bearers of the letter, and of Polyc. (ad Phil. xiv. 1), it is clear that Burrus also is simply

the bearer of the letter (cf. the writer's *Ignatius*, 242 f., 262).   So in the very common notes at the end of the Pauline Epistles, διὰ Φοίβης, etc. (Tischendorf, ii. 457, 568, etc.).   On the other hand, it is clear that the same words can be used to describe the composition of a letter.   Concerning the epistle which Clement wrote by commission and in the name of the Roman Church, without anywhere disclosing his own identity, Dionysius writes to the Romans (in Eus. *H. E.* iv. 23. 11): τὴν προτέραν ἡμῖν διὰ Κλήμεντος γραφεῖσαν (ἐπιστολὴν ὑμῶν).   Acts xv. 23 is ambiguous; for, while without any question Judas and Silas are described as the bearers of the communication from the Jerusalem Church (xv. 22, 25–27, 30), it is possible that they were also commissioned by the assembly to prepare it.   The expression γράψαντες διὰ χειρὸς αὐτῶν, and the fact that it is used independently along with πέμψαι (xv. 22, 25, 27), favour the latter view, which is also more in keeping with the character of the men and the commission given them.   The analogous understanding of 1 Pet. v. 12 is anticipated by Jerome, who undertakes to explain the difference in style between 1 Pet. and 2 Pet. by assuming that he made use of different *interpretes* (*Epist.* cxx. 11, *ad Hedib.*).   Jerome makes no mention of Silvanus, nor does he think of a subsequent translation of letters written by Peter himself in a different language; but of the writing of the letters by helpers having more linguistic ability than Peter, commissioned by him, and in his name (cf. *GK*, ii. 881).   In modern times a more or less strong influence upon the form and contents of 1 Pet. has been attributed to Silvanus by H. Ewald (*Sieben Sendschreiben des NT*, 1870, S. 3, 73), W. Grimm (*ThStKr*, 1872, S. 688 ff.), Spitta (*Der 2 Pt. u. Ju.* 1885, S. 531).

§ 39. TIME AND PLACE OF THE FIRST EPISTLE OF PETER.

The location of the Church from which greeting is sent to those in Asia Minor, and thus the locality where Peter was residing at the time, is described as Babylon.   This does not appear to be intended as news, by which the readers are informed for the first time of Peter's place of residence.   Such a communication would be without parallel in all other N.T. Epistles, and totally different in form from similar communications in other letters (n. 1). Assuming that the readers already know where Peter is staying, the name Babylon seems rather to be intended to describe the conditions by which he himself and the Church where he resides are surrounded.   In v. 9 it was suggested that the whole Church throughout the world had to endure the same sufferings as the readers.   So here attention seems to be called to the fact that the small portion of the "brotherhood" from whom Peter sends greeting, and Peter himself, are in the capital of the empire, and so just as much strangers, far removed from the land of promise and the city whose true citizens are Christians, as the readers, who are so sorely in need of consolation (above, p. 140 f.).   If, also, we take into consideration the fact that the Church sending greetings is personified, being represented as the sister of the Churches in Asia (above, p. 148), and that Mark is called the son of Peter only in a figurative sense, it follows, even on purely exegetical grounds, that it is Rome, the capital of the empire, which is called Babylon, the place of the writer's residence.   If the Babylon at the southern extremity of the Nile delta, or the ancient city of that name on the Euphrates, long destroyed (n. 2), be meant, it is impossible to explain how every trace of the tradition of the work of Peter on the Nile or the Euphrates could disappear from the Church as a whole, and, in particular, from the Churches of the lands in question.   And this difficulty is increased by the fact that it is not a question of an accidental sojourn, but, as the names of two such prominent missionaries as Silvanus and Mark along with that of Peter prove, of important missionary labours on the part of Peter in these countries.   The Church in Alexandria and Egypt never attributed its founding to Peter, but always to Mark (§ 51, n. 8).   And for centuries nothing was known in the tradition of the Syrian Church as to a residence of Peter in Babylon, until some scholars of the Middle Ages undertook to prove it from 1 Pet. v. 13 (n. 3).   If there had existed such traditions as made possible the literal interpretation of the name Babylon, which was also the most natural one, the interpretation that makes 1 Pet. v. 13 refer to Rome—which came more and more to be accepted, and which can be traced back to the beginning of the second century—could certainly not have been universally accepted; in fact, could scarcely have arisen at all. The entire absence of such traditions makes it impossible to believe—more so, in case the letter is spurious, than if the letter is genuine—that the writer would lead his readers to suppose that he was in Egypt or Babylonia. On the contrary, even assuming that the letter is spurious, the age and general acceptance of the interpretation of 1 Pet. v. 13, which makes it refer to Rome, are proofs that Peter visited Rome. Rightful opposition to the extravagant claims which for more than a thousand years the Bishops of Rome have made on the basis of this fact, ought not so persistently to mislead Protestant scholars into the denial of the well-attested fact itself (n. 4).

If, then, it be accepted as certain that 1 Peter was written in Rome, or purports to have been written there, the time of its composition is fixed within comparatively narrow limits. The story that Peter's Roman episcopate lasted from twenty to twenty-five years did not appear until after the beginning of the fourth century, and all the more ancient traditions affirm that Peter did not come to Rome until the time of Paul's activity there; while the few definite accounts which we have from the second century place the whole of Peter's residence and his martyrdom in the interval between Paul's first imprisonment in Rome and the second, which ended with his execution. To this are to be added all the indications that Peter was crucified late in the summer or in the autumn of the year 64 in the Vatican gardens, in order to satisfy the fury of Nero (n. 4). Moreover, with these ancient traditions agrees the negative testimony of the N.T. writings which cover this period. Leaving out of account Acts xxviii. 30 f., the silence of Paul concerning contemporaneous work in Rome on the part of Peter in the letters of the first Roman captivity, especially in passages like Col. iv. 10 f. and Phil. i. 14–18, would be inexplicable if Peter were preaching there at the time. It is even more inconceivable that

Peter, in a letter to the Churches in Asia Minor founded by Paul and his helpers, should send greetings from the Roman Church and from Mark, and say nothing about Paul, if Paul were living and working in the same community. Even assuming that the letter was written shortly after the death of Paul, Peter's entire silence regarding him could not be explained as due to tender regard for the Christians of Asia Minor, who were in so much need of comfort in other respects, but would have to be regarded as an extremely unnatural thing, no matter whether the readers learned of the apostle's death shortly before receiving Peter's letter, or were informed of it for the first time by the person who brought the same. On the other hand, everything fits together naturally, providing we follow the tradition, freed from later fictions. If Mark, who, up to the time when Colossians was written, was known in Colossæ only by name as the cousin of Barnabas, journeyed from Rome to Asia Minor shortly after the sending of Colossians, sometime during the autumn of 62 or the spring of 63 (Col. iv. 10), such a relation of Mark to the Asian Churches would have been then established as is presupposed in 1 Pet. v. 13. It is at least possible that this journey of Mark in the East was extended to Jerusalem, his native city, and that he informed his "father," Peter, of the condition of things in Rome. If Peter heard of the troubles which Jewish Christian preachers were making for Paul in Rome (vol. i. 442, 543), and learned of Paul's intention immediately after being liberated, as he expected to be, to go from Rome to the far West, it is possible that he felt called to go at once to the capital of the empire, now that Paul had left it. This was not in any sense a violation of the agreement made with Paul and Barnabas some twelve years before (vol. i. p. 266), since the Church in Rome from its beginning was anything but a Church founded by the apostle to the Gentiles, being composed largely of native

Jews, part of whom were Jewish Christians from Palestine
(vol. i. pp. 421–434). If Peter reached Rome, apparently
in company with Mark, in the autumn of 63, or even as
late as the spring of 64, Paul was no longer there. If
Paul had undertaken a missionary journey to Spain
of uncertain duration, it was all the more natural for
Peter, following Paul's example, to assume the care of the
Churches in Asia, as he does in writing 1 Peter. By
making use of the assistance of Silvanus, whom many of
the Christians addressed in the letter had come to know
in his capacity as Paul's helper, he was able the more
easily to strike the note that would find an echo in the
hearts of the Christians in Asia Minor who had been
instructed by Paul and his helpers. When Paul found
time again to visit the East, and long before he was
imprisoned again in Rome and executed, Peter had suffered
martydom in that city. Peter laboured there at most not
more than a year, possibly only part of a year. Since
there is nothing in 1 Peter to indicate that Peter had
recently come to Rome, and since, on the other hand, his
residence there seems to be already known to the readers
when he writes, it is probable that the letter was not
written until sometime in the course of the year 64, a few
months before its author's death.

1. (P. 158.) Paul always left it to the persons by whom his letters were
dispatched to say from what point they brought his letters to the readers.
Only in rare instances does he mention a city in such a way that his residence
there can be inferred, e.g. 1 Cor. xvi. 8. There is a certain hint in Rom.
xvi. 1, cf. xvi. 23, which can easily be as misleading as 1 Thess. iii. 1. On the
other hand, see Ign. *Magn.* xv. ἀσπάζονται ὑμᾶς Ἐφέσιοι ἀπὸ Σμύρνης, ὅθεν καὶ
γράφω ὑμῖν ; cf. *Eph.* xxi. ; *Trall.* xii. ; *Rom.* x. ; *Philad.* xi. ; *Smyrn.* xii.
2. (P. 159.) Babylon in Egypt, situated between Memphis and Heliopolis,
on the site which afterwards became Cairo, was a city of no small importance
(Strabo, xvii. p. 807), and is also occasionally mentioned in ecclesiastical
literature : Athan. *Hist. Arian ad mon.* 72 ; Theodoret on Ezek. xl. (Schulze,
ii. 929) ; Epiphanius (*Mon.*, ed. Dressel, p. 6) goes so far as to call it τὴν
μεγάλην Βαβυλῶν. Regarding the rapid decline of the ancient Babylon on the
Euphrates, see the review in *Pauly-Wissowa, RE*, ii. 2679 ff. Strabo (xvi. p.
738) applies to it the verse, " The great city has become a wilderness " ; Pliny
says (*H. N.* vi. 122) : *cetero* (*i.e.* with the exception of the temple of Bel, which

still remained) *ad solitudinem rediit* ; Pausanius says (viii. 33. 3 ; cf. i. 16. 3), speaking not with reference to his own time, but with reference to the time of the founding of Seleucia, that only the walls of Babylon were left. Of the Jews in Babylon, *i.e.* in Babylonia (cf. Philo, *Leg. ad Cai.* xxxi. 36), it is possible that some few found lodging among the ruins of the ancient city (Theodoret on Isa. xiii., Schulze, ii. 264) ; but the great majority of them dwelt in the neighbouring cities of Seleucia, Nehardea, and the villages (Jos. *Ant.* xviii. 9. 1–9).

3 (P. 159.) Probably Papias favoured the interpretation of Babylon which made it refer allegorically to Rome (*GK*, i. 888) ; for, according to Eus. *H. E.* ii. 15, the story told by Clemens Alexandrinus in the sixth book of his *Hypotyposes* about the origin of Mark in Rome during the time when Peter was preaching there, is supported by the testimony of Papias (see below, § 51, n. 10). The further tradition given by Eusebius in the same passage, that Peter wrote 1 Pet. in Rome, and that Babylon (1 Pet. v. 13) is a figurative expression for Rome, cannot be traced back to Clement, a witness named before and alongside of Papias ; for although in his comment on 1 Pet. v. 13 he takes advantage of the occurrence of the name of Mark in order to speak of the Roman origin of his Gospel, he says nothing about the place where 1 Pet. was written, either in this passage or anywhere else in his commentary. Indeed, elsewhere he identifies Babylon with the ancient city in the land of the " Parthians " (*Forsch.* iii. 83, 95, 102, 72 f. ; above, p. 157, n. 11). It was therefore probably Papias who interpreted Babylon in 1 Pet. v. 13 to mean Rome, as Rufinus understood him to do. With this agrees the fact that Papias quotes passages from 1 Pet. (according to Eus. *H. E.* iii. 39. 16) ; that he places high value upon the Apocalypse, which might easily suggest such an interpretation of Babylon ; and, finally, the fact that he interpreted other biblical passages allegorically (*Patr. apos.*, ed. minor, p. 74). This interpretation was from the first the prevailing one in the Church, and continued to be so ; cf. Jerome, *Vir. Ill.* viii. ; or Hilary (of Arles ?) on 1 Pet. v. 13 (*Spicil. Casin.* iii. 1. 241, where we have also the purely allegorical interpretation *in confusione gentium*) ; Andreas on Rev. p. 76, καὶ ἡ πρεσβυτέρα δὲ Ῥώμη Βαβυλὼν ἐν τῇ ἐπιστολῇ Πέτρου προσαγορεύεται ; Cramer, *Cat.* viii. 82 ; *Schol. in Matt.* pp. 80, 205 ; and Tischendorf. Similarly there does not exist any tradition worthy of credence concerning the residence of Peter on the Euphrates. That Clement was not familiar with any such tradition, is sufficiently proved by the fact that he says nothing about it in connection with 1 Pet. v. 13 and 2 John 1, 13 (above, p. 157). In the *Acts of Philip*, which were not written before 400, and which are absurd in character (*Acta apocr.*, ed. Lipsius et Bonnet, ii. part 2. 16. 7 ; cf. *Forsch.* vi. 18–24), it is related that Philip went to the land of the Parthians, and in a certain place (ἔν τινι πόλει) found Peter. If there were any connection between this story and 1 Pet. v. 13, it would be indicated by the use of the name Babylon. Nor is there any independent tradition behind the story ; for, in addition, Philip finds there John (*op. cit.* p. 162), who had just as little to do with the Parthians as did Philip himself. Cosmas Indicopleustes, who questioned the genuineness of the Catholic Epistles (*GK*, ii. 232), cites 1 Pet. v. 13 once (Montfaucon, *Coll. nov. Patrum*, ii. 147 f.), without so much as saying that it was written by Peter, making the reference apparently only in

order not to omit mention of the fact that there is in the N.T. an uncertain suggestion of an early spread of Christianity in Mesopotamia. He makes Thaddeus the missionary of Persia. According to the more ancient tradition, Thomas was the apostle to Parthia, to which territory Babylon belonged (Origen in Eus. *H. E.* iii. 1. 1 ; Clement, *Recogn.* ix. 29 ; Ephr. *Expos. ev. concord.* 286 ; Rufin. *H. E.* i. 6 ; Socr. *H. E.* i. 19). This is not contradicted by the other tradition, likewise ancient, which makes Thomas the apostle of India ; indeed, there is a certain connection between the two, since in the latter at least the bones of Thomas, who died in India, are represented as being brought to Mesopotamia, or more specifically to Edessa (*Acta Thomæ*, Supplement, *Cod. apocr.*, ed. Bonnet, 94. 10, 131. 18, 159. 15 ; *Acta apocr.*, ed. Lipsius et Bonnet, ii. part 2, 286. 11 ; Ephr. *Carm. Nisib.* xlii.; *Chron. Edess.* cc. xxxviii. lxi., ed. Hallier, 61 f., 103, 111 ; Rufin. *H. E.* ii. 5 ; also Chrysostom, Montf. xii. 237, makes reference to the same). On the other hand, neither are there traces of any tradition of Peter's activity in Babylon among the interpreters of the Antiochian school, nor in the Syrian national Church. The "Teaching of Addai," the essential parts of which were known to Eusebius (*H. E.* i. 13), makes Thomas the principal leader of missionary work in the East, who sent Addai, one of the seventy or seventy-two disciples, to Edessa (ed. Phillips, p. 5). On the other hand, it is Peter who sends the Epistles of Paul from Rome to the Syrian Christians (p. 46). This legend knows nothing of an Antiochian episcopate of Peter, but is familiar only with his Roman episcopate ; for it is only through the mediation of Peter's Roman colleague that Serapion of Antioch receives ordination as a bishop, an imprimatur which goes back ultimately to Peter. Among the places where Peter preached, Ephrem mentions besides Rome only the districts in Asia Minor mentioned in 1 Pet. i. 1 (*Expos. ev. conc.* 286 ; above, p. 154 ; cf. *Hymn.* ed. Lamy, i. 342, 712, Peter in Rome ; *Carm. Nisib.* lix. 2 f.; *Expos. ev. conc.* 231, 237, crucified head downward). The Syriac "Teaching of the Apostles," of a somewhat late date, mentions Addai as the missionary of northern Mesopotamia, and his follower Aggai as the founder of the Churches in "the regions about Babylon" and in the lands lying farther east. On the other hand, according to this same account, Peter founded Churches in Antioch and the parts of Syria adjacent, in Pontus and other provinces of Asia Minor, before he went from Antioch to Rome, where, with Paul, he suffered martyrdom under Nero (Cureton, *Ancient documents*, 33, 34, 35). It also quotes among the letters of the apostles, "What Simon wrote from Rome" (p. 32), *i.e.* 1 Pet., and interprets Babylon to mean Rome. Cf. the note at the end of a MS of the sixth or seventh century (Wright, *Catal.* p. 82), "The end of the letter of the apostle Peter, written from Rome." Similarly the confused views about *Rome* or *Rhode*, a daughter of Peter, of which Barhebræus gives an account in connection with 1 Pet. v. 13 ; Acts xii. 12, 13 (above, p. 157, n. 11), are to be traced back ultimately to the interpretation of Babylon to mean Rome. [Barhebræus himself understands the "Church," which he read in the Syriac text of 1 Pet. v. 13 (above, p. 157), to mean "The assembly of the apostles in Jerusalem"; and "Babylon" he takes as referring to the upper room, Acts i. 13, where he represents the Pentecostal miracle and many others to have taken place. Possibly with this view of Barhebræus is to be connected the no less remarkable statement about 1 Pet. to be found in

Syncellus, *ad A. M.* 5540 (ed. Bonn, 627), ἄλλοι δὲ ἀπὸ ᾿Ιόππης φασὶ γεγράφθαι, where there is an evident attempt to connect the letter with Acts ix. 36–x. 23.] The Syriac "Teaching of Simon Kepha" (Cureton, *Anc. doc.* 35–40) deals only with the twenty-five years of Peter's labours in Rome. The *Acta Maris* (ed. Abbeloos, 1885, dated by the editor in the fifth or sixth century) speak of Peter in Rome (pp. 31, 35), and describe the founding of the Church in Babylonia by Mare (47 ff.) without any suggestion of earlier, perhaps fruitless, preaching by the apostle in the same regions. George, bishop of the Arabians (translation by Ryssel, S. 58), writing in the eighth century, speaks of " Peter and Paul in Antioch and Rome and the regions adjacent," but says nothing more. Likewise Solomon of Bassora, writing in 1220 (translation by Schönfelder, S. 77), says, "In Antioch one year, in Rome twenty-seven." The only missionaries of Mesopotamia in general—particularly of Babylonia—known to Ebedjesu (Assemani, *Bibl. or.* iii. 2. 4) are Thomas, Bartholomew, Addai, and Mare. When, therefore, Amrus and Jeshujab (Assemani, iii. 2. 6 f.; cf. also Abbeloos, p. 10) claim with express reference to 1 Pet. v. 13 that Peter also was in Babylon, it is perfectly clear that this is not Syrian tradition, but only a product of later erudition. Lipsius' claim, based upon these quotations (*Apokr. apostelgesch.* ii. part 1. 3, n. 3, ii. part 2. 145), that from the first the Syrian Church was unanimous in its interpretation of 1 Pet. v. 13 to mean Babylon proper, and held the corresponding form of the tradition, is a strange perversion of the actual facts in the case, while his further conjecture that the tradition of Simon Peter's presence in Babylon was supplanted by the tradition of the work of Simon Zelotes in these regions (ii. part 2. 146, Supplement, S. 32) is without foundation, because the latter tradition was just as much unknown among the Syrians as the former. It should be mentioned also that the pseudo-Moses of Chorene (*Chron.* ii. 33, translated by Lauer, S. 94 ; A. Carrière, *La légende d'Abgar*, etc., 1895, p. 406), in his letter from Abgar to Nerseh in Babylon inserts a prophecy about the coming of Simon, *i.e.* Peter, to Babylon. Erbes (*ZfKG*, 1901, S. 18 f.), who blindly follows Lipsius in respect of the Syrian tradition, feels the insufficiency of his evidence against the Roman sojourn of Peter, and takes refuge in the desperate assumption that by Babylon (1 Pet. v. 13) Jerusalem is to be understood.

4. (P. 160.) Among the martyrs whose murder is to be avenged by the overthrow of Babylon are to be found, according to Rev. xviii. 20 (cf. xvii. 6, xix. 2), also apostles. Now it is true that Babylon in Rev. is not entirely synonymous with Rome, but is a metaphorical name for the imperial city in every age, especially in the last age. When, however, this book was written the imperial city was Rome. And if more than one apostle had not suffered martyrdom in Rome, then no apostles' blood had been shed in the imperial city, and the sentence is meaningless. What other apostle's name occurs so naturally in connection with Paul as that of Peter? Lipsius' argument against this interpretation (*Apokr. apostelgesch.* ii. 1) requires no refutation. The series of witnesses for Peter's presence in Rome, who mention him by name, begins with Clemens Romanus (above, 60, 68 ff.). The second witness is Ignatius ; for although the thought that he was not in a position to give commandments to the Church like an apostle is expressed elsewhere (*Thrall.* iii. 3 ; cf. *Eph.* xi. 2–xii. 2), only in his letter to the Romans does he

use these words, οὐχ ὡς Πέτρος καὶ Παῦλος ὑμῖν διατάσσομαι (iv. 3). Since, however, there is no suggestion of a letter from Peter to the Roman Church, Ignatius' statement must mean that Peter had had to do with the Romans in person. In all probability the third witness is Papias (above, p. 163, and below, § 51, n. 10). As the fourth, the present writer, with greater con- fidence, mentions Marcion. By changing the text of Phil. i. 15–18, especially by inserting the οὐδέν μοι διαφέρει of Gal. ii. 6, he forces the reader to his view that Paul is referring in this passage to Peter and his companions (*GK*, i. 592, A. 3, 648; ii. 528). In Marcion's text, Col. iv. 11 and Phil. i. 15–18 were written on the same page, so that he also maintained that the persons referred to in the former passage were there called Jewish preachers in Rome by Paul, who could not have recognised them as his fellow- labourers. No one claims that Marcion was ignorant of the composition of Phil. in Rome, or that he denied it, so that he must have held that Peter was actively engaged as a preacher of the gospel in the vicinity of Paul while he was a prisoner in Rome. Connected with the testimony of Marcion is that of Dionysius of Corinth, Irenæus, Canon Muratori (to the extent that it connects the *Passio Petri* with the departure of Paul from Rome to Spain), already discussed (above, p. 73 ff.), also that of Caius of Rome, Tertullian, Hippolytus, Origen, Petrus Alexandrinus, Lactantius, and all the later authors, including the Syrians, who made no effort to take Peter away from the Romans in order that they might claim him for them- selves (above, p. 163 f.). There is to be added also the testimony of Clemens Alexandrinus in two passages of his *Hypotyposes* mentioned above, p. 163, n. 3 (Lib. vi. fragments 15, 16 ; and on 1 Pet. v. 13, *Forsch.* iii. 72, 83, 95). This testimony is limited to the preaching of Peter in Rome and the origin of Mark, and contains no indication as to date. Of course, Eusebius' appeal to the authority of Clement (*H. E.* ii. 15. 2) cannot be made to cover the whole narrative from ii. 13 on. Even that which immediately precedes the appeal to Clement in Eusebius' account—leaving out of account the fact that he appeals at the same time to the authority of Papias—is only partly Clement's, since it contradicts Clement's own statements which have been accurately handed down to us (*Forsch.* iii. 72, A. 1, and below, § 51, nn. 8, 9). In addition, we have also the legends belonging between 160 and 190, especially the *Acts of Peter*, a Gnostic document (above, p. 73 f.). In all authors heretofore mentioned, when chronological data are given at all, it is no more than the general statement that the two apostles worked in Rome, and suffered martyrdom at about the same time ; while a few others, such as Tertullian, Origen, and Lactantius, affirm that the apostles were put to death by Nero. In the *Acts of Peter*, on the other hand, we have the more definite statement that the whole Roman residence of Peter and his martyrdom fell in the one year which, according to this same document, intervened between the first and second Roman imprisonments of Paul, and was occupied by his Spanish journey (above, pp. 62–67, 73–84). This same representation of the matter comes to view in the Canon Muratori, since this does not bring together the martyrdom of the two apostles, but the Spanish journey of Paul and the martyrdom of Peter. The fact that the *Acts of Peter* place the whole of Peter's Roman residence in the reign of Nero, and nevertheless make Peter leave Jerusalem for Rome twelve years after the beginning of the apostolic preaching (Lipsius, 49. 11), is not to be explained as due to an impossible chronological reckoning, but to the naïve combining—quite in keeping with the fantastic character of this work of Leucius—of the prevailing tradition, according to which both Peter and Paul worked in Rome and were put to death under Nero, with a saying of Jesus which the author took from a much older work, namely, *The Preaching of Peter* (Clem. *Strom.* vi. 43 ; *GK*, ii. 821). The latter writing, which claims to be a work of Peter himself, while possibly containing a prophetic reference to the death of Peter, naturally contains no account of the same (*GK*, ii. 820–832).   It is also to be observed that none of the writers mentioned considered Peter as bishop of Rome.   Leaving out of account Clemens Romanus, Ignatius, and Clemens Alexandrinus, who make no definite statements about the relation of Peter to the Roman Church, Dionysius (*Eus.* ii. 25. 8), Irenæus (iii. 1. 1, 3. 2, 3), Caius (*Eus.* ii. 25. 7) speak of Peter and Paul as the missionary preachers through whom the Roman Church was founded.   Linus and his successors on the Roman throne are not as bishops successors of Peter. Not Peter, but "the apostles," gave Linus his episcopal office (Iren. iii. 3. 3).   The Roman bishops were counted from Linus, who was reckoned as the first bishop ; they were not designated first, second, third after Peter, but from the time of the apostles (ἀπὸ τῶν ἀποστόλων).   The different reckoning to be found in Irenæus, i. 27. 1, iii. 4. 3, which presupposes that there was a bishop preceding Linus, namely, Peter, is a falsification, inconsistent with the fundamental views of Irenæus ; and that it is an error is confirmed by text tradition.   Even Epiphanius (*Hær.* xxvii. 6), who makes use in this passage among other authorities of reports of Hegesippus (cf. Lightfoot, *Clement*, i. 328 f., cf., however, *Forsch.* vi. 260), mentions as the first of the Roman bishops not Peter, but "Peter and Paul," beginning with these very clear words : ἐν Ῥώμῃ γὰρ γεγόνασι πρῶτοι Πέτρος καὶ Παῦλος ἀπόστολοι καὶ ἐπίσκοποι.   Even the ancient *Acts of Peter* and the *Acts of Paul* make the two apostles simply preachers of the gospel in Rome, labouring hand in hand ; there is no suggestion that Peter occupied the position of a bishop in Rome (*GK*, ii. 840).   And the same is true even of the late recensions of the legends, *e.g.* the so-called "Linus," and the combined *Acts of Peter and Paul*.   Obscure, to say the least, is the indication of Peter's bishopric in Rome to be derived from the fact that Tertullian makes Clement receive ordination from Peter alone (*Præscr.* xxxii. ; but cf. chap. xxxvi.). It is not until the middle of the third century that we find the Roman bishopric clearly represented as the *cathedra Petri*, *e.g.* in Cyprian (*Epist.* lv. 8, lix. 14), and in a sermon of practically the same date in Cyprian's name by a Roman bishop, *de Aleatoribus*, chap. i., and in the fabricated letter of Clement to James (*Clementina*, ed. Lagarde, 6), which can hardly be of an earlier date.   Leaving out of account the end of the *Teaching of Addai* (ed. Phillips, Syr. 52, Eng. 50), concerning which it may be questioned whether the conclusion belonged originally to this writing, the other parts of which are to be dated prior to Eusebius, Eusebius is the first known writer who states that Peter was bishop of the Roman Church for a definite number of years.   But in the ecclesiastical history and in other works where he speaks of Peter in Rome (*Demonstratio evang.*, *de Theophania*), he never calls him a bishop, and in speaking of the Roman bishops he always uses the ancient mode of expression already mentioned (*H. E.* iii. 21. 2). Nor does he say anything as to the time when Peter left Antioch and Euodius succeeded him there (iii. 22, 36. 2). The time of Peter's arrival in Rome he indicates very indefinitely (ii. 14. 6 under Claudius); and this disagrees with the date given in the *Chronicle*, which was written earlier. All this goes to show that Eusebius placed no reliance whatever upon the dates given in the *Chronicle*, which, though definite, are self-contradictory. In the *Chronicle* (Armenian version), under the date *anno Abrah.* 2055 (A.D. 39)=the third year of Caius, he remarks that Peter came to Rome after the founding of the Church in Antioch, and lived there as head of the Church for twenty years; but he does not make Euodius succeed Peter as bishop of Antioch until *anno Abrah.* 2058 (A.D. 42)=the second year of Claudius. Generally, the Roman episcopate of Peter is placed at "twenty-five years" instead of twenty; so, *e.g.* in the list of bishops in the Roman *Chronicle* of 354 (Catal. Liberianus in Duchesne, *Lib. pont.* i. 2). Incorporated in this *Chronicle* is a *depositio martyrum* (*op. cit.* p. 11), which shows that Peter's induction into the office of bishop was celebrated on viii. Kal. Mart.; see also the *Chronicle* of Eusebius as revised by Jerome under the date *anno Abrah.* 2058 (A.D. 42)=second year of Claudius (cf. *Vir. Ill.* i.); also the *Teaching of Addai* and the majority of later catalogues (cf., however, Duchesne, *Lib. pont.* i. 16, 34, 39, 40). This is not the place in which to investigate the origin of the sacred number 25, which possibly may be only an expression in round numbers for "something more than twenty years." It is perfectly evident, however, that Eusebius, who did not find and who does not give any definite tradition about the time of Peter's death (above, p. 78 f.), did not get his twenty years by counting back from the year of Peter's death. On the other hand, from the ecclesiastical history we learn what it was that led him to assume this long residence of Peter in Rome, in contradiction to the universal testimony of the early Church and the indirect testimony of the N.T. From Justin (*Apol.* i. 26) and Irenæus (i. 23. 1), Eusebius was acquainted with the tradition that Simon Magus came to Rome in the reign of Claudius, and was there deified (*H. E.* ii. 13. 2–5). Now, the tradition that Simon came to Rome in the reign of Claudius can hardly be due to a misinterpretation of the inscription on a statue of the Sabine god, Semo Sancus, which stood on the island in the Tiber, a misinterpretation reproduced in Justin, Irenæus, Tertullian, and many later writers (see Otto on Just. *Apol.* i. 26; Öhler on Tert. *Apol.* xiii.), and which in different form is made use of in the ancient *Acts of Peter* (ed. Lipsius, 57. 24). Rather does the misinterpretation of the inscription presuppose the tradition about Simon. There is nothing about the inscription to suggest the time of Claudius (*C. I. L.* vi. 1, No. 567), and there is nothing in the account in Acts viii. which could suggest its dating in this reign. Furthermore, only if it were already known from other sources that Simon Magus was once in Rome, could it possibly occur to anyone that this statue and its inscription had reference to him. Consequently, it follows that before the middle of the second century it was generally believed in Rome that Simon lived there, and carried on his work under Claudius; and the present writer knows no reason why this should not be regarded as a genuine tradition. Now, in the *Acts of Peter* (written between 160 and 170),

a book which was much read in the East as well as in the West (*GK*, ii.
843–848), we have the account of numerous contests in Rome between
Simon Magus and Peter, all of them connected more or less closely with
Acts viii. (*GK*, ii. 854). To be sure, these contests are said to have taken
place in the reign of Nero, while Paul was occupied with his Spanish journey;
but in this same story the tradition which connects Simon Magus with
Claudius has apparently a certain connection with the anachronistic statement that these took place twelve years after the beginning of the apostolic
preaching (above, p. 166, last line). With this tradition is to be connected
the story (*Acta Petri*, pp. 48. 19 ff., 49. 21 ff.) that immediately after the first
appearance of the Magician in Rome, Peter in Jerusalem received the divine
command to go to Rome in order to combat him. Under the influence of
this narrative, especially of the proofs there adduced of the divine guidance
in the whole matter (*Acta Petri*, pp. 49. 17–31, 51. 25–31, 52. 17), Eusebius
writes that shortly after the appearance of Simon Magus in Rome, while
Claudius was still on the throne (*H. E.* ii. 14. 6, παρὰ πόδας γοῦν ἐπὶ τῆς αὐτῆς
Κλαυδίου βασιλείας), Divine Providence sent Peter to Rome to oppose him.
When, on the other hand, the persecution of Christians by Nero was regarded
as the climax of his atrocities, and in consequence of this the martyrdom of
the two apostles was brought down toward the end of his reign (above, p. 78),
Peter's residence in Rome is made to cover more than a decade. Eusebius
was not the only writer—perhaps he was not the first one—who was led by
the *Acts of Peter*, through the combination of the tradition of Simon Magus'
residence in Rome under Claudius with the tradition of Peter's martyrdom in
Rome under Nero, to assume a long Roman episcopate of Peter. Once it had
arisen and become current, the story lost all connection with its sources. Even
in the *Chronicle* of the year 354 the twenty-five years' episcopate is treated as
an independent date, and incredibly enough is placed between 30 and 55 A.D.,
both in the list of bishops and in the Fasti Consulares (cf. Mommsen, *Chron.
min.* i. 57, 73). The later *Lib. pontif.* retains the twenty-five years, although
it places both the arrival of Peter in Rome and his death in the reign of
Nero, which covered only thirteen years (Duchesne, i. 50, 118). With
regard to the manner of Peter's death, in 2 Pet. i. 14 the expectation is
expressed, based upon a prediction of Christ's, that he will die a quick, *i.e.* a
sudden and violent, death. When John xxi. 18–23 was written, it must have
been generally known that Peter was crucified prior to the destruction of
Jerusalem. While Clement (*ad Cor.* v., see above, p. 68 ff.), Canon Muratori,
and many other writers merely say that he died a martyr's death, from
Tertullian on there is frequent mention of his crucifixion in Rome (above, p.
76 f.). It is not possible certainly to determine from Origen (*c. Cels.* ii. 14.
cf. Eus. *Chron.* under *anno Abrah.* 2048) whether this report had been heard by
Phlegon, a manumitted slave of Hadrian's. The legend that he was crucified
head downward is evidently an invention of the Gnostic *Acts of Peter*, which
date from about the year 170 (ed. Lipsius, p. 92 ff.),—an invention, however,
which is accepted by Origen as true (Eus. *H. E.* iii. 1. 2). The way is prepared
for this story by the conversation between Peter, as he was fleeing from Rome,
and Christ who appeared to him, in which Christ says first, εἰσέρχομαι εἰς τὴν
Ῥώμην σταυρωθῆναι, and then ναί, Πέτρε, πάλιν σταυροῦμαι (p. 88. 9, cf. *GK*,
ii. 846). The common source of this story and that of the crucifixion of

Peter head downward is evidently the ambiguous saying of Christ which Origen (*in Jo.* tom. **xx.** 12) quotes from the Catholic *Acts of Paul,* ἄνωθεν (*i.e. denuo,* but also *desuper*) μέλλω σταυρωθῆναι. Since, for chronological and other reasons, it is unlikely that the author of the *Acts of Peter* made use of the *Acts of Paul,* it is probable that the author of the Gnostic *Acts of Peter* and the author of the Catholic *Acts of Paul,* who wrote not much later, took the story from an older source, probably the "Preaching of Peter." For the original meaning of the saying, which possibly had nothing whatever to do with the death of Peter, see *GK,* ii. 878. In view of these facts, it is altogether unlikely that the story of Peter's crucifixion head downward is historical. On the other hand, there is no reason to call in question the Roman local tradition, firmly established by the year 210, and so certainly not due to a sudden new discovery or invention, that Paul was beheaded on the Via Ostiensis and Peter crucified near the Mons Vaticanus, and that both were buried near the places where they were executed (above, p. 81 f.). Had there been an inclination to supply by invention what could not be certainly known,—in view of the connecting of Peter and Paul, which was quite universal from the time of Clemens Romanus,—it would have been natural to think of them as united in death and burial. On the Mons Vaticanus, in the Ager Vaticanus, were the gardens of Agrippina and Domitia, both of which became the property of Nero. According to Tacitus (*Ann.* xv. 44), it was in these extensive pleasure-grounds that the terrible executions of Christians took place in the year 64 (*hortos suos ei spectaculo Nero obtulerat*), and among those sacrificed were also *crucibus affixi.* The agreement of this statement with the tradition about the manner and place of Peter's death has all the more weight, because the tradition of the early Church shows no connection between the martyrdom of Peter and the burning of Rome, much less does it show affinities with the description of Tacitus. Only by taking chap. **vi.** of Clement's letter in connection with chap. **v.** is it possible to infer any connection between the scenes described by Tacitus and the death of at least one of the apostles. To these considerations is to be added the fact that the entire Roman residence of Peter must fall in the interval between the first and second Roman imprisonments of Paul (above, p. 160 f.), *i.e.* between the autumn of 63 and the autumn of 66. There is consequently nothing in the way of the assumption, made so natural by traditions which there is no reason to suspect, that Peter perished late in the summer of 64 as a victim of Nero's attack upon the Christians in Rome. Baur (*Christent. der drei ersten Jahrh.* 2te Aufl. 86–93, 141–145 ; *Paulus,* 2te Aufl. 246–272) believed that the entire tradition of Peter's residence in Rome, which has just been examined, could be explained from the pseudo-Clementine Romance and so refuted ; and this view has been taken up and further developed especially by Lipsius (*Quellen der römischen Petrussage,* 1872 ; *JbPTh,* 1876 ; *Apocryph. Apostelges.* ii. part 1. 11, 28–69, 358–364 ; Supplement, 32–34). Since in this literature Simon Magus, with whom Simon Peter wages constant and successful contests, is only a mask for Paul, and not in any sense an historical person, the entire tradition about Peter in Rome is only the presentation in historical form of the thought that the Christianity preached in Rome by Paul was to be overcome by Jewish Christianity represented by Peter, or that it was to lose its detested peculiarities through union with its opposite. With regard to this view the following brief remarks may be made :—(1) The pseudo-Clementine Romance was not known in the West until Rufinus translated one recension of the same into Latin in 400 (cf. the same author's *Præfatio ad Gaudentium*). Even Jerome (*Vir. Ill.* xv.), speaking with regard to this literature, is able only to repeat in a very inaccurate way what he had read in Eus. *H. E.* iii. 38. 5. It is entirely inconceivable that the entire tradition of the Western Church concerning Peter in Rome should rest upon an appropriation and an entire misunderstanding of the Ebionitic legend as to the identity of Simon Magus and Paul. (2) Peter's presence and martyrdom in Rome were known to the Roman Church as early as the year 96 (above, pp. 61 f., 68 f.). The pseudo - Clementine Romance could not possibly have been written before 160, and in all probability originated in the course of the third century. (3) In both the existing recensions of the Romance it ends with the arrival of Peter in Antioch, whither Simon Magus had gone before him. That there was another recension of this Ebionitic legend, which included the work of Peter in Rome, and dealt with his contests with Simon Magus there, is merely a conjecture for which there is no proof. In the two existing recensions there are only two brief hints that in his preaching journeys Peter finally reached Rome (*Hom.* i. 16 ; *Rec.* i. 13, 74). Assuming that the letter of Clement to James is an integral part of the Homilies, this merely presupposes that Peter was a bishop in Rome, appointed Clement his successor, and died a martyr's death after having borne testimony to Christ publicly before the emperor (*Epist. Clem. ad Jac.* i.). There is no suggestion that the Magician went to Rome and was there overcome by Peter. According to *Hom.* xx. 13–17, 22, the Magician did not go from Antioch to Rome, but fled to Judea in order to escape the officers of the Roman emperor. We have the same testimony in *Rec.* x. 55–59. Quite inconsistently with this statement in *Rec.* iii. 63–64, cf. ii. 9 (*Hom.* ii. 27 is only remotely parallel to the latter passage), we have references to the miracles, the deification, and the statue of Simon in Rome. But not even here do we find any statements about contests in Rome between him and Peter. (4) In the Ebionitic literature, Simon Magus was not always the mask for Paul. In those portions which show the marks of greatest age, Paul is sometimes combated in his own name (Epiph. *Hær.* xxx. 16), sometimes opposed anonymously, being styled simply a "hostile man" (*Rec.* i. 70, 71 ; *Epist. Petri ad Jac.* chap. ii.) ; but he is distinguished from Simon Magus (*Rec.* i. 72). Even in the *Clementine Homilies*, in which alone Simon Magus stands as a veiled representative of Paul (*Hom.* xvii. 13–19; cf. ii. 22, xi. 35, xvii. 5, xix. 22), Paul is not the only person whom he represents. Simon Magus has a history, and teaches a doctrine which certainly cannot be regarded as simply a caricature of the life and teaching of Paul (*Hom.* ii. 22–32, xviii. 6, 12 ; *Rec.* i. 72, ii. 5–15, 38 f., 49 ff., iii. 47). On the contrary, there are essential points in which this picture of Simon Magus agrees with the statements of Justin (*Apol.* i. 26, cf. i. 56, ii. 15 ; *Dial.* cxx.), who was a Samaritan, and could have had no knowledge of the pseudo-Clementine Romance. The picture also has points of contact with the hints in Acts (viii. 9 f. ; cf. Klostermann, *Probleme im Aposteltext*, 15–21), which was written approximately a hundred years before the earliest possible date of the Clementine Romance. (5) The idea of representing and combating Paul under the figure of Simon Magus—which is carried out for the first time in the *Homilies* of Clement, but not as yet in other writings representing the same tendency—could not have arisen unless Simon Magus already stood for the type of religious teacher who was Christian in name but in reality was anti-Christian, and unless he was generally known in Catholic Christendom which this Ebionitic literature was designed to influence. (6) Even assuming that in Justin much that is unhistorical is combined with the ancient, genuine tradition, and suspecting as much as we will, the alleged writings of Simon Magus (Hippol. *Refut.* iv. 51, vi. 9 ff. ; Jerome *in Matt.* xxiv. 5, Vall. vii. 193 ; *Const. ap.* vi. 16 ; Maruta, *de synodo Nic.*, translated by Braun in Knöpfler's *Kirchengesch. Stud.* iv. 3. 47), we must nevertheless admit that in the middle of the second century and long afterwards there existed a sect which bore Simon's name, and which in a certain sense could claim to be Christian (Just. *Ap.* i. 26, speaking of Simon, Menander, and Marcion, πάντες οἱ ἀπὸ τούτων ὁρμώμενοι Χριστιανοὶ καλοῦνται). The first would have been impossible had Simon Magus existed only in imagination and in the partisan narratives of Ebionitic sects and writings. The second fact presupposes that the historical Simon Magus modified his original teaching, which was totally unchristian in character, through contact with Christianity and by the adoption of Christian elements, and that in this modified form it was promulgated by a party bearing his name. It is altogether likely that after his hypocritical conversion (Acts viii. 13-24) he taught the doctrine, the principal tenet of which is found in Iren. i. 23. 1. (7) The tradition concerning Simon Magus in Rome, which probably has some historical foundation (above, p. 168), as it appears in Justin, Irenæus, and Tertullian, has no connection with the tradition concerning Peter and Paul in Rome ; while, on the other hand, in Dionysius of Corinth, Irenæus, Tertullian, and Lactantius (probably also in the ancient *Acts of Paul, GK*, ii. 884), the tradition about Peter and Paul appears without any connection with that about Simon Magus. The first writer who to our knowledge combined these two traditions was the author of the *Acts of Peter* (*circa* 170 A.D.), who was a fabricator though not a finished one. His combination of these two independent traditions was not due to the influence of the Ebionitic legend. (*a*) The romance through which we learn of this legend was not yet written ; (*b*) it contains no narrative about the contests in Rome between Simon Magus and Simon Peter ; moreover, (*c*) the author of these Acts, who belonged to the school of Valentinus, was not at all likely to allow himself to be influenced by such a source. The attempt of Erbes (*ZfKG*, 1901, S. 1–47, 161–224) to prove that Peter never visited Rome, and that he was crucified not in Rome but in Jerusalem, gives no occasion for correcting or enlarging what was said above, pp. 68 f. and 162–172, nn. 2–4. It is sufficiently characterised by the manner in which Erbes agrees with the oldest witnesses. Concerning 1 Pet. v. 13, see above, p. 163, n. 3) ; with what Erbes (22 ff.) says concerning Clemens, Romanus, and Ignatius, cf. above, pp. 68 f., 165, n. 4. He does not think it worth while to take Rev. xviii. 20 (xvii. 6, xix. 2) and Marcion into consideration. On the other hand, we learn that neither Irenæus nor the author of the *Acts of Peter* was acquainted with John xxi. (p. 165), and that the one hundred and fifty-three fishes (John xxi. 11), under the tacit presupposition of the Dionysian Era, refers to the year 153 A.D., in which year Anicetus and Polycarp in Rome came to an agreement concerning the tradition of Peter's presence in that city, pp. 10, 219.

§ 40. THE GENUINENESS OF THE FIRST EPISTLE OF PETER.

The *external evidence* for the genuineness of the letter is strong; it is known and quoted as the work of the Apostle Peter by two men who were disciples of apostles, and also bishops of two of the Churches belonging to the group to which the letter purports to be addressed, Polycarp of Smyrna and Papias of Hieropolis (n. 1). Polycarp was baptized probably in the year 69, some five years after the probable date of the composition of the Epistle (*Forsch.* vi. 94 ff.). It is not at all likely that at this early date the Churches in Smyrna and Hieropolis could be deceived into accepting as an Epistle of Peter's written in the year 64 a letter forged in his name in the year 100.

As regards the *character of the letter*, we are unable to test it by comparison with writings of the same author regarding which there is no question. 2 Peter is one of the most suspected documents in the N.T.; and even if it should be proved genuine, its comparison with 1 Peter as regards point of view and style would not prove much, because of the important part that Silvanus took in the composition of 1 Peter, whereas in 2 Peter there is no evidence that the author made use of an amanuensis. While the discourses of Peter in Acts may faithfully reproduce his thought, and give a true picture of his manner of preaching, it is altogether unlikely that the form in which Luke reproduces them is derived from notes made at the time. But leaving out of account altogether the many changes which may have taken place in these discourses in the course of their transmission to Luke, and which may have been made by Luke himself in committing them to writing, and disregarding the influence which

Silvanus may have had in determining the form of 1 Peter, there is all the difference in the world between discourses which Peter delivered in the early days of the Church to the populace and the Sanhedrin in Jerusalem, in the house of Cornelius at Cæsarea, or later in Jerusalem before the Apostolic Council, and a letter which he directed Silvanus to write from Rome to the Gentile Christian Churches in Asia Minor at a much later time, and in altogether different circumstances (n. 2). All that can be claimed is that the impression of Peter's religious attitude and ecclesiastical position, which we get from Acts and the Epistles of Paul, agrees perfectly with the manner in which he conceives his new task in 1 Peter. Here we find the same unhesitating recognition of the divinely blessed labours of the missionaries among the Gentiles, and of the equal Christian standing of Gentile Christians and Jewish members of the mother Church (Gal. ii. 7–10; Acts x. 47, xi. 17, xv. 7–11; cf. 1 Pet. i. 4–12, ii. 3–10, v. 12); the same concentration of the gospel message upon the death on the Cross, the Resurrection, and the Second Coming of Christ (1 Cor. xv. 3–5, 11; Acts ii. 23–36, iii. 13–26, iv. 10, v. 30 f., x. 39–42; cf. 1 Pet. i. 3–7, 18–21, ii. 21–25, iii. 18, 21 f., iv. 1, 5, 13, v. 1, 4, 10). Finally, we observe also the consciousness of preaching as an eye-witness about the closing scenes of Jesus' life to others, who through this testimony are enabled to believe without having seen (Acts ii. 32, iii. 15, iv. 20, v. 32, x. 39–42; cf. 1 Pet. v. 1, i. 3, 8). But the modest reserve with which this consciousness is expressed in the letter (above, pp. 146, 155) is strong evidence against the suspicion that some later writer is here artificially and presumptuously assuming the rôle of Peter. Nor would such a writer, after having assumed this rôle, have again obscured the Petrine authorship, in which he wanted his readers to believe, by remarking that the letter was actually written by Silvanus, a secretary (v. 12). What could have been the motive of such a forgery? An "apology of Paulinism, written by a member of the Pauline party" at the time of the "persecution of the Church by Trajan, and intended for members of the Petrine party" (Schwegler, Baur, and others), would have been altogether superfluous in an age when generally throughout the Church Peter and Paul were looked upon as brothers closely united in their work (Clement, 1 *Cor.* v. 47; Ign. *Rom.* iv.). Possibly such an apology may have been needed by Jewish Christians in Palestine, but certainly not by the Churches in Asia Minor founded by Paul and his helpers. Consequently, if the writer had this or some similar purpose in view, he chose a very peculiar address for his letter. Just as strange are the means which he chooses to accomplish his end. Paul is not once mentioned by name, nor referred to in a way that would be intelligible, although i. 12, 25, v. 12 offered the amplest opportunity for such reference. Not a word is said about the opposition of Paul to the Judaisers in Galatia, who claimed to be followers of James and Peter, or to the Cephas party in Corinth; and yet the readers, whose knowledge of Peter's teaching, based as it was only upon verbal reports, must have been very indefinite, are to infer from certain resemblances to the Pauline Epistles that Peter has adopted the disputed teachings of Paul in order thereby to justify them!

The undeniable use of Pauline ideas in 1 Peter, when considered without prejudice, leads to an entirely different conclusion. It is in line with the relation of 1 Peter to James, already discussed (n. 3). The necessity of saying some word of encouragement to the Christians in Asia Minor, whose persecutions had recently grown very severe, recalled to the mind of Peter, or Silvanus, or of both, the letter of James, which some fifteen years before had been such a help to them as well as to other Christians, and which, as proved by Paul's letter to the Romans (vol. i. 127 f., 429), continued to be widely known. The result

was that a number of ideas and expressions found in
James were reproduced in 1 Peter. A writer thoroughly
original could not have permitted himself to follow so
closely an older model. But from all that we know of
Peter there is not the slightest reason to assume that he
was original, in the sense that James or Paul or John
was original. On the contrary, his nature was such as to
make him susceptible to influences from without; while
the fact that he recovered so quickly from the errors into
which this tendency led him, proves that in doing that
which was good and wholesome he did not have to contend with a strongly biassed character. Similarly, a
writer who was concerned to maintain a show or reputation of originality would have avoided these quotations
from another writer, or would have concealed them more.
Peter, who in v. 12 shows himself so little concerned in
this regard as to permit the readers to give Silvanus all
the credit for this beautiful letter, was not bound by such
considerations. The only thing which he was able to
claim for himself and put to his own credit was the intention of applying for the benefit of the readers what
Silvanus wrote in his name, and what James and others
before him had written. This inclination on his part is in
no sense external, interfering with the natural flow of his
own thoughts. The reader who is not familiar with the
originals does not observe the influence which they have
had upon the form of 1 Peter. The temper and tone of
the whole is independent and fundamentally different from
James. That there is no question here of slavish imitation of single passages, or of dishonest plagiarism, is proved
by the fact that earnest efforts have been made to reverse
the relation and make James dependent upon 1 Peter.

Exactly similar is the case of the undeniable agreement
between 1 Peter and some of the Pauline letters. The
only letters of Paul to which 1 Peter shows resemblance
in thought and language are Romans and Ephesians

(n. 4). But this fact finds no satisfactory explanation, if we assume that some author of a later time simply happened to make Peter use Paul's language. On the other hand, it is the most natural thing in the world, if this letter was actually written by Peter in Rome, in the year 64, with the assistance of Silvanus. When Peter went to Rome to fill up the gap made by the departure of Paul (above, p. 162), he must have had a very natural inclination to read the letter of Paul's preserved in Rome in which the apostle had made his first effort to establish relations between himself and the Roman Church; and when he found himself called upon to address the Churches in Asia Minor, with which up to this time he had remained personally unacquainted, in a letter which was to bear testimony to the genuineness of the gospel brought to them by Paul and his helpers, and to the truth of their Christian profession, he was under necessity of making the instruction which they had previously received his starting-point, and of adopting the tone of Christian address to which they were accustomed. But where could he find a better model than in the letter which Paul had written two or three years before to the same group of Churches, or to a large number of the Churches of the same group, namely, those in the province of Asia? The existence of a copy of Ephesians in the year 64 at Rome, where Paul wrote the letter, need occasion no surprise, since Ephesians was a circular letter of which possibly a number of copies were prepared immediately after it was written, and so were preserved in Rome (cf., moreover, vol. i. 249 f., n. 6).

The dependence of 1 Peter upon Romans and Ephesians is proof of its genuineness; since a pseudo-Peter, writing in the year 75 or in 110, would have had no occasion to imitate these particular letters of Paul. A pseudo-Peter of the time of Trajan would not probably have recognised the true character of Ephesians as a circular letter to the

Churches in Asia (vol. i. p. 479 ff.), and he would have been far more likely to use Galatians than Romans, since his alleged compilation is designed to pose as a letter of Peter among the Churches of Galatia as well as those of other regions.

If, on the other hand, it could be shown that the use of the name *Babylon* to designate *Rome* is explicable only if the writer is dependent upon Rev. xiv. 8, xvi. 19–xviii. 24, it would be a serious argument against the genuineness of the letter. But is it not possible that the relation is just the reverse? and, besides, what reason is there for supposing that such ideas arose and were spread simply through literary agencies? Just as the Jews called Rome and the Roman Empire Edom, and just as among Christians Jerusalem and Zion were typical designations of their commonwealth, which centres in heaven and has its future upon earth (Gal. iv. 25 f.; Heb. xii. 22, xiii. 14; Rev. xxi. 2), so Babylon, which among Greeks and Romans was the proverbial type of a great luxurious city, under the influence of historical tradition and O.T. prophecy, came to be used by Jews and Christians as the figurative name for the capital of the world-empire which was hostile to the Church of God, though no one was able to say who had used it first (n. 5). The name did not originate either with Peter or John, both of whom assumed rather that their contemporaries and fellow-believers were familiar with the Babylon of the present.

Moreover, there is nothing about the representation of *the situation of Christianity in the world* at this time which renders impossible the composition of the letter in the last years of Peter's life. Very frequently has it been supposed that the letter represented conditions in the time of Trajan; but this assumption is due to a misunderstanding of the interchange of letters between Pliny and Trajan, as if no attempt had been made by the Roman government before the year 112 to suppress Christianity

(n. 6). It is due equally to a misunderstanding of the statements in 1 Peter relative to persecution. It is true that in 1 Peter we have a representation of the relation of Christians to their heathen environment different from that of the earlier Epistles of Paul, with the exception of 1 Thessalonians, which presupposes a temporary and local persecution of Christians in Thessalonica. While in Paul's Epistles we do have suggestions of hostility to Christians on the part of Jews (Jas. ii. 6 f. ; 1 Thess. ii. 14 ; vol. i. 88 f.) and of Gentiles (Rom. xii. 14–21), there is also evidence that there were Churches of considerable importance which lived quite unmolested (1 Cor. iv. 8–10, viii. 10, x. 27, xv. 33 ; 2 Cor. vi. 14–16), and believed themselves able to get fair treatment even in heathen courts (1 Cor. vi. 1–8). Consequently, when we read that practically the same sufferings to which Christians were then being exposed in Asia Minor had to be endured by Christians throughout the world (1 Pet. v. 9), an entirely new situation is presented. Indeed, the readers themselves had not been accustomed to suffer in the way that they are now compelled to suffer (iv. 12). It is not a general experience of Christians—an experience they have always had—which is described in v. 8, but a present fact ; even now the devil is passing through the land like a lion roaring for his prey. The final consummation of things is at hand (iv. 7) ; the judgment begins (iv. 17). From beginning to end the letter is filled with references to a recent unfavourable change in the situation of Christians, especially those in Asia (i. 6 f., iii. 9–17, iv. 4 f., 12–19, v. 8–12). This impression is simply strengthened by the fact that in the later letters of Paul—in those that were written shortly before 1 Peter (64 A.D.) as well as in those that were written shortly after—there are various indications that the relations between Christians and their heathen neighbours were more strained than at the time when Romans and the Corinthian letters were written ;

cf. Col. iv. 5; Eph. iv. 27 f., v. 15 f., vi. 12; 1 Tim.
iii. 6 f. (in the last passage the best interpreters make
ὁ διάβολος refer to the class of slanderers), vi. 1; Tit.
ii. 5, 10.

When we inquire what these sufferings on the part of
Christians, which Peter felt it necessary to notice, actually
were, we observe at the very outset that nowhere in the
letter is there the slightest hint of bloody martyrdoms,
nor even of imprisonment and the confiscation of property.
Nor is anything said about judges before whom they were
brought, acts of worship which they were commanded to
perform, and recantations under the pressure of persecution. But we do find such hints in N.T. writings
of a later date and in the oldest portions of the post-
apostolic literature (n. 7). For this reason it is impossible to believe that 1 Peter was written at the time
of the Johannine apocalypse and of the letter of Clement
(90–100). Still less is it possible to believe that it was
written about 110, at the time of the Ignatian letters and
of Pliny's Epistles. The attacks upon the Christians at
the time of 1 Peter were various in character (i. 6); but
they were due mainly to and consisted primarily of slan-
derous and calumnious attacks upon them as Christians.
They were insulted "for the name of Christ" (iv. 14).
And, as is shown by what immediately follows (iv. 15), it
was this in which their sufferings consisted primarily if
not exclusively; whenever a specific injury is mentioned
which they suffered at the hands of the heathen, it is
always of this character:—καταλαλεῖν (ii. 12, iii. 16),
λοιδορεῖν (iii. 9), and ἐπηρεάζειν τὴν ἀγαθὴν ἐν Χριστῷ ἀνα-
στροφήν (iii. 16); βλασφημεῖν (iv. 4), and ὀνειδίζειν (iv. 14).
They are to silence their slanderers by their good conduct
(ii. 15); they are to put them to shame (iii. 16); above
all, they are not to answer reviling with reviling, but with
blessing (iii. 9). The very first condition of a comfortable
life is to refrain from evil and deceitful words (iii. 10).

Even in the passage where the suffering Christ is held up
as an example especially to slaves, it is not said that He
refused to use His power to defend Himself against violence
(Matt. xxvi. 51–55, xxvii. 40–44; John xviii. 36; Heb.
xii. 2 f.); but that when He was reviled He reviled not
again, and did not give vent to threatening words when
He was compelled to suffer (ii. 23). It is true that in
this same connection, besides the reviling, suffering is
mentioned which involved actual violence; but in the
foreground of the pictures stands the reviling, to which
one less patient would have replied with reviling and
threats. As a concrete example of the unjust treatment
which slaves, to whom these words are addressed, frequently had to endure at the hands of their heathen
masters, cuffing, not reviling, is mentioned (ii. 20). Of
course it goes without saying that a hostile feeling toward
the sect of Christians that had become general would not
be limited to insulting words. Every Christian had daily
to expect actual injury (iii. 14, εἰ καὶ πάσχοιτε; iii. 17, εἰ
θέλοι τὸ θέλημα τοῦ θεοῦ); but, according to Peter's opinion
and exhortation, the Christian ought not to fear it (iii. 13).
The form and extent of this persecution we are able to
infer only from casual hints. The designation κακοποιοί,
which was slanderously applied to Christians, is quite
general (ii. 12, iii. 17, iv. 15, n. 8); and equally general
is the exhortation to a virtuous walk among the heathen
and to good works which is contrasted with it. But this
is followed immediately by a special exhortation to silence
the ignorance of these unreasonable slanderers by obedience to the emperor and his officers (ii. 13 f.; cf. Acts xvi.
21, xvii. 7), and by the exhortation to show to all—
naturally to all to whom it is due (Rom. xiii. 7)—the
honour which their position demands, without prejudice
to their special love for their fellow-believers, and especially to honour the emperor, without prejudice to their
fear of God (ii. 17), all of which indicates that the Chris-

tians were accused of a hostility to the State which had
its source in their religion and in their close fellowship
with one another. The fact that the discussion of the
relation of Christians to the State is followed by a detailed
discussion of the relation of slaves to their masters (ii.
18–25), and of wives to their husbands (iii. 1–6), while
the conduct of husbands to their wives is touched upon
only briefly (iii. 7), and the character of the exhortations
to slaves and wives (cf. especially iii. 1 f. with ii. 12),
show that Christian slaves and wives were accused of
insubordination to their heathen masters and husbands.
Christians were looked upon as the enemies of social order
generally. The inner freedom from all earthly conditions
of which they boasted was regarded as a revolutionary
spirit. Every fault observed in the conduct of individual
Christians was laid to the charge of their peculiar views,
so that their fine words about freedom and the service of
God were regarded as cloaks for their hostility to social
order and the State (ii. 16). The inevitable result was
the defaming of the name of Christ Himself, whom they
confessed and after whom they were called (iv. 14, 16 ;
n. 10). The same was true with reference to the impression made by the earnest lives of the Christians, especially
by their abstinence from heathen worship and the festivities associated with it. Wonder at the peculiarities of
the Christians led to the blaspheming of the things that
they regarded as holy, and the source of their own sanctification (iv. 3–5). All the acts of the Christians, even
when they were not known, were construed in accordance
with their supposed views. They were looked upon as
κακοποιοί in the broadest sense of the word. They were
accused of everything bad. In cases of serious crimes,
like murder and theft, Christians would necessarily be the
first to be suspected (iv. 15). The natural consequence
was that they were accused of crimes, arrested, and
brought before magistrates ; and in the course of such

trials the fact that they belonged to the sect of Christians would be brought out, also the leading principles of their religion. Exhortations, like those which we read in Eph. iv. 28, Tit. ii. 10, 1 Thess. iv. 6, compel us to assume that not all the members of the newly organised Gentile Christian Churches abstained from acts which were punishable before magistrates. Persons so accused and so punished suffered as thieves, deceivers, and similar characters. Peter urges and expects that as the regular outcome of such trials the readers shall prove that there is no ground for suspecting them of acts which are criminal or subject to punishment; so that it shall appear that the only reason for suspicion against them, for their arrest, and for their unfair treatment by magistrates, is their Christian confession. In this case they suffered " as Christians," and were partakers of the sufferings of Christ, the innocent Lord, who was reviled, accused, and executed (iv. 13; cf. ii. 21, iii. 18), in the same sense that Paul was during his five years of imprisonment (Col. i. 24, iv. 3; Eph. iii. 1, 13, iv. 1, vi. 20; Philem. 1, 9; Phil. i. 7, 30, iii. 10), although as a result of Paul's trial "his bonds in Christ were made manifest" (Phil. i. 13); *i.e.* the trial brought out the fact that he was innocent of the offences against public order of which he was accused, and that he was indicted, imprisoned, and brought before the tribunal simply because he confessed and preached the Christian faith. It is really impossible to see how anyone can discover in 1 Peter a persecution of the Christian confession carried on by the imperial government or by any civil authority. The persecution of the Christians originated not with the authorities, but with the populace; and it consisted mainly of slanders and insults against the Christians, and blasphemous remarks about Christianity. In daily intercourse Christians were made to feel very strongly the hostility of their heathen neighbours; in particular, Christian slaves suffered at the hands of their

masters. When investigations were made by the police or
by the courts because of serious crimes, the general suspicion of the criminal character of Christians, particularly
of their hostile attitude toward the existing political and
social order, put them in a bad position at the very outset.
They were suspected first in connection with definite cases,
and in the accusations which followed they were charged
with general crimes and misdemeanours. If, in these trials,
their religious confession and their brotherhood came up
for discussion, it was nothing essentially different from
what happened in their daily private intercourse with
non-Christians. There was constant need for endeavour
to remove this suspicion by setting forth the nature of
Christian views. Christians must " be always ready with
an answer for every one and before every one who demanded of them a reason for their peculiar hope " (iii. 15).
There is nothing in the language which implies inquiry
by the police or officers of courts, but primarily only
what happened in daily intercourse (cf. Col. iv. 6). But
of course Peter's exhortation and the rule which he lays
down include also the cases where a Christian happened
to be brought before a judge, and where, as was unavoidable in view of popular feeling, the religion and morality
of the Christians came under discussion. But, in Peter's
opinion, here, as in daily life, the proof of pure intentions
and of moral conduct afforded by deeds was more weighty
and more effective than an apology in words.

In view of the contents of 1 Peter, it is impossible to
believe that Christians were brought to trial and sentenced
by magistrates to pay fines, or to undergo imprisonment,
banishment, or execution, simply on account of their confession (n. 9). And in this the situation of the Christians
at the time of 1 Peter is essentially different from that in
which they found themselves after Nero's attack upon the
Roman Christians—presumably for the first time during
the reign of Domitian, when the attitude of the imperial

government and of the provincial authorities was altogether changed. On the other hand, the representation of popular feeling toward the Christians as recently having grown more hostile, which we find in 1 Peter—written at the beginning of the year 64 or shortly before—is definitely confirmed by the words of Tacitus, written late in the summer or during the autumn of the same year (*Ann.* xv. 44): "Ergo abolendo rumori Nero subdidit reos et quæsitissimis pœnis affecit, quos per flagitia invisos vulgus Christianos (or *Chrestianos*) appellabat." The universal hatred which was heaped upon the Christians, and the opinion held by the vast majority of the populace that the Christians were a band of dangerous criminals, whose extermination would be for the good of the State and of society, a *utilitas publica*, were not, according to Tacitus, the result, but the presupposition of Nero's action against the Christians, on the charge that they were responsible for the burning of Rome in the autumn of 64. Even then the name *Christiani* was the object of popular hatred and of every evil suspicion (n. 10). This presupposition meets us as a simple fact also in 1 Peter. On the other hand, nothing is said in 1 Peter about the consequences of this popular feeling, such as were realised in Rome in the autumn of 64, not only in the execution of Christians, but their execution in large numbers and in a most gruesome manner. How is this omission to be explained, if the letter was written in 95 or 110 or even later? How inconceivable is the colourless description of the situation of Christians throughout the world in 1 Pet. v. 9, if this letter was written by Peter himself shortly after he had passed through the scenes of 64 in Rome upon the ground which had drunk the blood of saints and apostles (Rev. xvii. 6, xviii. 20, 24), or if it was written by some one in his name after his death ![1]

1. (P. 173.) For the chronology and historical position of Polycarp, cf. *Forsch.* vi. 1–157. Eusebius (*H. E.* iii. 39. 16) says of Papias : κέχρηται δ᾽ αὐτὸς

μαρτυρίαις ἀπὸ τῆς Ἰωάννου προτέρας ἐπιστολῆς καὶ ἀπὸ τῆς Πέτρου ὁμοίως
If not strictly proven, it has been shown highly probable (above, p. 163 ; cf.
also § 51, n. 10) that Papias interpreted 1 Pet. v. 13 as referring to Rome,
and used this passage in support of the tradition that Mark was written in
Rome. In Eus. *H. E.* iv. 15. 9, it is said of the Philippian letter of Polycarp :
κέχρηταί τισι μαρτυρίαις ἀπὸ τῆς Πέτρου προτέρας ἐπιστολῆς. While 1 Pet.
is not formally quoted in this letter, a number of passages in it show unmistakable resemblance to the same. Cf. the writer's *Ignatii et Polyc. epist.* 1876,
pp. 110–132 ; *GK*, i. 957 f. In *Polycarp*, i. 2, after a peculiar expression taken
from the speech of Peter in Acts ii. 24, the following words are found, which
suggest 1 Pet. i. 8, 12 : εἰς ὃν οὐκ ἰδόντες πιστεύετε χαρᾷ ἀνεκλαλήτῳ καὶ
δεδοξασμένῃ εἰς ἣν πολλοὶ ἐπιθυμοῦσιν εἰσελθεῖν, which makes it necessary
to assume either a most singular coincidence, or, that Polycarp knew that
Acts ii. and 1 Pet. originated with the same man, namely, Peter. For the
further testimony to 1 Pet. by Clemens Romanus, Hermas, Justin, Basilides,
and the Valentinians, see *GK*, i. 576, 759, 773, 958. In this connection it may
be observed that it is doubtful whether the citation from Justin, following
that of Iren. v. 26. 2 in Cramer, *Cat.* viii. 82, really belongs to Justin or is
an addition by the redactor of the catena, as is held by Otto, in his edition of
Justin, *Opp.* ii. [3rd ed.] 254, n. 7. For the impossibility of making 2 Pet.
iii. 1 refer to 1 Pet. see § 41.

2. (P. 174.) Worthy of notice, however, is the correspondence between
1 Pet. ii. 7 and Acts iv. 11 (cf. Matt. xxi. 42 ; Mark xii. 10), and between
1 Pet. iv. 5 and Acts x. 42 (cf. 2 Tim. iv. 1).

3. (P. 175.) For the relation of 1 Pet. to James, see vol. i. 133 f. The
thought of Jas. i. 3 (vol. i. 127), which is correctly understood and freely reproduced by Paul (Rom. v. 4 f.), necessarily takes another and more modest
place in 1 Pet. i. 7 ; since Peter, while he retains the word, gives it quite a
different meaning (vol. i. 133).

4. (P. 177.) In favour of the conscious dependence of 1 Pet. upon
Eph. is the fact that they begin with exactly the same words, εὐλογητὸς—
Χριστοῦ ὁ, followed by a participle,—a construction which does not occur in
this or similar form in any other N.T. Epistle. The participial clause which
follows is different, as is also the reason assigned for the thanksgiving. But
the reference to the future κληρονομία, 1 Pet. i. 4, is found also in Eph.,
only farther from the beginning, i. 14 ; while the thought which immediately follows Eph. i. 4 f. (cf. i. 9, 11), namely, that of election through the
divine foresight and predetermination, has been utilised already in 1 Pet. i.
1 f. The exhortations to a Christian life, in contrast to the former heathen life
of the readers, 1 Pet. i. 14–18, iv. 2 f., correspond to a whole series of expressions in Eph. : ὡς τέκνα ὑπακοῆς = ὡς τέκνα φωτός, Eph. v. 8 ; ἐν τῇ ἀγνοίᾳ
ὑμῶν = διὰ τὴν ἄγνοιαν τὴν οὖσαν ἐν αὐτοῖς, Eph. iv. 18 ; ἐκ τῆς ματαίας ὑμῶν
ἀναστροφῆς = ἐν ματαιότητι τοῦ νοὸς αὐτῶν, Eph. iv. 17 ; μηκέτι ἀνθρώπων
ἐπιθυμίαις . . . βιῶσαι = μηκέτι ὑμᾶς περιπατεῖν κτλ., Eph. iv. 17 ; οἰνοφλυγίαις
. . . εἰς τὴν αὐτὴν τῆς ἀσωτίας ἀνάχυσιν = μὴ μεθύσκεσθε οἴνῳ, ἐν ᾧ ἐστιν
ἀσωτία, Eph. v. 18. Eph. ii. 11–22 differs greatly from 1 Pet. ii. 4–10 in the
way in which the Gentiles are reminded of the fact that now, as Christians,
they are entitled to all the rights and honours of the people of God. This
renders all the more striking the fact that in both passages the figure used

is that of a building in which Christ is the corner-stone and Christians are the building stones. Paul develops the figure briefly at the end of the entire discussion ; Peter makes a varied and detailed use of the same, in connection with various O.T. expressions, and also sayings of Jesus. The building suggests the Lord of the building, who has chosen this particular stone for a corner-stone, and Himself has put it in place, after it had been rejected as worthless by the foolish master-builders. From the thought of the living character of the person of Christ, who is represented as the corner-stone, is argued the living character of the stones built upon this foundation, as well as the freedom of their attachment to Him. The comparison of the building with the temple suggests the thought of the priesthood and the offerings. The corner-stone is also the curb-stone (Prellstein), over which passers-by stumble. It would seem almost as if in 1 Pet. ii. 4–8 one were hearing the voice of a preacher making various applications of the figure suggested by his text, Eph. ii. 20–22. Nor is it strange that at the conclusion of both letters it is suggested that back of the men, through whose hostilities the readers are compelled to suffer, stands the devil, whom they are steadfastly to resist (1 Pet. v. 8 f.; Eph. vi. 11–13). Other resemblances in thought and language, *e.g.* that between 1 Pet. iii. 21 f. and Eph. i. 20–22, do not furnish positive proof, nevertheless they go to confirm the correctness of the observation that Peter and Silvanus had Eph. before them. Whether, as Hofmann holds (vii. 1. 206), they intended to suggest to the readers directly the circular letter which had been sent to them, is doubtful. The relation of 1 Pet. to Rom. is certainly quite different. While from the beginning to the end of 1 Pet. there are portions which are parallel to Eph., with Rom. there are only scattered points of contact. Cf. in this connection Hofmann's fine exposition (vii. 1. 207–212); on the other hand, the effect of Seufert's exposition (*ZfWTh*, 1874, S. 360–388) is to evoke the dissent of every intelligent reader of 1 Pet., rather than to convince him of its dependence upon Rom. It is especially the hortatory portion of Rom. to which 1 Pet. shows numerous points of resemblance : Rom. xii. 2 = 1 Pet. i. 14, μὴ συσχηματίζεσθαι, with substantially the same object in the dative ; Rom. xii. 17 = 1 Pet. iii. 9, μηδενὶ (μὴ) ἀποδιδόντες κακὸν ἀντὶ κακοῦ, in both instances standing between an exhortation to humility and the advice to preserve peace with non-Christians, while in the immediate context in both passages stands the command that they bless their persecutors instead of reviling them again (Rom. xii. 14). Taken in connection with such clear resemblances, a certain weight is to be given also to similarities in the same chapter, which cannot be used as positive proof, such as the similar use of λογικός,—not to be found elsewhere in the N.T. or LXX,—Rom. xii. 1, 1 Pet. ii. 2, and the conception of offerings, in a figurative sense, made by Christians, Rom. xii. 1 ; 1 Pet. ii. 5. In relatively close proximity to these parallels, Rom. xiii. 1–7 and 1 Pet. ii. 13–17, occurs an exhortation with regard to civil authorities. The sense is not only the same, but several expressions are alike, *e.g.* the aim for which civil authorities exist is described thus : εἰς ἐκδίκησιν κακοποιῶν, ἔπαινον δὲ τῶν ἀγαθοποιῶν, 1 Pet. ii. 14 = τὸ ἀγαθὸν ποίει καὶ ἕξεις ἔπαινον ἐξ αὐτῆς . . . θεοῦ γὰρ διάκονός ἐστιν ἔκδικος εἰς ὀργὴν τῷ τὸ κακὸν πράσσοντι (Rom. xiii. 3 f.). Notwithstanding, Peter's thought strikes one as independent. While Paul emphasises the thought of the divine institution of the civil order and the subserviency of the same to God, Peter represents it more broadly, describing it as πᾶσα ἀνθρωπίνη κτίσις. By this he does not imply that the civil power was created and endowed with its functions by men, which would be contrary to the whole Jewish (Dan. ii. 37) and Christian (John xix. 11 ; 1 Clem. lxi.) conception of the same, but means that government is an institution which belongs in the human realm and not in the domain of revelation. The adjective ἀνθρώπινος (Rom. vi. 19 ; 1 Tim. iii. 1 ; above, p. 124, n. 6) is not used in the sense of θνητός (e.g. in Rom. vi. 12), which suggests a conceivable motive for the conduct that Peter condemns,—a motive which he rejects,—so that the exhortation practically means, " Be subject to the government, and do not think that you are released from this obligation because this is only a human institution." But this word is meant to suggest to the readers that Christians are to honour and support everything that contributes to the maintenance of good order in human affairs, not less but more zealously than other people (cf. Rom. xii. 17 ; 2 Cor. viii. 4 ; Phil. iv. 8). The fact that Peter, writing from Rome, the seat of the imperial government, to provincial Christians who were governed by deputies sent from Rome, mentions not only the emperor, but also expressly the ἡγεμόνες sent by him into the provinces, while Paul, writing to Christians in Rome, speaks more generally of ἐξουσία, ἐξουσίαι, ἄρχοντες, is only another proof that we are not dealing with some man of letters who patterned what he wrote after more ancient models, but with Peter himself, who took account of the actual conditions under which he wrote.   Cf. an imperial decree of the third century in Grenfell and Hunt, *Fayûm Towns*, p. 120, τοῖς ἡγεμόσιν τοῖς κατ' ἐπιτροπείας παρ' ἐμοῦ ἀπεσταλμένοις.   That Rom. ix. 32 f. and 1 Pet. ii. 6, still more ii. 4–8, were not written independently of each other, is proved (1) by the fact that both apostles in quoting Isa. xxviii. 16 are practically agreed against the strongly variant reading of the LXX ; even the addition ἐπ' αὐτῷ (Rom. ix. 33, x. 11 ; 1 Pet. ii. 6) is certainly spurious in the LXX ; (2) from the fact that after the quotation of Isa. xxviii. 16, following a quotation from Ps. cxviii. 22, in 1 Pet. ii. 7 f. are added the words λίθος προσκόμματος καὶ πέτρα σκανδάλου, which are taken from Isa. viii. 14, but vary greatly from the text of the LXX, and which Paul inserts in the quotation of Isa. xxviii. 16. Here also Peter does not copy Rom.; he is familiar with the prophetic text from his own reading, since in ii. 6 he gives the characteristics of the stone,—as also earlier in ii. 3,—passed over by Paul.   But there remains in his memory also the form in which Paul had quoted the words of the prophet, and, following the cue suggested by Paul's combination of Isa. xxviii. 16 and Isa. viii. 14, he adds also Ps. cxviii. 22.   The relation of 1 Pet. iv. 1 to Rom. vi. 7 shows just as clearly an acquaintance on the part of the later author with the older writing ; for the thought that death annuls man's relationship to sin, which is only differently expressed in the two instances, is very boldly applied in both cases, first to the death of Christ and then as the ground of a moral obligation on the part of those who have been redeemed through His death. Similar relations do not exist between 1 Pet. and any other of Paul's letters. Gal. iii. 23 and 1 Pet. i. 5, quoted by Hilgenfeld, *Einl.* 633, agree only in the use of the word φρουρεῖν.   It would be more natural to compare the latter passage to Phil. iv. 7, which likewise would be to no purpose.

5. (P. 178.)   Regarding the use of Edom for Rome, cf. Weber, *Jüdische*

Theol. § 81, 8 ; Schürer, iii. 236, A. 55 [Eng. trans. II. iii. 99, n. 29]. Sc also in 4 Esdr. vi. 8 f. In 4 Esdr. iii. 1 f. (28, 31 in contrast to Zion) Babylon is certainly not the city on the Euphrates ; but if not Rome, at least the place which the writer knew to be the seat of the heathen power inflicting its burden upon Israel. Gutschmid, who held that the greater part of this book was written in 31 B.C., suggested Alexandria (*Kl. Schriften*, ii. 277). In spite of his evident interest for Egypt, the Jewish Sibyl of the years 71–73 claims to understand by Babylon Rome (*Sibyll.* v. 143, 159 ; cf. *ZfKW*, 1886, S. 39–45). Concerning Babylon-Rome in Rev. see below, § 75, n. 2. According-ing to the Midrash on Cant. i. 6 (translated by Wünsche, S. 35, cf. Sanhedr. 21b; Shab. 56b), Rome was called *Romi-Bablon*, because the clay out of which its first huts were built was mixed with water brought from the Euphrates. Paul does not use the word Babylon, but applies a prophecy concerning the departure of the exiles from Babylon (Isa. lii. 11 ; cf. xlviii. 20) to the separation of the Christians from the heathen world (2 Cor. vi. 17). For the proverbial meaning of Babylon among Greeks and Romans, see *Pauly-Wissowa, RE*, ii. 2667.

6. (P. 179.) The opinion that the rescript of Trajan to Pliny altered the legal status of the Christians—a view against which the present writer argues in an earlier work, *Hirten des Hermas*, 1868, S. 128 f.—is beginning to give way to a better view. With the position there advanced agree Arnold, *Stud. zur Gesch. d. plinian. Christenverfolgung*, S. 27, 39, 42, 47 ; C. J. Neumann, *D. röm. Staat u. die Kirche*, i. 17, 22 f. ; Mommsen, *HZ*, 1890, S. 395 f. ; Ramsay, *The Church in the Roman Empire*, pp. 212, 215 f., 226, notwithstanding many differences.

7. (P. 180.) Without distinguishing between what refers to the immediate present in the several writings and what is said with reference to past events, the following forms of punishment may be cited : imprisonment and con-fiscation of property, Heb. x. 32–34 ; banishment, Rev. i. 9 ; Hermas, *Sim.* i. (cf. the writer's *Hirten des Hermas*, S. 118–135) ; executions, Rev. ii. 13 (? see § 73, n. 3), vi. 9, 11, xii. 11, xvii. 6, xviii. 20, 24, xix. 2, xx. 4 ; Heb. xiii. 7 (?) ; Clem., 1 *Cor.* v. vi. ; Herm. *Vis.* iii. 2. 1 ; *Sim.* viii. 3. 6 f., ix. 28. 2–4. All these cases are prior to the time of the letters of Ignatius and Pliny.

8. (P. 181.) Κακοποιός, iv. 15, occurs in a list of offences of a more definite character, so that it is natural to take it in the more definite sense which *maleficus* (used to translate κακοποιός in Tert. *Scorp.* xii. and Cypr. *Test.* iii. 37) certainly came to have, = "sorcerer, witch," etc. Cf. the astrological term οἱ κακοποιοὶ τῶν ἀστέρων, Artemid. *Oneir.* iv. 59 ; also Suet. *Nero*, xvi. "Christiani genus hominum superstitionis novæ et *maleficæ*." The term is interpreted in this sense by Le Blant, *Les pers. et les martyrs*, 1893, p. 62. But there is no cer-tain proof of the corresponding use of κακοποιός, and if this were the meaning, we should expect rather μάγος (Acts viii. 9–11, xiii. 8 ; *Acta Theclæ*, cc. xv. xx.) or γόης (2 Tim. iii. 13 ; Orig. *c. Cels.* i. 6). Furthermore, the contrasted state-ments in 1 Pet. ii. 12, 14, iii. 17 show that the word was meant to be taken in an entirely general sense (cf. Mark iii. 4 ; Luke vi. 9 ; John xviii. 30 ; 3 John 11). The word appears to be weaker and not so definite as κακοῦργος, Luke xxiii. 32 f.; 2 Tim. ii. 9 ("transgressor," often with the special sense "rogue," "cheat"; cf. πανοῦργος). The list of misdeeds with which the Christians were charged is concluded almost immediately with a general expression

With a new ὡς, as something of especial importance, ἀλλοτριοεπίσκοπος is subsequently added. This word, which does not occur at all in the earlier literature, and only at a late date in ecclesiastical literature, and then not independently of 1 Pet., means one who acts as an overseer of things and persons that are foreign, *i.e.* a person who assumes to exert a determining influence and guardianship over men and affairs which do not concern him. While the word is omitted from the text altogether by Peshito, Tert. *Scorp.* xii. translates it *alieni speculator*; but in the oldest Latin Bible (see Cypr. *Test.* iii. 37) it is translated *curas alienas agens.* E. Zeller (*Sitzungsber. der berl. Ak.* 1893, S. 129–132) calls attention to the fact that this criticism was lodged against the Cynic philosophers, who made it their business to be the overseers (κατάσκοποι, ἐπίσκοποι) of the rest of mankind. Cf. especially the famous description Epict. iii. 22, and the answer to the criticism which it contains, § 97, οὐ γὰρ τὰ ἀλλότρια πολυπραγμονεῖ (the Cynic) ὅταν τὰ ἀνθρώπινα ἐπισκοπῇ, ἀλλὰ τὰ ἴδια ; and, on the other hand, the confession of the philosopher in Hor. *Sat.* ii. 3. 19, "aliena negotia curo, excursus propriis." Like the Cynics, the Christians were criticised for their inordinate zeal for making converts, for their unsolicited concern about the souls of others, and for their interference in the most intimate affairs of the heart and the home. But while the Cynics held that they were under obligation to exercise their preaching and pastoral office in the most decisive, authoritative, and defiant manner possible, only denying that in so doing they were meddling with things that did not concern them, the apostles (cf. also 1 Thess. iv. 11) condemn conduct which could be more or less justly described as ἀλλοτριοεπισκοπεῖν. Everywhere they exhort their followers in their intercourse with non-Christians to act with wisdom and modest reserve, to do good, and to suffer evil in silence (1 Pet. ii. 12, 18, 23, iii. 1, iv. 8–10, 15–17, v. 6 ; 1 Thess. iv. 12 ; Col. iv. 5 f. ; Phil. iv. 8), which, of course, did not mean that when it was a question of witnessing to the truth this witness should not be given boldly. What 1 Pet. iv. 15 omits is almost as instructive as what it contains. There is no trace in 1 Pet. of the three famous charges of ἀθεότης or ἀσέβεια, of the eating of flesh of children, and of unchaste orgies in connection with Christian worship. The first charge was in vogue as early as the time of Domitian (Dio Cass. lxvii. 14, lxviii. 1), and was noticed by Pliny, since he required Christians who were accused to perform heathen acts of worship (*Ep. ad Traj.* xcvi. 5). So also the second and possibly also the third charges came under his notice : inasmuch as, in the light of the confessions of persons who had been Christians, he describes their celebration of the sacrament in common as a "coire ad capiendum cibum, promiscum tamen et innoxium." After the time of Justin there is constant reference to all three charges.

9. (P. 184.) The opinion that 1 Pet. presupposes a persecution of the Christians at the instigation of the civil authorities (maintained still by Ramsay, *The Church in the Roman Empire,* pp. 279–302 ; *Exp.* 1893, pp. 285–296) is based primarily upon the words, ἐν ὀνόματι Χριστοῦ, iv. 14, and ἐν τῷ ὀνόματι (al. μέρει) τούτῳ and ὡς Χριστιανός, iv. 16. But ὀνειδίζεσθαι does not mean "To be accused before a court," and πάσχειν taken alone does not mean "To suffer punishment in consequence of a judicial sentence," still less "To be executed." A person convicted as a thief or ἀλλοτριο-

ἐπίσκοπος would certainly not be punished with death. The exhortation, "If anyone suffer as a Christian, let him not be ashamed," would be very strange indeed, if this suffering were execution. When one is on the point of being executed, there are matters of deeper concern than whether one is ashamed of his position and confession, or proud of it. It is self-evident that God can be glorified in the name of Christ without sacrificing life (cf. Phil. i. 20), and there are classic instances which show that arrests and trials which end with acquittal can be regarded as suffering for Christ's sake (see above, p. 183). But even granted that in iv. 16 the reference is to cases where Christians are executed as Christians, this is nothing essentially different from what happened in Rome in the year 64, Tac. *Ann.* xv. 44 ; for, according to Tacitus, with whom Suetonius (*Nero*, xvi.) and the Christian traditions agree, this was not a case of the punishment of a few Christians along with other suspected persons, but those who bore the Christian name in Rome were accused, sought out, and executed, first as incendiaries, and then afterwards many of them merely on account of the misanthropy due to their religion. Quite in agreement with this description, the readers of 1 Pet. would then have been executed primarily as murderers and thieves ; but where it was impossible to prove such charges, also as members of a dangerous society, *i.e.* as bearers of the Christian name. It would then foreshadow what happened some months later in Rome on a larger scale. The uncertainty which Pliny desired cleared up ("nomen ipsum—aut flagitia cohærentia") has in a certain measure always existed, and has really never disappeared entirely, and is repeated in analogous cases even to-day. Were the Armenians massacred in 1895 and 1896 because of their nationality, or their Christian confession, or anarchistic intrigues? One is reminded also of the vacillations of the anti-Semitic movement of our own day. But, as has been shown (above, p. 184 f.), there is nothing which indicates that even individuals who were Christians had up to this time suffered martyrdom, either in Asia Minor or in Rome, where the letter was written. This shows that the letter was written before July 64. It is true that the word ἀπολογία, iii. 15, does suggest a judicial process (Phil. i. 7, 16 ; 2 Tim. iv. 16 ; cf. Ramsay, *op. cit.* pp. 280, 294), but it is employed in the N.T. (1 Cor. ix. 3 ; 2 Cor. vii. 11, xii. 19 ; Rom. ii. 15) as elsewhere in literature quite commonly with reference to other conditions, and the context (ἀεί, παντὶ τῷ αἰτοῦντι ὑμᾶς λόγον) shows that it is used here in exactly the same sense as in Col. iv. 5 f. (πρὸς τοὺς ἔξω . . . πῶς δεῖ ὑμᾶς ἑνὶ ἑκάστῳ ἀποκρίνεσθαι). Ramsay, who (*op. cit.* p. 281) discovers in iii. 15, and even in v. 8, the spying out of Christians by Roman officials at the behest of the authorities with a view to their judicial punishment, is far from doing justice to the text, when in the *Expositor* (1893, p. 288) he substitutes for the Roman officials, private inquisitors—*delatores*.

10. (Pp. 182, 185.) To find in the use of the word Χριστιανός (1 Pet. iv. 16) an indication that the letter was written later than the year 64 is to contradict all existing sources, Christian and heathen. While Baur (*Christentum und Kirche der 3 ersten Jahrh.* 432) questions the account in Acts xi. 26 because of the genuinely Latin form of the name, and claims that the name originated in Rome, but without calling in question the correctness of Tacitus' statement in *Ann.* xv. 44 ("quos . . . vulgus Christianos appellabat"), that in 64 the

name was commonly used, Lipsius (*Über den Ursprung und ältesten Gebrauch des Christennamens*, Jena, 1873) endeavours to prove that the name is Greek in form, and probably originated in Asia Minor in the last decades of the first century. From the historical point of view, the following brief remarks may be made with reference to Lipsius' statements, which are confusing and too long to be considered in detail here :—(1) To begin with, there seems to be nothing whatever suspicious about the statement that in Antioch during the year 43–44, in consequence of the extraordinarily rapid growth of a Church consisting mainly of Gentile Christian converts, the Gentile populace came to apply to them the name Χριστιανοί (Acts xi. 26), for the reason that when Acts was written, even if this was as late as the year 110, this name was anything but a designation of honour of which its bearers were proud. On the other hand, the statement is rendered all the more trustworthy by the fact that, according to the original recension of the text, the narrator states immediately after xi. 27 f. that he was a member of the Antiochian Church of that time. The date of the origin of this name given in Acts is possibly confirmed by the reference of Jas. ii. 7 (vol. i. p. 99, n. 8). The incidental use of the name by king Agrippa II. some fifteen years later (Acts xxvi. 28) does not impress one at all as if Luke were trying in this way to confirm the historical invention which he had introduced in an earlier passage. If this had been his purpose, there were passages in Acts xii.–xx. better suited for it. (2) To explain the clear statement of Tacitus as an anachronism is unreasonable and purely arbitrary. Tacitus is not here referring conditions prevailing in the time of Trajan to the time of Nero, but is describing the events of 64 in their true historical setting (cf. Ramsay, 229, 241). Why, if this were the case, did he not use *appellat* instead of *appellabat*? But his whole account hinges upon the words "quos vulgus Christianos appellabat"; for, if the Christians were not known in Rome at that time as a society distinct from Jewish as well as heathen organisations, and if they were not designated by a special name, an intelligent man, who as a boy passed through the events of 64, could not relate that Nero accused the Christians. To this is to be added the testimony of Suetonius (*Nero*, xvi.), who describes the event from a different point of view, but also places the name *Christiani* in the time of Nero. (3) After all has been said, the fact remains that an inscription found on a wall in Pompeii in the year 1862, which became illegible shortly afterwards, contained at least the letters HPISTIAN ; and the common use of the name Christian in Pompeii prior to the year 79, when the city was buried, is proved by *C. I. L.* iv. No. 679 ; *Tab.* xvi. 2, 3 ; cf. de Rossi, *Bull. di arch. christ.* 1864, pp. 69 ff., 92 ff. Prof. Sogliano, who is opposed to this interpretation, reports, in an open letter to Prof. Chiapelli (*Giornale d'Italia* of October 11, 1905), concerning an earthen lamp, with a monogram of Christ in the form of a cross, which was found on July 3, 1905, between the strata of ashes and of stone in a Pompeian villa, and, from its location, probably in the rooms of the slaves. More accurate proof of this statement must be left to the proper archæologists. (4) Since the Christians were compelled, probably as early as 64 (cf. Ramsay, 238, concerning the meaning of *fatebantur* in Tac. *Ann.* xv. 44), and from that time on with more and more frequency, to answer the question, "Are you a Christian?" it is easy to see how gradually the name came to be used within the Church itself. The first traces of this usage are to be found in Ignatius (*Rom.* iii. 2 ; *Magn.* iv. ; more clearly *ad Polyc.* vii. 3 ; Χριστιανισμός, in contrast to Judaism and heathendom, *Magn.* x. 3 ; *Rom.* iii. 3 ; *Phil.* vi. 1). It occurs also in Justin. In contrast to this usage, in 1 Pet. iv. 16 it is employed in the original way, being used by heathen who condemned or persecuted the Christians, and occurs in no other sense. It is not necessary here to discuss the linguistic question whether the name as originally used among the heathen was incorrectly pronounced and written Χρηστιανός (thus cod. א, Acts xi. 26, xxvi. 28 ; 1 Pet. iv. 16 ; Suet. *Claud.* xxv. *Chrestus* ; Just. *Apol.* i. 4, 46, 49, ii. 6 ; Tert. *Apol.* iii. ; *Nat.* i. 3 ; Lact. *Inst.* i. 4 ; *I. Gr. Sicil. et Ital.*, ed. Kaibel, Nos. 78, 754 ; *C. I. Lat.* x. No. 7173 ; cf. Blass, *Hermes*, 1895, S. 465). It is of special importance to distinguish between adjectives ending in *ānós*, *ānus*, and the formation which we have before us here of adjectives in *ιανός* from a name (of a person, city, or country). The first formation is Greek as well as Latin, though much more frequently used in Latin than in Greek. Here belong naturally 'Ασιανός (Thucyd. i. 6, 138), Σαρδιανός (Xenoph. *Hellen.* iii. 4. 21 ; Ionic Σαρδιηνός, Herod. i. 22), Τραλλιανός, Σουσιανός, since in these cases the *ι* belongs to the stem. Consequently these words are not different from 'Αγκυρανός, and do not help in any way to explain formations in *-ιανός*. Just as little light is thrown upon the problem by the remarks of the older grammarians, who describe these and similar forms as τύπος τῶν 'Ασιανῶν (Lipsius, 13, A. 1), instead of which the modern grammarians remark more clearly, "The suffixes in *ānós, ηνός, ῑνός*, are formed only from names of cities and countries lying outside of Greece " (Blass-Kühner, i. 2. 296). But while these formations were used by the Attic writers of the best period, and to some extent were even borrowed by Latin writers (*e.g. Asianus* later than *Asiaticus*), adjectives in *iānus* derived from proper names are not a Greek, but a late Latin formation (*Archiv f. lat. Lexikogr.* i. 183). That they found their way from popular and provincial language into literature only gradually toward the end of the Republic, is illustrated by Gell. iii. 3. 10. While the learned Varro thinks that only *Plautinus*, and not *Plautianus*, ought to be derived from *Plautus*, he refers the *fabulæ Plautianæ* to a comic writer, *Plautius* ; and it makes no special difference whether there was an obscure poet by the name of *Plautius* (Ritschl, *Parergon Plaut.* 95) or not. This is confirmed by actual usage. While from names in *o, onis*, Cicero constructs such forms as *Milonianus, Pisonianus, Neronianus, Catonianus* (*ad Qu. fr.* ii. 4 [6]. 5 ; also *Catoninus, ad Fam.* vii. 25, cf. Liv. xxiii. 38. 9, *Varronianus*), he avoids *Cæsarianus* (since the true reading, *ad Att.* xvi. 10, is *Cæsarinus*), which is used by Auctor, *Bell. Afric.* 13 ; Nepos, *Attic.* 7—two writers whose style is said to be unrefined (Schwane, *Röm. Lit.*, 5te Aufl. S. 384, 386). Cicero ventures once to construct the form *Lepidianus* (*ad Att.* xvi. 11. 8) from a noun in *-us*. Under the influence of false analogies from the older period (*Æmili-anus Pompei-anus*), after the beginning of the imperial era these forms appear more and more frequently in literature; cf. Velleius Paterc. ii. 72, 74, 76, 78, *Brutianus* ; ii. 82, *Crassianus* ; Tac. *Ann.* ii. 8, *Drusianus* ; *Ann.* i. 109, 57, 61, ii. 7, 15, 25, *Varianus* ; *Ann.* xiv. 15 (cf. Suet. *Nero*, xxv.; *C. I. L.* vi. Nos. 8640, 8648, 8649, 12874), *Augustianus*, also *Augustalis* (*Ann.* i. 15, 54 ; *C. I. L.* vi. Nos. 909, 910, 913), *Augustanus* (*C. I. L.* vi. No. 8651). Inasmuch as these forms originated in the provincial speech of the Romans, and since their adoption into literature was resisted by the stylists, it is possible that through the intercourse of daily life they became familiar to Greek-speaking Orientals before they made their appearance in literature. There is no occurrence of the same in Greek literature earlier than Ἡρωδιανοί (Mark iii. 6, xii. 13 ; Matt. xxii. 16, and the names of heretical sects in Just. *Dial.* xxxv., cf. *Apol.* ii. 15 ?) ; but this does not prove that the word Χριστιανοί, which was of popular origin, was not used in Antioch as early as 44 A.D. (Acts ii. 26). A writer like Lucian (*de Hist. conscrib.* 21) makes fun of the Atticists, who in their zeal to Hellenise everything Roman changed Τιτιανός (which was possibly not formed from *Titus*, but from *Titius*) to Τιτάνιος. The less educated barbarians, Syrians, and Jews, who, through their intercourse with Roman officials and soldiers, must have taken over into their speech numerous Latin words and names, did not notice that Χριστιανός was not a genuine Greek word, and they did not concern themselves about this when they formed it. Regarding words borrowed from the Latin, see vol. i. p. 64 f. Attention may also be called to Latin words used by Ignatius, a native of Antioch, in the year 110 ; cf. the writer's *Ignatius*, S. 530–533.

§ 41. THE AUTHOR AND READERS OF THE SECOND EPISTLE OF PETER ACCORDING TO THE LETTER'S OWN TESTIMONY.

Whereas in his First Epistle Peter designates accurately the group of Churches which he is addressing (i. 1), and indicates in an unmistakable manner the place from which he writes (v. 13), in 2 Peter there are no geographical data whatever. The designation of the readers is extremely indefinite, even when compared to that of Jas. i. 1 (2 Pet. i. 1). In 1 Peter, aside from the mention of his name in the greeting, Peter lets his own person fall into the background in a way that seems strange, and only in three places (i. 3, 8, v. 1) does he make even slight reference to his own relation to the person and history of Jesus (above, pp. 146-156). On the other hand, in 2 Peter the writer calls attention repeatedly and emphatically to what he alone, or in company with others, heard Jesus say, and to what he had seen with his own eyes of Jesus' doings (i. 14, 16–18, also i. 3 ; see n. 10). In 1 Peter the apostle addresses the readers as one who is personally unknown to them, introduces himself to them, and in a sense lets himself be represented by Silvanus, one of their missionaries

(v. 12 ; above, pp.149, 175, 176); 2 Peter presupposes a relation between himself and the readers which was of long standing, and which is to be cultivated by continued intercourse until the death of the writer.

To begin with what is relatively clear, Peter calls this his second letter in which he designs to stir up his readers to keep in remembrance the prophecies of the O.T., and the commandment which originated with the Lord and Saviour, and which has been brought to the readers by their apostles (iii. 1, n. 1). This description of the purpose of the writer and the essential contents of his letter fits 2 Peter exactly. In the opening passage i. 5–11 emphasis was laid upon the active exercise of all Christian virtues, especially in view of the promised kingdom of Christ (ver. 11); and even in i. 4 attention was called to the great promises of Christ. Immediately after these exhortations to the practice of the Christian virtues in view of the coming of Christ, Peter speaks of his own obligation to keep the readers in remembrance of *these things* so long as he shall live, and of his earnest purpose shortly to fulfil this obligation again (i. 12–14),—all of which is in such entire agreement with what he says in iii. 1 ff. concerning the purpose and essential contents of this and his former letter to the readers, as to make it certain that in writing the second passage he had the first in view. In both cases he calls his exhortations a διεγείρειν ἐν ὑπομνήσει (i. 13, iii. 1 ; cf. ὑπομιμνήσκειν, i. 12, with μνησθῆναι, iii. 2), and emphasises and justifies the designation of his exhortations as mere reminders by recognising that the readers are already in possession of the truth (i. 12), or that their minds are pure (iii. 1 ; cf. Rom. xv. 14 f.). The lack in i. 12 f. of any specific description of the teachings, such as is found in iii. 2, is supplied by the περὶ τούτων (i. 12), which refers back to i. 5–11. And although in this passage the eternal kingdom of Christ is not expressly called a subject of O.T. prophecy, at the end of the first

section of the letter very explicit reference is made to
the prophetic utterances, the trustworthiness, value, and
intelligibility of which for Christians is dependent wholly
upon the self-revelation of Jesus (i. 19–21).

But iii. 1 f. is in no sense to be taken as referring
exclusively or even mainly to the preceding parts of this
letter. In that case the absence of any reference to the
whole of the second section of the Epistle (chap. ii.) would
be strange. Consequently what is said in iii. 3 f., which
follows iii. 2 without any break in the sentence, is part
of the description of what Peter intended to say to his
readers in this letter as well as of what he had said in
the one that preceded. At the same time, the participial
sentence, iii. 3 f., together with the explanatory clauses
that follow (iii. 5–7), mark the transition to a new reminder and exhortation (iii. 8–18), not previously discussed
with the same definiteness in this letter, to which new
passage the description in iii. 1 f. applies far more than
to i. 5–21. For, not only is reference here made to the
"Day of God" (ver. 12) predicted by the prophets, and
to the new world which they also predicted (ver. 13), but
the readers are very strongly reminded of their obligation
to live in accordance with these expectations, *i.e.* with the
"command" applicable to Christians (vv. 11 f., 14 f., 17 f.).
Thus in iii. 1 f. Peter not only describes the preceding
parts of the letter, but, as he clearly says, has in view all
that remains to be written. He describes in substance at
this particular point the meaning and the purpose of the
letter : because now, after the long discussion in chap. ii.,
which does not come directly under the description of
iii. 1 f., he is taking up again the thought of i. 5–21,
intending once more to exhort his readers more strongly
and indeed, after what has been said in chap. ii., more
definitely to the holy life enjoined by the prospect of
the prophesied end of the world. There was no more
necessity of proving in detail that the last things which

are recalled to mind in what follows were predicted by the O.T. prophets, than there was of showing that the moral requirements made in this same final section were in keeping with the command of Jesus and the moral recommendations of the apostles.   The mere fact that at the beginning of the third section (iii. 2) the writer says that the prophecies of the O.T. and the command of the apostles originating with Christ are what he desires to recall to the readers' minds in this letter, shows that the admonitions which follow go back to these sources.   Moreover, in i. 19 f. he had strongly urged upon his readers' attention prophetic prediction as this was confirmed and interpreted by the gospel history.

If, then, the description of the essential contents and purpose of the two letters of Peter in iii. 1 f. suits 2 Peter, it follows that the earlier Epistle of Peter to the same readers, referred to in this passage, was essentially the same as 2 Peter in the points mentioned.   This being so, it is impossible to suppose that Peter here refers to 1 Peter. For, while there are numerous exhortations to moral conduct in 1 Peter, these are nowhere referred to the command of Jesus and the teaching given by the missionaries to this group of readers.   Still less can it be said that 1 Peter is a reminder of prophetic utterances, more specifically of the end of the world, predicted by the prophets.   There is only one passage where reference is made to the prophets (1 Pet. i. 10 f.), and here they are represented as announcing beforehand the sufferings and glory of Christ, *i.e.* the contents of the gospel; but where mention is made of the objects of the Christian hope, the day of judgment, and the glorification of the Church (1 Pet. i. 3–7, ii. 12, iv. 13, 17, v. 4, 6, 10), there is no reference whatever to the O.T. prophets.

The fact that since the fourth century our 2 Peter has followed our 1 Peter in most Bibles, cannot be used to support the claim that these are the two letters mentioned

together in 2 Pet. iii. 1 ; for who can affirm that Peter did
not write twenty letters and send two or three letters to
more than one group of Churches ?   From this description
which covers both letters it follows that the earlier letter
in question—which, however, was sent to the same readers
—was not our 1 Peter, but a letter which has not come
down to us.

It is improbable, notwithstanding what is said in
iii. 15, that 2 Peter, like our 1 Peter, was directed to the
Gentile Christian Churches in Asia Minor.   The urgent
exhortation to live a life which shall be in harmony with
the trustworthy prophecy of the Day of the Lord, of the
end of the world, and of a new world, is concluded in
iii. 15 with an injunction to the readers, already intimated
in iii. 9, to regard as their salvation the patience shown
by the Lord Jesus in the deferment of His return.   This
injunction, which would be unintelligible apart from
what is said in the passage at the conclusion of which it
stands, and which, therefore, is not meant to be taken
apart from iii. 5–13, is now represented as being in
harmony with what Paul, the beloved brother of Peter
and his readers, wrote to these same readers according to
the measure of wisdom given him.   The readers of 1 Peter
were in large part at least identical with the readers of
Ephesians (vol. i. p. 479 ff.).   So long as it was maintained
that the earlier letter of Peter mentioned in 2 Pet. iii. 1 must
be the letter which precedes 2 Peter in the Canon, unavoid-
ably the letter of Paul referred to in 2 Pet. iii. 15 was
connected with this same circular letter, namely, Ephesians
(n. 2).   But Ephesians does not agree with what, according to 2 Pet. iii. 15, Paul wrote in his letter directed to
the readers of 2 Peter.   What is said of all of Paul's
letters (iii. 16, " As also in all his epistles, speaking
in them of these things ") might be justified by occasional remarks of Paul bearing upon the subject here
under discussion, but not the reference to a letter dealing

specifically with the same theme (iii. 15). The reference must be to a thoroughgoing exposition of this subject, from which Paul's specific teachings could be ascertained. The exhortations to a correct Christian life are throughout Ephesians based upon entirely different grounds (iv. 1, 20–25, v. 1–3, vi. 1–3, 8, 9), and the argument of the duty of sanctification, on the ground of the expectation of Christ's second coming, is much less frequent in Ephesians (iv. 30, v. 5 f.) than in other letters of Paul (1 Thess. v. 1–11; Rom. xiii. 11–14; cf. 1 John iii. 3). It would be more natural to suppose that the reference is to Hebrews than to Ephesians, although in Hebrews reference is made to the promise which is certain, only delayed in its fulfilment, in order to exhort the readers not so much to a virtuous life, as to a steadfast maintenance of faith and confession, which is not possible without struggle against sin (Heb. iii. 7–iv. 13, x. 35–39, xii. 1–17, 25–29). If only Paul had written Hebrews, or if the author of 2 Peter could have regarded Hebrews as a work of his! But this is impossible (§ 47); so that we are compelled to conclude that the letter of Paul mentioned in 2 Pet. iii. 15 is in existence quite as little as Peter's own earlier letter to the readers of 2 Peter mentioned in iii. 1.

Moreover, we have no knowledge of the carrying out of the intentions expressed by the author in i. 12–15 (n. 3). When he gives assurance that in the future he will be always ready to recall to the readers' minds such things as are to be found in the present letter, and goes on to explain that he feels this to be an obligation for the rest of his life,—all the more because he knows, partly through a revelation made by Christ to him, that he will die a sudden death (n. 3),—the language used can apply just as well to oral teachings as to future letters. Only, in case the reference were to oral teachings, we should expect the contrast between the present written and the later oral reminiscences to be expressed, or, if both were meant, we should expect a distinction to be made in this double form of teaching between the oral reminiscences which he would give when present and the written communications he would send when absent (n. 4). Apparently, therefore, Peter declares his intention of sending to the same readers in the future an occasional letter like this present one. To be clearly distinguished from this statement is what Peter says in the words that follow : " I will give diligence that at every time ye may be able after my decease to call these things (truths or teachings) to remembrance " (n. 5). Only, if Peter had previously expressed the intention or hope of visiting the readers again and impressing upon them once more orally the truths in question, could this statement be taken to mean that Peter, in view of the fact that *scripta litera manet,* is not satisfied with oral teachings, but when he leaves the readers, or afterwards, will put such teachings in written form, so that they may be permanently remembered by them, or will see to it that others do it for him. Since, however, there is nothing anywhere in the context to suggest this contrast between oral teaching and its embodiment in written form, the only contrast possible is that between such written communications as the present letter, the earlier letter mentioned in iii. 1, and similar letters which Peter intends to write in the future on the one hand, and a more extensive literary work on the other. The former are off-hand products, and are expected to have only a temporary effect ; the latter is designed to be of permanent value. No light is thrown upon the contents of this proposed work by the sentences that follow, in which Peter merely substantiates his right and the right of others, whom he mentions along with himself, to perform such literary work (vv. 16–18), but, at the same time, its character is indicated by the sentences that precede. The τούτων of ver. 15 resumes the περὶ τούτων of ver. 12, although the expression which intervenes—" the truth

which is with you (the readers)" (cf. Jas. i. 21)—and the
natural difference between letters of. a merely temporary
character and a book claiming to be of permanent value
forbid limiting the contents of the latter to exactly the
same topics as are discussed in 2 Peter. The work in
question was clearly designed to be doctrinal in character
like 2 Peter, not a historical work. Even if 2 Peter was
written as late as 170, the Gospel of Mark cannot be the
work in question ; for it was not until long after this date
that the story originated according to which Peter commissioned Mark to write his Gospel (n. 5) ; and even after
this opinion had grown up, Peter could not be represented
as expressing this intention in words applicable only to a
religious treatise. A writing which might claim to be the
product of the literary intention here expressed is not in
existence, and so far as we know never existed.

From the passages already considered it follows that
Peter has stood for a long time in an official relation to
the persons receiving this letter, which relation he feels
himself under obligation to maintain until his death
through instructions by letter, and after his death through
a treatise designed especially for them, just as he has
maintained it heretofore by a letter like 2 Peter. He had
also brought them the gospel, not alone, to be sure, but
in co-operation with other missionaries. For he can mean
nothing less than this when he says of himself and of the
companions whom he mentions along with himself, " We
have made known unto you the power and coming of
Christ" (i. 16, n. 6). Even assuming that the $\delta\acute{v}\nu\alpha\mu\iota\varsigma$
of Christ means only that power which Jesus obtained
through His resurrection and exaltation, in contrast to the
weakness in which He had previously lived and suffered
(2 Cor. xiii. 4 ; Rom. i. 4),—a view which has very little
in its favour,—this sentence cannot be made to refer to
the instruction of persons who are already believers concerning the exaltation to power and the coming of Christ

—instruction which presupposes a previous preaching of
the gospel—simply because there was and is no preaching
of the gospel which does not make known to the hearers
the resurrection, exaltation, and coming of Christ. All
subsequent teaching can be only the recalling of these
fundamentals of the gospel, or the indication of their
consequences in the life or thought of believers. Therefore it is impossible to suppose that Peter is here referring
to that earlier letter (iii. 1) and also to similar communications to the same group of readers by his fellow-workers,
or that he, in a manner so unclear as this, identifies the
original preaching of the gospel with all later oral and
written references to it. Our 1 Peter is quite out of the
question ; since the gospel was not preached to Christians
in Asia Minor by Peter, but by others from whom he distinguishes himself (1 Pet. i. 12). Furthermore, there is no
teaching in 1 Peter concerning the power and coming of
Christ which begins with the gospel and develops the idea
it contains. Those to whom 2 Peter is directed must be
persons among whom Peter laboured as a missionary, *i.e.*
persons belonging to the circumcision. The language
used to describe the gospel in i. 16 is applicable to it as
it was preached in Israel—in other words, among the contemporaries and countrymen of the Lord and His apostles,
who were more or less familiar with the facts of the
gospel history (Acts ii. 22, x. 37). They not only were
externally acquainted with the historical appearance of
Jesus, but also treated the same quite materialistically
(cf. 2 Cor. v. 6) ; they therefore needed to have it made
clear to them that in this weak man, who was denied,
reviled, and put to death by His fellow-men, there dwelt
a power which not only had found expression during His
lifetime in wonderful miracles (Acts ii. 22, x. 38), but
also had broken the bonds of death and raised Him to
the throne of God (Acts ii. 24–35, iii. 15, iv. 2, 10, 33,
v. 30), from whence He was to come again to finish His

work (Acts iii. 20, x. 42).   It would seem as if at times
the preaching of the gospel among the Gentiles was confined to the word of the cross (1 Cor. i. 17 ff., ii. 2); but
in the preaching to Israelites who were contemporaries of
Jesus emphasis was laid upon the resurrection of Jesus,
the revelation of His power and His return.   The faith of
Jewish Christianity was faith in the glory of Jesus (Jas.
ii. 1 ; cf. vol. i. p. 151, n. 7).

It is also impossible to assume that Peter here identifies himself with Paul and his missionary helpers, such as
Barnabas, Silvanus and Timothy, and connects his preaching with theirs.   For, in the first place, Peter distinguishes,
just as clearly as does Paul (Gal. i. 17, ii. 7–9 ; 1 Cor.
xv. 11, ix. 5), between the missionaries to the Gentiles
and the group to which he himself belonged (1 Pet. i. 12);
and although he calls Paul the beloved brother of himself
and of the readers (2 Pet. iii. 15), he does not intimate in
any way to them that Paul was one of their apostles
(2 Pet. iii. 2).   In the second place, in order to make
this identification, it is necessary to assume, against
the clear impression of the entire letter, that it was not
directed to a definite, homogeneous group of readers, but
to the whole body of Christians who owed their conversion
to the apostolic preaching, to which also Paul, according
to iii. 15, must on one occasion have addressed a letter.
But even then the identification of Peter with Paul and
his helpers in i. 16 ff. is inconceivable ; for the missionaries to the Gentiles could not claim what Peter here
claims for himself and his companions concerning their
personal relation to the gospel history.   This is the third
reason which prevents us from identifying Peter's work
with that of Paul and his helpers.   In preaching the
gospel, Peter and his companions have not followed fables
cunningly devised or artfully presented, but have preached
as those who were eye-witnesses of the majesty of Jesus.
Although Paul may have treated his experience near

Damascus as a substitute for the fact that he was not. like the earlier apostles, a personal disciple of Jesus (1 Cor. ix. 1, cf. xv. 8), he could not affirm with reference to himself, nor could anyone say of him, that he preached the gospel as one who was an eye-witness of the self revelation of Jesus which formed the content of the gospel. The comprehensive language which Peter uses is comparable only with what personal disciples of Jesus elsewhere affirm with reference to themselves (John i. 14, cf. ii. 11, xix. 35 ; 1 John i. 1 f., iv. 14 ; Acts x. 39–41) and with what Peter himself at least intimates in 1 Pet. i. 8, v. 1 (above, p. 147).

The group of preachers with which Peter identifies himself is indicated by the reference to the particular experience on which he bases his claim that he and his companions have declared the power and return of Jesus to the readers as former witnesses of His majesty, i. 17 f. If it be certain that the event referred to is the transfiguration on the mountain described in all three of the synoptic Gospels, then it is also to be assumed that the author of 2 Peter, like the evangelists, knew that the only eye-witnesses of this event were the three apostles, Peter, John, and his brother James (n. 6). Consequently these three are the preachers spoken of in i. 16, though, naturally, there is no exclusion in i. 16 of other apostles who stood in essentially the same historical relation to Jesus. Just as Peter here identifies himself with others of the twelve apostles by the use of " we," so he does also in iii. 2, where he uses the expression οἱ ἀπόστολοι ὑμῶν. " Your apostles " is not synonymous with " The apostles," but serves to distinguish from the entire class of men who may claim the apostolic name, those who have exercised the apostolic office among the readers here addressed, *i.e.* the missionaries to whom these Christians owe their conversion (cf. 1 Cor. ix. 2 ; Clem. 1 *Cor.* v. ; cf. above, 69, n. 6). The expression implies a contrast to other

apostles who were not the apostles of the readers, and
other Christians, to whom the apostles here intended were
not apostles.   It is thus quite impossible to suppose that
the expression "Your apostles" includes apostles who
laboured in fields that were widely separated, much less
can it include all the apostles without distinction.   The
suggestion that such language sounds strange on the part
of one who himself belonged to the group of missionaries
thus designated, is due to the misunderstanding of a mode
of speech which is constantly being used, and which is
sometimes extremely natural.   On the other hand, to
assume that the author does not identify himself with this
group is to make i. 16 stand in glaring contradiction to
iii. 2.   This is sufficient to disprove the correctness of
that interpretation of iii. 2, for which, in itself, there is
no sufficient reason (n. 7).   Taking these two passages
together, it seems clear that 2 Peter was not directed
to a single local Church, the origin of which was due to
the preaching of Peter alone (cf. 1 Cor. iii. 10, iv. 15,
ix. 2), but probably to a larger group of Christians, among
whom Peter had laboured with other missionaries in the
founding of Churches.   Chap. iii. 2 alone is insufficient to
prove that these were not Churches in Asia Minor, or any
other region within the sphere of Gentile missions, but
Churches within the sphere of Jewish missions, though
this is established by the unavoidable connection between
iii. 2 and i. 16.   The fact that later in the course of their
life Peter and others of the twelve apostles engaged in
missionary work among the Gentiles in Rome or in Asia
Minor, does not justify, on the part of one speaking in their
name, the use of such language as that in i. 16, to describe
their relation to the Churches founded by Paul and his
helpers, nor the distinction made in iii. 2 between them
and other apostles who had no official relation to these
Churches.   Nor can the beginning of this letter be used
in proof of this hypothesis, except by presupposing what

cannot be proved, namely, that 2 Peter followed 1 Peter, and was intended as a second letter to the same group of readers.

The statement of Peter in i. 1, that the readers, through the righteousness of our God and Saviour, Jesus Christ, have obtained faith of like value with that of Peter and his companions (n. 8), might be taken as implying a contrast between the Jewish Christians, in whose name Peter here speaks, and the Gentile Christians, whom he addresses; since by making no distinction in this regard between Jews and Gentiles, God shows Himself a fair-minded and just judge (Acts x. 34 f., 47, xi. 17 f., xv. 8 f.; Rom. ii. 11–29, iii. 22–30, x. 12). If there were only something in the context to indicate a distinction between Jews and Gentiles within the Church! The author begins by calling himself by the name which he had always borne, using the form most distinctively Jewish, and then adds the surname which Jesus gave him in token of his position among the disciples, and his place in the future Church (n. 9). Quite in harmony with the use of these two names, he calls himself, from one point of view, a servant of Christ, and, from the other, an apostle of Christ. The former title is appropriate to Simeon of Bethsaida, who, with his brother Andrew and many others after them, when they believed on Jesus, accepted Him as their Lord. On the other hand, the apostolic title corresponds to Cephas or Peter, to whom the Lord, by the bestowment of this surname, held out the prospect of a special calling, to which he was appointed when the twelve apostles were chosen, and which was confirmed subsequently more than once. But neither the position which Simeon occupies as the first of the personal disciples of Jesus, nor the position which Cephas has as foremost among the apostles, prevents him from recognising that the faith to which the readers have been brought through his own and his companions' preaching (i. 16) is of like value with his own faith and that of his companions. The distinction thus removed, or at least stripped of its religious significance, is simply that between personal disciples and apostles of Jesus, on the one hand, and, on the other, all those Christians who had not stood in such personal relation to Jesus, nor received the special calling corresponding to this personal relation, but had nevertheless been led, through the efforts of disciples and apostles, to believe on the Lord, who had bought them (ii. 1). The distinction is essentially the same as that between eye-witnesses of the majesty of Jesus and those to whom the eye-witnesses had brought the knowledge of it (i. 16; cf. John xix. 35, xx. 29, 31; 1 John i. 3). The same distinction is apparently expressed also in the sentences that follow, i. 3 f., which are not very clear, nor textually certain (n. 10). Here Peter identifies himself with the other disciples and apostles of Jesus, whom He called personally by the revelation of His glory, and by the demonstration of His moral power, to whom also through the knowledge of Himself He gave all that was needful for a true life and a pious conduct. He then contrasts himself and the other disciples and apostles with the readers to whom the Lord, through these disciples and apostles,—namely, through their preaching of the gospel, —has given very great promises, by virtue of which hereafter they may become partakers of the divine nature, having escaped the perishable pleasures of this world. While it is true that this distinction between the personal disciples of Jesus and other Christians, who have not seen and heard Jesus, is sometimes expressed where the former are addressing Gentile Christians (1 Pet. i. 8; 1 John i. 1–4; John i. 14, xix. 35), exactly the same distinction existed within Jewish Christianity from the beginning of the apostolic preaching.

Inasmuch, therefore, as there is not a single word in 2 Peter which suggests the Gentile character of the readers, and since it has also been shown that 2 Pet. iii. 1 cannot refer to 1 Peter nor 2 Pet. iii. 15 to Ephesians, the evidence of the statements in 2 Pet. i. 16–18, which are in perfect agreement with i. 1–4 and iii. 2, retains its full force. The letter is shown to be a hortatory writing of Peter's to a large group of Churches, who owed their Christianity to the preaching of Peter and other men from among the twelve apostles and the personal disciples of Jesus. From this it follows that the readers were, for the most part, if not altogether, Jewish Christians, and that they are to be sought in Palestine and the regions adjoining, but not in the regions north and north-west of Antioch ; because until the death of Peter (64 A.D. ; above, p. 161 f.) the agreement of the year 52 (Gal. ii. 7–9 ; cf. Matt. x. 23) was kept by all the missionaries, one of whom the writer indicates himself to have been (i. 1–4, 16–18). It was probably in Palestine and the adjoining regions that the preaching journeys of Peter and his companions, referred to by Paul in the year 57 (1 Cor. ix. 5), were made. The journey of Peter to Rome at the very end of his life, and the composition in Rome of his letter to the Gentile Christian Churches of Asia Minor (above, p. 158 ff.), did not make him a missionary to the Gentiles, and did not bring him into such a relation as that expressed in 2 Peter with any Church outside the "Land of Israel." In this entrance of Peter as an element in the life of the Gentile Christian Churches organised in Asia Minor by Gentile Christian missionaries, and as a factor in the development of the Roman Church, in the building of which Gentile Christian and Jewish Christian missionaries worked together, we have a foreshadowing— but only a foreshadowing—of the development which, at a date considerably later than the death of Peter and Paul, took men like John and Philip to Ephesus and Hierapolis.

There is no means of determining more definitely the

geographical position of the readers. The use of the
Greek language is no objection to the supposition that
2 Peter was intended for the whole circle to whom James
also wrote in Greek. Nor does the use of the name
" Simeon Petros " imply anything more (Acts xiii. 1,
xv. 14, n. 9). The reference to a letter of Paul's to the
same readers (iii. 15) does not help us, for the reason that
this letter has not come down to us (above, p. 198 f.). It
is very natural to suppose that during the two years of
enforced idleness in Cæsarea (from 58–60 A.D.), when his
arrest put an end to the exercise of all personal influence
among them, Paul took occasion to send some written
word to the multitudes of believing Jews (Acts xxi. 20),
on whose behalf he had made his last journey to Jerusalem. Or it may have been a smaller group of Churches,
mainly Jewish Christian, to which this lost letter of Paul's
and 2 Peter were directed, e.g. the Churches in Ptole-
mais, Tyre, and Damascus, with which Paul was personally
acquainted (Acts ix. 22–25, xx. 3–7 ; cf. xi. 19, xv. 3),
and others in the regions indicated of whose history we
know nothing.

The time at which 2 Peter purports to have been
written can be more accurately determined than the location of the readers. Although it is not directly stated
in i. 14 that Peter knows his death is near (n. 3), and
although we do not know that this expectation was fulfilled, even if Peter entertained it, i. 12–15 does convey
the general impression that it is an aged man who is
speaking. In iii. 16 mention is made not only of a letter
of Paul's to the readers of 2 Peter, but also of many other
letters of his which had found some circulation and had
been misunderstood. This could hardly have taken place
before the year 60. Furthermore, the way in which the
doubt as to the fulfilment of the prophecy concerning the
end of the world is expressed (iii. 4 ; cf. § 42, n. 5),
indicates the end of Peter's lifetime. The first generation

of Christians is beginning to disappear. On the other
hand, there is nothing to indicate that Peter had reached
Rome, the goal of his life-journey. It is natural to
suppose that, if Peter had recently come to the capital of
the world for the first time in his life, he would indicate
in some way his residence there, as he does in 1 Pet. v.
13. On the other hand, he is not in the immediate
vicinity of his readers. He has written them previously,
expects to do so soon again, and anticipates the sending
of frequent letters (above, p. 198 f.). He shows familiarity
with ecclesiastical conditions and movements outside the
world of the readers ; indeed, he shows familiarity with
the same within the sphere of Gentile Christianity. We
should probably be able to locate the place where the
letter was written more exactly, if we knew from what
point and by what route Peter went to Rome sometime
in the autumn of 63. It is natural to think of Antioch.
Taking everything into consideration, and assuming for
the time being that 2 Peter is genuine, we may date it
somewhere between 60 and 63. This makes it earlier
than 1 Peter.

1. (P. 195.) In view of the character of what precedes and follows, the
reference of iii. 1 f. to the entire Epistle yet unfinished—and in particular to
the third section of the Epistle which begins at this point—is quite as certain
as is the similar reference of ταῦτά σοι γράφω, 1 Tim. iii. 14 (see above, p. 39,
n. 2) ; and here the ταύτην . . . ἐπιστολήν makes the reference more definite
than the ambiguous ταῦτα in 1 Tim. iii. 14. That this description is meant
to apply equally to the first Epistle, to which reference is here made, is proved
by the use of ἐν αἷς instead of ἐν ᾗ. The difficult expression τῆς τῶν ἀποστόλων ὑμῶν ἐντολῆς τοῦ κυρίου καὶ σωτῆρος undoubtedly means the same as
that which in ii. 21 is described as the holy commandment handed down to
the Christians, or the same as διδαχὴ κυρίου διὰ τῶν δώδεκα ἀποστόλων, the
title of the so-called Didache. In form the expression finds a parallel in
Acts v. 32, if the correct reading there be αὐτοῦ μάρτυρες τῶν ῥημάτων τούτων
(cf. Winer, Gr. § 30. 3, A. 3 [Eng. trans. § 30. 3, A. 3]), as the present writer
believes to be the case. The expression is a harsh one, but even titles such
as Ξενοφῶντος Σωκράτους ἀπομνημονεύματα are quite as inelegant (GK, i. 475,
A. 2). In fact, the harsher the words (τοῦ κυρίου καὶ σωτῆρος), the more
arbitrary it is to strike them out as a gloss ; while to derive them from Jude
17 (Spitta, 224), where they are not found, is altogether impossible. No
mistake has been made in the transmission of the text of the passage, since

the Syrians ["The commandment of our Lord and Saviour, which" (*sc.* was communicated) "through the apostles"] were able to get over the difficulty only by a free translation, while the impossible combination of ὑμῶν with κυρίου, which occurs here as in the Sahidic, Coptic, and Ethiopic versions, is not made less difficult by the reading ἡμῶν instead of ὑμῶν—a variant found only in a few cursives. In this connection it may be remarked that the historical investigation of 2 Pet. is rendered difficult, not only by the style, which is often obscure, but also by the text handed down, which is in an especially bad condition. Readings which could not have been invented and which are certainly original, such as the order of words in i. 17 preserved by B alone (below, n. 6), and passages which can hardly be understood without resort to conjecture, such as i. 20, will suffice as illustrations. Tischendorf's apparatus in ed. viii. has been enlarged and corrected since its appearance, especially by *Le Palimpseste de Fleury*, ed. Berger, 1887, p. 41 f., and by Gwynn's investigation of the ancient Syriac version, which was probably a part of the Philoxenian text, in *Hermathena*, vol. vii. 1890, pp. 281–314. This translation (called in Tischendorf, Syr. bodl.) is designated S² by the present writer (see list of abbreviations). One source of the corruption of the text was the comparison of readings in 2 Pet. with Jude. This, however, can be used to correct the text. Whether we hold 2 Pet. to be dependent upon Jude or the reverse, the one document is certainly a very ancient witness for the text of the other. If the correct reading in Jude 12 be ἀγάπαις, then it must be that Jude read ἀγάπαις in 2 Pet. ii. 13, and that this, therefore, is the correct reading in the latter passage; or, if 2 Pet. is dependent upon Jude, then it is hard to conceive how Peter could change the clear ἀγάπαις of Jude to ἀπάταις, which does not make as good sense. So in this case also the original reading in 2 Pet. ii. 13 seems to have been ἀγάπαις.

2. (P. 198.) Most modern interpreters take the letter of Paul's mentioned in 2 Pet. iii. 15 to be Eph.—with especial positiveness Hofmann (vii. 2. 113 ff.). Grotius (p. 1060) and Dietlein (*Der zweite Petrusbrief*, 229–235) think that Rom. is meant; the elder Lightfoot (*Opp.* ii. 109, 116) and Bengel in his *Gnomon* think that the reference is to Hebrews. The last hypothesis would be impossible, even if 2 Pet. had been written at a time when Heb. had come to be regarded by part of the Church as an Epistle of Paul's; because a pseudo-Peter who undertook to compose an Epistle of Peter to the Ἑβραῖοι, to whom Paul had previously written Heb., could not have been content with a salutation, not a word of which refers clearly to the Ἑβραῖοι, nor would he have ventured in iii. 1 to lead the readers to suppose that 2 Pet. was meant for the same readers as 1 Pet. The credit for having broken radically with exegetical traditions regarding the letter of Paul mentioned in 2 Pet. iii. 15, and the letter of Peter mentioned in 2 Pet. iii. 1 belongs to Spitta (221–227, 286–288).

3. (Pp. 199, 209.) As to i. 12–15, μελλήσω with the present infinitive is hardly to be taken, as in Matt. xxiv. 6, or as μέλλω with the future infinitive (Acts xxiv. 15, xxvii. 10), as a mere periphrasis for the future; but is intended ɔ express the thought that the writer will be ready in the future, as often as necessity arises, to recall to the minds of the readers truths with which they are familiar, as he has done in the past, and as he does now throughout this entire letter. Copyists and translators, who knew nothing of the fulfilment

of the promise here made, found the expression too strong, and changed it in some instances to οὐ μελλήσω (in the sense of "I will not hesitate"—*non differam*, Palimps. Flor. and other Latin MSS), in other cases (the Antiochian recension and the Syriac versions) to οὐκ ἀμελήσω. The only other thing to be noted with regard to the variant readings is the fact that in ver. 15, besides ℵ, the Armenian version and one cursive also S² read σπουδάζω (see Gwynn, *op. cit.* 291). But this is an intentional alteration, designed to make it possible to connect the sentence with the letter which Peter was writing at the time. Even the σπουδάσατε of S³ and a few cursives, if taken as an aorist used in the graphic sense, tends, on the one hand, to confirm the reading σπουδάσω against σπουδάζω, and, on the other hand, shows, as does also the latter reading, that copyists and translators could not bring themselves to read here again a promise of Peter's which he seemed not to have fulfilled. What Peter says about his future literary plans is conceived altogether in the light of the end of his life. He refers to it three times in vv. 13, 14, 15. Only in ver. 14 is there a definite view expressed regarding its manner or time. His knowledge concerning his death, while not based exclusively upon a revelation of Christ, is due in part to this ; since it is inadmissible to take the καί here as the pleonastic καί which is common with particles of comparison (so Hofmann, Spitta), for καθώς does not here introduce a comparison, but a determining authority. With regard to the question what or what kind of a revelation is meant, it is to be observed : (1) That Peter refers to this revelation of Christ quite incidentally, and only in order to confirm an expectation certain on other grounds. In view of the fact that Peter was one of the missionaries who preached the gospel to the readers, and that there had been frequent intercourse between him and them, it is not likely that the readers were wholly unfamiliar with it, so that the reference is not to a communication from Christ which Peter had recently received. How great an interest these Christians who were intimately acquainted with Peter must have had in learning from him that the Lord had recently appeared to him in a vision, and made known to him that he was to die quickly, or soon, or suddenly ! As a matter of fact, however, the simple expression used, ἐδήλωσέν μοι, does not indicate any such wonderful revelation. (2) Taken alone, ταχινός, like ταχύς, does not mean either "soon" or "sudden," but "quick," "rapid." It may mean (*a*) the speedy termination of an action (John xx. 4 ; Jas. i. 19), and, taken in that sense here it would designate a quick death as contrasted with a death following long sickness. Since, however, the whole future may be conceived as something coming, approaching the subject, and since the rapid completion of this conceived movement involves the early appearance of the coming event, (*b*) the adverbial expressions ταχέως, τάχιον, τάχιστα, ταχύ, ἐν τάχει, especially when used with futures and imperatives, frequently mean "soon, without delay" (cf. Luke xvi. 6, xviii. 2 ; Matt. v. 25 ; 1 Cor. iv. 19 ; Phil. ii. 19, 24 ; 1 Tim. iii. 14 ; Heb. xiii. 19, 23). In all these cases the thing signified is not the quick termination of the action itself, writing, journeying, etc., but the immediate happening of the event in question. But (*c*) the approach of the future so conceived can itself be represented as a slow or rapid process, according as the future event is thought of as approaching gradually, or as coming without perceptible preparation and warning, like a bolt of lightning. So we get

the meaning "sudden"; cf. Rev. ii. 16 (=iii. 3; 1 Thess. v. 2–4; 2 Pet. iii. 10);
also Gal. i. 6; 2 Thess. ii. 2. It is in this sense that we say in the Litany,
"Deliver us from evil and sudden death." The first meaning (a) "quick" is
not applicable here; for, no matter whether he expects to die and be taken
from his work by a death struggle lasting only a few minutes, or only after
years of illness, this can hardly have any important influence upon his
valuation and use of the time remaining until he is called upon to meet this
quick or gradual death. The second meaning (b) "soon" suits better; since
the consciousness that only a short span of life remains, may make one
zealous in the performance of his calling, and remind him of the necessity of
providing for the time after his death. Cf. *Ep. Clem. ad Jac.* ii. (*Clementina*,
ed. Lagarde, p. 6). Against this interpretation there are the following objections: (1) This certain knowledge that he was soon to die Peter could have
obtained only through a revelation from Christ made to him recently, unless
recourse is had to the improbable supposition that Christ had told him long
before just how many years he was to live. In neither of these cases could
he refer as incidentally as he does to this revelation of Christ as something
with which the readers are already familiar. (2) The use of the adjectives
ταχύς and ταχινός in this sense is certainly rare. ταχὺς καρπός, Clem. 2 *Cor.*
xx. 2, cited by Spitta (87), is not a clear illustration of this usage. (3) ταχινὴ
ἀπώλεια (2 Pet. ii. 1), with which it is most natural to compare this passage, is
manifestly used in the third sense (c) "sudden," meaning a destruction
coming unexpectedly—unprepared for by sinners (cf. 1 Thess. v. 3; Luke
xvii. 27, xxi. 35; Mark xiii. 35; Matt. xxiv. 37–xxv. 13). It is not a catastrophe
coming soon, since there was no point of time from which this event could be
reckoned. Good illustrations of this usage are the examples cited by Hofmann (vii. 2. 29) from Thucyd. iv. 55. 1, πόλεμος ταχὺς καὶ ἀπροφύλακτος,
and Eurip. *Hipp.* 1044, ταχὺς ᾅδης ("sudden death"). Anyone knowing and
pondering the fact that he is to die a sudden death, will not in any given
instance put off what he regards as his duty until another day which seems to
him better adapted for its performance or which is more convenient; rather,
not knowing whether he may claim the next day as his, he will always be
ready to do what the present day demands. But it was just this which Peter
promised in ver. 12 with regard to the instruction of the readers during the
remainder of his life. We have seen how the certainty with which Peter
expected a sudden death is based only in part upon the revelation of Christ
to him, or, to speak more accurately, how he finds this knowledge to be in
harmony with the revelation of Christ, from which it is to be inferred that he
believed this to be certain quite apart from the revelation, which is practically the same conviction Paul had as to the martyr's death he was to die (see
vol. i. p. 546 f.). Furthermore, it is not to be assumed that Christ had said to
Peter in so many words what he here gives as his own conviction. In this
case his conviction would rest entirely upon the words of Christ, and nothing
could be said of Peter's independent knowledge about the same thing. There
is nothing, therefore, which prevents our taking the words of Jesus preserved
in John xiii. 36 and xxi. 18 f. as the foundation of 2 Pet. i. 14. The former
saying contains no clear statement as to the manner of Peter's death, but, in
the light of later reflection upon it, Peter could say that it did mean something more than that he was to die at some future time like other men, and

like all other disciples, through death to come into the presence of Jesus in heaven. If he came to feel that he was to die suddenly, then this word of Jesus must have been confirmation of the feeling; it could hardly mean to him anything else than that he, like Jesus, was to die a violent death. While it is true that sudden death is not always violent death, violent death, murder, or execution is always a sudden death, and stands in contrast to death which approaches gradually through sickness or old age. The other saying of Jesus, John xxi. 18, does convey primarily the idea that Peter, who is now young and impetuous, will become a helpless old man. But with this is connected the other thought that in his old age he shall fall into the hands of hostile men. The narrator of the story in John xxi. 19 takes the entire saying as a prophecy of Peter's martyrdom, and, in one feature of the picture (ἐκτενεῖς τὰς χεῖράς σου), he finds a reference to the definite manner of his death, namely, crucifixion. If this interpretation, like other interpretations of obscure prophetic utterances of Jesus (cf. John ii. 22, vii. 39, xii. 33), was not made until after the prophecy was fulfilled,—i.e. until after Peter's crucifixion,—it does not follow that Peter and the others who heard Jesus say this word had no thoughts about the prophecy. The reference to violence which he was to suffer at the end of his life (ἄλλος ζώσει σε καὶ οἴσει ὅπου οὐ θέλεις) was sufficient to enable Peter to say that his premonition of a violent death was confirmed by the Lord Himself, and at the same time to regard it as a second saying of this character (cf. John xiii. 36). Peter does not quote the word spoken by Christ to him, but says that his expectation is in accordance with a saying of Jesus. He describes the laying aside of his earthly tabernacle as sudden rather than violent, because the latter thought is appropriate in this context only as it is involved in the former. On the other hand, the language of Peter is extremely unnatural if the reference is to the legends already mentioned (see above, p. 168 f.). The saying of Jesus, ἄνωθεν μέλλω σταυροῦσθαι, quoted by Origen (tom. xx. 12 in Jo.) from the Acts of Paul, does not appear in this place to have reference to Peter at all; and, according to Origen's interpretation, it does not refer to the physical crucifixion of a disciple. In the Gnostic Acts of Peter, however, this saying is made to refer to the crucifixion of Peter in Rome—and that in the double sense in which ἄνωθει may be used ("again" and "from above"). In the crucifixion of Peter, Christ experienced His own crucifixion again; Peter was crucified head downwards (ed. Lipsius, 88, 92 f.; GK, ii. 846, 853, A. 3, 878 f.). Reference to this blunt μῦθος σεσοφισμένος is not in harmony with the delicate and modest recalling of the saying of Jesus in 2 Pet. i. 14. If this legend is based upon a saying of Jesus—specifically of the risen Jesus—preserved in the more original form in the Acts of Paul (GK, ii. 879), in the first place it is, to say the least, extremely doubtful whether it refers to Peter. But if it does, and describes his future crucifixion, then, from the critical point of view, it can be regarded only as a fanciful development of John xxi. 18 f. Whereas the canonical account distinguishes between the mysterious saying of Jesus and the interpretation of the same made in the light of the event, this fanciful story, and the later tale of the Acts of Peter, put into the mouth of Jesus Himself a prophecy exactly suited to the subsequent events. However, it is not with a fable like this that 2 Pet. i. 14 shows affinity, but with the words of Jesus preserved in John xiii. 36, xxi. 18.

4. (P. 200.) With what has been said above, p. 199 f., cf. 2 Thess. ii. 15 ; 2 Cor. x. 10, xiii. 10 ; Phil. i. 27 ; Polyc. *ad Phil.* iii. 2.

5. (Pp. 200, 201.) Michaelis (*Einl.* 1056), Schwegler, and others compare μετὰ τὴν ἐμὴν ἔξοδον, i. 15, with Iren. iii. 1. 1 : μετὰ δὲ τὴν τούτων (*i.e.* of Peter and Paul) ἔξοδον Μᾶρκος τὰ ὑπὸ Πέτρου κηρυσσόμενα ἐγγράφως ἡμῖν παραδέδωκεν. See also § 49. Inasmuch as the death of Peter is clearly spoken of in ver. 14, ἔξοδος in ver. 15 can be understood only as referring to him ; cf. Luke ix. 31 ; Heb. xiii. 7 ; *Acta Jo.* (ed. Bonnet, p. 184. 9), probably also Hermas, *Vis.* iii. 4. 3. Nor is Irenæus' meaning different in the passage cited. The strong emphasis of τὴν ἐμὴν ἔξ., used instead of τὴν ἔξ. μου, is to be noticed. After Peter dies others will teach and write ; but he desires that after *his* death it shall still be *his* voice that exhorts the readers.

6. (P. 201, 204.) With regard to i. 16 ff., it is to be borne in mind first of all that γνωρίζειν τινί τι means, " To make known to one something that he has not known before." This is its meaning even in 1 Cor. xv. 1, where, not without irony, Paul uses a certain *contradictio in adjecto.* Also in 1 Cor. xii. 3 and Gal. i. 11, truths and facts with which the readers could not have been wholly unacquainted are intentionally spoken of as if they were entirely unknown. The expression has the force of an emphatic οὐ θέλω ὑμᾶς ἀγνοεῖν or ἤ οὐκ οἴδατε. Furthermore, although παρουσία, like ἐπιφάνεια (see above, p. 133), can be used of the first as well as of the second coming of Christ (cf. Luke xii. 51 ; Heb. ix. 11), here, in accordance with the uniform usage of the N.T. (Matt. xxiv. 3, 27, 37, 39 ; 1 Cor. xv. 23 ; 1 Thess. ii. 19, iii. 13, iv. 15, v. 23 ; 2 Thess. ii. 1, 8 ; Jas. v. 7 f. ; 1 John ii. 28 ; cf. also 2 Pet. iii. 4, 12), it can refer only to the second coming, especially in view of the fact that otherwise it would have to precede δύναμις. But the interpretation of δύναμις as meaning the power manifested by Jesus while still upon the earth, is in keeping not only with the usage of the Gospels and of Acts in describing the miraculous work of Christ (Mark v. 30, vi. 2, 14, ix. 23 ; Luke iv. 14, 36, v. 17, xxiv. 19 ; Acts ii. 22, x. 38), but also with the usage of 2 Pet. itself (i. 3 ; see n. 10). There is no reason, however, why the conception should be limited to this power, and that power excluded which was shown by Jesus as He passed through death and resurrection to heavenly glory, which also will be fully manifested at His coming. It is just as arbitrary to limit ἐπόπται γενηθέντες τῆς ἐκείνου μεγαλειότητος either to the transfiguration upon the mountain, which is not mentioned until ver. 17, and then only in order to illustrate and confirm what has just been said (still advocated by Spitta, 97), or to the appearances of the risen Christ (as Hofmann, vii. 2. 33). There is nothing in the expression itself which would limit it in this way ; since Jesus' own μεγαλειότης comes to view, not only in these particular events, but in everything in which a θεῖα δύναμις of Jesus (i. 3) was expressed, or His ἰδία δόξα (i. 3) became manifest to those of His contemporaries who believed during His earthly life (John i. 14, ii. 11 ; cf. 2 Cor. iv. 6), in all those μεγαλεῖα τοῦ θεοῦ (Acts ii. 11) in which in and through Jesus God showed His μεγαλειότης (Luke ix. 43),—just as the glorification of God through Jesus is at the same time a glorification of Jesus (John xi. 4, 40, xii. 28, xiii. 31, xvii. 4, 10). The transfiguration upon the mountain and the appearances of the risen Christ are a part of these experiences of Peter and his fellow-disciples ; but only when what they witnessed is conceived of in the entirely

general sense implied by the absence of every specification, does the term serve as an adequate contrast to μῦθοι σεσοφισμένοι, and a suitable description of those experiences on which the preaching of the apostles was based. Nor does the ἐκείνου necessarily refer to one "beyond us," *i.e.* to the exalted Christ (Hofmann), but applies equally well to Him who lived once here upon the earth (1 John ii. 6, iii. 5, 16), but now can be no more seen even by His own. In this rests the peculiar significance of those preachers of the gospel who, by reason of the fact that they saw and heard what Jesus did and said in His earthly life, were able to declare what had happened as well as what was to take place in the future (John i. 14 ; 1 John i. 1 f., iv. 14 ; Acts x. 39–41). The interpretation of i. 17 f. is rendered difficult, but not made impossible, by the anacoluthon. If, as is certainly the case, vv. 17b, 18 refer to the event described in Matt. xvii. 1–13, Mark ix. 2–13, Luke ix. 28–36, λαβὼν παρὰ θεοῦ πατρὸς τιμὴν καὶ δόξαν cannot be taken in the sense in which Hofmann takes it, as referring to the glorification of Jesus completed at His resurrection (cf. 1 Pet. i. 21 ; John vii. 39, xiii. 32) ; for then there is no intelligible connection between this final glorification and the heavenly voice at the Transfiguration. Nor does the honour and glory received consist of the voice from heaven, which thought would necessarily be expressed by φερομένης, in the sense of an imperfect participle, instead of ἐνεχθείσης. The only other meaning possible is the visible glorification of Jesus in the scene upon the mountain. The dazzling light, by which the disciples saw the countenance and garments of Jesus illumined, can be called glory and honour which Jesus received at that moment from the Father (cf. Luke ix. 39, εἶδον τὴν δόξαν αὐτοῦ), with just as much appropriateness as the saying in Ps. viii. 6 about the crowning of mankind with δόξα καὶ τιμή can be applied in Heb. ii. 9 (cf. iii. 3, v. 4 f.) to the earthly life of Jesus while He had death yet before Him. Spitta's opinion (104, 496), that Peter, in contradiction to the Gospels, conceived the voice from heaven as preceding the visible transfiguration, cannot be justified from the text ; for even if the words be translated, "After a voice sounded," it is by no means certain that the genitive absolute is dependent upon the participle λαβών. It is rather like λαβών, dependent upon the principal clause of the sentence, which is left unexpressed. The latter is the more probable construction, for otherwise ἐνεχθείσης would certainly precede λαβών (cf. Heb. ix. 19). Furthermore, in the description of similar events, such as the appearance of the angels to the shepherds, the baptism of Jesus, the conversion of Paul, the visible phenomenon always precedes the audible. Why not here, as in the Gospels, without making Peter contradict these accounts? Nor does the present writer agree with Spitta when he claims that "it is possible to determine with entire certainty" (Spitta, 106) the originally intended continuation of the sentence beginning with ver. 17, though he regards it as quite possible that Peter did intend to say practically what is found in ver. 18 without breaking the construction of the preceding verse. Possibly he meant to write διελέχθη ἡμῖν περὶ τῆς παρουσίας αὐτοῦ, which is not expressly stated in the Gospels, but quite in harmony with Matt. xvii. 10–13 ; Mark ix. 11–13 ; cf. Matt. xvi. 28 ; Mark ix. 1 ; Luke ix. 27 ; or he may have meant to write διεστείλατο (ἐνετείλατο) ἡμῖν, ἵνα μετὰ τὴν ἀνάστασιν αὐτοῦ πᾶσι γνωρίσωμεν τὴν δύναμιν καὶ τὴν παρουσίαν αὐτοῦ, which might be suggested by Matt. xvii. 9 ; Mark ix. 9 f. ;

Luke ix. 36. These conclusions of the sentence agree better with the contents of ver. 16 than do ἡμᾶς εἶχε σὺν αὐτῷ ὄντας ἐν τῷ ὄρει τῷ ἁγίῳ (Spitta) and other similar expressions, which, moreover, leave the break in the construction unexplained. On the other hand, it is perfectly conceivable that, having expressed with vivid realisation in an independent sentence (ver. 18) the important circumstance that he and his companions themselves had heard the voice and been witnesses of the whole scene, Peter might leave the intended principal clause of the sentence unexpressed. Whatever the grammatical form of the intended principal clause, the clause itself was not necessary in order to complete the sense ; for the thing of chief importance—corresponding to the ἐπόπται γενηθέντες of ver. 16, which is the chief point to be established—Peter has already expressed. In fact, neither this nor any other passage in 2 Pet. can be shown to contradict the view of the events on the mountain, given in the Gospels. In Matt. xvii. 5, Mark ix. 7, Luke ix. 35, it is said that the voice sounded from the cloud which afterwards overshadowed the scene ; in 2 Pet. it is said that it came from heaven ; but these two passages are related in the same way as the narrative in Acts i. 9 is related to the reminiscence of the same in Acts ii. 34. In the Gospel passages the fact that it is God who speaks appears only from the contents of the call ; in 2 Pet., on the other hand, God is also expressly called the "majestic glory," i.e. God in His majesty is declared to be the efficient cause of this revelation ; but this would not imply a contradiction, even if the thought were here expressed that God in this phenomenon of brightness, νεφέλη φωτεινή (Matt. xvii. 5), became visible (cf. Ex. xiii. 21, xiv. 24, xvi. 10, xxiv. 16). But there is no ground for even this assumption. The attribute μεγαλοπρεπής can be used with reference to the audible voice itself (Ps. xxix. 4), and the μεγαλοπρέπεια of God (Ps. cxlv. 5, cxi. 3 ; Clem. 1 Cor. lx. 1, lxi. 1) or of His name (2 Macc. viii. 15 ; Clem. 1 Cor. lxiv ; cf. ix. 1, xix. 2, xlv. 7), also His δόξα (Rom. i. 23, vi. 4), or even the μεγαλοπρεπὴς δόξα (Clem. 1 Cor. ix. 2), are spoken of where there is no reference whatever to physical perceptibility. Further comparison with the Gospels brings out clearly the fact that the presentation by Peter is an independent one. Thus (1) the most interesting and remarkable features are omitted by Peter, e.g. the appearance of Moses and Elias, although, in view of the purpose expressed —to speak of the word of the prophets (i. 19 f.)—it was most natural to recall just these things. (2) The language of the heavenly call differs from the account given in all three of the synoptics in the following particulars :— (a) The omission of αὐτοῦ ἀκούετε at the close ; (b) the insertion of εἰς ὃν ἐγὼ εὐδόκησα, the only parallel to which is the ἐν ᾧ εὐδόκησα of Matt. xvii. 5 : the ἐγώ of Peter is not found in any of the parallels (Matt. iii. 17, xii. 18, xvii. 5 ; Mark i. 11 ; Luke iii. 22) ; (c) most unparalleled of all is the order of words, ὁ υἱός μου ὁ ἀγαπητός μου οὗτός ἐστιν, witnessed only by Cod. B, but rightly adopted by Westcott-Hort. The τοιᾶσδε (not ταύτης) is apparently designed to indicate that Peter does not claim absolute accuracy in his reproduction of the words spoken from heaven. (3) The twice-repeated φωνὴ ἠνεχθεῖσα, vv. 17, 18, seems to presuppose a φωνὴ ἠνέχθη in the underlying narrative, which, however, is not found in any of the Gospels (but cf. Acts ii. 2). (4) The fact that the place where the Transfiguration took place is here called τὸ ὄρος τὸ ἅγιον, but is not so designated in the Gospels, is explained by the fact that this mountain was not in itself holy, but was made a holy mountain for Christians by the knowledge of what Jesus, in company with His most trusted disciples, experienced there. Consequently in the narrative, in which the point of view is before the event, it is called a high mountain (Matt., Mark), or a (neighbouring) mountain (Luke), but in the retrospect of the eye-witness it becomes the holy mountain. If, on the other hand, Peter meant to refer to a mountain which was already venerated by the readers as a holy place, and even visited by pilgrims, he would not have failed to mention it by name, or in some other way to indicate its geographical location ; for if at the time when 2 Pet. was written there was any holy mountain so venerated by Christians, there were other mountains—*e.g.* the Mount of Olives, from which the ascension took place—that had at least as much claim to this designation as the mount of transfiguration. But the term which Peter chooses, taken out of its connection, is far more applicable to Zion (Ps. ii. 6, iii. 5 ; Joel iv. 17 ; Zech. viii. 3 ; Dan. ix. 16–20 ; Acts vi. 13 ; Rev. xiv. 1), or Sinai (Ex. xix. 3 ; 1 Kings xix. 8) than to any mountain in Galilee. The expression, therefore, is not due to the fame of the locality already established and expressed by use of the common name " The holy mountain," but grows out of associations of the event recalled. It is also to be observed that there is no ancient local tradition with regard to the place of the transfiguration. The tradition which makes Tabor the scene of this event is no older than that which places the temptation of Jesus upon the same mountain, and both traditions grew out of the almost identical designation of a mountain in Matt. iv. 8 and xvii. 2 (*GK*, ii. 690 f.). In the Gnostic *Acts of Peter* (ed. Lipsius, 67. 10), Peter speaks as follows in connection with a lesson just read from the book of the gospel (perhaps Mark ix. 2–13) : " Nunc quod vobis lectum est, jam vobis exponam. Dominus noster volens me *majestatem* suam videre *in monte sancto*, videns autem luminis splendorem eius cum filiis Zebedæi, cecidi tamquam mortuus et oculos meos conclusi et *vocem* eius audivi *talem*, qualem referre non possum, qui me putavi exorbatum ab splendore eius ; et pusillum respirans dixi intra me : ' Forsitan dominus meus voluit me hic adducere, ut me orbaret.' Et dixi : ' Et hæc tua voluntas est, non contradico, domine.' Et dans mihi manum elevavit me, et exsurgens iterum talem eum vidi, qualem capere potui." The words *majestatem* (cf. Palimps. Flor. 2 Pet. i. 1⁷, *de magnifica majestate*, Vulg. *a magnifica gloria*) and *in monte sancto*, perhaps also *vocem talem*, are taken from 2 Pet. i. 17 f. In the *Acts of John* also (ed. Bonnet, p. 195. 8–11) the event is described briefly, in order to connect with it a related story purely fictitious in character.

7. (P. 205.) For the impersonal designation of the apostles by one who belonged to the apostolic body (iii. 2), cf. Eph. iv. 11 ; 1 Cor. xii. 28 ; vol. i. p. 506 f. Every preacher or teacher is apt occasionally to say to his hearers or pupils, "Your preachers or teachers," without prefacing it with a " we." The aged preacher in Clem. 2 *Cor.* xvii. 3, 5, goes so far even as to employ a " we," including himself and listeners, and then to contrast the two together with the presbyters who preached to his hearers, although he himself is now preaching to them.

8. (P. 206.) The interpretation of πίστιν ἐν δικαιοσύνῃ κτλ., i. 1, to mean "Faith in the righteousness," etc., which led to the change of the reading in א to εἰς δικαιοσύνην, is to be rejected for the following reasons :

(1) Such a description of the essential element in Christian faith is unparalleled, and there is nothing in the rest of the letter that would occasion such a description here.   (2) δικαιοσύνη is without the article which would necessarily be used, if the reference were to a righteousness of Christ upon which the Christian based his hope of salvation.   Moreover, such a righteousness would be more properly described as that of the man Jesus, than as the righteousness of " our God and Saviour."   (3) There is a question about this construction of πίστις in all the N.T. passages where it is supposed to exist (Gal. iii. 26 ; Eph. i. 15 ; 2 Tim. iii. 15 ; cf. 1 Tim. i. 14 ; 2 Tim. i. 13).   ἐν δικαιοσύνη is therefore to be taken with λαχοῦσιν.   The assignment of human destinies has been made in righteousness (cf. Tit. iii. 5 ; Acts xvii. 31 ; Rev. xix. 11), and it is due to the righteous act of the Lord that those converted by the apostolic preaching, who have not seen nor heard Him, have come into the possession of a Christianity of no less value than that of the original disciples (cf. *Cat.*, ed. Cramer, 85), εἰς τὸ ἴσον αὐτοὺς τοῖς ἀποστόλοις ἀναφέρων χάρισμα.

9. (Pp. 206, 209.)   With regard to the use of Συμεών instead of Σίμων, see vol. i. p. 29 f.   Leaving out of account the thoroughly Jewish character of the name, the use of this original name along with Πέτρος proves that the writer did not intend his letter for the same group of readers for whom the greeting in 1 Pet. i. 1 was meant.   The Concordance shows how uncommon outside of Palestine was the use of Simon or Simeon to designate the apostle Peter, whether used in place of the latter name or along with it.   Paul calls him only Peter, or, what is the same thing, Cephas, which corresponds to Peter's own usage in 1 Pet. i. 1 (above, p. 155).   Mark calls him Simon until he is given a surname in iii. 16 ; from that point on only Peter is found in the narrative, which is all the more striking because Mark does not conceal the fact that Jesus called him Simon to the end (xiv. 37, λέγει τῷ Πέτρῳ Σίμων).   Luke also calls him regularly Simon until he is given another name (vi. 14) ; then he uses just as regularly Peter in both books, even when he is addressed by Jesus, Luke xxii. 34 (alongside of Σίμων, xxii. 31 ; cf. Mark xiv. 37) ; Acts x. 13 ; although he lets us know that he was generally called Simon (Luke xxiv. 34), or Symeon (Acts xv. 14), by his companions in Jerusalem.   Simon Peter occurs only once (Luke v. 8) ; " Simon with the surname Peter " is used in the Cornelius passages where Peter is thought of as being at a distance (Acts x. 5, 18, 32, xi. 13), though the simple designation Peter is found in the same narrative (fourteen times in the passage Acts x. 1–xi. 18, fifty-two times altogether in Acts).   In John, Simon alone occurs only in i. 41, Simon son of John in i. 42, xxi. 15–17 ; from i. 40 on, Simon Peter is used seventeen times, from xiii. 8 on it is used interchangeably with Peter fifteen times.   Except in address (xvii. 25, Simon ; xvi. 17, Simon Barjona), Matthew never uses Simon ; Simon with the surname Peter occurs only in the call and in the list of the apostles (iv. 18, x. 2), and on one other solemn occasion (xvi. 16) ; in all other cases Peter is used, occurring some twenty times.   There is no means of determining whether the person who translated this Gospel into Greek found uniformly in his original Kepha, or in passages where he found Simon replaced it by Peter, which was more familiar to his Greek readers.   With regard to the interchange of the Aramaic Kepha and the Greek Πέτρος, it may be said

that the latter once adopted as the translation was more natural to the Greek language. Just as Syrian translators and theological writers always wrote Kepha, so the N.T. writers used regularly Πέτρος. The former is found only once in the Gospels, John i. 42, where the writer, following an inclination which he often manifests, retains the original words of the saying which he is reproducing. All the cases where Paul writes Kepha are explained by the reference which he has to the " Hebrews," who, with appeals to the authority of Peter, were meddling with his affairs in Galatia and Corinth (above, p. 155, n. 8).

10. (P. 194, 207.) The present writer regards it as certain that ver. 3 f. follows ver. 2 without any break in the grammatical construction, as held by Lachmann and by Spitta (27 f.), who has proved this to be the case particularly by a correct interpretation of Ign. *Eph.* i., *Rom.* i., *Smyrn.* i., *Philad.* i., correcting fundamentally the writer's edition. He also holds that in ver. 2 τοῦ θεοῦ καὶ 'Ιησοῦ and similar words are to be omitted before τοῦ κ. ἡ. and τοῦ κυρίου ἡμῶν, read with P, Vulg. (in the best MSS.), to which S², S³, Aug. *Specul.* pp. 606. 16, 630. 1, and some cursives add simply 'Ιησοῦ Χρ. The same theme is dealt with here as in i. 8, ii. 20, iii. 18, namely, the knowledge of Christ. Therefore it is Christ who is referred to in i. 3. It is commonly held that in the N.T. only God, never Christ, is described as calling men ; but that this claim is erroneous is evidenced not alone by Gal. i. 6 and 1 Pet. ii. 9, regarding which there may be difference of opinion, but by the expression κλητοὶ 'Ιησοῦ Χρ., Rom. i. 6, and passages like Matt. ix. 13 ; Mark ii. 17 ; Luke v. 32. So also the expression κλητὸς ἀπόστολος Χριστοῦ, 1 Cor. i. 1, represents Christ as calling His disciples as well as sending them (1 Cor. i. 17), cf. *ZKom. Gal.* 43 f. If ver. 3 f. is thus closely connected with ver. 1 f. the ἡμᾶς (and ἡμῖν) of ver. 3 cannot be taken other than as ἡμῖν, ver. 1, namely, as referring to the apostles and personal disciples of Jesus, as distinguished from the Christians who were not called until they were called through their preaching. This distinction is also expressly made in ver. 3. Whereas God or Christ calls all other Christians through the preachers of the gospel, He called the apostles by the manifestation of (His) own glory and virtue. It was particularly natural for an apostle, whom Jesus Himself in the most literal sense of the word had called (Matt. iv. 19–22 ; Mark i. 17, 20, ἐκάλεσεν αὐτούς ; Matt. viii. 22, ix. 9 ; Mark ii. 14 ; Luke v. 10 f., 27, ix. 57–62 ; John i. 39, 43), to speak of Jesus as the one who called men, and to emphasise the fact that Jesus had called him and his companions directly through His own personal act, through the demonstration of His own glory and moral power, in contrast to the fact that all other Christians owed their call to the preaching of weak men, even that of Peter himself (i. 16). The words δόξα καὶ ἀρετή are intended to suggest the evidences of miraculous knowledge and power, which Jesus had shown at the time of these calls (John i. 42, 47–51 ; Luke v. 4), and the impression of His moral greatness (Luke v. 8 ; John i. 49), which rendered impossible or overcame any resistance on the part of the one who was called. Especially in the first word we have expressed the same view of Jesus, as He lived in intercourse with His disciples upon earth, that is found in i. 16 (above, p. 215) and in the words immediately preceding in ver. 3, τῆς θείας δυνάμεως αὐτοῦ ; for it may be regarded as certain that the reference in these expressions is to the supernatural power which dwelt in the man Jesus, and not to the power of God as the Creator and Ruler of the universe—

particularly in view of the fact that in ver. 1 Jesus is called our God and Saviour, and of the fact that, according to the more probable reading, God the Father is not mentioned at all in ver. 2.   The same Jesus who personally called the apostles, by reason of His own divine power and through the knowledge of Himself, to which He led them, also bestowed upon them all true blessings (τὰ πάντα, אA ; cf. Rom. viii. 32), especially the things necessary for the true life and pious conduct (Matt. xi. 25–30, xiii. 11–17, xvi. 16–19 ; Luke xxii. 28–35 ; John vi. 68 f.).   It is this personal experience (cf. John i. 16, xvii. 2 f., 6–18) from which the apostle derives the authority and the courage to express the wish for the readers in ver. 2.   To this he comes back in ver. 4.   With regard to variant readings, which are numerous, those affecting the order of the words are not of any great importance ; for even if ἡμῖν (or ὑμῖν) belongs between τίμια and καὶ μέγιστα, it must be taken with δεδώρηται (having here also the force of a middle—" He hath bestowed "). ὑμῖν does not have very strong MS. authority (AS², cursive 68), but the following may be said in its favour : (1) in the use of the N.T. Epistles in public worship, ὑμεῖς, which excluded the reader and preacher, was much more easily and frequently changed to ἡμεῖς, or entirely left out, than the reverse (cf. iii. 2) ; (2) the sudden transition to an address to the readers in ver. 4b without the insertion of a καὶ ὑμεῖς is intolerable, unless in 4a the readers are already clearly contrasted with the ἡμῖν, ἡμᾶς of ver. 3, through the use of ὑμῖν.   Moreover, δι' ὧν does not refer back to δυνάμει καὶ ἀρετῇ, which would require δι' ἧς ; still less does it refer to πάντα, which is far removed from the relative ; but it does refer to ἡμᾶς, i.e. the apostles.   Christ called the apostles in person, through whom, i.e. through whose preaching, He had bestowed upon the readers precious and very great promises.

§ 42. THE OCCASION OF THE SECOND EPISTLE OF PETER.

From i. 12–14 alone the impression might be gained that the only purpose which the writer had in this letter was to exhort now from a distance the readers to whom he had once preached the gospel, by sending them a letter intended to take the place of the oral instructions he would not fail to give them were he living among them. This he promises also to do occasionally in the future. That he had a more definite purpose than this, however, is evidenced, first of all, by the fact that the encouragement of the readers to a well-rounded moral life on the basis of their Christian faith (i. 5) and knowledge (i. 8, 12 ; cf. i. 2, iii. 18) is so variously reinforced by the prospect of the completion of their salvation.   Even in the restate-

ment of the apostolic preaching the fact is strongly
emphasised that in this preaching the return of Christ
was made known to the readers (i. 16), and that the Lord
had bestowed upon them through His disciples great and
precious promises (i. 4; above, p. 220). The purpose of
this revelation of the gospel is declared to be that the
readers may become partakers of the divine nature in the
future world, in contrast to the destruction which follows
the indulgence of pleasure in this world (i. 4). In view
of this glorious prospect, they are to spare neither pains
nor sacrifice to make their faith and knowledge fruitful in
the exhibition of all Christian virtues, in order that finally
they may experience in rich measure God's generous kind-
ness in that great day when it is decided whether entrance
is to be had into the eternal kingdom of Christ, or
destruction with the world and its pleasures (i. 5–11).
Reference is made to this day again in i. 19, and the
readers are exhorted to give heed, until this day comes,
to the word of the O.T. prophets, which the self-revelation
of Jesus has only served to make more trustworthy for
the apostles and all Christians, and which has lost none
of its usefulness. The same combination of the thought
of *moral obligation* and *the expectation of the end of the
world* meets us again in iii. 2, where the words of the
prophets are connected with the commandment of Jesus
handed down through the apostles, and is found also
throughout iii. 10–18 (above, p. 196).

There is also a *polemical* note to be observed in both
chap. i. and chap. iii. The moral requirements of i. 5–8 are
reinforced by the warning reference to those with whom
these Christian virtues are not to be found, and concerning whom it must be denied that they have the Christian
knowledge; since by their conduct they show that they
have forgotten the purification from their former sins
which they experienced in baptism (i. 9, n. 1). These
terrible examples do not seem to have belonged to the

circle of the readers; for although the readers are exhorted to growth in virtuous living (i. 8, iii. 18; cf. i. 2)
and to zeal in their own sanctification (i. 10), yet the
fact that they are addressed as brothers in this particular
passage and nowhere else in the letter, the even more
fervent ἀγαπητοί of iii. 1, 8, 14, 17, and the whole of the
remainder of the Epistle, make it evident that Peter had a
good opinion of them and full confidence in them.   They
not only possess and know the truth, but they stand fast
in it (i. 12; cf. iii. 17).   But among those who confess
Christianity there are persons who have learned nothing,
who are not firm in the truth, and who thus easily become
the prey of error and seduction (iii. 16; cf. ii. 14).   And
these persons who lack the Christian virtues, and are
therefore immoral in character, are not only evil examples
to the readers (i. 9), but also a threatening danger, against
whom the readers must be warned beforehand, in order
that they may not be led astray by them and so fall from
their own established position (iii. 17).

A third thing to be noticed is the *apologetic* tone in
the restatement of the apostolic preaching in i. 16–18.
This must be explained as due to opposition, either to
a depreciatory judgment of the apostolic preaching, or to
other teachers who actually followed invented stories, and
did not, like the disciples of Jesus, speak of the things of
Christianity from their own personal knowledge of Jesus'
self-revelation.   The latter view is favoured by the emphatic way in which Peter says of himself and his companions, that they are the persons who have heard with
their own ears the heavenly testimony concerning Jesus
(i. 18, ἡμεῖς, omitted in i. 16); the former view is supported
by the emphasis with which he assures the readers that he
and his fellow-apostles were called by Jesus Himself (i. 3;
above, p. 220).

Thus, in brief, almost every one of the more noticeable
statements of chap. i. points forward to the contents of

chap. ii. and chap. iii., and gets its full meaning in the light of these chapters. It is here that the occasion of the letter first comes clearly to view. After the mention of the O.T. prophets in i. 19–21, Peter goes on to say in ii. 1–3 that, just as in Israel the true prophets opposed those who wrongly claimed this name, so also among the readers, teachers will appear who do not deserve the name,—teachers who will smuggle in destructive heresies, find numerous followers, and covetously, by means of cunningly invented words, get gain at the expense of the Churches to which the letter is addressed (n. 2). The comparison with the false prophets of the O.T. does not imply that the persons in question claimed to be prophets ; but just as the false prophets in the O.T. were resisted by the true prophets, so in N.T. times the divinely commissioned teachers of the Church, that is to say, the apostles, oppose those who set themselves up as teachers, and affect the teachers' appearance and name—an opposition which we saw appearing earlier in i. 16–18 (see above). Just as the O.T. prophets and the apostles go naturally together (iii. 2 ; cf. i. 16–21), without their vocations being in any sense the same, so the false prophets of the O.T. and the false teachers in the Church are associated with each other. These false prophets originated in Israel itself : so the false teachers arise out of the Church. Once they knew the way of righteousness and the Lord Christ, and through this knowledge escaped the impurities of the worldly life. They have been washed from their former sins by baptism, have submitted themselves to the holy commandment, and for a time have walked in the straight way of truth and righteousness. Now, however, they have given up all this, and have become worse than they were before their conversion (ii. 15, 20–22, i. 9) ; by their deeds they deny the Lord who bought them that they might be His servants (ii. 2). In chap. ii. they are charged with various forms of immoral living,

especially unchastity (ii. 10, 14, 18, 20). It is in this
that they will find many followers, and so cause the
Christian doctrine to be blasphemed (ii. 2). The reference
to the trespass of the angels who before the Flood had
sexual intercourse with women (ii. 4; Gen. vi. 1–4), and
to the destruction of Sodom and Gomorrah (ii. 6 f.; Gen.
xix.), suggests the unnatural vices of which they were
the slaves. In particular, they made the love-feasts an
occasion not only for gluttonous eating, but for seducing
unsteadfast souls (ii. 13 f.; n. 3). They preferred to use
their seductive arts on those recently converted, who
were not yet firmly grounded in the Christian life (ii.
14, 18). In doing this they claim to be teachers of
Christianity (ii. 1). They make of their teaching a
prosperous business at the expense of the Churches (ii.
3, 14). This is one of the points in which they resemble
the heathen prophet Balaam (ii. 15). The other point in
which they are like him is in the evil counsel which
Balaam gave, *i.e.* the betrayal of the people of God into
unchastity, for which he was responsible (n. 3). The
cunningly chosen language by which they endeavour to
deceive the Churches and to lead individuals astray (ii. 3 ;
cf. Rom. xvi. 18), sounds like promises of freedom (ii. 19).
This same unbridled indulgence of the passions which
makes these persons themselves slaves of sin and destruction they recommend to others, who heretofore have lived
honourably, as the Christian freedom which they still lack
(cf 1 Pet. ii. 16). Another indication of the character of
their teaching is seen in the fact that they despise the
ruling powers of the other world, and revile them without
fear and trembling, even evil spirits against which angels
themselves do not dare to utter a reviling and disparag-
ing judgment (ii. 10 f., 18). While Peter accuses them
of ignorance, or at least insufficient appreciation, of the
evil spirits they blaspheme (ii. 12; cf. i. 9, iii. 16), they
themselves boast a full familiarity with them (Rev. ii. 24),

which accounts for the confidence with which they speak
so contemptuously of the devil and his servants, treating
them as harmless beings.   It is also to be observed that
they mock the vain waiting of Christianity for the return
of the Lord (iii. 3 f.).   For it is impossible to distinguish
between the libertines of chap. ii. and those who make light
of prophecy in chap. iii.   The latter also are immoral
in their lives, and from their immoral tendencies Peter
explains their denial of the prophecy concerning the end
of the world (iii. 3 f.); just as, on the other hand, he
derives the obligation to sanctification from the well-
grounded hope of the disappearance of this world and
the coming of another in which righteousness dwells (iii.
10–14).   In this same connection also he speaks once
more of seduction on the part of wicked men, against
whom he would have the readers forewarned (iii. 17).
The combining of moral demands with the expectation of
the end of the world, which comes to light in chap. i. and
runs through the entire letter, is due to the fact that
Peter designs to warn his readers against alleged teachers
of Christianity, who unite immoral theories and practices
with contempt for prophecy.

So long as the discussion of this Epistle proceeded on
the basis of the undemonstrable hypothesis that 2 Peter,
like 1 Peter, was directed to the Gentile Christian
Churches of Asia Minor, there remained the insuperable
difficulty that, while the appearance of the false teachers
and scoffers is prophesied to take place in the future
(ii. 1–3, iii. 3), and the readers are forewarned against
them, iii. 17 (ii. 10–22, iii. 4 f., 9, ὥς τινες βραδυτῆτα
ἡγοῦνται; cf. also i. 9, iii. 16), the same persons are described connectedly, accurately, and apparently from life
in the present tense.   The transition from the prophecy
of future phenomena to the description of present conditions in 2 Tim. iii. 1–9 and other passages of the last
Epistles of Paul, is not really parallel with the present case

above, p. 111 ff.).   Even less satisfactory is the citation of
such passages as Rev. xi. 4 ff. (Hofmann, vii. 2. 60).   On
the other hand, the explanation is simple, if it be recognised that 2 Peter was, or purported to be, directed to a
group of Jewish Christian Churches between 60 and 63
(§ 41), in addition to which there existed a widely spread
Gentile Christian Church.   The writer distinguishes clearly
between his readers who uniformly hold and steadfastly
maintain a true faith, which they need only to assert and
to put into general practice (i. 1, 5, 10, 12, iii. 1, 17 f.),
and the false teachers and the circles in which they exert
their influence.   The false teachers will not arise out of
their midst (cf. Acts xx. 30 ; 1 John ii. 19 ; Rev. ii. 14–16,
20–23), but will come from without—appear *among them*,
and seek to profit by them, and lead them astray (2 Pet.
ii. 1–3 ; cf. Acts xx. 29).   It is not their existence but
their appearance that pertains to the future.   The contrast
is not between the loyal and genuine Christians among
the readers, and others among them whose lives are unchristian and whose faith is wavering, as, for example, in
Rev. ii. 24, iii. 4.   Rather, the readers as a body, who are
regarded as having been up to this time faithful, and as
maintaining a correct faith and a true knowledge, are
contrasted not only with the immoral persons and false
teachers who will attack them in the future (iii. 17, i. 9),
but also with another group of Christians, or Churches,
in which conditions are to be observed that are as yet
foreign to the readers.   This is shown with especial clearness by the transition from iii. 16 to iii. 17.   Peter could
not address the readers as a whole with an emphatic ὑμεῖς
οὖν, nor speak of their ἴδιος στηριγμός, if the persons previously described (οἱ ἀμαθεῖς καὶ ἀστήρικτοι) as perverting
certain difficult passages in the Epistles of Paul to their
own destruction, had belonged to their own circle.   Paul
once wrote a letter to the readers of 2 Peter (iii. 15 ;
above, p. 199), which has not come down to us.   The

numerous other letters of Paul, concerning which Peter
has knowledge (iii. 16), were addressed to other Churches,
and, excepting only Romans of the letters known to us, to
Gentile Christians. It was among Gentile Christians that
they were read. Consequently it is here that we must
seek the Christians who lacked adequate knowledge of
Christianity, and requisite stability of moral or religious
training, and who therefore wrested difficult single statements in the letters of Paul from their natural connection,
perverted them, and applied them to life in a way that
was harmful to themselves.

It will be observed that this takes place in the present,
not in the future, concerning which prophecies are made
in ii. 1–3, and which is referred to in iii. 17 (προγινώ-
σκοντες). These persons belong in the future only in
relation to the readers, who are warned against them
beforehand. The two adjectives in iii. 16, which are used
with only one article, do not describe two distinct classes.
As regards their moral condition, these same persons are
portrayed in iii. 17 by a single word, οἱ ἄθεσμοι. But the
expression ἀστήρικτοι suggests immediately ii. 14, where it
is said that these false teachers prefer to entice unsteadfast souls. These unsteadfast souls are identical with
those who in ii. 18, according to the correct reading, are
called τοὺς ὀλίγως ἀποφεύγοντας, i.e. persons who are just
escaping the sinful life and its consequent destruction (cf.
i. 4, ii. 20), who are, in fact, only a few steps removed
from it, and therefore possessed of thoughts and habits to
a large extent such as held them before they became
Christians, or, in ecclesiastical language, catechumens or
neophytes (cf. 1 Cor. iii. 2 f., v. 1, 6, vi. 1–20, xv. 33 f. ;
2 Cor. vi. 14–18 ; 1 Tim. iii. 6). Thus ἀστήρικτοι refers
more to the persons enticed by the false teachers than to
the seducers themselves. Naturally the ἀστήρικτοι are
also ἀμαθεῖς ; since, if they had learned what was correct,
they would have been confirmed by the truth dwelling in

them, as were the readers of 2 Peter (i. 12, iii. 17). But when it is borne in mind that Peter does not charge those who allow themselves to be led astray by false teachers so much with ἀμαθία as with a lack of experience and confirmation in Christianity (ii. 14, 18), while, on the other hand, he uses various expressions for accusing the false teachers of an ignominious ignorance, a loss of their first knowledge of Christ, and a thoughtlessness about Christian things (ii. 12, 16, 20 f., iii. 5), it becomes apparent that it is especially for the latter that ἀμαθεῖς is intended, so that it quite appropriately precedes ἀστήρικτοι. Seducers and those enticed by them alike believe or pretend that in certain passages of Paul's Epistles, and in other writings which they similarly misinterpret, they find support for their immoral teachings.

In the same manner as in iii. 16, the present tenses in ii. 10–22 describe existing phenomena with which Peter had become familiar elsewhere than among the readers. In particular, what Peter says in ii. 13 f. about the misuse of the Agape by the libertines is inappropriate to a prophecy intended to describe future phenomena in large outlines or in a symbolic form. It is especially inappropriate to the prophecy of 2 Peter which deals with future phenomena among the readers of this Epistle. Moreover, according to the corrected text of ii. 13, these love-feasts, the name and holy purpose of which the libertines profane, are celebrated outside of the circle of the readers. Whether such feasts were common among the readers and called ἀγάπαι, it is impossible to say (n. 3).

Peter foresees and predicts that these teachers will find numerous followers in their immoral living, which implies that this was not yet the case (ii. 2). Since the region where they will gain this following is not named, and since this prediction is accompanied by another quite independent prediction that these teachers will make their appearance among the readers and endeavour to lead them astray (ii. 1, 3, iii. 17), it follows that ii. 2 refers to results in the same region where they have been active heretofore, *i.e.* outside the circle of the readers, or, in other words, among Gentile Christians. Eventually also these persons will bring their arts to bear upon the spiritual children of Peter and the other immediate disciples of Jesus. What the result will be is, to say the least, not clearly stated, not even in ii. 1 ($\alpha \acute{\iota} \rho \acute{\epsilon} \sigma \epsilon \iota \varsigma$). Peter makes every endeavour to prevent their gaining followers among his readers, and says simply that judgment upon them has long been impending and will not be delayed (ii. 3 ff.).

Of an altogether different character is the prediction of iii. 3. Here Peter himself is not directly the prophet. The manner in which the revelation of the end of the world is introduced ($\tau o \hat{v} \tau o \ \pi \rho \hat{\omega} \tau o \nu \ \gamma \iota \nu \acute{\omega} \sigma \kappa o \nu \tau \epsilon \varsigma$, iii. 3 ; cf. i. 20 ; 2 Tim. iii. 1 ; Rom. vi. 6 ; Jas. i. 3), shows that he does not intend to say here anything really new, but merely to remind the readers of the prophesied appearance of immoral scoffers, and of how they are to be answered, just as they are reminded of the commandment of Jesus and the prophecies of the O.T. prophets (iii. 2, n. 4). Here he appeals, just as Paul does (above, p. 111 ff.), to prophecy, which was still current in the Church. Not altogether independently of traditional sayings of Jesus, this foretold a falling away, and moral degeneracy within the Church in the last days. Probably also prophecy declared, following again predictions of Jesus (Luke xvii. 26 f. ; Matt. xxiv. 37 ff. ; cf. 1 Pet. iii. 20 ; 2 Pet. ii. 5, iii. 5), that, owing to the long time it would be necessary to wait for the parousia of the Lord (Matt. xxiv. 48, xxv. 5 ; Luke xii. 45), degenerate members of the Church, who were sunk in the life of the world, would go so far as to scoff at the promise. Prophecy declared this to be a sign of the last days ; but Peter does not say that for

him and the readers these are future days. In fact,
inasmuch as he uses direct discourse in quoting the scoffers,
—employing language which is apparently reproduced
from life (iii. 4, n. 5),—and inasmuch as he describes the
ignorance to which this insolent language is due in the
present tense (iii. 5), it is clear that he regards this prediction as already fulfilled in definite persons and events
existing in the present. The time which to him is present
is the last time (cf. 1 John ii. 18 ; Jas. v. 3, 7–9). But
since, as has been shown (above, p. 226), these scoffers,
whose scornful language concerning the parousia was only
one of their characteristics, are not different from the
libertines, we know also that Peter became acquainted
with them among the Gentile Christian Churches outside
the circle of his readers. That they, too, would make
their way to the readers, he does not need to repeat. The
earnest effort to guard his people against the treacherous
power of these particular ideas of the false teachers (iii.
8–13), shows that Peter did not expect the appearance
among them of harmful ideas of every kind, but of false
teachers of a definite character, who were both libertines
and despisers of prophecy. This, however, does not
exclude the possibility that those among whom they find
entrance will appropriate in some cases one, in other
instances the other side of their doctrine and view of the
world, and thus give rise to various movements or parties,
all of which would be harmful (ii. 1).

Although in this letter, as in the earlier one to which
reference is made in iii. 1, Peter may have met a pressing
need, and fulfilled his obligation to give to the Churches,
to which he along with others once brought the gospel,
the benefit of his fatherly instruction by writing to them
now from a distance, at the same time the occasion for
letters such as this and the earlier one like it, was the
experiences he had recently had in Churches outside that
were for the most part Gentile Christian. There he saw

the representatives of a dangerous tendency gaining an influence both by teaching and example,—a tendency which he, without being himself a prophet, but simply under the influence of prophecy as it existed in the Church, foresaw would increase in power and make its way into the Jewish Christian Church.

Whether it is really Peter who utters this warning against such a movement, or someone in the second century, who, under the mask of Peter as a prophet, describes what had actually taken place since Peter's time, cannot be decided until after the Epistle of Jude, which contains references to similar phenomena, has been investigated.

1. (P. 222.) Καθαρισμός, i. 9, cannot mean, as Spitta supposes, continuous self-purification, for the reason that this has not been forgotten (λήθην λαβόντες) by the persons here described, but left off by them at the present time. Moreover, τὰ πάλαι ἁμαρτήματα (אAK, etc.) are not the sinful habits formed before their conversion and not yet entirely overcome, which might possibly be called παλαιαὶ ἁμαρτίαι (cf. 1 Cor. v. 7 ; Rom. vi. 6, vii. 6 ; Eph. iv. 22), but their sins committed aforetime (Rom. iii. 25 ; Heb. ix. 15 ; cf. 1 Pet. i. 14, iv. 3 ; Eph. ii. 2 ; Justin, *Apol.* i. 61, τὰ προημαρτημένα ; Hermas, *Vis.* i. 3. 1 ; *Mand.* iv. 3. 3 ; *Sim.* viii. 11. 3). Accordingly, καθαρισμός can mean only the purification from the guilt of sin, which Christians experience once for all (Mark i. 44 ; Heb. i. 3) when they are called and chosen (2 Pet. i. 10), and are cleansed in baptism (1 Cor. vi. 11 ; Eph. v. 26 ; 1 Pet. i. 2 ; Heb. x. 22 ; Acts xxii. 16). Also in 2 Pet. ii. 20–22, where the word καθαρισμός is not found, the figurative λουσαμένη, ver. 22, refers to the washing of baptism, and the ἀποφυγόντες τὰ μιάσματα τοῦ κόσμου, ver. 20, to the salvation from the curse of sin which takes place once for all and accompanies baptism.

2. (P. 224.) As in the case of ἑτεροδιδάσκαλος (above, p. 126 f.), so in the case of ψευδοπροφήτης and ψευδοδιδάσκαλος (ii. 1), it is not permissible to separate the adjective from the verb (διδάσκειν, προφητεύειν), construing ψεῦδος, ψεύδη, as objects of the verbal idea. Analogies, such as ψευδάδελφος (Gal. ii. 4 ; 2 Cor. xi. 26), ψευδαπόστολος (2 Cor. xi. 13), ψευδόχριστος (Mark xiii. 22), absolutely determine the meaning. Even a ψευδομάρτυς is not so called because he makes false statements, but because he pretends to have seen or heard something which he has not seen or heard (Matt. xxvi. 60 ; cf. Acts vi. 11). The LXX does not read ψευδοπροφήτης in Isa. ix. 14 (" The prophet who teaches lies "), but does use it in Jer. vi. 13, xxvii. 9, xxviii. 1, xxix. 1, 8, Zech. xiii. 2, where the original text has simply נביא, the context making it clear that this title is wrongly borne. αἱρέσεις is here translated "separatist tendencies " (*Sonderrichtungen*), with Hofmann, vii. 2. 46, in order by the use of this ambiguous term to leave it undecided whether the word

is here used in the sense of sects, parties, as in Acts v. 17, xv. 5, xxiv. 5, 14,
1 Cor. xi. 19, Gal. v. 20, or in the sense of a general view contrary to Christianity, as possibly in Ign. *Trall.* vi. 1 ; *Eph.* vi. 2. In opposition to Spitta
(120 f.), it is to be remarked that αἵρεσις never means a single view or
tenet along with which as many other tenets as one chooses may be held (in
the literature of the ancient Church even the entire system of a Marcion or of
an Arius was regularly regarded as only a single heresy), and that in its
Christian usage αἵρεσις is never a neutral idea which comes to have a bad
sense only by the addition of some such word as ἀπωλείας,—for the following reasons : (1) Ignatius is not the first to use this word in a bad sense as
applying to conditions among Christians ; it is so used in 1 Cor. xi. 19 ; Gal.
v. 20 ; Tit. iii. 10. (2) According to the view of the apostolic age and of the
ancient Church,—and this is the basis of the ecclesiastical usage of the word,—
the Christian was not at liberty arbitrarily to choose from among existing
views and tendencies one that pleased him, but was bound to obey the gospel
as the truth. With regard to the much-disputed construction of ii. 1, it
may at the outset be considered certain that we cannot, with Spitta (123 ff.),
take the words καὶ—ἀρνούμενοι, ἐπάγοντες—ἀπώλειαν as referring to the O.T.
false prophets. After the important statement about the pseudo-Christian
teachers, it stands to reason that, in order to refer back to the O.T. prophets,
ἐκείνοι would be necessary. Further, there is nothing to explain the use of
the present participles, ἀρνούμενοι, ἐπάγοντες, instead of the aorists, which the
sense would require, nor to account for the break in the construction of the
sentence, which in this case it would be necessary to assume. Consistency
would require that also αὐτῶν (ver. 2) be taken to refer to the O.T. false
prophets, and the πολλοί, who are at least similar to the spurious teachers
of ver. 1,—so far as by Spitta's own confession, 128, they teach in a harmful
manner within the Church, ver. 3,—would be docile followers of the O.T. false
prophets,—for this is the relation expressed by ἐξακολουθήσουσιν, ver. 2 (cf. i.
16, ii. 15),—and not that the O.T. false prophets were merely types of the
immorality and the fate of these teachers. As a matter of fact, however, there
is very little to be learned from the O.T. about the teaching and conduct of
the false prophets, and nothing at all with regard to their final destiny. At
the latter point the lack is not supplied by the threat of destruction in Deut.
xiii. 2–6—a passage which Spitta thinks (126) Peter here had in mind ; indeed,
throughout the description of phenomena within the Church, which is given
us in 2 Pet. ii.–iii., there is no reference to the case under discussion in Deut.
xiii. 2–6, namely, betrayal into idolatry by a false prophet. Balaam, whose
followers the false Christians and teachers here referred to are declared to be
(ii. 15), was not a false prophet from among the people (ii. 1), but a heathen.
Neither in the LXX nor by Peter is he called a false prophet, but only a
prophet who sinned and led others into sin. Of his end (Num. xxxi. 8) Peter
makes no mention. If Peter had had a substantive at his command, such as
ἀρνηταί or ἀπαρνηταί, and had used this or προδόται instead of ἀρνούμενοι,
no one would find him obscure when he says : " Among you also there shall
be false teachers, who shall bring in destructive heresies, and deniers of the
Lord that bought them, who bring upon themselves swift destruction " (cf.
the co-ordination of participles, substantives, and adjectives in Rom. i. 29–31).
Just as ψευδοδιδάσκαλοι has dependent upon it the relative clause, so ἀρνούμενοι

governs the qualifying participial phrase that follows it. But there are not two different classes of persons described, only a double characterisation of one and the same class; although, of course, it is possible that in some individuals in this class teaching is more prominent, while the connection of others with the movement is mainly through their feelings and manner of life. This was true of the "Scribes and Pharisees" (Matt. v. 20). Nor is there any reason to complain about the lack of logical order in the passage. We have the statement about the disciples whom these teachers will gain followed by the relative clause of ver. 2b, which is logically independent, and then the discourse returns in an entirely natural way to the principal subject, namely, the ψευδοδιδάσκαλοι, the thought of whom is kept in mind by the use of αὐτῶν in ver. 2. In ver. 2, Peter speaks quite generally of a large following which these teachers will secure (πολλοί without ὑμῶν or ἐξ ὑμῶν); in ver. 3 he states how these same persons will endeavour to gain an entrance among the readers. Nor does it seem to the writer to be to the point to talk as Spitta does (122 f.) about the "logical folly" of putting what was intended from the start to be the principal statement into the comparative sentence, ὡς καὶ ἐν ὑμῖν κτλ. (ver. 1b); while the existence of false prophets in Israel, which is intended to be only an analogy, is expressed in the principal clause (ver. 1a). It is clear on any interpretation that not only in the words ὡς—ἀπωλείας, but also in ii. 2–22, the subject under discussion is not the false prophets of the O.T., but the analogous phenomena within Christianity. It is known that the Greek language can add in the form of a relative clause a logically independent and even strongly emphatic statement, which we express more clearly by the use of "and" and a demonstrative sentence (cf Rom. ii. 29, iii. 8; Gal. ii. 10; Acts xiii. 43, and all three of the relative clauses in 2 Pet. ii. 1–3; Kühner-Gerth, ii. 433 f.; A. Buttmann, 243 [Eng. trans. 282 f.]). So not infrequently ὡς or ὡς καί is equivalent to "and so" (cf. Kühner-Gerth, ii. 431, A. 4). The phrase "and so does Paul also in all his letters," in 2 Pet. iii. 16, is an independent statement concerning which more is said below. After the statements in i. 19–20, especially the last sentence of which might seem to imply that all prophecy in the O.T. era was inspired by the Holy Spirit, it was quite natural to state definitely that there were also false prophets in Israel. This would be the case even if there were no intention of making further mention of them, but simply of preparing the way for the further statement that in the realm of Christian revelation, besides the apostles whose message was true, there are and will continue to be false teachers against whom the Churches must be on their guard. In the case of the "prophetic word," a safeguard against error is found in the fact that it is only the messages of the true prophets of olden time which are found in Scripture (γραφῆς, i. 20; cf. Rom. i. 2), not those of the false prophets against whom the true prophets had to contend. In the realm of Christian teaching this was not yet true at the time when 2 Pet. was written. A Christian literature, produced by the true witnesses of Christ, was only in process of formation (i. 12–15, iii. 15, 16). This made it all the more necessary to remind the readers, that as there were false prophets in Israel, so there are or will be also false teachers in the Christian Church. If all that follows the first mention of the ψευδοδιδάσκαλοι refers to these persons, ὁ ἀγοράσας αὐτοὺς δεσπότης naturally refers to Christ (cf. Jude 4, and the use of the word δεσποσύνοι tα designate the relatives of Jesus, a manner of speech common in Palestine, Eus. *H. E.* i. 7. 14). For ἀγοράζειν, cf. 1 Cor. vi. 20, vii. 23—the latter passage in its context. They are legally "Slaves of Christ" (cf. 2 Pet. i. 1).

3. (Pp. 225, 229.) By the "Way of Balaam," as contrasted with the "Straight way" (ii. 15), the "Way of ϊruth" (ii. 2), and the "Way of righteousness"· (ii. 21), must be meant all that is recorded concerning his deeds in Num. xxii. 5–xxiv. 25, including the evil counsel he gave in Num. xxxi. 16 (cf. xxv. 1 f., 18), which in Rev. ii. 14 is called the "Teaching of Balaam"; cf. Didymus *in Jud.* 11 (Migne, 39, 1816). But it is to be observed that while the people did come to the point where they worshipped the gods of the Moabites (Num. xxv. 2 f., 5), it is always the unchastity connected with the feast that stands in the foreground (xxv. 1, 6–18, xxxi. 15 f., especially in Jos. *Ant.* iv. 6. 6–13). Consequently in Rev. ii. 14, 20, also the reference is not to idolatry, but to participation in idolatrous feasts and unchastity. In 2 Pet. the analogy seems to be even more limited. The reference is neither to the attendance upon idolatrous feasts nor to idolatrous worship. On the contrary, it is the meals eaten by Christians in connection with their worship in which the followers of Balaam take part at least with unchaste thought and looks (so according to ii. 13 f., especially if the correct reading in this passage be ἐντρυφῶντες ἐν ταῖς ἀγάπαις αὐτῶν, συνευωχούμενοι ὀφθαλμοὺς ἔχοντες κτλ.). If ἀγάπαις is to be accepted as the correct reading of Jude 12 on account of the close relationship of the two Epistles, it may be regarded almost certainly as the correct reading in 2 Pet. ii. 13; for ἀπάταις, which is more strongly attested here than in Jude 12, does not have the appearance of being, and certainly is not, an isolated paronomasia for love-feasts, but is a change made by a copyist who thought that he was correcting an error; and this is so whether the word stood in the original which Jude had before him, or was an alteration made by the author of 2 Pet. of the ἀγάπαις which he found in Jude; see above, p. 211, n. 1. Tischendorf's apparatus is misleading, in that it says nothing about the ὑμῖν after συνευωχούμενοι. It is not found in the earliest translations of the Syrians (S²), Egyptians (Sahidic Version, Woide-Ford, p. 213), and Latins (*Speculum pseudo-Augustini*, 640. 9; the pseudo-Cyprian *de Singularitate clericorum*, 28; unfortunately this part of the Palimps. Flor. is wanting), and is to be omitted here as in Jude 12 on the ground that it is an addition made to ϲυνευω-χούμενοι, being apparently required by the συν. In Jude 12 it is unnecessary after ἐν ταῖς ἀγάπαις ὑμῶν, because in thought everyone supplies ὑμῖν. The consequence is that the reading is much less strongly attested than in 2 Pet. ii. 13. But here also it can be omitted as unnecessary, since συνευωχεῖσθαι does not always necessarily mean "To feast with others," but can also signify, especially with a plural subject, "To feast with one another"; cf. συσσιτεῖν, συσσιτία, τὰ συσσίτια, or συμπίνειν παρά τινι, to take part in a symposium at the home of another (Xen. *Cyrop.* v. 2. 28). This is the meaning here, and ὑμῖν does not harmonise with ταῖς ἀγάπαις αὐτῶν, although the two are connected in B. This addition once accepted into the text must have helped to give currency to the reading ταῖς ἀπάταις αὐτῶν, if, indeed, it did not produce it. On the other hand, where ἀγάπαις was retained, αὐτῶν, which is undoubtedly genuine, was sometimes omitted, because it did not harmonise

with ὑμῖν, as, *e.g.* in Cod. Amiat. of the Vulgate. Peter says concerning these false teachers, these "spots and blemishes" of Christianity, these "Children of the curse": "they revel at their love-feasts, hold their banquets or common carousals with eyes full of adulterous desire, and entice the unwary with hearts practised in covetousness and hardened by it." Nothing is said which implies that unchastity itself was practised at these love-feasts. This enticement was not, as the accompanying characterisation shows, a direct temptation to impure actions, but a temptation to accept libertine principles (cf. ii. 3, 19). It would also be strange to speak only of lustful looks, and in a connection like this not so much as hint at what was worst in the conduct of these persons. But this leaves in full force the charge of sinful living, even of unnatural vices (above, p. 224 f.). The love-feasts are not described as meals eaten in company by an entire Church, but as meals eaten by the libertines. From this passage alone it might be inferred that these meals and their name were an invention of these persons, and that Peter rejects both the thing and the name, as does Clemens Alexandrinus (*Pæd.* ii. §§ 4–7 ; *Strom.* iii. §§ 10, 11, vii. § 98). But this view is made impossible by Jude 12, and by ecclesiastical usage elsewhere from Ignatius on (cf. *PRE*,[3] i. 234 ff.). But we also learn from Ignatius that, as early as the beginning of the second century, the meals (love-feasts) which ended with the Eucharist were not always eaten by the whole Church together under the direction of the officers of the Church, but that certain persons who did not accept the common faith of the Church availed themselves of this freedom and held private love-feasts (*ad Smyrneos*, vii.–ix. ; *ad Philadelphenos*, iv. ; cf. the writer's *Ignatius*, 342 f., 347 f., 363 f.).

4. (P. 230.) When iii. 3 is joined with iii. 1, 2, the possibility is not excluded that Peter had said something similar to iii. 3–7 in his earlier letter. But even in that case, especially if the form of the earlier communication is to some extent here retained, Peter does not himself prophesy anything distinctly new. Spitta (228–233) goes too far when he claims that because what is said in iii. 3 ff. has no sufficient basis in the preceding portion of 2 Pet., the earlier Epistle of Peter must have been "mainly eschatological in its contents," containing a reference to the scoffers of the last age. The statement concerning the essential contents and purpose of the two letters applies to what follows as well as to what precedes (above, p. 210, n. 1) ; while the break in the construction, by the use of the nominative γινώσκοντες, which renders the clause more independent, makes it all the more impossible to infer from the connection of iii. 3 with the μνησθῆναι of iii. 2, by the use of the word γινώσκοντες, that iii. 3–4 or iii. 3–7 is a recapitulation either of the preceding parts of 2 Pet. or of Peter's lost letter. μνησθῆναι introduces not an elaborate reminder of statements which have already been made, but an independent truth which needs to be impressed upon the readers' minds, only not a truth which needs to be preached to them as something entirely new. Cf. the parallel passages, above, p. 230.

5. (P. 231.) We should understand the actual language of the scoffers in iii. 4 better if they were quoted more often. Spitta (233) is right in rejecting the suggestion of Bengel, Hofmann, and others, that αὐτοῦ expresses irreverence on the part of the persons speaking. In this regard the expression is not different from the ἐκεῖνος of the apostles (above, p. 215 f.) and the αὐτός of

the Pythagoreans (Scholium on Aristophanes, *The Clouds*, 195, ed. Dindorf, i. 196). These persons do speak contemptuously of the devil and his servants (ii. 10–12 ; above, p. 225 f.), besides indulging in other extravagant language (ii. 18); but it is altogether unlikely that these clever teachers of Christianity would have spoken disrespectfully of Christ Himself or of God. That, however, the reference is to Christ and not to God, becomes all the more certain if it be held that the persons here speaking are Gentile Christians. The question, "Where is the promise of its coming?" arose simply in connection with the parousia, concerning which Jesus had spoken in a manner implying that His contemporaries would experience it (Matt xxiv. 34 ; Mark xiii. 30 ; Luke xxi. 32 ; Matt. xvi. 28 ; Mark ix. 1 ; Luke ix. 27). This determines also the meaning of οἱ πατέρες. Even if this word alone or with ἡμῶν can mean all the forebears of the persons speaking,—as, *e.g.* in the case of Jesus, the Israelites of the ancient dispensation (Heb. i. 1 = Matt. xxiii. 30),—the idea that these could or were expected to experience the parousia of Jesus is entirely incongruous. Only the immediate ancestors of the scoffers, and the men of that generation,—naturally only those of them who were at the same time members of the Church to which Christ promised His parousia,—could have expected, and actually did expect, to live until the parousia. The difference between the view of Spitta, who thinks that this word should be limited to the actual fathers of the scoffers (237), and that of the others, who think that it refers to all the first generation of Christians, is negligible. The absence of a ἡμῶν, and the unlikelihood that the false teachers consisted exclusively of the children of Christian parents, which even in the second century would have been a rare coincidence, favour the latter view. The older generation, which expected to live to share in the parousia, has passed away, and still it does not come ; all remains as it was in former generations. In view of this fact, the younger generation throws the entire promise overboard. It would imply a strange misunderstanding of the natural use of language in all ages to claim that before such an expression as this could be used, the first Christian generation must have entirely disappeared. What Christian in the second century, writing a letter in Peter's name, would not have known that the Apostle John, for example, outlived Peter, and have realised that Peter himself, in whose name he here speaks, was one of the πατέρες, all of whom are supposed to have died when 2 Pet. was written! As one after another of these ἀρχαῖοι μαθηταί (Acts xxi. 16) passed away without having had fulfilled the hope of living to see the parousia (Acts vii. 60, xii. 2 ; 1 Cor. xv. 6, xi. 30 ; 1 Thess. iv. 13 , it was extremely natural to declare the entire expectation a dream. The expression used is an unnatural hyperbole only if the letter purports to have been written between the years 30 and 50. If, on the other hand, it is to be referred to the years between 60 and 63, then an entire generation (from thirty to thirty-three years) had elapsed since Jesus had prophesied His parousia. This date is confirmed by the present passage. The difficulty arising from the fact that a double *terminus a quo* is given (ἀφ' ἧς . . . ἀπ' ἀρχῆς κτίσεως, cf. the repeated ἕως, Matt. v. 18), cannot be got rid of by assuming with Spitta (235) that the construction of the first ἀπό is pregnant (prior to which [*sc.* parousia], *i.e.* "before the coming of which, the fathers fell asleep"). This is evident for the following reasons : (1) there are no really analogous examples in the N.T. (cf. also the writer's *Hirt des Hermas* 490); (2) ἀφ' ἧς (1 Macc. i. 11 ; Acts xxiv. 11 ; Hermas, *Sim.* viii. 1, 4, vi. 6 ; cf. Acts xx. 18) is a frequent ellipsis for ἀφ' ἧς ἡμέρας (Col. i. 6, 9), or for ἀφ' οὗ (Ex. v. 23 ; Josh. xiv. 10 ; Luke xiii. 25, xxiv. 21). Apart from the above consideration is also the fact (3) that γάρ following ἀφ' ἧς would be impossible if it introduced a real relative clause, and if the phrase were not rather equivalent to ἀπ' ἐκείνης (ἡμέρας) ᾗ. The language used is very much compressed, but its meaning can hardly be mistaken : " Since the fathers fell asleep, (the expected world revolution has not taken place any more than during their lifetime, but) all remains (just as it was) from the beginning of the creation."

§ 43. EPISTLE OF JUDE.

The author of this Epistle introduces himself to the readers as " Jude, a servant of Jesus Christ, but brother of James." The order and connection of the two designations which he adds to the name show that the second of these additions was not a term in common use, and it might seem as if it were necessary in order to distinguish this Jude from numerous other persons bearing the same name (n. 1). But even if it were necessary to make such distinction, that is not the purpose of the addition here. For if this were the meaning, ἀδελφὸς ᾽Ιακώβου, which in this case could hardly have the article omitted before it (cf. Mark iii. 17, v. 37 ; John vi. 8 ; Acts xii. 2 ; Gal. i. 19), would necessarily stand directly after the name, and could not be placed in such evident contrast to the preceding designation of the writer as a Christian by a δέ. This contrast is very peculiar, since kinship with a Christian of whatever name does not stand in contrast to the relationship of service to Jesus, nor does the idea of kinship help to define the same (but cf. Tit. i. 1 ; above, p. 47). Even the earliest interpreters saw correctly that the one here speaking might have called himself a brother of some greater person, but preferred to designate himself his servant, using the title brother ; thus set free, as it were, to indicate his relationship to James (n. 2). Jude was one of the brothers of the Lord, who, like Peter and other apostles, laboured in

the year 57 as preachers of the gospel in various places
(1 Cor. ix. 5 ; Matt. xiii. 55 ; Mark vi. 3 ; John vii. 3–8 ;
Acts i. 14 ; vol. i. p. 105).   If reference to a brother instead of a father, in order to distinguish one from a companion of the same name, is unusual, and presupposes
great pre-eminence on the part of the brother in question,
such pre-eminence obtains peculiarly in the present instance, where James is mentioned for an entirely different
purpose.   He can be no other than the distinguished
James, who since the death of the son of Zebedee had
been regularly called simply James (Acts xii. 17, xv. 13,
xxi. 18 ; Gal. ii. 9, 12 ; 1 Cor. xv. 7), and who himself
uses this name only at the beginning of his letter, not
calling himself a brother of the Lord, as others called
him (Gal. i. 19), but a servant of God and of Christ.
Just as the absence of the apostolic title at the beginning
of James, a letter addressed to the entire Church of
the time, proves that the James who wrote it was not
an apostle, so the similar omission at the beginning of
Jude, which is also intended for a large circle of readers,
proves that this Jude was not an apostle.   This, if
anywhere, was the appropriate place for such mention,
and in the letters of Peter and Paul it regularly occurs
here at the beginning.   The conclusion thus drawn from
Jude 1 is confirmed by Jude 17 ; for, although the mere
mention of the apostles cannot of itself prove that the
person speaking is not an apostle (above, p. 218, n. 7),
nevertheless the solemn expression, " The apostles of our
Lord Jesus Christ," which is without parallel, would sound
very unnatural if spoken by an apostle.   In a passage
which seems to resemble this (Eph. iii. 5), Paul, whose
position was a peculiar one, does not identify himself with
the apostles (vol. i. p. 506 f.).   And there is nothing to suggest that Jude was one of the personal disciples of Jesus,
a fact so strongly emphasised by the writer of 2 Peter,
and at least not concealed by the writer of 1 Peter.

Of the history of Jude's life we know practically nothing. From Matt. xiii. 55, where he is mentioned last among the brothers of Jesus, and from Mark vi. 3, where his name occupies the place next to the last, it may possibly be inferred that he is the youngest brother of Jesus, or at least one of the younger brothers. In their relation to Jesus the development of all the brothers seems to have been the same (John vii. 3–8 ; Acts i. 14). There is no need to repeat here what has been said concerning James in this respect (vol. i. p. 105). While James, the unmarried ascetic, did not leave Jerusalem and the temple, and so is certainly not included among those mentioned in 1 Cor. ix. 5, Jude was one of the brothers of Jesus here mentioned, who, like Peter and other apostles, made preaching tours accompanied by their wives. Naturally, in the case of Jude as in the case of the older apostles, these tours were confined to the "cities of Israel" (Matt. x. 23 ; Gal. ii. 9 ; above, p. 208). If he was born several years later than Jesus, say somewhere near the tenth year of our era, he may have survived the destruction of Jerusalem a number of years. Hegesippus informs us that toward the end of the reign of Domitian, therefore about the year 95, two grandsons of Jude, who made their living by farming, were brought before the emperor charged with being descendants of David, and Christians. He says, moreover, that these charges were made by certain heretics. According to the same writer, they afterwards occupied a prominent place in the Church of Palestine until some time in the reign of Trajan (98–117), as did also the aged Simeon, a cousin of Jesus and of their grandfather Jude, who is mentioned as the second bishop of Jerusalem (Eus. *H. E.* iii. 19 f., 32. 5 f. ; cf. *Forsch.* vi. 238 ff.). The fact that Jude calls himself a brother of James shows that he is addressing Christians, among whom the latter was highly esteemed, or, if he was no longer living, among whom his memory was sacredly revered. Especially, if the latter were the case, the manner in which Jude mentions himself is natural. The lips of the leader so highly honoured in the Jewish Christian Church are sealed; a part of his duty, at least, is inherited by his brother, while another part falls to his cousin Simeon.

Notwithstanding the meagreness of the tradition concerning the brothers of Jesus, it is to be assumed that Jude had not laboured outside of the Jewish Christian world. There are no indications of it in his letter, such as are so abundant in 1 Peter. The designation of the readers would apply to the entire Church, or to any particular part of it; but there is not a single word to indicate that Jude was under necessity of first introducing himself to his readers, or of proving his right to address them. Like James, he addresses them as a teacher whom they are accustomed to hear. The verse immediately following (3) also shows that the relation in which the author stood to the readers was not created by this brief letter. He was already seriously considering, or had actually begun, writing to them concerning their common salvation, when conditions arose which necessitated the sending of this letter (n. 3). The purpose of his present letter he declares to be a summons to contend for the faith delivered to the saints once for all,—a description which corresponds to the contents of the Epistle. The fact that the readers' faith was imperilled at this time, what it was that imperilled it, and why Jude thought it necessary to write this brief letter at once, are indicated in ver. 4, and the exhortation that follows in vv. 5–23. The manner in which the faith for which they are to contend is characterised, indicates that this faith is not one thing to-day and another to-morrow, but a practically unalterable summary of religious convictions and teachings which has been communicated once for all to the Church, either by its Lord and Master, or by the preachers of the gospel (cf. Heb. xiii. 7–9, i. 1, ii. 3). This implies that, for the purposes of this letter, it is not necessary to expound and establish this faith anew. On the other hand, it would seem as if the writing, the preparation of which Jude had in mind when he received the information or made the observations which necessitated the preparation of this letter, was meant to be more didactic in character and of greater scope than the present one,—if we may judge from the statement of its subject, which, it must be admitted, is very general (περὶ τῆς κοινῆς ἡμῶν σωτηρίας). The mere fact that γράφειν ὑμῖν is used does not justify the assumption that this expression, like γράψαι ὑμῖν, refers to a letter. It does imply that the writing in question was intended for the readers, but beyond this it can refer to a work consisting of a number of parts quite as well as to a letter (cf. Luke i. 3). The expression certainly does not permit us to assume that Jude was about to address to the readers a didactic communication for which there was no special occasion, when the circumstances arose which led him to give his communication a different and more specialised content than it would otherwise have had. Rather is this brief letter to be taken as a temporary substitute for the more extended writing which he was intending to dedicate to the readers. Whether Jude ever carried out his intention of writing such a work, temporarily interfered with, or completed the work already begun, we do not know, any more than we know whether Peter carried out the similar intention expressed in 2 Pet. i. 15 (above, p. 199 f.). No writing has come down to us which could pass as the writing of Jude here referred to, or which might claim to be such a work.

Seeing that Jude had had in mind for some time the composition of a doctrinal work for the benefit of the readers, and now felt constrained by the danger threatening them to write this letter, it follows that he must have come in contact with them in his journeys as an evangelist

(1 Cor. ix. 5), and since then had kept them in mind Consequently he had the information which seemed tc him to necessitate the writing of a letter. Naturally, the readers themselves were in possession of the same facts. Nothing that Jude says implies that he is announcing new facts. On the contrary, assuming that the readers know what and whom he means, he characterises and condemns certain persons who have crept in among them and live in their midst (vv. 4, 12, 19). He calls them godless persons who pervert the grace of God into immorality, and deny the Christians' only Master and Lord, Jesus Christ (ver. 4). The first of these charges presupposes a teaching in which the fact that the Christians are under grace is used to justify an immoral life (n. 4). Since these persons claimed to be Christians, the latter charge must mean that they separated them-selves from Christ as Lord by their disobedience, denying Him, not in name, but in fact, by living a life inconsistent with the confession of Him (cf. Tit. i. 16; 2 Pet. ii. 1; above, p. 224 f.). They are described with greater detail in vv. 10–13, 16, 18, 19.

In the first place, it is everywhere assumed that they are outwardly members of the Church. They are like fruit trees in late autumn, when all the trees are bare; like good trees, they have had their spring, when possibly they bore blossoms, and a summer, when they could have borne fruit; but they have proved to be unfruitful, and the gardener has torn them up with their roots (ver. 12). If they have died twice, then once they must have been called from death to life (Eph. ii. 1, 5; Col. ii. 13; John v. 24), and have sunk back again into a state of death. They take part in the love-feasts of the readers as if they had a right to do so, and indeed this right cannot be contested outwardly on the ground that they are not members of the Church (ver. 12, n. 5 at end). Nor does the fact that they create divisions, while

lacking the Holy Spirit, and being still in bondage to
their own natural life (ver. 19, n. 6), argue against the
possibility of their regarding themselves as members of
the Church; it seems rather to indicate that they considered themselves pre - eminently men of the Spirit,
and made invidious distinctions between themselves and
ordinary Christians, which of itself indicates their separatist tendencies. It is this *second characteristic* which
is presupposed when among other things it is said
that they are followers of Korah, who with two hundred
and fifty prominent members of the congregation rebelled
against the authorities and the leaders of Israel whom
God had called, claiming that the entire congregation,
including themselves, were holy as well as Aaron, and
that God dwelt not simply with those who were in official
position, but with all the members of the congregation
(ver. 11 ; cf. Num. xvi. 2 f. with Num. xi. 16 f., 24–29 ;
1 Cor. xiv. 25). The comparison would be meaningless
unless the libertines of whom Jude is speaking had shown
themselves insubordinate to the heads of the Church, on
the ground that the whole Church was holy and in
possession of the Spirit. Following the common practice
of demagogues in every age, under the guise of an appeal
to the rights of all, they asserted their right to speak,
notwithstanding the regularly constituted order of the
Church, drawing comparisons between themselves, as
representatives of public spirit, and the spiritless officers
of the Church with the members of the Church who
blindly followed their authority. Moreover, the words
γογγυσταὶ μεμψίμοιροι, which are genuine only in ver. 16,
but at an early date were either added to ver. 11 or
inserted in ver. 12, being thus brought into direct connection with the name of Korah, serve in fact to recall
the fact that Korah and his company, dissatisfied with
their subordinate position, murmured against Aaron, and
against Moses also (Num. xvi. 11), all the more bitterly

because they chafed under the deprivations necessitated
by their departure from Egypt (Num. xvi. 13 f., xiv. 2,
27, 37 ; Ex. xvi. 2 f., xvii. 3). For similar reasons the
persons whom Jude describes are discontented murmurers
who complain of their fate. Dissatisfied with the renuncia-
tions which their Christian confession has compelled them
to make, and with the position in the Churches which has
fallen to their lot,—much lower than they feel they ought
to have,—they complain against the heads of the Church
(n. 5). Along with this murmuring, as in the case of
Korah and his companions and wherever elsewhere in the
Church similar conditions prevailed (cf. 1 Cor. x. 6, 10),
there went a longing for the comforts of life enjoyed
before redemption, and an actual falling back into the
pre-Christian life. This is the *third feature* in the
description of these persons. They walk according to
their wicked lusts (vv. 16, 18). This is evident from the
manner in which they conduct themselves at the love-
feasts (ver. 12). Without any reverence for the sacredness of these meals, they treat them as banquets, and
think only of securing for themselves the largest possible share of food and drink. There is even less indication than in 2 Pet. ii. 13 f. (above, p. 235) that they
made these meals an occasion for the practice of unchastity.
Indeed, that this was not the case is rendered certain by
the fact that Jude speaks of the love-feasts of the readers
(ἐν ταῖς ἀγάπαις ὑμῶν, ver. 12) ; for he nowhere charges
against them an intimacy with these wicked persons, or
a participation in their sins. But the readers, who allow
them to take part in their love-feasts, need to know that
the persons who sit with them at the table of the Lord
are polluted, and so take part in the love-feasts, not with
pure hearts, but with unchaste feelings which are manifest
in their looks (cf. 2 Pet. ii. 14). Jude does charge them
with unnatural sins when he compares the punishment
that awaits them with the punishment of the angels who

committed sins of the flesh and the destruction of Sodom and Gomorrah, describing the sins of these angels and cities much more clearly than is done in 2 Pet. ii. 4–10 (ver. 6 f.), and says expressly that the false Christians who have crept in among the readers corrupt the flesh in the same manner (ver. 8). Ver. 23 also indicates the practice of unnatural vice.

A *fourth characteristic* of these persons is their presumptuous talk (ver. 16), not only against the authority and heads of the Church, but even against God (ver. 15). They also set aside what should be recognised by men as a power superior to themselves, and blaspheme exalted spirits (ver. 8),—a term which, it seems natural to suppose from the following verse, includes also evil spirits. Since this conduct of theirs is associated directly with their impurity, it is to be assumed that they endeavoured to justify their unchaste conduct by a theory about the harmless character of evil spirits, or even by contemptuous remarks about the good angels, out of regard to whom other Christians felt under obligation to conduct themselves with especial modesty (1 Cor. xi. 10). The fact that all real knowledge of the spirits which they blaspheme is denied (ver. 10 ; see above, p. 225 f.), and that their blasphemies as well as their unchaste conduct are associated with visions and dreams (ver. 8), would indicate that they claimed to possess knowledge concerning the spirit world. From the single word ἐνυπνιαζόμενοι it is impossible to determine whether they claimed to have, through dream-visions, a deep insight into the spirit worlds, or whether Jude simply calls their confused ideas dreams. Even less certainly does this one word stamp them as false prophets ; nor does the reference to Balaam (ver. 11) prove them to be such ; for neither here nor in 2 Peter, nor in the O.T. is he called a false prophet (see above, p. 233). This reference serves rather to bring before us a *fifth characteristic* of these sinners. When it is said that for the sake of gain they gave themselves to the πλάνη of Balaam, the sin referred to cannot consist simply in expressions of their covetousness, but must be some activity in which for the sake of gain they engage with eagerness and all their strength. Since, now, in the O.T. Balaam is represented not as a man who was led or fell into error, but as one who gave treacherous counsel and thereby led the members of the Church of God into unchastity (above, pp. 225, 235), πλάνη cannot be taken in a passive, but only in an active sense (n. 7). At the same time, it is not said that in giving themselves up to the practice of heathen unchastity, as in fact they had done, though not for the sake of reward, these libertines had fallen victims to the seduction of Balaam, or to any seduction that can be compared to Balaam's counsel; but Balaam himself is their prototype, both in his πλάνος and in his acceptance of reward. It follows, therefore, as indicated in ver. 4 (above, p. 233 f.), that these persons are *teachers*, who endeavour to lead the members of the Church astray, not simply by their bad example, for which they would receive no reward, but by an exposition of their libertine theories designed to induce them to adopt the same views and indulge in the same practices, for which teaching they accept compensation (cf. 2 Pet. ii. 3, 14; above, p. 225; Tit. i. 11; 1 Tim. vi. 5; above, p. 101). The same situation is indicated in ver. 16. Their murmuring against the established order of the Church and its chosen leaders, and their presumptuous words, in which not even the holy God and superhuman spirits are spared, and which are also made to serve the purposes of their immorality, are not confined to their own circle, but are flaunted before such as have not yet been betrayed. They prefer to talk to persons who are prominent and rich, because of the material benefit which will accrue to them if they are successful in convincing such members of the Church. That they had already succeeded in gaining some following among the

readers through their teaching, is shown by the conclusion
of the letter. While it is true that here also, ver. 20 ff.,
the readers whom Jude expects to reach by his letter are
distinguished from the false teachers just as sharply as at
the beginning, still there are members of the Church who,
in varying degrees, have yielded to temptation, and are
commended to the pastoral care of the readers. There
are some who doubt, who have not decisively rejected the
pseudo-Christian teaching, but consider its pros and cons.
These the readers are to convince of the folly of their
hesitation, and of the untruth of the teaching so dangerous
to them. There are also some who have been scathed
by the fire of destruction, but can still be rescued.
Finally, there are those who must be treated with mingled
fear and sympathy; their unclean sins are to be hated
and shunned carefully, but they themselves are to be
shown that undeserved mercy which everyone himself
hopes to receive at the hands of the Lord Christ in the
day of judgment (vv. 21–23, n. 8).

A *sixth feature* in the description of these seducers is
the representation of their appearance in the present as
the fulfilment of a prophecy long since uttered and
written down. Immediately after the mention of their
appearance among the readers as the pressing occasion
for writing this letter, Jude goes on to say that these
persons had long before been the subject of a writing in
which this judgment was pointed out (ver. 4, n. 9). In
view of the fact that in what follows mention is made of
different cases of judgment in the O.T. typical of what
awaits these persons (vv. 5–7), and that the words of
Enoch about God's final judgment upon all godless persons
are quoted (ver. 14 f.), it is natural to consider the judgment to be described in the following passage, as one long
prophesied, especially since πάλαι suggests παλαιὰ διαθήκη
and προγεγραμμένοι recalls such passages as Rom. xv. 4;
Acts i. 16; 2 Pet. iii. 2. But this interpretation of τοῦτο

would be possible only if it were immediately followed by a statement as to the nature of the judgment that God was about to visit upon these persons. But this is not the case; indeed, one searches the letter in vain for any direct statement of this kind. The cited cases of divine judgment, actual and prophesied, are more suited to indicate the sinfulness of these unworthy Christians, whom God will certainly not leave unpunished, than to portray the judgment which eventually will overtake them. It is equally impossible to take τοῦτο as an introduction to Jude's description of these persons in ver. 4b (n. 9). If, as is generally the case, τοῦτο refers to what precedes, Jude conceives the appearance of these persons in the Churches to which he is writing as a judgment, and more than that, a judgment long since prophesied in some writing. Naturally it is not a judgment fulfilled upon them or by them, but a judgment upon the Churches in which they have appeared. Jude's thought is the same as John's when he represents the coming of Christ as bringing judgment into the world, although Christ Himself judges no one and is judged by no one (John ix. 39, iii. 19; but cf. iii. 17, xii. 47), and Paul's when he looks upon divisions into sects which he foresees, as a judgment appointed by God in the Church, in order to distinguish faithful Christians from the impure elements in its community (1 Cor. xi. 19). It is unfortunate that such persons are constantly making their way into new Churches, just as it is unfortunate that Christians are under necessity of being persecuted for their faith; but, looked at from the divine point of view, both are parts of the judgment which begins at the house of God (1 Pet. iv. 17) before it is fulfilled in the world; it is one of the signs of the last times (1 John ii. 18). The readers are enabled the more easily to assume the right attitude toward this saddening fact, because Jude, taking for granted that he is recalling only what the readers already know, is able to say that the godless persons who have come among them are those of whom it was long since prophesied in written form, not simply that they would come in general, but that they would creep in among Jude's readers. One seeks in vain for such a prophecy in the *Book of Enoch* or in the O.T., because at the time when they were written no Christian Churches were as yet in existence. On the other hand, in 2 Pet. ii. 1–iii. 4, we have a prophecy which exactly suits, namely, the announcement that false teachers, whose theory and practice exactly corresponds to those of the godless bearers of the Christian name in Jude, will appear among a certain group of Jewish Christian Churches. The narrative in which this is found shows verbal resemblances to Jude 4 at the very beginning. Assuming, then, that 2 Pet. ii. 1–iii. 4 is not copied from an older document which Jude also had before him, it is clear that Jude is referring to 2 Peter, and that this Epistle is addressed to the same Jewish Christian Churches as 2 Peter. This conclusion is confirmed by Jude 17 f. The readers are told to keep in remembrance the words of the apostles of Christ formerly spoken, namely, that "In the last time there shall be mockers walking according to their own ungodly lusts." Perhaps the direct form of speech in which the apostolic prophecy is here reproduced does not absolutely exclude the possibility of repeated and varied prophecies being summed up in this statement (n. 10). But if this were the case, the expression would be unnatural. Moreover, it is just as impossible here to leave out of account the ὑμῖν as in 2 Pet. i. 16 and iii. 15. The reference is to words which the apostles addressed to the readers of Jude, and so also to the readers of 2 Peter. Accordingly, in ver. 4 it is assumed that the readers are familiar with a written prophecy of the entrance among the readers of the libertines which has now taken place. That such a prophecy, having reference to their conditions, was ad-

dressed to this group of readers is almost as self-evident
as the fact that only a Christian could predict the appearance of false teachers among a definite group of Christian
Churches. Furthermore, according to the connection of
vv. 16–20, the mockers of ver. 18 are the same persons to
whom, according to ver. 4, this written prophecy referred.
Consequently the prophecy of ver. 4, only the general
contents of which are here indicated, and the prophecy of
ver. 18, which is verbally quoted, must have been contained in one and the same writing addressed to these
Jewish Christian Churches. But in 2 Peter, the same
Epistle which we recognise as the writing presupposed in
ver. 4 (2 Pet. ii. 1–3), we find almost exactly the words
quoted by Jude (ver. 18) from the same writing (2 Pet.
iii. 3). Unless recourse is had to very artificial assumptions (§ 44), here is positive proof that in ver. 18 and
ver. 4 Jude refers to 2 Peter, in both instances as a
writing addressed to the readers of his own letter, and in
ver. 18 as the writing of an apostle. Against this conclusion it cannot be argued that Jude attributes these
prophetic words not to a single apostle, but to the
apostles collectively. At most, a literal interpretation
could here draw only the improbable conclusion that all
the apostles had written a collective letter to the readers
from which this quotation was made. In the very nature
of the case, if he intended to use direct discourse, Jude
could quote what the apostles had said to the readers on
the point in question only as the saying of a single
apostle, naturally, of course, assuming that other apostles
had said or written similar things to the readers about the
same matter. It is this very presupposition which he
expresses when he mentions the apostles, and not Peter
alone, as the source of this prophecy. Although this
expression, in and of itself, is entirely intelligible, it is all
the more natural if Jude had 2 Peter before him ; since
in 2 Pet. iii. 3 Peter does not represent the prophecy

quoted by Jude as something new, expressed by him now
for the first time, but, in marked distinction from his own
prediction in ii. 1, he simply reminds the readers of this
prophecy as if it were something already known and
expected (above, p. 230). One apostle, who had once
written a letter to the same readers on related subjects,
expressing himself in the same way as Peter, is mentioned
in 2 Pet. iii. 15. Even if Jude knew no more than we
are able to infer from 2 Pet. iii. 3, 15, with this before
him he could write as he does; for he does not speak as
Peter does in 2 Pet. iii. 2 of the apostles of the readers, of
whom Paul was not one (above, p. 202), but of the apostles
of our Lord Jesus Christ, of whom Paul also was counted
one by the older apostles and the brothers of Jesus (Gal.
ii. 9). Jude makes use also of the words of 2 Pet. iii. 2
in introducing the quotation ($\mu\nu\eta\sigma\theta\hat{\eta}\nu\alpha\iota$ $\tau\hat{\omega}\nu$ $\pi\rho o\epsilon\iota\rho\eta\mu\acute{\epsilon}\nu\omega\nu$
$\dot{\rho}\eta\mu\acute{\alpha}\tau\omega\nu$), but does not copy them; rather he alters the
words and adapts them to his purpose. Neither in ver.
17 f. nor ver. 4 does he, like Peter, recall the prophecies
of the O.T. and Christ's commandment to the apostles,
but only an apostolic prophecy.

On the exegetical side this simple understanding of
the situation cannot be obscured by the remark, often
made, that $\pi\acute{\alpha}\lambda\alpha\iota$ (ver. 4) refers back to the remote past.
Taken in contrast to the recent appearance of the sinful
Christians, it can express an interval of weeks and months
just as well as of years and centuries (n. 11). How long
a time elapsed between the prophecy in 2 Pet. ii. 1–3
and the fulfilment of the same which was the direct
occasion for the composition of Jude, cannot be inferred
from the word $\pi\acute{\alpha}\lambda\alpha\iota$, "long ago," nor in general is it
possible to determine it; nevertheless, ver. 5 seems to in-
dicate a time subsequent to the great judgment of the year
70. Jude begins his statement in ver. 5 by saying that
he is recalling what the readers know; and this is emphasised by appeal to the comprehensive knowledge which the

readers already possess (cf. 1 John ii. 20 f., 27, and n. 12),
all of which implies that he is not only citing facts known
to the readers, but that he can also count upon their understanding of brief or obscure hints. How necessary this
preliminary remark was, is indicated by the history of the
interpretation of the closely connected sentences in ver. 5 f.,
which Jude must have had particularly in view when he
made the remark, since the connection of the third statement (ver. 7) is much more loose than that of the others.
The first thing he recalled is this, namely, " that God, the
Lord (this is the meaning of κύριος without the article), or
(according to the reading which is probably original, see
n. 12) that *Jesus*, after having saved a people out of
Egypt, the second time destroyed them that believed
not." That a fact from the O.T. is here meant is doubtful ; for then the order in which Jude cites his facts is
very remarkable, since in such a case he would pass
from the later books of the Pentateuch or O.T. back
to Gen. vi. and xix. (cf. the opposite order in Sir. xvi.
6–10). Against this understanding of the reference is
also the omission of the article before λαός (cf. Acts xv. 14 ;
Tit. ii. 14 ; 1 Pet. ii. 9 f. ; but ὁ λαός, Matt. ii. 4, iv. 23 ;
John xi. 50, 52, xviii. 14 ; Acts x. 2 ; 2 Pet. ii. 1 ; and
ὁ λαὸς αὐτοῦ, Matt. i. 21 ; Luke i. 68 ; Rom. xi. 1). But
the most important reason for rejecting this interpretation
is the impossibility of finding within the O.T. the familiar
second instance in which God destroyed those who were
redeemed from Egypt but remained unbelieving, in comparison to a first instance, equally well known, in which
He did the same thing ; for that the cases were parallel
is the natural presupposition, since otherwise it would be
necessary to indicate the contrast in the divine action in
the two cases (n. 12). The original readers readily understood that Jude was contrasting the judgment of the
generation of Israel that came out of Egypt, who, with a
few happy exceptions, perished in the wilderness for their

unbelief without having seen the land of promise (Num.
xiv. 11–38; Deut. i. 26, 32, ii. 14–16; Ps. cvi. 24;
1 Cor. x. 5; Heb. iii. 10, 19), with another generation,
which likewise, after having been redeemed as God's
people, was condemned and destroyed in punishment for
its unbelief. Throughout the N.T., from the discourses
of the Baptist to the visions of Revelation, we find
expressed, indicated, or presupposed, the idea that Christ
has accomplished a redemption comparable to the liberation of Israel from Egypt (n. 12). The object of this
redemption is not the Jewish people, but nevertheless a
people of God to whom the titles of Israel are applied
(vol. i. p. 82 f.). In neither case, after the redemption of
Israel out of Egypt and after the redemption by Christ,
were the redeemed people of God destroyed, but the
majority of those to whom redemption was offered—
those who were called first of all to the acceptance of
the redemption and the possession of the blessings which
it assured, i.e. the countrymen and contemporaries of
Jesus, who refused to have faith in Him—were condemned for their unbelief. Jude could say that Jesus
had visited this judgment upon the unbelieving mass of
the Jewish people, because they had been judged by the
testimony of Jesus which they rejected (John xii. 48,
xv. 22, ix. 39; Matt. xii. 39–45, xiii. 14 f.; Luke xx. 18),
and because the threatening prophecy of Jesus about the
evil and adulterous generation had been fulfilled by the
destruction of Jerusalem and the temple (John ii. 19 =
Mark xiv. 58, xv. 29; Acts vi. 14; also Matt. xxi. 19,
41–43, xxii. 7, xxiii. 35–xxiv. 2; Luke xix. 41–44,
xxi. 5, vi. 20–24, xxiii. 28–31). Jude, therefore, must
have written after this event. Among Jewish Christian
Churches especially, in whose minds the memory of this
catastrophe was fresh, no misunderstanding was possible,
and for them in particular was the judgment upon the
unbelieving majority of their own people the most powerful

incentive to hold fast their faith, and to maintain it
even against the temptation to which they had recently
been subjected,—the temptation to accept a so-called
Christianity, which really denied the only Lord of the
Christians, and perverted into heathen immorality the
state of grace in which His redeemed servants stood.

If Peter, who died in the year 64, toward the end of
his life predicted to the same Christian Churches to which
Jude is addressed, that teachers of an immoral type of
Christianity, and persons with whom he· had become
acquainted outside their circle, who scoffed at the promise
of the parousia, would appear among them ; and if Jude
believed, subsequent to the fall of Jerusalem, that this
prediction was fulfilled in the creeping in of dangerous
men, whose theory and practice were alike vicious, in
whom were to be discerned the essential features of the
prophetic description of 2 Peter,—he could say that this
had been written concerning them long ago (ver. 4), and
that their coming had been foretold to the readers by the
lips of apostles (ver. 17 f.).   Assuming the year 75 as the
approximate date for the composition of Jude,—since a
date much later is made impossible by the little we know
of the author's life history (above, p. 239 f.),—a period of
from ten to fifteen years had elapsed since Peter had
written 2 Peter to the same Churches.

1. (P. 238.)   In the time of Jesus and the apostles are to be distinguished,
(1) The apostle Judas, son of Simon, a man from Carioth (John vi. 71, xiii.
2, etc.); (2) the apostle Judas-Jacobi (son of a certain James, see *Forsch.*
vi. 344 f.), Luke vi. 16 ; Acts i. 13 ; John xiv. 22, probably to be identified
with Lebbæus or Thaddæus, Matt. x. 3 ; Mark iii. 18 ; (3) Judas [Jude], the
son of Mary, brother of James, Joseph, Simon, several sisters, and Jesus
(Matt. xiii. 55 ; Mark vi. 3 ; Jude 1, cf. Matt. xii. 46 ; Mark iii. 31 ; John ii.
12, vii. 3–8 ; Acts i. 14 ; 1 Cor. ix. 5 ; Hegesippus in Eus. *H. E.* iii. 19, xx.
1–8, xxxii. 5) ; (4) Judas Barsabas, a man of prophetic gifts, and the respected
representative sent by the mother Church to the Church in Antioch, Acts xv.
22–34, cf. vol. i. p. 31 (to be distinguished from Joseph Barsabas surnamed
Justus, Acts i. 23 ; Papias in Eus. *H. E.* iii. 39. 9).   Still another name
(§ 44, n. 1) is that of Judas, the last Jewish Christian bishop of Jerusalem in
the time of Hadrian (Eus. *H. E.* iv. 5. 3 ; *Chron., anno Abrah.* 2139 ; Epiph.

Hær. lxvi. 20), whom Schlatter (*Der Chronograph aus dem 10 Jahr. Antonins* 1894, S. 25–37) declares to have been the author of a chronology which he thinks Eusebius (*H. E.* vi. 7) refers incorrectly to the time of Severus (cf. *Forsch.* vi. 283, 291 ff.).

2. (P. 238.) Clem. *Hypot.* Lat. trans. (*Forsch.* iii. 83), "Judas, qui catholicam scripsit epistolam, frater filiorum Joseph exstans valde religiosus et cum sciret propinquitatem domini, non tamen dicit se ipsum fratrem eius esse, sed quid dixit? '*Judas servus Jesu Christi*, ut pote domini, *frater autem Jacobi*'; hoc enim verum est : frater erat ex Joseph." Clement holds to the view that the brothers of the Lord were sons of Joseph by an earlier wife. The pride of the relatives of Jesus, the δεσπόσυννοι, in their family, of which Africanus reminds us (Eus. *H. E.* i. 7. 14), was a later development (cf. vol. i. p. 109). Of more modern writers, cf. Bengel on Jude 1, but especially Hofmann, vii. 2. 145 f. The remarks of Spitta (300 f.), which are opposed to the view here advocated, are based, if the present writer understands them correctly, upon the untenable view that the title "Brother of James" is designed to establish the authority of the writer to send this letter of exhortation, having practically the same meaning as ἀπόστολος δὲ Ἰ. Χρ. (Tit. i. 1 ; cf. Rom. i. 1). Even if we be disposed to look upon the honour paid to the relatives of Jesus as one of the characteristics of the Jewish Christian type of thought,—of a kind not altogether spiritual, and contrary to the thought of Christ (Matt. xii. 49),—we are not to suppose that the Churches of Palestine had so far lost their reason as to pay special honour to Jude because he was a brother of James, or to Simeon because he was James' cousin, or, *vice versa*, to James because he was Jude's brother. On the contrary, after they believed they were known individually as "The brother of the Lord" (Gal. i. 19), and collectively as "Brethren of the Lord" (1 Cor. ix. 5 ; Acts i. 14); but they themselves make no use of this title in their Epistles. Here, as in Jas. i. 1, this negative conclusion is the only one that could be properly drawn from the writer's self-designation as a servant of Jesus Christ, even if it were not necessary in view of the chiastically constructed contrast between δοῦλος—ἀδελφὸς δέ and Ἰ. Χρ. and Ἰάκωβος.

3. (P. 241.) There is scarcely any doubt about the meaning of ver. 3. With regard to ἔσχον, cf. vol. i. p. 456, n. 3. From περὶ τῆς κ. ἡ. σωτηρίας we derive the impression that this is the central point or main subject of the proposed writing, since otherwise it would have to be further defined (cf. 1 Thess. v. 1 ; 1 John i. 1 ; 2 Pet. i. 12, iii. 16 ; Rom. i. 3). The strong expression, πᾶσαν σπουδὴν ποιούμενος γράφειν, means more than the eager turning over in one's mind of an intention which, in the case of a writing, would imply meditation preparatory to composition. Peter had such an intention in mind when he wrote 2 Pet. i. 15, but by the use of the future σπουδάσω he indicates that this intention has yet to be zealously carried out ; Jude was already engaged in the work. Cf. also Gal. ii. 10 ; 2 Pet. i. 5. By the ἅπαξ, ver. 3 (Heb. vi. 4), which is not essentially different in meaning from ἐφάπαξ (cf. 1 Pet. iii. 18 with Rom. vi. 10, or Heb. ix. 12 with ix. 26), it is clearly implied that a second παραδιδόναι is superfluous or inadmissible. Even in ver. 5, where ἅπαξ approaches the sense of "in general" (*überhaupt*) (Hermas, *Vis.* iii. 3. 4 ; *Mand.* iv. 4. 1 ; Didymus, Lat. *omnino*=ἅπαξ, *de Trin.* i. 19, cf. ἁπαξαπλῶς), it is correlated with ὑπομνῆσαι, in distinction from

διδάσκειν. τοῖς ἁγίοις without further definition can only mean the whole Church, or the Church of the Holy Land (vol. i. p. 455 f., n. 2). But since in the matter of faith the latter were not distinguished from the Gentile Christian Churches (cf. *e.g.* Gal. i. 22-24; 1 Thess. ii. 14; 1 Cor. xv. 11; 1 Pet. v. 9, 12; 2 Pet. iii. 15 f.), and since the Epistle shows no hostile feeling toward the Christianity of other Churches, it must mean the whole Church. The objections raised by Spitta (309) are to the present writer unintelligible, and Spitta's opinion (416), that through a misreading of 2 Pet. ii. 21 (τοῖς ἁγίοις instead of αὐτοῖς ἁγίας), Jude, contrary to all known usage, understood "the saints" to mean the apostles, seems hardly to require refutation. All Christians are here appropriately called saints (cf. 1 Pet. i. 15 f.); and this thought is somewhat emphasised by the relation of the word to the context, because in what follows the writer deals with persons who are or who have been reckoned among the "saints," and who, having received the same faith as the readers, have perverted it in a direction antagonistic both to the holiness of the Church and to its faith (ver. 20).

4. (P. 243.) Since παρεισέδυσαν is used in ver. 4 as παρεισῆλθον in Gal. ii. 4 without any indication of the region where the false teachers had crept in, it is necessary in both instances to supply this from the context. In Galatians it is the Church in Antioch (*ZKom. Gal.* 86 f.); here it is the circle of the readers among whom they are now found, ver. 12, and also in the latter passage their entrance into the Church through a purely sham conversion and hypocritical baptism is not called a παρεισδῦναι. Their teaching is that rejected in Rom. vi. 1. 15; Gal. v. 13; 1 Pet. ii. 16; and referred to in Rom. vi. 12; 1 Cor. vi. 12 ff., but described at greatest length in 2 Pet. ii. (above, p. 224 f.).

5. (Pp. 243, 245.) Even Didymus on Jude 11 (Latin version) interprets the typical significance of Korah as above, p. 244 f. Cf. 1 Cor. x. 1-11. In addressing the Church of Corinth, which was stirring up an insurrection against its founder, in 1 Cor. x. 10 Paul uses the words μὴ γογγύζετε, which are undoubtedly suggested by Num. xvii. 6-14, and so are intended to remind them of those complaints against the authorities which were instigated by Korah, and after his destruction were echoed throughout the entire congregation. Cf. 1 Cor. xvi. 16, also cf. Heb. xiii. 17 with Heb. iii. 7-iv. 11. The meaning of the comparison with Cain is more obscure. Being the first of three types, it may possibly express the more general thought that the false teachers are given over to unrighteousness; since, as contrasted with the righteous Abel, Cain is an unrighteous man (Matt. xxiii. 35). With this possibly is connected the thought of 1 John iii. 12, 15, that they, on account of their "evil works," are jealous of the righteous and their enemies, and are murderers of their own brothers. It is also possible that underlying the passage there is a traditional Jewish description of these "evil works" (cf. Siegfried, *Philo*, S. 150 f.). Spitta (352), following the example of Schneckenburger (*Beiträge z. Einl.* 221), attaches great importance to the embellishment of Gen. iv. in the Jerusalem Targum i., which represents Cain as disputing with Abel, and saying, "There is no judgment, and no judge, and no other world; the righteous will receive no good reward, and vengeance will not be taken upon the ungodly." This would suit perfectly the description in 2 Pet., but does not suit so well that in Jude, where no mention is made of the denial of the eschatological

hope which is especially noticeable in ver. 18. With regard to the text of ver. 12, see above, p. 235, on 2 Pet. ii. 13. Because in this instance ἀγάπαις ὑμῶν instead of ἀγάπαις αὐτῶν precedes, συν- in συνευωχούμενοι has a different force. The added ὑμῖν, which is poorly attested, is nevertheless correct in thought. There is much in favour of taking ἀφόβως with what follows, as in S² S³, and is done by Hofmann; for there is nothing inherently blameworthy about taking part in their feasts without fear. Nor can it hardly be the mere "feasting together" that is condemned, but rather the manner of their participation in the love-feasts, namely, the fact that they conduct themselves as σπιλάδες, which is clearly not here used in the sense of "rocks," "cliffs," but is intelligible only if taken as related etymologically and in sense to σπίλοι, 2 Pet. ii. 13 ("spots"), and, therefore, as equivalent to ἐσπιλωμέναι, Jude 23; μεμιασμένοι, as in Hesychius' gloss (cf. Jude 8; Tit. i. 15; Rev. iii. 4, xiv. 4). Didymus (Lat.) reads qui in dilectionibus vestris maculatis (but read rather with Lücke maculati) coëpulantur. Cf. Hofmann on vv. 12 and 23. This does not in any sense imply that they practised immorality at their love-feasts, but that they partook of them polluted by their unchastity, and wherever they went took with them the thoughts and passions corresponding to the character of their life.

6. (P. 244.) Ἀποδιορίζοντες, which is used in ver. 19 without the object, does not require the supplying of a single definite object any more than this is required when we speak of something that separates in distinction from something that unites. If διορίζειν is an emphatic ὁρίζειν, ἀποδιορίζειν is an emphatic ἀφορίζειν, and means a separation completely accomplished. The Pharisees, Gr. οἱ ἀφωρισμένοι (see vol. i. p. 68), separated themselves from the am ha arets and made sharp distinctions among the people of God, without withdrawing entirely from the people. These false teachers made even sharper distinctions, and created divisions along the lines of these distinctions. They are αἱρετικοί, Tit. iii. 10. In contrast to their practice stands the strong sense of unity in the Church, ver. 20 f. The Holy Spirit unites (ver. 20); the ψυχικοί, who are without the Spirit, divide (ver. 19), in the first place by their presumptuous judgments, and then by conduct tending to destroy the fellowship of the Church. That they claimed in exceptional measure to possess the Spirit, asserting that they were πνευματικοί, as distinguished from ψυχικοί, is at least probable. The misuse of Pauline phrases among these persons (2 Pet. iii. 16) reminds one of 1 Cor. ii. 10–iii. 3.

7. (P. 247.) Πλάνη is clearly used in an active sense ("leading astray," "seduction") in 1 Thess. ii. 3 (cf. 2 Cor. vi. 8); 2 Thess. ii. 11 (cf. ver. 9, τέρατα ψεύδους); also in Matt. xxvii. 64. The deceiver of the people (ὁ πλάνος, xxvii. 63) led them astray so long as he lived (John vii. 12; Luke xxiii. 2). His alleged resurrection will not increase the error of the people, but will make stronger and more injurious his power to lead them astray. Furthermore, cf. 1 John iv. 6 with 2 John 7; 1 Tim. iv. 1. In Eph. iv. 14 also the word can be taken only in an active sense, on account of the word with which it is connected, μεθοδία τῆς πλάνης, and the context.

8. (P. 248.) It is presupposed that in ver. 22 f. Tischendorf's critical apparatus is very imperfect, but that he nevertheless gives the correct reading (cf. Spitta, 377 f.). The reading is the same as that given by Clement (Lat.) in connection with ver. 23 (Forsch. iii. 85); while, on the other hand, ver. 22,

like so many other verses, is overlooked, this passage is carelessly quoted by Clement from memory in *Strom.* vi. 65. It is impossible for the present writer to escape the impression that *Didache* ii. 7 is dependent upon Jude 22 f. : οὐ μισήσεις πάντα ἄνθρωπον, ἀλλὰ οὓς μὲν ἐλέγξεις, περὶ δὲ ὧν προσεύξῃ, οὓς δὲ ἀγαπήσεις ὑπὲρ τὴν ψυχήν σου. The third clause is the least accurate reproduction ; but the preceding, "thou shalt hate no man," is in keeping with Jude's thought, who, while he requires hatred of the sins of the wicked (cf. Rev. ii. 6), requires also mercy toward the persons themselves.

9. (Pp. 248, 249.) In opposition to Spitta's contention (311 f.) that τοῦτο τὸ κρίμα = "this accusation," is used to introduce the words ἀσεβεῖς . . . ἀρνούμενοι, it is sufficient to suggest (1) that this syntactical relation can be expressed only by a complete sentence either in direct discourse (1 Cor. vii. 29 ; Gal. iii. 2, 17), or with ὅτι (Rom. ii. 3, xi. 25 ; 1 Cor. xv. 50 ; 2 Thess. iii. 10), or by an infinitive sentence (Rom. xiv. 13 ; 1 Cor. vii. 26 ; 2 Cor. ii. 1 ; Eph. iv. 17) ; (2) that κρίμα is hardly anywhere used in the sense of accusation. Nor is Hofmann's interpretation satisfactory, according to which τοῦτο refers to the judgment visited upon the intruders in the present ; for, although the sinner may be thought of as one who by his very act condemns himself (John iii. 18 f. ; Gal. ii. 11), this is not stated either in what precedes or follows ; so it is not a manifest fact to which τοῦτο might refer. But Hofmann states what is correct and really self-evident when he says that τοῦτο refers to what precedes, namely, to παρεισέδυσαν. Furthermore, Spitta reads more into the passage than it contains when he (314 f., 383 f.) concludes, from the article with προγεγραμμένοι, that acquaintance is here presupposed with a writing in which a still older prophecy, presumably from the O.T., is applied to the persons who now have crept in among the readers of Jude. Just as it is presupposed in John xi. 2 that the readers had heard or read of a woman who had anointed Jesus' feet, and that the information is there imparted that the woman, whose name they had not heretofore known, was Mary of Bethany ; so Jude assumes that the readers know that it has been previously written or prophesied in an older writing that certain persons, who are libertines in theory and practice, will make their appearance among them. What he says now is this, namely, that the persons who shortly before have appeared among the readers are those whose appearance among them was prophesied in the older writing. But Jude's reference is not to a commentary upon a prophecy, but to a writing whose prophecy is being fulfilled in the present, *i.e.* to 2 Pet. ii. 1–3, where we do not find an older prophecy applied to present phenomena, but where it is predicted that false teachers will come among the readers. Although not an independent sentence, the appositive clause expresses exactly the same thought as a sentence in the form οὗτοί εἰσιν οἱ προγεγραμμένοι κτλ., or something similar ; cf. Matt. iii. 3, xi. 10 ; John i. 46 (1 John ii. 22). By the use of this form of expression in vv. 12 and 19 is preserved the identity of the persons of unchristian character who have appeared among the readers with certain persons already described, except that the relation of subject and object is the reverse of that in ver. 4, as required by the different connections of the two passages. The mockers, whose appearance in the last age is prophesied by the apostles (ver. 18), are none other than the persons who, as the readers can daily observe, create divisions (ver. 19). In the same way, after a typical and typological **char-**

acterisation of them (ver. 10 f.), Jude identifies the persons who in the pre
sence of the readers take part in their love-feasts (ver. 12). Of an entirely
different character are the sentences in vv. 8, 10, 16, where the end sought is
not the identification of figurative with actual persons, but where mention
is made of different characteristics of the persons appearing among the
readers, who have already been described with sufficient definiteness in
ver. 4 (thus the use of οὗτοι).

10. (P. 250.) The language used in ver. 18 is not entirely comparable
with 1 Tim. iv. 1 ; for, although in this latter passage the ῥητῶς shows that
the reproduction of thought is intended to be as accurate as possible (see
above, p. 111), ὅτι, the formula of indirect discourse, which does not occur
before the words quoted in Jude 18, indicates that the quotation is not a
formal citation.

11. (P. 252.) With πάλαι, Jude 4, cf. Mark xv. 44 (according to the preponderance of evidence), also Soph. Philoct. 1030 = some hours before ; 2 Cor.
xii. 19 = since the time when Paul began to use the tone of self-defence, consequently somewhere about xi. 5, or possibly from the beginning of the
letter (i. 12)—from the point of view of the readers and hearers of the letter
about an hour before ; 2 Pet. i. 9 ; Matt. xi. 21 = within the lifetime of the
men in question ; Jos. Bell. iii. 8. 8, in contrast to ἄρτι, the time prior to
the captivity which has just taken place, or, if we read οὐ πάλαι = " not long
ago."

12. (Pp. 253, 254). The peculiar εἰδότας ἅπαξ πάντα has given rise to
numerous attempts to transpose ἅπαξ, and in some instances to its omission
altogether ; also to change πάντα into πάντας (S², but not in all MSS.), and into
τοῦτο, which is more common. Here the apparatus of Tischendorf, which is not
always without errors, and not very clear, is sufficient.   It is more difficult
to decide whether the correct reading is κύριος or Ἰησοῦς. Ὁ θεός (without a
preceding κύριος), which is badly attested by a careless quotation in Clement,
Pæd. iii. 44 (where λαόν also is arbitrarily put out of its place), S² and other
unimportant witnesses, is out of the question, because it suits any interpretation, and is found as an addition to κύριος in Clement, Hypot. (Forsch.
iii. 83). It is even less possible to assume with Spitta that the original
reading was θεός without the article, which is entirely unattested.   Certainly
the article which is placed before κύριος in the Antiochian recension (KL S³)
is not original, because it has against it all the authorities which support both
κύριος and Ἰησοῦς (for which ὁ Ἰησοῦς could have been written equally well),
also the dominus deus (i.e. κύριος ὁ θεός) of Clement (Hypot. Lat. trans.), and
because very frequently the article is inserted before the anarthrous κύριος
(Matt. i. 22, ii. 15 ; Jas. iv. 10, v. 10). The only choice left is that between
κύριος (א, perhaps C* and a Greek document attributed to Eph. Syr.) and
Ἰησοῦς. The latter reading is attested by AB, 66** (= Paul. 67**), Sahidic,
Coptic, Ethiopic, Vulgate versions ; also by Origen (both in the text and
scholion of the Cod. Laura 184, B 64, upon Mount Áthos ; see von der Goltz,
Eine textkrit. Arbeit des zehnten bzw. sechsten Jahrh. 1899, S. 51 ; cf. ThLb, 1899,
No. 16), and by Jerome, Vall. ii. 270, vii. 413. This was also Didymus'
reading, not only in his Latin commentary, ad loc., but also in de Trin. iii. 19,
although the text, as we have it, reads κύριος Ἰησοῦς. That the correct reading,
however, is Ἰησοῦς is proved by the fact that Jerome, vii. 412, is in verbal

agreement with Did. *de Trin.* Ἰούδας καθολικῶς γράφει ("Judas de omnibus generaliter . . . inquit"), so that Jerome in this passage of his commentary on Gal. must have copied from Didymus' commentary on the same book, which, p. 370, he mentions as one of his sources. There are also certain considerations of fact which support the much more strongly attested Ἰησοῦς as against κύριος. The mention of Jesus in a statement about the redemption out of Egypt is altogether strange and quite without parallel. The situation is not materially helped by assuming, as Jerome does, that Joshua is meant ; see *contra Jov.* i. 21 (Vall. ii. 270). This did not occur as a solution to the oldest interpreters, who substituted God for Ἰησοῦς (Clement ; see above). Didymus (Migne, 39. 1813) and Jerome, in the passage where he copies Didymus (Vall. vii. 412), and apparently also Origen in the seventh homily on Deut. (in the above quoted Athos MS.), use this passage to prove that it was Jesus Himself with whom the congregation in the O.T. had to do, a thought of very early date ; cf. Just. *Dial.* cxx., Ἰησοῦν τὸν καὶ τοὺς πατέρας ὑμῶν ἐξ Αἰγύπτου ἐξαγαγόντα. The name of Jesus did not prevent Didymus from making the sentence refer to the redemption of Israel from Egypt, without recourse to the impossible interpretation of the word to mean Joshua. Cf. also Cramer, *Cat.* viii. 155. 18, 157. 21, 158. 5–13, 161. 2. But whereas Clement understood correctly that Jude meant the judgment which came upon the Jewish people because of their failure to believe on Jesus (*Forsch.* iii. 83, 96), Didymus confines the meaning to the dying of Israelites in the wilderness ; cf. 1 Cor. x. 5 ; Heb. iii. 16–19. It hardly needs to be proved that the adverbial δεύτερον, τρίτον κτλ, both with the article (Mark xiv. 41 ; John xxi. 17 ; 2 Cor. xiii. 2) and without it (John iii. 4, xxi. 14, 16 ; Luke xxiii. 22 ; Rev. xix. 3 ; 2 Cor. xiii. 1), just as ἐκ δευτέρου (Matt. xxvi. 42 ; Mark xiv. 72 ; John ix. 24 ; Acts x. 15, xi. 9), shows that the action which it modifies is a repetition of an earlier action, no matter whether it is previously intimated or not that this action has already once taken place. Accordingly it is also explained how in late Greek τρίτον actually means τρίς, " thrice " (see the writer's *Acta Joannis*, pp. 256, 258 *sub voc.*). What happens a second or third time has happened twice or thrice. Recently F. Maier, *Bib. Z.*, 1904, S. 392, has confidently claimed that τὸ δεύτερον here as also often elsewhere is by no means a numeral adverb, but=*deinde, postea*, or even *ex contrario*. This meaning, however, should in any case be proved by the actual usage of language and not by appeal to the *Thesaurus* of Stephanus, or to other exegetes ; for example, to Hofmann, who (vii. 2. 159–161) has left not the slightest doubt concerning his contrary opinion in this matter. The only question is with what τὸ δεύτερον is connected. Through the position of the words it is impossible that τὸ δ. is to be taken with πιστεύσαντας, as if the reading were τοὺς τὸ δ. μὴ πιστεύσαντας. But also not with λαὸν . . . σώσας, for every intelligent author would have made this connection necessary for the reader by placing τὸ δ. before λαὸν or before σώσας. It belongs, therefore, to the principal verb ἀπώλεσεν. By this it is only indirectly said that also in the first instance on the part of many members of the nation which was to be saved, there existed unbelief to which that referred to in Jude is opposed as a similar second lack of faith ; and just as indirect is the statement that in the first instance as in the second (concerning which it is directly asserted) a deliverance of a nation out of Egypt had preceded the judgment on its unbelieving members. Only if τὸ δ. preceded σώσας or μὴ πιστ.—*i.e.* did not belong with ἀπώλεσεν—could the meaning be, that in fact the presuppositions of the main statement, namely, the deliverance of a nation or the unbelief of many of its members, were the same in both instances, but only in the second and not in the first could the divine action be an ἀπολέσαι. Even then the contrast would probably have been expressed; cf. Heb. ix. 28, ἅπαξ—ἐκ δευτέρου (=τὸ δεύτερον ἐρχόμενος); 2 Cor. xiii. 2, εἰς τὸ πάλιν (*i.e.* ἐλθὼν τὸ τρίτον), οὐ φείσομαι (*sc.* ὡς τὸ πρότερον). The only question is whether Jesus is to be thought of as the author of the first—only indirectly expressed—ἀπώλεσεν, which occurred in the wilderness, and so also indirectly of the first σώσας. In view of John xii. 41, 1 Cor. x. 4, 9 (τὸν Χριστόν in DGKL, Marcion; Iren. iv. 27. 3; Clement, *Ecl. proph.* xlix, and the ancient versions), this cannot be declared to be impossible. But from an exegetical point of view it is not possible. Since the action, with all its expressed presuppositions, is described only as a second one of its kind, the subjects in the two cases might be different; so that τὸ δεύτερον is an abbreviated expression for the thought, "And this was the second time that this happened." The comparison between the N.T. redemption and that of Israel from Egypt is presupposed in John i. 29, 36, and more clearly in 1 Pet. i. 15–21 (ii. 9; 2 Pet. ii. 1); 1 Cor. x. 1–11 (cf. v. 7 f.; Tit. ii. 14); Rev. i. 5 f., v. 9 f., xv. 3. Jude just after the judgment upon Israel speaks in the same manner as Paul prior to 70 (1 Thess. ii. 16; Rom. xi. 9 f.), merely alluding to the coming event. Above all, a comparison should be made with the typological expressions of Heb. in connection with the redemption of the people of God, and the judgment which is to follow upon the unbelieving of the redeemed generation; see below, § 46, n. 6; § 47, n. 9, with the amplifications belonging to them in the text.

§ 44. THE GENUINENESS OF JUDE AND THE TWO EPISTLES OF PETER (N. 1).

The question with regard to the genuineness of two of these Epistles is very sharply defined. It is even more impossible in the case of 2 Peter than of James or 1 Peter, by the assumption of later additions or by modifying the greeting, to get out of the letter an old writing, the author of which is not responsible for the claims that meet us in the document. The manner in which the beginning of the letter is connected with the greeting by the construction of the sentence, the repeated and definite references to experiences of Peter and his fellow-apostles, which are in keeping with the name in the greeting and declared to be experiences of the author (2 Pet. i. 3, 14,

16–18 ; above, pp. 194, 201–210, 215–221), make it clear beyond all question that the entire letter is meant to be represented as written by Peter.   If the letter is spurious, it is not pseudepigraphic in the narrower sense of the word, but from beginning to end a forgery.

In the same way, the author of Jude has not left us to guess which one of the many Jews and Jewish Christians of this name it was whom he represented himself to be ; he introduces himself to his readers as the well-known brother of the still more distinguished James (above, p. 238 f.).   If this introduction should prove to be false, then certainly we have no right to suppose that some other Jude is the author ; for the use of his own name on the part of a writer, in order to dispose of his wares under the mask of some older and more distinguished person of the same name, presupposes artificiality and boldness unparalleled in pseudepigraphic literature.   Until examples to the contrary have been found, we may assume as certain that a pseudo-Ezra, or pseudo-John, or pseudo-Hermas, or pseudo-Jude was not actually known as Ezra, or John, or Hermas, or Jude.   As regards its place in the Canon of the Church, Jude is better attested than 2 Peter, and even than James.   Although the Syrian Church, when it adopted some of the Catholic Epistles into its Canon, rejected Jude, 2 Peter, and 2 and 3 John, these four letters being translated apparently for the first time by Philoxenus (died 508), Jude was accepted about the year 200 without any question in Alexandria, Rome, and North Africa.   It is not necessary to investigate here the question to what extent the suspicions as to the genuineness of Jude and its place in the N.T. Canon, which developed later, led to its subsequent rejection in the Greek and Latin Churches.   On the other hand, there is no evidence that before the time of Origen, 2 Peter was accepted anywhere in the Church as a writing of the same rank as 1 Peter.   And throughout the whole of the fourth century we meet at most widely separated points in the Church very decided suspicion now of its genuineness, now of its place in the N.T. Canon. So long as it was presupposed that 2 Peter was addressed to the same Churches in Asia Minor as 1 Peter, the mere fact that the latter Epistle was early and very generally accepted was a strong point against the genuineness of 2 Peter ; for what prevented those who first received this letter, which must have followed 1 Peter after a short interval, from circulating it just as early and just as widely as they did 1 Peter ? (n. 2). If, however, it be proved that 2 Peter was not sent to the same Churches as 1 Peter, but to the Jewish Christian Churches in Palestine or neighbouring regions, it follows as a natural result that, from the beginning and for a long period, the history of the circulation and canonisation of these two letters followed entirely different lines. Just as the Nazarenes of the fourth century, notwithstanding their favourable opinion regarding Paul, and agreement with what is said in 2 Pet. iii. 15, thought that his letters to the Gentile Christian Churches did not concern themselves (*GK*, ii. 669 f.) ; so, for a long time, the Gentile Church took little account of 2 Peter, which was addressed to Jewish Christians. They treated James in practically the same way. But, in the case of both these letters, a limited circulation and early acquaintance of individuals with them are to be distinguished from acceptance of the same by the Catholic Church as books to be read in religious services (n. 3). There are points of resemblance between 2 Peter and a whole series of writings dating from 90 to 130, namely, the *Shepherd of Hermas*, the *Epistle of Clement to the Corinthians*, the so-called *Second Epistle of Clement to the Corinthians*, and the *Didache*, and it is very natural to suppose that several pseudo-Petrine writings are related to 2 Peter (see below, pp. 270 f., 273). In all these cases it cannot be so conclusively proved that 2 Peter is the source that no further objection is possible. Nor is this proof necessary, if it be admitted that Jude quoted 2 Peter at the beginning and end of his letter as an apostolic writing composed several years before (above, p. 250 f.).

One cannot but feel weary over the evasions by which the interpreters obscure the fact that not only in Jude 17 f., but also in Jude 4, an older Christian writing—the same which in Jude 17 f. is called apostolic—is quoted, in which Jude found predicted what he saw being fulfilled at the time when he wrote his letter. Since we now have a writing, purporting to be Peter's, which contains exactly what Jude quotes from the apostolic document cited by him, and since, besides these two express references of Jude, there are so many parallels between Jude and 2 Peter as regards facts, thought, and language as to necessitate the assumption of a literary relation between them, by the ordinary canons of criticism we should conclude that Jude knew and prized 2 Peter as an apostolic writing, and made it the basis of parts of his letter. The very artificiality of the present prevailing view, which reverses the relation, and represents the author of 2 Peter as copying from Jude, often unintelligently, requires that its exegetical proof should be all the stronger (n. 4). Certainly the style of Jude, which, in comparison with the obscure and clumsy style of 2 Peter, is clearer and generally better, cannot be used to prove the priority of Jude ; for what was there to hinder Jude from surpassing many of the original apostles in the use of the Greek language and in natural fluency of speech, as his brother James did ? Furthermore, it is only natural that in descriptions of actual and present phenomena, like those of Jude, the representation of the seducers should be more sharply outlined than in 2 Peter, which is so largely prophetic in character. If 2 Peter is genuine, it clearly cannot be dependent upon Jude ; for, in the first place, Jude did not write until after the year 70, *i.e.* after Peter's death ; and, in the second place, in representing as a prediction the appearance among the readers of false teachers, when from Jude he knew that they had already made their appearance among the readers of this Epistle, the writer of 2 Peter would necessarily have indicated clearly the difference between the historical presentation in his source and his own prophetic representation. He would also have distinguished between the region where, according to Jude, the seducers were already at work, and the region where, according to 2 Peter, they were to appear in the future.

But even assuming that 2 Peter is a forgery of the second century, and that Jude is a genuine writing of the late apostolic age, the view that the former is dependent upon the latter can be maintained only by a series of artificial hypotheses. If Jude 4, 17 f. has been correctly explained above (p. 250 f.), it is necessary to assume that the apostolic document which Jude quotes as his authority in both these passages was early lost, and that 2 Peter is a later caricature substituted for it. This lost apostolic writing must have resembled 2 Peter very closely. Like 2 Peter, it must have contained the prediction that persons who were libertines in theory and practice would appear as seducers among Jude's readers (Jude 4 ; 2 Pet. ii. 1–3). In it must have been found also a prediction regarding the scoffers of the last time, which is found in almost identical words in 2 Pet. iii. 3 and Jude 18, in the former without any definite indication as to its source, in the latter quoted as an apostolic word. The common assumption that the author of 2 Peter took these passages and all others parallel to Jude directly from this Epistle, is another hypothesis without any basis ; for what prevented the author of 2 Peter from copying them all from the lost apostolic document quoted by Jude ? In this case 2 Peter is not an independent writing, but, in part at least, the recasting of an ancient writing known to Jude as the work of an apostle. There is no doubt that such a writing, if it existed, bore the name of Peter, and had the form of a letter, since there is no reason why the later editor should have modified his original in these two respects. There is usually no difficulty in assuming such recasting of older genuine writings. Why in this case should we assume that the ancient and genuine document attested by Jude disappeared altogether, and that later 2 Peter was written on the basis of hints and quotations in Jude? But even assuming that this older writing was actually lost or destroyed, which is improbable, the origin of 2 Peter still remains inexplicable (n. 5). To reconstruct at a later time, from hints in Jude and from imagination, a lost apostolic prophecy concerning future errors, which, according to Jude, was actually fulfilled in the apostolic age, would have been a task as purposeless as it was difficult. It is much more conceivable that the old prophetic writing cited by Jude, and regarded by him as apostolic, was worked over in the light of more recent events to suit the spirit of the age, in order to make it more effective, and that in this way 2 Peter received all the peculiarities which have from the earliest times caused its genuineness to be questioned.

But the other assumption, namely, that both Jude and 2 Peter are spurious products of the post-apostolic age, involves the most unlikely consequences. They could not have originated independently of each other; but neither could they have been written by the same author, nor by two different forgers working together. Anyone desiring to oppose a tendency which sprang up in the post-apostolic time, on the authority of an apostle, might very well have done so in the form of an apostolic letter, in which, as in 2 Peter, the appearance of certain false teachers and scoffers is predicted. But it is difficult to understand how one who had written such a letter, or someone working in conspiracy with him, could have forged Jude also, in which the prediction of Peter regarding the future would be

represented as having been almost immediately fulfilled
Circumstances seemed rather to require a prediction, in
order that an apostle might be represented as prophetically
condemning later phenomena in the life of the Church.
It would be necessary to assume that the author of Jude
regarded 2 Peter as genuine, and that the later forger was
deceived by the older one.   But even in this case it has
yet to be explained why the person who thought that the
prediction of 2 Peter was fulfilled in certain phenomena
of his time used a pseudonym in order to express this
single fact, and further obscured the reference of his view
to his own times by putting it into the mouth of Jude,
the brother of James, who had long since died.

Passing now from these considerations of a hypothetical
nature to the examination of the genuineness of the letter,
the very manner in which the writer designates himself in
Jude 1 predisposes us in favour of the genuineness of this
Epistle.   According to historical tradition, Jude, the brother
of James, is a very obscure personality (above, p. 240 f.) ;
according to later tradition also, he was not an apostle,
and in the circle of the early Christian authors down to the
year 200, his name does not once appear (see Eus. *H. E.*
vi. 7).   What could have induced anyone desiring to defend
the common Christian faith and Christian morality to represent himself as Jude ?   Why was it necessary for him to
assume any character at all ?   Nothing that he says requires
any particular authority.   He refers to certain unpleasant
conditions in the present life of his readers ; describes
them, and condemns them severely, but only in such a
way as every earnest Christian was under necessity of
doing.   He declares that in these events of the present
an apostolic prediction written years before is finding its
fulfilment ; but this, again, could be recognised and
expressed by any ordinary Christian under the same conditions.   Nor does he claim any special authority.   He
does not call himself an apostle, and intimates only in

a very modest way that he is the Jude known to the readers as one of the brothers of Jesus (above, pp. 238f.,256). A further proof of genuineness is the manner in which he refers to one or to a number of apostolic writings. What forger, who could have had no other purpose in such a reference than to strengthen the authority of his own writing, would have been content with such hints as we find in Jude 4, 17 f. ? Would he not have mentioned the apostle, or apostles, by name ? If it be assumed that the letter is spurious, then the reference to another writing of the author, which was in the process of composition at the time this letter was written (ver. 3; above, pp. 241, 256), is wholly inexplicable. In case the letter is genuine, we have only to assume, either that the purpose of Jude there expressed, like so many other literary intentions, was never carried out, or that the writing contemplated at that time and later published, like so many other early Christian writings, has not come down to us (Luke i. 1 ; 1 Cor. v. 9, vii. 1). On the other hand, if the letter is spurious, it is necessary to assume that such a work of Jude regarding the Christian salvation existed at this time, and was generally known when this letter was written in Jude's name. But there is no trace of such a didactic writing of Jude's (n. 6). If such a writing in Jude's name did exist, it is wholly inexplicable why the author should speak of a writing which Jude intended to produce instead of the writing actually at hand. The fact that the author makes use of two pseudepigraphic writings bearing O.T. names, namely, the *Assumption of Moses* and the *Book of Enoch* (n. 7), lessened for a time the ecclesiastical reputation of the Epistle ; but this is no reason why we should question its genuineness. Except for the references in Jude, we do not know how these two books and other writings of like character were regarded by the older apostles and the brothers of Jesus. Nevertheless, what we find in Jude would seem to indicate that several of these writings, which do not stand the test of historical criticism, were regarded in this worthy circle as reliable witnesses of genuine tradition and true prophecy. It is, however, of critical importance that Jude apparently did not use the newly discovered Greek translation, but the Hebrew or Aramaic original of the *Book of Enoch* (n. 7). Jude is, like his brother James, a Hebrew who is also able to handle the Greek language with comparative ease. After what has been said above, vol. i. pp. 45, 113, the fact that Jude and Peter, if he is the author of 2 Peter, used the Greek language in addressing Jewish Christians, does not require further explanation. The other things that have caused objections to Jude, namely, its description of the libertines, and the resemblance it bears in thought and language to the letters of Paul, apply equally to 2 Peter. Therefore they can be best discussed with reference to the two letters together, taking into account, of course, their mutual relations and their differences.

If, on the one hand, it seems strange that a later author should write a letter in Jude's name, it is, on the other, entirely comprehensible that the name of the chief of the apostles should be misused in the writing of a spurious letter. Perhaps as early as the beginning of the second century a κήρυγμα Πέτρου was ascribed to him, and toward the middle of the same century an εὐαγγέλιον κατὰ Πέτρου, in both of which writings Peter himself assumes the rôle of author. The same is true of the ἀποκάλυψις Πέτρου, which is likewise old. Furthermore, in this same century, in the πράξεις Πέτρου, which are written from a Gnostic point of view, Peter is made the hero of a whole series of apostolic legends. Apparently in the third century he is made the principal figure in the Clementine Romance (*Homilies*), which is written in an Ebionitic spirit; while at the beginning of the Greek recension of this Romance we find a letter from him to James (n. 8). In view of all this, the mere occurrence of Peter's name in

an ancient writing is no proof of authorship. Furthermore, the view taken above regarding the authorship of
1 Peter (p. 149 f.) deprives us of one of the chief means of
determining the genuineness of 2 Peter. And yet it is
with the comparison of these two letters that our criticism
must begin. Notwithstanding the mention of Silvanus in
1 Pet. v. 12, 1 Peter was very early recognised and circulated as a genuine writing of the apostle. Anyone
desiring to ascribe a second Church letter to Peter at a
later date could not disregard the earlier and highly
prized first Epistle. According to the traditional opinion,
the author of 2 Peter actually made an explicit reference
to 1 Peter. But we have seen that 2 Pet. iii. 1 does not
refer to 1 Peter, and that 2 Peter does not, like 1 Peter,
claim to be directed to the Gentile Christian Churches of
Asia Minor, but to the Jewish Christian Churches of Palestine (pp. 194 f., 201–209). This, so far as the present writer
is able to see, is the conclusion of a perfectly sound
exegesis, and the conclusion is confirmed by the fact that
there are only a very few agreements in thought and
language between 1 and 2 Peter (n. 9). On the other
hand, there is something strikingly original about the
author's self-designation, Συμεὼν Πέτρος, which, so far as
we know, is unheard of elsewhere in Petrine and pseudo-
Petrine literature. The peculiar and often obscure style
of 2 Peter is in itself a strong argument against the suspicion that the letter was forged at a later time. The
fact that 2 Peter is entirely independent of 1 Peter, the
genuineness of which was widely accepted at a much
earlier date, is still stronger proof of the genuineness of
the former. Then the fact is to be considered that in
2 Pet. iii. 1 a letter of Peter is referred to which has not
come down to us. Now it must be admitted that the
reference in this place to a letter which never existed
would be meaningless, and a fiction entirely opposed to the
forger's purpose, namely, to win the confidence of his

readers.   Accordingly, those who deny the genuineness of
2 Peter must assume that the same pseudo-Peter, or one
before him, wrote another pseudo-Petrine letter.   But then
it is necessary to explain why only the second of this pair
of forged letters is preserved, although the author calls
attention in iii. 1 to the fact that he has addressed an
earlier letter to the same readers.   In like manner, the
announcement of Peter's intention to leave to the readers
a comprehensive and didactic writing (i. 15 ; above, p. 200 f.)
presents greater difficulties than the opponents of the
genuineness of 2 Peter seem to recognise.   The only purpose which a forger could have had in such a reference
would be to make his letter, which was as yet unknown,
seem more genuine by connecting it with a recognised
writing of Peter.   But how incredible it is that he should
assert merely his intention of composing such a writing,
and not the fact that he had actually done so !   And if
he meant a writing in Peter's name highly prized at the
time, such, e.g. as the ancient κήρυγμα Πέτρου, how aimless
it was on his part to omit all definite references to it !
But here again the assumption of genuineness removes all
the difficulties, as in the case of the writing which Jude
had planned but which has not come down to us (above,
p. 269).   The mere fact that Peter's letter, mentioned in
2 Pet. iii. 1, has not been preserved, needs no more explanation than the fact that the letter of Paul's spoken of
in 1 Cor. v. 9 was not made a part of the collection of his
Epistles.   The preservation of 2 Peter alone may be due
to the fact that it was only in this letter and not in the
earlier one mentioned in 2 Pet. iii. 1 that phenomena of
Church life were discussed which appeared first in the Gentile Christian Churches, and made their way thence into
the Jewish Christian Churches (above, pp. 223 ff., 242 ff.),
as Peter predicts would be the case, and Jude testifies
actually to have happened.   For this reason 2 Peter and
Jude had a certain value also for the Gentile Church, and

found some circulation there (above, p. 263 f.), while a hortatory letter written by the Apostle of the Circumcision to Churches belonging in the original sphere of his labours, which lacked such reference to the dangers threatening the whole Church, remained confined within this original circle. The fact that, so far as we know, the intention of Peter expressed in 2 Pet. i. 15 was never carried out, requires no special explanation. Yet it is hard not to think that the κήρυγμα Πέτρου was an invention suggested by 2 Pet. i. 15, and intended to supply the gap in the apostolic literature which this reference indicated. In the same way the emphasis upon the parousia as an integral element of the Petrine preaching (2 Pet. i. 16), and the prophetic character of 2 Pet. ii.–iii. probably supplied the impulse for the fabrication of the ἀποκάλυψις Πέτρου.

So long as it was assumed that 1 Peter was written by the apostle's own hand, and that 2 Peter was directed to the same readers as 1 Peter, the great difference between the two letters in thought and language was necessarily strong evidence against the genuineness of 2 Peter. These two presuppositions proving to be wrong, however, this argument against 2 Peter falls to the ground. That a letter to the Gentile Christian Churches of Asia Minor, written by Silvanus at Peter's request and in his name, would be different from a letter written by his own hand to Jewish Christian Churches who owed their Christian faith to him and his companions, is self-evident. In particular, it is clear that in the latter case he would necessarily betray an entirely different consciousness of his apostolic calling and official relation to the readers. While in the first letter he allows himself to be represented, and to a certain extent introduced, by a missionary prominent in the Churches of Asia Minor, in the second he speaks as the Apostle of the Circumcision to the flock over which Christ had made him shepherd (John xxi. 15–17 ; cf. x. 16). In speaking to these he

could say of himself what Paul said to the Corinthians in
1 Cor. ix. 2—and there was occasion for him to write in
this way if, as we saw above (pp. 222 f., 245), he had
become acquainted with a party which had sprung up in
the Gentile Christian Churches ; which spoke contemptuously of the simple Christians of the first generation
and condemned the apostles ; which was already threatening to bring this dangerous teaching also into the Jewish
Churches.   It is to be observed, however, that Peter does
not defend and magnify his apostleship in anything like
the severe and exalted tone of Paul (Gal. i. 1–ii. 14 ;
1 Cor. iii. 10–iv. 21, ix. 1–6, xv. 10 ; 2 Cor. x. 1–11, xi.
1–xii. 12, xiii. 1–3, 10 ; cf. 2 Pet. i. 1, 3, 16–18).   From
beginning to end the letter shows a brotherly spirit, and
is in keeping with Christ's exhortation to Peter in Luke
xxii. 32.   Anyone who regards the synoptic narrative of
the transfiguration and the words of Jesus in John xiii. 36 f.,
xxi. 18–22, as unhistorical, must, of course, take exception
to the reference in 2 Pet. i. 14, 16–18.   But it must be
remembered that when such prejudices, which in the last
analysis are dogmatic, are allowed to influence literary
criticism, the latter ceases to be worthy of its name.   On
the contrary, the manifest independence of this self-testimony of Peter, when compared with the Gospel accounts
(above, pp. 203, 211–218), is strong proof that it is not of
late origin, certainly not so late as 150 or 170.   Besides,
critics who are afraid of miracles need not be so seriously
embarrassed in accepting 2 Peter as genuine ; because the
feature of the synoptic account of the Transfiguration which
appears most mythical, namely, the appearance of Moses
and Elias, is omitted in 2 Peter.

Of more importance are the difficulties caused by the
statement about Paul and his letters in iii. 15 f.   The
chief thing to be noticed here is the fact that Peter speaks
of a single letter which Paul is represented as having once
sent to the Jewish Christian readers of 2 Peter, and the

fact that the letter is not only wanting, but also that there is no other trace of its previous existence in the early Church (above, p. 198 f.). Again, the assumption that 2 Peter is spurious, brings us face to face with the question, why again and again these persons writing in the name of Peter and Jude refer to writings, some of them already in existence and others in process of preparation, which no one else knows anything about? In reality, this appeal to a letter of Paul's, no longer to be found, is also proof of the age and genuineness of 2 Peter (cf. above, pp. 266 f., 271). In recalling to the readers' minds a single letter of Paul's with which they are acquainted, Peter mentions also a large number of other Pauline letters which, as the whole context shows (above, pp. 198 f., 227 f.), were addressed not to them, but to other Christians. There is nothing to indicate that the readers were acquainted with these letters also. Indeed, all that Peter says of them would seem to imply the contrary. He assures the readers, in the first place, that Paul in all his letters, whenever he speaks about the subject under discussion (λαλῶν, not λαλήσας), expresses himself in a similar way. Then Peter speaks of misinterpretations of certain passages in these letters (n. 10), not by his own readers, but by the false teachers and their followers, previously described in his letter, with whom he became acquainted in Gentile Christian circles (above, p. 227 f.). So far this statement contains nothing which precludes the possibility of Petrine authorship. There is nothing improbable in the supposition that from 60 to 64 A.D. many of Paul's letters had spread beyond the single Churches to which they were severally directed and were circulated in the Gentile Christian Church. Significant proof that Peter had read such letters is found in the fact that not very long after the composition of 2 Peter, when he wrote to the Churches in Asia Minor by the hand of Silvanus, he made use of Romans and Ephesians (above,

p. 177). Moreover, Peter had urgent occasion to express himself in this way regarding Paul and his letters. For, if the libertines who had made their appearance among the Churches founded by Paul justified their teaching and practice by an appeal to certain expressions of Paul's in his letters, they would have a very confusing effect upon the Jewish Christian Churches, if, as Peter expected, they made their way into these Churches in the near future. It was possible that the false teachers might be recommended to some Jewish Christians by their treacherous semblance of agreement with the great Apostle to the Gentiles, and this made their attempt at seduction all the more dangerous. In the case of the majority of Jewish Christians, however, such a connection would only serve to increase the feeling of mistrust toward the Apostle to the Gentiles which was not yet entirely overcome (Acts xxi. 20 ff.).

According to 1 Pet. i. 12, v. 12, and all reliable testimony regarding Peter, he endeavoured just as earnestly as did Paul (Gal. i. 22–24, ii. 7–10 ; 1 Cor. xv. 11 ; 1 Thess. ii. 14 ; 2 Cor. ix. 8–15 ; Rom. xv. 26–32) to promote harmony between the two branches of the Church and their respective leaders. Consequently he does not here call Paul simply his personal friend, but the beloved brother of himself and of his Jewish Christian readers (cf. Acts xxi. 20). For the same reason he reminds the readers of the letter which they had received from Paul, probably not long before (above, p. 209), and from which they can see that Paul and Peter are in agreement regarding the great essentials of Christian faith and hope and Christian morality. With this end in view he assures them that the same fundamental principles are held by Paul in all his other letters, and that, consequently, the appeal of the false teachers to his authority is just as false as is the mistrust of Paul by many Jewish-Christians.

The only thing that causes difficulty is the fact that

the false teachers are also said to pervert "the other scriptures" (2 Pet. iii. 16). Since elsewhere in the N.T. αἱ γραφαί is used only to designate the sacred writings of that time, *i.e.* the O.T. Scriptures, it might seem as if Peter included Paul's letters among these sacred writings. This would seem to bring us down to the time of Irenæus (n. 11). That this is a misunderstanding, however, is clearly proved by the fact that Peter here assumes a letter of Paul's as known, which is not anywhere mentioned in the literature of the Church among the canonical or apocryphal letters of Paul. Consequently the writer of 2 Peter did not have before him a collection of Paul's letters which were in general circulation in the second century. Furthermore, we are reminded here of the well-known Greek usage of ἄλλοι and ἕτεροι, which permits the following substantival designation to be limited to the group of words which these terms introduce (n. 12). A corresponding use of λοιποί might be possible, although examples of such use are wanting. But the very fact that the remaining writings in question are compared with the letters of Paul, or rather with certain passages in his letters hard to understand, in a way purely incidental and without any modifying adjectives such as ἅγιος (Rom. i. 2), ἱερός (2 Tim. iii. 15), θεοπνευστός (2 Tim. iii. 16), προφητικός (Rom. xvi. 26), παλαιός (2 Cor. iii. 14), ἀρχαῖος (Luke ix. 8, 19), proves that αἱ γραφαί is not here used in its technical sense, namely, "a collection of sacred writings." Among the Jews the technical use of הַסְּפָרִים = Bible did not prevent the application of the word ספר to all sorts of books and documents, as similarly among Greek-speaking Christians, the analogous technical use of αἱ γραφαί and τὰ γράμματα did not preclude the broader use of γραφή, γραφαί, and γράμματα (n. 12). The way in which the false teachers took obscure passages in Paul's letters out of their context and misinterpreted them, was only illustrative of their use of books in general. Of course, the reference is limited to books of a religious character naturally such as would claim recognition among Christian readers, either on account of the person who wrote them or of the use made of them in the service of the Church. Inasmuch as the libertines are nowhere represented as opposed in principle to the O.T., the sacred writings of the O.T. are not in any sense excluded, nor the apocryphal writings, such as Jude and Peter themselves read and used. We also do not know how large a body of Christian literature was already in existence by 60 or 64. As evidenced by 2 Peter and Jude in their time, some works had already been written, and others were projected, which have not come down to us, and in Luke i. 1 there is a definite reference to such literature ; so that we are entirely free to assume that in the years 50–70 other teachers, such as Barnabas, Apollos, Silvanus, and Timothy, occasionally prepared a didactic letter, or some other writing, out of which the false teachers took single passages and misinterpreted them, as in the case of Paul's letters.

So, then, 2 Pet. iii. 15 f. contains nothing which takes us beyond the period of Peter's life, while the mention of a letter of Paul's, unknown to the Church in the post-apostolic age, is proof that 2 Peter was written in apostolic times. We know that single passages in Paul's letters, and particularly passages dealing with the moral life and its relation to heathen immorality, were misunderstood even by the original receivers, and also interpreted unfairly (1 Cor. v. 9–13 ; 2 Cor. i. 13 f.; vol. i. pp. 261, 322). Furthermore, we saw that probably the libertines, whose entrance into the Jewish Christian Church was predicted by Peter and described by Jude after it had taken place, appropriated forms of speech such as Paul had used in 1 Cor. ii. 10–iii. 2 (Jude 19 ; above p. 258, n. 6). Jude seems to have found it worth while to read Paul's letters as Peter did. Along with 2 Peter, which is formally quoted, he mentions the utterances of other apostles which must

likewise have been addressed to his readers, since they
are exhorted to remember the same (Jude 17; above, p.
252). The reference, therefore, cannot be to letters of
Paul's addressed to Gentile Christian Churches or to individuals in these Churches, as has been assumed on the
basis of passages like 2 Tim. ii. 17 f., iii. 1 ff., iv. 3 f. It
is very natural, however, to suppose that he means that
letter of Paul's which, according to 2 Pet. iii. 15, was
directed to the same readers and was related in content to
2 Peter. If Jude read 2 Peter carefully, and ascertained
from it Peter's high opinion of the wisdom of Paul in his
letters, and that the false teachers misused numerous
passages in other Pauline letters, it is not astonishing
that he should endeavour to procure Paul's letters, and
that he should read them carefully. This was all the
more natural, in view of the fact that he felt it his duty to
summon his readers to oppose the libertines who used as
watchwords Pauline phrases which they misinterpreted.
So he himself could appropriate the Pauline distinction
between ψυχικοί and πνευματικοί which was misused by the
false teachers (Jude 19). There are also other resemblances
to Paul's letters which can hardly be regarded as accidental
(n. 13). Neither Jude nor 2 Peter shows evidence of the
use of literary works from the time after the destruction
of Jerusalem (n. 14).

Finally, the question arises as to the character of the
false teachers described in both letters. There is no
essential difference between the descriptions of 2 Peter
and Jude (above, pp. 224 f., 243 ff.). Though the word
ψευδοδιδάσκαλοι does not occur in Jude, the thing which the
word designates is found (above, p. 247 f.). While Jude
nowhere indicates that these intruders despised prophecy,
—an omission which is especially striking, because what
Jude leaves out in ver. 18 is found in the corresponding
passage in 2 Pet. iii. 3 f. which he cited,—the fact is not
to be overlooked that in 2 Peter also this side of the false

tendency depicted by Peter falls at once entirely into the background, and that Peter goes on to speak of the rise of various tendencies which will result from the intrusion of the false teachers which he foresees (ii. 1 ; above, p. 232, n. 2). It is in harmony not only with this prediction, but also with universal experience, that the representatives of the movement with which Peter had become acquainted in the Gentile Christian Churches did not reveal their whole "system" at once upon their entrance into the Jewish Christian Churches in Jude's time. They left untouched for the time being especially the teachings about the Christian hope which were so deeply rooted in Jewish Christianity, and, in general, strove to introduce their theory and practice, less by direct attack upon the common faith than by clever misinterpretation of the doctrine of grace (Jude 4), by depreciating judgments of the apostles and the simple Church officials (above, pp. 223, 243), by currying favour with the richer and more educated members of the Church (Jude 16), and by making the most of the opportunities afforded by the love-feasts for social, and yet at the same time religious fellowship (Jude 12).

It is not necessary to come down so late as the second century in order to find an illustration from other historical sources of the kind of false teachers described in Jude and 2 Peter. The essential features of this movement are to be found as early as the year 57 in the Corinthian Church (vol. i. pp. 273 ff., 298 f.). There a movement had temporarily gained a foothold which (1) advocated extremely dangerous principles with regard to sexual life, based upon the idea of the freedom of the Christian under the gospel (1 Cor. vi. 12–20), principles which were actually applied in the life of the Church. The Lord who had bought the Christians, that they might be His servants. was practically denied (1 Cor. vi. 20, vii. 23 ; cf. 2 Pet. ii. 1 ; Jude 4). From the hints in Romans, which was

written in Corinth in the year 58 (Rom. vi. 1 ff., 12, 14 ff.),
we also learn that an effort was made to find a theoretical
support for the continuance of heathen immorality in the
doctrine of the Christian state of grace, as well as in the
doctrine of freedom under the gospel (2) The same
movement in Corinth justified participation in the heathen
cultus acts, on the ground that all Christians, as a matter
of course, knew that the heathen conceptions about the
gods were false, and that the demons, who in the view of
Paul and all other Jewish Christians presided over the
idol worship, and were dangerous to Christians, were as
powerless and unreal as the gods of mythology (1 Cor.
viii.-x.; cf. 2 Pet. ii. 10 f.; Jude 8–10). (3) Exalted by
this feeling of superior knowledge, the representatives of
this movement assumed an attitude of insubordination and
irreverence toward the apostle Paul which he compares
to the rebellion of Korah (above, p. 257 f., n. 5). The
watchword ἐγὼ δὲ Χριστοῦ represented an attitude of scorn
toward all human authority in the Church (vol. i. p. 294).
(4) Those of the Corinthians who denied the most essential
point in the Christian teaching regarding the future life,
namely, the resurrection of the body (1 Cor. xv.), were
probably representatives of the same tendency. The expectation of the future kingdom of Christ (1 Cor. xv.
23–28), which is inseparable from belief in the resurrection,
was also practically denied in Corinth (1 Cor. iv. 8 ; vol. i.
p. 273 f.). (5) The libertines in Corinth are not described as
professional teachers ; but just as they endeavoured to find
a theoretical foundation for their practical views, so, being
" strong " spirits, they declared it to be their duty to bring
the " weak " to their point of view, and to impart to them
the knowledge which brings freedom, and to build them
up by their example (1 Cor. viii. 10 ; vol. i. p. 296, n. 1).
(6) One of the abuses of the common meals of the Church
(these meals are not yet called ἀγάπαι), which ended in the
celebration of the eucharist, was the fact that by many they

were degraded into occasions for revelling (1 Cor. xi. 21 f., 34 ; cf. 2 Pet. ii. 13 ; Jude 12). Here also the separative tendencies which threatened to destroy the unity of the Corinthian Church and its connection with the whole Church, came to view (1 Cor. xi. 18 f.; cf. Jude 19 ; vol. i. p. 284 f.). In short, all the elements of the prophetic picture of the false teachers in 2 Peter, and of the historical description of Jude, are to be found in 1 Corinthians, except that in the latter case they have not yet reached the same stage of development. In Corinth the libertines misinterpreted the written instructions of Paul (1 Cor. v. 9 ff.); they apparently applied passages which Paul had actually spoken in a way contrary to his meaning (1 Cor. vi. 12, x. 23, viii. 1, 4, x. 19); and they even boasted, when indulging in practices which Paul reproves, that they were following his instructions (1 Cor. xi. 2). All of these things are illustrations of 2 Pet. iii. 16. The only new feature is that Peter predicts that persons representing this tendency will appear among the Jewish Christian Churches as false teachers, and that Jude some ten years later testifies that this had actually happened. That these intruders are not charged, or at least not clearly charged, with participation in idolatrous sacrificial feasts, and with seducing others to such participation (above, p. 243 ff.), is not strange ; for in Jewish Christian Churches such demands would have met with insurmountable opposition. Furthermore, the environment of these Churches would perhaps hardly have furnished opportunity for such practices.

In view of the mention of Balaam's name (2 Pet. ii. 15 ; Jude 11), it is at least possible that Peter and Jude knew that many persons representing this tendency did not keep themselves aloof from idolatrous worship in their own home, *i.e.* in Gentile lands, to the degree that Peter and Jude and Paul himself felt to be necessary. From Rev. ii. 2, 6, 14 f., 20–25 we learn that between the years 90 and 95 representatives of a doctrine in which unchastity and participation in idolatrous feasts were justified among other reasons by appeal to a deeper insight into the nature of evil spirits (Rev. ii. 24), sought entrance into the Churches of Ephesus, Pergamos, and Thyatira, and were partially successful. The occurrence of the name of Balaam in Rev. ii. 14 (cf. 2 Pet. ii. 15 ; Jude 11) of itself almost compels us to assume a connection between this teaching and what is described in 2 Peter and Jude. The historical reports regarding the party and teaching of the Nicolaitans (Rev. ii. 6, 15) favour the assumption that in the last third of the first century they sent missionaries among the Jewish Christians in Palestine, as well as among the Gentile Christians in Ephesus (n. 15). While there were numerous parties and sects representing libertinistic theories and practices in the second and third centuries, there is none that so closely resembles the seducers described in 2 Peter and Jude as the libertinistic movement with which we become acquainted in 1 Corinthians, and as the Nicolaitans of whom we learn from hints in Revelation.

1. (P. 262.) The suspicions as to the genuineness and canonicity of 2 Pet. as of Jude current in the ancient Church were shared by the theologians of the sixteenth century. Erasmus, who thought that the reference in 1 Pet. v. 12 was to a letter earlier than our 1 Pet., written by Silvanus, was of the opinion that the statement that 2 Pet. was a second (instead of a third) letter could be explained only on the assumption that 2 Pet. was spurious, or, like the earliest, the lost letter, was written by Silvanus at Peter's direction (*Paraphr. in epist. can. Basil*, 1521, fol. A³, cf. A⁴ D²). Luther in the year 1524 (Erl. Ausg. Bd. 52, S. 271) quotes 2 Pet. iii. 15 as one of the passages on the basis of which its composition by Peter might be questioned, in so far as it indicates "that this Epistle was written long after those of Paul." 2 Pet. iii. 9 was objectionable to him on doctrinal grounds : " Doch ists gläublich, sie [die Epistel] nichts deste minder des Apostels sei " (still, it is credible that it may be an epistle of the apostle). Calvin in his *Argumentum* on 2 Pet. and on iii. 15 wavers between acceptance and rejection, but is inclined to believe that the letter was written by a disciple of Peter at his direction. Grotius (on 2 Pet. i. 1, 14, 17, iii. 1, ed. Windheim, ii. 1038, 1042 f., 1053, 1060), who is of the opinion that 2 Pet. could not have been written until after the destruction of Jerusalem, divides the letter into two letters, chaps. i.–ii. and chap. iii., making iii. 1 refer to chaps. i. and ii. as a first letter. They were both written not by the apostle Simon Peter, but by Simeon, the second bishop of Jerusalem in the time of Trajan (Eus. *H. E.* iii. 32). In

order to establish his theory, Grotios omitted the words Πέτρος . . . καὶ
ἀπόστολος, 1 Pet. i. 1, and ὁ ἀγαπητὸς ἡμῶν ἀδελφός, iii. 15, on the ground
that they are interpolations. He also conjectured that the heavenly voice in
i. 17 was an interpolation, so that the holy mountain may be understood as
referring to Zion, and the entire passage made to relate to John xii. 28.
Accordingly, Grotius, p. 1117, explained the words ἀδελφὸς δὲ Ἰακώβου, Jude 1,
as an interpolation, and declared this Epistle to be the work of the last Jewish
Christian bishop of Jerusalem in the time of Hadrian (§ 43, n. 1). Herder
(Briefe zweener Bruder Jesu, 1775, Opera, ed. by Suphan, vi. 471) regarded
both letters as genuine, but could not understand how the opinion could be
so long held that Jude is dependent upon 2 Pet., the opposite relation being so
perfectly apparent (S. 529). On the other hand, Semler (Paraphrasis ep. Petri
II. et Judæ, 1784, in the preface of fol. d¹ and p. 167 f.) declared both letters
to be pseudonymous forgeries of the second half of the second century ;
Jude he held to be an epitome of 2 Pet. While J. D. Michaelis (Einl., 4te
Auf. 1788, S. 1475 ff.) defends the genuineness of 2 Pet., and is inclined to
assume that Jude is fabricated on the basis of 2 Pet. (S. 1516), Eichhorn
(Einl. 1812, iii. S. 624–656) decides against the genuineness of 2 Pet., mainly
on the ground of the dependence of 2 Pet. upon Jude, which he thinks was
written perhaps before the year 70. And this is one of the main reasons for
the wide currency of a similar view to-day. Among the moderns who
advocate this view, special mention should be made of Mayerhoff (Hist. krit.
Einl. in die petrinischen Schriften, 1835, S. 149–217) ; among those who defend
the genuineness of 2 Pet., Weiss (see especially ThStKr, 1866, S. 255–308) ;
Hofmann, NT, vii. 3 (1875) ; Spitta, Der 2 Br. des Pt. und des Ju. (1885).
Nor have efforts been wanting since Grotius to find a genuine Epistle of Peter
in 2 Pet. by removing additions to the letter that are not held to be original.
Berthold (Einl. 1819, S. 3157 ff.) declared chap. ii. to be an interpolation based
upon Jude, holding chaps. i. and iii. to be an original letter of Peter's. C. Ull-
mann (Krit. Unters. des 2 Pt. 1821) accepted only chap. i. as the work of Peter.
Gess, Das apost. Zeugniss von Christi Person, 1879, ii. 2, S. 412 ff., is in favour
of striking out i. 20ᵇ (ὅτι πᾶσα)—iii. 3ᵃ (γινώσκοντες) as an interpolation.

2. (P. 264.) In explaining the entirely different reception of 1 Pet. and
2 Pet. in the ancient Church, appeal cannot be made to the lost letters of
Paul to the Corinthians (vol. i. pp. 261, 270, n. 9), to the Philippians (vol.
i. p. 535 f.) and to the readers of 2 Pet. (above, p. 198 f.), nor to Peter's own
letter, referred to in 2 Pet. iii. 1 (above, p. 199 f.) ; for the reason that, so far
as we know, these letters were very soon and for ever lost. On the other
hand, 2 Pet. was preserved and eventually came to be everywhere accepted
as a letter of Peter's. The real question is why the general circulation and
acceptance of 2 Pet. was so much later than that of 1 Pet.

3. (P. 264.) For traces of 2 Pet. and Jude in the literature of the early
Church, and their relation to the canon, see GK, i. 310–321, 759, 959–961, ii.
819, 853 ; Grundriss, 20, 21 f., 25 (A. 15), 42 f., 53, 54 f., 56, 60, 68 f., 71.
For the relation between 2 Pet. and Hermas cf. the writer's work, Hirt des
Hermas, 430–438 ; Hofmann, NT, vii. 3. 174 f.; Spitta, Der 2 Brief des Pet.
533 f. While in this work Spitta recognised only a certain general relation-
hip between the two writings in thought and language, later he came to
eel that the large number of close resemblances between them indicated a

literary relationship (*Z. Gesch. u. Lit. des Urchrist.* ii. 399–409).   According to Spitta, however, Hermas is not dependent upon 2 Pet., but in the year 64 the apostle Peter read in Rome the apocalypse which was written in Rome in the year 50 by a Jew named Hermas, and which in the year 150 was worked over by the Christian Hermas, the brother of bishop Pius of Rome (Can. Muratori, lines 73–80 ; Spitta, 434), into the *Shepherd*, afterwards so widely read in the Church.   Such a theory cannot be refuted in a passing remark.   But a protest is entered against the assumption of the accidental coincidence by which the original writer and the editor have the same names, thereby making the tradition and the theory agree (cf. above, p. 263).

4. (P. 265.)   Luther (in the year 1522, in the preface to James and Jude, Erl. Ausg. 63, S. 158) says : " No one can deny that the Epistle of St. Jude is an extract or a copy of St. Peter's second Epistle, inasmuch as almost all the words of the two are the same."   The view here expressed in an exaggerated form was held by Grotius, Bengel, Semler, Michaelis, and others without any more definite effort to establish it.   Herder opposed it as the prevailing view of his time (above, p. 284).   Eichhorn (*Einl.* iii. 637, 642 ff.) reversed this relation, and after his time the majority of critics made it one of the chief grounds of objection to the genuineness of 2 Pet.   This view finally became so general that it was accepted even by those who defended the genuineness of 2 Pet., as Hug, *Einl.*[3] ii. 556 ; Wiesinger, *Der 2 Pt.* 1862, S. 22 ff.; Weiss, *ThStKr,* 1866, S. 256 ff., 300 f. ; finally, Fr. Maier, *TQ,* 1905, S. 547–580 ; *ibid.* in *BbZ,* 1904, S. 377 on Jude 4 f., see above, p. 262, n. 12.   Into the discussion of this relation the question whether it was in accordance with Peter's dignity to follow closely the letter of Jude, who was not an apostle, should never have been allowed to enter, nor the conjecture that some pseudo-Peter objected to the apocryphal citations in Jude, and accordingly removed some of them and obliterated others.   This presupposes a precise dogmatic distinction between what was canonical and what was apocryphal, which was not to be found throughout the entire second century, especially with reference to O.T. matters.   Moreover, we cannot approve the efforts made on both sides to establish the dependence of one writer upon another, because of misunderstanding or clumsiness of expression.   Jude is not copied from 2 Pet. ; neither is 2 Pet. a working over of Jude.   The fact that Jude appealed to an apostolic prediction known to his readers, the beginning of the fulfilment of which he witnesses, made it natural for him to follow this prophecy in describing present realities.   He did so, however, only so far as the fulfilment of the same can be actually discerned.

5. (P. 267.)   It is impossible to conceive of 2 Pet. as being fabricated on the basis of Jude 4, 17 f., in the same way that the so-called *Third Epistle to the Corinthians* and the *Epistle to the Laodiceans* were fabricated on the basis of 1 Cor. v. 9, vii. 1, and Col. iv. 16 (vol. i. p. 270, n. 9, p. 488, n. 2).   As a matter of fact, the analogy between the two cases is very slight.   (1) There is no direct reference in Jude to a writing of Peter's.   (2) The reference in Jude 4, 17 f. would lead naturally to the fabrication of an apocalypse (above, pp. 270, 273) rather than to a letter in an apostle's name.   (3) 2 Pet. is too earnest and rich in thought to be due, like the letter to the Laodiceans entirely and 3 Cor. in part, to the mere desire to produce artificially at some later date the missing foundation in literature of a quotation found in some

apostolic writing. (4) How little attention was paid to these hints of Jude about other writings of the apostolic age is evidenced by the fact that the ancient interpreters either pass Jude 3, 4, 17 f. by altogether (Clem. *Hypot.* ; Didymus), or at most make Jude 17 refer to 2 Pet. and the Epistles of Paul (Cramer, *Cat.* viii. 168). So far as we know, a second, more detailed work of Jude was never written on the basis of Jude 3 (see above, p. 242).

6. (P. 269.) There is no high degree of probability in Spitta's conjecture (404) that the writing which, according to ver. 3, Jude was about to prepare, was the same for the composition of which Peter made himself responsible in 2 Pet. i. 15, without saying whether he would write it himself or commission someone else to do so. If Peter wrote in 63 or 64 and Jude in 75, then either Peter failed to keep his promise, or Jude was lax in carrying out his commission. The only thing indicated by the two passages is that the time had come when men in apostolic circles had begun to think about providing for the future by literary work; cf. 1 John i. 4.

7. (Pp. 269, 270.) Below are placed in parallel columns (1) the text of Jude 14 f. (Tisch. 8th ed.), with the omission of the first αὐτῶν after ἀσεβεῖς, which is due to an error in printing (see Tischendorf's apparatus for these verses, and Gregory, *Prolegomena*, 1285) ; (2) the Greek text of Enoch i. 9, edited first in 1892 by Bouriant (*Mém. de la mission archéol. au Caire*, ix. 1), following the edition of Flemming and Radermacher, p. 20 (cf. Lods, *L'évangile et l'apocalypse de Pierre*, p. 112 ; Charles, *The Book of Enoch*, 1893, p. 329): (3) an English translation of the Ethiopic Enoch, after the German of Flemming and Radermacher, which has been compared with Dillmann's German translation (S. 1) ; (4) the fragment of the Latin Enoch (Pseudo-Cypr. *ad Novat.* 16, Cypr. ed. Hartel, Append. p. 67 ; cf. *GK*, ii. 797-801 ; *Forsch.* v. 158, 438 ; James, *Apocr. anecd.* i. 146 ff.).

JUDE 14 f.

ἰδοὺ ἦλθεν κύριος ἐν ἁγίαις μυριάσιν αὐτοῦ, ποιῆσαι κρίσιν κατὰ πάντων καὶ ἐλέγξαι πάντας τοὺς ἀσεβεῖς περὶ πάντων τῶν ἔργων ἀσεβείας αὐτῶν ὧν ἠσέβησαν καὶ περὶ πάντων τῶν σκληρῶν λόγων, ὧν ἐλάλησαν κατ' αὐτοῦ ἁμαρτωλοὶ ἀσεβεῖς.

GREEK ENOCH.

ὅτι ἔρχεται σὺν ταῖς μυριάσιν αὐτοῦ καὶ τοῖς ἁγίοις αὐτοῦ ποιῆσαι κρίσιν κατὰ πάντων, καὶ ἀπολέσει πάντας τοὺς ἀσεβεῖς καὶ ἐλέγξει πᾶσαν σάρκα περὶ πάντων ἔργων τῆς ἀσεβείας αὐτῶν ὧν ἠσέβησαν καὶ σκληρῶν ὧν ἐλάλησαν λόγων καὶ περὶ πάντων ὧν κατελάλησαν κατ' αὐτοῦ ἁμαρτωλοὶ ἀσεβεῖς.

ETHIOPIC TEXT.

And lo! He has come [(Dill.) comes] with ten thousands of [(Dill.) with ten thousand] holy ones, to execute judgment upon them, and He will destroy the ungodly, and will reprove all flesh [(*Al.* and Dill.) will argue with all flesh] for all that which the sinners and (the) ungodly have wrought and committed [(Dill.) ungodly committed] against Him.

LATIN ENOCH.

Ecce venit cum multis milibus nunciorum suorum, facere iudicium de omnibus et perdere omnes impios et arguere omnem carnem de omnibus factis impiorum, quæ fecerunt impie, et de omnibus verbis impiis quæ de deo locuti sunt peccatores.

A number of different circumstances render difficult a definite judgment concerning this text. The original, which is commonly supposed
to have been Hebrew or Aramaic, is lost (Schürer, iii. 203 ; [Eng. trans.
II. iii. pp. 69, 70]). The text of Jude is not by any means fixed, and
it is quite possible that the text tradition of Jude was influenced by the
Greek text of the Book of Enoch, which was current in the second and
third centuries. Furthermore, we do not know when the Greek translation
of Enoch, from which the Ethiopic and Latin were derived, was made. If
it was made by a Christian after Jude was written, it is most likely that
in this passage the translator was influenced by the quotation in Jude,
just as copyists of the LXX were frequently influenced by N.T. quotations.
If, on the other hand, the Greek translation was made by a Jew before
Jude was written, Jude is hardly likely to have made use of the Greek
version. The peculiar ἰδοὺ ἦλθεν, instead of ἰδοὺ ἔρχεται, which alone suits
the passage, is a clumsy translation of the ambiguous הִנֵּה־בָא (cf. Isa. xxi. 9,
lxii. 11 ; Jer. l. 41 ; Zech. ii. 14 ; Mal. iii. 19, and, *per contra*, Ezek. vii. 12) ;
ἐν μυριάσιν is a Hebraism (Num. xx. 20 ; 1 Macc. i. 17 ; Luke xiv. 31),
which could never have been written by anyone who had the Greek σὺν
μυριάσιν before him. The agreement between Jude and the Greek Enoch
in the choice of words is, however, closer than is usually found between
two independent translators (ποιῆσαι κρίσιν κατὰ πάντων, ἐλέγχειν, ἀσεβεῖς,
ἀσεβεῖν, ἀσέβεια, σκληροὶ λόγοι), which compels us to assume that the Greek
translator of Enoch was a Christian familiar with Hebrew, and therefore
certainly a Jewish Christian, who, like so many Christians in later times,
became interested in the book through Jude 14, and was under the influence of the quite free citation of Jude when he translated the passage
cited by Jude, which stood at the very beginning of his original. It is
generally admitted by the Church Fathers that Jude quotes the *Book of
Enoch* : Clement, *Hypot.* (*Forsch.* iii. 85, 97), " his verbis (sc. *Judas*) pro-
phetam (not *prophetiam*) comprobat " ; Tert. *Cult. fem.* i. 3, " Enoch apud
Iudam apostolum testimonium possidet " (*GK*, i. 120 f.) ; Jerome, *Vir. Ill.* iv. ;
Comm. in Tit. Vall. vii. 708) ; August. *Civit.* xv. 23. 4, xviii. 38) ; Euthalius
(Zacagni, 480, 485). This has been vigorously denied by Hofmann, vii. 2.
187, 205–211 (cf. his *Schriftbeweis*, i. 420–424), and Philippi (*Das Buch Henoch*,
1868, S. 138–152), who advance the theory that Jude's only source was the
oral traditions of the rabbis, and that the *Book of Enoch* that has come down
to us was written by a Jewish Christian on the basis of Jude 14. Without
claiming that the pre-Christian origin of the whole of the *Book of Enoch* is
absolutely proved, it is possible entirely to reject this theory on the following
grounds : (1) The fact that Jude uses direct discourse in quoting *Enoch*
indicates that he has it before him in written form. Although in the
addresses in which the rabbis were accustomed to interpret and enlarge upon
the O.T. narratives in the synagogue certain mythical elements, including
the sayings and replies of the persons in the narratives, may have assumed
a relatively stereotyped form, it is inconceivable that one who was not a
disciple of the rabbis, but a brother of Jesus and a member of the first Christian
Church, should for this reason have quoted a somewhat long saying of the
patriarch Enoch in exactly the same way that men who held the same faith,
and were contemporaries of his, were accustomed to quote the prophecies of

Isaiah, as these were found in the O.T.   Other references in the N.T. tc
mythical additions to the O.T. history are confined to facts and names (Matt.
i. 5; Acts vii. 22 f., xiii. 20 f.; Gal. iv. 29 ; 2 Tim. iii. 8 ; Heb. xi. 37).   No
one would compare the citation of the words of Jesus at a time when the gospel
was as yet unwritten, but when numerous persons who had heard them were
still living in the Church (§ 48), with the apparently verbal quotation of a
prophecy supposed to have been spoken in patriarchal times.   To deny that
Jude 14 f. is taken from *Enoch* i. 9 is to deprive oneself also of the right to
affirm that Jude 17 f. is a quotation from 2 Pet. iii. 3 (above, p. 250 f.).   (2) If
the *Book of Enoch*, or even the passage which is parallel to what is found in
Jude, had been written on the basis of Jude 14 f., it would be evidenced by an
exact verbal quotation of Jude ; whereas, as a matter of fact, Jude, following
the example of the apostles and of the ancients generally, could reproduce
his citation quite freely, notwithstanding the fact that he quoted it in direct
discourse.   And this freedom would be all the greater if he had before him
the Hebrew *Enoch*, which he himself was under necessity of translating into
Greek.   If it be true that at least this part of the *Book of Enoch* was written
in Hebrew and is of Jewish origin, then it is impossible to believe that its
author borrowed from a Greek Christian writing.   (3) Besides the almost
verbal quotation, there are numerous other resemblances between Jude and
Enoch.   This is not confined to single quoted expressions such as σκληροὶ
λόγοι (*Enoch* v. 4, xxvii. 2), ἕβδομος ἀπὸ Ἀδάμ (*Enoch* lx. 8, xciii. 3), which
recur in other parts of the book.   It is to be particularly observed that the
fall and punishment of the angels who before the Flood had intercourse
with women (Jude 6 ; cf. ver. 7) is described in such a way that what is said
could not have been derived from Gen. vi. 1–4 or 2 Pet. ii. 4.   Jude's source
is rather, for the fall, *Enoch* vi., vii., ix. 7–9, xii. 4–6, xv. 3–xvi. 4 ; for the
punishment, *Enoch* x. 11–14, xiv. 5–6, xviii. 14–xix. 2 ; cf. especially xii. 4
(also xv. 3), ἀπολιπόντες τὸν οὐρανὸν τὸν ὑψηλόν, and x. 12, δῆσον αὐτοὺς
ἑβδομήκοντα γενεὰς εἰς τὰς νάπας τῆς γῆς μέχρι ἡμέρας κρίσεως αὐτῶν κτλ.
Cf. Spitta, 324 ff., 360–367.   It is not so easy to establish the correctness of
the opinion of the Church Fathers that Jude 9 is related to the ἀνάληψις
Μωϋσέως, since the fragment of the Latin translation of this Jewish apocryphal writing (Fritzsche, *Libr. apoc.* 700–730) is broken off before the burial
of Moses is reached, and so contains nothing corresponding to the passage in
Jude.   But what reason is there for disbelieving the Fathers, who had the
Greek text of this book, when they say that Jude quoted from it; cf. Clem.
Hypot. (*Forsch.* iii. 84, 96 f.), "hic confirmat assumptionem Moysi"; Orig. *de
Princ.* iii. 2. 1 ; Didymus, Lat. trans. (Migne, 39. 1815) ; Euthalius (Zacagni,
480, 485).   In particular, we are justified in assuming that there was something in this book corresponding to the passage in Jude, by a quotation in
Gellasius Cyzicus (Mansi, ii. 857 ; cf. Apollinaris in Nicephor. *Cat. in octa-
teuchum,* i. 1313 ; Cramer, *Cat.* viii. 161, 163 ; Matthæi, *Epist. cathol.* pp.
170, 238, 244).   There is nothing in the parallel passage 2 Pet. ii. 10 f.
referring to the same event, and so no reference to the *Assumptio Mosis*.   It
is uncertain whether Peter had in view Zech. iii. 2 (Hofmann, vii. 2. 65), the
passage upon which the author of the *Assumptio Mosis* is supposed to have
based the passage in his work used by Jude, or whether Peter thought of
Enoch x. 4–8, 11–14. xii. 4–xiii. 2 (Spitta, 170 ff.).   It is altogether likely

that in 2 Pet. ii. 4–11 use is made, not only of unwritten Jewish tradition, but of apocryphal books, such as *Enoch* cited by Jude.

8. (P. 270.) With reference to the pseudo-Petrine writings, cf. *GK*, i. 199 f., 308–311, 758, 802, ii. 742–751, 810–855 ; *Grundriss*, 25. The *Epistle of Peter to James* (*Clementina*, ed. Lagarde, p. 3) cannot be regarded as a type of the pseudo-Petrine letters to Churches for the following reasons : (1) It is not a letter addressed to a Church. (2) It was written by a man who took a view of Peter antagonistic to that of biblical and ecclesiastical tradition, whereas the view of the author of 2 Pet. is in direct accord with the same. (3) This *Epistle of Peter to James* was certainly not written before the third century. The subordination of Peter to James, which is part of the fundamental idea of this work, renders Peter's apostolic consciousness less prominent (p. 4. 16, κύριέ μου). This is more strongly expressed in the *Epistle of Clement to James* (Lagarde, 6. 12 ff.).

9. (P. 271.) As to the resemblances between 1 Pet. and 2 Pet. in language and content, cf. Schott, *2 Petrusbrief*, S. 167–188 ; Hofmann, vii. 128–139. In view of the fundamentally different character of the greetings of the two Epistles of Peter, both as regards the designation of the writer and of the readers, which precludes the possibility of intentional imitation, the correspondence in the greeting itself (χάρις—πληθυνθείη) is of no great significance ; since it is limited by the phrase which follows in 2 Pet. i. 2, and by the connection made by this phrase with the text that follows (above, p. 220). Moreover, εἰρήνη ὑμῖν (or ἡ εἰρήνη ὑμῶν) πληθυνθείη is a common Jewish formula (vol. i. p. 32, n. 18). It is found in a somewhat altered form in Jude 2, and in Clem. 1 *Cor.*, and Polyc. *ad Phil.*,—in the last two cases clearly influenced by 1 Pet. i. 2,—and in the communication of the Smyrneans in the year 155 (*Martyr. Polyc.*), in this case closely following Jude 2. More worthy of notice is the fact that both in 1 Pet. iii. 20 and 2 Pet. ii. 5 the number of those saved in the Flood is given as eight, though in Gen. vi. 18, vii. 7, 13, viii. 16, no number is mentioned. Moreover, that interpretation of 1 Pet. iii. 19 is in all probability correct, according to which a preaching of Christ at the time of the Flood is referred to, *i.e.* a preaching through Noah, so that Noah is here represented as a preacher of righteousness, as in 2 Pet. ii. 5. In such a connection the fact that the deferment of the judgment is explained by the μακροθυμία of God in 1 Pet. iii. 20 and 2 Pet. iii. 9, cf. iii. 5 f., deserves notice, although the thought is itself a very natural one (Rom. ii. 4). There are, moreover, a few words and phrases which in the whole N.T. are found only in 1 Pet. and 2 Pet. or practically nowhere else : ἀρετή, 1 Pet. ii. 9, 2 Pet. i. 3, is used as an attribute of God or Christ when represented as calling men (above, p. 220) ; also twice found in 2 Pet. i. 5 of human virtue, and elsewhere only in Phil. iv. 8 ; ἄσπιλος καὶ ἄμωμος (or ἀμώμητος), 2 Pet. iii. 14, in reverse order in 1 Pet. i. 19 ; σαρκὸς ἀπόθεσις ῥύπου, 1 Pet. iii. 21 ; ἀπόθεσις τοῦ σκηνώματος, 2 Pet. i. 14 ; ἐποπτεύειν, 1 Pet. ii. 12, iii. 2 ; ἐπόπται γενηθέντες, 2 Pet. i. 16. Cf. 2 Pet. ii. 14, ἀκαταπαύστους ἁμαρτίας, and 1 Pet. iv. 1, πέπαυται ἁμαρτίας ; also ψυχαί to designate persons, 1 Pet. iii. 20 (ii. 25) and 2 Pet. ii. 14, found elsewhere only in Rom. xiii. 1. It is also to be observed that certain ideas, which recur with special frequency in one of the letters, are found also in the other : ἀναστροφή six times in 1 Pet., twice in 2 Pet., elsewhere in the whole N.T. only five times ; ἀσέλγεια, 2 Pet. ii. 2.

7, 18; 1 Pet. iv. 3; ἐστηριγμένος, 2 Pet. i. 12; ἀστήρικτος, ii. 14, iii. 16; στηριγμός, iii. 17; but also in 1 Pet. v. 10, στηρίξει. Notwithstanding such details, which may serve to suggest that, when Silvanus wrote 1 Pet. by Peter's directions and in his name, he was influenced by Peter's thought and language, we get from the letters the impression of a totally different style, which even in antiquity tended to make questionable the composition of 2 Pet. by the writer of 1 Pet. (Jerome, *Vir. Ill.* i.; *ad Hedibiam, Ep.* cxx. 11).

10. (P. 275.) It may be accepted as certain that the correct reading in iii. 16 is ἐν αἷς (אAB, many cursives, S² S³), not ἐν οἷς (CKLP and the majority of cursives). It is equally clear that we are to read πάσαις ἐπιστολαῖς (ABC) without ταῖς inserted in א and the Antiochian recension. It makes an important difference in the sense. With the article the Epistles are represented as a definite whole, and the statement made covers all parts of the collection without exception. With the article omitted the one letter of Paul's known to the readers is contrasted with letters of all kinds which he has written. In other words, one may take any one of them he chooses and he will never find the libertine view, but everywhere the same moral earnestness.

11. (P. 277.) Cf. *e.g.* Iren. ii. 30. 7: "universæ clamant scripturæ, et Paulus autem testimonium perhibet"; ii. 28. 7, "et dominus manifeste dixit et reliquæ demonstrant scripturæ."

12. (P. 277.) For ἄλλοι in the above-mentioned sense (above, p. 277), cf. Kühner-Gerth i. 275. The Latins, French, and Italians also use this illogical form of speech (see Thiersch, *Versuch.* 423); ἕτεροι is used in the same way less frequently, Luke xxiii. 32; Thucyd. iv. 67. 2; cf. also ἕτερος δὲ τῶν μαθητῶν, Matt. viii. 21, where the meaning is a second person who is already one of the disciples, in distinction from the first who was one of the scribes, and had just declared his readiness to become a disciple (viii. 19). An analogous use of λοιποί must first be pointed out and is extremely improbable, because this word does not, like ἄλλος, ἕτερος, carry with it the idea of distinctive difference. Unfortunately there is wanting the original of sentences as found in Orig. Lat. trans. (Delarue, iii. 877, 888 *in Matt.*) § 61, *apostolos certerosque episcopos et doctores,* § 72, *Christi . . . ceterorumque discipulorum* ejus. Cf. also the second quotation in n. 11, above. Even if λοιπά were genuine in Eph. iv. 17, it could not be cited as proof of this usage; since the Gentile Christians are Gentiles, cf. Eph. iii. 1. That γραφή in its common sense does not occur in the N.T. is accidental. On the other hand, we find γράμματα, which in John vii. 15 undoubtedly means the ἱερὰ γράμματα (2 Tim. iii. 15) from which the Jewish γραμματεῖς derive their title, used of writings of the most diverse character (Luke xvi. 6, 7; Acts xxviii. 21), even of letters and characters (Gal. vi. 11). Cf. the frequent use of βιβλίον referring to other than sacred books along with τὰ λοιπὰ τῶν βιβλίων in the prologue of Sirach. For γραφή see 2 Chron. ii. 10; Neh. vii. 64; Dan. v. 7 ff.; 2 Macc. xiv. 27, 48; and in Christian Literature, Iren. iii. 6. 4, 17. 4; v. prologue (regularly *hæc scriptura* of Irenæus' own work); Clem. *Strom.* vi. 32 (προϊούσης τῆς γραφῆς followed immediately by κατὰ τὴν γραφήν, meaning "according to the Holy Scriptures"), *Strom.* vi. 131; Eus. *H. E.* ii. 11. 1 (τὴν περὶ τούτου παραθώμεθα τοῦ Ἰωσήπου γραφήν, cf. ii. 10. 1, 2). Furthermore, ἡ γραφή and αἱ γραφαί are never used in the Epistles of Peter of the O.T., the anarthrous γραφῆς in

2 Pet. i. 20 means "written"; and ἐν γραφῇ, 1 Pet. ii. 6, which, according tc אBA, is also without the article, signifies only "in a writing," although the reference is to a quotation from one of the prophets indirectly through Rom. ix. 33 (above, p. 188).

13. (P. 279.) Particularly striking is the resemblance between Jude 24 f. and Rom. xvi. 25, 27, τῷ δὲ δυναμένῳ φυλάξαι ὑμᾶς ἀπταίστους καὶ στῆσαι (in Rom. στηρίξαι, but Rom. xiv. 4, δυνατεῖ γὰρ ὁ κύριος στῆσαι αὐτόν) . . . μόνῳ θεῷ σωτῆρι ἡμῶν (Rom. μόνῳ σοφῷ θεῷ) διὰ 'I. Χρ. τοῦ κυρίου ἡμῶν δόξα (Rom. διὰ 'I. Χρ. ᾧ ἡ δόξα) . . . εἰς πάντας τοὺς αἰῶνας (Rom. εἰς τοὺς αἰῶνας τῶν αἰώνων), ἀμήν. With regard to the genuineness and original location of Rom. xvi. 25-27, cf. vol. i. p. 379 ff. Cf. also Jude 20, ἐποικοδομοῦντες ἑαυτοὺς τῇ ἁγιωτάτῃ ὑμῶν πίστει, with Col. ii. 6 (Eph. ii. 20 ; 1 Pet. ii. 5), ἐποικοδομούμενοι ἐν αὐτῷ καὶ βεβαιούμενοι τῇ πίστει ; also with Rom. xiv. 19, xv. 2, and all the passages where Paul uses the figure of building. See also Spitta, 389 ff., who discovers in οἱ ἀποδιορίζοντες a reference to the lost letter of Paul's (see above, pp. 252, 258, n. 6) ; but this view is hardly tenable.

14. (P. 279.) For the *Assumptio Mosis* and the *Book of Enoch* in Jude, see above, p. 286 ff. Edw. Abbot (*Expos.* 1882, vol. iii. 49–63) endeavours to show that Jude and 2 Pet. are dependent upon the *Antiquities* of Josephus (completed in 94 B.C.) ; but cf. *per contra*, Salmon, *Hist. Intro. to N.T.* (1885) pp. 638–653. While F. W. Farrar holds to the view (*Expos.* 1888, vol. viii. 58–69) that 2 Pet. is not dependent upon Josephus, but that the reverse is the case (cf. *Expos.* 1882, vol. iii. 401–423), Krenkel goes back to the other view, *Jos. u. Lucas*, 1894, S. 350. Single expressions such as τοῖς μύθοις ἐξακολουθήσαντες (Jos. *Ant.* procem. iv., cf. 2 Pet. i. 16), οἷς ποιήσετε καλῶς μὴ προσέχοντες (*Ant.* xi. 12. 6, cf. 2 Pet. i. 19), πᾶσαν εἰσηνέγκατο σπουδήν (*Ant.* xx. 9. 2, cf. 2 Pet. i. 5 ; Jude 3 ; also *C. I. Gr.* 2715a–b ; Deissmann, *Bibelstudien*, 278 [Eng. trans. p. 361 ff.] ; Prologue to Sirach, προσενέγκασθαι σπουδήν) would have value as proof only if they were found in similar contexts, which, however, is by no means the case. But that the writer of 2 Pet. studied the work of Josephus as a model of style and imitated it, is an assumption altogether absurd. When 2 Pet. ii. 5 calls Noah a δικαιοσύνης κῆρυξ (cf. 1 Pet. iii. 19 ff., above, p. 289, n. 9) ; and Jos. *Ant.* i. 3. 1 declares that Noah, incensed by the sins of his contemporaries, preached repentance to them before the Flood ; and when we read in a Midrash on Gen. vi. 9 that Noah was a herald for God (Beresch. rabba, translated by Wünsche, S. 129, cf. bab. Sanhedr. 108b), —the only thing proved is that, in the synagogues where Josephus and Peter went, it was customary to enlarge upon the O.T. history. Of a different character, however, are the statements of 2 Pet. ii. 15 (cf. ii. 13 f.) and Jude 11 when they accuse Balaam of covetousness, and the statement of Philo (*Vita Mosis*, i. 48) and Josephus (*Ant.* iv. 6. 5) when the one says and the other suggests that Balaam allowed himself to be tempted by bribes ; because the basis for all that is said is found in Num. xxii. 7, cf. xxii. 17 f. Nor does the statement require any explanation when it is expressly said in 2 Pet. ii. 16 (ἐν ἀνθρώπου φωνῇ) and in Josephus (iv. 6. 3, φωνὴν ἀνθρωπίνην ἀφεῖσα) that the ass spoke with a human voice, since that was what any child must say, if he meant to imply that the ass was understood by a man. It would be much more natural to assume that the writer of Rev. ii. 14 is dependent upon Jos. *Ant.* iv. 6. 6 for the statement that Balaam gave evil counsel to

Balak, which is not stated in Num. xxxi. 16, except for the fact that the same is found in Philo, *Vita Mosis*, i. 54. The form Βοσόρ for בְּעוֹר, which is certainly the correct reading in 2 Pet. ii. 15, is not yet explained. It is taken neither from the LXX, which everywhere has Βεωρ or Βαιωρ, nor from Josephus nor Philo, who do not use the name at all. To assume an accidental error in the original MS., or in one of the ancient copies of 2 Pet., is less natural than to suppose that Peter made a mistake either through imperfect pronunciation or defective hearing. The Hebrew ש is frequently interchanged with the Aramaic ע (אַרְעָא=אֶרֶץ earth), and so it was possible for a fisherman from Bethsaida, who heard Num. xxii. 2 ff. read in Hebrew in the synagogue and interpreted in Aramaic, to make the opposite mistake (cf. C. B. Michaelis in Gesen. *Thesaur.* 227; Hofmann, vii. 2. 74). The use of a slight vowel—a composite shewa, having the same sound as the full vowel preceding—before or with ע is not infrequent (Gesen. 977), and has a parallel in Βοανηργές (vol. i. p. 16). Cf. above, p. 287, regarding the relation of Jude to the Hebrew *Enoch*.

15. (P. 283.) If the context of Rev. ii. 2 and ii. 6 shows that the false apostles who had come to Ephesus were wandering teachers, who spread the teaching of the Nicolaitans in the Churches of Asia Minor, this is one point of resemblance between them and the false teachers in 2 Pet. and Jude. If ἐνυπνιαζόμενοι, Jude 8, refers to visions (above, p. 246), it is natural to associate the same with the prophetess Jezebel, Rev. ii. 20, who favoured the Nicolaitan teaching. With regard to time, the statement of Hegesippus to the effect that heresy did not appear in the Palestinian Church until after the death of James (Eus. *H. E.* iv. 22. 5), notwithstanding the fact that his report is anything but clear, may be taken as indicating that 2 Pet., which predicts the near approach of this development, was written before this date, *i.e.* before the year 66, and that Jude, which represents it as having taken place shortly before, was written some years later (cf. above, p. 246). If this be true, then light is thrown upon the report that the grandchildren of Jude were denounced by heretics (above, p. 240). It was done out of revenge. The remark with which Clement (*Strom.* iii. 11) introduces an abbreviated quotation of Jude 8–16, namely, that Jude is here making predictions about the sect of Carpocratians and other similar parties, is to be placed in the same category with the similar statements of Irenæus and others with regard to the false teachers of the Pastoral Epistles (above, p. 128, n. 14), or the claim of Epiphanius (*Hær.* xxvi. 11) that the Holy Ghost through Jude referred to certain parties that existed in the fourth century. What led Clement to make the citation was the parallel between Jude 12 and the report of unseemly orgies in the lovefeasts of the Carpocratians (*Strom.* iii. 10). This itself shows that the description in 2 Pet. and Jude does not suit this party ; for what is said in 2 Pet. ii. 13 f., Jude 12, about abuses practised in connection with the lovefeasts (above, pp. 236, 243 f.) is not to be compared with the reports which, according to *Strom.* iii. 2, Clement had heard concerning the Carpocratians, and with what Irenæus declares to be hardly credible (i. 25. 5), namely, that a community of wives was actually in practice among them in connection with the love-feasts. Of the distinctive teachings of Carpocrates and of his son Epiphanes (Iren. i. 25. 1–6, 28. 2 ; Clement, *Strom.* iii. 5–11, cf. iii. 25– 27 ; Hippol. *Refut.* vii. 32 ; Pseudo-Tert. ix. ; Philaster, xxxv. ; Epiph. *Hær.*

xxvii.), there are no traces in 2 Pet. and Jude : (1) creation of the world by subordinate spirits, of whom the chief was the devil ; (2) the contention that Jesus was the son of Joseph ; (3) instead of emphasising the doctrine of grace and the freedom that went with it, they taught that every man must save himself, as Jesus did, by doing the will of the devil as enjoined in Matt. v. 25, and by undergoing all human experiences ; for only in this way does the soul escape from the prison of the body and so from the rule of spirits, and only in this way is it kept from entering another body. (4) In the measure that they were able in this way to get the better of the spirits in the world, they attained the power to perform miracles like Jesus, and perhaps in greater degree than many of the apostles. It was for this reason that they practised magic arts. (5) Only faith and love have value ; all external actions are indifferent. The imaginary distinction between good and evil, and between the ideas of ownership and theft, are due entirely to the prejudices of men and arbitrary laws, among which the decalogue is particularly ridiculous, because of the statement in Ex. xx. 17. Grotius' identification of the false teachers of 2 Pet. and Jude with the Carpocratians cannot be accepted (ed. Windheim, ii. 1045, 1047, 1049, 1053, 1058, 1117, 1120).

§ 45. THE TRADITION CONCERNING THE EPISTLE TO THE HEBREWS.

The writing which, from the earliest times, has been transmitted as a letter " to the Hebrews " was, like 2 Peter and Jude, intended for Jewish Christians. There are reasons for supposing that it was written about the same time as Jude, or somewhat later. This makes the investigation of Hebrews all the more in place at this point ; because, as we have seen from 2 Pet. i. 12–15, Jude 3 (above, pp. 200 f., 241 f., 286, n. 6), this was a time when the apostles and other teachers of their circle felt it necessary, in order to promote the undisturbed growth of the original Christian faith, not only to preach and write occasional letters, but also to prepare writings doctrinal in character. Hebrews is such a didactic writing, although in its form and content it is a letter directed to a definite group of readers.

Inasmuch as the letter has no greeting from which we can ascertain the name of the real or alleged author, and the character of the original readers, it seems advisable to begin with a review of the tradition concerning both these points (n. 1). Even if the investigation of these questions should be without positive results, it would be worth while to free the historical investigation of the letter from the burden of false opinion. The fact that the tradition regarding the readers is not as clear, and regarding the author not so unanimous, as we could wish, is due merely to the absence of any greeting ; for we must remember that most of the ecclesiastical tradition regarding the writings of the N.T. is only the echo of the testimony of the documents regarding themselves ; and this tradition is good or bad according as this self-testimony was correctly understood or not. Nevertheless, the history of an Epistle like Ephesians shows us that even such traditions as had no support from the document itself became dominant in the Church at a very early time (vol. i. p. 481 ff.). As regards the age and unanimity of the tradition supporting it, the title πρὸς ᾽Εβραίους stands on the same level with the title πρὸς ᾽Εφεσίους. It is found not only in all the Greek MSS. and the versions, but there is not the slightest trace of evidence that Hebrews was ever known by another title in ʿany part of the Church, or that any ancient critic ever suggested another title on critical grounds, as Marcion did in the case of Ephesians. The title ad Hebræos was accepted by the Alexandrian theologians Pantænus, Clement, and Origen, to whom the letter was transmitted as a writing of Paul, and as a part of the collection of Paul's letters used in the Churches ; also by all the Eastern Churches of the subsequent period which held the same traditions as the Alexandrians, and even by the African Tertullian, to whom Hebrews was known only as a work of Barnabas, and whose native Church did not include Hebrews in its Canon. Moreover, when the historians Eusebius, Stephanus Gobarus, and Photius speak constantly of ἡ πρὸς ᾽Εβραίους ἐπιστολή in reports which are in other respects trustworthy, and

according to which Irenæus and Hippolytus knew and
quoted Hebrews, though denying its composition by Paul
(n. 9), it is presupposed that Irenæus and Hippolytus
called the document by the same name. Otherwise the
historians would either not have spoken at all of Irenæus'
and Hippolytus' mention of Hebrews, or they would certainly have given the different title of the letter employed
by them, if from citations and other references this were
clear. Thus, although there was the greatest diversity
of opinion regarding the author and canonicity of Hebrews
at the close of the second century, Churches and writers
were unanimous in accepting the title of the book.

From the facts incidentally mentioned above, it would
seem that the traditions concerning Hebrews reached
Irenæus, Pantænus, and Tertullian from very different
sources, so that their common root must lie very far back.
This renders it most questionable whether the common
element in these traditions, which vary so much among
themselves and thus are independent of one another, can
be explained as due to a scribal error, or whether it is
permissible to assume that Hebrews is really referred to
under any other than the traditional title, *e.g.* under such
titles as *ad Alexandrinos* or *ad Laodicenos* (n. 2). On
the other hand, it is self-evident that the title πρὸς
Ἑβραίους did not originate with the writer ; nor, in this
very brief form, which, however, is correct (n. 3), could it
very well have originated with someone who merely copied
the letter, or had numerous copies of it made for the
purpose of circulation ; but it is probably due to the circumstance that Hebrews was bound with other letters
variously directed, and so was provided with a short title,
in the same way as the other parts of the collection, in
order that it might be more readily found and quoted.

The exact date when the Epistle was given this title is
even more impossible of determination than the time when
the collection of the four Gospels or of the Pauline letters

was made. Nevertheless, this one common element in all
the traditions concerning Hebrews is of such antiquity
that it is worth while to inquire as to the meaning of the
title. Since it is clear to every reader that the letter is
directed to Christians, only those instances throw light
upon the meaning of the title in which the name Ἐβραῖοι
is applied to certain Christians in order to distinguish
them from certain other Christians. This is done in two
ways (n. 4). In Churches in which different languages
were spoken, as, *e.g.* that in Jerusalem, the Jewish Christians who retained the use of the mother-tongue, most of
whom were born in Palestine and continued to reside there,
were called Hebrews, in distinction from the Hellenistic
Jewish Christians, who were born abroad and had adopted
the Greek language (Acts vi. 1 ; vol. i. pp. 39, 42 f., 47 f.,
60, 67 f.). This was a distinction within the Jewish
nation due to historical developments much older than the
Christian era, which simply continued to exist in that
part of the nation which became Christian as well as in
the part that remained non-Christian. Besides this, however, all Christians within the Church who were Jews by
birth were frequently called Hebrews, without reference to
difference of language, owing to the fact that there was an
aversion to calling them Jews (n. 4). The first meaning
is inapplicable here ; for no one could infer from Hebrews,
which is written in Greek, that it was directed to Hebrew-
speaking Jewish Christians and not to Hellenistic Jewish
Christians. The opinion of Clement of Alexandria, that
Hebrews was written by Paul in Hebrew and translated
into Greek by someone else (n. 5), is palpably a false
inference from the title πρὸς Ἐβραίους, and cannot be
regarded as an authentic interpretation of this title, which
at that time was possibly a hundred years old. The only
other interpretation possible is that the title was intended
to designate the readers as Jews by birth ; and it is a
question whether it is meant to signify more than this—

something that every reader can infer from the letter itself. It is comparable to the title of 1 Peter, *ad gentes*, which originated in the West, and later became attached also to 2 Peter (*GK*, ii. 274 ; *Forsch.* iii. 100).

The title of Hebrews contains no geographical statement such as we find in the titles of Paul's letters, in the old Latin title of 1 Peter, *ad Ponticos*, and in a sense also in the Latin title of James, *ad dispersos*.　In particular, the error that this title taken alone indicates Palestine, cannot be too often contradicted.　If Ἐβραῖοι be taken to mean those who retained the Hebrew language, there were almost as many such in Mesopotamia as in Palestine, and there were persons of this character even in the Greek Diaspora, as in Tarsus and Rome (vol. i. p. 47 ff.).　If it be taken as a designation of Christians of Jewish origin, then there were considerable numbers of such, both in the apostolic time and certainly also at the time when this title originated, who were members of Churches in places widely differing, as Rome and Antioch, Asia Minor and Egypt.　It is easy to understand how almost universally, so far as we know, ancient scholars sought the readers of Hebrews in Palestine ; but this fact throws no light upon the original meaning of πρὸς Ἐβραίους.　In their own time it was only there and in the adjoining regions that entire churches of Christian Jews still existed ; and, so far as they knew, this had always been the case (n. 6).

That, however, Hebrews was not intended for all the Jewish Christians scattered throughout the world, but for a group of readers in a definite locality, is clear to every intelligent reader at least from Heb. xiii. 7–25.　This does not imply that the author of the title πρὸς Ἐβραίους himself understood it in the same way as later interpreters did.　It is possible that he knew from the tradition that Hebrews was intended for the Jewish portion of a large local or provincial Church outside of Palestine.　But it is also possible that in ignorance of the local destination

of the letter he gave Hebrews a title resembling in form
the titles of other letters, while actually expressing only
the self-evident fact that the persons addressed in the
letter were Jewish Christians.

The Alexandrian Church, so far as we are able to go
back into its early history, always regarded Hebrews as
one of Paul's writings.   On the basis of this tradition,
which was undisputed in his circle, Pantænus undertook
to explain why Paul did not introduce himself in this
letter as in his other letters by name and as the apostle
of the readers (n. 5).   Clement does not question this
tradition, for he handles the same problem as Pantænus,
solving it in a way which necessarily presupposes the
Pauline authorship of the Epistle.   He also asserts this
directly, and apparently without any doubt as to its
truth, in numerous quotations from Hebrews, as well as in
the two passages where he speaks of the beginnings of
questionings about the tradition (n. 5).   The idea that the
Greek Hebrews was a translation, was, of course, an inference from the title as it was understood at that time ; but
why was not the same inference drawn regarding James, or
why were not the conjectures regàrding the translator of
the Gospel of Matthew just as definite as those regarding
the translator of Hebrews, especially in view of the fact
that it was known from tradition in the case of Matthew
that Matthew wrote the Gospel in Hebrew ?   When
Clement twice positively affirms that Luke is the translator of Hebrews, and in this way explains the alleged
similarity of style between Hebrews and Acts, we are not
to infer that his assertion is based upon a tradition to this
effect, but only that the observation of the great difference
in style between Hebrews and Paul's letters had given
rise to doubts in the Alexandrian School about the local
tradition.   It was thought that criticism and tradition
could be reconciled by assuming that the Greek Hebrews
was a translation from Hebrew.   It was natural to make

Luke the translator, because a close connection between the Gospel of Luke and the oral preaching of Paul was usually assumed ; moreover, resemblances in style between Hebrews and Acts seemed to corroborate this view. Whether also views of other Churches gave impulse to these scholarly efforts we do not know. But Origen's judgment concerning Hebrews is evidently influenced by the difference of opinion which existed in the various parts of the Church regarding the authorship and canonicity of Hebrews (n. 7). He had learned that in certain quarters an unfavourable opinion was expressed regarding a Church like that in Alexandria, which had accepted Hebrews into its Canon as a letter of Paul's ; for, as the result of his criticism, he concludes : a Church should be allowed to retain its good name, even when it holds such opinions regarding Hebrews, *i.e.* it should not be condemned on this account as unscrupulous or without critical judgment ; "for the men of the olden time did not without good reasons transmit Hebrews as a letter of Paul's." Inasmuch as he is protecting his native Church against unfair criticisms, he defends also its tradition ; but he does so with a full appreciation of the current objections to the same. Everyone who is capable of judging differences in style must admit that the Greek of Hebrews is better than that of the generally accepted letters of Paul, and that it does not show the lack in literary skill to which Paul in 2 Cor. xi. 6 confesses. Origen, however, did not find the reconciliation between the result of his observation and the tradition of the Alexandrian Church, as did Clement, in the hypothesis that Paul wrote Hebrews in Hebrew and that a disciple of his translated it. He does not even mention this hypothesis, so confidently proposed by Clement ; but, after a full discussion of the various views, which unfortunately is only incompletely preserved for us, he finally adopts as the most probable conclusion, that the apostle, *i.e.* Paul, furnished the ideas, but a

disciple of his put them into the form of a letter according
to his instructions. Therefore, Origen's question is not
who the translator was, but who wrote the Epistle working in the spirit and under the direction of his teacher
Paul. Origen holds a definite answer to this question to
be impossible—" God alone knows," he says ; yet he is not
willing to pass by altogether the learned tradition that
had come to him, in which now Clement of Rome and now
Luke is made the author of the Epistle. It would seem,
then, as if Luke, whom Clement of Alexandria mentions as
the translator of Hebrews, was mentioned by others before
the time of Origen as its author. Besides him, however,
Clement of Rome was mentioned in the same capacity.
The numerous resemblances between Clement's letter to
the Corinthians and Hebrews make the latter conjecture
more natural than the supposition that Luke was the
translator or author of the letter. The only thing that
can be asserted with certainty is that Origen found both
these names mentioned either in the oral or written
tradition. Whether the representatives of these views
called Clement of Rome or Luke the author of Hebrews
in the limited sense in which Origen discussed the question concerning an author of the letter, associated with
Paul in its production, or in the fullest sense of independent authorship, or like Clement of Alexandria called
them authors in the sense of translators, we do not know
(n. 5). When Origen expressed his judgment, the Alexandrian Church seems to have stood quite alone in the
tradition of the Pauline source of Hebrews ; he defends a
single Church holding this view (εἴ τις οὖν ἐκκλησία κτλ.)
against the judgment of the other Churches. It cannot
be shown that this opinion was held at that time anywhere
outside of Egypt, nor subsequently in any place not under
the influence of Alexandrian scholars. In the fourth century we find it dominant throughout the Greek and Syrian
Churches as well as in the Churches dependent upon

them ; the belated opposition of several Arians could not change this general opinion. The modifications in the Alexandrian tradition which Clement and Origen made when they accepted it were dropped ; the tradition itself which they found and which Origen defended was adopted.

Regarding the opinion which prevailed among the Greek Churches in Syria, Asia Minor, Macedonia, and Greece in the time of Clement and Origen with reference to the origin of Hebrews, we have no direct information. In the West, Hebrews was not unknown from early times, but until after the middle of the fourth century it was excluded from the collection of Paul's letters and from the N.T. in general (n. 8). This fact is of itself significant. A letter, which to all appearances was regarded as an important ancient didactic writing by Clement of Rome, Justin, who wrote in Rome, the younger Theodotus, a disciple of the Theodotus who came from Byzantium to Rome, Irenæus, Hippolytus, and Tertullian, but which nevertheless was persistently excluded from the N.T. in Italy, North Africa, and Gaul, could not have passed as a work of Paul's in these regions, since the objections to its reception into the collection of books read in the religious services which might be raised on the ground that it was intended for "the Hebrews," could not have had more weight in Rome than in Alexandria. These objections must have been outweighed by the influence of Paul's name, if it had been connected with it. Moreover, the Gospel of Matthew, which was originally designed for Jews and Jewish Christians, was accepted into the Canon of the entire Gentile Christian Church. We also have the testimony of persons who had access to the writings of Irenæus and Hippolytus which are no longer extant, that both these teachers denied the Pauline authorship of Hebrews (n. 9). On the part of Irenæus this denial was probably only indirect, Hebrews being quoted by him without mention of Paul's name. Hippolytus, on the other hand, to all appearances protested formally against the appeal of the Theodotians to Hebrews às a work of Paul's and as a part of Holy Scripture. If in this connection Hippolytus and Irenæus had mentioned some-one else as the author of Hebrews, the silence of three independent reports on this point (n. 9) would be incomprehensible. It may be regarded as certain, therefore, that Hebrews as Irenæus and Hippolytus knew it was anonymous.

There were, however, Churches in which Hebrews was transmitted as an epistle of *Barnabas*. It is not a conjecture or personal opinion that ·Tertullian expresses, as Jerome declares (*Vir. Ill.* v.), but simply a reproduction of a current tradition, evidently just as found in the manuscript before him, when he writes as follows (n. 10): " Extat enim et *Barnabæ* titulus *ad Hebræos*, a deo satis auctorati viri, ut quem Paulus juxta se constituerit in abstinentiæ tenore . . . (1 Cor. ix. 6) ; et utique receptior apud ecclesias *epistola Barnabæ* illo apocrypho Pastore mœchorum."

From what has been stated above concerning the indifference of the Western Church toward Hebrews, it is evident that Tertullian does not set forth in the passage cited the tradition and public opinion of the catholic Church of his African home, or of the Church of Rome. Tertullian himself proves this by the way in which he introduces the quotation. After giving proofs, taken from the apostolic writings, he cites, as something wholly superfluous (*ex redundantia*), Heb. vi. 4–8, as evidence of some companion and disciple of the apostles. For the catholic clergy of Rome and Africa, who controverted the Montanism of Tertullian, after the final separation of the Montanist Church, Hebrews was not a sacred writing to be used for proof texts, whereas they appealed to the *Shepherd of Hermas* for the principles of their lax discipline,

although both Catholic and Montanist Churches had excluded it from the Bible (*de Pudic.* x.). As far as the
West is concerned, the Churches in which Hebrews received greater consideration than the *Shepherd*, and in
which it was handed down as a writing of Barnabas, could
have been only the Montanist Churches. Since, however, Montanism was introduced into the West from the
province of Asia, there is the greatest probability that the
tradition concerning Barnabas as the author of Hebrews
originated there, and that it was not confined to the
Montanist Churches of that region. This same tradition
appears again in the Latin sermons, published by Batiffol
(1900), which wrongly bear· the name of Origen. In
them it is set forth not as the conjecture of an individual
scholar, but as a fact accepted in the preacher's circle
(n. 11). The discussion concerning the origin of these
sermons is not yet settled, and will not come to an end
without a new investigation, which fairly considers every
particular. If the preacher is not Novatian, as the present
writer, following others and along with them, thought he
might claim, he must have belonged to a Novatian Church,
and nothing is more probable than that the tradition of
Barnabas as author of Hebrews was handed down from
the Montanists to the Novatians, as were the polemical
use of Heb. vi. 4–8, and the high value placed upon the
Epistle, things which we have long known.

It appears, therefore, from the above discussion, that
there existed, between the years 180 and 260, three
more or less widely diffused opinions regarding the
authorship of Hebrews which stood over against each
other—(1) Paul (held by the Alexandrians, and perhaps
the Theodotians in Rome); (2) Barnabas (held by the
Montanist Tertullian, evidently already by the Phrygian
Montanists and also by the catholic Churches of the province of Asia, as well as by the Novatians); (3) some
unknown person (Irenæus, Hippolytus, and probably still

other Catholics of the West). The common source of this threefold tradition can only be the third view (n. 12), for in each of the other two cases it is incomprehensible how a tradition originally associated with Hebrews, whether it were ascribed to Paul or to Barnabas, in the circles from which Irenæus came, could have given way to entire ignorance in regard to the matter. It is equally incomprehensible how Βαρνάβα could arise from an original Παύλου, or *vice versa*. The history. of early Christian literature offers elsewhere examples of how writings, originally anonymous in the tradition, were ascribed to definite authors on insufficient grounds (n. 13). The receivers of the letter certainly knew the name of the author ; he himself indicates in Heb. xiii. 18–24 that he was known to them, and this knowledge would surely be preserved for some time. But when Hebrews began to be circulated, it could no longer have existed in the place from which it was sent out into the Churches. In view of the fact that, so far as we are aware, Hebrews was never known to any Church writer without the title πρὸς Ἑβραίους (above, p. 295 f.), it is probable that it was connected with the collection of Paul's letters either from the beginning or through a later addition. It is therefore very easy to understand how in Alexandria the letter was attributed to Paul. The Παύλου (ἐπιστολή) which it was necessary to supply with πρὸς Κορινθίους, πρὸς Ἐφεσίους κτλ. was also very naturally supplied with πρὸς Ἑβραίους, in the title of the appended anonymous writing (n. 13). The mention of Timothy (Heb. xiii. 23), the author's knowledge of the Scripture, the reading τοῖς δεσμοῖς μου συνεπαθήσατε (Heb. x. 34, n. 14), which, though certainly false, is perhaps very old, all tended to strengthen this view. If Hebrews was not appended to the Pauline letters until later, it is not surprising that the Churches which had received the original collection of Paul's letters without Hebrews were afterwards unwilling to accept the anonymous letter and to recognise it as a letter of Paul's. The individuals into whose hands it came regarded it either as an anonymous writing from ancient apostolic times, or resorted to conjecture. If Paul did not write it, then it must have been written by some other distinguished teacher of the apostolic age. Barnabas was such a man. It is possible that 'this assumption was furthered by the fact that an ancient document with many allegorical interpretations of O.T. legal regulations, our so-called *Epistle of Barnabas,* was circulated in the Oriental Churches under Barnabas' name. One who was seeking for the author of Hebrews might be influenced by this document to ascribe Hebrews also to this Barnabas. This same development of the Barnabas idea is also conceivable in case Hebrews was a part of the original collection of Paul's letters. Even if ἄλλου πρὸς ʿΕβραίους was not in the title, the report could have been circulated with the collection that the document was not written by Paul, but was added to the collection of his letters because of its instructive and edifying character. In Alexandria this tradition disappeared, while in other regions it was preserved, and resulted either in the separation of this letter from those of Paul, or in the conjecture that it was written by Barnabas. In brief, there is no tradition regarding the author of Hebrews which compares with the traditions regarding the authors of the other N.T. writings in age, unanimity, and an originality, hard to invent.

1. (P. 294.) For the canonical history of Heb. see *GK*, i. 283–302, 379, 577 ff., 759, 963–966, ii. 85, 160 ff., 169–171, 238, 275, 358–362, also *PRE*³, vii. 492–506.

2. (P. 295.) Klostermann (*Zur Theorie der bibl. Weissagung und zur Characteristik des Hb,* 1889, S. 55) conjectures that πρὸς ʿΕβραίους is an incorrect copy of πρὸς Βερναίους = Βεροιαίους, and holds that Apollos, who, according to Acts xviii. 27 f., laboured in Macedonia (Where is this statement found ?) and Achaia, wrote this letter to the Church in Berœa, the original constituency of which, according to Acts xvii. 11, was certainly Jewish. A more natural supposition would be Berœa in Syria (Aleppo), which was the main centre of Jewish Christianity in the time of Jerome. Harnack, *ZfNTW*, 1900, S. 21, had an idea of πρὸς τοὺς ἑταίρους as the original title. Semler (cited in

Öder's *Freie Untersuchung über d. Off. Joh.* 1769, S. 29), followed later by Hug in his *Einl.*[3] ii. 482 ; Wieseler, *Chronol.* 483 ff., *Untersuch. über den Hb,* 1861, i. 26 ff. ; Hilgenfeld, *Einl.* 104, 354, was the first to advance the view that Heb. was really the epistle *ad Alexandrinos,* which, according to Can. Mur. line 64, was fabricated like an epistle *ad Laodicenos,* under Paul's name in the spirit of the Marcionite heresy. There were also many critics who believed that in Philaster the statement was to be found (*Hær.* lxxxix.) that in his time (380 to 390) Hebrews was quite generally regarded as a letter to the Laodiceans. This led to the further hypothesis that the words following the Epistle to Philemon at the end of the Cod. Bœrn. of the Pauline letters, *ad Laodicenses incipit epistola,* πρὸς Λαουδακήσας ἄρχεται ἐπιστολή, are the title of Heb. which ought here to follow in the MS. This was the opinion of Credner (*Einl.* 560), Anger (*Über den Laodicenerbr.* 29), and Wieseler (*Unters.* i. 34 ff.). The *Epistle to the Laodiceans* referred to in Can. Mur. and in Cod. Bœrn. is the apocryphal letter of this title which is still in existence. With regard to the *Epistle to the Alexandrians,* we know nothing definite or certain ; cf. *GK,* i. 277–283, ii. 82–88, 238, 566–592.

3. (P. 295.) For the meaning of *titulus* see vol. i. p. 488, n. 3. In the oldest MSS. (אABCK) the only words found in the title at the beginning or in the title at the end are πρὸς Ἑβραίους without ἐπιστολή, first L, and in the title also P, have this addition, and this is apparently all that Tertullian found, for he writes (*de Pud.* xx.) : *extat et Barnabæ titulus* (not *epistola*) *ad Hebrœos.* This title cannot be compared with those of writings which were circulated independently, such as Κλήμεντος (λόγος) προτρεπτικὸς πρὸς Ἕλληνας or Τατιανοῦ λόγος πρὸς Ἕλληνας (Eus. *H. E.* vi. 13. 7). When titles of this kind are found in MSS. without λόγος, this is to be supplied from the title of a preceding writing by another author with a different address, *e.g.* in Eus. iv. 16. 7 from the preceding συγγράμματα. Different still is the case of Τατιανὸς ἐν τῷ πρὸς Ἕλληνας in Clem. *Strom.* i. § 101. Moreover, comparison with all these titles is rendered impossible by the fact that they contain the name of the author, whereas the common source of the divergent titles *Barnabæ* (*titulus*) *ad Hebrœos* and Παύλου (ἐπιστολή) πρὸς Ἑβραίους could not possibly have contained the name of an author.

4. (P. 296.) Ever since the time that the Jews began to call themselves Jews (Jer. xxxii. 12), they designated their race and their ancestors Hebrews (1) in a retrospective view of the patriarchal and ancient Israelitish period, particularly where there was occasion to mention Israelites from the point of view of those who were not Israelites. This is found even in Jeremiah, where reference is made to a Mosaic ordinance (Jer. xxxiv. 9, 14, along with the more modern העברי, Jer. xxxii. 12, xxxiv. 9). Cf. also Philo (*Vita Mos.* i. 2, 4, 26, 27, 48, 50), where the term Hebrews is used along with Ἰουδαῖοι without any distinction of time (*op. cit.* i. 1, 2, 7, ii. 7), Josephus (*Ant.* i. 6. 2, 4, 5, ii. 5. 4, 9. 1 ff. ; *Bell.* iv. 8. 3, v. 9. 4), and the poet Ezekiel (in Eus. *Prœp.* ix. 28 f.), in reproductions of the ancient history, or occasional references to the same. For the same reason it is also found regularly in the *Sibyllines,* the alleged predictions of an ancient prophetess. The usage in Judith x. 12, xii. 11, xiv. 18 ; 2 Macc. vii. 31, xi. 13, is also archaic. The Jews are very seldom mentioned by Greek and Roman writers. Once Plutarch uses along with the regular Ἰουδαῖοι (*Apophthegm. regum,* p. 184 ; *Is. et Osir.* 31, p. 363 ; *Quest.*

conv. iv. 4. 4, 5. 1, 2, pp. 669, 670), τὰ Ἑβραίων ἀπόρρητα, p. 671, in reference to their ancient institutions ; once Tac. *Hist.* v. 2 has *Hebraeas terras* (cf. Jos. *Bell.* v. 4. 3). The term is used more frequently by Pausanius of land and people without distinctions as to time, i. 5. 5, v. 5. 2, 7. 4, vi. 24. 8, x. 12. 9. (2) The Jews regularly use Ἑβραῖοι (also ἐβραϊκός, ἐβραΐς, ἐβραϊστί) when speaking of their language and literature ; cf. Philo, *de Conf. Ling.* xxvi. ; *Migr. Abrah.* iii. ; *Vita Mos.* ii. 6 (of the seventy translators) ; *Somn.* ii. 38 ; *Congr. Erud. Gr.* viii. ; Jos. *Ant.* i. 1. 1 f., iii. 6. 7, x. 10. 6. Cf. the lexicons of Levy or Jastrow, for example, Jer. Baba Bathra, 17c, " A Hebrew and a Greek witness." So the word came to be used in contrast to Hellenistic (see vol. i. pp. 39, 48 f., 67, n. 14). (3) While the Jews with pride called themselves Jews (Rom. ii. 17 ; *C. I. Gr.* 9916, 9926 ; *JHSt*, 1891, p. 269; cf. Berliner, *Gesch. der Juden in Rom.* i. 72 ff., nr. 12, 81, 109), the name assumed a different significance to Christians, and even to Jewish Christians, after the majority of this people had rejected the gospel, and Ἰουδαϊσμός (Gal. i. 13, 14 ; Ign. *Magn.* viii. 1, x. 3 ; *Phil.* vi. 1 ; Inscription from Portus given by Dérenbourg in *Mél. Renier*, 1887, p. 440) came to stand for a religion hostile to Christianity—a religion, acceptance of which made those who were not Jews Jews (Dio Cass. xxxvii. 17. 1). The time soon came when the term οἱ Ἰουδαῖοι no longer sufficed to distinguish genuine from false Jews (Rom. ii. 28 f. ; Rev. ii. 9, iii. 9), inasmuch as it was used for the nation which excluded the Christian Church from itself (1 Thess. ii. 14; 1 Cor. x. 32 ; 2 Cor. xi. 24; Matt. xxviii. 15 ; John xiii. 33, xviii. 14, xx. 19; Acts xii. 3, xx. 3, xxi. 11, xxvi. 2). It is only very rarely and always with an evident purpose that Christian Israelites are called Jews by themselves and others ; cf. Gal. ii. 13–15 ; Acts x. 28, xxi. 39, xxii. 3 (in Acts xxi. 20 the text is uncertain, still more so in Acts vi. 7). Cf. also the comparatively late catholic *Acts of Peter and Paul*, ed. Lipsius, 122. The more favourite expression is οἱ ἐκ περιτομῆς (Gal. ii. 12 ; Col. iv. 11 ; Tit. i. 10 ; Acts x. 45, xi. 2 ; cf. Phil. iii. 3 ; 1 Cor. vii. 18), or the simple statement of Jewish origin, ἐξ Ἰουδαίων (Rom. ix. 24 ; Just. *Dial.* xlvii. 48 ; cf. *GK*, ii. 671, A. 2). In the post-apostolic age (2 Cor. xi. 22 ; Phil. iii. 5 ; Acts vi. 1 cannot be cited in favour of this usage ; cf. vol. i. p. 48), they were called also Ἑβραῖοι. Although in numerous instances the linguistic meaning of the word exerted a strong influence,—as, for example, in the case of the Aramaic-speaking Nazarenes and their Hebrew gospel, as it was apparently called by Hegesippus (Eus. *H. E.* iv. 22. 7; cf. *GK*, ii. 643, 649 ff.),—in the vast majority of cases it indicates a contrast between Jews and non-Jews, without any reference to the contrast between Hebrews and Hellenists within the Jewish race itself, as in Acts vi. 1. When Clement (*Pæd.* i. 34 ; *Strom.* i. 11), speaking of Paul and one of his own teachers, calls them Ἑβραῖοι ἀνέκαθεν or ἄνωθεν, or when Eusebius (*H. E.* i. 11. 9, ii. 4. 3, iv. 5. 2) uses the same expression with reference to Philo, Josephus, and the first bishops of Jerusalem (cf. *H. E.* iv. 22. 7, with regard to Hegesippus), the only thing indicated is their ancestral connection with the Jewish people and faith. Clement (*Pæd.* i. 34) uses along with Ἑβραῖος, Ἰουδαῖος to designate their religion ; and Eusebius (*H. E.* iv. 5. 4) uses the same word interchangeably with ἐκ περιτομῆς. In speaking of the destination of Matt., Irenæus uses once, iii. 1. 1, ἐν τοῖς Ἑβραίοις, and in a second instance (*Fragm.* 29, ed. Stieren, p. 842) πρὸς Ἰουδαίους. Eusebius also calls the gospel, " which gave special

joy to those of the Hebrews who accepted Christ" (*H. E.* iii. 25. 5), τὸ καθ
Ἑβραίους εὐαγγέλιον, both in the passage here cited and elsewhere (iv. 22. 7) ;
occasionally also "The gospel which is among the Jews" (*de Theophania syr.*
iv. 12). The most decisive proof is that furnished by the Ebionites, whose
entire literature, so far as we know it (their gospel, the pseudo-Clementine
writings, the translation of the O.T., and the commentary of Symmachus),
was Greek, but who, notwithstanding, always called genuine Jews and Jewish
Christians Hebrews (Clement, *Epist. ad Jac.* i. ; *Hom.* i. 9, viii. 5, 6, 7, x. 26,
xi. 35, xviii. 4 ; *Recogn.* i. 7, 32, v. 35), and who, according to Epiph. *Hær.*
xxx. 3, 13, occasionally spoke of their Greek gospel as a ἑβραϊκόν and καθ'
Ἑβραίους εὐαγγέλιον. "Hebrews" means here, as in Tert. *Marc.* iii. 12, *Hebræi
Christiani*, Jewish Christians.

5. (Pp. 296, 298, 300.) Eus. *H. E.* vi. 14. 2 ff. (cf. Cramer, *Cat.* vii. 286 ;
cf. Severianus, p. 115 ; Jn. Damasc., ed. Lequien, ii. 258 ; *Forsch.* iii. 71, 149)
gives the following account taken from the *Hypotyposes* of Clement : καὶ τὴν
πρὸς Ἑβραίους δὲ ἐπιστολὴν Παύλου μὲν εἶναί φησι, γεγράφθαι δὲ Ἑβραίοις
ἑβραϊκῇ φωνῇ, Λουκᾶν δὲ φιλοτίμως (*sic*) αὐτὴν μεθερμηνεύσαντα ἐκδοῦναι τοῖς
Ἕλλησιν, ὅθεν τὸν αὐτὸν χρῶτα εὑρίσκεσθαι κατὰ τὴν ἑρμηνείαν ταύτης τε τῆς
ἐπιστολῆς καὶ τῶν πράξεων· μὴ προγεγράφθαι δὲ τὸ "Παῦλος ἀπόστολος" εἰκότως·
"Ἑβραίοις γάρ, φησιν, ἐπιστέλλων, πρόληψιν εἰληφόσι κατ' αὐτοῦ καὶ ὑποπτεύ-
ουσιν αὐτόν, συνετῶς πάνυ οὐκ ἐν ἀρχῇ ἀπέτρεψεν αὐτοὺς τὸ ὄνομα θείς." Εἶτα
ὑποβὰς ἐπιλέγει· "Ἤδη δέ, ὡς ὁ μακάριος ἔλεγε πρεσβύτερος, ἐπεὶ ὁ κύριος
ἀπόστολος ὢν τοῦ παντοκράτορος (Heb. iii. 1) ἀπεστάλη πρὸς Ἑβραίους, διὰ
μετριότητα ὁ Παῦλος, ὡσὰν εἰς τὰ ἔθνη ἀπεσταλμένος, οὐκ ἐγγράφει ἑαυτὸν
Ἑβραίων ἀπόστολον διά τε τὴν πρὸς τὸν κύριον τιμήν, διά τε τὸ ἐκ περιουσίας
καὶ τοῖς Ἑβραίοις ἐπιστέλλειν, ἐθνῶν κήρυκα ὄντα καὶ ἀπόστολον." It may be
regarded as certain that "The sainted presbyter" Pantænus is the principal
teacher of Clement (cf. *Forsch.* iii. 157–161, 168–176). Clement expresses
himself just as definitely in his comment on 1 Pet. v. 13 (*Forsch.* iii. 83) :
" sicut Lucas quoque et actus apostolorum stilo exsecutus agnoscitur et Pauli ad
Hebræos interpretatus epistolam." While Origen speaks of persons who called
Luke not the translator, but the author of Heb., and of others who said the
same of Clement of Rome (above, p. 299, and below, p. 309, n. 7), Eusebius
(*H. E.* iii. 38. 2) changes this ἱστορία, as Origen calls it, into another, according to which some made Luke, others Clement of Rome, the translator of
Heb. The latter assumption Eusebius considers particularly probable because
of the resemblance in style and thought between Heb. and Clement's *Epistle
to the Corinthians* (§ 3), although he does not deny that this relationship was
due to the fact that Clement was dependent upon Heb. (§ 1). Jerome in his
usual fashion mixes everything up (*Vir. Ill.* v. ; *Ep.* cxxix. 3, *ad Dardanum*).
Tertullian says that Barnabas is the author of Heb. (see n. 3), while others
attribute it to Luke or Clement of Rome. But the authorship of Clement
is represented as affecting only the literary form, or as perhaps confined to a
translation from the Hebrew. Philaster (*Hær.* lxxxix.) states that the opponents of the Pauline authorship were divided in their opinion as to whether
Barnabas, Clement, or Luke was the author (below, n. 11). Ephrem (*Comm.
in Pauli epist.*, ed. Mekith. p. 200) reproduces the two opinions that Clement
of Rome was the author and that he was the translator, without accepting
either. Severianus of Gabala (Cramer, *Cat.* vii. 115), on the authority of

Eusebius, mentions Clement and Luke as possible translators. Theodorus, who rejected the idea of the intentional anonymous authorship of Heb., remarks incidentally that Timothy acted as Paul's amanuensis (Cramer, vii. 113 f.). According to Theodoret, *in Heb.* xiii. 23, Timothy was only the messenger who delivered the letter.

6. (P. 297.) Pantænus (see preceding note) assumes it as self-evident that Heb. was directed to the same persons to whom Jesus preached, *i.e.* the Jewish Christians of Palestine. This was also the view of Clement, who agrees with the opinion of his teacher, which he reports ; for it is only on this presupposition that Clement could assume as self-evident that Heb. was written in Hebrew, since he must have known that the Jews in Alexandria, Rome, and other places were entirely Hellenistic. Ephrem asserts very positively, p. 201, that Heb. was written shortly before the destruction of Jerusalem to the Christians of that city, the disciples of the original apostles who were probably still living there. He represents it as being a counterpart of the letter of the Jerusalem Church to the Gentile Christians in Antioch (Acts xv. 23). The same view is expressed by the genuine Euthalius (Zacagni, 526), only less definitely, when he represents Heb. as being an epistle to the Jewish Christian Churches mentioned in 1 Thess. ii. 14 ; by Chrysostom (Montfaucon, xii. 2, ποῦ δὲ οὖσιν ἐπέστελλεν ; ἐμοὶ δοκεῖ ἐν Ἱεροσολύμοις καὶ Παλαιστίνῃ), and Theodoret (Noesselt, 543). The pseudo-Euthalius (Zacagni, 668) thinks that Heb. was addressed to the whole body of Jewish Christians.

7. (P. 299.) According to Eusebius (*H. E.* vi. 25. 11–14), Origen in his homilies on Heb. says : "Ὅτι ὁ χαρακτὴρ τῆς λέξεως τῆς πρὸς Ἑβραίους ἐπιγεγραμμένης ἐπιστολῆς οὐκ ἔχει τὸ ἐν λόγῳ ἰδιωτικὸν τοῦ ἀποστόλου, ὁμολογήσαντος ἑαυτὸν ἰδιώτην εἶναι τῷ λόγῳ, τουτέστι τῇ φράσει, ἀλλά ἐστιν ἡ ἐπιστολὴ συνθέσει τῆς λέξεως Ἑλληνικωτέρα, πᾶς ὁ ἐπιστάμενος κρίνειν φράσεων (al. φράσεως) διαφορὰς ὁμολογήσαι ἄν· πάλιν τε αὖ ὅτι τὰ νοήματα τῆς ἐπιστολῆς θαυμάσιά ἐστι καὶ οὐ δεύτερα τῶν ἀποστολικῶν ὁμολογουμένων γραμμάτων, καὶ τοῦτο ἂν συμφήσαι εἶναι ἀληθὲς πᾶς ὁ προσέχων τῇ ἀναγνώσει τῇ ἀποστολικῇ (Eusebius here interrupts the narrative with the remark, τούτοις μεθ᾽ ἕτερα ἐπιφέρει λέγων). Ἐγὼ δὲ ἀποφαινόμενος εἴποιμ᾽ ἄν, ὅτι τὰ μὲν νοήματα τοῦ ἀποστόλου ἐστίν, ἡ δὲ φράσις καὶ ἡ σύνθεσις ἀπομνημονεύσαντός τινος τὰ ἀποστολικὰ καὶ ὡσπερεὶ σχολιογραφήσαντός τινος τὸ εἰρημένα ὑπὸ τοῦ διδασκάλου. Εἴ τις οὖν ἐκκλησία ἔχει ταύτην τὴν ἐπιστολὴν ὡς Παύλου, αὕτη εὐδοκιμείτω καὶ ἐπὶ τούτῳ· οὐ γὰρ εἰκῆ οἱ ἀρχαῖοι ἄνδρες ὡς Παύλου αὐτὴν παραδεδώκασι. τίς δὲ ὁ γράψας τὴν ἐπιστολήν, τὸ μὲν ἀληθὲς θεὸς οἶδεν, ἡ δὲ εἰς ἡμᾶς φθάσασα ἱστορία ὑπό τινων μὲν λεγόντων ὅτι Κλήμης ὁ γενόμενος ἐπίσκοπος Ῥωμαίων ἔγραψε τὴν ἐπιστολήν, ὑπό τινων δὲ ὅτι Λουκᾶς ὁ γράψας τὸ εὐαγγέλιον καὶ τὰς πράξεις. This is copied inaccurately in Cramer, *Cat.* vii. 285 f., but accurately and almost entire in a scholion in one of the Athos MSS. (von der Goltz, S. 85). For the interpretation see *GK*, i. 287, A. 1. To take αὕτη with ταύτην τὴν ἐπιστολήν instead of with εἴ τις οὖν ἐκκλησία, as Hofmann suggests, v. 46, is impossible, both in view of the construction and of the sense.

8. (P. 301.) The Canon Muratori, which mentions by name and rejects two pseudo-Pauline letters, and takes account of differences in opinion concerning a writing of Peter's and the *Shepherd of Hermas*, has nothing to say concerning Heb. The same is true also of the African canon, *circa* 360

(*Grundriss*, 83). There are no citations from Heb. in Cyprian and contemporaries, in Optatus of Milevi and in the Acts of the Donatist controversy
In Rome, furthermore, the number of Paul's Epistles was limited to thirteen
by Caius (*circa* 210), and Eusebius makes the statement, that even in his day
the Roman Church, or many Romans, *i.e.* Westerners, objected to Heb. as un-
Pauline (*H. E.* iii. 3. 5, vi. 20). On the other hand, clear traces that Heb. was
read with great esteem in Rome are first found in Clement of Rome and
Hermas (*GK*, i. 963 f., also 577 f. on Justin, and 295 ff. on Theodotus). Additional matter in nn. 9 and 11 ; also § 47, n. 7.

9. (Pp. 295, 301, 302.) Stephanus Gobarus says in the year 600 (see Photius,
Bibl. 232) : ὅτι Ἱππόλυτος καὶ Εἰρηναῖος τὴν πρὸς Ἑβραίους ἐπιστολὴν Παύλου
οὐκ ἐκείνου εἶναί φασι (whereas Clement of Alexandria and Eusebius reckon
it among the Pauline letters). Photius says the same thing, *Bibl.* 121, about
Hippolytus, the author of the work against the thirty-two heresies. Since
Stephanus mentions Hippolytus before he does Irenæus,—although the latter
is older,—it is probable that his information about Irenæus is derived solely
from a remark of Hippolytus with regard to Irenæus' views concerning
Heb. Evidently Hippolytus was the first who had occasion expressly to
deny the Pauline authorship of Heb. in opposition to the Theodotians, while
Irenæus appears to have quoted Heb. without naming the author (Eus. *H. E.*
v. 26 ; cf. *GK*, i. 296–298).

10. (P. 302.) Tert. *de Pud.* xx. ; cf. *GK*, i. 290 ff. Inasmuch as there was
no Latin Bible in Tertullian's time, he must have had before him a Greek
copy of Heb. with the title, Βαρνάβα πρὸς Ἑβραίους (ἐπιστολή). Merely
oral traditions which are associated with the text of the books Tertullian is in the habit of reproducing in a different way, *e.g.* with regard to
the relation of Mark to Peter and of Luke to Paul, *contra Marc.* iv. 5, he uses
the words *affirmatur adscribere solent*. The attempt has been made incorrectly
to discover the same tradition in the index of Cod. Clarom. of the letters of
Paul, where, after the seven catholic Epistles, we have the words, *Barnabæ
epist. ver.* 850. This view is supported by Westcott, *Ep. to the Hebrews*, 1889,
p. xxviii, with overmuch emphasis upon the idea that the numbers suit
Heb. better than the so-called *Epistle of Barnabas*. Cf. *per contra, GK,* ii.
169 f., 950 ff.

11. (P. 303.) *Tractatus Origenis de libris ss. scripturarum*, ed. Batiffol, Paris,
1900. Up to the present time the result of the discussion seems to be the conclusion that these twenty sermons are not the work of Origen, and that they are
not translations from the Greek. The view that they were written by Novatian is supported by Weyman (*Archiv f. lat. Lexicographie*, xi. 467, 545–576),
Hausleiter (*ThLB*, 1900, Nos. 14–16), Zahn (*NKZ*, 1900, S. 348–360), Jordan
(*Die Theologie der neuentdeckten Predigten Novatians*, 1902). Some of the objections raised to this view demand earnest consideration. In *Tract.* 10, p. 108,
between a saying of the *beatus apostolus Paulus* quoted from Rom. xii. 1,
and a quotation from 1 Cor. iii. 16, is found the following : "Sed et Sanctissi-
mus Barnabas, 'Per ipsum offerimus,' inquit, 'deo laudis hostiam labiorum
confitentium nomini eius'" ; cf. Heb. xiii. 15. According to Epiphanius (*Hær.*
lix. 2), Philaster (*Hær.* lxxxix. 3–8), Ambrose (*de Pœnit.* ii. 2), the Novatians,
like Tertullian (*de Pudit.* xx.), used Heb. vi. 4–8 to justify their rejection
of the "second repentance." About the opinion of the Novatians of the

fourth century concerning the author of Heb. there is no tradition, but it
is probable that they also followed the Barnabas tradition, and that it
was with reference to their opinion on this matter that Philaster wrote at
the beginning of the chapter in which he deals with the misuse of Heb.
by the Novatians : " Sunt alii, qui epistolam beati Pauli ad Hebræos non
adserunt esse ipsius, sed dicunt aut Barnabæ esse beati apostoli aut Clementis
de urbe Romæ (Roma ?) episcopi, alii autem Lucæ beatissimi evangelistæ
aiunt." This was probably written somewhat earlier than the kindred
statements of Jerome, *Vir. Ill.* v., and much earlier than Jerome's letter to
Dardanus (above, p. 308, n. 5 ; *GK*, ii. 234 f.). Philaster does not copy Jerome,
nor does he, like him, attribute the Barnabas tradition to an individual,
namely, Tertullian, but to a party of his own day. Pacian, *Epist.* i. 2,
mentions the Montanist Proculus (*al.* Proclus) as holding a position midway
between Montanism and Novatianism. When now Caius of Rome, in his
dialogue with Proclus, charges the Montanists with making new Holy
Scriptures, and in this connection mentions the thirteen letters of Paul
exclusive of Heb. (Eus. *H. E.* vi. 20), it is extremely probable that
Proclus had quoted Heb. as Holy Scripture, which Caius and the other
Catholics in Rome (Can. Mur. and Hippolytus) did not accept as such. But
it does not in any sense follow that Proclus quoted Heb. as a work of Paul's.
It is much more probable that Proclus, like his admirer and fellow-Mon-
tanist, Tertullian, regarded Barnabas as the author of Heb., and, like Tertullian, quoted this Epistle as an authority, only he gave it more weight
than Tertullian did.

12. (P. 304.) The hypothesis of Fr. Overbeck (*Zur Gesch. des Kanons*,
1880, S. 1–70), according to which Heb. at the time of its canonising in
Alexandria (160–170), and with a view to its being canonised, was artificially
made an Epistle of Paul's by the omission of the original greeting of the letter
and the addition of Heb. xiii. 22–25, cannot be presented here with all the
absurdities which it involves (cf. *GK*, i. 300 f., A. 1). The main difficulty
with it is its failure to explain how Irenæus, Hippolytus, and the other
Western writers, who did not like the Alexandrians, have Heb. in their
Canon, and who were in general independent of Alexandria, came to lose
the greeting. Neither does it explain the rise of the Barnabas tradition,
which could originate only when and where the letter was received as anonymous, without any greeting and without any association with the name of
Paul. If the alleged original greeting contained the name of Barnabas, the
desire on the part of the Alexandrians to canonise the letter was no reason
why they should omit the greeting ; since for a time in their Church they
accepted as canonical the letter which by themselves, and afterwards in
Christian literature, was attributed to Barnabas (*GK*, i. 347–350, ii. 159,
169 f., 948–953). Even if a less distinguished name had stood in the greeting, it is inconceivable that men who were willing to make Heb. an Epistle
of Paul's in an underhanded manner, and who were bold enough to set
aside the greeting that stood in their way, and to insert a closing paragraph
obscurely referring to Paul, should have lacked the courage and intelligence
required by their undertaking to replace the original greeting with another
which met their wishes.

13. (P. 304.) A parallel is found in the tradition concerning the so-called

Second Epistle of Clement to the Corinthians. For some reason this ancient sermon, preached probably in Corinth, became associated with the letter of the Roman Church to the Corinthians, which, according to tradition, was written by Clement. After the writings became associated, both the address, πρὸς Κορινθίους, and the author's name, Κλήμεντος, were applied to the second writing also. As a result, in the time of Eusebius the *Second Epistle of Clement* (*H. E.* iii. 38. 4), and in both Greek MSS. and in the Syriac version in which these two writings are found, the sermon is called a second letter of Clement to the Corinthians. It is due simply to the fact that in the MSS. of certain spurious writings of Justin as they were handed down, there was added a τοῦ αὐτοῦ, which perhaps was at first supplied only in thought, but which is found written in the one existing MS., that the *Epistle to Diognetus* came to be regarded as a work of Justin's (Otto, *Just. opp.*[3] ii. p. xiv).

14. (P. 304.) The reading δεσμίοις, Heb. x. 34, is supported by AD* 67** (a marginal reading of the Vindob. *Gr. theol.* 302, which very often agrees with the uncials BM in which Heb. x. is wanting), Coptic, Vulgate, Armenian, versions S¹ S³, Ephr. Lat. trans. 229 (otherwise he would not have omitted this sentence, p. 201, in his discussion of the Pauline authorship of Hebrews). In favour of the reading δεσμοῖς μου are אHLKP (also the scribe who corrected D, hence also E), most cursives, Clem. *Strom.* iv. 103 ; Orig. *Exh. mart.* 43 (but without μοῦ) ; Theodoret *in Heb.* x. 34 and *in Isa.* v. 17 (Schulze, ii. 202, iii. 611) ; Cramer, *Cat.* vii. 241 ; pseudo-Euthalius (Zacagni, 670). Hofmann, v. 416 f., is the last writer who vigorously defends the latter reading. The reading of Origen and of the Latin text Clarom. (*vinculis eorum,* referring to the οὕτως ἀναστρεφόμενοι mentioned in ver. 33) would seem to indicate that first δεσμίοις was changed to δεσμοῖς in a purely mechanical way, and the attempt was made later to make this reading clear by the addition of μοῦ or αὐτῶν. The latter word was inserted from the text, without thought of supporting any theory of the letter's origin, but the former word is suspiciously connected with the tradition of its Pauline authorship. Where this tradition prevailed the reading was accepted ; it may also have helped to confirm and to give currency to the tradition, if the reading was in existence before Clement's time ; the pseudo-Euthalius, *op. cit.*, uses this text as proof of the Pauline authorship of Heb.

§ 46. THE LITERARY FORM AND THE HISTORICAL PRESUPPOSITIONS OF THE EPISTLE TO THE HEBREWS.

It is not only the lack of a greeting which makes the beginning of Hebrews seem more like an essay than an Epistle. In all the writings of the apostolic and post-apostolic age, whose epistolary character is indicated at once by the greeting, the sentences which follow the greeting are very different from those in Heb. i. 1–14.

In every case, even where a connected doctrinal exposition
is intended and presented later in the course of the letter,
the Epistle begins with personal remarks often very closely
connected with the greeting. These vary in character,
consisting sometimes of an expression of the feeling of the
author toward the readers ; sometimes of a remark about
the occasion of the letter, or the relation between the
author and the readers ; or it may be some request or
admonition addressed to the readers (n. 1).

The assumption that Hebrews originally had a greeting which was later intentionally removed (above, p. 311,
n. 12), or accidentally lost, does not adequately explain
the peculiarity of the letter's beginning. If the beginning
of Hebrews was ever intended to give the impression of
a letter, much more than an opening greeting must have
been lost. But in this case it is incomprehensible, and
without analogy in the early Christian literature, that the
didactic body of the letter, which has been preserved,
should begin with a fully-rounded rhetorical sentence,
which does not permit of logical or stylistic relation to
something that preceded. Comparison may be made with
Romans, if Rom. i. 1–15 (or –16a τὸ εὐαγγέλιον) had been
lost ; or the experiment may be tried of cutting out the
introductory part of any letter of Paul's which is predominantly didactic, to see whether it is possible to obtain
something comparable to the beginning of Hebrews. The
assumption that the beginning of Hebrews was intentionally or accidentally mutilated, is just as untenable as the
supposition that the same thing was done to 1 John, the
introduction to which seems at first sight to resemble that
of Hebrews. It will be observed at once, however, that
while 1 John shows in a more distinct way an epistolary
character at the beginning than Hebrews, in the further
course of the letter and in the conclusion it is less so.
The author of Hebrews describes his production as a short
letter (xiii. 22, διὰ βραχέων ἐπέστειλα ὑμῖν). He charges

the readers to greet their officers and all the Christians in their locality, and he conveys to them the greetings of the Christians from among whom he writes (xiii. 24). He expresses the hope that he may in the near future visit them, or rather return to those among whom he had formerly lived. In this journey he hopes to be accompanied by Timothy, who has recently been released from imprisonment, if the latter can reach him in time (xiii. 19, 23). But even leaving out of account xiii. 18–24, Hebrews is not an essay, but, as the author himself says, an exhortation directed to the heart and conscience (xiii. 22, ἀδελφοί, ἀνέχεσθε τοῦ λόγου τῆς παρακλήσεως). The longer as well as the shorter theoretical discussions always end in practical exhortations (ii. 1–4, iii. 1–4, 16, v. 11–vi. 12, x. 19–39, xii. 1–xiii. 17). Nor do these exhortations give the impression of being an appended moral. The intensity of their language and the detail with which they are frequently worked out, would seem to indicate that they express the main purpose of the letter to which even the most artificial and detailed discussions are subordinate. From the first exhortation to the readers in iii. 1 (cf. ii. 1–4) on, it becomes more and more evident that Hebrews is not an essay meant for whoever may chance to read it, but a letter addressed to a group of Christians living at a particular time in a definite locality. It is also apparent that they are living under practically the same conditions as before conversion; that they have been and are still exposed to the same inward and external perils; consequently that they are a homogeneous and harmonious body. Hebrews is really an Epistle in the same sense as the letters of Paul to particular Churches, but less than any one of these an Epistle designed for some specific occasion. Hebrews is accurately described by what Jude says regarding the didactic writing which he planned, and for which, on account of the pressing need, he temporarily substituted a short practical letter (Jude 3; above, p. 242 f.).

Of the extant writings next to 1 John, Hebrews most
resembles James in point of style. But both James and
1 John omit all direct personal communications, and indicate at once in the salutation the distinction between
their written address to a wide circle of readers and oral
preaching in a local Church. The author of Hebrews, on
the other hand, leaves it to the bearer of his letter to
indicate to the readers for whom it was intended, that it
is his word to them, *i.e.* the word of their well-known
teacher.

Even without entering deeply into the content and
the development of the thought of Hebrews, it is possible
to gather from the letter much that throws light upon the
character of the readers and the author. The N.T. proclamation of salvation which Jesus Himself, the great
original Apostle, was the first to proclaim (iii. 1, cf. i. 1),
was brought to the readers and writer alike by those who
heard the preaching of Jesus, and had been confirmed among
them by the accompanying witness of signs and wonders,
by works of healing, and by manifold manifestations of the
inspiring spirit (ii. 3 f.). The author himself was not a
personal disciple of Jesus, but owed his Christian faith to
the preaching of such disciples. The same must also
have been true of all his readers. They are represented as
standing in exactly the same historical relation to Jesus
and the apostles as the readers in 2 Pet. i. 16, iii. 2 ; cf.
i. 4 and Jude 17 f. Though the language shows points
of resemblance to passages like 1 Cor. i. 6, 1 Thess. i. 5,
a difference comes at once to view. It could not be said
of Churches founded by Paul and his helpers that they
received the gospel—the first announcement of salvation—
from those who heard the preaching of Jesus, nor is this
anywhere said by Paul or by Peter, where he speaks to
such persons (1 Pet. i. 12, 23–25, ii. 25), or by John
(1 John ii. 7, 24, iii. 11). On the other hand, among the
readers there could not have been personal disciples of

Jesus; or those who were such must have been so few in number and so unimportant as to be left out of account. Those disciples of Jesus who had brought the gospel to the readers no longer live among them. They have either gone elsewhere in the prosecution of their missionary labours, or they are no longer alive. The latter is certainly true of the men to whom primarily the readers owed their conversion (xiii. 7). In order to emphasise their obligation to the leaders, of whom they are to be mindful, these are described as those who spoke to them the word of God, which means simply that they brought the gospel to them and were instrumental in their conversion (cf. Phil. i. 14; 1 Thess. ii. 16; Mark iv. 33; Acts iv. 29, viii. 25, xi. 19). When the readers are exhorted further to consider with admiration the end of their life and to imitate their faith, it is implied that the missionary preachers died as martyrs. The description of these deceased teachers as οἱ ἡγούμενοι ὑμῶν is justified only if they occupied, at least temporarily, an official position in the Church to which the readers belonged (above, p. 124, n. 5). The same must have been true also of the author. From xiii. 18 f. (cf. xiii. 23) it follows that prior to this time the author had lived among the readers, and hoped that his return in the near future would be a gain to them. Moreover, the general tone of the letter, and especially such passages as v. 12–vi. 3, vi. 9, xii. 4 f., 12 f., show that he was accustomed to teach, and enjoyed a certain reputation as a teacher, not only among other Christians, but also among the readers. That he was one of their ἄνδρες ἡγούμενοι (Acts xv. 22) while he lived among them, and that he will resume this position, is conclusively proved by the transition (xiii. 17 ff.) which he makes from his exhortation that the readers obey their leaders and not render their pastoral work difficult, to the request for their prayer on his behalf, the avowal of his effort to live a blameless life, the expression of his hope through the intercession of the readers to be restored to them, and, finally, the reminder that, while human teachers may come and go, Christians have always with them their great Shepherd, Jesus (n. 2).

The unconditional recognition of the preaching and life of the apostles and disciples of Jesus, who brought the word of salvation to them, carries with it a similar recognition of the original religious life of these Christians. This is also expressed directly. The foundation of Christian knowledge was rightly laid among them (vi. 1 f.); they have only to hold fast the confidence of their first faith (iii. 14); at present they are in a state of doubt and discontent, and in serious danger of falling away; and everything that the author must lament in their condition, and must fear for them, is an indication of the relaxation of the religious energy which they had shown earlier and possessed from the beginning (cf. especially xii. 12). Previously this energy had manifested itself in various ways. Its *first* fruit had been charity toward " the saints," which they displayed earlier and have not ceased to exercise even now (vi. 10). They must have distinguished themselves in this matter above other Churches, since the author bases his confidence that after all his worst fears of their final apostasy will not be realised, on the righteousness of God which will not permit Him to forget their labour and love in rendering this service to the saints in God's name. The language used plainly indicates that this was not mutual aid among the readers themselves, nor the charity of the well-to-do toward the poor around them, nor even charity on the part of the whole body of readers to Christians generally outside their circle. It can only mean that the readers had a prominent part in the great collection for the mother Church in Jerusalem which was begun in Antioch as early as 44, and had since been carried forward by the earnest and repeated efforts of Paul (n. 3). In the *second* place, the faith of the readers had been maintained considerably earlier in the face of severe persecution (x.

32–34, n. 4). It is an error to conclude, as has been often done, from xii. 4 that this persecution was bloodless; for the reference in this passage is not to suffering for the sake of the Christian confession (Phil. i. 29 f.), nor, in general, to the struggle for the faith (Jude 3), but to the conflict of the believers with their own sins (cf. Heb. xii. 1; 1 Cor. ix. 25 f.). This struggle does not, therefore, like that of x. 32, belong to the past, but extends throughout the whole earthly life. At the time when the letter was written the readers had grown weary in this struggle. They had not resisted "unto blood" the sin besetting them through manifold temptations, especially those arising through the hostility of persons not of their faith, and the necessity of life in the world (Heb. xii. 3, 5–11, ii. 18, iii. 13, iv. 15). Rather have they yielded to the same. On the other hand, in the great tribulation now long past (x. 32, ἀναμιμνήσκεσθε δὲ τὰς πρότερον ἡμέρας), they stood the test nobly. The fact that nothing is said of the taking of life, but only insults and oppressions, imprisonment and confiscation of property, are mentioned, does not justify the assumption that the persecution was a bloodless one. The author is not here giving a chapter of Church history in which the Church of a city or province is represented as a permanent corporate body outliving its individual members (n. 4), his object rather is to speak to the conscience of the Christians to whom he writes, by recalling the courage and willingness to make sacrifices which they once had manifested. Certainly they were not put to death at that time; in which case the author could not write to them. Nevertheless they must have been in great distress, from which they escaped only with their lives. In their sufferings they presented to the world and the Church at the time a notable spectacle (θεατριζόμενοι, cf. 1 Cor. iv. 9). Furthermore, when they themselves escaped with life and liberty, they were not ashamed of the fellowship of those who fared worse (cf. 2 Tim. i. 8, 16 f.), but visited and comforted them in prison. When forcibly deprived of their possessions they gladly sacrificed them. A reference to those who had actually suffered as martyrs in the persecution would have been out of place here, where the author's object is, not to make the sufferings and services of the survivors seem small by comparison with those of the martyrs, but to represent them as great as possible. It is natural to assume that the teachers who laid the foundations of the faith among them, whose martyrdom is referred to in xiii. 7 (above, p. 316), lost their lives in the same persecution. In all probability the μνημονεύετε in xiii. 7 refers to the same event as the ἀναμιμνήσκεσθε in x. 32.

The author's remark, that the readers endured this great tribulation after they were enlightened (n. 5), *i.e.* after their conversion, does not in any sense imply that the persecution took place immediately after their conversion. It is only intended to guard against the possible misunderstanding of the phrase " earlier days," which might be made to refer to the time prior to their conversion. Whether this remark was occasioned by the peculiar character of the earlier history of these Christians remains to be considered later. It is perfectly clear that the author intends to speak only about what they suffered as Christians, though this was at a period considerably earlier. What is here indicated incidentally is expressly stated in v. 12, namely, that the readers have behind them a long Christian experience. Because of this fact one might expect that they would teach Christianity to others; but, as a matter of fact, they have grown so dull as to seem in need again of instruction in the most elementary principles of Christianity. This blame, like the praise in x. 32 ff., shows how incorrect it is to suppose that Hebrews was addressed to the second generation of a Christian Church. In this case it would have been necessary to remind the readers not simply of their original confidence

in the faith (iii. 14), of their own earlier days (x. 32), of
the spirit of sacrifice which they themselves manifested
at that time, and of the long period that had elapsed
since they were first instructed in the principles of Christianity, but primarily of the faith, sufferings, and ripe
knowledge of their deceased fathers (cf. 2 Pet. iii. 4) and
mothers (2 Tim. i. 5). It is self-evident that in the
interval between the first preaching of the gospel to the
readers and the present, other Christians of their circle, as
well as their apostles (xiii. 7), have died ; but in the main
the same generation is still living which had heard the gospel
from the lips of the disciples of Jesus (ii. 3 ; cf. n. 4).
Besides these indefinite hints, which indicate the date of
the Epistle only relatively, there is another, disputed, to be
sure, which, rightly understood, fixes the time of the composition of the letter absolutely (n. 6). The writer does
not quote Ps. · cv. 7*b*–11 as scripture in iii. 7–11 to prove
some statement which precedes or follows, but he puts
rather what he himself has to say to the readers into the
language of the Psalm. This is indicated by the formula
of introduction and the manifestly intentional alteration of
the text of the Psalm. Furthermore, the words thus freely
quoted from the Psalm are referred to the Holy Spirit by
the parenthetical remark, καθὼς λέγει τὸ πνεῦμα τὸ ἅγιον,
not in order to say incidentally that they are taken from
the Holy Scripture,—for this it was customary to use
simpler formulæ,—but in order to soften the harshness of
the sudden transition from his own words in iii. 9 to those
of God, as is also the case in Ps. xcv. 9 (cf. x. 15). The
warning which the Psalmist once uttered to his own
generation, in view of the wanderings in the wilderness,
the author utters anew to the Hebrews of his time. Since
it is only in proportion as they hold fast the Christian
hope to the end that Christians have a right to feel themselves members of the household of God (iii. 6), the readers
should not harden their hearts to-day when they hear

God's voice, as was the case in the provocation in the day of testing in the wilderness, where their fathers saw and proved the works of God for forty years. It was because this generation, notwithstanding their experience, failed to acknowledge His ways that God's wrath burned against them, and that He swore that they should not enter into the rest promised by God to His people. To us it may seem that the author is only recalling events from the history of Israel, just as the Psalmist, whose words he appropriates, did in his time. But if this were the case, it is surprising that he adds further exhortations (vv. 12–14) without expressly comparing the facts of O.T. history with the present, and without a formal application of them to the conditions of the readers, returning at the close to the thought of ver. 6. Not so with the readers who were familiar with the author's typological mode of teaching. Although here as elsewhere (xiii. 13) he clothes his own thoughts in language borrowed from the description of conditions long past, which, taken literally, do not apply to the present, still he is not, like the Psalmist, speaking of *that* generation which came out of Egypt with Moses, but of *this* generation, namely, the generation to which he and his contemporaries belonged. To this evil generation of the Jewish people who hardened themselves against the Son of God (Matt. xi. 16, xii. 39–45, xxiii. 32–38, xxiv. 34), and who for forty years (from 30–70 A.D.) witnessed God's redeeming work, first in the person of Jesus and then in the preaching of the apostles, accompanied as it was by miracles, and yet failed to acknowledge God's ways, God has sworn in His wrath that they should have no part in the rest promised to the people of God. This does not apply to the readers, since they suffered themselves to be saved from *this* generation through the preaching in which they believed (Acts ii. 40). But they understood perfectly what was meant when the author, using the language of the Psalmist, called this unbelieving Israel their fathers (Heb. iii. 9), instead of employing the prosaic expression their "brothers after the flesh" (Rom. ix. 3), or their "brothers and fathers" (Acts vii. 2). Those referred to are the Jewish people from whom they descended, and the decisive acts in which the hatred of the Jewish people against the final revelation of God found expression were committed by persons no longer living.

A second allegory (iii. 15–iv. 11) begins with what seems to be a purely historical exposition of the passage from the Psalm, which previously the author had used to express his own thoughts. But this interpretation ends by showing how, in its typical significance, the history of the wanderings in the wilderness applies also to the present and the future (cf. 1 Cor. x. 1–11). The entrance of God's people into the Promised Land, from which the unbelieving contemporaries of Moses were excluded, was, according to the testimony of Ps. xcv., still future in David's time. It was the same in the author's time. It is not stated in so many words that between David's time and the present a second redemption of God's people had taken place,—which was always considered the counterpart of the deliverance from Egypt (above, p. 262, n. 12), and which, like the latter, was connected with a promise. Nor is it expressly said that in Jesus Christ reappeared a more perfect antitype of Moses (Heb. iii. 2 f.), of Jesus, i.e. of Joshua the son of Nun (iv. 8), and also of David (vii. 1–17). But both are taken for granted as known by the readers, and simply recalled by a mere suggestion (iv. 2). It is presupposed throughout the whole letter that the readers understood this reference, and saw in it an allusion to the fact that as at the time of the wandering in the wilderness, so now in their own time a separation had taken place between the majority of the Jewish people hardened by their unbelief and a minority who had believed (iv. 2 f. ; cf. vi. 18). It is also assumed that they understood that, while the Jews who had accepted Christ, including the author and his readers (iv. 3,

vi. 18), are on the way toward the realisation of the promise, the wrathful oath of God has been fulfilled upon the rebellious majority (especially iii. 19, iv. 6). The fact that such typological and allegorical treatment of the O.T. history and the corresponding changing picture of present events does not suit our occidental taste, does not alter the fact that it was much employed in the apostolic age (cf. Gal. iv. 21–31 ; 1 Cor. x. 1–11 ; 2 Cor. vi. 16–18 ; Rom. ix. 14–24, xi. 2–10, especially Jude 5 ; above, p. 260 f.). From Heb. iii. 7–iv. 11 we conclude that Hebrews was written after the year 70, and that both author and readers were of Jewish origin.

The latter statement has been comparatively seldom disputed, but is questioned by some even to-day (n. 7). The title πρὸς Ἑβραίους does not prove that the readers were native Jews ; since, whatever the age of the title, it does not necessarily reflect a yet older tradition, but may be due solely to a misunderstanding of the letter itself (above, p. 295 f.). Nor is it absolutely proved by the fact that the author calls the ancient Israelites his own and the readers' fathers (i. 1, iii. 9), nor by the fact that he calls the Church whom Christ redeemed Abraham's seed (ii. 16 ; cf. vi. 12–18). The former expression is found also in 1 Cor. x. 1 ; the latter, in Gal. iii. 7–29, iv. 21–31 ; Rom. iv. 11–18 (cf. vol. i. 81). And yet there is a difference between Hebrews and these thoughts of Paul's and such statements as are found in Eph. i. 13, ii. 1–iii. 12 ; Col. i. 21 f., ii. 11 ff., iii. 8–11 ; 1 Thess. i. 9 ; 1 Cor. xii. 2 ; 1 Pet. ii. 10, iii. 6, iv. 3 ; for Hebrews does not contain a single sentence in which it is so much as intimated that the readers *became* members of God's people who descended from Abraham, and heirs of the promise given to them and their forefathers, and how they became such. It follows, therefore, that they were the people of God through birth and training. If iii. 9 has been correctly interpreted, this is true beyond doubt. The difference

between the godly of the O.T. and the Christians whom
the author addresses, or with whom he identifies himself, is throughout only that between Past and Present
(i. 1, xi. 2, 39 f., xii. 23). It is nowhere said in early
literature intended for Gentile Christians that God spoke
to them directly through His Son (i. 1 ; n. 8). Although
the author states plainly the significance of the work of
redemption for all men (ii. 9, 15 ; cf. v. 9, ix. 26–28), still
he views and discusses it so entirely from the point of
view of the pre-Christian Jewish congregation, as almost
to make it seem that he was limiting the atoning effect of
the death of Jesus to the sins of Israel (ix. 15, xiii. 12 ;
cf. Matt. i. 21), and the significance of the New Covenant
entirely to the people of the Old Covenant (viii. 6–13, x.
16 f.). That both the readers and the author belong to
the Jewish people is proved directly by xiii. 13. After
showing that the Christians cannot expect any material
advantages from their acts of worship, because the one
sacrifice upon which their salvation rests is of the nature
of a sin-offering,—which, according to the law, must be
burned without the camp,—and, after recalling how this
idea is in keeping with the history of Jesus' life, since He
was crucified outside the gates of Jerusalem,—a criminal
rejected by His people,—the author adds this exhortation,
" Let us therefore go forth unto Him without the camp,
bearing His reproach. For we have not here an abiding
city, but we seek after the city which is to come " (n. 9).
That this is figurative language is, of course, apparent ;
since the camp in which the Israelites dwelt at the time
of the wanderings in the desert has long since ceased to
exist. Nor is it possible to supply in its place the city of
Jerusalem, since in ver. 12, where Jerusalem is meant, the
author does not name it, and nothing is said of a city.
On the other hand, there was nothing to hinder him from
naming the city instead of the camp in ver. 13. Moreover,
there was no moral profit in journeying from the Holy City

to the place before the gates of the city, particularly since it certainly would not lead to Jesus, who was no longer to be found before the gates of Jerusalem. What we have is therefore a figurative expression in keeping with the symbolic language of the entire letter, meaning that the readers were to renounce fellowship with the Jewish people who had rejected Jesus, to confess the crucified Jesus, and to take upon themselves all the ignominy that Jesus met at the hands of His countrymen. This demand is essentially the same as that in Matt. x. 24–39 ; Luke xiv. 26 f. ; John xii. 25 f. ; cf. Gal. vi. 14. But in its present form it was not applicable to Gentiles. These could be exhorted not to be ashamed of Christ and the gospel, or to imitate Jesus in bearing injustice (1 Pet. ii. 21 ff.), or to follow the example of Jewish Christians in enduring the hostility of their countrymen (1 Thess. ii. 14 f.). But where they are urged to renounce race affiliations, it is in the form, "Come forth from Babylon" (2 Cor. vi. 17 ; cf. Isa. lii. 11, xlviii. 20 ; Rev. xviii. 4 ; Jer. li. 6). The summons, on the other hand, to go forth without the camp of Israel, presupposes that those exhorted have always dwelt there.

It has been maintained that the Gentile origin of the readers is proved by the fact that their conversion in time past to the Christian faith is described as a turning from dead works, and as faith in God (vi. 1 ; n. 7). With reference to the second characterisation, it is not to be overlooked, in the first place, that the author elsewhere describes the same experience as believing in the gospel which they had heard (iv. 2 f. ; cf. ii. 3), as a fleeing for refuge (vi. 18), as receiving the knowledge of the truth (x. 26), as a coming to the heavenly Jerusalem and to the blood of Jesus by which they were sanctified (xii. 22–24, x. 29). Furthermore, in the experience of the Israelites the time came, in connection with the gospel, when faith took the place of the law (Gal. iii. 23–25), which up to this time had dominated their religious life. This is faith in the ordinary sense, which is, primarily, faith in God (Mark xi. 22 ; John xiv. 1). So deeply had the emphasis which Jesus laid upon faith as the saving power impressed itself upon the Jewish Christians, that it gave rise to a false application of this truth which was opposed by James (ii. 14 ; vol. i. p. 126). It cannot be proved that ἔργα νεκρά —an expression occurring nowhere in the Bible except in Heb. vi. 1, ix. 14—means sinful conduct of every kind, in particular the sins of heathen life or even idolatry (n. 10). Universally, the opposite of dead is not pious or good, but living. Only those works are living which are animated by faith and done under the influence of the life-giving Spirit. On the other hand, everything is dead, even the conduct which outwardly has the appearance of being pious, which lacks spirit and faith, and is therefore vain (cf. Jas. i. 26, μάταιος ; Matt. xv. 9, μάτην). The author, who universally represents the O.T. cultus as of divine establishment, although incomplete, cannot any more than Paul or Jesus treat the conscientious observance of the law as dead works, from which it was necessary to turn to God (vi. 1) and to be cleansed by the blood of Jesus (ix. 14). But he could speak in this way of conduct in accordance with the forms of legal piety, void of faith and without spiritual power. Those common human sins of which Jews and Gentiles alike must repent, and from which they must have their consciences cleansed, are manifestly not excluded. But it was only among the Jews that these sins had become connected with the observance of a formal religion of such a character that the renunciation of sin could be called a renunciation of dead works (cf. Rom. vii. 4–6).

In contrast to these dead works are those acts of worship (ix. 14)—for this is the meaning of λατρεία and λατρεύειν in Hebrews (viii. 5, ix. 1, 6, 9, x. 2), as everywhere else in the N.T. (1 John xvi. 2 ; Luke ii. 37 ; Rom. i. 9, 25, ix. 4, xii. 1)—which the Christians must render to the living God throughout their whole life. This worship of the Christians is based upon the high-priestly work of Christ performed once for all, and consists in constant prayer and thanksgiving, in works of mercy, and, generally, in a life well-pleasing to God, bearing testimony of the gratitude for grace experienced (xii. 28, xiii. 15 f.). The work of Christ is everywhere contrasted with the sacrificial system of the O.T. and the whole Mosaic ceremonial law, being represented as a living service which was performed through the Spirit (vii. 16, 25, ix. 14, x. 20), which satisfies the deepest needs of heart and conscience, and which truly corresponds to the relations existing between men and God. While, on the one hand, in the same way true Christian conduct is described in figures borrowed from the Mosaic sacrificial system (xii. 28, xiii. 10, 15 f.), on the other it is represented as being the only form of religious service (ix. 14) in keeping with faith in the living God and membership in the commonwealth of the living God, the heavenly Jerusalem (xii. 22). By the use of similar figures Paul also describes the Christian life to the Jewish Christians of Rome as a spiritual service, the offering of a living sacrifice (Rom. xii. 1; cf. Phil. iii. 3). Jesus condemned the legalistic piety of His fellow-countrymen as impious hypocrisy, and compared those who devoted themselves to this life to whited sepulchres, and, in contrast to the ceremonialism of the temple in Jerusalem or of Gerizim, He demanded a spiritual worship in keeping with the spiritual nature of God (Matt. xv. 7 ff., xxiii. 27; John iv. 20–24). In the same way Paul bids the Jewish Christians in Rome to consider that, while under the letter of the law, they brought forth fruit unto death, and reminds them that it was only through their conversion, new birth, and baptism that they were enabled to render a true and living service to God (Rom. vii. 6, vi. 11, 17). Now it was just as possible for the author of Hebrews as it was for Jesus and

Paul to contrast the dead works in which the readers lived before conversion, while under the law, with the service consisting of spiritual sacrifices, which it is their duty as Christians now to render to the living God. In both these cases the characterisation is applicable only to those who were Jews by birth.

The Jewish character of the readers is also apparent from the contents of the entire letter, in so far as the epistle is designed to save the readers from deserting their Christian confession. Apostasy from Christianity is a personal matter, and it does not need to be said that it is for individuals that the author is always primarily concerned. (This explains the use of τὶς in iii. 12, iv. 1, 11, xii. 15, 16.) These the others are not to leave to their fate, but they are to guard them from apostasy by exhortation and good example (x. 24 f., xii. 13, 15 ; n. 11), in order that the evil may not increase (xii. 15). But it already had such a hold upon the entire Christian community that the writer warns all the readers most earnestly against open and complete apostasy from the living God and from their Christian confession (ii. 3, iii. 7–iv. 2, vi. 4–8, x. 26–31, 35–39, xii. 17, 25), with frequent reference to the judgment of destruction that will inevitably follow such a course. The same condition of things also makes him lament their spiritual dulness (v. 11–vi. 2) and their religious and moral apathy (xii. 3–13), and leads him constantly to exhort them to hold fast their Christian confession (iii. 1, iv. 14, x. 23). They are especially exhorted to hold fast their hope in the certain though delayed fulfilment of the promises of God made to His people (iii. 6, 14, iv. 1–10, vi. 11–20, x. 35–39, xi. 40, xii. 26–28). There is scarcely a word of recognition of what was good in their conduct at the time (vi. 10, καὶ διακονοῦντες) to soften the severity of this judgment. They all lack that ideal power of faith which is illustrated by a long series of witnesses from the O.T. and by the perfect example of Jesus (xi. 1–xii. 3), *i.e.* a faith the essential quality of which is patient waiting for hoped-for blessings, and which finds in itself sufficient proof of invisible realities (xi. 1).   It is for this reason that they find it so hard to bear the adversities arising from their Christian confession (xii. 4–11, xiii. 13 ; above, pp. 314 f., 324), so insignificant in comparison with what they endured in an earlier persecution (x. 32).   This explains why, like their fathers in the wilderness, they make regretful comparisons between what they have lost and gained by the acceptance of the gospel (iv. 1 ; cf. iii. 7–iv. 10).   In their disappointment they are on the point of giving up, as did Esau for a mess of pottage, their birthright which belonged to them as Christians (xii. 23) for a mere temporary improvement in the conditions of their life (xii. 16).   They are about ready to treat, what for the Christians must always be most sacred, the Son of God and His atoning blood as a common thing, and thereby to make themselves guilty of the sin of the murderers of Jesus (vi. 6, x. 29).   They have not yet reached this extreme, but the dissatisfaction with which they have necessarily been seized, as their faith in the unseen blessings and the hope of future blessings has grown less and less, has come to affect their belief in the Redeemer Himself (cf. 1 Cor. xv. 19).   They found it impossible permanently to regard Jesus, who died a common and ignominious death and then disappeared from the world, and whose promises have remained so long unfulfilled, either as God's final and complete revelation, or as the Saviour from sin and death, or as the head of an eternal kingdom.   It is necessary to show them that Jesus perfectly fulfils for them all these three functions, if only they hold fast their faith and profession.   The Son of God through whom God spoke His final word to them is the *true apostle* of God ; since He surpasses in dignity, not only all the prophets from Moses on, but even the angels through whom the law was given (i. 1–ii. 4 : cf. iii. 1–6.

xii. 18–29). In order to cleanse the seed of Abraham and through them the entire race from sin, to save them from death and sustain them in all their weaknesses, He must enter fully into fellowship with human life, temptation, and mortality (ii. 5–18; cf. iv. 15 f.). It was necessary at the close of such a human life, subject to temptation and weakness, for Him to offer His life to God, taking the place both of *priest* and *sacrifice*, and with His own blood to enter the Holy Place in the heavens, in order perfectly to perform the service which the *high priest* by his official acts had only incompletely foreshadowed, and in order, at the same time, to fulfil the promise of a priestly *kingship* and a *royal* priesthood (iv. 14–x. 18). From the material out of which these thoughts are developed, it is plain that the readers not only knew the law (Rom. vii. 1; vol. i. 374 f), but that they were accustomed to measure everything of the nature of a Divine act or institution by the standard of the O.T., especially of the O.T. law. This also proves that they were Jews by birth.

The danger against which the writer endeavours to guard the readers is not a possible falling back into their pre-Christian state, *i.e.* into a legalistic Judaism, or a Judaism in which the coming of the Messiah was expected. This idea is precluded by the elaborately developed comparison with the Israelites who wandered in the desert (iii. 7–iv. 10), and the short but impressive allusion to Esau (xii. 16), and the expressions used to describe the threatened apostasy. It would be an apostasy from the living God, brought about by the deceitfulness of sin, consisting in a state of unbelief (iii. 12 f., x. 26); a falling of such as are now standing (vi. 6); a cowardly abandoning of all hope in the fulfilment of the Divine promise (x. 35–39; cf. iv. 9, vi. 12–20); a renunciation of the sacrifice which alone has atoning power, without hope and prospect of another (x. 26 f.); a reviling and crucifying of the Son of God without hope of a better king (vi. 6, x. 29). If in spite

of all this they still clung to their Jewish institutions, of
which we cannot think apart from religion, what they
possessed would be only a shadow of Judaism, a Judaism
like that of Caiaphas and his companions (John xix. 15).
It is not a false belief, but unbelief, into which they are
in danger of sinking. All this makes it clear that the
readers have not been misled, or are not in danger of
being misled, by some false gospel, and by teachers of
such a gospel. If this were the case we should certainly
have a clear reference to such a danger, such as we find
throughout Paul's letters, and also in 2 Peter and Jude.
It is not until toward the end of the letter, when the
main discussion gives place to exhortations, the substance
of which would be appropriate in a letter to any Christians
whatsoever (xiii. 1–8), that we find this warning : " Be not
carried away by diverse and strange teachings, missing
your goal ; for it is good that the heart be established "
(n. 12). In expressing this thought the author suggests
that this takes place by grace. Then follows the rejection
of the erroneous view that steadfastness of heart is secured
by the use of certain foods, from which, nevertheless, those
accepting this doctrine have reaped no profit. This is all
the data we have for determining what sort of doctrines
are referred to. It is impossible to derive further material
for determining the character of these teachings, or the
specific teaching mentioned by way of example from the
following section (xiii. 10–16 ; n. 9), which is both grammatically and logically independent. As contrasted with
the self-consistent word of God which their deceased
apostles had brought to the readers, and the word of the
one immortal Master Teacher, who still abides with them
(xiii. 7 f.), these teachings are a motley assortment, and
foreign to the nature of the Christian Church. This could
not very well be said, especially to Jewish Christians, of the
regulations of the Mosaic law, e.g. of the Mosaic prohibi-
tions of the use of certain foods. Nor is it very probable

that abstinence from these would be said to establish the heart. Still less does the description suit the religious meals, such as the Passover meal, or the sacrificial meals following the peace-offerings. Taking part in the sacrificial ceremonies, against which it would certainly have been necessary to warn the readers, could not be called a περι-πατεῖν ἐν βρώμασιν, as has been claimed in the light of ix. 10. The language indicates rather a prescribed manner of life (n. 12). Now we know that Jewish Christians in Rome regarded abstinence from meat and wine as a means of imparting steadfastness to the Christian, and keeping him from falling (Rom. xiv. 4; cf. xiv. 13, 20, 21, xvi. 25; vol. i. p. 365 f.). In Colossæ also such rules were recommended as indispensable means of sanctification where men lived in a heathen environment (Col. ii. 8–23; vol. i. p. 463 f.). Paul also characterises such abstinence as incapable of accomplishing this end, and as generally unprofitable (1 Tim. iv. 1–8; Tit. i. 15 f.), while he describes the recommendation of such abstinence as foolish human commandments and laws (Col. ii. 6–8, 20–22). The description of such a manner of life by the positive expression ἐν βρώμασιν περιπατεῖν, which to some has seemed peculiar, has a parallel in Paul's statement to the effect that ascetics in Rome are vegetarians (Rom. xiv. 2), in his holding up before them and their opponents the truth that eating and drinking do not constitute the essence of the kingdom of God (xiv. 17), and his warning to both not to injure a brother for the sake of food (Rom. xiv. 15, 20). Both the one who from principle abstained from certain foods and the one who used all without question (1 Cor. viii. 8) moved in the sphere of the βρώματα. It is evident, therefore, that an ascetic teaching of the character represented by Jewish Christians and Jewish Christian teachers in Rome, Colossæ, Ephesus, and the island of Crete had made its appearance also among these Hebrews. With this conclusion agrees the exhortation

(xiii. 4) τίμιος ὁ γάμος ἐν πᾶσιν, which does not mean that those in the married state are to *regard* it as *holy*,—this is not considered until the following sentence,—but that all, especially those who are unmarried and are inclined to despise marriage, are to *honour* this state. There were, therefore, those among the Hebrews who from principle despised the married life, and consequently all relations between the sexes.

With the assumption that the readers of Hebrews are to be sought for in Jerusalem has always been connected the idea that they took part in the temple worship after as well as before their conversion, and that the author is endeavouring to separate them from it, or, if they were on the point of resuming it after having broken it off, to warn them against it. So deeply rooted was this idea, that there were scholars who believed that the readers, who were to be found in Alexandria, assumed a similar relation to the schismatic worship in the temple at Leontopolis (n. 13). With reference to the Christians in Jerusalem, we know that from the beginning until their flight from Jerusalem shortly before the destruction of the temple, under the leadership of their apostles and of James, they continued to participate in the temple worship, and generally to observe the forms of the Jewish law. But if, in the opinion of the author, this constituted a forty years' resistance of the will of God revealed through Jesus, he could not have praised the beginning of their faith and their earlier Christian life (iii. 14, vi. 10, x. 32 ff.). Nor could he have represented the teachers and leaders who left the impression of their personality upon them (xiii. 7, ii. 3) as models of faith, but must have pictured them as warning examples of that stubborn self-will which clings to dead works and brings punishment upon itself. Naturally, on this hypothesis there could be no question of an actual or possible relapse of the readers into Jewish worship,—of which, to be sure, there is not the slightest

hint in the whole letter,—because the Christians in Jerusalem had never ceased to take part in the temple services.
The author is not dealing at all with the question as to
how the Christian confession was to be combined with
temple worship, and how, generally, life under the law is
to be judged,—a question which every Christian before
the destruction of Jerusalem had to meet, because of the
existence of the Church there. If that had been his purpose, consistency with the theories developed by him
would seem to demand that he condemn the whole attitude of the mother Church; and yet, in view of the
position which Paul took toward the Church in Palestine,
this would appear to be historically impossible. Nor
during the first decades after the destruction could it be
forgotten that until recently thousands of the Jewish
Christians in Palestine had been zealous for the law (Acts
xxi. 20), or were still so. If the author believed that this
was no longer right, he must, in the first place, have
demanded expressly that the readers cease from all observance of the law, now that worship according to the law
was made impossible by the destruction of the temple.
But he does not refer to this fact, of so much importance
in determining the attitude of the Palestinian Jewish
Christians toward the law, nor does he make any such
demand of them, not even in xiii. 13 (above, p. 324).
In the second place, if he did not wish to condemn the
legalism of the mother Church and of the apostles, which
he would have the readers give up, he must have excused
it, either on the ground that it was a weakness, pardonable in their time, or a peculiarity for which there were
good reasons. In the third place, it would have been
necessary for him to state that what was accepted as right
by the entire Church prior to 70, and what was practised
by an important part of the same, was now no longer to
be recognised, and for the change of attitude he must have
given reasons. The fact that none of these things are

found in Hebrews, and that none of these questions entered the author's mind, proves that he did not have the mother Church in view, and that he is writing to Christians who prior to conversion had no connection with the Jewish sacrificial worship. Throughout the letter we find him speaking, not of a temple or system of worship existing in his time at Jerusalem or Leontopolis, but of the tabernacle and the worship appointed for it in the Pentateuch. It is by this that he and his readers are to measure the service of Christ. Once he speaks of that system of worship, and the whole institution of which it was a part, as a thing of the past which was already ended by Jeremiah's time (viii. 7–ix. 10); but, as a rule, he uses the present tense, which in a theoretical discussion is most natural (n. 13). To conclude from this that the system of worship, *mutatis mutandis*, still existed, would be as wrong as to infer from xiii. 11, 13 that when Hebrews was written the Jewish people did not dwell in towns and villages, but in tents. Here, however, we touch questions which cannot be answered from Hebrews alone.

1. (P. 313.) Paul, as well as Peter in 1 Pet. i. 3, begins his letters to the Churches regularly with an expression of thanks to God on behalf of the readers immediately after the opening greeting. An exception to his habit is afforded by Gal., where he uses an expression of indignation at what is happening among the readers. The expression of thanks in 2 Tim. i. 3 and Philem. 4 passes immediately into a description of his mood toward the recipients and an exhortation to them. Paul begins with similar expressions of feeling and of exhortation, but without any expression of thanks, in 1 Tim. i. 3; Tit. i. 5. In Jas. i. 2 and in 2 Pet. i. 3–5 ff.—in the latter without making any grammatical separation—there is in close connection with the greeting, a transition to an exhortation of the readers (vol. i. 146, n. 1; above, p. 220, n. 10). Jude 3; 2 John 4; 3 John 3 (for the greeting is not completed till ver. 2); Clem. 1 *Cor.* i.; Philem. 1; *Ep. Smyrn. de mart. Polyc.* i., and all the letters of Ignatius, are begun with a statement of the circumstances which led to the writing of the letter. The *Epistle of Barnabas*, also, which begins by prefacing "All hail!" a form of greeting absolutely divergent from what is customary, follows it by an address to the readers, and an expression of the feeling of the author toward them.

2. (P. 317.) Even without the καί before ἡμῶν, xiii. 18, attested by D* and its Latin translation and by Chrysostom, there arises the impression which is repeated above, p. 316 f. The sudden transition from the plural of the

first person, xiii. 18 (cf. ii. 5, v. 11, vi. 9, 11)—elsewhere a common expression of the author's—to the singular, xiii. 19 (cf. xi. 32, xiii. 22 f.), must have been caused by the fact that from ver. 17 on he considers himself to be one of those who watch over the spiritual welfare of the readers,—often with sighing, —and so, for that reason alone, he keeps the plural; but he also finds the " I " more natural, where he comes to speak of his outward circumstances and of his impending journey. Just as in xiii. 8 the eternally living and unchangeable Christ is presented as the immortal teacher in contrast to the preachers who pass away, so the Jesus who has been raised to heaven from the world of the dead is contrasted with the earthly readers and ministers who come and go, as the great Shepherd of the sheep, xiii. 20 (cf. 1 Pet. ii. 25, v. 4; John x. 11–18), *i.e.* as the ever-present regent and minister of His whole Church on earth. The author was and is still to a certain extent one of these.

3. (P. 317.) With vi. 10, διακονήσαντες τοῖς ἁγίοις καὶ διακονοῦντες, cf. the expressions used with reference to the collections for the Jerusalem congregation, 2 Cor. viii. 4, ix. 1, τῆς διακονίας τῆς εἰς τοὺς ἁγίους; ix. 12 (cf. also ver. 13), ἡ διακονία τῆς λειτουργίας ταύτης . . . τὰ ὑστερήματα τῶν ἁγίων; 1 Cor. xvi. 1, τῆς λογίας τῆς εἰς τοὺς ἁγίους, evidently also xvi. 15, εἰς διακονίαν τοῖς ἁγίοις ἔταξαν ἑαυτούς; furthermore, Rom. xv. 26, κοινωνίαν τινὰ ποιήσασθαι εἰς τοὺς πτωχοὺς τῶν ἁγίων τῶν ἐν Ἱερουσαλήμ; xv. 31, ἡ διακονία μου ἡ εἰς Ἱερουσαλὴμ εὐπρόσδεκτος τοῖς ἁγίοις, perhaps also Rom. xii. 13, ταῖς χρείαις τῶν ἁγίων κοινωνοῦντες (on the contrary, not Philem. vv. 5–7; vol. i. p. 455, n. 2); also Acts xi. 29 f., xii. 25, xxiv. 17; Gal. ii. 10; vol. i. p. 310 f. According to the usage well attested here, οἱ ἅγιοι, even without any geographical reference, signifies the Christian community of the " Holy City" (Matt. iv. 5, xxvii. 53; Rev. xi. 2, xxi. 2, 10, xxii. 19), without the words necessarily having ceased to signify the Christians generally in distinction from the non-Christians (1 Cor. vi. 1 f.; Col. i. 12; Jude 3; Rev. xiii. 7), especially with πάντες (Eph. i. 15, iii. 18, vi. 18; 1 Cor. xiv. 33). This attribute would also not be wanting in Heb. vi. 10, if, in contrast to the mutual support of those addressed, the extension of their practical love to the whole of Christendom was to be praised; cf. 1 Thess. iii. 12 f.; Col. i. 5; Philem. 5. The ἅγιοι without an article in 1 Tim. v. 10 is not a parallel case.

4. (Pp. 318, 320.) Clemens Romanus, *circa* 96, includes in the address to his readers the Corinthians of the years 52–57 with the members of the "old Church of the Corinthians" of that time (1 *Cor.* xlvii., cf. chap. i.); similarly also Polycarp, *circa* 110, includes the Philippian Christians of his time with those of the time of Paul (Polyc. *Phil.* xi. 3; cf. *Forsch.* iv. 251 ff.); while at the same time he very clearly distinguishes "the men of that time" from the people of the present. In this respect there is nothing to be compared with the expression of Heb., save the way in which Paul, without taking account of single deaths and new conversions, identifies the Christians who were converted by him at the founding of a congregation with the members of the same congregation at the time of writing the letter (1 Cor. ii. 1–5, iv. 15; 2 Cor. i. 19; Phil. iv. 10–16).

5. (P. 319.) Heb. x. 32–34. On the text of ver. 34 see above, p. 312, n. 14. Aside from the false δεσμοῖς μου instead of δεσμίοις the text is given by Clemens Alexandrinus exactly as by the modern textual critics. Accord-

ing to vi. 4 (cf. Eph. iii. 9 ; Just. *Dial.* cxxii., twice ; especially of baptism φωτισμός and φωτίζεσθαι, *Apol.* i. 61), φωτιζθέντες signifies conversion to Christianity. But inasmuch as no ἄρτι (1 Thess. iii. 6 ; Matt. ix. 18 ; cf. 1 Pet. ii. 2) or προσφάτως (Acts xviii. 2) accompanies it, it cannot have also the meaning of νεόφυτοι (1 Tim. iii. 6) or νήπιοι ἐν Χριστῷ (1 Cor. iii. 1).

6. (P. 320.) For the exegesis of Heb. iii. 7–19, very little can be remarked here : (1) The stylistic ability of the writer forbids the hypothesis that the clause beginning with διό is not to be continued until ver. 12, so that all that is between would be a parenthesis, or that the clause introduced by διό has been left out altogether. The parenthetic insertion is limited to the words καθὼς λέγει τὸ πνεῦμα τὸ ἅγιον, beyond which, just as with a parenthetical καθὼς γέγραπται, John vii. 38, Rom. iii. 4, xv. 3, 21, 1 Cor. i. 31, ii. 9, the statement before begun—in this instance the statement begun by the author with διό—is resumed. The situation here is not essentially different from that in passages where a καθὼς γέγραπται and similar expressions without a following citation are joined on to the statement proper (Rom. ii. 24 ; John i. 23), or, where the author does not say at all that he is employing words from other writings, 1 Pet. i. 24, ii. 7, iii. 10–12 ; Rom. x. 6–8. (2) For this reason the author, contrary to his custom of using formal quotations, reproduces the O.T. text with conscious freedom. Without alluding to what is doubtful, he has, by the insertion of a διό, given the chronological reference to what precedes ; furthermore, by changing ἐκείνῃ after τῇ γενεᾷ to ταύτῃ, he has shown that he means not the Israelites of the Mosaic age, but a generation of the Jewish people much nearer him and his readers. The former change seems so much the more intentional from the fact that the author, in explaining the words of the psalm according to their original historical sense, restores also the original connection of the words (προσώχθισεν τεσσεράκοντα ἔτη, iii. 17). (3) If we recognise, *e.g.* with Bleek, *Heb.* ii. 436 ff., 440 ; Delitzsch, *Komm.* 119 f.; Grimm, *ZfWTh*, 1870, S. 31, that the author refers to the forty years since the death of Jesus, which Hofmann, v. 167, has called a venturesome exegesis, we must not conclude that the letter was written *circa* 70, and that the readers have had opportunity for forty years to contemplate the works of the N.T. redemption. The latter is impossible, because this is said not of the readers, but of their forefathers, *i.e.* of the Jewish people ; the former, because the end of the forty years and the visible realisation of the Divine oath against the unbelieving, which was manifested in the destruction of Jerusalem, must have been behind the author, if he is supposed to have spoken in this sense, or in this double sense, of the forty years and of the exclusion of the unbelieving Jews on account of their forty years of unbelief, from the Sabbath rest of the people of God. It is unlikely that, among other notions of the old rabbis, the idea of a forty years' duration of the days of the Messiah, depending in part on Ps. xcv. 10 (Bleek, ii. 439 ; Delitzsch, 119 ; Weber, *Jüd. Theol.*, § 82) should have been in the mind of the author ; for the "days of the Son of Man" (Luke xvii. 22, cf. Heb. v. 7) were terminated for him, on the one hand, by the death of Jesus ; on the other hand, they were still in the future, and in yet another sense endless (xiii. 8). But the utilisation of the forty years of Heb. iii. 9 for the chronology seems to the present writer to be much better justified by the character of Heb. as a whole and especially by the character of this section,

than when it is concluded from Shakespeare's *Romeo and Juliet*, Act I. Scene 3, "'Tis since the earthquake now eleven years," that this drama was written in the year 1591.

7. (Pp. 323, 325.) "Epist. vulgo ad Hebræos inscriptam non ad Hebræos, sed ad Christianos genere gentiles et quidem ad Ephesios datam esse demonstrare conatur," E. M. Roeth, 1836. This thesis is maintained with characteristically confused and extravagant rabbinical learning, and with a profusion of new interpretations of N.T. passages (sixty-three of which are enumerated in a special index, S. 265 f.); cf. below, n. 10. Roeth, p. 256 f., was led to think of Ephesus by the words θέατρον, Acts xix. 29, and θεατριζόμενοι, Heb. x. 33. V. Soden (*JbfPTh*, 1884, S. 435 ff., 627 ff.) also contested the Jewish nationality of the readers, and thought that Heb. could be understood as a circular letter to the preponderatingly Gentile Christian congregations of Italy, including those of Rome (especially S. 647–652). Cf. *per contra*, Grass, *Ist der Hb. an Heidenchristen gerichtet?* Petersburg, 1892.

8. (P. 324.) It follows from ἐλάλησεν ἡμῖν ἐν υἱῷ (i. 1) that the author and the readers, who as individuals have not heard the preaching of Jesus (ii. 3), belong to the people of the circumcision, whose servant Jesus was all through His ministry; cf. Rom. xv. 8. God, or Christ, speaks to the heathen through the apostles. Cf. 2 Cor. v. 19 f.; Eph. iii. 7; Rom. x. 12–15; also Clem. 1 *Cor.* xlii. 1. Christ is in a way the mouth by which God has spoken, and the word which He has caused to go forth into the world (Ign. *Rom.* viii. 2; *Magn.* viii. 2); but the Gentile Christians of the old time do not say: "Christ has spoken to us." He is to them always the Christ preached, and even the idea that He was the apostle sent of God into the world (Heb. iii. 1) is noticeably unobtrusive.

9. (Pp. 324, 331.) A fundamental condition of the correct exegesis of xiii. 10–16 is a recognition of the fact that the tabernacle must be of the same importance as the altar; in other words, that it is not definitely stated that the Jewish priests, or indeed the Jews who cling fast to the Mosaic cultus, had no part in the Christian institution of salvation. Inasmuch as Christ is considered here not as a priest officiating at the sanctuary (viii. 2), but simply as a sacrifice, only those Christians whose altar is concerned can be called οἱ τῇ σκηνῇ λατρεύοντες, *i.e.* priests who there offer sacrifice (cf. ix. 14, xii. 28, xiii. 15 f.; Rom. xii. 1; 1 Pet. ii. 5, 9; Rev. i. 6, v. 10, viii. 3). They are to bear in mind that they, in contrast to the O.T. priests who derived their support also from their altar (1 Cor. ix. 13), have no such advantage to expect from their cultus; for the offering, upon which their whole relation to God is based, is like that of the Day of Atonement, from which no priest and no layman had anything to look for but forgiveness of sins (see above, p. 324). The expression for the N.T. facts which are brought to mind, and for the demand which is based upon them, is borrowed, on the one hand, from the gospel story, and, on the other hand, from the Mosaic age and its institutions, and, in so far as the latter is the case, is quite as consciously anachronistic as xi. 26 is the opposite. Moses bore the shame of Christ in that he renounced the honourable position among the Egyptians which he possessed from earliest childhood, and attached himself to his own people. The Hebrews of the present are to take upon themselves the shame of Christ, by renouncing their connection with the Jewish people, to whom they belong

by birth, and by their confession of the crucified Christ to take to themselves the same hatred and the same abuse which this people had heaped upon Jesus (cf. xii. 2 f.; Rom. xv. 3).

10. (P. 326.) In the misinterpretation of Heb. v. 12–vi. 2, Roeth, 218–239, has gone the furthest astray. By the λόγια τοῦ θεοῦ he understood the Messianic prophecies, while the whole revelation of the Word of God, including that of the N.T., is meant (cf. Heb. i. 1, ii. 3, iv. 2, vi. 5, xiii. 7 ; Rom. iii. 2), and found it inconceivable that those who were Jews by birth had first to be instructed in them. Cf. *per contra*, *e.g.* Matt. ix. 13, xii. 3–8, xxii. 29, 42 f.; Luke xxiv. 26 f., 44 f.; John v. 46, xx. 9 ; Acts ii. 16–35, iii. 21–25, vii. 2–53, xiii. 16–39, xvii. 3, xxviii. 23. But, as far as the words ἔργα νεκρά are concerned, it is well known that the gods of the heathen, not in the N.T. to be sure, but elsewhere, are said at times to be dead (Ps. cvi. 28 ; cf. cxv. 4 ff. ; Wisd. Sol. xiii. 10 ; *Didache* vi. 3) ; and one is reminded of the instances in which God, in contrast to the idols, is called the Living God, 1 Thess. i. 9 ; 2 Cor. vi. 16 ; Acts xiv. 15. But He is also so called even where the contrast with unbelieving or legalising Judaism obtains or is obvious, Matt. xvi. 16 ; Rom. ix. 24 ; 2 Cor. iii. 3–11 ; cf. Matt. xxii. 32 ; Luke xx. 38 ; John vi. 57. In Heb. ix. 14, also, any thought of the λατρεία τῶν εἰδώλων is far from the intent of the passage, as the whole context shows. On the contrary, it is rather the O.T. λατρεία (ix. 1, 9, 21) that underlies the thought. Furthermore, in Heb. xii. 22 the heavenly Jerusalem is called a city of the Living God, not in contrast to Babylon or Rome, but to the earthly Jerusalem, in which God no more reveals Himself as the Living One. In Heb. iii. 12, x. 31, 1 Tim. iii. 15, iv. 10, the contrast with false gods is as impossible as in Ps. xlii. 3. Besides, the condition of men who remain in heathendom and in heathen sinfulness of life may perhaps be characterised as spiritual death (Col. ii. 13 ; Eph. ii. 1, 5, v. 14) ; but so also is the condition of the Jews who do not yet believe in Jesus (Matt. viii. 22, cf. xxiii. 27 ; John v. 24, 40, viii. 21, 52), and essentially the same is said of Jewish Christians in Rom. vi. 4–11 as is said of Gentile Christians in Col. ii. 12 f. But the former depraved life of Christians who had come from a state of heathendom is nowhere characterised as a dead or lifeless way of living, but always alluded to in other terms, *e.g.* 1 Cor. vi. 9–11 ; Gal. vi. 16–21 ; Col. ii. 5 ff., v. 3–14 ; 1 Pet. i. 14–18, iv. 2–5.

11. (P. 328.) The μὴ ἐγκαταλείποντες τὴν ἐπισυναγωγὴν ἑαυτῶν of Heb. x. 25 by way of contrast has both before it and after it, on the part of those who are still firm in faith, an exhorting and inciting of others who are in danger of falling away. It cannot be said, therefore, that in many cases the tendency toward falling away had already shown itself in the habit of neglecting to attend the Christian assembly. The contrast would then have been : "Neglect not the assembling of yourselves together, but visit the services of the congregation and listen there to words of exhortation." This habit of neglecting attendance upon the gatherings shows itself much more in the case of those who perhaps would be in a position to strengthen the wavering and "to heal that which is lame" (xii. 13). Instead of fulfilling this duty and of taking the part of the weak (cf. Rom. xv. 1 f.), they abandon the assembly to which they belong, and the brethren who meet there ; for their action is called ἐγκαταλείπειν (2 Tim. iv. 10, 16 ; 2 Cor. iv. 9 ; Heb. xiii. 5),

in distinction from καταλείπειν. What they do is from lack of love and from ill-feeling toward those with whom they have to associate, and in a spirit against which the author himself has to be upon his guard in his relations with the readers (cf. v. 11–vi. 9),—a spirit which he holds to be possible in the case of their leaders also (xiii. 17). The result of this is that the purpose of ἑαυτῶν after τὴν ἐπισυναγωγήν—a term which at all events is not the equivalent of ἡμῶν, or, in the sense of τινές, equal to αὐτῶν—is not to affirm that those Christians absent themselves from the *Christian* meetings, while they visit the *Jewish* synagogues. Those who had departed so far from the faith could not be called upon to exhort the others. The contrast to that assembly to which the Christians in question belong can lie only in other Christian assemblies of the same place ; as to these see below, § 47. Furthermore, ἐπισυναγωγή (2 Macc. ii. 7) means, at any rate, not the place of meeting, for which συναγωγή is the technical expression, nor perhaps the individual assembly (or as 2 Thess. ii. 1, the union in a passive sense), for which only the plural would be natural, but the assembled congregation (cf. vol. i. p. 94), to which ἐγκαταλείπειν is most appropriate.

12. (Pp. 331, 332.) Heb. xiii. 9. Luther's otherwise masterful translation fails only in rendering the aorist ὠφελήθησαν incorrectly. Along with this the present περιπατοῦντες is, with א*AD*, to be retained—the idea being that there are at the present time people of this manner of life, though it has already become evident that they do not attain their purpose. In the N.T. περιπατεῖν is used of the daily manner of life thirty-two times in Paul's writings, ten times in the letters of John (cf. Acts xxi. 21)—in fact, always in this sense in the N.T.—apart from the passages where it is used in its literal meaning.

13. (Pp. 333, 335.) In regard to the description in the present tense of the ceremonial acts prescribed in the Mosaic law, and all that is connected with them (Heb. v. 1–4, vii. 5, 8, 20, viii. 3–5, ix. 6–10, 22, x. 1–4, 8, 11, xiii. 11), it is to be noticed that (1) the same form of expression is quite commonly found in writings which, without any doubt, were written after the year 70. It is so in Josephus' works, where he portrays the Mosaic institutions, *Ant.* iii. 7. 1 ff., 9. 1 ff.; indeed, it is so in his apology on behalf of Judaism (*Contra Apion.* ii. 23), where he even speaks in imperative futures and imperatives, as though the service of the high priest and the priests would continue still in time to come. So Clement, 1 *Cor.* xl. xli. ; Plutarch, *Quæst. conviv.* iv. 6. 2, and the Talmud. (2) Pressing the use of the present tense would lead to the absurdities that the priests, according to ix. 6 f., still serve in the tabernacle, as they are described together with their utensils in ix. 1–5, and that the sin-offering of the Day of Atonement is still burnt before the tents in the wilderness (xiii. 11), and that Melchizedek still serves as priest-king (vii. 3). (3) Preceding and together with these expressions in the present tense, occur in decisive passages, imperfects and other forms which show that what is described as present really belongs to the past (ix. 1 f., ii. 2). (4) From ix. 9, where an especially strong proof of the continuance of the temple cultus has been found, rather the contrary is to be concluded. Of course, much in this connection is yet in debate among commentators. But, according to the definite statements of ix. 2 f., 6 f., the " first tabernacle " of ix. 8 can only be the Holy Place in contrast to the Holy of Holies, and τὰ ἅγια means not

(contrary to the usage of ix. 2) the Holy of Holies, the entrance to which was by no means unknown or closed (ix. 7), but only the true sanctuary into which Jesus was the first to find and open the way (vi. 20, viii. 2, ix. 12, x. 19 f.). The time when the approach to the true sanctuary was not yet known, because the Holy Place still existed (ix. 8), is for the author time past, because he knows and believes that Jesus has entered into that true sanctuary, that He has opened the way to it, and made it known (ix. 11 f., x. 19 f.). He calls this, for the Christians, past time ὁ καιρὸς ὁ ἐνεστηκώς from the standpoint of the Holy Spirit, who uses the legal cultus as a means of instruction, and in the sense of all the presents in ix. 6–9. This period of the legal cultus has its limits at the καιρὸς διορθώσεως (ix. 10). If, beyond all question, however, this epoch has already begun through the high-priestly function of Christ, then the καιρός which, from the standpoint of the Holy Spirit who taught through Moses (ix. 9) was spoken of as present, has thereby reached its close. The Holy Place, or the division of the sanctuary by its separating curtain, is no more. To be sure, this is understood primarily in an ideal sense, *i.e.* for the faith of the Christians. But the expression in ver. 8, especially the ἔτι which, according to vv. 10–12, has become for the Christians an οὐκέτι, must seem very unnatural to us, if in the author's day a temple with that division into a Holy Place and a Holy of Holies, still existed. The hypothesis that the readers of Heb. were still connected with the temple of Leontopolis which Wieseler, *Unters.* ii. 81 ff.; *ThStKr*, 1867, S. 665 ff., has zealously defended, hardly finds a representative to-day. All the presuppositions upon which it is based are untenable, namely (1) that the readers had anything at all to do with any temple cultus ; (2) that the author describes, or has in mind, a Jewish temple and cultus, still existing somewhere in his day ; (3) that the alleged contradictions between the statements in Heb. regarding the tabernacle and the arrangement of the temple in Jerusalem, find their solution in the supposition of a reference to the temple in Leontopolis, concerning whose interior arrangement and cultus we know very little (cf. the literature in Schürer, iii. 99 [Eng. trans. II. ii. 287]) ; (4) that in Philo, who never mentions this temple, but, on the contrary, looks upon the temple at Jerusalem as the only sanctuary of the Jewish people (*de Mon.* ii. 1–3, and in Eus. *Præp. ev.* viii. 14, 64), there should occur for the same reason—that he has in mind the temple in Leontopolis—departures from the ordinances of the Pentateuch and from the cultus at Jerusalem similar to those in Heb., cf. *per contra*, *PRE*[3] vii. 500 f.; Grimm, *ZfWTh*, 1870, S. 57–66, who, however, has misjudged the " literary carelessness " in Heb. vii. 27, ix. 4 f., x. 11 ; on which cf. below, § 47, n. 14.

§ 47. READERS, DATE, AND AUTHOR OF THE EPISTLE TO THE HEBREWS.

It is so clear from § 46 that Hebrews was not directed to the Church in Jerusalem shortly before or shortly after the year 70, that it is only necessary to summarise a number of observations. (1) If Hebrews was written to the Church in Jerusalem shortly before or shortly after the year 70, the legalism practised by the Jewish Christians in Palestine, and particularly the participation of the mother Church, its teachers and leaders, in the temple worship, would not have been passed over so lightly, while at the same time they are so severely condemned, *i.e.* if the letter is supposed to answer the question as to how the Christian confession was to be combined with the cultus of the Jewish temple, which as a matter of fact it does not ask (above, p. 333 f.). (2) The very great poverty of the mother Church, which necessitated the frequent sending of money for its relief by Christian Churches abroad, proves that they could not have exercised charity to other Churches in the noteworthy way for which they are praised in vi. 10. On the other hand, it is clear that it was the mother Church which was so largely benefited by the charity of the readers of Hebrews (above, p. 337). (3) Until it was banished from Jerusalem, the mother Church had in its membership not a few persons who heard the preaching of Jesus. Consequently the Church could not be treated as one which owed its faith to the preaching of the disciples of Jesus (ii. 4, xiii. 7 ; above, p. 315 f.). (4) It could not be said of the Church in Jerusalem by way of reproof, that because of its age it ought to be capable of instructing others in the knowledge of salvation, and was under obligation to do the same, since in rich measure the Church had always done so (Acts viii. 4, xi. 19 ff.). Even after Antioch became an independent centre of missionary effort among the Gentiles, missionaries continued to go from Jerusalem to Galatia, Corinth, and Rome (vol. i. pp. 167 f., 288 f., 442, 540); and Paul, who had reason enough to be dissatisfied with many of these wandering teachers, nevertheless regarded the Church in Jerusalem as the source of the gospel, to which the Gentile Church was under obligation out of grateful love to send back their gifts (Rom. xv. 27 ; cf. *per contra*, 1 Cor. xiv. 36). (5) On the supposition that the letter is addressed to the Church in Jerusalem, it is necessary to assume that the persecution referred to in x. 32 ff. is that in which Stephen lost his life, and that in xiii. 7 reference is perhaps made to Stephen, James the son of Zebedee, and James the brother of the Lord. But how is it possible to speak, as in x. 32, of these martyrdoms which took place in the years 35, 44, and 66 respectively, and of the accompanying sufferings of the Church (cf. Acts viii. 1–3, xi. 19, xii. 1–4 ; 1 Thess. ii. 14), as a single persecution belonging to the comparatively remote past ? If Hebrews were directed to the Church which reassembled in Jerusalem after the year 70 under Simeon, the cousin of James, the temporary banishment of the Church from Jerusalem, and the sufferings which the Christians undoubtedly experienced in withdrawing "from the camp" of Israel, would be included. But a letter to this Church, written before the year 90, as was certainly the case with Hebrews (see below), must have taken cognisance of the events of the year 70, which affected so deeply the life of the Church.

It would be more plausible to assume that Hebrews was addressed to a group of Jewish Christian Churches outside of Jerusalem, but in Palestine or the adjoining regions, possibly the readers of 2 Peter and of Jude, who are partly identical with the readers of James (n. 1). But there is no suggestion in these letters of any dispositions or propensities existing in this Church from which the state of mind among the readers apparent in Hebrews could have developed. These Christians were threatened only by influences from without coming from Gentile Christian circles ; and the libertines, who also despised prophecy, seem not to have ventured to criticise it directly among Jewish Christians (above, p. 279 f.). Moreover, the first two reasons given above against the supposition that

Hebrews was intended for the mother Church, hold also against its having been intended for any other Church in Palestine. The poverty, relief of which was laid as an obligation upon the liberality of the Gentile Christian Churches, could hardly have been confined to the city of Jerusalem (Acts xi. 29, τοῖς κατοικοῦσιν ἐν τῇ Ἰουδαίᾳ ἀδελφοῖς), and we have no knowledge that the Jewish Christian Churches south of Antioch took part in that collection.

Only when it is assumed that Hebrews is addressed to Gentile Christian readers is it possible to suppose that it was meant for the Church in Ephesus (above, p. 338, n. 7). Others have assumed that it was intended for the Church in Antioch (n. 2). But, according to Acts xv. 1, 23, Gal. ii. 1–14, this Church, even before the council in Jerusalem, must have become so thoroughly Gentile in character, that the Jewish Christian minority had adopted both the morals and the views of the Gentile Christian majority. Judging from analogy, the Church in Berœa (above, p. 305, n. 2), like the other Churches in Macedonia, must have been at an early date one of the "Churches of the Gentiles" (Rom. xvi. 4, xv. 26 f.). For a long time more favour was accorded the suggestion that the readers were to be sought in or near Alexandria (n. 3). When, however, the additional hypothesis that the readers were adherents of the temple at Leontopolis is rejected as being inconsistent with the contents of Hebrews (above, pp. 333, 341), this view has nothing left to support it. Of the history of the Egyptian Church before the time of Pantænus and Clement we know practically nothing. It is possible that in the first century it contained larger Jewish Christian elements, and that influences from Palestine were stronger than we are able to discover from the later development (n. 4). But this conjecture remains only a bare possibility.

On the other hand, the conjecture that Hebrews was

intended for Jewish Christians in Italy, or more specifically in Rome, can be said to be probable (n. 5). The
reasons which support this hypothesis are as follows :
(1) It is possible if necessary to take the words in xiii. 24,
ἀσπάζονται ὑμᾶς οἱ ἀπὸ τῆς ᾿Ιταλίας, to mean that the author
was at some point in Italy, and that only Italian Christians
were about him, from all of whom he sends greeting to
the readers. However, if this is the case, it is strange
that he does not designate these Christians either as the
brethren or saints about him, or as the Church of the place
where he is staying (1 Pet. v. 13), but instead calls them
persons from Italy, thus simply indicating their nationality.
Such an expression would be natural only if, from among
the Christians who are about him, the author distinguishes
those from Italy. But this would presuppose that at the
time both he and they were outside of Italy, and that
these Christians from Italy were closely related to the
readers, or that the readers had a special interest for those
sending greeting because the latter were Italians (cf. Phil.
iv. 22). This interest is most naturally explained if those
to whom the greeting was sent were also Italians. They
are greeted by their countrymen (n. 6). (2) At the
beginning of the year 58, when Paul wrote to the Romans,
the Church was made up of a large majority of native
Jews and a small minority of Gentiles, so small that the
whole Church could be uniformly addressed as a Jewish
Christian Church (vol. i. pp. 421–434). When this relation between Jews and Gentiles was reversed we do not
know. But we do know that while Paul was in prison in
Rome, Jewish Christian missionaries of various kinds were
at work in the city (Col. iv. 11 ; Phil. i. 14 ff. ; vol. i. pp.
442, 540), and we may assume that these laboured especially for the conversion of their own countrymen. It is
hardly likely that the large Jewish majority in the Roman
Church was completely reversed before the year 80. It
has been conjectured, not without reason, that Clement,

the author of the letter of the Romans to the Corinthians about the year 96 was a Jew by birth ; and this was even more probable in the case of Hermas, the contemporaneous author of the *Shepherd* (n. 7). Assuming as proved that these two Roman writers were familiar with James, and that Paul saw fit to take cognisance of this letter in Romans (vol. i. 126 f., 131 f.), more than ordinary importance attaches to the fact that beyond question Clement of Rome was familiar with Hebrews, and in all probability Hermas also (n. 7). A knowledge of James, which was addressed to Christians of Palestine and the neighbouring regions about the year 50, was brought to Rome by these Christians, who constituted the nucleus of the Roman Church (vol. i. 126, 428 f.). The exact acquaintance which Clement and Hermas have with Hebrews, which was written much later, and which was not accepted and circulated in Rome as an Epistle of Paul (above, p. 301 f.), is explained naturally only on the supposition that Hebrews was first received by the Roman Christians. In the year 58 the Jewish majority of the Roman Church clung with fondness to their people, and were deeply grieved that the Jewish people, the majority of whom persisted in rejecting the gospel, were losing ground in Christendom just as they were declining nationally and politically. They were still open to many Jewish prejudices against the gospel. It was possible for the feelings which Paul contends against throughout the whole of Romans, especially those encountered in Rom. ix.–xi. 12, to subside, but they could also have developed to that degree of bitterness which we meet in Hebrews. As early as the year 58 there was a party among the Roman Christians who regarded abstinence from flesh and wine as necessary for steadfastness in the Christian life. We encounter exactly the same tendency again in Heb. xiii. 9 (above, p. 331 f.), while the related movement of which we are informed in Col. ii. 8–13 is based upon different ideas.

The view here advocated, namely, that Hebrews was intended for Roman Christians, is also supported by the fact
that in Romans the Romans (vol. i. p. 427), and in Hebrews
the Hebrews (above, pp. 328 f., 339, n. 11), were not in any
way associated in worship with the Jews in their localities.
It also deserves notice that the use of the word ἡγούμενοι
(Heb. xiii. 7, 17, 24) to designate the heads of the congregation, which was not common among the Pauline
Churches, was retained in Rome (above, p. 124, n. 5).
The use of the expression ἐπισυναγωγή τινων (Heb. x. 25)
to designate the separate assembly of Christians, finds a
parallel in the words used by the Roman Hermas (*Mand.*
xi. 9), συναγωγή ἀνδρῶν δικαίων (cf. vol. i. 94). (3) What
is suggested in Hebrews with regard to the history of its
readers suits the Roman Christians.   If the gospel was
brought to Rome for the first time about the year 50 by
Jewish Christians who came hither from Jerusalem (vol. i.
p. 428 f.), if these were followed in the succeeding decade
by other Christians of the same nationality (Col. iv. 10 f.),
and if, finally, Peter came to Rome as a missionary
preacher, there is ample foundation for what is said in
Heb. ii. 3.   The reference in Heb. xiii. 7 is primarily to
Peter, but also to Paul, and perhaps to others of the
numerous Roman teachers (Col. iv. 10 f. ; Phil. i. 14 ff.)
with whose end we are not acquainted.   The days of severe
persecution, which after their conversion the " Hebrews "
so bravely endured (x. 32–34), are the days of Nero.   In
view of the descriptions of Tacitus (*Ann.* xv. 44) and of
Clement (above, pp. 61 f., 68 f.), and the echoes of this
persecution in Rev. xvii. 6, xviii. 20, 24, the expression
used in Hebrews (x. 33, θεατριζόμενοι) is not too strong, nor
when rightly understood is it too weak (above, p. 318 f.).
This hypothesis also explains why the writer remarks
expressly that they endured this persecution after their
conversion, thereby implying a contrast to other sufferings
which they encountered *before* their conversion (above,

p. 319). Some twelve years before Nero's persecution of
the Christians, the Jews were driven from Rome by
Claudius (vol. i. pp. 427 f., 433). Among these the Jews
who subsequently became Christians, as Aquila, had suffered
(Acts xviii. 2). Why should we stretch our imaginations in
order to find a Church to which these allusions in Hebrews
will apply, when in the events preceding the founding of the
Roman Church and the history of the Church we can find
the requisite facts. It is also very easy to understand
how the members of the oldest Roman Church, because of
their close relation with the Christian communities in
Palestine (vol. i. p. 428 f.), exercised charity toward the
poor Christians in Palestine without it being necessary for
Paul to urge them (Rom. xii. 13, cf. xv. 25–32) to do so,
and so deserved the praise accorded them in Heb. vi. 10.
(4) If Heb. x. 25 has been correctly interpreted (above,
p. 339 f.), it is necessary to seek the readers in a large
city where the Christians were wont to assemble in
several places. Many of the readers are beginning to
absent themselves from those places of worship which
they had always been accustomed to attend, not because
they intended to leave off attending Christian worship,
and also not because they wished to attend the Jewish
synagogues instead, but in order that they might visit
some other Christian assembly in the same city where
they could find greater edification. The author condemns
this, because he thinks that those Christians whose religion
is vital ought rather to stay at their post and strengthen
and encourage their brothers who are weak in faith, and
not to withdraw from them in discontent, leaving them to
their fate in a loveless spirit, in order selfishly to connect
themselves with another Christian congregation where
they found more satisfaction. Hebrews was not directed
to the entire Church of a large city. Were this the
case, it would be difficult to explain the lack of a greeting if this were originally a part of the letter (above,

p. 312 f.), and also the history of Hebrews in the Church, especially the ancient title πρὸς Ἐβραίους. According to the analogy of all N.T. and post-apostolic language (2 Cor. vi. 11 ; 1 Thess. i. 1 ; 2 Thess. i. 1 ; Phil. iv. 15 ; Clem. 1 *Cor.* xlvii. 6 ; Ign. *Eph.* viii. 1, xi. 2 ; *Magn.* xv. ; *Trall.* xiii. ; *Philad.* xi.), and especially in keeping with the external titles of letters, the readers of Hebrews would have been described as the inhabitants of their city if they had been the only Christians in their locality. The same would have been true if these Hebrews had lived scattered over a whole country, but had constituted the whole body of Christians in the region (cf. Gal. i. 2, iii. 1 ; 1 Cor. xvi. 19 ; 2 Cor. i. 1, viii. 1, ix. 2 ; Rom. xv. 26). The whole body of Christians in a province or large city could hardly have been so homogeneous as regards their condition of faith and their frame of mind as the readers of Hebrews are everywhere represented as being, especially in passages like v. 12 ff., xii. 4 ff. What differences Paul had to take into consideration in the Corinthian and Roman Churches ! Nothing of this appears in Hebrews. That this undeniable fact should be made an argument against the position that Hebrews was intended for a part of a Church (Grimm, *ZfWTh*, 1870, S. 33 ; von Soden, *JbfPTh*, 1884, S. 439), is one of the most incomprehensible things that have been said about Hebrews. The Roman Church as a whole must have been the principal starting-point for missionary work in the West ; at the time of Paul's imprisonment there were many members of the Church zealously engaged in missionary work ; in the year 96, in the letter of Clement, the Church takes an active part in adjusting the disturbed state of affairs in Corinth, with an apology for having delayed so long in the matter (Clem. 1 *Cor.* i. 1) ; finally, in the year 110, Ignatius praises the Church in this language (*ad Rom.* iii.) : " You have taught others ; but I desire that you keep yourself what as a teacher you have imparted to your pupils." Such a Church as this could

hardly at any time be reproved on the ground that its age
ought to enable it to be a teacher of others (Heb. v. 12).
The readers of Hebrews were a smaller group of persons
who had been Christians for a long time, and who constituted a part of the whole Church of a large city. It
was a congregation attached to some household, besides
which there were in the same city one or several other
similar household congregations. This conclusion is confirmed by the injunction to the readers to greet *all* their
officers and *all* the saints (xiii. 24). Since the πάντας
which is used twice cannot be explained here as elsewhere
to mean that they were to greet all as distinguished from
certain individuals or a small group of persons (Gal. i. 2 ;
1 Cor. xvi. 20–24 ; 2 Cor. i. 1 ; Phil. iv. 21 ; 2 Tim. iv.
21 ; Ignatius, *Smyrn.* xiii. 2 ; *ad Polyc.* viii. 2), the contrast
must be that between the particular and the general, *i.e.*
between the readers who are to convey the greeting and
the whole Church whom they are to greet. Special
significance attaches to the πάντας in xiii. 24, where the
heads of the Church are mentioned a second time, in view
of the fact that the leaders of the Church upon whom the
pastoral care of the readers devolves are called simply
ἡγούμενοι in xiii. 17 (cf. 1 Thess. v. 12 ; 1 Tim. v. 17 ;
1 Pet. v. 1). The readers, who constitute a separate ἐπισυναγωγή (x. 25), perhaps with their own officers (xiii. 17),
are, nevertheless, a part of the collective Church of the
great city in which they live. The history of the whole
Church is their history also (vi. 10, x. 32 ff., xiii. 7), and its
officers are theirs as well. Therefore the greeting is sent to
all the officers and *all* the saints. It is difficult to find in
the first century of Church life conditions which correspond
more perfectly to these exegetical observations than the
conditions of the Christians in Rome. Paul in his time
distinguishes three groups in the Church there. In addition to the Church in the house of Aquila to which all
persons in close relation to Paul belonged (Rom. xvi.

3–13), there were a second and a third (cf. xvi. 14, 15 ;
vol. i. p. 430, n. 1). Whether one of these, *e.g.* the one
mentioned in xvi. 14, is identical with the readers of
Hebrews, or whether in the interval between Romans and
Hebrews new groups were formed in the Roman Church,
we do not know. Neither are we informed as to how the
separate ἐπισυναγωγαί were related to the whole Church.
But it is not unlikely that Hebrews was directed to a
group of the Roman Christians consisting entirely of
Jews (n. 8).

The *terminus ad quem* of Hebrews is determined by
three facts : (1) the use of the letter by Clement of Rome
(96 A.D.) ; (2) the mention of Timothy (xiii. 23) ; (3) the
circumstance that the author is dealing with readers who
in the main belong to the first generation of Christians.
Timothy, who was born about the year 25 (above, p. 37),
may have lived until the end of the century. The character of Clement's dependence indicates that Hebrews was
written before 90. The *terminus ad quem* fixed by the
third fact varies with the place in which the readers are
sought. If this place be Rome, where Christians had lived
since about the year 50 (vol. i. p. 427), we are compelled
to date the letter somewhat before 90. On the other
hand, according to x. 32, a considerable time must have
elapsed since the persecution of the year 64. If the preceding interpretation of iii. 9 (above, p. 320 ff.) be correct,
the destruction of Jerusalem and the temple had certainly
already taken place. In writing to Roman Christians, the
author had even less occasion to refer more definitely to
this event than did Jude, who wrote to readers so much
nearer Jerusalem (n. 9). There was even less occasion
if the event had taken place a number of years before.
In this case also the fall of Jerusalem could make the
Jewish Christians all the more doubtful about the entire
Christian hope. It did indeed happen in fulfilment of
a prophecy of Jesus ; but where was the fulfilment of

the accompanying promise of the second coming of Jesus which was so intimately connected in the thought of the early Church with the judgment upon Jerusalem ? We shall not be far wrong if we place the composition of Hebrews about the year 80.

We shall be least successful in determining the origin of Hebrews. It is not necessary to refute the idea that some unknown person wrote Hebrews with the deceitful intention of passing it off as a work of Paul's (n. 10). A writing which has always been anonymous in form (above, pp. 304 f., 312 f.) cannot be also pseudonymous. The genuineness of the writing is proved fully by the subordination of the author's personality to his subject, by the earnestness of his purpose—apparent in every line—to save a definite body of readers, distinctive in character, from shipwreck, and by an eloquence born out of the depths of an inspired soul. Of the two names between which the inharmonious tradition of the second century gives us choice, those of Paul and Barnabas, the first is certainly to be rejected (n. 11). Aside from the fact that Hebrews was not written until after 70, *i.e.* several years after Paul's death, he could not have been its author. He could not be called one of the Christians who received the word of salvation from those who heard the preaching of Jesus (ii. 3). It is not a question here of mere external knowledge of the gospel history, of which Paul also had received the tradition from older Christians where he was not familiar with the facts before his conversion, but the author is speaking of the Word of God, preached with signs and wonders, implanted in the hearts of believing hearers, and bringing salvation—the word which Paul calls the gospel of God and of Christ (cf. Heb. iv. 2, vi. 5, xiii. 7). This, however, was not received by Paul from men, nor through human teachers (Gal. i. 12), but it had enlightened him like a stroke of lightning from heaven. The matter is also settled by Origen's judgment, that the style of Hebrews precludes its Pauline authorship (above, p. 309). The fact that we have such a large number of Epistles from Paul's hand, covering a period of some fifteen years, produced under the most varying conditions and in very different states of mind, and on this account showing the greatest variety in thought, in form, and in language, compels us to affirm positively that he could not have been the author of Hebrews, which in that case must have been written before 2 Tim. The author of Hebrews is no ἰδιώτης τῷ λόγῳ (2 Cor. xi. 6), but a teacher rhetorically trained, who, notwithstanding all the earnestness of his concern for the salvation of his readers, nevertheless makes it a point to put his thoughts into artistic and rhythmical language, as appears from the very first sentence, i. 1–4 (n. 12). It would be rash to affirm that the versatile Paul could not, if occasion demanded, have developed the ideas peculiar to Hebrews. But if Paul is the author, it is incomprehensible that he should never have been led by the development of thought in Hebrews and by its contrasts to suggest the thoughts which dominated him to the end, namely, that men are justified and saved by faith and not by works of the law (cf. among other passages, Eph. ii. 8 f. ; Phil. iii. 9 ; 1 Tim. i. 12–16 ; Tit. iii. 5–7), and that in Christianity all national differences lose their religious significance (cf. among other passages, Col. iii. 11 ; 1 Tim. ii. 4–7 ; Tit. ii. 11, iii. 4). Furthermore, it is inconceivable that Paul, who mentions the Saviour more than 600 times in his Epistles, either as Christ, or Jesus Christ, or our Lord Jesus Christ, or simply the Lord,—only very rarely as Jesus (Rom. iii. 26, viii. 11 ; 2 Cor. iv. 10–14, xi. 4 ; Eph. iv. 21 ; 1 Thess. i. 10, iv. 14 ; cf. Rom. x. 9 ; 1 Cor. xii. 3), and never in his last letters, Philemon, 1 and 2 Timothy and Titus,—should in Hebrews suddenly change his usage and regularly employ the simple name "Jesus" (ii. 9, iii. 1, vi. 20, vii. 22, x. 19, xii. 2, 24, xiii. 12, cf. iv. 14)—"Jesus Christ" only three times (x. 10, xiii. 8, 21)—more rarely simply "the Lord" (ii. 3, not in viii. 2, xii. 14), but never the full Pauline formula, "our Lord Jesus Christ" (not even in xiii. 20). Moreover, the use of the plural to designate the writer (ii. 5, iv. 13, v. 11, vi. 1, 3, 9, 11, xiii. 18), which is replaced by the singular only in xi. 32, xiii. 19, 22, is contrary to Pauline usage (vol. i. 171, n. 1, 209, n. 3, 316, n. 3). An author does not assume for one writing a usage which he never afterwards employs. The hypothesis that Paul is the writer of Hebrews is not only not supported by the tradition, but rendered impossible; for although it is easy to understand how, in Alexandria, Hebrews, which was associated with Paul's letters, was ascribed to him, it is difficult to understand how the tradition of Pauline authorship, if it was originally connected with Hebrews, could have been lost in most of the Churches, or indeed replaced by another name (above, p. 298 f.).

More can be said in favour of the Barnabas tradition (n. 13). In the first place, we know so little about Barnabas that we can form no exact conception of how he would have expressed himself as an author. We possess no writings of his by comparison with which his production of Hebrews might be disproved. It is not impossible that Barnabas, who entered the Church in Jerusalem before the year 35, who, as early as the year 38, enjoyed a certain distinction (Acts ix. 27), and was sent shortly afterward on an important mission to Antioch (Acts xi. 22), was still alive in the year 80, an old man of about fourscore years, although Hebrews does not give the impression of having been written by an old man. Just as Mark, his cousin and helper, in spite of early differences with Paul, worked hand in hand with him later (Col. iv. 10; 2 Tim. iv. 11), so it is possible that Barnabas may have been on the best of terms with Timothy, the disciple of Paul (Heb. xiii. 23). There are some traces of a tradition according

to which Barnabas once came to Rome (vol. i. 432 f., n. 5).
The fact that he soon showed himself inferior to Paul as a
preacher (Acts xiv. 12) does not prove that he was not
proficient in the use of language, although a Levite born
in Cyprus and living in Jerusalem (Acts iv. 36 f.) is not
likely to have possessed the very great rhetorical skill
which the author of Hebrews shows. Ignorance of the
ritual regulations of the temple at Jerusalem, which some
think is apparent in a number of passages in Hebrews,
would be neither more nor less surprising in the case of
Barnabas than of Paul. This objection is not serious,
however, for the simple reason that the author is speaking
throughout the letter not of the contemporaneous worship
in Jerusalem, but of the worship in the tabernacle which
was prescribed in the law (n. 14); so that in any case the
author can be charged only with lack of a technical knowledge of the law. How much or how little of such knowledge Barnabas possessed no one can say. On the other hand,
it could hardly be explained how a man, who like Barnabas
had been a prominent member of the mother Church, could
have lost so fully from his mind its attitude toward the Jewish
cultus and the ceremonial law (above, p. 334 f.); this would
remain inexplicable, even if he were writing to Jewish
Christians outside of Palestine. Although all of these
comparisons of the little we know about Barnabas with
Hebrews do not absolutely exclude the possibility of the
hypothesis that this λόγος τῆς παρακλήσεως (Heb. xiii. 22)
was written by the υἱὸς παρακλήσεως (Acts iv. 36), yet
it is improbable when the tradition is considered. If the
tradition that makes Barnabas the author goes back to
the time when the letter began to circulate, which must
have been the case if it is true, it is impossible to
explain its disappearance, especially in circles where Paul's
name was not allowed to take its place. We conclude,
therefore, that the Barnabas authorship of the letter, like the
Pauline, is unsupported by a real and genuine tradition,

but is an ancient hypothesis (above, p. 303 f.). It is not likely that the future will ever take us beyond hypotheses. The conjecture, probably first made by Luther, that Hebrews was written by Apollos, has, not without reason, always been regarded with favour (n. 15). The union of Greek rhetorical skill with Jewish knowledge of the Scriptures for which he was distinguished, and the fiery zeal with which he testified to his faith, particularly among his countrymen, both appear in Hebrews (Acts xviii. 24–28 ; vol. i. 262 f., 270 f., 286 f.). The faith in Jesus which Apollos brought with him from his native city of Alexandria to Ephesus, without having previously belonged to a Church whose members were baptized, he may have owed to persons who had been led to believe through the preaching of Jesus Himself (n. 4), even before Pentecost, possibly while visiting the feast in Jerusalem. Apollos could have written Heb. ii. 3. What is said in xiii. 23 would be in harmony with his friendly relations with Paul (cf. Tit. iii. 13); also xiii. 7, if Paul as well as Peter is referred to in this passage. Luther's hypothesis has a twofold advantage over all the others: (1) among the teachers of the apostolic time, so far as we are able to form a conception of them, there is no one whom our impression of the author of Hebrews suits better than Apollos; (2) in the little that we know of his history there is nothing directly opposed to the hypothesis. But the outcome of every thoughtful discussion of the origin of Hebrews is likely to be the same as Origen's conclusion : τίς δὲ ὁ γράψας τὴν ἐπιστολήν, τὸ μὲν ἀληθὲς θεὸς οἶδεν.

1. (P. 343.) W. Grimm, ZfWTh, 1870, S. 19–77, who refutes (S. 46–53) the theory yet held by Bleek, Lünemann, Riehm, and others, that Heb. is intended for Jerusalem, still retained Palestine as the home of the readers, and suggested (S. 71) Jamnia as their residence. Westcott does not wish to dispute this, but contents himself with the supposition that it is a congregation in the neighbourhood of Jerusalem (p. xlii).

2. (P. 344.) Böhme, Ep. ad Hebr. 1825, p. xxxii ff., held the Antiochian community to be the circle of readers of Heb. ; and Hofmann, v. 531 ff., with

the added supposition that Paul is the author, believed them to be the Jewish Christians of Antioch and vicinity.́ But the very fact that in Antioch as late as 63, at the time when Hofmann believes Heb. to have been written, the Jewish portion of the congregation was still separated from the Gentile portion, is, according to Acts xv. and Gal. ii., inconceivable. That Timothy had any very close connection with Antioch is nowhere proved; and that he, profiting by the opportunity offered by the journey of Acts xviii. 22, stayed there with Paul for any length of time (Hofmann, 532), is a theory incompatible with Acts xviii. 18. At the time of Paul's leaving Corinth, Timothy was not with him, and we do not meet him again with Paul until very much later in Ephesus (Acts xix. 22 ; 1 Cor. iv. 17 ; cf. vol. i. 265, n. 2).

3. (P. 344.) The readers of Heb. were sought in Alexandria by Wieseler, *Chron.* 479 ff. ; *Unters. über den Heb.*, Heft ii. 1861 ; Köstlin, *ThJb*, 1854, S. 388 ff. ; Ritschl, *ThStKr*, 1866, S. 89 ff. ; Hilgenfeld, *Einl.* 385 ff., and others. It is possible that the author was a native Alexandrian ; but there is nothing to make it likely that he belonged by birth to the circle of the readers. It would not be possible, therefore, from the origin of the author to draw any conclusion as to the residence of the readers. Concerning the alleged reference to the temple at Leontopolis see above, p. 341. The attempt of Köstlin (*ThJb* 1854, S. 395 ff.) to refer the οὕτως ἀναστρεφόμενοι, Heb. x. 33, to the sufferings of the non-Christian Jews of Alexandria under Caligula, is unsuccessful. Cf. especially, Grimm, *op. cit.* 67 ff.

4. (P. 344.) If Apollos in 54 brought with him from his home in Alexandria a belief in Jesus which made him an ardent preacher of the gospel in the synagogue of Ephesus ; and if, on the other hand, he knew nothing of the ecclesiastical baptism, and did not as yet possess the Christian knowledge which had developed in the Church (Acts xviii. 24-26 ; cf. xix. 1-7), then the conviction that Jesus was the Messiah must have spread to the Jews of Egypt independently of the organised Church, and perhaps before the rise of a Church in Jerusalem, *i.e.* in the days of John the Baptist and of Jesus Himself. It is to these Jews that Mark in the first instance must have turned, if he is to be rightly considered the founder of the Alexandrian Church (Eus. *H. E.* ii. 16. 1 and 24), and Barnabas also if he went to Alexandria (Clem. *Hom.* i. 9-14 ; cf. vol. i. 432 f., n. 5). The Jewish population of Egypt is estimated at one million (Philo, *contra Flaccum*, vi.) ; and the Samaritans, who wished to be reckoned as Jews (Jos. *Ant.* xi. 8. 6), were also represented there in large numbers (Jos. *Ant.* xii. 1). There was, as a matter of fact, in the neighbourhood of Arsinoë, a city which was either by them or after them named Samaria (*The W. Flinders Petrie Papyrus*, ed. Mahaffy, ii. 14, 88, 93, 94). Cf. Schürer, iii. 19-25 (Eng. trans. II. ii. 226-230). There was, consequently, no lack of material for Jewish Christian communities in Egypt. If the *Didache* was written in Egypt about 110 (vol. i. 304), we might conclude that there was a connection between the primitive Egyptian Church and that of Palestine. The very fact that there were originally twelve presbyters of Alexandria (Eutych. Alex., ed. Pococke, i. 331 ; cf. Clem. *Hom.* xi. 36 ; *Recogn.* vi. 15) might point in the same direction. Further evidence may be found in the traces of a knowledge of Jewish Christian Gospels, which appear in many of the fragments of apocryphal Gospels

found in recent years in Egypt (*ThLb*, 1897, col. 426, 430 ; *NZK*, 1900, S. 361–370; 1905, S. 171–175). The present writer refrains from expressing any opinion concerning the Epistles of St. Anthony (especially *Ep. 2 ad Arsinoïtas*, Migne, 40, col. 981). As a matter of fact, we have no certain knowledge of Jewish Christian commun ies in Egypt.

5. (P. 345.) Wettstein was the first to think of Christians in Rome, *Novum Testamentum*, ii. 386 f. ; and more recently Holtzmann, Kurz, and the present writer (*PRE*², v. 666 ff. ; ed. 3, vii. 501 f.). Erroneous notions concerning the composition of the Roman congregation have been the chief hindrance to the spread of this view.

6. (P. 345.) It should not be denied that expressions such as οἱ ἀπὸ τῆς Ἰταλίας, xiii. 24 ; οἱ ἀπὸ Κιλικίας καὶ Ἀσίας, Acts vi. 9 ; ὁ ἀπὸ Ναζαρέθ, Matt. xxi. 11 ; John i. 46 ; Acts x. 38, denote origin, whether that of birth, or the place from which one has just arrived (cf. *e.g.* Acts xxi. 27 ; Matt. xv. 1, if οἱ is genuine here = Mark iii. 22, vii. 1), and that such a description of persons can only have arisen outside of the places where they were born, or where they customarily resided. This is not in any way altered by the transfer of the formula to other expressions than those of place, such as οἱ ἀπὸ τῆς ἐκκλησίας, Acts xii. 1 ; or οἱ ἀπὸ σκηνῆς and similar ones ; nor by the cases in which, by virtue of a sort of attraction (Kühner-Gerth. *Gr.* i. 546), the departure from a place is combined with the preceding residence in it, Acts x. 23, xvii. 13 ; cf. *per contra*, xvii. 11. As an instance of this is the case where a messenger sent from Sparta to Thessaly speaks in Herodotus, viii. 114 (cf. in connection also Polyb. v. 86. 10) of Ἡρακλεῖδαι οἱ ἀπὸ Σπαρτῆς. On the other hand, it must be admitted that a narrator, who as such is generally removed from the standpoint of the events narrated, might on occasion so express himself as to introduce a person by his title of origin, although at the time of writing the person is within his own place of residence. As the Lazarus whom Jesus raised from the dead is generally called the Lazarus of Bethany to distinguish him from others of that name, he is so called in John xi. 1, which, inasmuch as the narrative is centred at Lazarus' own home, is a not very elegant form of expression. Still worse is the ἀσπάζονταί σε . . . πάντες οἱ ἀπὸ Φιλίππων, ὅθεν καὶ ἐπέστειλά σοι, which the pseudo-Ignatius, *circa* 370 or 400, makes Ignatius in Philippi write (*ad Her.* viii.). It would be hard to point out anything of this sort in a real letter, even of a man of much less education than the author of Heb. The theory of a similar clumsiness of expression in Heb. xiii. 24 would in no wise explain why the writer designates by their origin, or place of residence, those who are sending greetings, instead of characterising them as Christians of his vicinity (Gal. i. 2 ; Phil. iv. 21 ; Tit. iii. 15). If he wished, however, in a manner similar to 1 Cor. xvi. 19, Rom. xvi. 16, to extend greetings, not expressly entrusted to him to deliver, in behalf of all the Christians of the country in which he was living, he would have written αἱ ἐκκλησίαι τῆς Ἰταλίας, or something similar. It will probably have to be granted, then—(1) that the author and the Italians who send greeting are outside of Italy. (2) The Italians alone, of the Christians of his vicinity, have commissioned him to extend greetings, because they most naturally have a greater interest in the readers who live in Italy.

7. (P. 346.) Lightfoot, *Clement*, ii. 205, holds Clement to be a Hellenistic

Jew. The present writer attempted to prove the Jewish origin of the author of the *Shepherd of Hermas* in his *Hirt des Hermas*, 485–497. Spitta, *Urchrist.* ii. 243–437, makes the greater part of the *Shepherd* the work of a Jew, Hermas, who had not yet become Christian. After attention had been called, even before Origen's time, to the points of contact between Heb. and Clem. 1 *Cor.* (above, pp. 299 f., 308 f.), Eusebius noticed that the latter betrayed the borrowing from Heb. not only of thoughts, but also of words. "The fact is unmistakable," writes Overbeck (*Zur Gesch. d. Kanons*, S. 3), "that this letter of Clement's makes use of Heb. without acknowledgment, at times copying it outright." For details, cf. *GK*, i. 963 f. The present writer attempted to demonstrate the dependence of the *Shepherd* upon Heb. in his *Hirt des Hermas*, 439–452, cf. Hofmann, v. 45. Spitta, ii. 412–414, allows nothing more than the possibility that the author of Heb. was acquainted with the original purely Jewish writing of the *Shepherd*.

8. (P. 351.) As the Roman Christians, since the time of Claudius, had been cut off from the fellowship of the synagogue (vol. i. 427), the division of the Roman Jews into a considerable number of synagogue congregations furnishes merely the analogy and not the basis for the division of the Roman Christian congregations into smaller circles, meeting at different places. Least of all is it to be imagined that one of those Jewish synagogue congregations, which during the first centuries remained such (vol. i. 47 f., 67, n. 14 ; 433 f., n. 6), had been transformed, at so early a period as the apostolic age, into a Christian congregation, and that the particular assembly to which the readers of Heb. belong, and which they are not to leave (x. 25 ; above, p. 339, n. 11), is one of these Jewish synagogues. Nestle's question (*ET*, 1899, p. 422), whether the title πρὸς Ἑβραίους might not be connected with the name of the συναγωγὴ Ἑβραίων (vol. i. 67, n. 14), is on this account to be answered in the negative ; and all the more decidedly as the historical significance which Ἑβραῖοι had in the name of that synagogue was not applicable to the first recipients of Heb. (above, pp. 296, 306 f.).

9. (P. 351.) On Jude 5, where, not the destruction of Jerusalem or of the Temple, but, as in Heb. iii. 7–19, iv. 6, the ruin of the generation of the Jewish people which had sinned against Jesus is expressed, in a form borrowed from the history of Mosaic times, see above, pp. 253 f., 320 f. If Jerusalem and the Temple were in ruins, the readers must have thought of this fact when they came to Heb. viii. 13, xii. 22, xiii. 14, as the Corinthians must have done in reading Clem. 1 *Cor.* vi. 4 (ζῆλος καὶ ἔρις πόλεις μεγάλας κατέσκαψεν καὶ ἔθνη μεγάλα ἐξερίζωσεν) ; and they must have understood the author's reason for using in xiii. 13 παρεμβολῆς instead of πόλεως or πύλης, as he has it in xiii. 12. Jerusalem and its gates were no longer standing. If the readers found in xiii. 14 a contrast between the Christians, who had no enduring city upon earth, and the Jews, who in Jerusalem still possessed one, it was only because they failed to take into account the fact that (1) this contrast would have had to be expressed at least by an emphatic ἡμεῖς ; (2) that a Christian, *circa* 66–70, in view of the prophecy of Jesus and of the actual conditions, could not possibly have said, even indirectly, that Jerusalem was a πόλις μένουσα. The Jews who have imagined this, through their unbelief, have lost the city, which they held to be enduring ; the Jewish Christians, through the faith in which they have followed their forefathers (xi. 10, 13–16), have won for them-

selves an eternal city. That the author would have had to direct attention more clearly and strongly to the judgment of the year 70 than he does in iii. 7–19, iv. 6, ix. 8–12 (above, pp. 321 ff., 339 f.), xiii. 14, and that he would have had to use—particularly in viii. 13—the annihilation of the temple-cultus which had occurred as a most powerful argument for his position, instead of saying, from the standpoint of Jeremiah, that the end of the old covenant was near at hand, in that a new one was opposed to it by the prophets,—these and other similar challenges would be in place only if it had been necessary to combat a false devotion to the Temple and its cultus. But there is no trace of this in Heb. If a Jewish Christian addressing Jewish Christians, who viewed with a sad heart their ruin and the ruin of their people, had allowed "the brutal logic of facts" to speak more loudly and decisively, he would have been open to the reproach against which Paul guards himself in Rom. ix. 1 ff.

10. (P. 352.) Schwegler, *Nachapost. Zeitalter*, ii. 304 f., declares Heb. to be a pseudo-Pauline forgery. Baur, *Christ. u. Kirche der drei ersten Jahrh.* (2 Aufl.) 109, who viewed it as a product of Jewish Christianity, believed, however, that in xiii. 23 he had discovered the author's fraudulent purpose to introduce "his writing as one which had come from among the associates of Paul." Köstlin wrote against Schwegler from within the circle of his own school, *ThJb*, 1853, S. 420 ff.; 1854, S. 437, so that Overbeck also (S. 6) viewed the hypothesis of a fiction as permanently disposed of.

11. (P. 352.) Among those who more recently represent the theory of the Pauline authorship may be mentioned Hug, *Einl.*[3] ii. 461–496; Hofmann, v. 42–52, 520–561; Biesenthal, *Das Trostschreiben des Ap. Pl. an die Hebräer*, 1878; Holtzheuer, *Der Br. an die Ebräer*, 1883.

12. (P. 353.) On the language and style of Heb., especially in comparison with the writings of Paul, cf. Seyffarth, *De ep. ad Hebr. indole*, 1821; Bleek, i. 315–338; Hofmann, v. 555–561. In regard to the rhythm, see Blass, *ThStKr*, 1902, Heft 3, also his "(Barnabas) Brief an die Hebr. Text mit Angabe der Rhythmen," 1903. The idea of Hofmann that Paul, freed from a five years' imprisonment, and awaiting the return of Timothy in an Italian port, must have had leisure to bestow a care in the execution of Heb. which is not his custom, is not obvious. Torn from an environment in Rome which had been familiar to him for two years past, and which was in no way oppressive, in the discomfort of a seaport city, where there could hardly have been a Christian community, and in the impatience of awaiting the arrival of Timothy, or a suitable chance of obtaining passage, Paul would have been much less in a position to bestow a conscious care upon his style than when, in the bosom of the reconciled Corinthian congregation, he wrote to the Romans; or when from Rome, surrounded by friends and helpers, after he had become accustomed to the local customs, and previous to the opening of the exciting trial, he wrote the Col. and Eph. letters. A conscious effort to attain elegance of expression and a euphonious rounding out of clauses was contrary, in any case, to the character of Paul. Such an effort is also not to be ascribed to the real author. He who would write in the style in which Heb. is written, with such great care and such ardent desire to produce an effect upon the hearts and consciences of his readers or hearers,—and the "readers" of that time were always for the most part hearers (Rev. i. 3),—to him such a

style of writing must have become second nature; he could no longer do otherwise. Besides periods, everywhere grammatically transparent, symmetrically formed, and rhythmically rounded (i. 1–4, ii. 2–4, v. 1–3, vi. 16–20 vii. 18–25, x. 19–25, xii. 1, 2), in the carrying out of which the author does not allow himself to be disturbed by lengthy citations (iii. 7 ff. ; above, p. 337)—besides these, alliterations and paranomasia are conspicuous (i. 1, πολ-, πολ-, παλ-, πατ-, προφ ; ii. 1, περ-, προσ-, παρ-; ii. 10, παν-, παν-, πολ-, παθ-; v. 8, ἔμαθεν—ἔπαθεν ; vii. 3, ἀπάτωρ, ἀμήτωρ ; xi. 4, πισ-, πλει-, παρ-, προσ-). The hexameter, xii. 13, καὶ τροχιὰς ὀρθὰς ποιήσατε τοῖς ποσὶν ὑμῶν, has evidently arisen by chance (cf. vol. i. 118, n. 5). According to אP (ποιεῖτε instead of ποιήσατε) it does not exist; but comparison with the original (Prov. iv. 26, ὀρθὰς τροχιὰς ποίει σοῖς ποσίν) shows, nevertheless, the author's sense of rhythm. The correct verdict of Origen (ἑλληνικωτέρα, above, p. 309) has been sadly exaggerated when, e.g. Kurz, Komm. S. 19, "praises" Heb. "for using a Greek idiom free from any sort of Semitic colouring." Absolutely Semitic is the adjectival use of the genitive in Heb. ix. 5, Χερουβεὶν δόξης, "glorious cherubs" (in which the Aramaic and therefore modern Hebrew form of the name is to be noticed, which the Antiochian recension has changed to the old Hebrew Χερουβίμ) ; iii. 12, καρδία ἀπιστίας ; xii. 15, ῥίζα πικρίας ; iv. 2, ὁ λόγος τῆς ἀκοῆς ; also iv. 16, ὁ θρόνος τῆς χάριτος. No Greek, not even a Philo, would have written ἐπ᾽ ἐσχάτου τῶν ἡμερῶν τούτων, i. 1 ; ἐν ταῖς ἡμέραις τῆς σαρκὸς αὐτοῦ, v. 7 ; τῷ ῥήματι τῆς δυνάμεως αὐτοῦ, i. 3 ; cf. per contra, Col. i. 20, 22 ; Rom. vii. 24. ἧς τὸ τέλος εἰς καῦσιν, vi. 8, cf. Num. xxiv. 20, Ps. cix. 13, Isa. v. 5, is thoroughly Hebrew in conception, and still no part of a citation. The Hebraic ἐνώπιον with the genitive, iv. 13, xiii. 21, the pleonastic ἑαυτοῖς with ἔχειν, x. 34 (DKL), which badly applied pedantry has cancelled (P) or emended to ἑαυτούς (אAH) or to ἐν ἑαυτοῖς (min.), and other examples of the same sort, would not have been passed over by the stylists which a Josephus made use of. The complete correspondence with the LXX the author has in common with Paul; whether he had a knowledge of the Hebrew text also, and used it (cf. Hofmann, v. 522 f.), is as much a matter of dispute as in the case of Paul, and the proof of the theory that he had before him a different text of the LXX than Paul possessed (Bleek, i. 369–375, cf. per contra, Hofmann, v. 522 f.)—proof, which is presented in a manner far from convincing—is really of no importance, when, apart from this, it is certain that Paul is not the author. The opinion that Heb. is a translation of a Hebrew or Aramaic original, was held at a very early date, but on very unsubstantial grounds (above, p. 298), and has been maintained, moreover, by Michaelis, Einl. 1356–1384, very learnedly, and by Biesenthal, S. 43 ff., very superficially. It seems unnecessary to refute it again.

13. (P. 354.) The theory which makes Barnabas the author has been defended most energetically by Weiseler. Without exactly advocating his exaggerated presentation of the tradition in favour of Barnabas, Ritschl, ThStKr, 1866, S. 89, among others, has agreed with him. Recently also Blass in his edition, cited in n. 12, above, S. 9, with unsatisfactory proof from tradition.

14. (P. 355.) There has been a disposition to find, especially in vii. 27, an ignorance of the regulation of the cultus, in so far as it is held that the

passage indicates a *daily* offering of the twofold sacrifice for his own sins and for the sins of the people as the duty of the high priest. No account is to be taken of x. 11, where ἱερεύς is better attested than ἀρχιερεύς, and indicates nothing as to a definite kind of sacrificial procedure. On the contrary, in vii. 27 the twofold offering of the high priest on the Day of Atonement is unmistakably referred to, concerning which a similar expression is used in v. 3, ix. 7, and of which it is said expressly in ix. 7 (cf. ix. 25, x. 1, 3) that the high priest has to offer it only once a year. It is therefore inconceivable that vii. 27 should mean that the high priest was bound to offer this sacrifice daily. To this yearly twofold sacrifice of the high priest corresponds what Jesus has done once for all in offering Himself as a sacrifice. The limiting of the τοῦτο to the second part of the twofold sacrifice, which previously without repetition of the ὑπέρ is joined with the first part, is not permissible, any more than limiting it to the first part of the sacrifice,—a proposition which, as a matter of fact, is advanced by A. Seeberg (*NJbfDTh*, iii. 367, 370). If it were intolerable to the author to think that Jesus, like the high priest, made offering also for Himself, he could not have brought out this point prominently three different times (v. 3, vii. 27, ix. 7); at best he could have called attention in passing to the fact that this part of the function of the high priest was not applicable to the sinless Jesus (iv. 15), *i.e.* that in this respect the typical comparison was incomplete. Instead of this, in v. 3 he lays the greater emphasis precisely upon the offering of the high priest in his own behalf, and shows in ver. 7 f. that Jesus, in spite of His innate dignity, and in contrast to His present exaltation as heavenly priest-king, nevertheless in His earthly life did offer a sacrifice, which was evidence of His weakness, His fear of death, and His unreadiness for the dread experience, and which corresponds, therefore, *mutatis mutandis*, to the yearly offering of the high priest for himself. In so doing the author can have in mind nothing but the struggle in prayer in Gethsemane, which he looks upon as the act of Jesus introductory to the function of high priest. In offering up His will in Gethsemane, His body upon the cross (x. 10), and His blood in the heavenly sanctuary (ix. 12), He offers Himself continually. If these three points are included in the ἑαυτὸν προσενέγκας of vii. 27, it cannot be denied that Jesus had to make an offering for Himself, or for His own sins. It is denied only that He was under the necessity of making daily the offering which corresponds to the twofold offering of the high priest; for this might seem necessary in so far as Christ has to discharge His function of high priest, not merely now and then, but continually (ii. 18, iv. 15 f., vii. 23-25, ix. 14). But this is not necessary, because Christ's offering of Himself once for all, as distinguished from that which is accomplished by the typical service of the legal high priest, has secured an eternally valid atonement and redemption (vii. 27 f., ix. 12, 26, x. 10). If the author, by his negation, in contradiction of his repeated and correct statement, wished to advance the erroneous assertion that the legal high priest was bound to offer the twofold sacrifice daily, he would have had to choose (1) another word-grouping, and write perhaps: οὐχ ὡς οἱ ἀρχιερεῖς καθ᾽ ἡμέραν or οὐ καθ᾽ ἡμέραν ὥσπερ οἱ ἀρχιερεῖς ἔχει ἀνάγκην κτλ. ; and (2) after he had just designated Jesus in vii. 26 as the high priest, he would have had to characterise the O.T. high priests, in contrast to this true and perfect high

priest, as οἱ κατὰ νόμον ἀρχιερεῖς (vii. 16), or something similar. The phrase
ὥσπερ οἱ ἀρχιερεῖς, unobtrusive because of its position and brevity (cf. *per
contra*, iv. 10, ix. 25), opens the infinitive clause, which is dependent upon ἔχει
ἀνάγκην, and serves merely to call to mind the fact that the action whose
daily repetition is unnecessary for Jesus, inasmuch as He has completed it
once for all, is precisely that which belongs to the office of high priest.
Hofmann has already given what is essentially a correct interpretation of
the passage. When one remembers that καθ' ἡμέραν expresses proverbially
the frequent and constant recurrence of a process, no matter whether it takes
place once a day or three times a week (cf. 1 Cor. xv. 31 ; 2 Cor. xi. 28 ; Heb.
iii. 13, x. 11), he will not easily understand why A. Seeberg, *op. cit.* 368,
demands πάντοτε instead of the preceding explanation. If this demand were
justified, it would have precisely the same value over against the new
explanation, according to which the καθ' ἡμέραν, which is excluded in spite
of the position of the negation, is to be translated "in his daily recurring
acts," by which would be meant the intervention of Christ for His own
people (S. 369 f.). This, too, may be necessary a hundred times a day, if all
the Christians on earth are to find help seasonably for their needs (iv. 16). But
this new interpretation goes beyond most of the earlier ones in the obscurity
of its assumed modes of expression (S. 368). In ix. 4 the error was discovered that the incense altar is made to stand in the Holy of Holies. χρυσοῦν
θυμιαστήριον surely cannot refer to anything but this, which Symmachus and
Theodotion (Ex. xxx. 1) as well as Philo (*Rer. Div. Hær.* 46 ; *Vita Mos.* iii. 9)
and Josephus (*Ant.* iii. 6. 8) regularly call by that name, though LXX, Ex.
xxx. 1 and elsewhere regularly substitutes for it θυσιαστήριον θυμιάματος ;
neither can an incense pan, or a censer, be meant, for which, in Ezra viii. 11,
2 Chron. xxvi. 19, 4 Macc. vii. 11, and, according to one translator, Lev. x. 1,
θυμιατήριον is used, but elsewhere πυρεῖον (Ex. xxvii. 3, xxviii. 3 ; Lev. x. 1,
xvi. 12). The reference cannot be here to a vessel of secondary importance,
which in the descriptions of the tabernacle is mentioned only incidentally
among other vessels, and which is described, not as being of gold but of
bronze, and which, furthermore, inasmuch as it was to be handled by the
priests daily, every child must have known was not kept in the Holy of
Holies—a place accessible only to the high priest, and to him but once
a year. Even the consideration of a golden censer mentioned in the Mishna
(Joma iv. 4), which was used only on the Day of Atonement by the high
priest, could not lead the author astray ; for this was kept, as a matter of
course, outside of the Holy of Holies (Joma vii. 4). If, however, the golden
incense altar is meant, it could have been no more a matter of doubt to the
author, according to Ex. xxx. 1-10, xl. 1-5, 22-27, Lev. xvi. 12, than to a
Philo or a Josephus, that the incense altar, as well as the table and candle-
stick, stood in the Holy Place. Furthermore, from the law, without any
knowledge of the Jewish cultus of his time (Luke i. 8-23), he must have
known that the service of the incense altar belonged to the daily duties of the
priesthood (Ex. xxx. 7 f. ; cf. Heb. ix. 6, x. 11), consequently that it did not
stand in the Holy of Holies, which only the high priest entered once a year
(Heb. ix. 7). Accordingly, in ix. 4 the special inclusion of the golden censer,
or incense altar, within the Holy of Holies, cannot be what is affirmed,—a
meaning which is not required by the expression (ἔχουσα ; cf. ix. 1, x. 1, 35,

xiii. 10, and *per contra*, ἐν ᾗ, ix. 2, 4),—but merely an ideal relation to it, as in 1 Kings vi. 22, which corresponds to the service connected with the altar on the Day of Atonement; cf. Delitzsch, 356–360; Riehm, *Lehrbegr. des Hb.* 489 f.; Hofmann, 318 f.; Westcott, 246 f.   The author follows a tradition voiced in LXX, Ex. xvi. 23, and therefore followed by Philo (*Congr. Erud. Gr.* 18), when he makes in ix. 4 the manna jar to be of gold; and it is upon the basis of the traditional exegesis of Ex. xvi. 34 and Num. xvii. 25 that he transfers the manna jar and the staff of Aaron to the ark of the covenant, a tradition whose age is rather corroborated than controverted by 1 Kings viii. 9. What, aside from this, has been actually believed, and the fictions that have been invented concerning the whereabouts of these articles and of the ark itself, do not concern us, since the author describes (ix. 1) here, as unequivocally as anywhere, the legal regulations of the O.T. cultus specified in the Thora, and does so without any regard for possible changes of a later day, or for a cultus existing in his time.

15. (P. 356.)   Luther in the *Vorrede zum Heb.* of 1522 (Erl. Ausg., Bd. 63, S. 154 f.), by a comparison of Heb. ii. 3 and Gal. i. 1, 12, declared a Pauline origin of the Epistle to be out of the question, and maintained that it was the work of a disciple of the apostles, " perhaps long afterward." He called attention, furthermore, to the passages vi. 4–8, x. 26–31, xii. 17, as in their thought dogmatically questionable, closing his discussion with the words : " But whoever wrote them is unknown, and wishes perhaps to remain unknown for a time." In the *Kirchenpostille* (Bd. vii. S. 181) he calls their Pauline origin a " credible delusion. They are not the work of St. Paul, for the reason that they have a diction much more ornamental than St. Paul elsewhere is accustomed to use. Some believe them to be St. Luke's, some St. Apollo's, whom St. Luke praises " (Acts xviii. 24). Similarly, *Enarr. in Gen.* xlviii. 20 (*Op. exeg.* xi. 130) : " Auctor epist. ad Hebr. quisquis est, sive Paulus sive, ut ego arbitror Apollo." Finally, in a sermon of the year 1537 on 1 Cor. iii. 4 f. (Bd. xviii. S. 181), he says, " This Apollo(s) was a man of great intelligence, the Epistle of the Hebrews is indeed his." This hypothesis was recommended especially by Bleek (i. 423–430) and adapted by many ; also by Klostermann, who, *op. cit.* 47–51, aptly portrays the characteristics of the author. The conjectures of H. Ewald (*Der Heb.* S. 30), that the N.T. Apollos fell later into bad ways, and might be identical with the swindler Apollonius of Tyana, has no more value than the fanciful identification of the N.T. Apollos with the martyr Apollonius, *circa* 180–185, in the title of his *Apostelgeschichte* (ed. Klette, S. 92).   As proof of the Alexandrian origin of the author, which would be an additional reason for ascribing the letter to Apollos, special emphasis has been laid upon the points of contact between Heb. and the writings of Philo. Parallels have been diligently collected by J. B. Carpzov, *Sacræ Exercit in S. Pauli ep. ad Hebr. e Philone Alex.*, Helmstädt, 1750 ; some also by Siegfried, *Philo*, 321–330. Intelligent discussions are to be found in Riehm, *Lehrberg. des Heb.* 855 ff., and briefly also in Hofmann, v. 530. There exists between Philo and Heb. an occasionally apparent similarity of expression and a common basis of rabbinical and rhetorical training. It remains unlikely, however, that such a gifted Christian as the author of Heb. would have found pleasure in such terribly tiresome writings as those of the Alexandrian Jew; cf. Michaelis, 1385. This has no bearing, of course, upon the origin of the

letter, which statement applies also to the incidental points of contact between Heb. and the remaining writings of the N.T. The citation of Heb. x. 30, in its similar departure from LXX and from the original also, as in the case of Rom. xii. 19, is the foremost proof of the author's knowledge of Pauline writings. And it is easily conceivable that, when the author wrote to the Christians in Rome, he had in mind Paul's letter to the Romans. The rest that has been collected (Brückner, *Chronol. Reihenfolge der ntl. Schriften*, 1890, S. 239–241) is unimportant. The alleged undeniable dependence of 1 Pet. and Jas. upon Heb. (Brückner, 35–41, 291) would compel us to accept the composition of Heb. before the year 50 ; and the alleged use, on the part of the author, of the *Antiquities* of Josephus, completed in the year 94 (Hitzig, *Zur Krit. der paul. Briefe*, S. 34–36), would bring us down to the year 100. The latter assertion does not seem to have found any favour even with Krenkel, who in his *Josephus und Lucas*, 1894, S. 345–353, would not otherwise have silently passed over the matter. As far as the relation to James is concerned, observations must be limited to the seemingly contradictory treatment of the sacrificing of Isaac and the deed of Rahab in Heb. xi. 17, 31 and Jas. ii. 21–25. To return to serious questions : the wholly original theory put forward by Luther, has the advantage over all others which have arisen in earlier and later times. Luke, whom Clemens Alexandrinus regarded as a translator, and others of about the same period, as a secretary under Paul's direction (above, pp. 298, 308), was declared by Grotius in *Praeloquium zum Heb.* to be the independent author. Delitzsch also, in the course of his learned commentary and at its close (S. 701–707), has attempted to prove that Luke "wrote" Heb. "by order and according to the directions of Paul." Against Harnack's conjecture, that Aquila and Priscilla wrote Heb., but that the larger portion of the same should be ascribed to the more capable Priscilla (*ZfNTW*, 1900, S. 16–41), the following is to be noted—(1) The variation between the *we* and the *I* of the author (above, p. 354) which Harnack explains by stating that formally two persons are introduced as authors, but that in fact only one of the two wrote the letter, would by just this hypothesis be fully unintelligible. In case Aquila and Priscilla are the speakers in xiii. 18 (vi. 1–3, 9, 11, but then also ii. 5, iv. 13, v. 11), and, on the other hand, only one of them the speaker in xiii. 19, 22 f., the readers of the letter could not guess whether Aquila or Priscilla wished to be considered the actual and only author of the letter, and which of the two, who everywhere else in the N.T. form an inseparable pair, was intending soon to visit them without the other consort. While the information is given that Timothy will travel in company with the author, there is lacking in xiii. 19, 22 f. the much more necessary information that Priscilla, whose name could not have been wanting here (cf. 1 Thess. ii. 18 ; 2 Cor. x. 1), was planning shortly without Aquila to visit the readers, and the explanation why this was so. (2) It is inconceivable that a Jewish artizan, and especially his wife, who, according to Acts xviii. 3, regularly shared the work of her husband, should have possessed a rhetorical culture, like that of which Heb. gives evidence. (3) This hypothesis explains no better at least than the Apollos-hypothesis the disappearance of the true tradition (in opposition to Harnack, 24, 32, 38). The prejudice against the thought that the rôle of a Church teacher should fall to a woman as co-author of the letter, could at all events have led to the striking out of her name from the opening greeting, if indeed Hebrews ever had a greeting.   If, however, an intentional omission of the "Address" (above, pp. 311, n. 12, 312 f.) is not to be considered as possible, as also Harnack seems to realise (16, 21), it is therefore not conceivable by what other means the names of both authors, or the name of Priscilla should have been "suppressed."   Memory cannot be controlled by force; its gradual extinction is a process of nature.   The latest hypotheses, according to which Aristion is said to be the author both of Mark xvi. 9–20 and of Heb. (Chapman, *Revue. Bénéd.* 1905, pp. 50–62) will scarcely need to be seriously controverted even when the promised proofs appear in full.   A μαθητὴς τοῦ κυρίου, such as Aristion was, according to the evidence of his disciple Papias (Eus. *H. E.* iii. 39. 4, cf. *Forsch.* vi. 138 ff., 218 ff.) could not have written Heb. ii. 3 f.

IX.

THE FIRST THREE GOSPELS AND ACTS.

§ 48. THE UNWRITTEN GOSPEL.

THE writings investigated up to this point have been, without exception, letters. Some of these (Ephesians, James, 1 and 2 Peter, Jude, Hebrews) were found not to be letters in the strict sense in which nearly all that we possess from Paul's hand are, but gave the impression, rather, of a written sermon or of an essay. Still in every instance what the absent teacher wrote was intended for a definite circle of readers in the same locality, predominantly of the same origin, and living under similar conditions. In these writings we found repeated reference to other Christian writings belonging to the same class. From Paul himself we learned of other letters of his, which have not come down to us, written to the Corinthians and Philippians, also of a letter which the Corinthian Church had sent to him (vol. i. pp. 261, 524 f.). In 2 Pet. iii. 15 we learned of a letter of Paul's to the Jewish Christians in Palestine, which has not come down to us, and in 2 Pet. iii. 1 of an epistle of Peter's to the same readers, now lost. Furthermore, it was clear from 2 Pet. iii. 16 that numerous letters of Paul's were read outside the circle of readers for which they were originally intended, and that Peter himself had read not a few of these (above, pp. 198 f., 209, 274 f.). In agreement with this last statement is the fact that 1 Peter betrays familiarity on the part of its author with Romans and Ephesians (above, p.176 f.); while Jude and the author of Hebrews appear to have been acquainted with Romans (above, pp. 279, 291, 365, line 2 ff. Paul had read James when he wrote to the Romans, and he took cognisance in his letter of its peculiar teaching (vol. i. 126 f., 428 f.). We saw that 1 Peter was likewise influenced by James (vol. i. 133; ii. 186, n. 3). Jude appeals to the authority of 2 Peter, although he does not mention the author by name, but characterises him merely as an apostle (above, pp. 250 f., 266 f.). From what we learn in 2 Pet. i. 13–15 and Jude 3 of the literary intentions of these two authors, we conclude that their writings were to be in part letters and in part more comprehensive didactic compositions, but that they were still to retain the essential character of letters (above, pp. 199 f., 242).

The question arises whether during this whole period there was no other form of Christian literature in existence—in particular, whether what Jesus had "done and taught" (Acts i. 1) was committed to writing quite as little as the revelations of the prophetic spirits in the Churches. Jesus' words and deeds certainly could not have been forgotten, and the existence of a comprehensive body of gospel literature is of itself sufficient proof that the recollection of both was fostered in many ways. Much that Jesus desired to be left unpublished during His earthly ministry His disciples were to proclaim in all the highways and upon the house-tops. What they had experienced in fellowship with Him they were to testify openly before the world (John xv. 27; Acts i. 8, 22; Matt. x. 27; Acts x. 39, 42). His words, which are to outlast the world (Matt. xxiv. 35; Mark xiii. 31; Luke xxi. 33; John vi. 68), which taken separately are words of God, and which in their totality constitute God's Word (John xvii. 8, 14, 17),—particularly His commands and prophecies,—they were not merely to lay up in their own hearts and to exemplify throughout their whole life (Mark iv. 20, xiii. 23; Luke viii. 21; John viii. 31, 51, xiv. 15,

21, 23, 26, xv. 7, 10, xvi. 4, 14 f.), but were to impart to others also. And they were to do this because what Jesus says to them applies to all men (Mark xiii. 37 ; Matt. x. 27, xxviii. 20). In fact, without proclamation of the deeds, the sufferings, and the resurrection of Jesus the missionary preaching was impossible, and teaching within the Church necessitated that the sayings of Jesus be recalled. Nor could one of these functions ever be fulfilled without in some way involving the other. So far as we are able to form a conception from Acts ii.–x. of the missionary preaching among the Jews and Jewish prose-lytes in Palestine, it was possible during the first years, at least, to take for granted a certain familiarity with the gospel history. The preachers needed only to recall it in order to set it at once in its true light. But even when recalled in this way the principal events of Jesus' public ministry as preacher and miracle-worker, from the days of the Baptist until the crucifixion, were brought out and made the basis of the testimony regarding His resurrec-tion and second coming (n. 1). Among the Jews of the diaspora and the Gentiles, however, not even acquaintance with the main features of the history of Jesus' life could be presupposed. In the case of such hearers even these had to be imparted (n. 2). Here also the missionaries appear to have begun their historical account with the preaching and baptism of John (n. 1). Naturally the chief emphasis was laid upon the death on the cross and the resurrection, but the missionaries could not preach about these facts without making statements about Jesus' place in the history of His people, His Davidic descent,— which was the presupposition of His appearance as the Messiah,—His submission to the Jewish law, His activity as a preacher of the kingdom of God, and an undaunted witness to the truth, — which brought upon Him the deadly hatred of His own people,—the truly human life which He lived in spite of all the halo of miracle gathered about it, and His sinlessness. Where one who had seen and heard Jesus appeared quite outside of Jewish circles among the Greeks, and proclaimed the gospel to the latter, those who became converts must have been eager to learn the whole truth about Jesus' life,—a desire which must have been satisfied by the missionaries (cf. 1 John i. 1–4, iv. 14). Nor could the elementary regulations of Church life and religious worship be established in the newly founded Churches without reference to what Christ had prescribed and instituted. How far Paul went into the details of Jesus' life and sayings in his missionary preaching we are unable to determine from the scanty hints of Acts and the references to it in his letters, which are always incidental (n. 3).

That abundant details of this character were not wanting, is evident from the very necessity which every intelligent missionary must have felt who desired to arouse faith in the Founder of a religion and enthusiastic love for a Saviour on the part of hearers who had never heard of this person before. Furthermore, the expression "gospel of Christ," so frequently used by Paul to characterise the gospel preached by him, rightly understood (n. 2), shows that Paul always remained conscious of the connection of all true preaching of the gospel with what Jesus Himself had preached and taught (Rom. xvi. 25). Though Paul's position in this regard was not so favourable as that of the personal disciples of Jesus, it is not to be overlooked that, quite apart from his visits to Jerusalem, which were always short, Paul from his conversion in 35 A.D. onwards frequently had intercourse, lasting for years, with earlier members of the mother Church. Thus, during his three years' stay in Damascus, which was only temporarily interrupted by a journey into the dominion of Aretas, and the six or seven years when he was engaged in teaching in the Antiochian Church,—the nucleus of which consisted of refugees from Jerusalem,—there were

abundant opportunities of this kind. On his missionary
journeys he was accompanied and supported in his preaching
by persons who had been members of the mother Church
in the early stages of its growth, at first by Barnabas and
Mark, later by Silas, which arrangement was manifestly not
accidental, but due to careful forethought. At the time
of his Roman imprisonment also, we find him again in close
relations with Mark, together with a certain Jesus Justus,
who was his companionable fellow-labourer in missionary
work (Col. iv. 10 f.); and again in his last imprisonment
the personal ministrations of this native of Jerusalem
seemed to him to be almost as indispensable as the books
which he had left behind (2 Tim. iv. 11–13). It is clear,
therefore, that the Churches founded by Paul and his
helpers did not lack from the first opportunity and means
of becoming acquainted with the history of Jesus' life in its
details, and their members could not have been like other
men if they failed to make diligent use of this material.
If, in the judgment of the greatest of the missionaries to
the Gentiles, the missionary preaching was to continue to
be the "gospel of Christ," in spite of the changes effected
in the gospel by the death, resurrection, and exaltation
of Jesus, and to retain a close relation to Jesus' own
preaching, the view held regarding the relation of instruction within the Church to Jesus' teaching must have been
at least equally strict (n. 2). It is "the word of Christ"
Himself which is to be fully appropriated in the Church
where it has found permanent lodgment, and to be reproduced in various forms of teaching and in spiritual song
(Col. iii. 16). It is the very "words of our Lord Jesus
Christ" which are to be followed in all religious teaching
and all sound discourse designed for the instruction of the
Church (1 Tim. vi. 3). In the passage in which Paul
boasts that at the time of the founding of the Ephesian
Church he had preached the whole counsel of God without
omissions, and that he had given them besides full instruc-

tion how they ought to walk, he counts it a part of his work also that he exhorted them to remember the words of the Lord Jesus, one of which he quotes (Acts xx. 27, 35 ; cf. *GK*, i. 916, n. 1). Though unable to distinguish sharply between what was communicated originally with the missionary preaching and what was imparted later, we do, nevertheless, recognise that very early a considerable body of information concerning the history and sayings of Jesus had been circulated in Gentile Christian (n. 4) and Jewish Christian (n. 5) circles. Though, on account of the meagreness of the sources, no cautious investigator would venture an opinion as to what parts of the gospel tradition familiar to us were unknown in the Churches between 50 and 80, nevertheless it is clear that parts of the tradition then current in the Church were not embodied in the canonical Gospels (n. 4 under i. 8, 12 *c, e, f,* ii. 1 ; n. 5 under i. 13). It is also to be noticed at this point that, judging from the facts disclosed by a comparison of our Gospels with the tradition which the other N.T. writings show to have been current in the Church, the claims of the first three Gospels to be an accurate or even full reproduction of the traditions concerning Jesus' deeds and sayings current in the apostolic Church are no greater than those of the Fourth Gospel (n. 4 under i. 10, 11, ii. 5 ; vol. i. 121 f.).

It is a peculiar though undeniable fact that, apart from the Gospels and the first sentence of Acts, which connects it with the Gospel, and with the single exception of 1 John i. 4 (§ 70)—and this is not altogether clear—there is nothing to show throughout the literature of the N.T. that the memory of Jesus' life and words in the Church was aided by written records of the same. " Remember the words of the Lord Jesus" (Acts xx. 35); " Keep His word and testimony, His commandment and teaching, which ye have heard from the beginning" (*e.g.* 1 John ii. 5, 7); " Remember the command of the Saviour trans-

mitted and taught to you by your missionaries " (2 Pet.
iii. 2, ii. 21 ; above, p. 210, n. 1) : so we read everywhere.
What the witnesses saw of His life and heard from His lips
they preach to others, that they might come to believe and
to love Him whom they had not seen and heard (1 John i.
1–3, 5, iv. 14 ; 2 Pet. i. 16–18 ; Heb. ii. 3 ; cf. 1 Pet. i.
8, 12, v. 1 ; above, p. 147 f.).   The great missionary to the
Gentiles, who did not belong to the circle of Jesus' disciples, did not fail when occasion required to say to his
converts in so many words, that he had delivered to them
the account of Jesus' life and words, when he preached to
them, just as it had been handed down to him, the gospel
on which their faith was founded.   The tradition spread
by Paul in his work as a missionary and organiser of
Churches came from the Lord Himself, whose words and
life were the theme of his preaching.   Nevertheless he
received his knowledge of both through men (n. 6) quite
as much as the Churches to whom he brought it ; and
when he desires to substantiate the trustworthiness of
this tradition, he does not appeal to a book or to several
books whose credibility is acknowledged, but to the Twelve
and the hundreds of witnesses still living (1 Cor. xv. 5–7).

The opinion which arose in the third century, that
where Paul speaks of " his gospel " he has a book in view,
possibly Luke's Gospel (n. 7), no longer requires refutation.
Throughout the whole N.T., even in Rev. xiv. 6 and
Mark i. 1, the word εὐαγγέλιον means the oral proclamation
of God's plan of salvation as made known and realised by
Jesus ; not until after the beginning of the second century
do we find the word used to designate written records of
the gospel history.   But of the existence of such records,
if we leave the Gospels out of account, there is no evidence
whatever anywhere in the N.T. with the exception of Acts
i. 1 mentioned above, and, if it be insisted, 1 John i. 4.
Still, too much weight is not to be laid upon this fact.   In
the first place, we must remember that in antiquity books

were much more frequently read by a single person to a large body of hearers than in modern times, and in this way were made known to many. Private reading was confined for the most part to the learned. It happened even in the realm of heathen literature that where one person gained his knowledge of a book by reading, often hundreds became acquainted with it through hearing, which was still more true on Christian soil in the Churches for whose use primarily the Gospels, like the other N.T. books, were written (n. 8). Therefore it is impossible, on the basis of the statements which represent the Christians of the apostolic age as receiving their information about Jesus' words and deeds only through hearing, to conclude at once, and for the whole period covered by the N.T. documents, that the anagnost, *i.e.* the lector, who read to them, was not one of those through whom they received this information. In the second place, we still meet such formulæ as "remember the words of the Lord Jesus," even when there is no longer any question not only as to the existence of the Gospels, but also as to their use in religious worship (n. 9). And there are times even at present when the preacher makes use of the same expression. The only thing that can be concluded from the preceding observations is that, during the lifetime of Paul and Peter, the beginnings of gospel literature which may have been in existence were without perceptible influence upon the life of the Church, and that, until toward the end of the first century, the gospel literature then existing, or in process of formation, was not regarded as the chief source from which the Church was to derive its knowledge of the words and deeds of Jesus—at least in regions where there were persons still living who had seen and heard Him.

The tradition regarding the origin of our Gospels places them all later than the year 60. And this tradition must appear *a priori* credible when it is borne in mind that in a later age the desire for trustworthy information about Jesus, together with the circumstance that these four books were the only sources from which such information was to be had, must have produced a disposition to furnish these books, which came more and more to be treated as sacred original documents, with every possible guarantee of their trustworthiness, and to put back their composition as close as possible to the facts which they recorded. The *Protevangelium of James*, which was written before the middle of the second century, is represented as having been written directly after the death of Herod, when Jesus was still a child (*GK*, ii. 775). The apocryphal literature connected with the name of Pilate, the beginnings of which belong to the same period, purports to be based upon an official report of Pilate contemporaneous with Jesus' trial and death, as shown by its ancient title (Justin, *Apol.* i. 35, 48, τὰ ἐπὶ Ποντίου Πιλάτου γενόμενα Ἄκτα). The tradition regarding the origin of our Gospels, which goes back at least as far as the time when these apocryphal accounts were written, and puts the first steps in their preparation thirty or more years after Jesus' death, stamps it as essentially genuine. Independently of this, however, the tradition is confirmed by the silence of the other N.T. writings regarding the existence of a gospel literature. That this generation (from 30 to 60 A.D.), living as it did in constant expectation of Jesus' return, should have taken little thought of the coming generations for whom the memory of the gospel history must be preserved, is less strange than that men should have felt so long that the necessities of the present could be met without written records of Jesus' words and deeds. In comparison with the multitude of those who wished and had to know more of the details of Jesus' earthly life, the number of original witnesses who could narrate what Jesus had said and done was none too great to begin with, and grew less with every decade. Moreover, must not the original witnesses themselves have felt the necessity of giving their own memory the definite support which the recollection of a large number of sayings heard only once, and of a multitude of events differing in character and following in rapid succession, usually finds only in written records? The single express statement which we have about numerous writings treating of the gospel history, composed before at least a part of the gospel literature that has come down to us (Luke i. 1), contains no indication of the date when these writings began to make their appearance, nor is anything definite said about their purpose and character. Notes which were intended simply to meet the personal necessities of those who prepared them can be meant or at least included. The statement can cover also such books as Luke's own Gospel, designed primarily for individuals who desired fuller information concerning Jesus. The only thing that the negative testimony of the other N.T. writings does exclude is the possibility that the Gospels were regularly read in the religious services of the Christians before the death of Peter and Paul, and the possibility that they were employed as the basis for instruction in the Church. Accordingly we are free to use our imagination and to fill even the period before 60–70 with manifold beginnings and attempts in the direction of a gospel literature. However, it is to be remembered that the imagination has a place in historical science only in so far as it serves to set in a clear light the possibility and probability of the presuppositions which are demanded by the actual facts. Nor has the imagination any rights over against a tradition, be this as meagre as it may, until it is shown that the latter is without basis in fact, and therefore false. Finally, the imagination must guard itself carefully against postulates which have possible support only in the narrow experience of scholars whose vision is bounded by the four walls of a study.

1. (P. 369.) Acts ii. 22, καθὼς αὐτοὶ οἴδατε ; x. 37, ὑμεῖς οἴδατε τὸ γενόμενον ῥῆμα καθ᾽ ὅλης τῆς ᾿Ιουδαίας. The apostolic testimony, strictly considered, begins with the fact of the resurrection of Jesus (Acts ii. 32–36, x. 40–43. Cf. Luke xxiv. 18–21, Acts iii. 13b–15a, on the one hand, and Acts iii. 13a, 15b, iv. 2, 10, v. 30–32, 2 Pet. i. 16 [see above, p. 203 f.] on the other). That the preaching of conversion confined itself to the public ministry of Jesus, which in turn was connected with the work of John the Baptist, appears most clearly in Acts x. 37 f., but also in ii. 22, and indirectly in i. 22. The preaching among the dispersion was essentially the same in this respect (xiii. 23–25).

2. (Pp. 369, 371.) The difference between the preaching outside of Palestine and that in Palestine (see note 1) is well characterised (Acts xiii. 23–29). We get also an expressive phrase in τὰ περὶ τοῦ ᾿Ιησοῦ (Acts xviii. 25, xxiii. 11, xxviii. 31), which does not differ in conception from the corresponding usage with reference to other persons (Eph. vi. 22 ; Col. iv. 8 ; Phil. i. 27 ; cf. Luke vii. 3, 17, xix. 9, xxiv. 19). It is the events, circumstances, and historical conditions that have to do with Jesus which, in the missionary proclamation, naturally become the subject not of communication merely, but of a preaching which aims at conviction and of an instructional discussion (Acts xviii. 25, xxviii. 23, viii. 12), forming thus an element, and a very essential element, in the εὐαγγέλιον θεοῦ . . . περὶ τοῦ υἱοῦ αὐτοῦ (Rom. i. 1, 3). Quite different from this designation of the gospel in terms of the centre about which it moves is the phrase τὸ εὐαγγέλιον τοῦ Χριστοῦ, Gal. i. 7 ; Rom. i. 9. 16 (the reading in this instance not well supported), xv. 19 ; 1 Cor. ix. 12, 18 ; 2 Cor. ii. 12, ix. 13, x. 14 ; Phil. i. 27 ; 1 Thess. iii. 2 ; cf. 2 Thess. i. 8. The translation, "Evangelium von Christo" [Gospel about Christ], upon which Luther ventured only in Mark i. 1, Rom. i. 9, 16, but avoided everywhere else, is to be rejected—(1) because it is the construction with περί which Paul uses (Rom. i. 3 ; cf. 1 John i. 1) to express the thought that Christ is the chief object of the Christian preaching (cf. 1 Cor. i. 23, xv. 12 ; 2 Cor. i. 19, iv. 5, xi. 4 ; Phil. i. 15 ; Acts v. 42, viii. 35, ix. 20, xix. 13) ; (2) because the analogy of εὐαγγέλιον τοῦ θεοῦ (Rom. i. 1, xv. 16 ; 2 Cor. xi. 7 ; 1 Thess. ii. 2, ii. 8, 9 ; 1 Pet. iv. 17), which cannot possibly mean the glad tidings of the existence or the attributes of God, is decisive against construing τοῦ Χριστοῦ in connection with εὐαγγέλιον as objective genitive, and for its construction as subjective genitive. The gospel can be named from God as the original author and sender of this message of salvation, and also from Christ as its first herald in the world. In Mark i. 1 this latter usage may be inferred directly from the opening (i. 14) of the narrative thus entitled, but it also holds good in general for the simple reason that the gospel was first proclaimed by Jesus (Heb. ii. 3, iii. 1 ; cf. i. 1). The "preaching of Jesus" Himself, to which Paul refers in Rom. xvi. 25, is the original form of the gospel, which no more ceases to be the gospel of Christ because, after His departure, it is proclaimed by the apostles and other sinful men, than it ceases to be the gospel or word of God. (3) The same conclusion follows from the analogy of τὸ μαρτύριον τοῦ Χριστοῦ, 1 Cor. i. 6 (cf. 2 Tim. i. 8), which does not, and cannot grammatically, mean anything different from τὸ μαρτύριον τοῦ θεοῦ, 1 Cor. ii. 1 ; and, further, from the equivalence of ὁ λόγος τοῦ κυρίου and τοῦ θεοῦ as a designation of the gospel (cf. Acts viii

25, xiii. 48, 49, xv. 35, 36, xix. 20; 1 Thess. i. 8; 2 Thess. iii. 1, on the one hand, and Acts iv. 31, vi. 2, 7, viii. 14; 1 Cor. xiv. 36; 2 Cor. ii. 17, iv. 2; Col. i. 25, on the other), where there can be no question that the gospel, like every revelation and proclamation similarly designated (Rom. ix. 6; Heb. iv. 12; Ps. xxxiii. 4; Hos. i. 1, iv. 1; Amos v. 1), can be called the word of God or of the Lord simply because in the last analysis God or the Lord is the speaker in it. (4) That every genitive of a person with εὐαγγέλιον is with Paul himself a subjective genitive (or *genitivum auctoris*), is shown further by τὸ εὐαγγέλιόν μου (Rom. ii. 16, xvi. 25; 2 Tim. ii. 8; cf. 1 Cor. ii. 4) or ἡμῶν (2 Cor. iv. 3; 1 Thess. i. 5; 2 Thess. ii. 14). When Paul, Rom. xvi. 25, sets τὸ κήρυγμα Ἰησοῦ Χριστοῦ beside this gospel of his as a second norm, the preaching of Jesus Himself and the truth which He preached are undoubtedly intended (cf. Matt. iv. 17; Mark i. 14; Luke iv. 18; also vol. i. 412, n. 17). While the gospel of Paul and the preaching of Jesus can be mentioned side by side as two things to be historically distinguished, all true gospel, no matter who proclaims it or to whom it is proclaimed (Gal. ii. 7), falls in the category of the one indivisible εὐαγγέλιον Χριστοῦ (Gal. i. 7, *ZKom, Gal.* 47 f.)—the gospel of Christ as its author and its first herald. (5) The necessity of this interpretation becomes especially clear in 2 Thess. i. 8 : τῷ εὐαγγελίῳ τοῦ κυρίου ἡμῶν Ἰησοῦ, where the use of the proper name "Jesus" (cf. Acts xx. 35) shows that the apostle had in mind the historical appearance of the Lord as the pioneer preacher of the gospel. Nevertheless here, as in the passages where the εὐαγγέλιον Χριστοῦ is mentioned, the reference is not directly, as in Rom. xvi. 25 (τὸ κήρυγμα Ἰησοῦ) to the preaching of Jesus in the historic past, but to the one message of salvation brought into the world by the preaching ministry of Jesus, and afterwards further proclaimed by His apostles and others. This message can be named from its historical origin and author, because on the lips of the apostles it is not essentially different from the message of the great First Apostle (Heb. iii. 1), the beginner of the preaching (Heb. ii. 3). (6) In the same way, too, are we to understand ὁ λόγος τοῦ Χριστοῦ, Col. iii. 16, and the similar plural te·m, 1 Tim. vi. 3. It is evident that this can as little signify "the word about Christ" as can ὁ λόγος τοῦ κυρίου, where it denotes the gospel (see under (3) above), or a single word of Jesus (Acts xx. 35; 1 Thess. iv. 15; cf. vol. i. p. 223, n. 4). It is rather the content of that which Jesus first proclaimed, and which has since lived on in the Christian community—gospel and commandment, promise and teaching. Where it is necessary to emphasise—as he must emphasise again and again—the application of Christ's word to the life of the believers and the Churches, Paul calls it the commandment outright (1 Tim. i. 5, 18, vi. 14). In this he does not differ from the older apostles (1 John ii. 7, iii. 23, iv. 21; 2 Pet. iii. 2). He could not speak in this way, if he did not know as well as they that Jesus Himself had given this command or law (Gal. vi. 2, τὸν νόμον τοῦ Χριστοῦ; cf. 1 Cor. vii. 10, 25, ix. 21); for men's commands and doctrines have no weight in the Church of Christ (Col. ii. 22; Tit. i. 14). In view of all this, it should be self-evident—and may be mentioned here—that ἡ μαρτυρία τοῦ Ἰησοῦ in Rev. is primarily the testimony which Jesus Himself, the true witness (Rev. i. 5, iii. 14), gave during His life on earth (cf. John iii. 11, v. 31, vii. 7, xviii. 37; 1 Tim. vi. 13). This fundamental meaning occurs in Rev. xix. 10; in i. 2 it is transferred to that which the exalted Jesus testifies to the Churches through John.   At the same time, this passage shows that that which God has spoken or Jesus has testified does not cease to be considered God's word and Jesus' testimony where it is represented that, on this ground, a man acknowledges this word and testimony, and bears witness to it before others.   Even when thus mediated by men (Rev. i. 9, xii. 17, xix. 10a, xx. 4 ; cf. vi. 9, ii. 13, xvii. 6) it is the testimony of Jesus, as it is the word of God, though elsewhere it is spoken of as the testimony of the men who hold it and confess it before the world (Rev. xii. 11).   Just as one may not translate ὁ λόγος τοῦ θεοῦ (Rev. i. 9, xx. 4 ; cf. i. 2), "the word or doctrine concerning God," so μαρτυρία τοῦ Ἰησοῦ may not be rendered "the testimony concerning Jesus."   The derivation of all Christian preaching from the lips of Jesus Himself is very clearly affirmed in the Johannine Epistles (1 John i. 5 ; cf. i. 1, 3).   The Christian teaching is the teaching of Christ Himself (2 John 9).   The one all-inclusive command of God (1 John iii. 22-24, v. 2 f.) is the command and word of Christ (ii. 3-8).

3. (P. 370.)   We have examples of the missionary preaching among the Jews of the dispersion, Acts xiii. 16-41, xxviii. 23-28, and a few hints, Acts xvii. 3, 7, 11, xviii. 5, 25, 28, xix. 8, 13.   We cannot form a similar idea of the preaching addressed to the heathen from Acts xiv. 15-17, xvii. 22-32, for these were occasional addresses called forth by peculiar circumstances, and followed the missionary preaching ; cf. Acts xiv. 9, xvii. 17.   For Paul's support by helpers from Jerusalem, cf. the writer's *Skizzen*, 2te Aufl. S. 82-85. With regard to the content of Paul's missionary preaching and the instructions connected with it, more light is to be had from the occasional references in the Epistles, Gal. iii. 1 ; 1 Thess. i. 9 f., ii. 12, iii. 4, iv. 1 f., 6, 11, v. 2 ; 2 Thess. ii. 5, 15, iii. 6, 10 ; 1 Cor. i. 6, 17-25, ii. 1-5, iii. 1 f., 10 f., iv. 17, vi. 2 f., 9 ff., ix. 21 f., xi. 2, 23-25, xv. 1-11 ; 2 Cor. i. 18-20 (ii. 14-iv. 6), v. 11, 18-21, xi. 2-5 ; Eph. iii. 4-12, iv. 20-24 ; Col. i. 5-7, 25-29, ii. 6 f., iv. 3 ; 1 Tim. i. 12-16, ii. 3-7 (iii. 15 f.), vi. 3, 12-16 ; 2 Tim. i. 8-11, 13, ii. 8 (iii. 10-17), than from Acts (see also Acts xvi. 21, xvii. 18).

4. (P. 372.)   Paret, "Paulus und Jesus," *JbfDTh*, 1858, S. 1 ff. ; Keim, *Gesch. Jesu*, i. 35 ff. ; Roos, *Die Briefe des Ap. Paulus und die Reden Jesu*, 1887, where as an appendix, S. 250 ff., the relation of the other N.T. writings to the Gospels is discussed.   These questions, especially with reference to the Fourth Gospel, are treated with more suggestiveness and penetration, if sometimes a trifle boldly, by P. Ewald, *Das Hauptproblem der Evangelienfrage*, 1890, S. 57-97, 142-160.   Cf. further Feine, *Jesus Christus und Paulus*, 1902 ; Resch, *Der Paulinismus und die Logia Jesu*, 1904.   Here only a brief statement of the material can be given, first from the Pauline Epistles, and, further, not only from the discourses of Paul in Acts, but also from 1 Pet., which is addressed to a circle of Churches founded by Paul and his associates, and from the Johannine Epistles and Rev., of which the same is true. Rom. and Heb. occupy a peculiar position, inasmuch as the former was addressed to the preponderantly Jewish Christian community in Rome, and the latter, some twenty years later, to a part of it consisting of Christians, who were Jews by birth.   For the present purpose these also may be included here :—I. THE HISTORY OF JESUS: (1) His Davidic descent, Rom. i. 3 (as an element in the missionary preaching, cf. Acts xiii. 22 f., 32-37) ; 2 Tim. ii. 8 (as an element in the Church confession,

cf. the writer's *Das apost. Symb.* 40, 42); Rom. xv. 12 ; Heb. vii. 14 ; Rev
iii. 7, v. 5, xxii. 16.　(2) His entrance into the common life of men, Gal.
iv. 4 (γενόμενον ἐκ γυναικός without mention of a human father, cf. the writer's
Das Apost. Symb. 64) ; Rom. i. 3 (τοῦ γενομένου . . . κατὰ σάρκα, for interpretation see vol. i. 338, n. 8), viii. 3. 29 ; Phil. ii. 7 ; 2 Cor. viii. 9 ; Heb. ii.
9–18, iv. 15, v. 2, xii. 2 f. ; 1 John i. 1, iv. 2 f. ; 2 John 7.　(3) His position
under the law, Gal. iv. 4 ; presupposed, Gal. iii. 13 ; Rom. vii. 1, 4 ; Eph.
ii. 15 ; Col. ii. 14.　(4) His baptism with water, 1 John v. 6 ff., according to
the most probable meaning of ὁ ἐλθὼν δι' ὕδατος and οὐκ ἐν τῷ ὕδατι μόνον.
On this occasion, though not only then, God testified concerning His Son
(v. 10, 11).　Referred to in John i. 33 f., but narrated only in Matt. iii. 17 ;
Mark i. 11; Luke iii. 22.　(5) His sinless life in obedience to God, Phil. ii. 7 f.;
2 Cor. v. 21; Rom. v. 19 ; 1 Pet. ii. 22 ; 1 John ii. 6 ; Heb. iv. 15 (χωρὶς
ἁμαρτίας), v. 8, vii. 26.　(6) His preaching work in Israel, Rom. xv. 8, xvi.
25 ; Eph. ii. 17 (with reference to the Gentile world, cf. John x. 16, xii. 32 ;
Matt. viii. 11 f. ; Luke xiii. 29) ; Heb. i. 1 (see p. 338 above), ii. 3, iii. 1.
(7) His institution of the Lord's Supper, 1 Cor. xi. 23–25, with which
Luke xxii. 19 f. would correspond exactly, but for the omission of vv. 19b–20
in accordance with the Western text.　That this event occurred on the night
in which Jesus fell into the power of His enemies, or was arrested (for no
more than this is affirmed in παρεδίδετο, cf. Rom. iv. 25, viii. 32 ; Mark i. 14 ;
Matt. iv. 12), accords with the synoptic Gospels, which alone report the
institution ; likewise the indication that it took place on the occasion of the
Passover Supper (xi. 24, 25, εἰς τὴν ἐμὴν ἀνάμνησιν, twice strongly emphasised,
cf. Ex. xii. 14 ; also x. 16, τὸ ποτήριον τῆς εὐλογίας).　(8) The struggle in
Gethsemane, Heb. v. 7 f., see above, p. 362.　If this passage is taken to refer
to the prayer on the cross, we obtain, at least, no greater correspondence with
the Gospels ; for we read, it is true, in Matt. xxvii. 46, Mark xv. 34, that
Jesus prayed with a loud voice in the words of the Psalm, and in Matt.
xxvii. 50, Mark xv. 37, Luke xxiii. 46, that with His last breath He once
more cried aloud ; but there is no mention of *repeated, urgent request, with
strong crying and tears, for deliverance or protection from death.*　An independent
tradition, therefore, must be represented here.　If Epiph. *Ancor.* xxxi. was
right in asserting that in the supposably uncorrected MSS. of Luke xxii. 44
the words about sweat like drops of blood were preceded by the statement
that Jesus wept aloud (ἔκλαυσε), this reading, which is otherwise unsupported,
must have crept into some MSS. of Luke from Heb. v. 7, or else from an
apocryphal source.　But Epiphanius' appeal to Irenæus, who is said to have
cited this phrase, casts suspicion upon his whole account ; for Iren. iii. 22. 2
does indeed mention Jesus' weeping before the bloody sweat, but derives it
from John xi. 35 ; while Epiphanius, as so often, by reading carelessly what
lay before him, has for the first time come upon the interesting fact of which
he informs us as of something new.　Massuet (see in Stieren, p. 543) has not
succeeded in defending him against Petavius.　(9) His trial before the
Sanhedrin, Acts xiii. 27 f. (cf. Matt. xxvi. 59 f. ; Mark xiv. 55 f. ; Luke
xxii. 66 ff.) ; 1 Pet. ii. 23 (cf. John xviii. 22 f. ; Matt. xxvi. 65 ff. ; Mark
xiv. 63 ff., xv. 4 f.).　(10) His testimony before Pilate, Acts xiii. 28 ; 1 Tim.
vi. 13 (John xviii. 37 corresponds most nearly, cf. Rev. i. 5, iii. 14).　(11) His
execution by the secular authorities, 1 Cor. ii. 8 ; the Jews the real murderers,

1 Thess. ii. 15, who besought Pilate to put Him to death, Acts xiii. 28. Then the crucifixion (cf. John xviii. 32), 1 Cor. i. 17-23, ii. 2; Col. ii. 14; Phil. ii. 8; 1 Pet. ii. 24, cf. Heb. vi. 6; in Jerusalem, Rev. xi. 8; more precisely, before the city gate, Heb. xiii. 12; shedding His blood, Rom. iii. 25, v. 9; Eph. i. 7, ii. 13; Col. i. 20; 1 Pet. i. 2, 19; 1 John i. 7, v. 6; Rev. i. 5, v. 9; Heb. ix. 12, 14, x. 19, 29, xii. 24, xiii. 20 (recorded only in John xix. 34, and to be inferred from John xx. 20, 25, 27, but not from Luke xxiv. 39); removal from the cross, Acts xiii. 29 (by the Jews? cf. *Gosp. of Peter* vi. 21, also Matt. xxvii. 57 ff.; Mark xv. 43 ff.; Luke xxiii. 50ff.; John xix.˙38 ff.); burial, 1 Cor. xv. 4; Acts xiii. 29, as an element in the missionary preaching—perhaps alluded to in Rom. vi. 4; sojourn in the abode of the dead, Eph. iv. 9; Heb. xiii. 20; Rev. i. 18 (also 1 Pet. iii. 19, iv. 6?). (12) His resurrection, as an element in the missionary preaching, 1 Cor. xv. 3-20; Acts xiii. 30-37, xvii. 3, 18, 31; and in Church confession, 2 Tim. ii. 8, cf. Rom. i. 4, iv. 24 f.; Gal. i. 1; Col. i. 18; 1 Pet. i. 3 (see p. 156 above), iii. 18, 21; Heb. vi. 2, xiii. 20; Rev. i. 5, 18. Details brought out are (*a*) τῇ ἡμέρᾳ τῇ τρίτῃ, 1 Cor. v. 4; (*b*) appearances during a somewhat extended period, Acts xiii. 31, cf. i. 3; 1 Cor. xv. 5-8; (*c*) an appearance to Peter—this as an item in the missionary preaching, which is not distinctly affirmed of the remaining instances, 1 Cor. xv. 5 (presupposed in Luke xxiv. 34, but narrated neither there nor elsewhere, nor referred to in Mark xvi. 9-13); (*d*) an appearance to the twelve apostles, 1 Cor. xv. 5 (probably identical with Luke xxiv. 36 ff.; John xx. 19-23); (*e*) an appearance to more than 500 brethren at once, 1 Cor. xv. 6 (otherwise not reported); (*f*) an appearance to James, 1 Cor. xv. 7 (not recorded elsewhere in the N.T.; in the *Gosp. of the Heb.* set back to the morning of the resurrection day, *GK*, ii. 700); (*g*) an appearance to all the apostles, 1 Cor. xv. 7 (perhaps identical with Matt. xxviii. 16-20, or with Acts i. 2-8; Luke xxiv. 44-51). (13) His exaltation to heaven or the right hand of God, Rom. viii. 34; Eph. i. 20; Col. iii. 1; Phil. ii. 9; 1 Tim. iii. 16; 1 Pet. iii. 22; Heb. i. 3, iv. 14, vii. 26; Rev. v. 6, ii. 26 f. (narrated only in Acts i. 9, implied Luke xxiv. 51, even according to the shorter text, cf. Acts i. 2; alluded to, John vi. 62, xx. 17). II. WORDS OF JESUS. (1) Acts xx. 35, πάντα ὑπέδειξα ὑμῖν, ὅτι οὕτως κοπιῶντας δεῖ ἀντιλαμβάνεσθαι τῶν ἀσθενούντων μνημονεύειν τε τῶν λόγων τοῦ κυρίου Ἰησοῦ, ὅτι αὐτὸς εἶπεν· "μακάριόν ἐστιν μᾶλλον διδόναι ἢ λαμβάνειν." All the variations from this fundamental reading (p. 372 f. above) can be reasonably accounted for; thus τὸν λόγον in the Antiochian recension, and τοῦ λόγου in others (Sahidic and Vulgate versions, some min.), because only a single saying is cited. So also with the somewhat widespread form of the saying itself, "Blessed is the giver more than the receiver," Peshito, and in indirect quotation, *Ap. Const.* iv. 3, Anast. *Quæst.* 13, μακάριος, Cod. D (in the direct form), may be a trace of this alteration, so easily suggested by the recollection of the uniformly personal subjects of the Beatitudes. More important is the proposal of Lachmann and Blass to connect πάντα with what precedes. The Peshito has altered the whole construction by inserting a καὶ before πάντα and omitting ὅτι. It begins a new sentence with οὕτως, in which μνημονεύειν also depends upon δεῖ. A misunderstanding of the connection of this infinitive with ὑπέδειξα gave rise also to the alteration μνημονεύετε. Paul admonished the elders of his time to be mindful in the conduct of their office

not of this single saying only, but of all the words of Jesus (cf. 1 Tim. vi. 3). That these constitute a suitable standard for them in particular is shown by the citation of a single saying. It is not found in our Gospels. That Luke quoted it "from the *Apostolic Constitutions*" (see above) was a bit of naïve folly on the part of the pseudo-Euthalius (Zacagni, 420), which found currency as a marginal gloss. On the other hand, Clement, 1 Cor. ii. 1 ($\eta\delta\iota\nu$ $\delta\iota\delta\acute{o}\nu\tau\epsilon s$ $\mathring{\eta}$ $\lambda\alpha\mu\beta\acute{a}\nu\nu\tau\epsilon s$), may have known the saying from Acts, or independently of it. (2) 1 Cor. vii. 10, $\tauo\hat{\iota}s$ $\delta\grave{\epsilon}$ $\gamma\epsilon\gamma\alpha\mu\eta\kappa\acute{o}\sigma\iota\nu$ $\pi\alpha\rho\alpha\gamma\gamma\acute{\epsilon}\lambda\lambda\omega$ $o\mathring{\upsilon}\kappa$ $\grave{\epsilon}\gamma\grave{\omega}$ $\grave{a}\lambda\lambda\grave{a}$ $\acute{o}$ $\kappa\acute{\upsilon}\rho\iota os$ "$\gamma\upsilon\nu\alpha\hat{\iota}\kappa\alpha$ $\grave{a}\pi\grave{o}$ $\grave{a}\nu\delta\rho\grave{o}s$ $\mu\grave{\eta}$ $\chi\omega\rho\iota\sigma\theta\hat{\eta}\nu\alpha\iota$ . . . $\kappa\alpha\grave{\iota}$ $\mathring{a}\nu\delta\rho\alpha$ $\gamma\upsilon\nu\alpha\hat{\iota}\kappa\alpha$ $\mu\grave{\eta}$ $\mathring{a}\phi\iota\acute{\epsilon}\nu\alpha\iota$" (cf. Matt. xix. 6 ; Mark x. 9, for the phrase, Luke xvi. 18, $\mathring{a}\pi\nu\lambda\epsilon\lambda\nu\mu\acute{\epsilon}\nu\eta\nu$ $\mathring{a}\pi\grave{o}$ $\mathring{a}\nu\delta\rho\acute{o}s$). The words which the present writer has omitted stand outside the construction, and so do not belong to Jesus' command. That a traditional saying of Jesus is intended is shown by the reverse expression, 1 Cor. vii. 12, $\tauo\hat{\iota}s$ $\delta\grave{\epsilon}$ $\lambda\iota\pio\hat{\iota}s$ $\lambda\acute{\epsilon}\gamma\omega$ $\grave{\epsilon}\gamma\acute{\omega}$, $o\mathring{\upsilon}\kappa$ $\acute{o}$ $\kappa\acute{\upsilon}\rho\iota os$, and vii. 25, $\pi\epsilon\rho\grave{\iota}$ $\delta\grave{\epsilon}$ $\tau\hat{\omega}\nu$ $\pi\alpha\rho\theta\acute{\epsilon}\nu\omega\nu$ $\grave{\epsilon}\pi\iota\tau\alpha\gamma\grave{\eta}\nu$ $\kappa\upsilon\rho\acute{\iota}o\upsilon$ $o\mathring{\upsilon}\kappa$ $\mathring{\epsilon}\chi\omega$. We are still in the same position to-day with regard to the marriage of hitherto unmarried persons and of widows (vii. 39 f.), and with regard to mixed marriages (vii. 12–16). Matt. xix. 10–12 also contains no command. (3) 1 Cor. ix. 14, $o\mathring{\upsilon}\tau\omega s$ $\kappa\alpha\grave{\iota}$ $\acute{o}$ $\kappa\acute{\upsilon}\rho\iota os$ $\delta\iota\acute{\epsilon}\tau\alpha\xi\epsilon\nu$ $\tauo\hat{\iota}s$ $\tau\grave{o}$ $\epsilon\mathring{\upsilon}\alpha\gamma\gamma\acute{\epsilon}\lambda\iota\nu$ $\kappa\alpha\tau\alpha\gamma\gamma\acute{\epsilon}\lambda\lambdao\upsilon\sigma\iota\nu$ $\grave{\epsilon}\kappa$ $\tauo\hat{\upsilon}$ $\epsilon\mathring{\upsilon}\alpha\gamma\gamma\epsilon\lambda\acute{\iota}o\upsilon$ $\zeta\hat{\eta}\nu$. Cf. Matt. x. 9–11 ; Luke x. 7 f., for the phrase, Matt. xi. 1, $\delta\iota\alpha\tau\acute{a}\sigma\sigma\omega\nu$ $\tauo\hat{\iota}s$ $\delta\acute{\omega}\delta\epsilon\kappa\alpha$. 1 Tim. v. 18, $\mathring{a}\xi\iota os$ $\acute{o}$ $\grave{\epsilon}\rho\gamma\acute{a}\tau\eta s$ $\tauo\hat{\upsilon}$ $\mu\iota\sigma\thetao\hat{\upsilon}$ $a\mathring{\upsilon}\tauo\hat{\upsilon}$, corresponds more closely with the wording of Matt. x. 10, and exactly with that of Luke x. 7, but it is not quoted as a saying of Jesus, and only apparently as Biblical ; cf. above, p. 118 f. (4) 1 Cor. xi. 23–25, the words of Jesus at the institution of the Lord's Supper, see above, under i. 7. (5) Here may be added Col. ii. 11, $\grave{\epsilon}\nu$ $\tau\hat{\eta}$ $\pi\epsilon\rho\iota\tauo\mu\hat{\eta}$ $\tauo\hat{\upsilon}$ $X\rho\iota\sigma\tauo\hat{\upsilon}$, as Paul calls the ecclesiastical rite of baptism. This, of course, could not be described as the circumcision which Christ underwent (Luke ii. 21 ; Gal. iv. 4, cf. Rom. xv. 8), for this was just what was not to be imposed upon the Gentile Christians, but the circumcision commanded by Christ in distinction from that appointed by the law. Nor can $\tauo\hat{\upsilon}$ $X\rho\iota\sigma\tauo\hat{\upsilon}$ be regarded as a substitute for the adjective " Christian," —a term not yet found in the apostolic vocabulary,—for Paul uses the formula $\grave{\epsilon}\nu$ $X\rho\iota\sigma\tau\hat{\omega}$ in that sense; as in the construction with $\tau\grave{o}$ $\epsilon\mathring{\upsilon}\alpha\gamma\gamma\acute{\epsilon}\lambda\iota\nu$, etc. (see above, p. 377 f.), it can only be genitive of subject and author. So Eph. v. 25 f. ; Paul knows, consequently, a command of Jesus by which baptism was ordained in the Church. Such a command we find only in Matt. xxviii. 19 (cf. John iii. 22, iv. 1). 1 Cor. i. 17 is not inconsistent with this, for Paul is not speaking there of preachers in general, nor of the twelve apostles, but declares for his own part that the command to baptize was not included in his commission by Christ. To this declaration, indeed, he was impelled by those Jewish Christians who laid stress on the fact that they had been baptized by Peter (vol. i. 303, n. 11). Peter certainly was bidden to baptize, but not so Paul, according to all accounts. (6) 1 Thess. iv. 15, $\tauo\hat{\upsilon}\tauo$ $\gamma\grave{a}\rho$ $\mathring{\upsilon}\mu\hat{\iota}\nu$ $\lambda\acute{\epsilon}\gammao\mu\epsilon\nu$ $\grave{\epsilon}\nu$ $\lambda\acute{o}\gamma\omega$ $\kappa\upsilon\rho\acute{\iota}o\upsilon$ $\kappa\tau\lambda$. Paul not only wishes to have the eschatological teaching which follows received as reverently as if it were a word of the Lord, but will have it understood as the Lord's own word. This by no means guarantees a verbal citation, but only a conscious dependence on reported sayings of Jesus. If what is thus introduced seems to close with iv. 18, this is simply because the teaching up to that point is chiefly occupied with the answer to the questions of doubt (iv. 13) ; in fact, it is only in v. 1–5 that conscious dependence on the discourses of Jesus becomes unmistakable. The parallels have already been indicated in detail, vol. i. 223, n. 4. Suggestions of Johannine character are also present, especially v. 4 f., οὐκ ἐστὲ ἐν σκότει, ἵνα ἡ ἡμέρα ὑμᾶς ὡς κλέπτης καταλάβῃ· πάντες γὰρ ὑμεῖς υἱοὶ φωτός ἐστε, cf. John xii. 35 f. This completes the references to specific words of Jesus in the writings designated. There are other passages, e.g. 1 Thess. iv. 2, which imply a reference to Jesus' words, though it cannot be directly proved. The profusion of thoughts and statements in the Epistles, especially 1 John, which may have been influenced by words of Jesus living in the recollection of the writers and the Churches, cannot be indicated here. The fancies of Resch, who sees in 1 Cor. ii. 9, ix. 10, xi. 26, Eph. v. 14, 1 Tim. v. 18 formal citations from a precanonical gospel (Agrapha, S. 162, 172, 178, 222), from which Paul is supposed to have drawn in many other passages also, have not become more worthy of belief through the more detailed elaborations in his later work, Der Paulinismus und die Logia Jesu. As it is only in the second century, with Ignatius, Barnabas, and Justin, that we find it gradually becoming customary to quote from the Gospels used in the Churches with γέγραπται, it is self-evident that Paul cannot have referred to a Gospel when he used this or a similar formula. Cf. also Ewald, Hauptproblem, 143 f., 202-208; the writer's GK, ii. 790 ff., and many other passages; Ropes, Die Sprüche Jesu, S. 8 f., and the remarks there noted.

5. (P. 372.) In the writings designed for the Jewish Christians of Palestine (aside from Matthew), James, 2 Pet., Jude, and in the corresponding discourses in Acts i. 15–xi. 18, we find references to the following gospel material :—I. HISTORICAL : (1) Davidic descent, Acts ii. 30, and, indirectly, Acts iv. 25–27. (2) "That Jesus was of Nazareth," Acts ii. 22, iii. 6, iv. 10, vi. 14, x. 38, cf. xxiv. 5, xxvi. 9. (3) The continued intercourse of Jesus with His disciples, and His public ministry from (ἀπό) or after (μετά) the baptism by John, Acts i. 22, x. 37. In addition to His preaching (Acts x. 36), His miraculous work is also particularly emphasised, and viewed as a result of His anointing with the Spirit and power, x. 38, ii. 22 (cf. iv. 27; and for δύναμις, δόξα, ἀρετή, 2 Pet. i. 3, 16; above, p. 220, line 11 from end); the baptism of Jesus is to be recalled in this connection. Galilee is mentioned as the first field of this activity, x. 37, but "His deeds in Judea and Jerusalem" are also spoken of, x. 39, cf. 37. (4) The prediction of Jesus regarding the destruction of the Temple and of Jerusalem, and that in the form in which it is given, John ii. 19, and only assumed in Matt. xxvi. 61, xxvii. 40, Mark xiv. 58, xv. 29, evidently underlies Acts vi. 14; cf. also Jude 5; see above, p. 254. (5) The call and choice of the apostles by Jesus Himself, 2 Pet. i. 3; see above, p. 220 f.; presupposed, Acts i. 17. (6) The Transfiguration on the mount, 2 Pet. i. 16–18, see above, p. 215 ff. (7) Jesus' prediction of the martyrdom of Peter, 2 Pet. i. 14, see above, p. 212 f. (8) The treachery of Judas, Acts i. 16 ff., with peculiar details. (9) The crucifixion of Jesus, as the act of the Jewish nation, especially its rulers, who used the Gentile Pilate as a tool, Acts ii. 23, iii. 13, 17, iv. 10 f., v. 30, vii. 52. (10) The choice between Jesus and Barabbas before Pilate, Acts iii. 13 f. (11) Herod's participation, Acts iv. 27. (12) The resurrection from the grave, Acts ii. 24–32, iii. 13, 15, iv. 2, 10, v. 30, and that, too, on the third day, x. 40. (13) The appearances of the risen Christ, with whom the apostles ate and drank,

Acts x. 41 (cf. i. 4 ?); this is not actually stated in the Gospels, as Luke xxiv. 41–43 speaks only of Jesus' eating before the disciples, and John xxi. 12 f. only of the disciples' eating before Jesus. It is on the ground of these appearances that they are witnesses to His resurrection, Acts ii. 32, iii. 15, v. 32. (14) The exaltation to heaven, Acts ii. 33–36, iii. 21, v. 31. II. WORDS OF JESUS are not explicitly cited. With regard to the echoes of them in James, see vol. i. 114, 121 f. That the apostles, in particular, transmitted the commands of Jesus also is shown 2 Pet. iii. 2, see above, p. 210. With regard to the reference to John xiii. 36, xxi. 18 f. in 2 Pet. i. 14, see above, p. 214. From Acts x. 42 it seems that the apostles were commissioned by the risen Christ to testify to the nation that Jesus was the divinely appointed judge of the living and the dead (cf. 2 Pet. i. 16, παρουσίαν ; i. 4, ἐπαγγέλματα ; iii. 9, ἐπαγγελία).

6. (P. 373.) The chief passages to indicate the form in which the gospel tidings were transmitted are 1 Cor. xv. 1–3 (τὸ εὐαγγέλιον ὃ εὐηγγελισάμην ὑμῖν, ὃ καὶ παρελάβετε—παρέδωκα γὰρ ὑμῖν ὃ καὶ παρέλαβον) and 1 Cor. xi. 23 (ἐγὼ γὰρ παρέλαβον ἀπὸ τοῦ κυρίου, ὃ καὶ παρέδωκα ὑμῖν). From these it appears (1) that the παραδιδόναι of the apostle with regard to the gospel facts was included in the εὐαγγελίζεσθαι, as was an oral communication, like this ε 'αγγελίζεσθαι and every other παραδιδόναι in the planting of the faith. Cf. on παραδιδόναι, παράδοσις, and the corresponding παραλαμβάνειν, 1 Cor. xi. 2 ; 1 Thess. ii. 2, 8 (μεταδοῦναι τὸ εὐαγγέλιον), ii. 13 (παραλαβόντες λόγον ἀκοῆς παρ' ἡμῶν), iii. 4, iv. 1 (παρελάβετε παρ' ἡμῶν), iv. 2 (ἐδώκαμεν ὑμῖν), iv. 11; 2 Thess. ii. 5, iii. 6 (τὴν παράδοσιν ἣν παρελάβοσαν παρ' ἡμῶν) ; cf. also the distinction between the later written communication and the earlier oral, 2 Thess. ii. 15, iii. 14 ; further, Rom. vi. 17 (vol. i. 374); Gal. i. 9 ; Col. ii. 6 ; Phil. iv. 9. It appears (2) that the earlier παραλαβεῖν on Paul's part was like the subsequent παραλαβεῖν of the Corinthians, that is, the hearing of oral παράδοσις ; and (3) that, without prejudice to the correctness of Gal. i. 12, 16, which has to do not with the external details of the gospel history, but with the truth of redemption and the knowledge of Christ (cf. above, p. 352, on Heb. ii. 3), Paul obtained his acquaintance with the individual historical facts (τὰ περὶ τοῦ Ἰησοῦ, see above, p. 377, n. 2), as the Corinthians did, from the narrations of others who knew them before him, and not through any extraordinary revelations from God or Christ, whether once, at his conversion (Gal. i. 16 ; 2 Cor. iv. 6), or oftener, subsequently (2 Cor. xii. 1 ff.). For, apart from the absurdity of such a superfluous revelation, a communication and instruction received directly from the Lord would necessarily have been expressed by παρέλαβον παρὰ τοῦ κυρίου (cf. 1 Thess. ii. 13, iv. 1 ; 2 Thess. iii. 6 ; 2 Tim. i. 13, ii. 2, iii. 14; Gal. i. 12 ; John i. 41, vi. 45, vii. 51, viii. 26, 40, xv. 15 ; Acts xx. 24). By ἀπὸ τοῦ κυρίου (which is unquestionably the correct reading in 1 Cor. xi. 23 against D, which alone has παρά, and G, which alone has θεοῦ) Paul means to say neither more nor less than that the tradition which he brought the Corinthians from three to five years before, and of which he now reminds them, is not only identical with that which he himself received after his conversion some twenty-two years earlier, but descended from Jesus Himself to him, or, to put it otherwise, can be traced back to Jesus Himself, with whose acts and words on the night before His death we have here to do. Who were the

human media of transmission between Jesus and Paul may be gathered from the story of Paul's life (Acts ix. 17–30, xi. 25–30, xiii. 1 ; Gal. i. 17–ii. 14).

7. (P. 373.) Marcion probably wrote τὸ εὐαγγέλιον without μοῦ in Rom. ii. 16 (*GK*, ii. 516), and his disciples in the time of Origen and the centuries following did not emphasise this μοῦ, but the singular in Rom. ii. 16 and the assertion of the oneness of the gospel in Gal. i. 6–8, in order thus to lodge a complaint against the Church, which had not one Gospel, but several (tom. v. 7 *in Jo.*, ed. Preuschen, p. 104. 24 ; Adamantius, *Dial. c. Marc.* ed. Bakhuyzen, p. 10 f. ; Chrysost. *in Gal.* i. 6 f., Montf. x. 667). In these passages they thought of a book, and in their dispute with the Catholics now and then asserted, on this ground, that Paul was the author of their Marcionitic Gospel, after their claim that Christ Himself had written it had been disproved (*Dial.* 808 ; Caspari, *Anec.* p. 11 f.). Marcion himself was not responsible for this. On the other hand, Origen was already acquainted with the application of 2 Cor. viii. 18 to Luke as evangelist as an accepted and traditional interpretation (*Hom. I. in Luc.* : " Unde et ab apostolo merito collaudatur dicente ' cuius laus in evangelio est per omnes ecclesias.' Hoc enim de nullo alio dicitur et nisi de Luca dictum traditur." This is the proper punctuation, and not *traditur*, as introduction of the following citation from Luke i. 3 ; Delarue, iii. 933). This tradition is continued by Ephrem, *Comm. in Ep. Pauli*, 103 ; Jerome, *Vir. Ill.* vii. ; Præf. *Comm. in Matth. ; Comm. in Ep. ad Philem.* 24. Origen, too, does not dispute the right of the Marcionites to refer Rom. ii. 16 to a book (see above), and has no scruple in calling the Book of Luke " the Gospel praised by Paul " (in Eus. *H. E.* vi. 25. 6). Eusebius (*H. E.* iii. 4. 8) reports it as a common opinion that wherever Paul says κατὰ τὸ εὐαγγέλιόν μου, he means the Gospel of Luke. Cf. *GK*, i. 156, n. 3, 619, 655. This would apply to Rom. ii. 16, xvi. 25, 2 Tim. ii. 8, and logically also to τὸ εὐαγγέλιον ἡμῶν, 2 Cor. iv. 3 ; 1 Thess. i. 5 ; 2 Thess. ii. 14 ; and this seems to have been Ephrem's opinion (*ThLb*, 1893, col. 471). The absurdities to which one would thus be led even in Rom. ii. 16, xvi. 25, hardly need to be stated. The idea that the missionaries immediately after their oral preaching handed the Gospels to their believing hearers may fit the time of Trajan, of which Eus. *H. E.* iii. 37. 2, speaks. To carry it back into the time of Paul and Peter is an anachronism. On the other hand, what is said of Bartholomew's bringing the Gospel of Matthew into India or South Arabia may be true (§ 54, n. 7).

8. (P. 374.) For a contrast of the one reading the book in the assembly and the many hearers, cf. Rev. i. 3. In 1 Tim. iv. 13, also, ἀνάγνωσις is not to be understood of private study, but of the public reading to the congregation which was included in the teacher's duty. The exhortation and other forms of teaching followed the reading (Luke iv. 20 ; Acts xiii. 15; Just. *Apol.* i. 67). Reading aloud in a circle of friends was a preliminary to publication, Plin. *Epist.* i. 13, ii. 19, iii. 7. 5, 18. 4, v. 3. 7–11, 12 (*al.* 13), 17, vi. 15, vii. 17. 7, viii. 12 ; Tac. *de Orat.* 9 ; Luc. *Hist. Conscr.* 9. A public reading, at which those interested gathered in large numbers, often served also to bring into more general notice books already published ; cf. August. *Retract.* ii. 58.

9. (P. 374.) Clem. 1 *Cor.* xiii. 1, μεμνημένοι τῶν λόγων τοῦ κυρίου Ἰησοῦ ; cf. xlvi. 7 ; Polyc. *ad Phil.* ii. 3, cf. *GK*, i. 841 ; Orig. *Exhort. Mart.* 7, μνημον-

ευτέον τοῦ διδάξαντος, "ἐγὼ δὲ λέγω"; *Vita Polyc.* xxiv. 31, ed. Duchesne, pp. 30, 36. But the Christians are also expressly "reminded" of the contents of the O.T. Scriptures, with which they were well acquainted, Clem. 1 *Cor.* liii. 1.

§ 49. THE COMMON TRADITION IN THE CHURCH REGARDING THE ORIGIN OF THE GOSPELS.

The history of the Canon shows that by 130 at the latest our four Gospels were read in the Church services throughout the extent of the "Catholic Church" of that time (Ign. *Smyrn.* viii. 2). A definite opinion regarding the composition of these books by particular authors was equally common, as was also apparently a judgment regarding the time when they were written. We begin at once with a statement of this general tradition, and an estimate of its worth.

I. In the period between 180 and 220, Matthew and John, who were apostles, and Mark and Luke, disciples of apostles, were everywhere regarded as the authors of the four books which, even as early as 150, were commonly called Gospels (Just. *Apol.* i. 66, ἃ καλεῖται εὐαγγέλια). The occasional designation of the Gospels briefly as writings of the apostles, and of the evangelists as apostles (*e.g.* Iren. iii. 11. 9; *GK*, i. 154 ff.), is explained, so far as it requires any explanation at all, in the first place, by the fact that later writers, influenced partly by the analogous usage in the N.T., employed the title apostle, not only for the Twelve and Paul, but also to designate their helpers in preaching, as Barnabas, Luke, and others (*Forsch.* vi. 6–8). In the second place, it is explained by the fact that even the Gospels written by Mark and Luke were associated more or less intimately with their teachers, Peter and Paul (see below). It was only this tradition of the Church regarding the composition of the Gospels by Matthew, Mark, Luke, and John which at that time found embodiment in the Greek MSS., and soon afterwards also in the MSS. of the

Latin translation, even in the titles, *i.e.* the superscriptions, the subscriptions and column-headings of the separate Gospels,—the original form of which in all probability was κατὰ Ματθαῖον, κατὰ Μᾶρκον, etc. (n. 1). To be sure, the Manichean Faustus, who referred this κατὰ Ματθαῖον, etc., to the authors of the Gospels themselves, found in it, at the same time, the admission that the Gospels were not written by the apostles and followers of the apostles, but composed later by unknown persons, on the basis of alleged traditions, from the apostles and their disciples (n. 2). This opinion has been very commonly circulated up to the present time, only with the difference that it is no longer the evangelists themselves, but the Church gathering and circulating the Gospels, which is made to say in this peculiar way that the Gospels were not written by the four persons named, but by others writing in their spirit and under their names. The absurdity of this view is perfectly apparent. For, in the *first* place, the oldest witnesses for the κατὰ Ματθαῖον, namely, Irenæus, Clement, and the author of the Muratori fragment (n. 3), state as explicitly as do Origen and all the other later authors, that Matthew, Mark, Luke, and John wrote the Gospels bearing their respective names. In the *second* place, the Church teachers of this period had received, and transmitted as trustworthy, the tradition that the ultimate source of Mark's Gospel was Peter's oral preaching (§ 51), and it was a very common supposition that a similar relation existed between Luke's Gospel and Paul. After this tradition regarding Mark's Gospel, which reaches back to the first century, had become general, a title intended to designate not the author of the Gospel, but the person who was its guarantee and final security, could only have read εὐαγγέλιον κατὰ Πέτρον, not κατὰ Μᾶρκον. In the same way, κατὰ Παῦλον would have taken the place of κατὰ Λουκᾶν. Nor, on the other hand, is this κατὰ Ματθαῖον a book-title in the usual sense in which the term is used, *i.e.* to designate simply the name of the author, but is to be explained, especially in its original form, without εὐαγγέλιον, from the peculiar character of these books and their place in the Church. Sayings of Jesus were cited generally with the formula, " The Lord says " or " said," or " The Lord says in the Gospel," or " It is written in the Gospel," or " The Gospel says." The name used in the apostolic age to designate the oral preaching of salvation was transferred to the documents in which later generations possessed this preaching, without any distinction being made between the separate books in which the one and only gospel of Christ was found. Indeed, the singular τὸ εὐαγγέλιον was probably used before the plural τὰ εὐαγγέλια as a general designation of all such writings. It was not until later that εὐαγγέλιον came to be used of a single writing of this character, and εὐαγγέλια to denote a number of them. When, however, it became necessary to say on what authority the claim was made that the Lord had spoken this or that single word in the Gospel, or that the Gospel testified this or that fact, following common usage, the expression was employed : " According to Matthew, the Lord said " ; " According to John, on one occasion Jesus changed water into wine " ; " The Gospel testifies, according to Mark, that Jesus was asleep in the ship upon a pillow." The apostolic conception of the uniqueness of the Gospel—a thought which the Church could not give up to the Marcionites (above, p. 385, n. 7) —produced necessarily in the Church the concept on of the inseparable unity of the four Gospels. This idea explains not only these formulæ of citation, which were in use early, and which continued current also in the centuries that followed, but also such titles as κατὰ Ματθαῖον κτλ. These last presuppose, as a general title of the collection of Gospel writings, εὐαγγέλιον, in exactly the same way that πρὸς 'Ρωμαίους presupposed that the single writing so entitled was part of a collection of Παύλου ἐπιστολαί.

Leaving out of account the denial of the genuineness of the Fourth Gospel, made at a comparatively late date, *circa* 170, by the Alogi, who declared it to be the work of the heretic Cerinthus, the tradition of the Church embodied in the titles of the Gospels was contradicted by no one in the second century, whether members of the Church or heretics. Justin calls the Gospels regularly "memoirs of the apostles," and remarks incidentally in connection with the account of Jesus' baptism, "The apostles of this our Christ (or His apostles, *i.e.* apostles of this our Christ) themselves have written this" (*Dial.* lxxxviii.); and on one occasion, when quoting something a parallel to which is to be found only in Luke xxii. 44, *i.e.* in a Gospel written by a disciple of one of the apostles, he uses the more exact expression, "It is written in the memoirs which I claim were composed by the apostles and by their disciples" (τῶν ἐκείνοις παρακολουθησάντων, *Dial.* ciii.). When we take into consideration also that in two other passages, where Justin introduces material peculiar to Luke's writings, he is careful not to say unconditionally that the Gospels were written by the apostles (*Apol.* i. 33, οἱ ἀπομνημονεύσαντες πάντα τὰ περὶ τοῦ σωτῆρος ἡμῶν Ἰ. Χρ. ; *Dial.* cv., ὡς ἀπὸ τῶν ἀπομνημονευμάτων ἐμάθομεν), it is practically certain that, like Irenæus and all the later authors, Justin distinguishes between Gospels written by apostles and Gospels which originated from their disciples; and that he knew the third Gospel to be a work of the latter kind, which did not, however, prevent him from speaking generally of the "memoirs of the apostles" (*GK*, i. 476, 478 ff., 497). Even the Gnostics, the disciples of Valentinus and Marcion, never ascribed the Gospels used in the Church to any other authors than those to whom they were ascribed by the Church itself. The preparation of a collection of Gospel traditions, under the title *Evangelium Veritatis*, by Valentinus or his disciples (Iren. iii. 11. 9 ; *GK*, i. 748 ff.), implied a certain criticism of the Gospels used by the Church. They claim that in their common form the Gospels do not contain the full truth concerning Jesus and without knowledge of the secret tradition, their reports, which are contradictory in many points, cannot be correctly understood. Nevertheless, the Valentinians cite and comment upon the Gospels used in the Church as apostolic writings (*GK*, i. 732 f., 741 f., 744, n. 1). The *Acts of Peter*, written *circa* 170 by a member of the Valentinian school, or by a man in close touch with it (above, p. 73, n. 7), represent the book of the Gospel read in the Church assembly to be an apostolic work in the composition of which Peter also seems to have had a part. John xxi. 25 and 1 John i. 1–4 are adduced to show the need of interpretation and enlargement ; but still no fault is found with the book directly, much less is it ascribed to less notable and later authors (*Acta Petri*, ed. Lipsius, p. 66 f. ; *GK*, ii. 848, n. 2, 849 ff.). Others went further than the Valentinians in their criticism of the Gospels used by the Church, and claimed that much of a Jewish legalistic character was to be found in them. Still, they did not attack the tradition regarding their origin, but charged the apostles, whom they also accepted as authors of the Gospels, with having combined those elements that did not belong in the Gospel with the words of Jesus ; and this was explained to be due to Jewish prejudices, by which they were still influenced, and to the misunderstanding of Jesus' manner of teaching, which was to a large extent accommodative (n. 4). Marcion, the boldest of these critics, who did not hesitate to criticise the tradition of the Church in other points, including literary matters (vol. i. p. 481), left the Gospels unassailed as regards their authorship. According to him, the apostles, who were of Jewish origin themselves, went so far as to deliberately falsify the Gospel in the books which they wrote, and this evil work was completed by others of kindred spirit through the insertion of later interpolations (*GK*, i. 591–594, 656–680). It

cannot here be pointed out in detail how Marcion criticised
the separate Gospels.   The important remnants of his own
Gospel extant show very clearly the thoroughgoing criticism
which he thought necessary in the case of Luke's Gospel
(*GK*, i. 680–718, ii. 455–494).   He was thoroughly dissatisfied, not only with the details of this Gospel, which he
could have cut out as later interpolation,—just as he had
removed similar elements from the Pauline letters,—but
with its whole plan and spirit as well, and so necessarily
with its author.   It is not, therefore, surprising that, in
the single passage of Paul's letters (Col. iv. 14 ; Marcion
rejected 2 Timothy altogether) where Luke is mentioned in a
significant manner, he cut out the words ὁ ἰατρὸς ὁ ἀγαπητός,
which expressed the author's esteem of Luke ; so that Luke
was left in this passage, as in Philemon 24, without any
distinguishing characterisation, in the suspicious company
of the ill-famed Demas (*GK*, i. 665, 705 f., ii. 528).   Unless
we are disposed to assume a very singular coincidence in
explanation of this omission, it proves that Marcion knew
Luke's Gospel, which he made the principal basis of his
own Gospel, to be the work of Luke, the disciple of Paul,
and that, far from attempting to dispute this tradition,
he calumniated Luke, whom he, too, recognised to be the
author of the Gospel current in the Church under his name.
An oral tradition which was accepted so early and so
universally by friend and foe alike as was the tradition
that the Gospels used by the Church were written by
the Apostles Matthew and John, and by Mark and Luke,
the disciples of the apostles, hardly needs in support of
itself a documentary tradition, which was later doubted.

The rise of this tradition from actual facts adequate to
explain its origin is all the more necessary, because there
is nothing in the books themselves which would necessarily
have given rise to the unanimous tradition regarding their
authors.   In the case of the Gospels which pass under the
name of Matthew and Mark, the personality of the authors

is nowhere betrayed by the use of an "I." In Matt. ix. 9, x. 3, the name of the apostle to whom the first Gospel is ascribed occurs, but without any hint of the author's special interest in this apostle. The names of Mark, Luke, and John are not found at all in the books bearing their respective names. From the preface to the third Gospel and the "we" which occurs in several passages of Acts, it possibly could be inferred that this work in two parts was written by the disciple of an apostle, and by a man who was for a time a companion of Paul. But there is nothing in the work to lead one to suppose that the author was Luke rather than Titus. From several passages of the Fourth Gospel it is possible to infer that its author belonged to the apostolic circle; but, judging from our present knowledge of exegesis in the ancient Church, the cleverest scholar of that time could not have guessed that the author was John and not James the son of Zebedee, or Alphæus, or Bartholomew, or Simon Zelotes. It follows, therefore, that the tradition associated with the four Gospels from the time when they began to circulate, which was not once attacked during the entire period from 70–170 even by hostile critics, of whom these books had no lack even at this early date, is based not upon learned conjectures, but upon facts which at that time were incontrovertible.

II. Origen claims to have learned as tradition that the four Gospels of the Church were written in the order in which we are accustomed to find them in our Bibles (n. 5). In order to estimate properly this tradition and other statements which possibly could seem to us ambiguous, it must be borne in mind that in the ancient Church the separate parts of the collection of Gospels were arranged in various orders, and that until the third century the Holy Scriptures were not written in book form in our sense of the word book, *i.e.* in the form of a codex which could contain a large number of writings, but in rolls which were

of limited though for the most part of quite uniform size.
Books of the average compass of our Gospels, Acts, and
Revelation required each a roll. The only way in which
it was possible to indicate externally that a number of
such writings belonged together was by placing the rolls
belonging together in one holder or the same drawer of a
bookcase (n. 6). At the time, when this method was in
use there could be no question about the order of the
Gospels. The transition began to be made from the roll to
the codex in Origen's lifetime, and it is probable that he
himself saw codices in which all four Gospels were written.
But the order in which he found them seems to have been
that which prevailed in Egypt for a long time, John,
Matthew, Mark, Luke. Neither this nor any other
arrangement could have had influence upon the tradition
stated above regarding the order in which the Gospels
were written, or upon the statements of writers before
Origen's time, because the codex did not come into general
use until during the course of the third century, and then
only gradually. What Origen gives as a tradition, without
any thought of a divergent view, is expressed also by
Irenæus and the author of the Muratorian fragment without
the least indication of uncertainty (n. 7). It continued to
be the prevalent view in antiquity (n. 8), and it was this
more than anything else which brought it about, that the
arrangement of the Gospels familiar to us displaced more
and more the other arrangements in the East from the
beginning of the fourth century on, and after Jerome also
in the West. But Irenæus makes further statements of a
more definite character (n. 7). According to him, the time
when Peter and Paul were preaching the gospel in Rome,
and engaged in laying the foundations of the Church there,
Matthew, who lived among the Hebrews, issued a gospel
writing in their language. After the death of the two
apostles, Mark, the follower and interpreter of Peter,
delivered to the Church in written form what Peter had

preached. Irenæus makes Luke's Gospel follow that of
Mark, but without more exact indication of the time when
it was written. So, with reference to the Fourth Gospel,
he says merely that John issued the same after the appearance of the other Gospels, during his residence in Ephesus.
According to Irenæus' idea of the chronology (above, p. 76),
the Hebrew Matthew appeared between 61–66, Mark not
long after 66 or 67, and Luke somewhat later ; while John,
who, according to Irenæus (v. 30. 3), wrote Revelation
toward the end of Domitian's reign (died 96), and was still
alive in the first years of Trajan's reign, 98–117 (Iren.
ii. 22. 5, iii. 3. 4), must have composed his Gospel sometime between 75 and 95. It is to be noticed, further, that
Irenæus had read Papias' work (v. 33. 4), which contained
notices regarding the origin of Matthew and Mark, and,
according to a doubtful report, also of John. With reference to Mark, Papias preserved a statement of his teacher,
John, whom Irenæus held to be the apostle of this name,
in which Mark is represented as having reproduced faithfully in his Gospel his recollections of Peter's narratives
(§ 51). This statement seems to exclude the possibility that
Mark wrote his Gospel in the vicinity where his teacher
Peter was staying, or it seems to presuppose that Peter
was no longer alive when Mark wrote. Since Irenæus uses,
among other expressions of the teacher of Papias, the same
peculiar phrase which the latter employed to express the
relation in which Mark stood to Peter (ἑρμηνευτὴς Πέτρου),
it is perfectly clear that Irenæus was aware that his view
regarding the time of the composition of Mark's Gospel was
in agreement not only with that of Papias, but also with
that of his teacher John the presbyter, who, according to
Irenæus, was the apostle John. This is to be kept well in
mind in considering a statement of Clement of Alexandria,
which appears to be directly to the contrary (n. 9). Clement
claims to have received from his teachers the tradition that
the Gospels containing a genealogy of Christ were written

before the others.   Inasmuch as Clement reports, also in
the same connection, that John wrote last, with the incompleteness or one-sided character of the other Gospels in
view, his chronology agrees with the only other tradition
handed down in making Matthew write first and John
last.   But his report varies from the other tradition—if
his short statement is to be taken literally—in representing not only Matthew, but also Luke, which likewise has a
chronology, to have been written earlier than Mark, which
lacks such a chronology.   In line with this variation
would be the supposition that Clement, following some
older source, placed the composition of Mark in the lifetime of Peter, and not, as Irenæus, after the death of Peter
and Paul.   This last difference would not be very considerable, since, according to the older tradition, Peter's stay in
Rome was very brief, lasting at longest only a year
(above, p. 165 ff.; above, pp. 68–84); and, on the other hand,
Irenæus manifestly means to say that Mark issued his
Gospel soon after the death of Peter and Paul.   Following
Clement, Mark would have to be dated in 63 or 64, while,
according to Irenæus, it was written somewhere about 67.
Inasmuch, also, as the tradition concerning the time and
circumstances in which Luke's Gospel was written was not
so definite as that concerning Mark, the opinion that Luke
was written before Mark could have been merely an
inference from the close of Acts.   If it was assumed, as is
still done by numerous scholars, that Luke wrote Acts
immediately after the close of the two years (Acts xxviii.
30),—which would imply that his Gospel was written
somewhat earlier,—and if the fact was also considered that
Luke makes no note of Peter's residence in Rome at the
time, or if it was known from the tradition that Peter did
not come to Rome until after Paul's departure from the
city (above, p. 165 f.), the conclusion must have been drawn
that Luke wrote earlier than Mark, *i.e.* if the latter wrote
his Gospel in Rome under Peter's supervision.   But closer

scrutiny of Clement's own words shows that he knows and says nothing of the completion of Mark's Gospel in Peter's lifetime (§ 51).   In any case, Clement's isolated statement, which seems to say that Luke was written before Mark, must give way before the tradition which represents the two Gospels as having been written in the order Mark–Luke, not only because the witness for the latter view is incomparably stronger, but also because Clement's view might have been the result of critical reflection, which is inconceivable in the case of the opposing tradition. Learned hypotheses, however, no matter how old they may be, do not deserve the name of tradition ; all that they show is the greater or less degree of intelligence possessed by those by whom they are made, regarding which it is not the purpose of this text-book to judge.

1. (P. 387.)   Cod. B has as titles of the four Gospels and as headings of the columns simply κατα Ματθαιον κτλ.; so also ℵ in the headings of the columns, but in the subscriptions of Mark, Luke, John ευαγγελιον κατα Μαρκον κτλ. In the uncials the latter is the rule, only sometimes ευαγγελιον is written once instead of twice in succession, e.g. Cod. D, ed. Scrivener, p. 262, ευαγγελιον κατ λουκαν επληρωθη· αρχεται κατ μαρκον.   So also in the Latin MSS.   That the Latins did not originate their *secundum Matthæum*, but took it at first hand from the Greek MSS., is shown by the Greek form *cata Marcum, Lucam*, etc., in the MSS. of the Old Latin version, Cyprian, Firmicus Maternus, Lucifer, Priscillian (*GK*, i. 164, n. 5 ; also the true Victorinus of Pettau, cf. Haussleiter in *ThLB*, 1895, S. 194 ; Marius Victorinus, *contra Arianos*, iv. 4, 8, 18, see note 3 below ; Jerome, *in Gal.* iv. 4, Vall. vii. 449 ; *Onomast.*, ed. Lagarde, p. 99. 23).   The same is true of the Egyptian versions.   The Syrians, on the other hand, in all forms of their translation of the Gospel have simply "of Matthew " instead of " according to Matthew."   Tertullian also, who did not as yet have a Latin Gospel, avoided κατά, *secundum*.

2. (P. 387.)   Faustus, in August. *contra Faustum*, xxxii. 2, appeals to the criticism which the Catholics also apply to the Mosaic law, and then inquires : " Solius filii putatis testamentum non potuisse corrumpi, solum non habere aliquid, quod in se debeat improbari ?   Præsertim *quod nec ab ipso scriptum constat nec ab eius apostolis, sed longo post tempore a quibusdam incerti nominis viris*, qui ne sibi non haberetur fides scribentibus, quæ nescirent, *partim apostolorum nomina, partim eorum, qui apostolos secuti viderentur, scriptorum suorum frontibus indiderunt, adseverantes secundum eos se scripsisse quæ scripserint*.   Quo magis mihi videntur injuria gravi affecisse discipulos Christi, quia quæ dissona idem et repugnantia scriberent, ea referrent ad ipsos *et secundum eos hæc scribere se profiterentur evangelia*, quæ tantis sint referta erroribus, tantis contrarietatibus narrationum simul

ac sentent: .rum, ut nec sibi prorsus nec inter se ipsa conveniant." Quite similarly again xxxiii. 3. The replies of Augustine, especially xxxii. 16, 19, 21, 22, xxxiii. 6–8, are also worth reading. Even Lagarde (*Mitteilungen*, iv. 109) could write : "The Gospels in the earliest sources bear the title, Gospels according to Matthew, etc.; except in the interpolated MSS., then, they are not given out as Gospels of Matthew," etc. It is not surprising that Jews like Hamburger, *Jesus von Nazareth*, 1895, S. 8, go still further in the same direction.

3. (P. 387.) Iren. i. 26. 2, 27. **2**, iii. 11. 7, 8, 9, 14. **4**; Clem. *Pæd.* i. 38 ; *Strom.* i. 145, 147 ; *Quis Div.* v ; *Hypotyp.* on 1 Pet. v. 13 ; 1 John i. 1 ; Can. Mur. line 2 (*GK*, ii. 5. 21 f., 140). For the old formulas of citation, cf. *GK*, i. 162 f. On those in which the original significance of the κατά M. still appears (*GK*, i. 167, note 2), cf. also Victor. *contra Arianos*, iv. 18, "Idem (*sc.* Christus) tamen, ut ostenderet suam præsentiam semper, κατὰ Ματθαῖον sic loquitur " (Matt. xxviii. 19 f. follows) ; *ibid.* iv. **4**, "colligamus igitur κατὰ Ἰωάννην dictum" (John iv. 24 follows). Also iv. 8, "in evangelio κατὰ Ἰωάννην " (Migne, viii. 1115, 1119, 1126). With regard to the conception of the unity of the Gospels, cf. *GK*, i. 161 ff., 185 f., 477–481, 842–848, ii. 21 f., 32 f., 40 f. In all transferences of this εὐαγγέλιον κατά, followed by name of a person, to other gospels, as κατὰ Πέτρον (Orig. tom. x. 17 *in Matt.*; Serapion in Eus. *H. E.* vi. 12), κατὰ τοὺς δώδεκα, κατὰ Θωμᾶν, Βασιλείδην, Ματθίαν (Orig. *Hom. 1 in Lucam*, *GK*, ii. 627), these names denote the supposed writers, not the authorities standing behind them.

4. (P. 390.) Iren. iii. 2. 2, "apostolos enim admiscuisse ea, quæ sunt legalia, salvatoris verbis"; iii. 12. 12, "apostolos quidem adhuc quæ sunt Judæorum sentientes annuntiasse evangelium," have to do formally and primarily with the oral preaching and tradition ; but, as the context of both passages shows (iii. 2. 1 before the words quoted, and iii. 12. 12 after), the intention is to show the object of the criticism directed against the Gospels by the heretics, and its justification from their standpoint. When Irenæus (iii. 1. 1) maintains, in opposition to this criticism, that the apostles did not preach and write the Gospel till after the resurrection of Jesus and the gift of the Spirit, he too connects the composition of the Gospels immediately with the oral preaching.

5. (P. 392.) Eus. *H. E.* vi. 25. 3, says of Origen : ἐν δὲ τῷ πρώτῳ τῶν εἰς τὸ κατὰ Ματθαῖον (al. add. εὐαγγέλιον), τὸν ἐκκλησιαστικὸν φυλάττων κανόνα, μόνα τέσσαρα εἰδέναι εὐαγγέλια μαρτύρεται ὧδέ πως γράφων· Ὡς ἐν παραδόσει μαθὼν περὶ τῶν τεσσάρων εὐαγγελίων, ἃ καὶ μόνα ἀναντίρρητά ἐστιν ἐν τῇ ὑπὸ τὸν οὐρανὸν ἐκκλησίᾳ τοῦ θεοῦ, ὅτι πρῶτον μὲν γέγραπται τὸ κατὰ τόν ποτε τελώνην, ὕστερον δὲ ἀπόστολον Ἰησοῦ Χριστοῦ Ματθαῖον, ἐκδεδωκότα αὐτὸ τοῖς ἀπὸ Ἰουδαϊσμοῦ πιστεύσασι, γράμμασιν ἑβραϊκοῖς συντεταγμένον· δεύτερον δὲ τὸ κατὰ Μᾶρκον, ὡς Πέτρος ὑφηγήσατο αὐτῷ, ποιήσαντα, ὃν καὶ υἱὸν ἐν τῇ καθολικῇ ἐπιστολῇ διὰ τούτων ὡμολόγησε φάσκων : "ἀσπάζεται ὑμᾶς ἡ ἐν Βαβυλῶνι συνεκλεκτὴ καὶ Μᾶρκος ὁ υἱός μου." καὶ τρίτον τὸ κατὰ Λουκᾶν, τὸ ὑπὸ Παύλου ἐπαινούμενον εὐαγγέλιον τοῖς ἀπὸ τῶν ἐθνῶν πεποιηκότα· ἐπὶ πᾶσι τὸ κατὰ Ἰωάννην. Cf. Origen's introduction to the *Homilies* on Luke in Latin and Greek, *GK*, ii. 625, 627 ; also tom. vi. 17 *in Jo.*, ἀρξάμενοι ἀπὸ τοῦ Ματθαίου, ὃς καὶ παραδέδοται πρῶτος τῶν λοιπῶν τοῖς Ἑβραίοις ἐκδεδωκέναι τὸ εὐαγγέλιον, τοῖς ἐκ περιτομῆς πιστεύουσιν. Cf. tom. i. 6; as ἀπαρχὴ τῶν εὐαγγελίων, John

is written not first but last (cf. i. 2), and before it Matt., Mark, Luke write in the order named.

6. (P. 393.) With regard to roll and codex, see *GK*, i. 60–83 ; v. Schultze in *Greifswalder Studien*, 1895, S. 149–158. For the order of the Gospels in the codices, cf. *GK*, ii. 364–375 ; for those especially in Egypt, and for Origen's, cf. ii. 371 ff., 1014.

7. (P. 393.) Iren. iii. 1. 1 ; in Greek, Eus. *H. E.* v. 8. 2 : Ὁ μὲν δὴ Ματθαῖος ἐν τοῖς Ἑβραίοις τῇ ἰδίᾳ αὐτῶν διαλέκτῳ καὶ γραφὴν ἐξήνεγκεν εὐαγγελίου, τοῦ Πέτρου καὶ τοῦ Παύλου ἐν Ῥώμῃ εὐαγγελιζομένων μαὶ θεμελιούντων τὴν ἐκκλησίαν. Μετὰ δὲ τὴν τούτων ἔξοδον Μᾶρκος, ὁ μαθητὴς καὶ ἑρμηνευτὴς Πέτρου, καὶ αὐτὸς τὰ ὑπὸ Πέτρου κηρυσσόμενα ἐγγράφως ἡμῖν παραδέδωκεν. Καὶ Λουκᾶς δέ, ὁ ἀκόλουθος Παύλου, τὸ ὑπ' ἐκείνου κηρυσσόμενον εὐαγγέλιον ἐν βιβλίῳ κατέθετο. Ἔπειτα Ἰωάννης, ὁ μαθητὴς τοῦ κυρίου, ὁ καὶ ἐπὶ τὸ στῆθος αὐτοῦ ἀναπεσών, καὶ αὐτὸς ἐξέδωκε τὸ εὐαγγέλιον, ἐν Ἐφέσῳ τῆς Ἀσίας διατρίβων. The differences between this Greek text of Eusebius and the Latin version of Irenæus are unimportant. The *Ita Matthæus* attaching to the preceding context (οὕτως ὁ Ματθαῖος with or without μέν and δή), Eusebius has not unnaturally changed. The Latin translator, on the other hand, has omitted the καί before γραφήν, which is contrasted with the oral preaching of the apostles (cf. *GK*, ii. 22, n. 1). When later compilers (Cramer, *Cat.* i. 263, 264), following Irenæus or Eusebius' quotation from Irenæus, spoke of the time of the composition of Mark as μετὰ Ματθαῖον or μετὰ τὴν τοῦ κατὰ Ματθαῖον εὐαγγελίου ἔκδοσιν, they were right. Very far from right, however, is the attempt to correct in accordance with this the text of Irenæus (see Eus. *Hist. Eccles.* ed. Heinichen, v. 8. 2, S. 198). The only reading which has been handed down, τὴν τούτων ἔξοδον, without mention of any place or locality which they left (cf. on the other hand, Ps. cxiv. 1 ; Sir. xl. 1 ; Heb. iii. 16), can only denote the death of Peter and Paul, cf. Luke ix. 31 ; 2 Pet. i. 15 (see above, p. 215, n. 5) ; Wis. iii. 2, vii. 6 ; Philo, *de Carit.* iv. ; *Epist. Lugd.* in Eus. *H. E.* v. 1. 36. It is the same as ἔξοδος τοῦ βίου. Just. *Dial.* cv., or τοῦ ζῆν, Jos. *Ant.* iv. 8. 2 (189), or ἔκβασις τῆς ἀναστροφῆς, Heb. xiii. 7, or ἀνάλυσις, which also needs no nearer definition, 2 Tim. iv. 6 (cf. Phil. i. 23 ; Luke ii. 29 =the Modern Hebrew פטירה). E. Grabe, on Iren. iii. 1. 1 holds that the departure of Peter and Paul from Rome is meant ; but, in the first place, the simple ἔξοδος could not be so understood by any reader (cf. Can. Mur. line 38, *profectio Pauli ab urbe in Spaniam*, Acts xviii. 1, iv. 15) ; and, second, so far as we know, Peter never left Rome at all after he had once entered the city (see above, p. 165ff.). For Paul, too, the period of his preaching in Rome, though it was not uninterrupted, came to its final close in his second imprisonment and execution, and not in a departure from the city (above, p. 66). Of other misinterpretations of the passage the present writer would mention only that of A. Camerlynck, *St. Irenée et le Canon du NT*, Louvain, 1896, pp. 27–31. In Camerlynck's opinion the words τοῦ Πέτρου—ἐκκλησίαν cannot denote the time of composition of Matt., because this construction would require an adverb (p. 31). What adverb we are not told : probably ἔτι, which Camerlynck gratuitously introduces into his paraphrase of the preceding words (*Matthieu encore en Judée*, p. 30, which would be ἔτι ὢν ἐν τοῖς Ἑβραίοις). By ἔξοδος he would understand the departure of Peter and Paul to preach in the whole world, instead of which Irenæus mentioned the preaching in Rome by way of

example ! Whereas (tandis que, not pendant que) Peter and Paul preached the gospel in Rome, i.e. in the wide world, Matthew remained at home and wrote a book ; and after they had set out, no one knows where, Mark did the same thing. Few will agree with the conclusion, Cette explication nous paraît très logique. Occasion for such fancies can hardly be found in the circumstance that Clement puts the composition of Mark a little earlier than Irenæus (see above, p. 394 and n. 9), or that Eusebius (H. E. ii. 15), in a very inexact reproduction of statements by Papias and Clement, adopts the latter's view of the composition of Mark during Peter's lifetime, and seems to assign it to the time of Claudius along with the fable of Peter's contest with Simon Magus (cf. above, p. 168 f.). Eusebius, who was conscientious enough to report faithfully traditions concerning the chronological order of the Gospels from Clement (H. E. vi. 14. 5) and Origen (vi. 25. 3 ff.), which were apparently or actually contradictory, also reproduced exactly the testimony of Irenæus as to the composition of Mark after the death of Peter and Paul (H. E. v. 8. 3), though Clement's view appealed to him more strongly (ii. 15, v. 14. 6). Moreover, Irenæus' intention in iii. 1. 1 of giving the chronological order is so evident from the indications of time in connection with Matt., Mark, and John (ἔπειτα), that his other enumerations cannot be counted against it. The order in iii. 9. 1–11. 6, Matt., Luke, Mark, John, which is repeated in iii. 11. 7, is occasioned by the desire to emphasise the two Gospels in which Jesus' affirmative attitude towards the O.T. is most apparent. The order in iii. 11. 8, John, Luke, Matt., Mark, depends on the arrangement of the apocalyptic symbols. The distribution of the four animal figures of Ezek. i. 5, 10 and Rev. iv. 6 f., which Irenæus did not invent, but found as a tradition, has of itself nothing to do with the chronological order of the Gospels, nor with their arrangement in the codex ; cf. Forsch. ii. 257–275, iii. 222 f.; v. Schultze, Greifswalder Studien, S. 158. The two oldest and commonest arrangements are — (1) Matt. = man, Mark = eagle, Luke = ox, John = lion (so Irenæus and the true Victorinus of Pettau ; cf. Haussleiter, ThLB, 1895, Col. 194) ; (2) Matt. = man, Mark = lion, Luke = ox, John = eagle (so Theophilus Lat., Epiphanius, Jerome).

8. (P. 393.) The chronological succession of the Gospels given by Irenæus without any notice of divergent opinions, and by Origen as an old tradition (see above, p. 397 f.), is clearly indicated in Can. Mur. lines 1–16, in spite of the incompleteness of its beginning (GK, ii. 14 ff.) ; also Eus. H. E. iii. 24. 6 f. ; Epiphan. Hær. li. 4 (Ματθαῖος πρῶτος ἄρχεται εὐαγγελίζεσθαι). 6 (εὐθὺς δὲ μετὰ τὸν Ματθαῖον ἀκόλουθος γενόμενος ὁ Μᾶρκος τῷ ἁγίῳ Πέτρῳ ἐν Ῥώμῃ ἐπιτρέπεται τὸ εὐαγγέλιον ἐκθέσθαι καὶ γράψας ἀποστέλλεται ὑπὸ τοῦ ἁγίου Πέτρου εἰς τὴν τῶν Αἰγυπτίων χώραν). 7 (Luke wrote an account of misinterpretations of Mark), xii. 19 (finally, John, when more than ninety years old). Further, Jerome, Præf. Comm. in Matth., Vall. vii. 3 ff.; cf. Vir. Ill. iii. ; Ephrem, Expos. ev. Conc. p. 286 ; Chrysost. Hom. 4 in Matth., Montfaucon, vii. 46 ; August. Cons. Evv. i. 2. That John was the last to write is involved in every tradition that has specially to do with the Fourth Gospel. The remark of Tertullian (contra Marc. iv. 2), that the disciples of the apostles among the evangelists wrote " cum apostolis et post apostolos," and the further words, "ex apostolis Joannes et Matthæus, ex apostolicis Lucas et Marcus," express no particular opinion as to the chronological order of the Gospels. or

at most only the presupposition, which no one in the ancient Church disputed, that the earliest Evangelist was an apostle, not a pupil of the apostles. The old Latin prologues to the Gospels also give the order, Matt., Mark, Luke, John ; *Prol. in Luc.* (*N.T. Lat.*, ed. Wordsworth, i. 269) : "Qui cum iam descripta essent evangelia per Matthæum quidem in Judæa, per Marcum autem in Italia, sancto instigante spiritu in Achaiæ partibus hoc scripsit evangelium, significans etiam ipse, ante alia esse descripta." The improbable opinion of Corssen (*Monarchianische Prologe*, 1896, S. 37), that the same writer in his prologue to Mark represents that Gospel as written after Luke, rests upon two misunderstandings. The words (Wordsworth, i. 172) "perfecti evangelii opus intrans et a baptismo domini deum prædicare inchoans" evidently refer to Mark i. 9 ff. in distinction from "initio evangelicæ prædicationis," Mark i. 1 ff. The complete Gospel comes first through Christ, in distinction from the Forerunner, whose preaching Mark has termed the beginning of the Gospel. And when it is said of the physical birth, that Mark saw it *in prioribus* and therefore did not think it worth while to narrate it again, it is very arbitrary to supriy *evangeliis* (*sc.* Matt. and Luke). The phrase probably stands for the common ἐν τοῖς πρὸ τούτων, cf. for example, Orig. tom. ii. 1, *in Jo.* where to be sure but a single *tomus* has preceded, or ἐν τοῖς ἔμπροσθεν, or similar expressions. The author of the prologues, which are hardly so old as Corssen would have them, had before him the codex in which Matt. i. stands before Mark i. ; and he had not forgotten that according to his express statement Matt. indeed, but not Luke, was written before Mark.

9. (P. 394.) Eusebius, *H. E.* vi. 14. 5 (*Forsch.* iii. 72), quotes from the Hypotyp.: αὖθις δ' ἐν τοῖς αὐτοῖς ὁ Κλήμης βιβλίοις περὶ τῆς τάξεως τῶν εὐαγγελίων παράδοσιν τῶν ἀνέκαθεν πρεσβυτέρων τέθειται, τοῦτον ἔχουσαν τὸν τρόπον· "Προγεγράφθαι ἔλεγον (*al.* ἔλεγεν) τῶν εὐαγγελίων τὰ περιέχοντα τὰς γενεαλογίας." The less supported reading, ἔλεγον, which has the presbyters for its subject, and in tense is quite in accord with the way in which Clement usually speaks of his teachers (*Forsch.* iii. 161, A. 1), is to be preferred to ἔλεγεν, instead of which one would sooner expect ἔφη, as indeed one MS. has it, or φησίν, or nothing at all. For τάξις cf. the old chapter title of Eus. *H. E.* iii. 24, and the writing of Galenus (ed. Kühn, xix. 49), περὶ τῆς τάξεως τῶν ἰδίων βιβλίων ; cf. *GK*, ii. 365, A. 5. Clement means an historical account of the composition of the writings, observing the chronological order. If, in consideration of the general currency of the tradition that the order was Matt., Mark, Luke, John (n. 8), one may assume that it was known to Clement's teachers and to himself, it is noteworthy that their divergent statement is given without any hint of its opposition to the common view. It is not impossible, then, that the presbyters simply meant that Matt. was written before Mark and Luke before John.

§ 50. HISTORY OF THE "SYNOPTIC PROBLEM."

Whoever reads the first three Gospels in order for the first time, with a fair degree of attention, must have been reminded constantly, in going through the second and third, that he had read essentially the same narratives and discourses once or twice before, partly in the same order, and in language which in all cases was very similar, and often exactly the same. Since the authors themselves say nothing of the sources and helps of which they made use, and since, further, the ancient tradition contains no notice of the use of the work of one evangelist by another, we have the so-called "Synoptic Problem," a problem which has been in existence ever since the Gospels were read alongside of each other. The facts have been very often represented to the eye by editions of the text designed to show the similarities and variations of the first three, or of all four Gospels (n. 1). As early as the third century, a certain Ammonius, of whom nothing more definite is known, prepared an edition of Matthew in which the sections of the other Gospels agreeing more or less closely with Matthew were arranged alongside of the Matthew text, which was given in full. Ammonius gave his work the same title—*Diatessaron*—which the Syrian Tatian used earlier in the second century for his work, though this was of an entirely different character, being, in fact, a Gospel history compiled from the words of the four Gospels : τὸ διὰ τεσσάρων εὐαγγέλιον. Eusebius speaks highly of the careful scholarship of Ammonius' *Diatessaron*, but felt the breaking up of the text of all the Gospels, except Matthew, into small fragments to be a defect. This led him to invent a new method, which left the text of the Gospels intact, but which divided it into small sections (κεφάλαια, περικοπαί), successively numbered in each Gospel. Then through tables preceding the text, in which the numbers of the corresponding sections were arranged together (κανόνες), and to which references were made by means of figures written in red on the margin of the text, the reader was enabled easily to find the parallels to any passage in any one of the Gospels (n. 1). In spite of the widespread use of this arrangement of the text in the Greek, Syrian, and Latin Churches, the problem under discussion was scarcely realised by the scholars of the ancient Church. The thing which caused surprise was not the similarity of the Gospels in form, but the differences which existed between their contents. Attempts were made to explain and to harmonise these differences, especially where such harmonisation was demanded by ecclesiastical, dogmatic, or even apologetic interests (n. 2). With reference to the origin of the Gospels, no information was sought beyond that furnished by the scanty reports of the oldest traditions. It was only because the tradition reported that John wrote his Gospel later than the other evangelists, with their books in view and for the purpose of supplementing them, that this fact was recalled occasionally in connection with the discussion of single points, regarding which the accounts of the Gospels differed. Only in very isolated cases do we find similar expressions regarding a conscious relation of the other evangelists to their predecessors, made, of course, on the basis of the generally accepted view that the Gospels originated in the order in which they are arranged in our N.T. (n. 3). This was the case with Augustine, who was the first to be led, by the observation of similarities of language in the Gospels, to what was at least the beginning of a definite view regarding the origin of this phenomenon. He thought it could be proved that Mark was consciously dependent upon Matthew, which in part he repeated word for word, in part reproduced in abbreviated form (n. 4). The matter was not pursued further, either in the Middle Ages or at the time of the Reformation, either by the harmonists of the orthodox period or by the pioneers of a critical history of the N.T. It seems to have required the great revolution in the entire way of thinking about Christianity and its original documents, which began with the middle of the eighteenth century, to produce an appreciation of the problem presented by the similarities and differences of the first three Gospels. In what follows the principal attempts made at its solution are described briefly.

1. G. E. Lessing was led, by the strife which the publication of the Wolfenbüttel fragments produced, to propound what was really a "new hypothesis" concerning the manner in which the synoptic Gospels originated (n. 5). Starting with the fact that the earliest Christians were called Nazarenes (Acts xxiv. 5),—a name retained by the Jewish Christians of Berœa until Jerome's time,—and the various names which the Gospel, or rather the Gospels, of the Jewish Christians bore in the confused reports of the Church Fathers, he conjectured that the root of the entire Gospel literature, the *original Gospel*, was the Aramaic *Gospel of the Nazarenes*, the kernel of which originated in the time immediately following Jesus' death, and which underwent a number of changes in the early Christian period. By means of a bold interpretation of Eusebius' account of the origin of Matthew (*H. E.* iii. 24. 6), Lessing arrived at the conclusion that when Matthew left Palestine to preach among the Greeks or Hellenists, he made an abstract of the original Aramaic Gospel in Greek for the benefit of his new hearers, which abstract is our canonical Matthew. That Matthew's name was transferred to the original also should not be considered surprising. By a similar handling of Papias' testimony (§ 54), it was made to appear that numerous individuals translated excerpts from this original Gospel into Greek, just as Matthew had done, always from their own points of view and for different purposes. Among these translators belong the many writers of Luke i. 1,—in particular, Luke himself, and Mark also. "In a word, Matthew, Mark, and Luke are nothing but translations, partly different, partly the same, of the so-called original Hebrew Matthew, which each made as best he could" (Lessing, § 50). We possess only two Gospels,—a Gospel of the flesh in a

threefold Greek recension, and a Gospel of the spirit, that according to John. This unelaborated thought of Lessing contained suggestions which were bound to develop.

While Lessing left it to the reader to apply his hypothesis for the explanation of the varied way in which the Gospels agree at one point and then differ from each other again, J. G. Eichhorn in Göttingen (n. 6) reversed the method, beginning with the fact that in forty-four sections the three synoptic Gospels are in essential agreement, in content, form, compass, and point of view. This is not to be explained on the supposition that one Gospel was used in the composition of another, but only on the hypothesis that all are dependent upon a common source. This source he declared to be an Aramaic Gospel, written as early as the year 35 by a disciple of one of the apostles, containing a biography of Jesus which covered the time from the appearance of the Baptist to the resurrection. During the decades which followed, this Gospel was frequently recast, enlarged, and abbreviated, first in Aramaic and then also in Greek. The Gospels which originated in this manner between 35 and 60—practically countless in number— constitute in their manifold combinations the sources from which were drawn the Gospels accepted by the Church, as well as the various Gospels used by Jewish Christians and Gentile Christian heretics, Justin's citations, and Tatian's *Diatessaron*. On this point Eichhorn accepted in the main the tradition regarding the origin of the Gospels in use by the Church. It was, in fact, through this tradition that he came to suppose, in opposition to it, that the Greek trans- lator of the Aramaic Matthew, compiled as it was by the apostle Matthew from a number of sources, modified the same by important additions of his own, some thirty-five in number, smaller and greater, *e.g.* chaps. i.–ii., which he prefixed to the Gospel. The artificiality of Eichhorn's hypothesis, and the impossibility of proving the numerous accessory hypotheses upon which it was based, led inevitably to attempts in the opposite direction. It was not Eichhorn's hypothesis, but Lessing's idea, which Eichhorn appropriated without acknowledgment, that continued to live, and that was revived later (see below, No. 7).

2. In 1783 and later, J. J. Griesbach, working in the spirit of Lessing's genuine historical method, and in conscious agreement with him,—in fact, differing from him only in his results,—and in strong opposition to Eichhorn and his followers, advanced a hypothesis the simplicity of which seemed especially to commend it (n. 7). According to this view, the apostle Matthew wrote his Gospel in Greek from his own acquaintance with the facts, and without the use of earlier sources ; Luke composed his on the basis of his investigations of the oral tradition still uncrystallised, and with the help of Matthew ; Mark's Gospel was made up of excerpts from Luke and Matthew. Mark's own additions—in all not more than twenty-four verses— show that in his home in Jerusalem he had heard much of the history, related with more vividness and in greater detail than he found in the narratives of Matthew, which he made the basis of his work, or in Luke, which he employed as a help. He designed his book to serve as a handy compendium of the Gospel history for readers unacquainted with Jewish conditions and views, and without interest in much that Matthew had recorded. The tradition, according to which a close relation exists between Mark's Gospel and the discourses of Peter, is a conjecture, and simply an invention of Papias. Also the opinion that Matthew wrote in Hebrew is an improbable conjecture, since even Mark had a Greek Matthew before him. While the tradition regarding the authors of the Gospels is to be preferred to all modern hypotheses, all the reports of the ancient Church which go further, and purport to give an account of the origin of the Gospels, are worthless fables.

3. At about the same time G. Chr. Storr and G. Herder declared Mark to be the oldest of the extant Gospels (n. 8).

Starting with the name "Gospel," which as a matter of fact no one of our evangelists gave his own work, but which was applied by the Church to the Gospels in the second century, Herder postulated as the common basis of the entire gospel literature a Gospel existing at first in an unwritten form, which was, nevertheless, quite thoroughly fixed. In content it was limited to a definite series of narratives and discourses, covering the period from the baptism of John to the ascension of Jesus (Acts i. 1 f., 22), and was a compendium of the historical content of the missionary preaching intended especially for the guidance of the missionary preachers of the second order, the evangelists, or "ministers of the word" (Luke i. 2). This Gospel, which originated in Palestine between 35 and 40, and which was thought out and, so to speak, composed in Aramaic, was communicated orally to the helpers engaged in preaching, of whom Mark was one, but committed by them to writing for their own convenience, and probably at once. In this way a multitude of private writings arose. Several decades later Mark published his copy, essentially unchanged, probably in Rome, and accordingly reproduces for us in a Greek form, but nevertheless faithfully, the original unwritten Gospel which originated under the eyes of Peter, James, and John. In 60, or somewhat later, a fuller Gospel in Aramaic was prepared in Palestine on the same basis, and was immediately published. In modified form this Gospel survived in the Hebrew *Gospel of the Nazarenes*, and in the Greek Matthew, which was not written until after 70. Finally, Luke, who wrote his historical work not for the Church, but for an individual belonging to the upper classes, used this elaborate Aramaic Gospel, which was afterwards recast in the Greek Matthew as an auxiliary source. He also used, in addition, the outline of the apostolic preaching which he had had in hand for the twenty years that he had been engaged in assisting with the preaching work, and also the information which he had gathered from persons who had heard and seen Jesus.   While Herder left it undecided whether any one of the three Synoptists had in hand the work of the other two, Storr, who was gifted with less imagination than Herder, confined himself strictly to given data, and explained the similarities among the Gospels on the supposition that the two later evangelists used the work of the earlier one.   According to his view, the Gospel of Mark, which was drawn chiefly from Peter's narratives, was written in Jerusalem at a very early date, before Mark became engaged in foreign missionary work. This oldest Gospel the apostle Matthew did not hesitate to make the basis of his own Gospel, which otherwise was based upon independent knowledge of the facts, and was written from a peculiar point of view.   Mark was worked over also by Luke, who, however, was unacquainted with Matthew.

Later, Chr. G. Wilke (1838), Bruno Bauer (1841), and G. Volkmar (1870) undertook to prove that Mark was the original Gospel, but in a sense differing entirely from that of Herder and Storr (n. 9).   Although Wilke left the tradition entirely untested, and made no attempt whatever to explain and thereby to remove its errors, and although he omitted all discussion of the leading thoughts of the separate Gospels and of the historical conditions under which they were written, he believed that in his voluminous work he had established for all time, from the agreements and variations of the texts of the synoptic Gospels, the fact that our Mark is the original Gospel, except for a number of interpolations, part of which he believed could still be removed by the application of commonly accepted critical principles.   This original Gospel was worked over in an arbitrary way in Matthew and Luke, supplemented by the addition of later legends and adapted to serve particular ends.   The agreements between Matthew and Luke in passages not derived

from Mark is to be explained on the ground that, in
addition to his principal source Mark, Matthew also used
Luke.

4. Fully recognising that the solution of the synoptic
problem is to be sought through a study of the documents
in their historical connection, but at the same time making
the tradition of the ancient Church regarding the origin of
the Gospels and the order in which they were written his
starting-point, J. L. Hug (n. 10) undertook to show that
Mark had in his possession and made use of Matthew.
The same was true of Luke in relation to Mark and
Matthew, while John had and used all three Synoptics.
In all cases the sources employed were supplemented and
corrected by independent information. Regarding the
sources used by Matthew, there is no necessity of inquir-
ing; only it was natural that a person so accustomed to
writing, as was the tax-collector Matthew, should have
noted down at a very early date the discourses and sayings
of the Master to aid him in his own work as a teacher,
and also that he should have made use of these collections
of his own in the elaboration of his Gospel, traces of which
are actually to be found in it (*Einl.*[3] i. 179). Whether
and to what extent Luke used others of the writings
which he mentions in Luke i. 1, and the oral tradition in
addition to Matthew and Mark, we are no longer able to
determine (*op. cit.* S. 186). Hug accepts the tradition as
correct at every point, with the exception that he holds
the unanimous tradition of antiquity by which Matthew
is represented as having been written in Hebrew to be a
scholastic fable.

5. Opposed to Eichhorn's hypothesis of an original
written Gospel which originated early in the apostolic age,
is that of J. C. L. Gieseler (n. 11), which makes the
common basis of all three Synoptics, as well as of numerous
apocryphal Gospels of the second century, an original
Gospel which was entirely oral. The silence of the other

N.T. writings and of the oldest post-apostolic literature regarding the use of written Gospels, the way in which the words and deeds of Jesus are introduced in this literature, further, the fact that comparatively little writing was done in the apostolic age (S. 35, 60 ff.), and the simple character of the culture possessed by the early Christians in Palestine, render it impossible that records of the Gospel should have been made so soon, also that such documents, after they originated privately, should have been circulated so widely and have had so much influence in the Church. Material for the construction of Gospels was drawn from the oral tradition until within the second century; still more in the apostolic age was the tradition fixed enough to make the use of written helps seem unnecessary. Entirely without design, frequent repetition produced a fixed form of the narrative and an outline of the Gospel history from the appearance of the Baptist on, in which the most important events and sayings were reproduced with the greatest uniformity by all narrators and teachers. The history of the liturgy and of the creed, which were unwritten for so long, anecdotes from the history of the ancient Church, and analogies from the history of heathen religions and of Jewish Rabbinism, should enable us moderns to form a conception of the tenacity of memory which, under conditions of ancient culture, characterised groups of like-minded men, especially in cases where the sayings were regarded as sacred, and where the things recalled were of an historical nature. When the Gospel passed from Palestine to the Greeks, it necessarily took on a Greek form, but continued oral. Though so flexible that the order, emphasis, and application could be changed according to varying necessities, this Gospel was still able, in spite of all these modifications, to survive in its original stereotyped form. Here belong, *e.g.* among other things, passages quoted freely from the O.T. Comparison of 1 Pet. ii. 6 f. with Rom. ix. 33 proves that the recurrence of such citations in several different writings is not to be explained by supposing that one is dependent upon another, or both of the extant writings upon an original now lost (p. 260, n. 12). It is easy to see that this and many other of Gieseler's proofs are inconclusive; but for all that it is not to be denied that Geiseler made a more serious attempt than did Herder to treat the problem from a thoroughly historical point of view, and that he called attention to facts which deserve more consideration than the doubtful speculations of a critique which does not get beyond counting words, and which does not have even a perverted historical sense. G. Wetzel (n. 11) called his theory an improvement upon Gieseler's "tradition-hypothesis." Unlike Gieseler, who accepted the tradition regarding the origin of the Gospels, Wetzel rejected it altogether; and without any attempt to explain its origin he replaced it with the following imaginary picture. The necessity came to be felt in the mother Church of giving the Hellenists (Acts vi. 1) who came to Jerusalem from outside Palestine, and who were therefore unfamiliar with the Gospel history, regular instruction in the same. This task was entrusted to the former tax-collector, Matthew, who was especially proficient in Greek. After this instruction had been continued for years, it took on a fixed form, which was partly memorised by the hearers, and finally was committed to writing by not a few of them. In this way the numerous books of Luke i. 1 originated, of which three have been preserved to us. This explains the agreements among the Gospels; the differences, on the other hand, are exactly such as exist at the present time among the notes made of academic lectures. Even the most industrious student at times absents himself from lectures, and not every student comprehends with entire correctness what he hears. Recently, K. Veit (n. 11), who rejects Wetzel's "improvement," has supplemented Gieseler's hypothesis in several points.

Thus, he brings the analogy of rabbinic methods of teaching to bear with greater definiteness upon the problem as to how the disciples were taught by Jesus Himself, and how the apostles and other missionary preachers and the teachers in the local Church instructed the new converts. Further, he attempts to show, through numerous examples, how the tradition-hypothesis can be applied, not without trenchant critical remarks about current criticism of the Gospels.

6. Fr. Schleiermacher's analysis of Luke (n. 12) was not planned to answer the whole question regarding the origin and relation of the synoptic Gospels, though this work is based upon a complete view of the problem. It made little impression, for the simple reason that Schleiermacher's fundamental idea, which involved a discussion also of Acts, was only incompletely worked out in this first publication upon the subject, and because the exposition of the general theory from the detailed observations, and even a discussion of the same in relation to Luke's preface, was for the time being postponed. According to Schleiermacher, the bond of connection among the Gospels—the basis and the beginning of the entire Gospel literature— was neither an oral nor a written Gospel, nor the use of earlier Gospels in the composition of later ones, but a large number of short written narratives. Schleiermacher's new interpretation of Papias' testimony regarding Matthew and Mark had more effect. That up to the year 1832 no one had doubted that Papias meant our Matthew and Mark, Schleiermacher found incomprehensible. All that Papias knew of Matthew was a collection of Jesus' sayings which Matthew wrote down in Hebrew. Papias says nothing of a translation of Matthew's Gospel into Greek, but speaks only of a number of recensions of this collection of sayings,—the Λόγια, so celebrated later. One of these recensions is preserved in our Matthew, and others, as for example the different Gospels used by the Jewish

Christians, are known to some extent from several reports of the Church Fathers. Of Matthew, chaps. v.–vii., x., xiii. 1–52, xviii. 23–25 belong to the collection of sayings. Besides these chapters, there are other scattered fragments not so easy to separate from their context. Nor was Papias acquainted with our Mark, which does not suit his description, but with a writing of Mark much less complete, and showing much less order. This writing of Mark was worked over by a later hand into our Mark, apparently also by another hand into the apocryphal *Gospel of Peter.* Thus Schleiermacher discovered an original Matthew and an original Mark, which opened the way for new combinations for the solution of the synoptic problem.

7. After the question raised by D. F. Strauss' *Leben Jesu* (1835–36) as to whether the whole body of traditions gathered in our Gospels was essentially mythical or historical, had awakened wide theological interest, F. Chr. Baur (n. 13), dissatisfied with the dogmatism of Strauss as well as of his opponents, also with the "quantitative method" of Wilke, and all attempts to solve the problem in an artificial manner, undertook "to conceive the relation of the Gospels to one another as something which grew up naturally, the working out of a principle of inner development." So long as the relation of the narrative to the consciousness of the narrators—the dominating idea, the *tendenz* of each one of the Gospels—is not made clear, "the discussion remains vague and uncertain." Baur began with the Fourth Gospel, which presupposed the historical material of the Synoptists, but which nevertheless was subordinated and accommodated to the new conception of Christ as the eternal Logos by the selection of such parts of the same as were suited to the author's purpose. From John he proceeded to the consideration of Luke, which was certainly older than John. Luke was edited, according to Baur, about 150,

on the basis of an original Luke written in the spirit of Paul and retained by Marcion in his Church. Matthew was also used in its preparation, against which Gospel the original Luke was also supposed to have polemicised—the purpose of the redaction being to remove the sharp opposition between the extreme Paulinism of Marcion and the surviving Jewish construction of the Gospel, so far as this was possible from the point of view of a modified Paulinism. The only sources employed by Mark, who proceeds from the opposite, originally Judaistic point of view, and who represents less a harmonising tendency than the disposition to remain actually neutral with reference to the great conflicting tendencies of the apostolic age, were Matthew and Luke, or the original Luke. The small amount of new material which Mark introduces, and the numerous small additions which he scatters here and there throughout his book, are merely amplifications, and have no historical value, being due partly to the author's misunderstanding of his predecessors, and being partly inventions of the author, intended to create the impression of independent knowledge. Of the canonical Gospels, Matthew is the most original. It presents a picture of Christianity as it existed while still under the dominance of national ideas, which is the original form of Christianity as it emerged from Judaism. But the Gospel itself appears not to have been edited until during the Jewish rebellion under Hadrian, between 130 and 134, and is the result of a long process of literary development, the single steps of which can no longer be distinguished. The immediate predecessor of Matthew was a Hebrew Gospel which the Church tradition ascribed to the apostle Matthew, and which in a great variety of forms and under changing names was the only Gospel in existence until toward the middle of the second century. To use a short inaccurate expression, this was the *Gospel of the Hebrews*. Like Schwegler, Baur declined to refer the particularistic Jewish features of Matthew to the Hebrew Gospel, and to assign the words and narratives universal in tone to the redactor of the Gospel, on the ground that even the Hebrew Gospel may have contained "purer elements" and because the principle by which "the apparently disparate elements of Matthew" could be united was to be found in early Christianity itself (*Unters. der kan. Evv.* S. 578 f., 613 ff.). Hilgenfeld, on the other hand, undertook to distinguish in our Matthew an original apostolic document written in a thoroughly Jewish spirit, which he supposes to have been worked over in a more universalistic spirit by a Hellenist, apparently in Egypt, after the year 70 (n. 13). At first Hilgenfeld rejected the ancient tradition of a Hebrew Matthew as purely legendary, holding even the original document to have been a Greek work, which was the basis also of the Aramaic *Gospel of the Hebrews*. Later, however, he became convinced of the original character of the *Gospel of the Hebrews*, which he then made the real original Gospel. While Mark, which Baur treated so contemptuously, is, to be sure, wholly dependent upon the Greek Matthew, it is nevertheless to be restored to its old place between the Greek Matthew and Luke. This is also the opinion of C. Holsten, who abandoned all effort to determine more exactly the character of the document at the basis of the canonical Matthew, which he also assumed, and attempted to explain the origin of the synoptic Gospels from the conflicting dogmatic tendencies of the apostolic age (n. 13).

8. Without any knowledge of Wilke's work, which appeared at about the same time, Chr. H. Weisse (n. 14), who was influenced by Strauss' *Leben Jesu* to make a new investigation of the sources of the Gospel history, undertook to show that our Mark is none other than the work commented upon by Papias and the presbyter John. Though at this particular point Weisse rejects entirely Schleiermacher's interpretation of Papias' testimony, and

does not leave uncriticised his interpretation of what
Papias says regarding Matthew, he appropriates, never-
theless, the essential result of Schleiermacher's critique,
namely, his discovery of the collection of Jesus' sayings in
Aramaic from Matthew's hand. From these two original
works Luke, the disciple of Paul, compiled his Gospel
without much independent knowledge of the tradition,
while somewhat later the Greek redactor of the original
Matthew enlarged the collection of sayings into our
Matthew by the use of material borrowed from Mark.
After the number of those accepting the originality of
Mark and its priority to Matthew had become greater, and
after A. Ritschl had broken with his master Baur, in his
view of the Gospels, as in other points, and gone over to
the Mark hypothesis, H. J. Holtzmann, following up this
hypothesis, was courageous enough to describe minutely
the sources from which the synoptic Gospels are supposed
to have been put together,—their character and compass,—
and also to attempt practically a verbal restoration of the
same (n. 14). One of the original documents at the basis
of all three Gospels, employed by each of the evangelists
without the knowledge that the others had used it, is preserved in our Mark in practically complete form and
throughout in its proper order. This we may call the
original Mark: since the only changes which the author
made in his original was to abbreviate the same at the
beginning, i. 1–13, and at certain other points, and to
omit certain passages, such as the Sermon on the Mount
and the account of the centurion (Luke vi. 20–vii. 10) after
Mark iii. 19 (no one knows why), and, because of its objectionable character, the narrative found in John vii. 53–viii.
11, which Hitzig places after Mark xii. 17. Also a large
part of the material peculiar to Mark, which is not great,
is taken from the original Mark—particularly the accounts
of healing, Mark vii. 31–37, viii. 22–26, but also many of
the little details which enliven Mark's narratives. Unless

interpreted too strictly, Papias' testimony regarding Mark suits this original Mark in a general way. Also what Papias says of a collection of sayings by Matthew meets the requirement of the hypothesis, and gives a show of appropriateness to the expression Λόγια, chosen to designate the second principal source, the use of which on the part of Matthew and Luke is supposed to explain agreements between these two Gospels which are not due to their common dependence upon the original Mark. This remarkable book contained only a number of the discourses, for the most part the shorter discourses, of Jesus. Moreover, these discourses, part of which were provided with titles and short historical introductions, belonged exclusively to the later Galilean ministry, and were subsequent to the call of Matthew, and the choosing of the apostles (Holtzmann, *Synopt. Evv.* 1863, S. 252, cf. S. 365 f.). But the very first long discourse, which is supposed to have followed the choosing of the apostles in the original Mark, was wanting in the Matthew Logia. In contrast to the original Mark, this did not begin with the testimony of the Baptist concerning Jesus, but with his doubting question (Luke vii. 18–35 ; Matt. xi. 2–19), and ended with a series of parables ; at the very close stood probably the saying which we find in Matt. xiii. 52. As in the case of the earlier Galilean ministry, so from the period of Jesus' activity in Jerusalem and the Passion the author preserves no sayings. He is extremely careful in other respects, also, not to repeat anything already contained in the original Mark. Although we are able to form a much better idea of the arrangement and original wording of the Logia from Luke than from Matthew, still, without exception, the apostolic Church transferred Matthew's name from the Logia, of which he was the author, not to Luke's Gospel, but to Matthew. Material in Matthew and Luke, derived neither from the Logia nor from the original Mark, was produced for the most part by the evangelists themselves, being either put into writing by them for the first time from the oral tradition, as Matt. xvii. 24–27, or worked over on the basis of older and shorter documents—as the genealogies and several parts of the Sermon on the Mount—or pure invention—as the sending out of the Seventy (Luke x. 1), which Luke fabricated because he did not want the same commission, which he found in both his sources, to be addressed twice to the same hearers. These are the main features of the hypothesis. Later modifications of details by Holtzmann himself, Weizsäcker, and others cannot be presented here.

9. Finally, the independent view of B. Weiss, which, during an entire generation, its author, with great persistence, has worked out in all its details, deserves notice (n. 15). The original Gospel, so vainly sought since Eichhorn, is a book written by the apostle Matthew in Aramaic, but very soon translated into Greek. Though consisting for the most part of discourses and sayings of Jesus, naturally with the indispensable historical setting, this document contained also a considerable number of narrative pieces, even groups of such, and so in its original form was a work very much like our Gospels, covering the period from the appearance of the Baptist to the beginning of the history of the Passion, concluding somewhere about Matt. xxvi. 2–13. The question arises at once why the history of the Passion, where, so far as we can see, the narratives in Matthew, Mark, and Luke are related to each other in essentially the same way as in the preceding parts of the history, should have been omitted from the original apostolic document. Practically the only answer which Weiss gives to this question is the statement that a presentation of the Passion history, differing so radically from that of the Fourth Gospel as do all three synoptic accounts, could not have originated from an apostle. The original document, already translated into Greek, was one of the sources used by Mark; the others were the oral

narratives of Peter. The author of the canonical Matthew used as sources the original Gospel and Mark. Mark had therefore always the choice between two apostolic authorities, one written, the other oral; whereas the author of the canonical Matthew must select between the statements of an apostolic document and the work of a disciple of one of the apostles. The reason for this entire theory is the observation that sometimes Matthew, sometimes Mark, gives the impression of the greater originality; for this is supposed to be explained by assuming that in some cases Matthew preserved the original apostolic document more faithfully than Mark, while in other instances he followed Mark's account. Finally, Luke, who knew nothing of the canonical Matthew, and who, therefore, could not possibly have used the same, made copious use of the original apostolic document in addition to Mark, which he made the basis of his Gospel, and another source, probably written, which can no longer be distinguished with exactness. Particularly in vi. 20–viii. 8, and ix. 51–xviii. 14, large sections of the original documents were adopted by Luke; and, so far as we are able to make comparisons with Matthew, these are reproduced for the most part in a more original form.

Up to the present time no one of the investigations of the synoptic problem can be said to have produced results which have been generally accepted, or that can lay well-grounded claims to such acceptance. In one point only is there agreement, namely, that it is impossible to set forth the history of the origin of the first three Gospels in a satisfactory manner on the basis of reliable reports and trustworthy observations; that, rather, gaps remain in our knowledge based upon these two classes of data, which must be filled up by conjecture. There is no hope that the question as to which one of the conjectures made heretofore or to appear in the future comes nearest to the truth will be decided by a new display of cleverness on the part of representatives of one of these hypotheses in working it out in detail, so that it shall appear to all capable judges to be the simplest solution of the problem. On the other hand, there is no reason to despair of a solution, at least not on the part of one convinced of these two sets of given facts, which can be ascertained without the help of hypotheses, namely, (1) that the tradition regarding the origin of the Gospels goes back to the time of their origin, (2) that the three books in our possession are as yet far from being adequately understood and estimated. With reference to the tradition, the boldest of the critics, with a few unhappy exceptions, have shown enough historical sense to seek support for their hypotheses in the oldest notices regarding the origin of the Gospels, though, to be sure, for the most part selecting arbitrarily what suited their own purposes. Thanks also to fortunate discoveries and the investigations stimulated by such discoveries, we are in possession of more thorough knowledge of the Gospel literature of the second century than was possible for Lessing and Herder, Schleiermacher and Baur, Credner and Bleek. We really know more than did these investigators about Marcion's *Gospel*, Tatian's *Diatessaron*, the *Gospel "according to the Hebrews,"* and the *Gospel "according to Peter."* Nevertheless, it is true that many critics do not seem to have kept abreast of the advances in knowledge indicated above. Besides, very often it has not been appreciated that the tradition is either to be accepted as a whole, or the error of such parts of the same as do not deserve acceptance plausibly shown. With reference to the second point mentioned above, namely, the proper valuation of the Gospels as literary products, it is true that serviceable work in this direction has been done. But little use has been made of these results in the investigation of the origin of the Gospels, because of a one-sided tendency in this investigation to make conjectures regarding the sources supposed to be at

the basis of the Gospels, without adequate knowledge of
the characteristics of each separate Gospel.   On the other
hand, the method of a comparative interpretation of the
géneral content of the synoptic Gospels—a method employed in the earlier period by Calvin and Gerhard, and
among the pioneers of the new criticism of the Gospels used
and recommended especially by Griesbach, and absolutely
demanded by Wilke—had a positively harmful effect with
reference to this question, tending especially to confuse and
to bewilder those beginning the investigation for the first
time.   How is it possible to understand an author when he
is interrupted after every third word!   How can one writing be compared with another when each is not known by
itself as its author intended, and consequently not understood in its details!   Irenæus speaks of teachers who read
to their hearers from unwritten books, and calls such a
procedure "making ropes out of sand" (i. 8. 1).   In our
time we have commentaries on books, the existence of
which, to express the matter mildly, can be proved only
by means of conjecture.

1. (P. 401.) In connection with Burgon's pioneer investigation in *The
Last Twelve Verses of St. Mark*, 1871, pp. 126–131, 295–312, the writer has
carefully discussed the *Diatessaron* of Ammonius, *Forsch.* i. 31–34, cf. S. 1,
99, 101–104, 293 ; *ThLb*, 1896, S. 3 f.   Cf. also Schmidtke, *Die Evv. eines
alten Uncialcodex*, 1903, S. xxxii. ff.   The only direct source of our knowledge
of the work of Ammonius is Eusebius' introduction to his edition of the four
Gospels—an introduction composed in the form of a letter to Carpianus, and
arranged according to the method developed in the Gospels themselves.
This is printed in many editions of the N.T., *e.g.* the Tischendorf-Gregory
edition, *Prol.* p. 145.   The κανόνες, arranged by Eus.—*i.e.* catalogues, tabular
statements (*Grundriss*, 6 f.), are ten in number ; the first embraces the
sections which are common to all four Gospels, 2–4 those which are
contained in three Gospels, 5–9 those contained in two Gospels, and 10, in
four subdivisions, those which are found in but one Gospel.   The κεφάλαια
or περικοπαί (Eusebius uses both expressions), which were long mistakenly
called *sectiones Ammonianæ*, are 355 in Matt., 233 in Mark (later increased
to 241 or 242 in consideration of the spurious additions), 342 in Luke,
and 232 in John, in all 1162—a number which is given also by Epiphanius
in his *Ancorites*, chap. l., and Cæsarius in his *Dialogue*, i. 39 ; cf. Gregory,
143.   Eusebius reckoned 74 sections which were found in all the Gospels,
111 only in Matt., Mark, Luke ; 22 in Matt., Luke, John ; 25 in Matt.,

Mark, John ; 82 only in Matt., Luke ; 47 only in Matt., Mark ; 7 in Matt., John ; 13 in Mark, Luke ; 21, in Luke, John ; 62 in Matt. ; 19 in Mark ; 72 in Luke ; 96 in John alone.   The so-called Gospel harmonies, at the head of which stands Tatian's Syriac *Diatessaron*, were primarily for ecclesiastical use, and not for scholarly purposes, like the works of Ammonius and Eusebius ; cf. *PRE*³, v. 653–661.   That of J. Clericus, however (*Harmonia Evangeliorum*, Amstelod. 1699, reprinted without the Greek text, Lyon, not Leyden, 1700), forms a transition to the synopses, in so far as it prints the text of the four Gospels in parallel columns.   The real beginning in this direction was made by J. Griesbach, *Synopsis Evangeliorum Matth. Marc. Luc.* 1776, which was intended to serve as a basis for exegetical lectures on these three Gospels, which were then called synoptic Gospels.   Among many subsequent works should be mentioned the *Synopsis Evangelica* of Tischendorf, first published in 1851, in which the entire text of the fourth Gospel is again included ; that of Anger (1851), which takes from John only the few real parallels to the text of the first three Gospels, and is, moreover, distinguished by a wealth of citations and parallels from the apocryphal and patristic literature of the second century (a book which deserves as do few to be reissued, with such alterations and extensions as time demands) ; and, finally, the handsomely printed *Synopticon, An Exposition of the Common Matter of the Synoptic Gospels*, by W. G. Rushbrooke, London, 1880, and a supplementary volume (without mention of the year) with appendices—(*a*) The Double Tradition of St. Matthew and St. Luke ; (*b*) The Single Tradition of Matthew ; (*c*) The Single Tradition of Luke.   Finally, A. Wright, *The Synopsis of the Gospels in Greek*, with various readings and critical notes, 2nd ed., London, 1903.

2. (P. 402.)   Famous examples of the harmonistics of the ancient Church are the discussions of the Last Supper in the Easter controversies about 190 ; Africanus' letter to Aristides on the genealogies of Matt. and Luke ; Eusebius' work, *de Evangeliorum* διαφωνίᾳ (Jerome, *Vir. Ill.* lxxxi. ; Eus. *Quæst. ad Stephanum, ad Marinum*) ; the unfortunate attempts of Epiphanius in many places in his writings, especially in his article on the Alogi (*Hær.* li.) ; and Augustine, *de Consensu Evangeliorum*.

3. (P. 402.)   When Eusebius remarks that one evangelist supplements another (*e.g.* in a Syriac fragment in Mai, *Nova P. Bibl.* iv. 1. 279 : "What Matthew omitted and did not say Luke relates, and what the latter does not tell the former does" ; cf. pp. 229, 265 f.), he simply states the actual conditions, not the conscious procedure of the evangelists.   Epiphanius does speak of the supplementing of each Gospel by the one following, but it is the Spirit which "compels" the writers to all their work, and to this connection with their predecessors (*Hær.* li. 7, 12, cf. 6).   Chrysostom, who emphasises the chronological succession of the Gospels, is the first to explain the brevity of Mark as designed in view of the already extant, fuller, and in many ways exhaustive presentation of Matt., though he gives it also as an additional reason that Mark depended on Peter, a man of few words, while Luke reproduced the fuller current of Paul's speech (*Hom.* iv. *in Matt.*, Montf. vii. 46).   He has no thought of an actual use of the earlier Gospel in the composition of the later ; on the contrary, he finds the little discrepancies between them a valuable proof that they were not written according to some

questionable agreement, but that each evangelist told the simple truth to the best of his knowledge (*Hom.* i. p. 5 f.).   Augustine (*de Consensu Ev.* i. 2. 4) goes further : " Et quamvis singuli suum quemdam narrandi ordinem tenuisse videantur, non tamen unusquisque eorum velut alterius præcedentis ignarus voluisse scribere reperitur vel ignorata prætermisisse, quæ scripsisse alius invenitur, sed sicut unicuique inspiratum est, non superfluam cooperationem sui laboris adiunxit.   Nam Matthæus suscepisse intelligitur incarnationem domini secundum stirpem regiam et pleraque secundum hominum præsentem vitam facta et dicta eius.   Marcus eum subsecutus tamquam pedissequus et breviator eius videtur.   Cum solo quippe Ioanne nihil dixit, solus ipse perpauca, cum solo Luca pauciora, cum Matthæo vero plurima, et multa pene totidem atque ipsis verbis, sive cum solo, sive cum ceteris consonante (*al.* -ter).   Lucas autem, etc.   § 5 : Non autem habuit tamquam breviatorem coniunctum Lucas, sicut Marcum Matthæus.   Et hoc fortasse non sine aliquo sacramento," etc.   With regard to Matt., Mark, Luke (iii. 4. 13) : " Tres igitur isti eandem rem ita narraverunt, sicut etiam unus homo ter posset cum aliquanta veritate, nulla tamen adversitate."   Mark's close connection with Matt. is often further mentioned, *e.g.* iii. 4. 11.   For the understanding of this work (written about 400) it is essential to bear in mind that, as Burkitt has shown (*The Old Latin and the Itala,* 1896, pp. 59, 72–78 ; cf. *ThLb,* 1897, col. 374), Augustine had before him Jerome's revision of the text of the Gospels, which was furnished with the Eusebian canons and sections.   This arrangement of the Gospels, introduced by Jerome among the Latins, was plainly used by Augustine in his harmonistic work, as in Books II. and III. he compares Matt. with the parallels by means of the double figures noted upon it and Canons i.–vii., and then in Book IV. goes through the portions peculiar to each Gospel according to Canon x.   When he says of Mark (see above), *cum solo Ioanne nihil dixit,* it is not the result of study, but simply of the fact that in Canons v.–ix. Eusebius provided for all possible combinations of two Gospels except Mark-John.   Also, the remarks which follow were written with reference to the canons of Eusebius, or rather to a codex of the Gospels in the Vulgate, which lay open before him, and at the beginning of which he found Jerome's letter to Damasus and the canons which it explained. This very circumstance is a new proof that Augustine used the Vulgate as the basis of his *de Consensu Evangeliorum.*

4. (P. 402.)   Calvin in the argument of his commentary on the harmony of the synoptic Gospels (ed. Tholuck, i. p. 6), besides an incorrect statement about Jerome and an unfair judgment of Eusebius, delivers, quite without proof, his own opinion that Mark never saw Matt. and that Luke never saw Matt. or Mark.   Much sounder was the judgment of H. Grotius, who wrote of the title of Matt. (ed. Windheim, i. 13) : " Sicut autem Marcus usus est Matthæi Ebræo, ni fallor, codice, ita Marci libro Græco usus mihi videtur, quisquis is fuit, Matthæi Græcus interpres."   On this R. Simon (*Hist. du Texte du NT,* 1689, p. 108) remarked that only conjectures were possible.

5. (P. 403.)   Lessing, *Neue Hypothese über die Evangelisten als bloss menschliche Geschichtschreiber betrachtet,* 1778 ; first published 1784 in *Theol. Nachlass. Werke,* ed. Lachmann-Maltzahn, xi. 2. 121–140.

6. (P. 404.)   Eichhorn first developed his view in 1794 in the *Allgemeine Bibliothek der biblischen Literatur,* v. 759 ff., then in amended form in his

Einleitung, i. 1804, 2te Aufl. 1820. In the latter was included a defence against hypotheses which had appeared meanwhile. Aside from the artificiality and pettiness of the treatment, which contrasts strongly with the broad conception of Lessing's sketch, one is painfully impressed by two particulars—first, the statement of the advantage of "this discovery of the original Gospel" in the "simplification of Christian doctrine for which German theology has been so earnestly striving for fifty years" (*Einl.* 2te Aufl. i. 445); and, secondly, an absolute silence with regard to Lessing, from whom Eichhorn derived the best of his material. After Herder (*Vom Erlöser der Menschen*, 1796, S. 174) had explained the true state of the case, it was not so much in order to herald Eichhorn as the founder of modern Gospel criticism, as to lament, with Herder, that Lessing did not work out his hypothesis himself.

7. (P. 405.) J. J. Griesbach first set forth his view briefly at the end of the Jena Easter Program for 1783 (Griesbachii *Opusc. Acad.*, ed. Gabler, ii. 241–256 : "Inquisitio in fontes, unde evangelistæ suas de resurrectione domini narrationes hauserint"), and then developed it in detail in two Programs, 1789 and 1790 : "Commentatio, qua Marci ev. totum e Matthæi et Lucæ commentariis decerptum esse monstratur." A revision, with a defence against criticisms which had been made meanwhile, appeared in Velthusen, Kuinoel, Ruperti, *Comm. Theol.* i. (1794), and was reprinted in Gabler, *op. cit.* 358–425. For his attitude toward Lessing, cf. S. 425.

8. (P. 405.) G. Herder, *Vom Erlöser der Menschen nach den drei ersten Evv.* 1796, 4 Abschnitt, S. 149–233 ; with more detail and definiteness in *Von Gottes Sohn, der Welt Heiland nach Johannes' Ev.* 1797, S. 303–416 (Herder's *Werke*, ed. Suphan, xix. S. 194–225, 260 f., 380–424). The theory is presented in brilliant and yet shifting lights, which make a brief and accurate restatement difficult. For instance, it is not clear how Herder could decide so positively against an original writing no longer extant (xix. 417), and yet hold that the primarily oral *evangelium commune* was at once written down by many, if only for private use (xix. 205, 207 f., 394 f., 408 f.). He seems also not to have determined definitely in his own mind what part was to be assigned to Matthew in the first writing of the original Hebrew Gospel, or of the later Palestinian Gospel, written about 60, which underlay the Greek Matt. and even the last form of our present Matt. (xix. 205, 401). The later discussion no longer speaks of the original unwritten Gospel as a "sacred epic," as does the earlier (199—in distinction from myth, 2 Pet. i. 16), nor of the evangelists, whose narrations are in part oral, as rhapsodists (214, 217). Herder's protest against the idea of an "apostolic gospel-office" in Jerusalem (209 f.), and much of what he says of the character of the individual Gospels, is excellent. G. Chr. Storr (1746–1805), *Ueber den Zweck der ev. Geschichte und der Briefe des Johannes*, 1786 ; *De Fonte Evv. Mat. et Luc.* 1794. F. Hitzig, *Ueber Johannes Marcus und seine Schriften*, 1843, should be named here rather than among those mentioned in note 9. Without attempting to solve the synoptic problem, he undertook the defence of Mark against the unfavourable criticism which began with Griesbach, and by means of the supposition that 2 Cor. viii. 18 refers to Mark as the author of a Gospel, and that 1 Cor. vii. 10 presents a citation of Mark x. 1–12, was able to maintain that Mark had already begun to be circulated in 57 A.D., from which it then followed

naturally that it served as a source for Matt. and Luke (37–62, 167–173). The chief object of the book was to show that John Mark was the writer not only of the Gospel, but of Rev. also.

9. (P. 407.) Chr. G. Wilke, *Der Urevangelist oder exeg.-krit. Untersuchung über das Verwandschaftsverhältnis der drei ersten Evv.* 1838. The number of those who have had the patience to read through this large book—almost 700 pages in extent—is probably not great. In its lack of historical perspective and vital ideas, as well as in its crude and self-sufficient spirit, which Wilke first introduced into the Gospel inquiry, it has not been without successors. Its only service is its opposition to Gieseler's hypothesis (26–152). The short sections peculiar to Mark which he wished to excise as later interpolations (672 ff. ; cf. 323 ff., 463 ff., 552 f.) are for the most part the very ones which show us the individuality of Mark. Others are set aside in the most violent fashion. In Mark i. 13 the words πειραζόμενος ὑπὸ τοῦ σατανᾶ are an interpolation from Luke iv. 2 and not proper to Mark ; the interpolators were "clever enough," however, to write the Markan σατανᾶς instead of the Lucan (*e.g.* 12) διάβολος (664 f.). "We give our hand and seal for all eternity that our result is correct" (684). Thus Wilke thought "to win the applause of impartial investigators of truth," which he states (694) to be the object of his work. Bruno Bauer, *Kritik der ev. Geschichte*, Bde. i.–iii. 1841–42, 2te Aufl. 1846. G. Volkmar, *Die Evv. oder Marcus und die Synopse*, 1870, and a supplement with continuous paging, *Die kanon. Synoptiker in Uebersicht mit Randglossen und das Geschichtliche vom Leben Jesu*, 1876. "The Gospel books are allegorical narrative elaborations of the one Gospel of Jesus and the apostles" (S. vii). The chronological summary (viii) is quite convenient : (1) Mark, *circa* 73 ; (2) *Genealogus Hebræorum*, *circa* 80 ; (3) perhaps *Evangelium Pauperum, Essenorum, circa* 80 ; (4) Luke, *circa* 100 ; (5) Matt. (the last of the Synoptists, as shown by Wilke, S. xi), *circa* 110 ; (6) *Gospel of Peter, circa* 130 ; (7) Marcion, 138 ; (8) *Gospel of the Nazarenes* according to the Twelve Apostles, *circa* 150 ; (9) *Gospel of the Logos according to John, circa* 155 ; (10) *Gospel of the Egyptians,* 160–170. On the other hand, Primitive Matt., Primitive Mark, Primitive Luke, Book of Maxims, etc., are mere fancies.

10. (P. 408.) J. L. Hug (1765–1846), after an uncompleted first attempt which the present writer knows only from the preface of 1808, published his *Einleitung* entire in that year, 3te Aufl. 1826, on the Gospels, ii. 1–243.

11. (P. 408, 410.) J. C. L. Gieseler, *Historisch-kritischer Versuch über die Entstehung und die frühesten Schicksale der schriftlichen Evv.* 1818 ; substantially published in 1817 in Keil and Tzschirner's *Analekten*, vol. iii. To illustrate the evangelists' accuracy of memory, Gieseler adduces (105 f.) Plato, *Phædrus,* p. 380 ; Cæsar, *Bell. Gall.* vi. 14 (the Druids and their pupils); August. *Doctr. Christ.* i. 4 (St. Anthony); Gregor. *Magn. Dial.* iv. 14. He also calls to mind (60) the Rabbinic method of teaching before the writing of the Mishnah ; cf. Schürer, ii. 321–325, (Eng. trans.) ii. 1. 323–326. On the possibility of the oral perpetuation of whole books, cf. also Spiegel in *ZDMG*, ix. 178 ff. Wilke's criticism (see note 9 above) appealed particularly to the Johannine parallels of the synoptic Gospels (John vi. 1–21, xii. 1–xiii. 30, xviii. 1–xx. 23), but also to the materials peculiar to John, which show that neither in the choice of materials nor in the form of their presentation had any such fixed and uniform type of narration been developed among the apostles as a com-

parison of the three synoptic Gospels on the supposition of their mutual independence would indicate to be their common basis. The Gospel fragments in Paul (1 Cor. xv. 3–7 and xi. 23–25 compared with the corrected text of Luke xxii. 15–20 and with Matt. xxvi. 26–29, Mark xiv. 22–25) afford similar evidence (see above, p. 380 ff.). Wilke was also right in observing (119) that from Papias' comments on the discourses of Peter (Eus. *H. E.* iii. 39. 15) one obtains a very different idea of the Gospel narratives of an apostle from that involved in an unwritten primitive Gospel.   G. Wetzele, *Die synoptischen Evv. eine Darstellung und Prüfung der wichtigsten über die Entstehung derselben aufgetretenen Hypothesen mit selbständigem Versuch zu Lösung der synopt. Evangelienfrage*, 1883.   K. Veit, *Die synopt. Parallelen und ein alter Versuch ihrer Enträtselung mit neuer Begründung*; two parts in one volume, 1897, Part i. the text arranged in an interlinear synopsis, Part ii. an elucidation of the synoptic parallels.

12. (P. 411.) Fr. Schleiermacher, *Ueber die Schriften des Lucas, ein krit. Versuch*, first part (only), 1817 ; *Werke, Zur Theol.* vol. ii. 1–220. Schleiermacher began with Hug and Eichhorn, who, in his opinion, admirably refuted each other ; before concluding he also noticed Gieseler's work in its earliest form (note 11). He left uncertain especially whether and how far Luke found the single narratives already combined in larger groups, and so used collections which came into existence before our Gospels (S. 13 = 10). In the lectures on introduction, also (*Werke, Zur Theol.* iii. 233, 239), we are left in the dark as to how these detached fragments and the incomplete collections arising from them were related to the "combining Gospels," of which, according to his prologue, Luke must already have known several.   More important is "Ueber die Zeugnisse des Papias von unsern beiden ersten Evv.," *ThStKr*, 1832, S. 735–768 ; *Werke, Zur Theol.* ii. 361–392.

13. (P. 412, 414.) F. Chr. Baur, *Kritische Untersuchungen über die kanon. Evv., ihr Verhältnis zu einander, ihren Charakter und Ursprung*, 1847 ; *Das Marcusev. nach seinem Ursprung und Charakter*, 1851 ; *Christentum und Kirche der drei ersten Jahrhunderte*, 2te Aufl. S. 23 ff., 73 ff. In several respects Baur depended on the preliminary work of his pupils, such as Schwegler, *Nachapostol. Zeitalter*, 1846 ; A. Ritschl, *Das Ev. Marcions und das kanon. Lucasev.* 1846, and various dissertations by E. Zeller. Following Baur, Hilgenfeld (*Die Evv. nach ihrer Entstehung und geschichtlicher Bedeutung*, 1854) sought to lessen the emphasis on the ecclesiastical and dogmatic tendency of the Gospels, and to push their origin further back, the document underlying Matt. about 50–60 (S. 115), our Matt. about 70–80 (103), Mark shortly before 100 (148), Luke about 100–110 (224). The discussions in which he developed and partly modified his view are indicated in his *Einl.* 462. While Dr. Fr. Strauss in his new *Leben Jesu für das deutsche Volk*, 1864, S. 98 ff., and Th. Keim, *Gesch. Jesu von Nazara*, i. 1867, S. 44–103, agreed substantially with Baur's view and Griesbach's conclusion with regard to Mark, Hilgenfeld did Mark more justice, and also recognised the traditional account in so far as he allowed that Mark was written in Rome "under the influence of Petrine tradition," and even held it possible that, if Mark was still living at the time when the Gospel named for him was written (in the early part of Domitian's reign, say 81–85, *Einl.* 517), he was, not perhaps its author, but its author's sponsor (*Einl.* 518). C. Holsten, *Die drei ursprünglichen, noch ungeschriebenen*

Evv. Zur synopt. Frage, 1883 ; *Die synopt. Evv. nach der Form ihres Inhalts*, 1885, again undertook to explain the dissimilarity of the first three Gospels wholly on the basis of the dogmatic principles which dominated the apostolic time, and their agreement in material and form on the theory that Mark remodelled Matt. and that Luke worked over Matt. and Mark together. The three forms of the unwritten Gospel are : (1) the Jewish-Christian, which Peter preached until he lapsed into Judaism, A.D. 52–53 ; (2) that of Paul ; (3) the anti - Pauline Gospel of the Judaisers. Our Matt. corresponds throughout with the first. Only Matt. v. 17–19 comes of a Judaising spirit foreign to that of Matt., perhaps from a Greek adaptation of the Λόγια of which Papias speaks, or from the original Gospel of Matt. or *Gospel of the Hebrews*, which was written at the time when Judaism was dominant in Jerusalem (53–70 A.D.), perhaps as early as 55, and apparently by the apostle Matthew (*op. cit.* 1883, S. 63, A. 2 ; 1885, S. 174 ff.). How and where the original Petrine Gospel maintained its existence after Peter's own lapse, so as to be revived after the destruction of the temple and reduced to writing in our Matt.; how the fertile author of this much more anti-Judaistic than anti-Pauline book could commit the folly of putting crass Judaism and the bluntest condemnation of lawless Paulinism in the mouth of Jesus, in only one passage, to be sure, but so significant a passage as v. 17–19 ; how the name of Matthew became affixed to a Gospel which with respect to the discourses of Jesus stands in sharp contrast to Matthew's Judaistic collection, and betrays its dependence on such a source in but one passage ; how as early as 100 not this Petrine Matt. but Mark was connected with Peter,—these and other questions are not even raised. Matt. would be unacceptable to the Gentile Christian Churches, which would not abandon Paul's Gospel. To leave room for this, Mark is composed about 80 from the material of Matt. In place of the legal Sermon on the Mount appears the διδαχὴ καινή, Mark i. 27, *i.e.* the Gospel of Paul, while ix. 30–32 betrays the opinion that by their failure to understand Jesus' death on the cross the first apostles were hampered in any complete understanding of the Gospel as a whole. At the beginning of the second century, when, through the simultaneous use of Matt. and Mark, Jewish Christian as well as Pauline ideas had struck root in the Churches, Paulinism had weakened, and circumstances called for the union of all Christians, a typical representative of these conditions worked Matt. and Mark into one, making use also of the oral tradition, which was not yet quite spent. This is the origin of Luke.

14. (P. 414, 415.) The more important works referred to under No. 8 above (p. 414 f.) are : Chr. H. Weisse, *Die ev. Geschichte kritisch und philosophisch bearbeitet*, 2 Bde. 1838 ; *Die Evangelienfrage in ihrem gegenwärtigem Stadium*, 1856. A. Ritschl, "Ueber den gegenwärtigen Stand der Kritik der synopt. Evv." in the *Theol. Jahrbb.* of Baur and Zeller, 1851, S. 481–538. H. J. Holtzmann, *Die synopt. Evv., ihr Ursprung und geschichtlicher Charakter*, 1863 ; he also pursued the subject in a number of later essays, and gave a convenient summary in his *Hand-Commentar*[2], i. 1892, S. 1–13. C. Weizsäcker, *Untersuchungen über die ev. Geschichte, ihre Quellen und den Gang ihrer Entwicklung*, 1864. In independent acceptance of the "two source theory," Wendling, *Urmarkus, Versuch einer Wiederherstellung der ältesten Mitteilungen über das Leben Jesu*, 1905, has recently undertaken an analysis of Mark according to

which three elements are to be clearly distinguished: (1) M¹=a collection of sayings of Jesus in a brief but distinct narrative setting, beginning with i. 9, 16 (ἦλθεν Ἰησοῦς ἀπὸ Ναζ. τ. Γαλιλαίας καὶ παράγων κτλ.) and ending with xv. 34, 37 (καὶ τῇ ἐνάτῃ ὥρᾳ ὁ Ἰησοῦς ἀφεὶς φωνὴν μεγάλην ἐξέπνευσεν) (2) M²=narratives of miracles of Jesus in extended description, which is in part highly poetical, beginning with i. 4, closing with xvi. 8; (3) additions of the editing evangelist, e.g. i. 1–3, 14, 15, iii. 6–30, iv. 10–25, etc., naturally also xiii. 3–27.

15. (P. 417.) B. Weiss first developed his view in *ThStKr*, 1861, S. 29 ff., "Zur Entstehungsgesch. der drei synopt. Evv."; *JbfDTh*, 1864, S. 49 ff. "Die Redestücke des apostolischen Mt."; *ibid.* 1865, S. 319, "Die Erzählungsstücke des apostolischen Mt."; then in his commentaries: *Das Marcusev. und seine synopt. Parallelen*, 1872; *Das Matthäusev. und seine Lucas-Parallelen*, 1876, and in his comprehensive works, e.g. in his *Einl.*³ 1897, S. 453–560.

§ 51. THE TRADITION REGARDING MARK AND HIS GOSPEL.

John, with the surname Mark (n. 1), was the child of a Christian household in Jerusalem. In this home a large body of Christians were gathered for prayer at the time of the Passover—probably on the night of the Passover feast in the year 44 (Acts xii. 12). Since Mark's mother, Mary, is mentioned as the owner of this house, it may be regarded as certain that his father, whose name we do not know, was no longer living. Mark must have been grown up at the time and a member of the Church, since Paul and Barnabas, who visited Jerusalem shortly afterward, took him with them to Antioch, evidently with the intention of making use of his services in their work (Acts xii. 25). According to the usage of the apostolic age, the characterisation, "my son," employed by Peter some twenty years later (1 Pet. v. 13), can hardly mean anything else than that Mark was converted through Peter's influence, and possibly also baptized by him (n. 2). With this agrees the express statement of Papias, that Mark did not hear the Lord's preaching, nor accompany Him as a disciple, but that he sustained a relation of this kind only to Peter (see below in text, and n. 14). This proves that the view which appeared in the fourth century, according to which Mark was one of the Seventy (Luke x. 1), is a fable (n. 3). If the statement which Paul makes incidentally, to the effect that Mark was a cousin of Barnabas (Col. iv. 10), is to be taken to mean that they were cousins on their fathers' side, Mark, like Barnabas, was a Levite (Acts iv. 36), and, from this point of view, there would be nothing to prevent us from accepting the ancient tradition that Mark cut off his thumb in order to make himself ineligible to priestly service. The nickname " stump fingered," given Mark on this account, was commonly known at the beginning of the third century in Rome, where we should most naturally expect to find genuine traditions concerning Mark (n. 4). In this same quarter, according to the most probable emendation and interpretation of the beginning of the Canon Muratori, we meet the report that Mark had become acquainted with a number of the facts recorded by him through personal experience, though in general he had not heard Jesus' words nor witnessed his deeds (n. 5). The Fragmentist adds that Mark also presented these facts as he learned them. When we reflect how slightly noticeable the traces of first-hand knowledge in Mark really are,—if indeed they exist at all,—further, how late and with how much uncertainty it came to be suspected that the author was concealed in xiv. 51 (n. 6), and, finally, how little inclination and capability the commentators of the ancient Church showed in following up hints of this character in the N.T., it must be regarded as extremely improbable that the definite statement of the Fragmentist is the result of clever exegesis. It is far more likely to have been a reproduction of a tradition still current in Rome about the year 200. And, then, what is there to prevent the son of a Christian household in Jerusalem, who, in 44, was perhaps thirty or thirty-five years of age, from having witnessed some of the scenes in Jesus' life in the year 30,

without his having been at the time one of those who
heard and believed Jesus' preaching? According to
another tradition (n. 7), the beginnings and development
of which are as yet only imperfectly cleared up, Jesus
celebrated His last Passover with His disciples (Mark xiv.
14) in the home of Mark and his mother (Acts xii. 12),
where also the apostles were gathered with the women on
the day of the ascension (Acts i. 13), and where the Spirit
was poured out (Acts ii. 2).   Without any legendary help
concerning the place where these events occurred, this
combination might have been made by a comparison of
the texts, beginning with Acts xii. 12 and going backwards
in the accounts.   But this furnishes no occasion for
suspecting the tradition of the Canon Muratori or the
interpretation of Mark xiv. 51 f., which identifies the
individual there mentioned with the evangelist.   In
the stories about the house of Mark the latter is occasionally identified with the person referred to in xiv. 13, but
not with the youth in Mark xiv. 51 (n. 7).

If Mark came to Antioch in 44 with his cousin Barnabas and Paul, and if they took him along on their first
missionary journey perhaps in the year 50 (Acts xiii. 5),
we may assume that he helped them during the intervening
years in their work as missionary preachers and teachers in
the Church of Antioch (Acts xi. 26, xiii. 1), just as he did
on the first missionary journey.   He is not mentioned in
Acts xiii. 1 among the teachers and prophets of the
Antiochian Church, nor is he characterised in xiii. 5 as a
preacher of the gospel having the same rank as Paul and
Barnabas, but as one helping these two missionaries in
their preaching in a comparatively subordinate position.
He had a part in the work of missionary preaching (Acts
xv. 38 ; Philem. 24), but as a servant of the missionaries,
who "took him with them" (Acts xv. 37 f.).   The representation of Mark's relation to the missionaries in Acts
differs manifestly from the manner in which the part

taken in Paul's preaching by Silvanus and other helpers
is described in Acts xvi. 6, 10, 13, 32, xvii. 4 ; 2 Cor. i.
19 ; 1 Thess. i. 5 ff. On the other hand, it is in very
striking agreement with what Paul says of Mark shortly
before his own death, ἔστιν γάρ μοι εὔχρηστος εἰς διακονίαν
(2 Tim. iv. 11, above, p. 371). The best way in which to
explain this peculiar relation is to suppose that Mark, the
spiritual son of Peter, and the son of a Christian household in Jerusalem in which a part of the mother Church
was accustomed to assemble, could supply something which
Paul lacked and which Barnabas, who left Jerusalem and
entered the foreign missionary work much earlier than
Mark, did not possess in the same measure, namely, a
treasure of narratives from the lips of Peter and of other
disciples of Jesus, who were accustomed to come and go
in his mother's house. This knowledge of the details of
the Gospel history (τῶν περὶ τοῦ Ἰησοῦ, above, p. 377, n. 2)
must have been an invaluable help to the missionaries.
Mark was better suited to be their ὑπηρέτης than were
others, but appears to have lacked the dash and courage
for the prosecution of the missionary work. When it was
decided to press forward from Cyprus into Asia Minor, he
separated himself from the missionaries and returned to
his mother in Jerusalem (Acts xiii. 13), apparently from
Paphos. A year later, however, we find him again in
Antioch, though it is not indicated who it was that
induced him to return thither (Acts xv. 37–39). Here a
separation took place between Paul and Barnabas on
Mark's account, Paul holding that his conduct on the first
journey showed him to be unfitted for missionary service,
and construing Barnabas' milder judgment in the case as
due to his partiality for his cousin. In consequence, Paul
took Silas and went to Asia Minor, while Barnabas and
Mark returned to Cyprus, Barnabas' home. Here we lose
trace of them ; in fact, we do not hear of Barnabas again
(vol. i. 433, n. 5). In the year 62 or 63, Mark appears

again in Rome as one of the two Jewish missionaries, the
method of whose work gave the apostle joy, in contrast to
that of the other Jewish missionaries there (Col. iv. 10 ;
vol. i. 450, n. 4).   Paul is able to count him among
his fellow-workers in Rome (Philem. 24).   All traces of
a strained relation between the two men has vanished.
Since Mark had planned for some time to travel to the
East, and on the occasion of this journey to visit also the
interior of Asia Minor, Paul had commended him to the
kindly reception of the readers of Colossians, to whom
Mark had remained personally unknown, even before the
letter was despatched in which the commendation is repeated (Col. iv. 10).   We have no reason to doubt that
Mark actually made this journey.   A year or two later he
is again in Rome along with Peter (1 Pet. v. 13).   The
fact that, with the exception of the greeting from the
whole Roman Church to the Christians in Asia Minor,
Mark's is the only greeting which Peter sends, proves that
in the interval between his two residences in Rome, Mark
had become acquainted with at least part of the Churches
in Asia Minor.   Whether he made his second journey to
Rome in company with Peter, and whether he left Rome
again after Peter's death in consequence of the Neronian
persecution, we do not know ; but that he did both it is
only natural to conjecture (above, p. 161 f.).   At all events
he was again in the East, apparently in Asia Minor, in 66,
when Paul wrote his last letter to Timothy, in which he
commissioned him to bring Mark with him to Rome,
thinking that he could make further use of his services,
even in his present condition (2 Tim. iv. 11).   The tradition, according to which Mark preached the gospel in
Egypt and became the first bishop of Alexandria, is ancient
and very little contradicted, so that it is to be given a
certain amount of credence ; though its date and circumstances cannot be determined with exactness (n. 8).

In two passages of his *Hypotyposes* which are mutually

supplementary, Clement of Alexandria gives us an account
of the origin of Mark's Gospel with numerous details,
which he had learned, probably, from one of his teachers
(n. 9).   Although one of these reports is only a Latin
translation and the other is preserved only in indirect
discourse, still they suffice to show the inaccuracy of an
account of Eusebius (n. 10) for which the latter quotes the
authority of Clement and also of Papias.   According to
Clement, during the time that Peter was engaged in
publicly preaching the gospel in Rome, persons of equestrian rank belonging to the royal court, who had heard
Peter's preaching, requested Mark to write down what
Peter had spoken, inasmuch as he had been associated with
Peter from an early date, and therefore had his discourses
in memory, in order that they too might impress the same
upon their memories, and when the Gospel was completed
to give the same over to those who had made this request
of him.   When Peter learned of this he neither hindered
nor encouraged Mark in the undertaking.   Notwithstanding this attitude of Peter, Mark complied with the request
and wrote his Gospel, following Peter's narratives.   On the
other hand, according to Eusebius' presentation, Peter
learned of the matter through a special revelation, where-
upon he expressed his gratification at the zeal of those
with whose wishes Mark complied, and, finally, approved
of the Gospel after its completion, formally appointing it
to be read in the Churches (n. 10).   In contrast to this
account of Eusebius, that of Clement is especially noticeable, on account of the very indifferent attitude which it
makes Peter take toward the committing of his Gospel to
writing by Mark.   Eusebius' presentation belongs to the
time when the word " Gospel " suggested at once a book,
and when no effort was spared to exalt the authority of
the written word ; whereas Clement's account is in harmony
with the spirit of an age when the unwritten form of the
Gospel was dominant, and when the beginnings of a written

Gospel in existence at the time were scarcely noticed (§ 48). Further, according to Clement, Peter's judgment did not have reference to the book after its completion, but to Mark's work in its inception.   Even if it were possible grammatically to take Clement's account to mean that Peter did not learn of the matter until after Mark had written his Gospel and placed it in the hands of those who had requested its composition (n. 9), what is said of Peter's attitude is entirely against this construction of the passage.   After a book has been composed and published it is possible to commend or to blame the person responsible, but not to hinder (κωλύειν) or encourage him (προτρέπεσθαι).   What Peter noticed or learned from others were the transactions between those who heard his preaching and his disciple Mark leading up to the composition of a Gospel by Mark, and besides this, at most, the inception of the work by Mark.   Then it was possible for Peter either to forbid the writing of such a book, or to add his request to that of his hearers and encourage Mark to compose a Gospel.   He did neither, but let things take their own course.

So understood, this account is not in irreconcilable contradiction with the statement of Irenæus, that Mark published or gave his Gospel to the Church after the death of Peter and of Paul (pp. 393 f., 398, n. 7). Although the expression which Irenæus uses with reference to Mark (τὰ ὑπὸ Πέτρου κηρυσσόμενα ἐγγράφως ἡμῖν παραδέδωκεν) does not indicate so clearly as what he says about Matthew (γραφὴν ἐξήνεγκεν εὐαγγελίου) and John (ἐξέδωκε τὸ εὐαγγέλιον), the publication of the completed Gospel, still this is in every respect the most natural way in which to understand his words.   It may therefore very well be the case that Mark was requested to write his Gospel during Peter's stay in Rome, which possibly did not cover an entire year, and actually began the preparation of the work during this time, and that he did not complete it until three years later, or, if the book was never finished (§ 52), that he did not decide until then to publish it, *i.e.* did not direct or allow the multiplication of copies for wider circulation. Irenæus does not say expressly that Mark was written in Rome, but he takes for granted that this fact is known; for only on this presupposition can we understand why he sets its date after the death of the two apostles who laboured in Rome. At any rate, the tradition that Mark was written in Rome is not an invention of Clement or of his authorities. Evidently Papias had already borne witness to this fact (above, p. 163, and below, n. 10). This, for good reasons, was accepted generally (n. 11). The same is true of the connection between Mark's Gospel and the narratives of Peter. The earliest witnesses for this connection are not Irenæus, Clement, Tertullian, Origen, and later authors (n. 11), but, as will be shown immediately, it is attested as early as the close of the first century. Moreover, it is misleading to judge of this relation from short, incidental references, which because of their fragmentary character are easily misunderstood, instead of from the oldest accounts concerning it. What Clement says is not to the effect that Mark wrote down the sermons which Peter preached in Rome; any attentive hearer, who was able to write, could have done that equally as well as Mark. The reason why the request was made of Mark especially was rather because, unlike the Romans, who had become followers of Peter only recently, he had been his disciple for a long time, *i.e.* at a much earlier period had been associated with him, and had had abundant opportunity to hear and have impressed upon his memory Peter's narratives. This account is not, therefore, in any way contradictory of Mark's personal history, according to which from 44 on he was constantly in the company of Paul or Barnabas, and, so far as we know, was not again in the constant companionship of Peter until 63 or 64 in Rome. In spite of this separation, he was and continued to be a "son" of

Peter, as it is quite possible that for a decade prior to his entrance upon foreign missionary service he had heard Peter's narratives and addresses in his mother's house (Acts xii. 12–17 ; cf. ii. 42, 46, v. 42).   When he was privileged, two decades later, to rejoin Peter in Rome, all these recollections of his earlier years must have been renewed, and of this experience his presentation of the Gospel facts must show traces, if the narrative was written in Rome at that time.   The designation of the Gospel specifically as the *Gospel of Peter*, to be found as early as the time of Justin (n. 12), and employed by numerous writers of Tertullian's time, was an abbreviated expression for this relation of Mark's Gospel to Peter's preaching and narratives.   This form of expression did not, however, become established in the usage of the Church, and disagrees entirely with the oldest testimony concerning Mark, namely, that of Papias and of his teacher John, or simply "the Presbyter," as Papias calls him in the passage where he reproduces his opinion concerning Mark.

The question, so long disputed, as to the identity of the presbyter John—whether he is the apostle John, as Irenæus thought, or, as Eusebius claims to have discovered, a person bearing the same name, but to be distinguished from the apostle John—cannot be decided here in this incidental connection (n. 13).   Every reader of Papias' fragments, and everyone acquainted with the other traditions regarding the apostle, the author, and the teacher John, may be asked to give unconditional assent to the following statements : (1) Until toward the close of the first century there was living in Ephesus a John, who had attained an extreme old age, and who enjoyed the greatest distinction in the Church of the province of Asia, exercising a decisive influence upon its development.   (2) Prominent among the personal disciples of the same were Polycarp, the bishop of Smyrna, who likewise lived to a very great age, and was put to death by burning on the 23rd of February 155 ; and

Papias, the bishop of Hierapolis, who lived at least until
Hadrian's time (117–138), and who apparently in his
extreme old age, somewhere about the year 125, wrote
his work, entitled λογίων κυριακῶν ἐξήγησις, in five volumes.
(3) According to the unanimous tradition—whether this be
biographical, having relation to his disciples; or of a
literary and historical character, dealing with writings
attributed to him ; or legendary, concerning his own person,
—this teacher of Polycarp and of Papias was the only
person bearing the name of John who, during the last
decades of the first century, was in any way distinguished
in the Churches of Asia Minor. Eusebius attempted to
prove that, in addition to the apostle and evangelist John,
whom with all the older tradition he identifies with the
John of Ephesus and the teacher of Polycarp, there lived in
Asia Minor a presbyter John, who was not an apostle, but
the teacher of Papias. However, he went only half way
with his criticism. The single John of Ephesus, whom the
tradition knows, cannot be divided into two : the teacher of
Polycarp cannot be separated from the teacher of Papias.
Whether, on the other hand, the one John of Ephesus
was one of the twelve apostles, *i.e.* the son of Zebedee, or
whether, in consequence of the similarity of name, he had
been confused with him by the entire tradition before
Eusebius' time, cannot be decided merely by the interpretation of a fragment of Papias' preface. The tradition of
the Church concerning John of Ephesus is always open to
different interpretations, so that it must be left out of
consideration, and the question decided primarily from the
testimony of the writings themselves which are ascribed to
this John (Part X.). (4) As is shown by the very first mention of his name in Papias' preface (ὁ πρεσβύτερος Ἰωάννης,
Eus. *H. E.* iii. 39. 4 ; twice repeated by Eusebius in this
form, §§ 7, 14, not Ἰωάννης ὁ πρεσβύτερος), and still more
clearly in Papias' statement concerning Mark (καὶ τοῦτο ὁ
πρεσβύτερος ἔλεγε), the John to whom Papias refers was so

commonly called "the elder" among his disciples that this
expression, used as a title of honour for the aged teacher,
could at times be employed instead of his own name. This
fact is confirmed by the greetings of 2 John and 3 John ;
and the case is entirely analogous to that of Clement of Alexandria, who was in the habit of citing one of his teachers—
all of whom were dead, and whom he designates collectively
as "the Elders"—simply as ὁ πρεσβύτερος or ὁ μακάριος
πρεσβύτερος, without name or other definite designation.
(5) The John of Papias, like a certain Aristion whom
Papias mentions in the preface together with John, and
who is frequently cited with him in the course of the work
as authority for various traditions (*op. cit.* §§ 4, 7, 14), was
a μαθητὴς τοῦ κυρίου. As is self-evident, this expression does
not mean "a Christian" or "a true Christian," but a
personal disciple of Jesus. This is made clear beyond all
doubt by the context ; for immediately preceding is a
list of names, beginning with Andrew and ending with
Matthew, the whole concluding with the words ἤ τις ἕτερος
τῶν τοῦ κυρίου μαθητῶν. This is the only interpretation
which corresponds to the usage of the second century.
The reason why Papias does not call even Andrew and
Peter apostles, is the fact that their significance for him—
namely, their confirmation of the Gospel tradition as those
who had heard and seen Jesus—had nothing to do with
their apostolic office ; for him, Aristion, who was not one
of the apostles, was just as important a witness as the
apostle Thomas, or indeed more so, since Papias had had
no opportunity to see or hear Thomas, as he had Aristion.
His point of view is that of one seeking trustworthy
tradition concerning Jesus ; consequently he makes no distinction between those who were apostles and those who
were not apostles, but designates those who had seen and
heard Jesus μαθηταὶ τοῦ κυρίου or πρεσβύτεροι respectively,
according as he thinks of them in relation to Jesus or in
relation to himself and the generation in which he lived.

The individual in question is therefore a Palestinian
Jewish Christian settled in Asia Minor, and called John—
in other words, according to the unanimous tradition of
the second century, the apostle John, whose statements
Papias cites in numerous passages of his work, partly as
he heard them from John's own lips, partly as they had
come to him through other disciples of his.

One of these citations made by Papias reads as follows :
" This also the Presbyter said (or, was accustomed to say),
' Mark, who was (or, who became) an interpreter of Peter,
wrote down accurately all that he remembered of what the
Lord had said or done, though this was not (set forth) in
order ' " (n. 14).   Not only the formula with which the
words of the Presbyter are introduced ($\kappa a\grave{\iota}$ $\tau o\hat{v}\tau o$ $\acute{o}$ $\pi\rho\epsilon\sigma$-
$\beta\acute{v}\tau\epsilon\rho o\varsigma$ $\acute{\epsilon}\lambda\epsilon\gamma\epsilon$), but also the way in which the Presbyter
introduces Mark's name ($M\hat{a}\rho\kappa o\varsigma$ $\mu\acute{\epsilon}\nu$), shows that in the
preceding account by Papias there were other sayings of
the Presbyter, which while dealing with related topics,
having reference possibly to earlier records of Jesus'
sayings, did not concern Mark in particular.   He is introduced in contrast to what precedes.   The understanding
of the concise opinion of the Presbyter is rendered somewhat easier by the explanatory remarks which Papias
adds directly after his teacher's words.   These would be
of still greater use to us if Eusebius had copied also the
passage preceding the citation from the Presbyter, to
which Papias refers expressly in this passage.   Papias
says as follows : " He (Mark) neither heard the Lord nor
followed Him (as a disciple); but later, as remarked
(he heard and followed) Peter, who constructed the discourses which he used in teaching as necessity required,
but not as he would have done in preparing a written
account of the Lord's sayings.   So, then, Mark made no
mistake when he wrote down some things as he remembered them, since he was concerned only for one thing,
namely, to omit nothing that he had heard, and not

to say anything in his account that was false." It
is clear from the words of John, as well as from the
explanation which Papias adds, that unfavourable
opinions had been expressed concerning Mark's book
in the circle to which Papias and John belonged. Only
the purpose to counteract such opinions enables us to
understand John's ἀκριβῶς ἔγραψεν and Papias' οὐδὲν
ἥμαρτεν. What had been particularly noticed in John's
vicinity, what John himself admitted in the words οὐ
μέντοι τάξει, and what Papias apologised for at length,
was the lack of order. Variation from the order of
another Gospel cannot be here meant ; for in this case
the point of criticism and defence would have to be the
contradiction between Mark and the recognised authority
of another evangelist, and not want of order in general,
more specifically, as Papias' apology shows even more
clearly than John's statement,—want of an order such as
might be expected in the case of one who had been a
witness of Jesus' words and deeds. The John who spoke
with his disciples concerning Mark was such an αὐτόπτης
καὶ αὐτήκοος. Whether or not at this time he himself had
already written a Gospel, or wrote one later, his disciples
at all events were accustomed to hear his narrative concerning Jesus' words and deeds. Judged by this standard,
Mark's book seemed to them to lack plan, and to present
things out of their proper chronological order. That a
personal disciple of Jesus, in speaking of the correct order
of Jesus' words and deeds, could mean no other order than
that in which he remembered them, is self-evident. If a
book were the standard by which a man of letters, ancient
or modern, judges another book for himself and his
readers, he could not fail to cite such a work, whether it
was his own or that of another. The lack in Mark's
Gospel, which John and Papias both admit, they explain
and condone by pointing out that Mark was not a disciple
of Jesus, but a disciple of Peter ; on this account he was

not able to narrate what he himself had seen and heard,
but was bound by Peter's discourses, which from their
very nature were not adapted to give a connected and
chronological view of Jesus' work as a teacher, consisting
as they did always merely of separate stories, intended, as
the case might be, for instruction or edification. Even
though we do not possess the preceding section of Papias'
work, to which he refers in ὡς ἔφην, and in which he had
spoken, probably, of the origin of Mark's Gospel in
Rome (n. 10), we see that Papias is not thinking here
of Mark's relation to Peter as that of a missionary
helper, but as that of a disciple under the instruction of
his master, as shown by the fact that he does not speak of
Peter's preaching, but of the discourses delivered by him
in teaching. The memory upon which Mark draws goes
back to his youth. He owes it to the relation in which
he stood to Peter prior to his entrance upon foreign
missionary work, a relation the existence of which we
infer from 1 Pet. v. 13 and from Acts xii. 12–17, and
which is noticed also in Clement's account (above, p.
431 f.). Now Papias does not say that Mark wrote down
Peter's oral Gospel word for word, as might possibly
be inferred from Irenæus, Clement, Origen, and Eusebius
by a prejudiced interpretation of their statements (above,
p. 398 ; below, n. 11). According to Papias, the responsibility of authorship is entirely Mark's ; and this responsibility he is able to bear, if only unreasonable demands
be not made of him, and if it be borne in mind that
he was not a disciple of Jesus, but only a disciple of
Peter.

Papias expressly limits the dependence of Mark's
Gospel upon the discourses of Peter to *some* portions of
the Gospel. Papias' judgment, οὐδὲν ἥμαρτε Μᾶρκος, οὕτως
ἔνια γράψας, ὡς ἀπεμνημόνευσεν, has been interpreted to mean
that he is attempting to defend Mark against the charge
of having reported only part of the Gospel history in his

book ; but this has against it not only the wording of the
passage which emphasises οὕτως—ὡς and not ἔνια, but common sense as well.   At the time when John xx. 30, xxi.
25 was written, or shortly afterward, and in the circle
of Papias, who, dissatisfied with the information supplied
by the Gospel literature already in existence, was constantly searching for traditions that were as yet unwritten,
the criticism of a single Gospel on the ground that it was
incomplete would have been laughed out of court.   What
Papias defends is the method of Mark's presentation.   It
is not the account of one who saw and heard Jesus, but
that of a disciple of one of the apostles, dependent upon
the discourses of one who was an apostle and an original
witness.   More than this, the discourses upon which he
was dependent were not designed to give an historical
survey of Jesus' life, but were intended for an entirely
different purpose.   With reference to these is to be judged
also the one purpose which, in positive and negative form,
Papias indicates Mark to have had in view.   Under
similar circumstances an unscrupulous author might have
yielded to the temptation to add to the discourses which
he heard all sorts of invention of his own, with a view to
rendering the stories more interesting or pleasing, or in
order to remove also single features which might make an
unfavourable impression.   Mark did neither, but reproduced Peter's discourses, naturally in so far as he recorded
them at all, accurately, without leaving anything out or
making additions of his own. · Incidentally, however, we
learn that in Papias' opinion this close dependence upon
Peter's narratives was to be noticed in *some* passages of
Mark's Gospel.   This observation is of a character exactly
similar to that of the Canon Muratori (above, p. 428 f.), to
the effect that here and there in Mark's account there are
passages which might lead one to suppose that he narrated
as an eye-witness of certain events, which he had experienced.   When Papias claims that Mark was not a disciple

of Jesus, but a disciple of Peter, he does not deny this observation and claim of the Fragmentist; quite as little does Papias' opinion that in numerous passages Mark appears to be dependent upon the discourses delivered by Peter in teaching invalidate the observation of later critics that he is largely dependent upon an older document containing an account of the Gospel history. In the light of Papias' full explanation is to be understood also the statement of his teacher John, which is so brief as to be enigmatical. According to John also, Mark drew upon his memory, and in his opinion, as in Papias', this must have been his recollection of Peter's narratives. When John praises the accuracy of all that Mark remembered of what he had heard Peter say, and when in his closing sentence Papias declares with reference to this accuracy that Mark was careful not to omit or arbitrarily to change anything that he heard, their words do not in turn imply that Mark's book contained nothing else than reproductions of Peter's narratives. On the contrary, John hints that where this source of memory failed him Mark's presentation actually shows want of accuracy. For this very reason he fails to reproduce exactly the order of events in the Gospel history. John does not mention expressly whose the account was in dependence upon which Mark wrote his accurate narratives, which would be incomprehensible, if he had not thought that this point was clear to his followers from the words ἑρμηνευτὴς Πέτρου γενόμενος. This very omission on John's part is of itself decisive proof that the expression does not mean that on Peter's missionary tours Mark acted as his interpreter, a misunderstanding which comes to light in a half uncertain way for the first time in Jerome, who is the only writer in antiquity to advocate the view (n. 12 end). Furthermore, if this were the meaning of the words, it would be incomprehensible that Papias, in his comparatively full explanation of the words of his teacher, should not refer in any way to this

office of Mark, or say anything about the language in
which Peter taught, and the language into which Mark
translated the words of Peter, either orally or in writing,
but that he should speak only of the close connection
between Peter's narratives and Mark's account of the
same, and of Mark's relation of discipleship to Peter as
explaining this close connection.   The same is true of all
those who after Papias' time repeat John's expression
(ἑρμηνευτής, interpres), namely, Irenæus, Tertullian, and
Jerome (above, p. 398, and below, n. 12).   Equally noteworthy is the fact that Clement, Origen, and also Eusebius,
to whom we are indebted for John's testimony, never say
anything about Mark's being Peter's interpreter, and
especially when speaking of the dependence of Mark's
Gospel upon Peter, they avoid the word ἑρμηνευτής ; and, on
the other hand, always emphasise the one fact that Mark's
relation to Peter was that of a disciple (n. 12).   Ancient
scholars were safe against this error, because they knew
that, except for his work among the "Hebrews" in
Palestine, Peter, like Paul, needed only the Greek language
in all the places to which the ancient tradition represents
him to have gone—Palestine, Antioch, and Rome.   Inasmuch as he was proficient in this language, they knew also
that he did not need an interpreter, which was actually
the case (vol. i. pp. 34–72, 112 f. ; above, p. 112).   Even
though Mark, who had lived since the year 44, where
Greek was the dominant language, may have acquired
greater readiness in the use of the Greek idiom than Peter,
—of which, however, his Gospel in comparison with 2 Peter
shows no evidence,—the idea that Mark performed the
office of an interpreter, translating Peter's Aramaic discourses into Greek, or what is still more impossible, his
Greek sermons into Latin, cannot be held by anyone
having any knowledge at all of language conditions in the
apostolic age.   For this reason, therefore, this view is not to
be attributed to the presbyter John.   With his disciples,

who did not need to be informed by him, to begin with, what language Peter used in Antioch and Rome, or what the personal relation was in which Mark stood to Peter, John could speak of Mark's reproduction of Peter's narratives figuratively, and say that it was by virtue of the composition of his book he became Peter's interpreter (n. 15). To those who had not heard Peter tell the story concerning Jesus, he supplies these narratives. Herein lay the strength of Mark's Gospel, but likewise its pardonable weakness.

Of greater weight even than this *estimate* of Mark's writing by a disciple of Jesus is the *fact* that, between the years 75 and 100, a book dealing with the words and deeds of Jesus, and written by a disciple of Peter, was in existence in the province of Asia, and had attracted the attention of Christians in that region. This is attested also by other facts. Our Fourth Gospel, which originated in this same region, and which is assigned by the unanimous tradition to John of Ephesus, shows clear traces of its author's acquaintance with Mark (§ 66). Furthermore, there is a credible tradition that Mark was the favourite Gospel of the school of Cerinthus, who lived in Ephesus in John's old age (n. 16). Finally, it is self-evident that there was no doubt in Papias' mind as to the identity of Mark's book, of which he had heard his teacher speak, with the one used in the Church of Asia Minor at the time when he wrote (125 A.D. or somewhat later). Papias' testimony and the wide circulation which the above mentioned facts show that Mark had among the Christians in and about Ephesus even before the close of the first century, exclude the possibility that in the interval between the days of John and the time when his opinion was recorded by his disciple Papias, Mark had been recast into what was practically another book, and the original edition replaced by this modified form of the Gospel after the former had been already widely circulated without this change having been noticed. John's judgment has reference, therefore, to the canonical Mark.

1. (P. 427.) Acts xii. 12, Ἰωάννου τοῦ ἐπικαλουμένου Μάρκου, cf. xii. 25, xv. 37, might mean that at the time of the composition of Acts, and in the circle for which Acts was written, Mark regularly bore this Roman praenomen as a cognomen, while at the time of the events here related, and especially in Jerusalem, he was known only as John. In Acts xiii. 5, 13 the Hebrew name corresponding to that early period would be retained, while in Philem. 24, Col. iv. 10, 2 Tim. iv. 11, 1 Pet. v. 13, the Roman name is used which was given him later, and was the only one current among the Gentile Christians. But as ἐπικληθέντα has the weight of evidence in Acts xii. 25, the present in xii. 12, xv. 37 cannot be pressed, but is to be regarded as an imperfect participle. Moreover, the name Mark is too unimportant to receive later an additional name, as in Acts iv. 36. John, then, doubtless bore a Latin name along with his Hebrew name from the beginning, like Joseph Barsabbas, surnamed Justus (Acts i. 23), Jesus—Justus (Col. iv. 11), Silas—Silvanus (vol. i. 31 f., 207 f.), Saul—Paul (vol. i. 69 f.). The attempts to distinguish two Marks in the N.T. hardly need refutation in these days; cf. Schanz' Kom. über Mk. S. 2.

2. (P. 427.) 1 Pet. v. 13, Μάρκος ὁ υἱός μου; cf. 1 Tim. i. 2 ; 2 Tim. i. 2 ; Tit. i. 4 ; Philem. 10 ; 1 Cor. iv. 15, 17.

3. (P. 428.) Adamantius, Dial. contr. Marcion (ed. Bakhuyzen, p. 10, written circa 300–313 ; ZfKG, ix. 238), in opposition to the Marcionites, includes Mark and Luke among the seventy or seventy-two disciples. So Epiph. Hær. xx. 4 (with Justus, Barnabas, Apelles, Rufus, Niger) ; with reference to Mark, in particular, cf. Hær. li. 6, with the further embellishment that Mark was one of those disciples who, according to John vi. 66, deserted the Master, but was afterwards reconverted by Peter.

4. (P. 428.) Hippol. Refut. vii. 30, says, in an argument against Marcion : τούτους (τοὺς λόγους) οὔτε Παῦλος ὁ ἀπόστολος οὔτε Μᾶρκος ὁ κολοβοδάκτυλος ἀνήγγειλαν—τούτων γὰρ οὐδὲν ἐν τῷ κατὰ Μᾶρκον εὐαγγελίῳ γέγραπται— ἀλλὰ Ἐμπεδοκλῆς. It is not a sufficient explanation of the designation of Mark as κολοβοδάκτυλος to say that by its use Hippolytus indicated the incompleteness of Mark's gospel,—the lack of an introductory history and a proper ending,—and at the same time accounting for the mutilated gospel of Marcion. This is the view of Duncker and Schneidewin ad loc., who also accept a biographical tradition concerning the meaning of the epithet ; also of Bartlet (JThS, 1904, Oct. pp. 121–124) in the sense that this passage of Hippolytus was the source of the later legends. Hippolytus assumed that the Gospel of Mark was, like Paul, an authority on which Marcion relied, and so held, mistakenly, that Marcion's Gospel, which depends on Luke, was an adaptation of Mark. So it is not the fact that Marcion, as Wordsworth is inclined to suppose (N.T. Lat. sec. ed. Hieron. i. 173), once called Mark stumpfingered, in order to characterise him as indolent or cowardly ; on the contrary, Hippolytus gives him this title, as he gives Paul the title of apostle, as an honour. The incidental way in which this is done presupposes about 230 in Rome a general acquaintance with this epithet of Mark's. This may be read in the old prologue to Mark (Wordsworth, N.T. Lat. sec. ed. S. Hier-

onymi, i. 171 ; Corssen, *Monarchianische Prologue*, 1896, S. 9 f.) : " Marcus evangelista dei et Petri in baptismate filius atque in divino sermone discipulus, sacerdotium in Israhel agens, secundum carnem Levita, conversus ad fidem Christi evangelium in Italia scripsit . . . " (p. 172 f.). " Denique amputasse sibi post fidem pollicem dicitur, ut sacerdotio reprobus haberetur, sed tantum consentiens fidei prædestinatæ (Corssen, S. 10, 16, prædestinata) potuit electio, ut nec sic in opere verbi perderet, quod prius meruerat in genere ; nam Alexandriæ episcopus fuit." According to the Targum on Ps. cxxxvii. 4, to which Nestle calls attention *ZfNTW*, 1903, S. 347, the Levites tore off their thumbs with their teeth, and said : " How shall we sing a hymn of thanksgiving to Yahweh on foreign soil." The thumb and especially that on the right hand (Ps. cxxxvii. 5) is as essential for playing the accompaniment of a hymn on a harp or zither (Ps. cxxxvii. 2 ; 1 Sam. xvi. 23 ; 1 Kings x. 12 ; Jos. *Ant.* vii. 12. 3), as is the tongue for singing. Both duties were laid upon the Levites. Moreover, cf. the story of the hermit Ammonius (*Hist. Laus.* ed. Butler, p. 33), who cut off his left ear in order that, in accordance with the Jewish law, he might incapacitate himself for the office of bishop. The account about Mark, which is found in essentially the same form in Arabic MSS. (*ZDMG*, viii. 586, xiii. 475) is not incredible. Harnack's appeal (*ZfNTW*, 1902, S. 165 f.) to ἱερέων Acts vi. 7 (see vol. i. p. 66, n. 12), which is textually doubtful, signifies little. It is, moreover, possible that κολοβοδάκτυλος was originally applied as an epithet to Mark, because of a congenital shortness of the fingers or a finger, which was noticeable, and then later was explained as referring to an intentional mutilation. The matter is thus represented in an old MS. of the Vulgate in Toledo (Wordsworth, p. 171) : " Marcus, qui et *colobodactilus* est nominatus, ideo quod a cetera (ad ceteram) corporis proceritatem digitos minores habuisset." Cf. concerning James "the less" and Barsabbas Justus "with the flatfoot" *Forsch.* vi. 345 f., 349 f.

5. (P. 428.) The only words which remain of the account of Mark in Can. Mur. (line 1, " quibus tamen interfuit et ita posuit ") express the idea above mentioned, if we read [*ali*]*quibus* (*GK*, ii. 5, 15–18, 140). Even without assuming that the words used (line 6) with reference to Luke, " dominum tamen nec ipse vidit in carne," compare him with Mark and not with Paul (cf. *per contra*, *GK*, ii. 30), we may infer that the Fragmentist knew the older tradition, according to which Mark was not a disciple of Jesus, and conclude from *tamen* that he repeated it, and maintained, on the other hand, "aliquibus tamen interfuit."

6. (P. 428.) With regard to the fleeing youth, Mark xiv. 51 f., various opinions were current even in early times. (1) Some would see in him the apostle John. So, without any justification, Ambrose (on Ps. xxxvi., ed. Bened. i. 801) and Peter Chrysologus (*Sermo*, 78, 150, 170, Migne, 52, col. 421, 600, 645). That this view originated on Greek soil is evident from the opposition of an anonymous writer in the *Catena Patr. Græc.*, ed. Possinus, p. 327. Epiph. *Hœr.* lxxviii. 13, in a more precise reference, shows that he was acquainted with this view, and accepted it as correct as a matter of course. The lack of clearness in his statement, however, led to a misunderstanding as early as the Middle Ages, and also in the first edition of this Introduction, namely, that he identified the fleeing youth with James, the

Lord's brother. His meaning is rather that James, who is said to have worn only linen clothing, is to be compared in this particular with the sons of Zebedee; and he appeals to Mark xiv. 51 for support, assuming as well known that the youth there mentioned was one of these latter; cf. *Forsch.* vi. 231. This cannot be an original tradition, for it is plain that the young man is not one of the circle of apostles. At the same time the view, in this form, can hardly have arisen through mistaken exegesis; for the old tradition that John was the youngest of the apostles (cf. the writer's *Acta Jo.* cxxviii., cxxxiv.; also Theod. Mops. *In Ev. Jo.*, ed. Chabot, pp. 3, 15), and a combination of this tradition with the word νεανίσκος, is not a sufficient explanation. On the contrary, we cannot avoid the conjecture that the evangelist John Mark has here been confused with the evangelist and apostle John, as has happened in other cases also (see note 7 below). (2) The original tradition, which is found in Epiphanius and Ambrose, but obscured by this confusion, presents the view that *John Mark*, who did not belong to the Apostolic circle, was the fleeing youth. The same is presupposed in Can. Mur. (see above, note 5). It is instructive to notice, in this connection, that the Cyprian monk Alexander, of the sixth century, who had access to many old books, in his encomium on Barnabas (*Acta SS. Jun.* tom. ii. 440, § 13), gives it as an old tradition that Mark was the man with the pitcher of water, Mark xiv. 13, whereas the monk Epiphanius (ed. Dressel, p. 36) states that in the opinion of many the master of the house, Matt. xxvi. 18, was the youth James John. (3) The idea that the young man was James the Just, the Lord's brother, is mentioned by Theophylact and Euthymius (Migne, 123, col. 657; 129, col. 693), and rests, as is particularly plain in Theophylact's case, simply on the misunderstanding of Epiphanius of which we have already spoken. (4) According to *Cat. in Ev. sec. Marcum*, ed. Possinus, p. 326, Victor of Antioch commented on Mark xiv. 51 : ἴσως ἀπὸ τῆς οἰκίας ἐκείνης, ἐν ᾗ τὸ πάσχα ἔφαγον, καὶ οὐδὲν ξένον. Casaubon, *Exerc. ad Baronii Ann.* (1663), p. 524, made use of this statement, and argued from the young man's singular costume that he must have risen from his bed, comparing appropriately Dionys. Alex. in Eus. *H. E.* vi. 40. 7 : μένων ἐπὶ τῆς εὐνῆς, ἧς ἤμην γυμνὸς ἐν τῷ λινῷ ἐσθήματι, τὴν δὲ λοιπὴν ἐσθῆτα παρακειμένην αὐτοῖς ὤρεγον. Cf. Herodotus, ii. 95, ἣν μὲν ἐν ἱματίῳ ἐνειλιξάμενος εὕδῃ (sc. ὁ ἀνὴρ) ἢ σινδόνι.

7. (P. 429.) The complicated tradition concerning the house mentioned in Acts xii. 12 is carefully investigated in the article on "Die Dormitio S. Virginis und das Haus des Johannes Markus" in the *NKZ*, 1899, S. 377–429 (also published separately, Leipzig, 1899). According to Epiphanius, *De Mens. et Pond.* 14, a small Christian church stood in the time of Hadrian on the plot of ground before what is now the Zion Gate, a portion of which was presented by the Sultan to Emperor William II., and transferred by him to the German Catholics on October 31, 1898. On its site a larger church was built, probably about 340, which Cyril, about 348, called "the church of the apostles in the upper city" (*Catech.* xvi. 4), but which by the end of the same century was usually known as ἡ ἀγία Σιών. According to numerous testimonies from the period 380–420, this was regarded as the place, (1) of the institution of the Lord's Supper, the *cœnaculum* (Mark xiv. 14–25), (2) of the outpouring of the Spirit (Acts ii. 2), (3) of the appearances of the risen Christ in Jerusalem (John xx. 19–28; Luke xxiv. 36 ff.), (4) of the gathering

in Acts i. 13 f., and also (5) as the regular meeting-place of the primitive Church under its first bishop, James. Not till the pilgrim Theodosius, about 525 (*Itin. Hieros.*, ed. Geyer, p. 141. 7, " ipse fuit domus sancti Marci evangelistæ "), and the monk Alexander, several decades later (*Encom. in Barn.* §§ 12, 13 ; see the preceding note), do we find an explicit identification of the "Holy Zion " with the house of Mary the mother of Mark (Acts xii. 12), but it appears then not as a conjecture, but as an unquestioned tradition. Only after the conquest of Jerusalem by the Persians in 614 was the opinion gradually, and at first quite timidly, advanced among the patriarchs and festival preachers of Jerusalem, that the "Holy Zion " was rather the house of the apostle John, in which he received his adoptive mother, Mary the mother of Jesus (John xix. 26). Apart, too, from the disagreement of older traditions with regard to the dwelling of the mother of Jesus and the house in which she died, it is clear that after 614 the evangelist and apostle John and his adoptive mother began to displace the evangelist John Mark and his own mother.

8. (P. 431.) Eusebius, *H. E.* ii. 16, notices as a report that Mark was a preacher in Egypt of the Gospel which he had already committed to writing (according to ii. 15, in Rome), and the first to found Churches in Alexandria. Cf. Jerome, *Vir. Ill.* viii. In *Chron. ad anno Abrah.* 2057, Eusebius also refrains from calling him bishop outright, though he begins the succession in that city with Mark (*anno Abrah.* 2077 ; *H. E.* ii. 24). Nothing more than this is affirmed by Theophilus in John Malalas, lib. x. p. 252, ed. Bonn., who is perhaps no other than the old Antiochian bishop and apologete about 180 (cf. *Forsch.* ii. 6 f., iii. 58 f.). According to Eusebius, *Theoph.* iv. 6, ed. Gressmann, p. 20 Greek, p. 174 according to Syriac ; cf. the Hypothesis of Victor or of Cyril in Combefis, *Auct. Noviss.* i. 436 ; Cramer, *Cat. in Matt. et Marc.* p. 265 ; as well as Epiph. *Hær.* li. 6, Nicetas in Combefis, *op. cit.* 431, and others, Peter sent Mark as his substitute from Rome to Egypt. The tradition which brings him to Alexandria without touching Rome sounds still less historical (*Acta Barnabæ*, xxvi., ed. Tisch. 73 ; *Acta Marci*, Migne, 115, col. 164 f. ; the Armenian Bibles, cf. Conybeare in *Exp.* 1895, Dec., p. 419).

9. (P. 432, 433.) Clem. *Hypotyp.* on 1 Pet. v. 13 (*Forsch.* iii. 82 f. ; this portion is unfortunately lacking in the Troyes MS.) : " Marcus, Petri sectator, prædicante Petro evangelium palam Romæ coram quibusdam Cæsareanis equitibus et multa Christi testimonia proferente, petitus ab eis, ut possent quæ dicebantur memoriæ commendare, scripsit ex his quæ Petro dicta sunt evangelium quod secundum Marcum vocitatur." In immediate connection with the words from Eusebius, *H. E.* vi. 14. 5, transcribed above, p. 400, note 9 (*i.e.* if ἔλεγον is admitted as the correct reading, and we have a statement of the presbyters put by Clement and not first by Eusebius into *oratio obliqua*), we read further : τὸ δὲ κατὰ Μάρκον (*sc.* εὐαγγέλιον) ταύτην ἐσχηκέναι τὴν οἰκονομίαν· τοῦ Πέτρου δημοσίᾳ ἐν Ῥώμῃ κηρύξαντος τὸν λόγον καὶ πνεύματι τὸ εὐαγγέλιον ἐξειπόντος, τοὺς παρόντας πολλοὺς ὄντας παρακαλέσαι τὸν Μάρκον, ὡσὰν ἀκολουθήσαντα αὐτῷ πόρρωθεν καὶ μεμνημένον τῶν λεχθέντων, ἀναγράψαι τὰ εἰρημένα, ποιήσαντα δὲ τὸ εὐαγγέλιον μεταδοῦναι τοῖς δεομένοις αὐτοῦ· ὅπερ ἐπιγνόντα τὸν Πέτρον προτρεπτικῶς (Vales. conj. προφανῶς) μήτε κολῦσαι μήτε προτρέψασθαι. πόρρωθεν is, of course, to be understood temporally, not spatially (Rufinus, *olim.* ; Niceph. Call. ἐκ πολλοῦ) ; πάλαι or ἄνωθεν might

be substituted for it. The words ποιήσαντα to αὐτοῦ, which Rufinus omitted are to be construed as subordinate to παρακαλέσαι, and not as a co-ordinate statement of the reporter. Aside from the logical grounds stated above, pp. 432 f., the latter construction is inadmissible, because we ought in that case to have τὸν δὲ Μᾶρκον or τοῦτον δὲ ποιήσαντα, and instead of the present τοῖς δεομένοις, something like τοῖς παρακαλέσασιν αὐτόν. The *Cæsareani* (Καισαριάνοι, Epic. *Diss.* i. 19. 19, iii. 24. 117, iv. 13. 22, or καισάρειοι, Dio Cass. lx. 14. 1, 16. 2, 17. 5, 31. 2, lxix. 7. 4) are not in themselves *equites* also (cf. *per contra*, Dio Cass. lxxviii. 18. 2 : οὐχ ὅτι δοῦλοι καὶ ἐξελεύθεροι καὶ Καισάρειοι, ἀλλὰ καὶ ἱππεῖς, βουλευταί τε καὶ γυναῖκες τῶν ἐπιφανεστάτων). But many of these court attendants were raised to equestrian rank. One is reminded of Phil. iv. 22 ; *Act. Pauli*, ed. Lipsius, 105. 8 (vol. i. p. 550, n. 1). According to the *Acts of Peter*, that apostle had to do with much more distinguished company ; ed. Lipsius, 54. 33, 73. 33, 84. 15, 86. 2. But aside from this, we are not to think that Clement derived his account from the *Acts of Peter*, however natural the conjecture may be in some ways. In the *Hypotyposes* Clement cites the *Acts of John* (*Forsch.* iii. 87, 97), which are from the same hand as the *Acts of Peter* (above, p. 73, note 7), and the cool attitude toward the written Gospel which the Peter of the legend assumes (ed. Lipsius, p. 66 f. ; *GK*, ii. 849) would fit in with Peter's hesitancy with regard to Mark's undertaking in Clement's story. But in the legend the Gospel which the Roman Christians read is already in existence when Peter comes to Rome, and in the unbroken progress of the narrative, from his arrival in Rome to his death, there is no mention of the origin of a Gospel nor of the person of Mark.

10. (Pp. 432, 434, 440.) In connection with the account of Peter's contest with Simon Magus in Rome, Eus. in *H. E.* ii. 15 (*Forsch.* iii. 72) writes : Τοσοῦτο δ' ἐπέλαμψεν ταῖς τῶν ἀκροατῶν τοῦ Πέτρου διανοίαις εὐσεβείας φέγγος, ὡς μὴ τῇ εἰσάπαξ ἱκανῶς ἔχειν ἀρκεῖσθαι ἀκοῇ, μηδὲ τῇ ἀγράφῳ τοῦ θείου κηρύγματος διδασκαλίᾳ, παρακλήσεσι δὲ παντοίαις Μᾶρκον, οὗ τὸ εὐαγγέλιον φέρεται, ἀκόλουθον ὄντα Πέτρου, λιπαρῆσαι, ὡς ἂν καὶ διὰ γραφῆς ὑπόμνημα τῆς διὰ λόγου παραδοθείσης αὐτοῖς καταλείψοι διδασκαλίας, μὴ πρότερόν τε ἀνεῖναι ἢ κατεργάσασθαι τὸν ἄνδρα, καὶ ταύτῃ αἰτίους γενέσθαι τῆς τοῦ λεγομένου κατὰ Μᾶρκον εὐαγγελίου γραφῆς. Γνόντα δὲ τὸ πραχθέν φασι τὸν ἀπόστολον ἀποκαλύψαντος αὐτῷ τοῦ πνεύματος ἡσθῆναι τῇ τῶν ἀνδρῶν προθυμίᾳ κυρῶσαί τε τὴν γραφὴν εἰς ἔντευξιν ταῖς ἐκκλησίαις. Κλήμης ἐν ἕκτῳ τῶν ὑποτυπώσεων παρατέθειται τὴν ἱστορίαν· συνεπιμαρτυρεῖ δ' αὐτῷ καὶ ὁ Ἱεραπολίτης ἐπίσκοπος ὀνόματι Παπίας, τοῦ δὲ Μάρκου μνημονεύειν τὸν Πέτρον ἐν τῇ προτέρᾳ ἐπιστολῇ, ἢν καὶ συντάξαι φασὶν ἐπ' αὐτῆς Ῥώμης, σημαίνειν τε τοῦτ' αὐτόν, τὴν πόλιν τροπικώτερον Βαβυλῶνα προσειπόντα διὰ τούτων· "ἀσπάζεται ὑμᾶς ἡ ἐν Βαβυλῶνι συνεκλεκτὴ καὶ Μᾶρκος ὁ υἱός μου." Rufinus translates the last sentence : " Simile dat testimonium etiam Hieropolites episcopus nomine Papias, qui et hoc dicit, quod Petrus in prima epistola sua, quam de urbe Roma scripsit, meminerit Marci, in qua tropice Romam Babyloniam nominarit." Eusebius did not write very clearly here ; but probably Rufinus was right in supposing that everything that follows Papias' name was taken by Eusebius from Papias, for this cannot be discovered in Clement (see above, 163 n. 3). The supposition that the words Κλήμης—Παπίας form a parenthesis, after which the report continues, and that φασίν following συντάξαι, is a resumption of

the first φασίν after πραχθέν, has against it : (1) that there is then no reason
why Eusebius broke off his account which was almost finished with an
appeal to his two witnesses, instead of placing this appeal at the end of the
entire report. (2) That in this case Eusebius would surely have used the
second φασίν immediately after he had resumed the account, perhaps after
μνημονεύειν, and not in a relative sentence dependent upon it. It therefore
remains probable, that following Papias, who gave the tradition in connection
with 1 Pet. v. 13, and explained it by a figurative interpretation of the name
Babylon, Eusebius reported that this letter which was often cited by him
(Eus. H. E. iii. 39. 16) had been written in Rome. Furthermore, in the same
connection he probably in all essentials confirmed (ἐπιμαρτυρεῖ) the account
of Clement, also concerning the origin of Mark's Gospel in Rome. Papias, in
his testimony with reference to Mark, which has been preserved for us in its
general meaning (see below, n. 14) refers to an earlier passage of his work,
in which he had already expressed himself concerning the relation of Mark's
Gospel to the addresses of Peter. Consequently in that passage which in its
wording has not been preserved, he probably stated what according to Eus.
ii. 15 he in all probability said concerning 1 Pet. v. 13 and the Roman origin
of Mark's Gospel. That Eusebius does not repeat the account of Clement
unchʰ ʲnged is shown not only by a comparison with Clement's own words
(above, n. 9), but also in the phraseology of Eusebius himself ; for at the
point where his account begins to go beyond Clement (γνόντα δὲ τὸ πραχθέν
. . . ἀποκαλύψαντος κτλ.) he introduces a formula (φασί) which points to
an uncertain tradition ; and, furthermore, he does not make Clement responsible for all the details which are given (as, for example, in ii. 23. 19, iii. 19),
but merely in a very general expression says that he included the ἱστορία
in question in his Hypotyposes. Eusebius' unhistorical account was repeated,
and in some respects still further exaggerated, e.g. Jerome (Vir. Ill. viii.) :
" Quod cum Petrus audisset, probavit et ecclesiis legendum sua auctoritate
edidit"; Alexander Mon. Encom. Barnabæ, cap. xx. (Acta SS. Jun. ii. 443).
In Liber Pontificalis (ed. Duchesne, i. 50, 118) the influence of Peter on the
Gospel of Mark and on the ecclesiastical use of the Gospels in general appears
still more noteworthy.

11. (P. 434.) Rome is named as the place of composition by Papias (see
preceding note), and in addition to him Clement Alex. expressly (n. 9),
Eusebius (H. E. ii. 15), Epiph. (Hær. li. 6 ; see above, p. 400), Jerome (Vir.
Ill. viii.), Ephrem Syr. (Expos. Ev. Conc. p. 286, cf. Forsch. i. 54 f. ; Prol. Lat.
in Ev. Marci (N.T. Lat., ed. Wordsworth, i. 171, "evangelium in Italia
scripsit "); Alexander Mon. op. cit. cap. xx. p. 443. The statement of Chrysostom (Hom. i. in Matt., Montf. vii. 7), that Mark wrote his Gospel in Egypt
at the request of hearers there, stands quite alone. The fable that he wrote
the Gospel in Latin appears first in Ephrem, Expos. Ev. Conc. p. 286, and
elsewhere among the Syrians also, e.g. Wright, Catal. p. 70 ; in a Peshito MS.
of the 6th century ; among the Armenians, Forsch. v. 149 ; also in several
Greek minuscules (Tischendorf, i. 410); later in the West; defended by
Baronius, Annales, anno 45, xli.

12. (Pp. 435, 442, 443.) After Papias, the first witness to be considered for
the relation of Mark to the preaching of Peter is Justin, Dial. cvi : καὶ τὸ
εἰπεῖν μετωνομακέναι αὐτὸν Πέτρον, ἕνα τῶν ἀποστόλων, καὶ γεγράφθαι ἐν τοῖς

ἀπομνημονεύμασιν αὐτοῦ γεγενημένον καὶ τοῦτο μετὰ τοῦ καὶ ἄλλους δύο ἀδελ·
φοὺς υἱοὺς Ζεβεδαίου ὄντας, μετωνομακέναι ὀνόματι τοῦ Βοανεργές, ὅ ἐστιν υἱοὶ
βροντῆς κτλ. According to Justin's regular usage, αὐτοῦ cannot refer to
Christ, but only to Peter, cf. *GK*, i. 510 ff. ; and, further on in this note, the
phraseology of Eusebius, *Dem.* iii. 5. 89, 95. Mark iii. 16 f. is the basis of the
statement. Connected with this is the representation in the *Acts of Peter*,
according to which Peter was associated with other apostles in the composition of the Gospel book (see above, p. 390). Iren. iii. 1. 1 follows (see above,
p. 398), cf. iii. 10. 6 : " Quapropter et Marcus, interpres et sectator Petri,
initium evangelicæ conscriptionis fecit sic, ' Initium evangelii Jesu Christi,' "
etc. Further, Clemens Alexandrinus (see above, p. 449) ; Tertullian, *contra
Marc.* iv. 5 : " Licet et Marcus quod edidit (sc. evangelium) Petri affirmetur,
cuius interpres Marcus ; nam et Lucæ digestum Paulo adscribere solent."
Origen in Eus. vi. 25. 5 (p. 397, above) : δεύτερον δὲ τὸ κατὰ Μάρκον, ὡς Πέτρος
ὑφηγήσατο αὐτῷ ποιήσαντα. Out of this, later writers like pseudo-Athanasius,
Synops. (Montf. ii. 202), made a ὑπαγορεύειν = to dictate. Further, Victorinus of Pettau (*circa* 300), according to the original text of his commentary
(Haussleiter, *ThLb*, 1895, col. 194) : " Marcus interpres Petri ea quæ in
munere docebat commemoratus conscripsit, sed non ordine." He had read
Papias therefore, for Eusebius' *Church History* was not yet written. Eusebius,
H. E. iii. 24. 14, refers to the information from Clement and Papias, which
he had already given and elaborated somewhat (ii. 15 ; see above, p. 449,
n. 10). Quite definite also is *Dem. Ev.* iii. 5. 89 : τούτου Μᾶρκος γνώριμος
καὶ φοιτητὴς γεγονὼς ἀπομνημονεῦσαι λέγεται τὰς τοῦ Πέτρου περὶ τῶν πράξεων
τοῦ Ἰησοῦ διαλέξεις ; cf. §§ 91–94, 95 : Μάρκος μὲν ταῦτα γράφει, Πέτρος δὲ
ταῦτα περὶ ἑαυτοῦ μαρτυρεῖ· πάντα γὰρ τὰ παρὰ Μάρκῳ τῶν Πέτρου διαλέξεων
εἶναι λέγεται ἀπομνημονεύματα. Similarly in *Theophania Syr.* v. 40. Only
hints exist in Epiphanius, *Hær.* li. 6 ; Chrysostom, *Hom.* i. *in Matt.*
Jerome, *Vir. Ill.* i. : " Sed et evangelium iuxta Marcum, qui auditor eius
et interpres fuit, huius (sc. Petri) dicitur." A statement regarding the
pseudo-Petrine writings follows, as the first of which stands the *Gospel of
Peter*, cf. *Vir. Ill.* viii. : " Marcus, discipulus et interpres Petri iuxta quod
Petrum referentem audierat, rogatus Romæ a fratribus breve scripsit evangelium." As to what follows, cf. p. 450, above, n. 10. Further, cf. Jerome,
Ep. lvii. 9, cxx. 11 (of Paul : " Habebat ergo Titum interpretem, sicut et
beatus Petrus Marcum, cuius evangelium Petro narrante et illo scribente
compositum est "). With regard to the equivocal use of the term *interpres* in
the latter passage, cf. *GK*, i. 881 f. It is very significant that in the only
place where Eusebius uses the expression " Marcus evangelista, Petri interpres " (*Chron. ad anno Abrah.* 2057), there is no reference to his activity in
Peter's company, for it is his independent activity in Egypt which is reported. Eusebius has no thought of an interpreter's service rendered to Peter.
Mark became his interpreter by writing the Gospel, and also by preaching as
his representative in Egypt. See below, n. 15.

13. (P. 435.) What the present writer maintained and attempted to
prove in a somewhat youthful essay on Papias of Hierapolis (*ThStKr*, 1866,
S. 649–696 ; 1867, S. 539–542), and occasionally in other connections (*Der
Hirt des Hermas*, S. vi–x ; *Acta Joannis*, pp. cliv–clxxii ; *Forsch.* iii. 157 ff. ;
GK, i. 155, 800, ii. 33), with regard to Papias' " presbyter " named John, he

has again set forth briefly in an essay on "Apostel und Apostelschüler in der Provinz Asien" (*Forsch.* vi. 1–224, especially 112–147), in a wider connection and, he hopes, in a more convincing way. This hypothesis does not at all suit Mommsen, who (*ZfNTW*, 1902, S. 156 ff.) is of the opinion that Eusebius controverted Irenæus "in his thorough way." Also dissatisfied with Harnack's and Corssen's interpretations, he *strikes out* (on the basis of the Syriac Version) κυρίου μαθηταί, the inconvenient characterisation of both of Papias' teachers, against all Greek MSS., as also against the testimony of Jerome (*Vir. Ill.* xviii.) and of Rufinus (who only freely and wrongly translates the words by *ceterique discipuli*). Concerning the essays by E. Schwartz, see below, § 64, n. 2. To what has been said in the text (p. 435 f.) the present writer will add here but three remarks—(1) the use of οἱ πρεσβύτεροι, which we find in Papias, is the same in form as that which occurs in Irenæus and Clement, and occasionally also in Origen and Hippolytus. The term, which of itself may denote the men of the distant past (Heb. xi. 2, οἱ πρεσβύτεροι=i. 1, οἱ πατέρες=Matt. v. 21, οἱ ἀρχαῖοι), comes to signify the teachers of the next preceding generation only when the speaker characterises those to whom he applies it as his own personal instructors. The succeeding generation calls them the old men or the fathers when their ranks begin to be thinned, and also after they have altogether given place to the younger. *In concreto*, of course, they are very different persons, according to the period of the respective speakers. (2) That the πρεσβύτεροι, from whom Papias claims personally to have received much information, were themselves personal disciples of Jesus, not only follows from the fact that he calls his teachers, Aristion and John, disciples of the Lord,—just as he does the apostles Andrew, Peter, Thomas, etc.,—but is at once evident to every sound sense of interpretation of his sentence : εἰ δέ που καὶ παρηκολουθηκώς τις τοῖς πρεσβυτέροις ἔλθοι, τοὺς τῶν πρεσβυτέρων ἀνέκρινον λόγους· τί Ἀνδρέας ἢ τί Πέτρος εἶπεν, ἢ τί Φίλιππος ἢ τί Θωμᾶς ἢ Ἰάκωβος ἢ τί Ἰωάννης ἢ Ματθαῖος ἤ τις ἕτερος τῶν τοῦ κυρίου μαθητῶν, ἅ τε Ἀριστίων καὶ ὁ πρεσβύτερος Ἰωάννης (al. οἱ) τοῦ κυρίου μαθηταί, λέγουσιν. The indirect question (τί εἶπεν) and the co-ordinate relative clause (ἅ τε—λέγουσιν) explain τοὺς τῶν πρεσβυτέρων λόγους. The text was so understood by the early and entirely competent translators, the Syrian about 350, Rufinus about 400, and Jerome (*Vir. Ill.* xviii.). But the classical witness for the correctness of this interpretation is Eusebius himself, who disputes it. In order to show that Papias was not himself a disciple of the apostles, he says (§ 7) : "Papias acknowledges that he received the words of the apostles from their disciples (τοὺς τῶν πρεσβυτέρων λόγους παρὰ τῶν αὐτοῖς παρακολουθηκότων), but claims that he was a hearer of Aristion and the presbyter John." That is, he substitutes τοὺς τῶν ἀποστόλων λόγους for the τοὺς τῶν πρεσβυτέρων λόγους of Papias, and αὐτοῖς referring back to τῶν ἀποστόλων, for the τοῖς πρεσβυτέροις of Papias. Thus Eusebius suppresses the obvious fact that Papias spoke first of such traditions as he received from the presbyters directly (or from the apostles, as Eusebius puts it) — ὅσα ποτὲ παρὰ τῶν πρεσβυτέρων καλῶς ἔμαθον—before saying that he *also* inquired concerning the words of the presbyters ("apostles") in case he fell in with others who like him had been their disciples. (3) The mention of a presbyter and disciple of Jesus named John between James and Matthew, and again a presbyter and disciple òf Jesus named John after Aristion, on which Eusebius based his self-contradictory interpretation, is indeed remarkable. The conjecture suggested by Renan (*L'Antechrist*, 1873, p. 562) and ingeniously argued by Haussleiter (*ThLb*, 1896, col. 467), that the words ἢ τί Ἰωάννης in the enumeration of apostles were interpolated in the text of Papias before Eusebius' time, is venturesome and inadmissible since it is needless. The questions which Papias at the time of his investigations in the course of his earlier years was accustomed at every opportunity to ask (ἀνέκρινον) of visiting disciples of the apostles fall into two classes, which are distinguished even in the formation of the sentence. The inquiries, τί εἶπεν, he asked of such as had lived in Palestine for a long time and had had there opportunity to hear many apostles and other disciples of Jesus: the inquiries, ἅ τε λέγουσιν, he made of such, like Papias himself, as had had for a time intercourse with the disciples of Jesus, then living in the province of Asia, or also still had intercourse with them, while it was denied him. The apostle John belonged to both groups of the disciples of Jesus, whose words Papias wished to ascertain from their own disciples. This accounts for the double mention of the name. There remains only a certain clumsiness, rhetorically considered, on Papias' part.

14. (P. 438.) After Eusebius (*H. E.* iii. 39. 14) has referred the reader to Papias' work for other traditions of Aristion and John the presbyter, he continues: ἀναγκαίως νῦν προσθήσομεν ταῖς προεκτεθείσαις αὐτοῦ φωναῖς παράδοσιν, ἣν περὶ Μάρκου τοῦ τὸ εὐαγγέλιον γεγραφότος ἐκτέθειται διὰ τούτων· ʻ καὶ τοῦθ᾽ ὁ πρεσβύτερος ἔλεγεν· Μᾶρκος μὲν ἑρμηνευτὴς Πέτρου γενόμενος, ὅσα ἐμνημόνευσεν, ἀκριβῶς ἔγραψεν, οὐ μέντοι τάξει τὰ ὑπὸ τοῦ κυρίου (al. Χριστοῦ) ἢ λεχθέντα ἢ πραχθέντα. οὔτε γὰρ ἤκουσε τοῦ κυρίου οὔτε παρηκολούθησεν αὐτῷ, ὕστερον δὲ ὡς ἔφην Πέτρῳ, ὃς πρὸς τὰς χρείας ἐποιεῖτο τὰς διδασκαλίας, ἀλλ᾽ οὐχ ὥσπερ σύνταξιν τῶν κυριακῶν ποιούμενος λογίων (al. λόγων). ὥστε οὐδὲν ἥμαρτε Μᾶρκος, οὕτως ἔνια γράψας ὡς ἀπεμνημόνευσεν· ἑνὸς γὰρ ἐποιήσατο πρόνοιαν, τοῦ μηδὲν ὧν ἤκουσε παραλιπεῖν ἢ ψεύσασθαί τι ἐν αὐτοῖς.ʼ Ταῦτα μὲν οὖν ἱστόρηται τῷ Παπίᾳ περὶ τοῦ Μάρκου. Only the words Μᾶρκος μὲν . . . πραχθέντα constitute the statement of the presbyter John: what follows (at once distinguished by its fulness from the enigmatical conciseness of the preceding sentence) is from Papias. ὡς ἔφην is decisive on this point. That Eusebius, in his quotation from Papias' book, transcribed these words also, although he does not give his readers the earlier passage to which they refer, simply testifies to the faithfulness of his copy. One need not even call to his support the fact that ii. 15 in all probability alludes to the earlier passage in Papias to which Papias himself here refers (see above, p. 449f., n. 10). On the other hand, it is inconceivable that Papias, who did not have a book by John before him, but drew upon his recollection of John's oral instructions, should have set down a portion of what the presbyter John said about Mark, and should have sought to characterise it as a fragment of some record by a parenthetic ὡς ἔφην. How one can assert, in view of the concluding words of Eusebius (not, "This was the presbyter John's opinion of Mark, according to Papias," but, "This is what Papias reports about Mark"), that he took all of what he transcribes to be the language of the presbyter, the present writer does not understand (Link, *ThStKr*, 1896, S. 414). The ἔλεγε which introduces the

words of the presbyter (not εἶπε or ἔλεξε) shows that Papias is not giving a stenographic report of a discourse delivered at some time by John, but that, from his recollection of his conversations with his teacher, he means to report fully what John *used* to say about Mark as he had occasion. It is the more certain that this is the meaning of the imperfect here, since no long address follows and no situation is being described. Cf. Kühner-Gerth, i. 143 f. ; Blass, *N.T. Gr.* § 57. 5 (Eng. trans. § 57. 5) ; more specially a remark of Birt (*Das antike Buchwesen*, 483 ; *GK*, i. 872 ; and, in general, the whole discussion, 871–889), which is largely dependent on Klostermann, *Das Marcusev.* 1867,—by far the most important work on this Gospel,—326–336.

15. (P. 444.) The right interpretation of ἑρμηνευτὴς Πέτρου γενόμενος which almost alone found favour in the early Church (above, pp. 442 f., 450 f., n. 12) is represented by Michaelis, *Einl.* 1052 ; Fritzsche, *Ev. Marci*, xxvi ; Thiersch, *Versuch*, 181 ; Klostermann, 329, with whom the present writer expressed his agreement ; *GK*, i. 878–882. The older view, again contended for by Th. Mandel, in opposition to the present writer, *Vorgeschichte der öffentlichen Wirksamkeit Jesu*, 1892, S. 325–332, namely, that Mark, as Peter's interpreter in Rome, translated his sermons into *Latin*, rests upon untenable premises which cannot be indicated here in passing. What had this office of interpreter on the part of Mark, which lasted for only a few months, to do with his Gospel, concerning which " the presbyter John " speaks ? This also has weight against the view of Schlatter (*Die Kirche von Jerusalem vom J. 70-130*, s. 52) that Mark in Jerusalem, *i.e.* before the year 44, interpreted into Greek the Aramaic discourses of Peter for the Hellenistic portion of the Jerusalem Church. To the opposition to the writer's view by A. Link, *ThStKr*, 1896, S. 405–436, it may be briefly replied : (1) Since John, using ἑρμηνευτὴς Πέτρου γενόμενος without the article, does not say that Mark was *the* interpreter of Peter, but that he was or became *an* interpreter, Link's remark (410) that Mark was by no means the only channel of acquaintance with the narratives of Peter, and hence could not be called Peter's interpreter outright in the sense which the present writer maintained, is little to the point. John's statement leaves room for ten other interpreters besides Mark, and also for the fact that in numberless instances Peter spoke in public without the help of any interpreter whatever. One hesitates to refer to such passages as Eph. iii. 7 ; Col. i. 23, 25 ; Gal. iv. 16. (2) The remark (411) that on the writer's interpretation the words in question, "become perfectly useless and meaningless," seems of no greater value. For without them the following ὅσα ἐμνημόνευσεν hangs in the air, as no man could guess what or whom Mark remembered in his writing. He might just as well have been a disciple of Jesus, the lack of order (τάξις) would remain unexcused, and the praise which accompanies the admission of this deficiency would be unjustified. Even if one adopts (as does Link, 414) the impossible construction which makes Papias' added explanation the words of John, John's first complete sentence is still meaningless without ἑρμηνευτὴς Πέτρου γενόμενος rightly understood. (3) As to the claim that the words in question, on the writer's interpretation, should follow the main proposition (413), he must decline to discuss the point with a scholar who thinks it necessary (413, note 1) to inform him that in Acts i. 24 (προσευξάμενοι εἶπαν) the praying is indicated as the medium of the saying ! See examples in Kühner-Gerth, i. 197 f., 199, n. 8, and Blass, § 58. 4 (Eng. trans. § 58. 4). (4) When,

in *GK*, i. 879, the writer questioned whether Mark of Jerusalem would have been a suitable interpreter for the Galilean Peter, he intended, of course, that everyone acquainted with the subject should recall that a knowledge of *Greek* was at least as general, and probably much more general, in Galilee, with its large non-Jewish population, than in Jerusalem and Judæa. To be confuted with the information (Link, 419) that the differences between the Aramaic dialect of Galilee and that of Judea were insignificant, is something of a surprise. (5) The idea that Mark accompanied Peter as interpreter on all his missionary journeys (418, 426 ff.) is inconsistent with the little that we know. Until about the year 63, Peter was, so far as we know (pp. 165-172, above), a preacher of the circumcision in the Holy Land and the neighbouring regions, and certainly went no farther than Antioch, and there only on a visit. Mark, on the other hand, after 44, was a missionary helper in the company, first, of Paul and Barnabas, then of Barnabas alone, and then again of Paul ; and it is highly improbable that he was ever long in Peter's company before 63, when Peter came to Rome. The expressions παρηκολουθηκώς τινι (Papias in Eus. iii. 39. 15, in relation to Jesus or Peter ; cf. xxxix. 4, 7 ; Just. *Dial.* ciii.), or ἀκολουθήσας τινι (Clement in Eus. vi. 14. 6, p. 448, above), or ἀκόλουθός τινος (Eus. ii. 15, p. 449, above), or ἀκόλουθος γενόμενός τινι (Epiph. *Hær.* li. 6)=*sectator* (Iren. iii. 1. 1, 10. 6 ; Clem. (Latin trans.), p. 448, above), denote, not a travelling companion but a disciple, who has for some time enjoyed the instruction of a teacher and lived in familiar intercourse with him, and are occasionally replaced by μαθητής (Iren. iii. 1. 1 ; Chrysost. *Hom.* i. *in Matt.*), ἀκουστής (Iren. v. 33. 4), γνώριμος καὶ φοιτητὴς γεγονώς (Eus. *Dem.* iii. 5. 89), and similar expressions. But when such a disciple imparts the instructions of his teacher to others, he becomes his interpreter, because through him the absent or departed teacher addresses those who would otherwise not hear or understand him. This conception, which is presented by the real signification of the word (Xenophon, *Anab.* ii. 3. 17, ἔλεγε πρῶτος Τισσαφέρνης δι᾽ ἑρμηνέως), is everywhere adhered to, whether the term is applied to the disciple who hands on the instruction of his teacher, to the poet in relation to the Muse, or the prophet in relation to the Pythia or to Apollo, or to Hermes the messenger and interpreter of the gods, or, as among us, to the musical performer, the actor, and the reciter in relation to the composer and the poet (*GK*, i. 878 ff.). (6) What Clement, *Strom.* vii. 106, says of the founders of sects who appeared in the post-apostolic time is undoubtedly instructive : καθάπερ ὁ Βασιλείδης, κἂν Γλαυκίαν ἐπιγράφηται διδάσκαλον, ὡς αὐχοῦσιν αὐτοί, τὸν Πέτρου ἑρμηνέα· ὡσαύτως δὲ καὶ Οὐαλεντῖνον Θεοδᾷ διακηκοέναι φέρουσιν, γνώριμος δὲ οὗτος γεγόνει Παύλου. With regard to the text, cf. *Forsch.* iii. 125. When Link (432) claims, in opposition to the present writer, that Glaukias is called the interpreter of Peter, not by the Basilidians but by Clement, this also must be considered an error ; for after κἂν ἐπιγράφηται, which already shows that Basilides claimed Glaukias as his teacher in order to recommend his doctrines, ὡς αὐχοῦσιν αὐτοί would be quite redundant, if it referred to the same relation. The phrase serves, therefore, to introduce the following τὸν Πέτρου ἑρμηνέα. Moreover, Clement does not omit to show by αὐτοί, which otherwise would be meaningless, that they do indeed boast that this Glaukias was *the* or *an* interpreter of Peter, but that he for his part by no means cares to guarantee the claim. Mark, too, is never so designated by Clement (p. 448 above). The Παύλου γνώριμος of the Valentinians with reference to Theodas (*Forsch.* iii. 122–126) corresponds to the ἑρμηνεύς of the Basilidians regarding Glaukias. Now it is evident that both these alleged disciples of the apostles are brought forward as bearers of a secret tradition, and that this can be brought into rational connection with Glaukias' possible service as interpreter to Peter, even less readily than the composition of a Gospel can be connected with Mark's supposed service in a similar capacity. Here too, then, ἑρμηνεύς is figuratively meant. It cannot be an accident, however, that the term is applied to the medium of the secret tradition between Peter and Basilides, and not to Theodas who stands similarly between Paul and Valentinus. In the school of Basilides, as in that of Valentinus, there was a peculiar Gospel (*GK*, ii. 748, 771). Neither was ascribed to an apostle, but each school believed that it could appeal to a disciple of Peter, or a disciple of Paul, as the transmitter of Gospel narratives, just as well as the Church could. Theodas corresponded to Luke, and Glaukias to Mark. The Basilidians, who boasted that their Glaukias was *the* or *an* interpreter of Peter, knew the Church tradition of Mark's relation to Peter, and imitated it. In another way this was done about 150 A.D. by the author and admirer of the εὐαγγέλιον κατὰ Πέτρον, in which Peter does not use an interpreter, but speaks in his own person (*Grundriss*, S. 30 f.).

16. (P. 444.) Iren. iii. 11. 7: "Qui autem Jesum separant a Christo, et impassibilem perseverasse Christum, passum vero Jesum dicunt, id quod secundum Marcum est præferentes evangelium, cum amore veritatis legentes illud, corrigi possunt." Comparing i. 26. 1 (cf. iii. 11. 1; vol. i. 515, n. 4), there can be no doubt that the Cerinthians are meant; and it is obvious why they preferred the Gospel of Mark, which begins with the bap' 3m. The misunderstandings which have been occasioned by Epiphanius, *Hær.* xxviii. 5, xxx. 3, and Philaster, *Hær.* xxxvi., who in this instance depends on Epiphanius, require no discussion here (cf. *GK*, ii. 730; Hümpel, *De Errore Christolog. in Epist. Jo.*, 1897, p. 68 ff.).

§ 52. TITLE, PLAN, AND CONCLUSION OF MARK'S GOSPEL.

The words ἀρχὴ τοῦ εὐαγγελίου Ἰησοῦ Χριστοῦ (n. 1), with which the author of the Gospel according to Mark begins his book, are of such a character that they must have given rise to the attempt, even at a very early date, to construe them as the subject or predicate of a sentence concluded in vv. 2–3, or, if ver. 2 was taken parenthetically, in ver. 3, or, in case the whole of vv. 2–3 was treated as a parenthesis, in ver. 4. The very number of such attempts to construe the words argues against them

all. Further, while it must be admitted that the Greek
of the Gospel is far from classical, it must nevertheless be
regarded as improbable that an author, who in the rest of
his book does not show any inclination to write periodic
sentences, should, without any apparent necessity, begin
the same with such an ambiguous and at best extremely
clumsy construction. A decisive argument against all
these attempts is the fact that they are based upon the
impossible presupposition that εὐαγγέλιον can be used to
designate the Gospel history, and that not in the sense of
"a recording or accounting" of the facts (*historia*), but
of "recorded facts" (*res gestæ*). The baptism and preaching of John the Baptist might possibly be treated as the
beginning of the gospel history in the latter sense, namely,
as the first one of the facts which it was the business of
the Gospel, *i.e.* the Christian preaching, to report and to
proclaim (Acts x. 37, xiii. 24 ; cf. § 48). But it could
never be considered the beginning of the proclamation of
those facts. But the latter is the only sense in which
εὐαγγέλιον was used in the apostolic age.

It may therefore be considered as certain that the
first five words of the Gospel are to be taken independently, and to be treated as a title prefixed to the book by
the author; since to suppose that Mark meant to say,
"Herewith I begin the Gospel of Jesus Christ," involves
a whole tangle of anachronisms. It is a well-known fact
that among the Latins, the Greeks, and the Syrians, it
was a habit among the scribes of the Middle Ages to mark
the transition from one document to another in the same
codex by inserting ἐτελέσθη or ἐπληρώθη (*explicit*) and
ἄρχεται (*incipit*) before or after the customary title (n. 2).
That in this case the ἄρχεται or ἀρχή, which means the
same thing, was not the author's own statement, requires
no proof. Leaving out of account the fact that these
formulæ are not found in the oldest MSS. extant, they
presuppose the binding together of separate writings in

one codex. In the present case, however, it is not a question of the particular way in which a copyist indicated the fact that a new book was begun at a certain point, but, if we may accept the unanimous tradition, we are dealing with words which were always a part of Mark's Gospel. But to suppose that an author should have begun his book by saying to his readers, " Here my book begins," or " Now I begin," would be an absurd conjecture. Such an idea is also impossible, because then Mark would have called his book not only *a* Gospel, but *the* Gospel of Jesus Christ. Even if he had said "*a* Gospel" it would have been an anachronism, because the name εὐαγγέλιον was not used to designate a writing, or a number of writings, until after the beginning of the second century, certainly not in the apostolic age (above, p. 387 f.). But even granting that here the individual author may have anticipated the general development of ecclesiastical language, or that Mark i. 1 was not written until 120, still, in designating his work "*the* Gospel," *i.e.* the only Gospel which exists or has a right to exist, and, more than this, in calling it "the Gospel of Jesus Christ," the author would make himself guilty of a presumption which is incomprehensible. The title which Mark gives his book is not εὐαγγέλιον 'Ι. Χρ., but ἀρχὴ τοῦ εὐαγγελίου 'Ιησοῦ Χριστοῦ ; for it is entirely self-evident that, if the words are to be taken as a title, they have reference to the whole book and not to any one of its chapters, be it longer or shorter. Aside from the fact that the title applies very inappropriately to what follows it immediately (i. 2–13), if the title covered only part of the book, we should expect a number of chapters, each with its own special title ; this, however, is not what we find. Accepting the words as a title, they are not to be compared with titles like *Bereshith* or Γένεσις κόσμου at the beginning of the first book in the O.T., which were invented at a late date by learned editors or ignorant scribes. It is rather to be ascribed to the

author himself, or perhaps to the redactor or editor of
our Mark, like the titles of the prophetic books of the
O.T., of the Proverbs, of Revelation, of the *Antiquities*
of Josephus, and of the work of Irenæus against heresies.
In the case of such titles it does not matter at all whether
or not the author mentions his own name in the title, or
whether a name which may occur in the title be that of
the real or only of an alleged author, or whether it is only
represented as such. It must be taken for granted that
such a title characterises rightly the content of the book,
and indicates the subject which the author intended to
discuss, at least when he began his work ; only, of course,
due allowance must be made for the *a potiori fit denomi-
natio* in a title designed to sum up in a word the varied
contents of a comprehensive work.

Mark purposes, therefore, to set forth in his book the
beginning of the Gospel of Jesus Christ. Since his work
is in the form of a narrative, ἀρχή cannot be meant in the
sense of "cause, principle, ground" (Prov. i. 7, viii. 22 ;
Sirach xxix. 21 ; Col. i. 18 ; Rev. iii. 14), but is to be
understood only in the usual sense of "beginning." The
conception of origin is, however, involved ; for how is it
possible to describe the beginning of a thing without
indicating its origin ? An ἀρχή is always an ἀρχὴ γενέσεως
(Wisdom of Solomon vi. 23, vii. 5). In his account he
intends to answer the question how the Gospel of Christ
began, and therewith also the question how the Gospel of
Christ originated. In a certain sense the question is
answered at the outset by the very terms which Mark
chooses to designate the Gospel, for Gospel of Jesus Christ
means in this passage, as everywhere else in the N.T., the
message of salvation brought into the world by Jesus,
which was preached by Him first, and which now, when
it is no longer proclaimed by Jesus Himself but by His
ambassadors, bears upon it the seal of its author (above,
p. 377 f.). A fuller answer of the same character is to be

found in Heb. ii. 3 ; the Gospel began with its first proclamation by Jesus, the Apostle of God (Heb. iii. 1), and
after He ceased to speak to men directly it was continued
by those who had heard the preaching of the great original
Evangelist. This same idea, which is common to the
whole of the N.T., is given noteworthy expression in Acts
i. 1, where all of Jesus' work and teaching set forth in the
third Gospel is characterised as the beginning of a continuous work. The same thought is to be found in Acts
x. 36 f., though presented from a different point of view,
—the beginning of the proclamation of the good tidings
which God sent to the people of Israel was not through
John and his preaching, but after the baptism and preaching of John, through Jesus Christ, the original Evangelist
(cf. Eph. ii. 17). This is exactly Mark's thought. In the
apostolic preaching there was never wanting some reference
to Jesus' forerunner and something showing the relation
between Jesus and John, who in his turn was connected
with the O.T. revelation. Nor could this backward reference be omitted in an historical account of the beginning
of this preaching. It is wanting in no one of our Gospels ;
but what Mark says about the Baptist in i. 2–8, and his
notice, showing the connection between Jesus' history and
the work of the Baptist in i. 9–13, is so outlinear and so
brief that it cannot possibly be the form in which the
tradition was used for the instruction of converts and in
the missionary preaching. He makes it so, because what
he set out to portray was not the preliminaries, but the
beginning of the Gospel of Jesus.

The discussion of the subject proper begins in i. 14
with the sentence, " After John was delivered up, Jesus
came into Galilee, *preaching the Gospel of God*, and
saying, ' The time is fulfilled and the kingdom of God
is at hand, repent ye and *believe the Gospel.* ' " This
sentence, which gives an outline view of Jesus' entire
ministry, is in keeping with the title of the book, and

goes to confirm the interpretation of the same given above. Jesus' mission is represented to be the proclamation to men of God's good tidings, and He Himself urges upon them faith in this message. While it is true that, according to other traditions, Jesus in quoting from Isa. lxi. 1 makes use of the word translated by the Greek εὐαγγέλιον or of the corresponding verb (Luke iv. 18, vii. 22 ; Matt. xi. 5), nevertheless, in comparison with similar passages in the other Gospels, Mark's use of the word in his description of Jesus' life-work (ver. 14) and in the summary which he gives of the essential contents of Jesus' preaching (ver. 15), also the comparatively frequent recurrence of the word in the further course of this Gospel (n. 3), all go to prove that in using it Mark had in mind always the purpose of the book indicated in its title. This is to be seen also in the separate narratives which show how the program indicated in i. 14 was carried out. In contrast to the brevity which characterises the sketch that precedes the verse in which Jesus' ministry is outlined,—a brevity which renders single passages in the same so obscure as to be scarcely intelligible (especially i. 13),—from i. 16 on the narratives are remarkable for their graphic clearness and for a fulness of detail which is certainly not essential (n. 4). Even if such a conclusion were not necessary from a comparison of Mark's account with the presentation of the same facts in the other Gospels, the careful reader would still be compelled to admit from a comparison of Mark's style with that of accounts presenting different material — as for instance the Fourth Gospel or Josephus—that Mark has not only a predilection for vivid and clear narrative, but possesses distinguished ability in this direction. His description of the features and movements of those speaking or acting, the constant use of direct discourse in reporting chance remarks and replies, the use of numerous synonyms in the discourses, repetition in full of words repeated in spoken discourse, and the use of elliptical expressions

customary in conversation but not in written discourse,—
all tend to give Mark's style a dramatic quality. If all
this is artificial and not natural, then certainly Mark was
an adept at *artem arte celare*. That this was the case
is, however, quite improbable, in view of the thoroughly
clumsy way in which Mark uses language. These little
touches never make the impression of being designed ; to
write in this way is the author's second nature. What he
did keep clearly before himself, however, was his purpose
to set forth the history of the beginning of the gospel.

In the *first* section (i. 16–45) we see how the preaching
which Jesus declared to be His essential vocation (i. 38 f.)
was accompanied from the first by miracles which attested
the effective power of His word, and which contributed
much to the spread of the conviction throughout all Galilee
that Jesus was a teacher with full authority from God, and
that His teaching, in contrast to the instruction of the
rabbis based upon the traditions, was a new and powerful
doctrine (i. 22, 27 f.).   At first Jesus alone is the preacher;
He silences the demons who proclaim Him the Holy One
of God (i. 24 f., 34, cf. iii. 11 f.), and forbids the man
whom He has healed to publish what had been done for
him (i. 44).   But just as He Himself discloses, at the very
beginning (i. 16–20), His intention of winning helpers in
His ministry, so He is totally unable to hinder those who
have been helped by Him from becoming at once tireless
proclaimers of His deeds (i. 45, cf. vii. 36).   Every word in
the concluding sentence of this first section is consciously
chosen—ἤρξατο, which is not altogether without significance
(cf. v. 20, also i. 1) ; κηρύσσειν, everywhere else used of the
preaching of the gospel (cf. i. 14, 38, 39, iii. 14, v. 20, vi.
12, xiii. 10, xiv. 9, cf. i. 4, 7) ; the added πολλά, which indicates that when the preaching is begun it is not to end
at once ; and, finally, τὸν λόγον without any addition, used
elsewhere of the gospel (ii. 2, iv. 14–33), to describe the
report which the man who had been healed circulated where-

ever he went. The *second section* (ii. 1–iii. 6) shows how
Jesus' preaching, attested as it was by His works, especially
His proclamation of the forgiveness of sins, and the freedom of His life and teaching from asceticism and slavish
observance of the law, induced constant opposition on the
part of the religious teachers whose influence had been
dominant up to this time, and made Him more and more
the object of their deadly hatred. The *third section*
(iii. 7–vi. 13) begins with a general description of the
spread of Jesus' fame throughout all Palestine and the
adjoining regions, and of the effect which this had in
widening the circle of those among whom Jesus had to
work (iii. 7–12). This seems to have influenced Jesus to
make free choice from among His hearers of twelve, with
a view to sending them out as *preachers* (iii. 13–19).
The section thus begun is concluded in a general way with
the account of the first mission of these twelve (vi. 7–13).
It is noteworthy that in both these accounts the name
apostle, which is only used by Mark once (vi. 30), is
avoided ; also, that the commission of the disciples here
described is expressly declared to be the first of its kind,
and is called the beginning of the sending out of twelve
preachers. Finally, in the account of their choosing, the
fact is not to be overlooked that, while its ultimate purpose
is indicated to be their later commission to preach, and
though they engaged in this work at once (vi. 12), the
immediate purpose and the one first mentioned is that
they may be constantly with Jesus (iii. 14, ἵνα ὦσιν μετ'
αὐτοῦ καὶ ἵνα ἀποστέλλῃ αὐτοὺς κηρύσσειν). Through their
intercourse with the first preacher of the gospel they
were to be trained for their future vocation as preachers.
Thereby Jesus intends to make true in the case of these
men the words He had spoken to some at the beginning
of His preaching in Galilee (i. 17). What is recorded
between the choice of the apostles and their first commission to preach, shows how Jesus trained the Twelve in

that independence of judgment and knowledge requisite
for the exercise of their calling.   When on one occasion
His relatives, apparently His nearest kinsmen, expressed
the opinion that the immoderate zeal with which He gave
Himself to His work was deranging His mind, and His
opponents declared Him to be possessed by an evil spirit
(iii. 21 f., cf. ver. 30), He declares those to be His true
relatives who, notwithstanding these opinions, give heed
to His word (iii. 31–35); and, while He preaches the
secret of the kingdom of God to the multitude in parables,
to His disciples—among whom, as is evident from the
peculiar wording of iv. 10, the Twelve primarily are meant
—He not only interprets the individual parables spoken to
the people (iv. 14–20, 34), but declares them to be those
chosen ones to whom this secret is entrusted (iv. 11).
This secret they are to learn to understand, even when it
is concealed in figurative language (iv. 13), and one day
are to reveal it to the world (iv. 21–25).

Of the parables spoken on this particular day, the
great number of which is referred to repeatedly (iv. 2, 33),
three are recorded, among them one that is peculiar to
Mark's Gospel (iv. 26–29).   The first parable explains the
differing reception which the word—used thus alone, and
referring, therefore, to the gospel preached by Jesus and
to be preached by the apostles—receives among men as
due to the different qualities of heart to be found in the
hearers.   The second parable shows that the kingdom of
God, once it has been brought into the world through
Jesus' preaching, has within itself germs which will develop
to the harvest, and that, too, without direct intervention
on His part.   The third parable shows that the small
beginnings of this kingdom are no reason for doubting
that ultimately it will compass the entire world. · In the
narratives which follow, iv. 35–vi. 6, the relation to the
apostles and their future calling remains in the background, though attention is called repeatedly to their

presence or participation in the work (v. 31, 37, vi. 1,
otherwise in Matt. ix. 22–26, xiii. 54). Not until the
account of the commission and instruction of the Twelve
(vi. 7–11) is the reader again reminded that the "being
with Jesus," which was their special privilege (iii. 14) and
which was denied to others, without their being forbidden
on this account to make known the grace that they had
received (v. 18–20), was intended primarily to prepare
the disciples for their vocation as preachers of the gospel.

This relation of the history to the apostles and their
future calling comes out more clearly in the *fourth section*
(vi. 14–x. 52). Jesus appears here not so much engaged
in work as a preacher and prophet among the people, as in
training His apostles. He avoids the principal scene of
His earlier labours, moves frequently, and changes constantly His place of abode, though there are times when
His sympathy for the multitudes leads Him to mingle
with them, or to help individuals among them who are
in need (vi. 34, 45, viii. 2, 10, 13). He removes to the
boundaries of Jewish territory and goes beyond the same
(vii. 24, 31, viii. 27), not with the intention of preaching
to the Gentiles, but in order to escape contact with the
crowds and His enemies, that He may devote Himself
entirely to the instruction of His disciples, as expressly
stated in ix. 30 f. In the accounts of the miraculous feeding the part taken by the disciples is emphasised more
strongly than in the parallel accounts, especially those of
Matthew and John (vi. 37–39, 41, viii. 6). In vi. 52,
which has no parallel in the other Gospels, and the account
in viii. 14–21, which is much more detailed and more
emphatic than in Matt. xvi. 5–12, these occurrences are
treated altogether from the point of view of a practical
instruction of the disciples. They are to learn not only
to believe in Jesus' miraculous power, but out of what
Jesus furnishes them also to satisfy thousands of those
who hear the word. Where the superstitious opinions

concerning Jesus, produced by His work so far, are mentioned for the first time (vi. 14 f.), the occasion is made
use of to introduce an episode about the death of the
Baptist (vi. 17–29). When we compare this account,
which is very full, with the exceedingly brief notice in
i. 2–8, it does not seem that it is inserted for its own sake,
but as a prophecy with reference to the death of the
mightier preacher (cf. ix. 12 f.). In the second instance
where these superstitious opinions are mentioned—this
time by the apostles in answer to a question by Jesus
(viii. 27 f.)—the design is to bring out strongly the independence of faith and knowledge developed in the disciples
under the influence of Jesus' teaching and work.

But progress in this development is slow and painful.
Although it was not necessary any longer for Him to ask
the reproving question, "Have ye not yet faith ?" (iv. 40,
cf. *per contra*, ix. 23 f.), He did, nevertheless, have constantly to lament their lack of insight (vi. 52, viii. 17–21),
their failure to understand His purposes (viii. 33, ix. 32),
their want of determination and presence of mind (ix.
18 f., 28 f.), and their failure to make unselfish sacrifice of
themselves (ix. 33–50, x. 28–31, 35-45). They are still
much affected with the hardness of heart, the unbelief, and
the superstition that characterised their countrymen (vi.
49–52, viii. 11–15, ix. 19). It is not to be denied, however, that the governing thought, which in the earlier
sections is everywhere noticeable, in the whole of the
plan, in the details of its elaboration, and especially in
the choice of material, becomes less and less prominent as
the narrative proceeds. Especially in the *fifth section*
(xi. 1–xvi. 8), where the closing scenes of Jesus' life are
described, does interest in the material itself, without
which no history of Jesus' public ministry would be
possible, predominate over the particular point of view
from which this material is handled in Mark's Gospel. A
certain parallelism is noticeable between Jesus' work in

Galilee and in Jerusalem, which shows itself sometimes in the use of similar language. Jesus begins His work in Jerusalem with deeds (xi. 1–10, 15–18) and teachings (xi. 18 = i. 22, cf. xi. 17, xii. 14, 35, 37, 38, xiv. 49) which arouse the enthusiasm of the people, only to fall back upon the use of parables, of which but one example is recorded. Here, as there, He encounters an alliance between the Pharisees and the Herodians (xii. 13 = iii. 6). Here also in these circles there are those who are drawn to Jesus, and in whom He finds something to commend (xii. 34 = x. 21). And finally, in Jerusalem as in Galilee, He devotes Himself to the instruction of His disciples (xiii. 1 ff.). In this instruction a prominent place is given to a series of statements about the call of the apostles to preach (xiii. 9–13), which are introduced by Matthew—in part also by Luke—in a different connection. Repeatedly notice is taken of the presence of the disciples, or of the impression which something has made upon them (xi. 11, 14, 20 f., xiii. 1–5), and the fact recalled that their task is the commission of Jesus' word to others (xiii. 37), and that the Gospel is for the whole world (xiv. 9). But notwithstanding all this, one observes that the material is not subordinated to the governing thought of the book. Very possibly this thought would have become more prominent again at the close. But the book was never finished.

It may be regarded as one of the most certain of critical conclusions, that the words ἐφοβοῦντο γάρ, xvi. 8, are the last words in the book which were written by the author himself (n. 5). How early and how generally it was felt to be unfortunate that Mark had broken the thread of his narrative with these words in the midst of his account of Jesus' resurrection just as this account was begun, is attested by the existence and circulation of two additions, which were attached to the Gospel in order to supply this lack. The first positive witness for the former of these—xvi. 9–20 in the *textus receptus*, designated

in what follows by A—is that of Irenæus (iii. 10. 6 ;
GK, ii. 924). That it was a part of Mark, however, is
presupposed also in Tatian's *Diatessaron*, in which the
substance of the pericope was incorporated (n. 5) ; for it
has not been shown as yet that a passage of any considerable length was taken by Tatian from a source other
than one of the canonical Gospels. Apparently Justin also
was familiar with the passage (*GK*, i. 515). It must
therefore have been appended to the Gospel as early as
the first half of the second century. While there is no
trace of the pericope, or of a substitute for it, to be found
in Tertullian and Cyprian, Clement of Alexandria and
Origen, Cyril of Jerusalem and Athanasius, and numerous
other authors who would have had occasion to make use
of it had it been known to them, nevertheless from the
middle of the fourth century on it became more and more
widely circulated. Whereas in Eusebius' time it was to
be found in only a few Greek MSS. (*GK*, ii. 913), in
those that have come down from the fifth century (Codd.
ACDE, etc.) it is found regularly, also in the different
Syriac versions, with the exception of Syr. Sin. and in
the Gothic and later Egyptian (Memphitic) translations.
It is witnessed, further, by Chrysostom, Epiphanius, Marcus
Eremita, and the *Apostolic Constitutions*. The first to
testify to its existence in Alexandria is Didymus ; in
Latin North Africa, Augustine ; in Italy, apart from
Justin and Tatian, who in a sense are to be reckoned
here, and some doubtful notices (n. 5), Ambrose, the
Latin MSS. of the Gospels used by Jerome, and Jerome
himself, who gave the A text a fixed place in the West
by adopting it in his revision of the Latin N.T.

Besides this addition, there is another much shorter
conclusion to the Gospel designated here by B, which was
circulated somewhat widely at a comparatively early date
(n. 6). This text is found (1) as an integral part of
Mark's Gospel in a fifth century MS. (k), which represents

the oldest form of the Latin text of the Gospels, showing much agreement with Cyprian's citations.   (2) In
several Greek uncials of the seventh to ninth centuries
(LT¹Ψ) and several Greek cursives and Ethiopic MSS.,
only that here as if giving a choice between the two, the
A text is added also partly with introductory and inter-
posed remarks which give evidence that these additions
are doubtful and circulated only here and there.   (3) On
the other hand, it appears on the margin of a Greek cursive
of the tenth century (Ev. 274), A being inserted in the
text.   This is the case also in the latest Syriac version
made in Alexandria in the seventh century by Thomas
of Heraclea, who compared Greek MSS. (*GK*, ii. 922).
(4) Finally, it is probable that the scribe who copied the
Codex Vaticanus was familiar with B, not A.   There is
also a Coptic MS. which seems to depend upon an original having the B text (*GK*, ii. 912, 921).   A third
recension (C), namely, that in which Mark's Gospel is
concluded with xvi. 8, is found (1) in the two oldest
Greek MSS. extant (אB); (2) according to Eusebius'
testimony in " almost all," and these the " accurate " MSS.
of his time, which Jerome also declares to have been the
case still in his time (*GK*, ii. 919); (3) in one of the two
oldest forms of the Syriac translation (Ss).   To the above
is to be added (4) the silent witness of authors who betray
acquaintance with neither A nor B, and (5) the indirect
witness of the B recension.   From the witnesses cited
above under 2, 4, for the B text, it is clear that in the
regions where B originated and was circulated A did not
become known until later; nor is it hardly conceivable
that B should have been invented where A had been
handed down by the tradition.   The B text cannot be
traced back beyond the fourth century, although it may
have originated in the third century, and apparently in
Egypt, whence it found its way into single MSS. in Latin
Africa.   The A text, which was the only one known to

Irenæus, originated probably in Asia Minor before the middle of the second century, whence it spread without resistance to Italy and Gaul, whereas in Palestine though known it was rejected by scholars. And in Syria, where its contents were very early made known by its incorporation in the *Diatessaron,* it had to struggle for its existence.

The way in which both the additions harmonise with the beginning of the book, show that they were written after careful consideration. The statement with which both A and B conclude, namely, that the apostles, authorised by the risen Christ, preached the gospel throughout the world, is a suitable conclusion for a book which, according to its title, was intended to set forth the beginning and origin of the gospel of Christ. In B this is all that is said, and at the same time expressed in ecclesiastical language which has a comparatively modern sound. The only thing it contains in the nature of a conclusion to the interrupted narrative is the brief statement that the women fulfilled the commission given them by the angel. The apparent contradiction with xvi. 8—which, after all, is only apparent—was partly removed, as in codex k, by changes made later in xvi. 8 (*GK,* ii. 920 f.). The contradiction was, however, little felt, because the passage was written more with reference to xvi. 7 (cf. Luke xxiv. 9 f., 23 ; John xx. 18). The A text is of an entirely different character. To begin with, it is very easy to see that the text is made up of different elements. In vv. 9–13 and vv. 19–20 there is no narrative such as we find elsewhere in the Gospels, especially in Mark. Compared with these sentences, the meagre sketch in i. 2–13, which precedes the account of Jesus' preaching, shows ample breadth of description, and is full of graphic detail, while the use of direct discourse (i. 7 f., 11) lends it a certain dramatic vigour. In the addition, on the other hand, not a single word spoken by the risen Christ

at the time of His appearances to His disciples is reproduced, nor is an account given of a single act.   In short,
it is not *narrated*, but *chronicled*, that Jesus appeared
first to Mary Magdalene, and then to two unnamed
persons going into the country, with the statement in
both cases that their tidings were not credited by the
others (xvi. 9–13).   At the close, moreover, (xvi. 19–20),
in the fewest possible words, the ascension, Jesus' exaltation to the right hand of God, and the entire missionary
work of the apostles are outlined.   The sources from
which these statements are taken are not hard to find :
xvi. 9–11 is from John xx. 1–18, with the insertion
of a phrase from Luke viii. 2 ; xvi. 12–13 is from Luke
xxiv. 13–35, the dependence being in part verbal (Luke
xxiv. 13, δύο ἐξ αὐτῶν . . . πορευόμενοι εἰς κώμην), but with
omission of all details.   The language of ver. 19 is that
of the Apostolic Creed, not of the Gospels, while that of
ver. 20 resembles the apostolic teaching (Heb. ii. 3 f. ;
Rom. x. 14 f., xv. 18 f. ; Col. i. 6 ; 1 Tim. iii. 16 ; Acts
xv. 12).

Vv. 14–18 are strikingly different from the verses
between which they stand (vv. 9–13, 19–20).   This is
a real narrative, being in its substance an address to
the apostles by the risen Christ, with a brief statement
of the circumstances under which they were spoken.
Further, there is nothing in the passage betraying its
dependence upon a canonical Gospel ; while, on the other
hand, its style does not, like that of vv. 19–20, differ
from the classic style which characterises the Gospels.
xvi. 14 is cited in Latin by Jerome from a Greek MS.
with a very original addition (n. 7).   When the Lord
reproaches the disciples for their unbelief and hardness of
heart, they excuse themselves, saying, "This unrighteous
and unbelieving world is under Satan (Satan's power),
who by the agency of unclean spirits prevents (men) from
laying hold of the true power of God.   Therefore reveal

now thy righteousness." Everyone sees at once that this
is not a gloss written by some copyist, but that it is a
bit of conversation handed down by the tradition, which
is not only in perfect accord with the spirit of that time
(Acts i. 6), but which suits also the context in the
Textus receptus. Whereas in the latter the account
passes very abruptly from reproof of the disciples' unbelief
to the commission in which they are bidden to preach the
gospel to the whole world, in the passage as cited by
Jerome the necessary transition is supplied. In the excuse
which they offer, the apostles confess themselves guilty (cf.
Mark ix. 24), so that it can be taken for granted without
any statement to this effect that the exhortation, "Be not
faithless, but believing" (John xx. 27), is already more
than half realised. And the request of the apostles that
Jesus reveal His righteousness at once, i.e. set up His
kingdom, thereby destroying the power of Satan and
his emissaries in the world, is followed naturally by the
promise with which He sends them out into the wide and
wicked world (xvi. 17 f., cf. Mark vi. 7, 13, ix. 1, 28 f. ;
Luke ix. 1 f., x. 17–20). This fragment, which Jerome
preserved but did not incorporate among the variants in
his revision of the Latin Bible, restores the original
connection of the passage. The words are not, however,
original in Mark, and could not have been written by the
author of the A text ; for then it would be impossible to
explain why they have disappeared from all the Greek
MSS. and from the Syriac and Latin texts which have A.
That Satan and his emissaries have power in the world
(John xii. 31, xvi. 11 ; 2 Cor. iv. 4 ; Eph. vi. 11 f. ;
1 Pet. v. 8), that the world is lying in wickedness
(1 John v. 19), and that the apostles longed for the
coming of the kingdom of Christ and the future world in
which righteousness dwells (Acts i. 6 ; 2 Tim. iv. 8), were
certainly not thoughts so offensive to Bible readers and
copyists of the second century that they felt constrained,

when they found such thoughts in their copies of the
Gospels, to cut them out of the text.   Then there is the
other difficulty of explaining the incredible thoroughness
with which this was done in all quarters.   The original
form of this narrative which is preserved by Jerome must
have been taken from the very source from which the
author of A took this part of his compilation.   It found
its way into the Greek MS. of the Gospel, in which
Jerome found it apparently first as a gloss and then as a
part of the text.   Unless all appearances are greatly
deceptive, this source was rediscovered some years ago
(n. 8).   In an Armenian Evangelistarium belonging
to the year 989, and purporting to be copied from
MSS. of a much earlier date, after Mark xvi. 8 there is
a space left large enough for two lines; then follows the
title written with red ink—" Ariston's, the Presbyter's."
Since the Armenian translation of Eusebius, *H. E.* iii.
39. 4, and the Syriac original on which the Armenian
translation is dependent, transcribe Ἀριστίων with *Ariston*,
and since this Aristion was one of the presbyters who
were Papias' teachers,—from whom also Papias became
acquainted with numerous sayings of Jesus which did
not become canonical and with other gospel traditions, all of which he preserved in his work,—there
is little reason to doubt that this notice has reference
to the Aristion whom Papias makes a personal disciple of Jesus (above, p. 452 f.).   In so far as it states
formally, or seems to imply, that Aristion is the author
of the whole A text, the notice is misleading.   In the
first place, as already shown, the A text is made up
of fragments which are totally different in style; but
neither Papias' fragments nor the account of Eusebius in
which they are incorporated give the impression that
Aristion was engaged at all in literary work, and in
making compilations from the canonical Gospels.   Apart
from this, however, if Aristion were the author of A, it

would be quite impossible to explain how the original form of the narrative could disappear from all the Greek MSS. having the A text, to turn up again suddenly in a Greek MS. in the hands of Jerome. So the fact of the matter must be, rather, that Mark xvi. 14–18 is one of those narratives and traditions (cf. Luke i. 1) of the disciple Aristion which Papias incorporated in his work (Eus. *H. E.* iii. 39. 7, 14). This is confirmed in the most striking manner by a marginal gloss to Rufinus' translation of Eusebius, *H. E.* iii. 39. 9, though inserted by a later hand, which connects Aristion's name with the story taken by Eusebius from Papias, that Justus, called Barsabbas (Acts i. 23), once drank a deadly poison, but was preserved by the grace of the Lord from all harmful effects. Here is an actual case where the promise of Jesus in Mark xvi. 18 is fulfilled. This promise and the narrative of its fulfilment are referred independently to the same Aristion by two different persons acquainted with Papias' work. Papias' work is therefore the source from which the author of A took the middle part of this addition, combining it with material from Luke and John into an indifferent unity. The way for the Lord's rebuke of the disciples' unbelief (ver. 14) is prepared by the statement that the reports of Mary Magdalene and of the two going into the country were discredited (vv. 11, 13), while the sketch of the apostolic missionary work (ver. 20) follows naturally the command and promise of the Lord (vv. 15–18). The fact that the redactor of A left out the sentence, of which we gain our first knowledge from Jerome, does not need special explanation ; since, in constructing a suitable close for Mark's Gospel, he did not need to copy his sources, but to excerpt and to compile them. The very originality of the sentence, which makes it interesting to everyone who is fond of the antique, may have made it appear to him too peculiar and too obscure to form a part of an epilogue so entirely outlinear in character. These

last statements also go to strengthen the conjecture that
the A text was appended to Mark's Gospel in Asia Minor,
where this Gospel was highly esteemed at an early date
(above, p. 444 f.), and that this was done before the middle
of the second century, since, outside of Asia Minor, acquaintance with Aristion's oral narratives and Papias' work
in which these narratives were recorded cannot be presupposed at such an early date.

After what has been said, further proof that A does
not belong to the author of the book is scarcely necessary.
Defenders of this view have undertaken to explain the
later setting aside of this alleged concluding section, on the
ground of objections to the contradictions between its
contents and the other Gospels.   To be sure, the learned
harmonists, from Eusebius on, busied themselves with
these differences along with others (*GK*, ii. 913–918).
But, after all, what do they amount to compared with
those which exist between the evangelists' narratives in
other parts of the gospel history.   The attempt was made,
from the second century on, to modify or to remove such
differences by means of exegesis, more or less artificial, and
by small changes in the text, consisting of removals and
additions ; that, however, a section of this compass, above
all this section, to which authors like Irenæus, Epiphanius,
Chrysostom, Ambrose, and Augustine made no objection,
should have been cut out for such reasons, and the Gospel
of Mark thereby simply mutilated in a passage where
it would be particularly noticeable to every reader and
copyist, is inconceivable, quite as much so as that the work
of the mutilator should have been accepted so widely for
centuries.   To begin with, there are two points in the
language which show that Mark could not have been
the author of A.   (1) Instead of (ἡ) μία (τῶν) σαββάτων, the
only usage current in the Apostolic Church (Mark xvi. 2 ;
Matt. xxviii. 1 ; Luke xxiv. 1 ; John xx. 1, 19 ; Acts xx.
7 ; 1 Cor. xvi. 2), we find in Mark xvi. 9, πρώτη σαββάτου.

which is better Greek (vol. i. p. 19, n. 14), but which does not occur elsewhere in the N.T. (2) Jesus is twice called "The Lord" (xvi. 19, 20), an expression which does not occur elsewhere in the book, and which is not to be found in Matthew, and only rarely in Luke and John. Attention has already been called to the fact that the whole character of the narrative is foreign to Mark, certainly that of xvi. 9–13, 19–20 (above, p. 470 f.). That Mark could not have excerpted portions from Luke and John, as the author of A evidently did, will appear when these Gospels are investigated. They are later than Mark. The content of A is, moreover, of such a character that Mark could not have written it as the conclusion of the narrative begun in xvi. 1, and so as the conclusion of his book. After making the angels repeat the promise of Jesus recorded earlier in xiv. 28 so near the close of the Gospel as xvi. 7, he could not have omitted to mention that the risen Jesus appeared to the disciples in Galilee, and to tell how this took place. But in A the reader thus made expectant does not hear a word about Galilee. Cf. *per contra*, Matt. xxviii. 16 in relation to Matt. xxvi. 32, xxviii. 7. Nor could Mark have omitted to narrate how the women so far recovered from the terror which at first sealed their lips (xvi. 8) as to be able to carry out the angel's commission (xvi. 7), which was undoubtedly the case with Mary Magdalene, whom Mark mentions for the first time in xvi. 1, if we may believe Mark xvi. 10 and all the other traditions.

If it be accepted as proved from what has been said that A is in the same position as B, which no modern scholar is bold enough to claim as original with the author of the book, and that both are later additions, it follows that C is the original text. The same result follows even from the application of the critical canon that, where two mutually exclusive longer texts are opposed to a shorter text from which their origin can be explained, the shorter reading is to be preferred, especially if it has good witnesses

(n. 9). The canon is entirely applicable to the case in
hand; for, in the *first* place, it is perfectly evident that a
text breaking off suddenly with the words ἐφοβοῦντο γάρ,
as does C, must have given rise to attempts to supply the
book, so manifestly incomplete, with a suitable conclusion.
Presupposing, therefore, that C is original, the origin of A
and B is entirely conceivable. In the *second* place, C
is strongly supported by direct and indirect witnesses
(above, p. 469). In the *third* place, we cannot understand
how C could have originated from either A or B. The
assumption that originally C was followed by another
conclusion—here called X—written by the author, which
afterwards disappeared altogether from the tradition (n. 8),
is to be rejected as fanciful, because, as shown, it is unnecessary in explanation of the facts. Whatever form it
may take, this hypothesis, which we may indicate briefly
as C + X, is improbable. Though the N.T. text can be
shown to have met with varying treatment, it has never as
yet been established from ancient citations, nor made really
probable on internal grounds, that a single complete sentence of the original text has disappeared altogether from the
text transmitted in the Church, *i.e.* from all the MSS. of the
original and of the ancient translations. Quite as little
has the opposite been shown to be the case, namely, that
there is a single sentence of the text, transmitted in the
Church and witnessed by all existing sources, which did
not belong originally to the text (n. 9). Here, however,
it is not a question of a short sentence, but the part which
is wanting—which must, therefore, have been lost if
originally in the text—must have been a narrative of
considerable compass (see above, p. 475). Nor is it a case
where the section was of such a character that it could
disappear without notice, because an intelligible connection
remained after it was left out; it is rather the question
of the concluding section, which the reader must await
with interest after what precedes, and the loss of which

must leave the book noticeably incomplete. The most inconceivable supposition of all would be that some one, who was displeased with this alleged genuine conclusion (X), removed the same intentionally, and that this mutilated copy succeeded in entirely replacing the complete exemplars. The mutilation must have been made immediately after the appearance of the book and before it began to circulate, consequently in the region where it was written, and, if the author did not die at the very moment when his work was completed, in the vicinity where he was. Such an intentional setting aside of X would have been a senseless and hopeless undertaking, if the critic who ventured it did not at once furnish a suitable substitute, *i.e.* if the person who mutilated Mark were not at the same time the author of A, the most widely circulated of the spurious conclusions. But if X was set aside by the author or the redactor of A, how are we to explain the origin of all those exemplars, widely circulated until after the fourth century, which at that time were, and in their existing form are, without either the original conclusion (X) or the conclusion which it is alleged was intentionally substituted for it (A)—in other words, all the witnesses for B and C ? It is, of course, conceivable that a recension, C + X, was objected to in various quarters, and that the recension A won friends earlier than we know—before it came into general use in the Church ; but it is absurd to assume that entire Church provinces should have adopted the negative part of this new recension—a mutilation of the Mark which they possessed originally—but not the positive part of the same, *i.e.* the new conclusion. The absurdity is not helped by the assumption (n. 8) that, while the intentional setting aside of X and the appending of xvi. 9–20 took place in the same circles and from similar motives, a period of twenty years or more elapsed between the two processes, during which time the Gospel was widely circulated in its

mutilated form, without as yet having been completed
again.   It is inconceivable that one who had read critically
the original in its completed form should have been satisfied
with the production of such an unsightly torso, and that
persons in possession of the completed book in circulation
as early as the first century in Rome, as well as Asia
Minor,—certainly also in many other places,—should have
exchanged the same for the mutilated work.

The conclusion stands, therefore, that Mark was circulated from the beginning only in its incomplete form C
(i. 1–xvi. 8), and the question arises as to the origin of this
abnormality.   An accident to the original MS. has been
suggested, which must have taken place before any copies
were made.   But if this happened before the book left
his hands, why did not the author correct it before he
permitted his book to be copied, *i.e.* before it was issued ?
More probably death, or some other compelling circumstance, arrested his pen.   If he died before the completion
of the work, the friends for whom it was originally intended
would have felt it their duty to copy and issue the
posthumous work without additions.   If, however, as the
tradition seems to show (above, p. 433), Mark published
the book himself, its incompleted form would be incomprehensible only in case that a few lines were wanting
which the author and editor could have added at any
time.   On the other hand, the small compass of the work,
in comparison with the other historical books of the N.T.,
leaves room for the conjecture that Mark intended to add
several portions to his work (n. 10).   Other things besides
the resurrection appearances could have been included.
For, carrying out the idea expressed in the title, a mass
of material remained which could have been appropriately
used, such as we find utilised in Acts (cf. *e.g.* 1 Pet. i. 12
with Acts ii. 1–14).   If he began to write the Gospel
before the death of Peter (64), but did not publish the
same until after the death of Paul (67), things enough

could be mentioned which must have interrupted the pen
of this spiritual son of Peter and younger friend of Paul
in the city where both the apostles had died as martyrs,
and which also in the time immediately following must
have prevented him from at once completing his book as
he desired. If, in these circumstances, he yielded to the
request for its issue, it would not have been something
unheard of or irrational. It is perfectly possible also
that during the months and years while he and others
were hoping for the completion of the interrupted work he
had given the unfinished book to friends to read, and that
they had made several copies without his being able to
prevent it (n. 11). At all events, the incomplete character of the book is proof that it was handed down in the
Church in the form in which it came from the author's
pen, since the first attempt to recast the work would have
been directed toward furnishing it with a conclusion. The
varied and slow success of the later attempts in this
direction show how difficult it was to change the form of a
book after it had once found a circle of readers in the
Church. Nor is the result different if we assume that it
is not the original work of Mark which has had the
misfortune, either by accident or intention, of losing its
conclusion, but only a later working over of the same ; for
how could a new working over of the Gospel, which was
never completed, have replaced the original work, which
was complete, and which had already come to be highly
esteemed by many ?

1. (P. 456.) The question whether υἱοῦ θεοῦ is to be read after 'Ιησοῦ
Χριστοῦ in Mark i. 1 need not be raised here. Iren. iii. 10. 6, 11. 8, 16. 3,
seems to have construed i. 1 as subject of the predicate contained in ver. 2, as if
it read, ἡ ἀρχὴ τοῦ εὐαγγελίου Ἰ. Χρ. ἐγένετο κατὰ τὸ γεγραμμένον ἐν τῷ Ἡσαίᾳ.
Origen, however, without expressing himself definitely as to the grammatical
construction, interprets the passage (in Jo. tom. i. 13, vi. 24) as if ver. 1
with ἐγένετο of ver. 4 were the predicate and 'Ιωάννης the subject. This construction, so popular in later times, was deliberately excluded by ℵ*, καὶ
ἐγένετο, and Copt. ἐγένετο δέ in ver. 4. The fundamental error of the still
dominant interpretations appears in Bengel's Gnomon, though at the same

time he rejects a still more mistaken construction : " Initium tamen appellat Marcus non libri sui, sed rei gestæ." For further details we must refer to the commentaries.

2. (P. 457.) That the indication of the close of a book serves to set off one complete literary production from another writing following it in the same codex is shown as early as Hier. *Ep.* xxviii. 4 : " Ut solemus nos completis opusculis ad distinctionem rei alterius sequentis medium interponere 'explicit' aut 'feliciter' aut aliquid istiusmodi." The same, of course, is true of the corresponding *incipit.* It may be mere chance that these formulas appear earlier in Latin Gospel books (*e.g.* in Vercell. sæc. iv., Veron. and Bobb. sæc. v., cf. Bianchini, *Ev. Quadr.* i. 262 ff., 474 ; *Old Latin Biblical Texts,* ed. Wordsworth, ii. 23) than in the Greek. The oldest Greek text of the Gospels in which such formulas are found is that of the Græco-Latin Cantabrigiensis (sæc. vi., ed. Scrivener, p. 95, ευαγγελιον κατα Ματθαιον ετελεσθη, αρχεται ευαγγελιον κατα Ιωαννην ; p. 262, ἐπληρώθη, ἄρχεται). That τέλος and ἀρχή were also customary at an earlier period needs first to be proved. With regard to τέλος, cf. *GK,* ii. 933. The comparison with Hos. i. 2 which has been suggested,—by whom first the present writer does not know,—is not apt. Aside from the fact that the Hebrew ought probably to be translated, " As Yahweh began to speak with Hosea," the ἀρχὴ λόγου κυρίου προς Ὡσηέ of the LXX is not the beginning or the title of the book, but comes after it (Hos. i. 1), and refers only to the succeeding portion,—say chaps. i. and ii.,—or perhaps only to the command of i. 2 itself.

3. (P. 461.) In the Johannine writings we do not find εὐαγγέλιον and εὐαγγελίζεσθαι, except in Rev. x. 7, xiv. 6—where it is not applied to the Gospel usually so called—and a suggestion of the word in ἀγγελία, 1 John i. 5, iii. 11. Even Luke, who shows most clearly the derivation of the idea from Isa. lxi. 1 (Luke iv. 18, cf. vii. 22 ; Matt. xi. 5), and who uses the verb with some frequency, putting it in Jesus' own mouth (iv. 43, vii 22, xvi. 16), besides applying it to the preaching of His disciples (viii. 1, ix. 6, xx. 1 ; Acts v. 42, viii. 35, x. 36, etc.) and to other announcements connected with it as well (i. 19, ii. 10, iii. 18), does not use the noun in the Gospel, and in Acts only in the mouth of Peter (xv. 7, cf. Mark i. 15) and of Paul (xx. 24, cf. 32) with a designation which is characteristic of his teaching. Matthew uses εὐαγγέλιον four times, twice in words of Jesus (xxiv. 14, xxvi. 13), and twice referring to Jesus (iv. 23, ix. 35), three of these times with the addition, peculiar to him, of τῆς βασιλείας (for in Mark i. 14 τοῦ θεοῦ is certainly to be read instead of τῆς βασιλείας). But Mark in his much shorter Gospel has the word seven times ; he alone of the evangelists uses it in connection with Ἰησοῦ Χριστοῦ (i. 1), as is common with Paul, or τοῦ θεοῦ (i. 14) ; and among the five passages in which he puts the word without addition in Jesus' mouth (i. 15, viii. 35, x. 29, xiii. 10, xiv. 9), there are two where comparison with the parallels (Mark viii. 35 = Matt. x. 39 ; Mark x. 29 = Matt. xix. 29 ; Luke xviii. 29) shows that the expression is peculiar to Mark.

4. (P. 461.) We find in Mark's narrative a number of details lacking in Matt., and for the most part in Luke also, which are not indispensable to the understanding of the story, but which describe the situation more exactly or the action more graphically : i. 19 (ὀλίγον), 20 ("the hired servants"), 29 (particular designation of the house and of Jesus' companions), 33 ("the whole

city was gathered at the door"), 36, ii. 1b, 2, 16 (ἰδόντες ὅτι ἤσθιεν), 18 (it was a fast-day), iii. 9 f., 20 f., 34 ("looking about Him at the multitude which surrounded Him," cf. ver. 32), iv. 36, 38 (ἐν τῇ πρύμνῃ ἐπὶ τὸ προσκεφάλαιον), v. 3–vi. 13 (the number of the swine), 15 f., 26, 29–33, 40 (Jesus' company), 41 (the exact words), 42 (the age of the girl), vi. 13 (anointing with oil), 20 f., 37 (cost of the bread), 38, 39 (" the green grass "), 40, vii. 26, viii. 3b, 14 (the one loaf), 27 (ἐν τῇ ὁδῷ, and often besides, ix. 33, x. 17, 32, 52), ix. 3, 14–16 (see § 53), 17 f., 21–26, 28 (εἰς οἶκον), 33 (ἐν τῇ οἰκίᾳ), 34, 35 (καθίσας), 36 (ἐναγκαλισάμενος, so also x. 16), x. 10, 32a, 46, 49–51, xi. 4, 13 (first what Jesus saw from a distance, then what He noticed on the spot), xiv. 7b, 30 (δίς, τρίς, cf. xiv. 72), 44 (καὶ ἀπάγετε ἀσφαλῶς), 51 f., 54 (ἔσω πρὸς τὸ φῶς), xv. 21, 24 (τίς τί ἄρῃ), 29 (οὐά), 44. It is often noted that Jesus looked about Him, noticed objects, or looked at persons, and sometimes the effect is also mentioned, iii. 5, 34, v. 30, 32, x. 21, 23, 27, xi. 11.   The feeling and manner, too, of Jesus' words and actions is sometimes noticed by Mark alone, i. 41, iii. 5, x. 14.   It is frankly stated that Jesus failed to hear something, inquired about something that He did not know, and looked for something that was not to be found, v. 30–32, 36, vi. 38, xi. 13, cf. xiii. 32 ; and that His relatives and disciples spoke of or to Him with disrespect or reproach, iii. 21, iv. 38, v. 31 (v. 40), viii. 32.   Mark likes to give a precise note of time, sometimes by an addition to the less definite expression found in the other accounts, i. 32, 35, xvi. 2, cf. i. 21, ii. 1, iv. 35, vi. 2, 35, 47, 48, viii. 2, ix. 2, xi. 11, 19, 20, xiv. 12, 17, xv. 1, 25 (hour of the crucifixion, Mark only), 33, 34.   He likes strong forms of expression : ἐξέστησαν εὐθὺς ἐκστάσει μεγάλῃ, v. 42 ; λίαν ἐκ περισσοῦ ἐν ἑαυτοῖς ἐξίσταντο, vi. 51, cf. vii. 37, x. 26 ; πολλοὶ πλούσιοι πολλὰ—μία χήρα λεπτὰ δύο, xii. 41 f. (cf. in comparison with this Luke xxi. 1 f.).   The merely adverbial πολλά, i. 45, iii. 12, iv. 2, v. 10, 23, 38, 43, vi. 20, 34, ix. 26, he alone of the evangelists has ; vii. 8, 13 also belongs here, while v. 26, viii. 31, ix. 12, xv. 3 belong in the same category as Matt. xvi. 21, xxvii. 19 ; Luke ix. 22, xxii. 65.   A comparison with the parallels shows that μόνους, ix. 2, πάντων, x. 44, ὄντως, xi. 32, πολύ, xii. 27, are the sharpening of other simpler and sufficient terms.' For him πάντα ὅσα εἶχεν is not sufficient, he adds ὅλον τὸν βίον αὐτῆς, xii. 44.   The much repeated καὶ εὐθύς (often amended by transcribers to εὐθέως) and the likewise frequent πάλιν and καὶ πάλιν will perhaps weary a reader attentive to the style, but on the other hand show the vivacity of the narrator.   Some proper observations on this point occur in Mandel, Kephas der Evangelist, 2–6.   Like other narrators from among the people, Mark seems rather to favour than to avoid the repetition of the same circumstantial expression within the single narrative, instead of an abbreviation of similar meaning, iii. 1, 3, iii. 31, 32, v. 9, 15, v. 30, 31, vi. 14, 16, x. 47, 48, xiv. 13, 72, xv. 37, 39 (ἐξέπνευσεν), xiv. 28, xvi. 7.   In the discourses and conversations, moreover, he likes refrain and recapitulation, vii. 8 (even according to the shorter text), 13, vii. 15, 18–20, x. 23, 24, xii. 24, 27 (πλανᾶσθε), xii. 29–31, 32–33.   Consequently ix. 44, 46 are not to be removed from the text on the ground of tautology.   He uses direct discourse even where unspoken thoughts (v. 28, ix. 10), or remarks of several persons, or words spoken on different occasions, are reproduced, i. 37, iii. 11, vi. 14, 16, and also where other narrators do not find it necessary to repeat the words at all, vi. 24, x. 49.   Mark is not afraid of ellipsis, iii. 30. (he spoke in view of the fact) " that they said " ; ix. 11, (how is it related with the fact) "that the Pharisees say ?" ix. 23, (how can you say) "If thou canst ?" ix. 28, "That we could not cast it out" (how is that to be explained ?) ; xiv. 49, "but (it must happen so), in order that the Scriptures might be fulfilled." The impression of accuracy is also heightened by the frequent retention of the Aramaic phrase ; see § 53.

5. (Pp. 467, 468.) The most detailed and scholarly arguments for the authenticity of Mark xvi. 9–20 are those of Burgon, *The Last Twelve Verses of the Gospel according to St. Mark*, ˙871 ; Martin, *Introduction à la Critique Textuelle du N.T.*, Partie Pratique, tome ii. 1884. Among those who dispute the authenticity of these verses, special mention may be made of the critical apparatus of Tischendorf, that of Westcott and Hort, *N.T. Appendix*, 28–51, the investigation of Klostermann, *op. cit.* 298–309, and the writer's discussion *GK*, ii. 910–938, which cannot be fully repeated here. With regard to the evidence for the text which closes with xvi. 8, we might add that the *Gospel of Peter* (*circa* 150) should probably be included ; cf. the writer's work on the subject, 1893, S. 53. The dependence of this Gospel upon Mark in general, and especially in the account of the resurrection morning, is undeniable. An ἦν, which is proper only in the mouth of the narrator, Mark xvi. 4, is in *Gospel of Peter* xii. 54 attributed to the women, on whose lips it is meaningless. From Mark xvi. 5 the *Gospel of Peter* xiii. 55 takes νιανίσκον . . . περιβεβλημένον στολήν κτλ., whereas in xi. 44 it had called the same angel ἀνθρωπός τις ; from Mark xvi. 8 it borrows φοβηθεῖσαι ἔφυγον. But the *Gospel of Peter* concludes the account of the resurrection day at this point. This coincidence with the original conclusion of Mark would be a very remarkable circumstance if xvi. 9–20 had also been before the author. Lods, *L'Ev. de St. Pierre*, p. 64, compares *Gospel of Peter*, vii. 27, πενθοῦντες καὶ κλαίοντες ; Conybeare, *Expos.*, Dec. 1895, p. 413 ; *Gospel of Peter*, xiv. 59, ἐκλαίομεν καὶ ἐλυπούμεθα, with Mark xvi. 10, πενθοῦσιν καὶ κλαίουσιν. But the first passage belongs to a different historical connection, and the second is not particularly similar. The combination πενθεῖν καὶ κλαίειν is quite usual, Jas. iv. 9 ; Luke vi. 25 ; Rev. xviii. 11, 15, 19 ; and also John xvi. 20,—a prediction which was not to fail of literal fulfilment. Rohrbach (*Der Schluss des Marcusev.* 27–33 ; *Die Berichte über d. Auferstehung Christi*), following up a conjecture of Harnack's (*Bruchstücke des Ev. und der Ap. des Petrus*, 2te Aufl. 33), has attempted to show that the *Gospel of Peter* derived its conclusion from the lost original ending of Mark. But, granted that there was such an ending, how is one to show what it contained ? We must assume that Mark, if he had finished his work, would have told of an appearance of the risen Lord in Galilee, as would probably *Gospel of Peter*, xiv., also—where, however, the name Galilee does not appear, and there is no account of an appearance of Christ. But Matt. xxviii. 16–20 and John xxi. also tell of an appearance in Galilee, and the connection of the *Gospel of Peter* with the latter chapter is evident. That Levi the son of Alphæus is mentioned there, only shows that the writer knew Mark and used it here as in other passages ; cf. Mark ii. 14. Horn, *Abfassungszeit, Geschichtlichkeit und Zweck von Jo.* xxi. S. 94–156, has given an extended criticism of the Harnack - Rohrbach hypothesis. With regard to the authorities for Mark xvi. 9–20, we must notice also that the fact that the section was worked over by Tatian (*Forsch.* i. 218 f. ; *GK*, ii. 554) has been still further confirmed ; cf. *NKZ*, 1894, 106. On the other hand, one may not with Harnack (*TU*, xiii.

4. 51) adduce Novat. *Trin.* viii., in connection with which Gallandi, *Bibl.*[2] iii.
292, had inappropriately cited Mark xvi. 15, or the writing *Ad Novat.* (Cypr.,
ed. Hartel, App. p. 56) attributed by Harnack (*op. cit.* xiii. 1) to Pope
Sixtus II. and the year 257–258 ; for *evangelizate gentibus,* also in an inexact
quotation of Matt. xxviii. 19, does not correspond exactly with Mark xvi. 15
(*prædicate evangelium omni creaturæ*).   Conybeare, *op. cit.* 402, shows that
the Armenian Eznik, in his work against heresies (ed. Venet. 89), quotes
Mark xvi. 17, 18 verbatim according to the usual Armenian translation, but
without attributing the words expressly to Mark.   The principal conclusion
which Conybeare draws is that Mark xvi. 9–20 always belonged to the
Armenian translation of the Gospels, but was afterwards set aside because the
addition was known to the Armenians from the beginning as a work of the
presbyter Ariston (see n. 8), and so, with stricter views regarding the Canon,
could not be permanently admitted as a part of Mark.   The history of the
Armenian translation of this section, of which Martin, *op. cit.* 325 ff., gives a
different account and opinion than Conybeare, 403 f., 417 f., cannot be
followed further here.   But see n. 8.   For an extended variant of the longer
form see Freer MS.

6. (P. 468.)   The most important witnesses for the shorter addition B
are—(1) L. (sæc. 8, ed. Tischendorf in *Monum. sacra ined.* 1846, p. 206) ;
(2) Ψ (sæc. 8 or 9, in Gregory, *Textkritik des NT"s,* i. 94) ; (3) T¹ (sæc. 7 or 8,
in Gregory, *op. cit.* 70, a Coptic-Greek fragment) ; (4) Ol (so called by
Schmidtke, *Die Evv. eines alten Uncial codex,* 1903, the text is given S. 29 ;
it is Miniscule 574, according to Gregory's enumeration = Paris, Bibl. nat. gr.
97, used by the present writer in discussion of the question [*GK*, ii. 921]
following Martin, *Description techn.* p. 91–94 ; Nestle, *ZfNTW,* 1903, S. 255,
is mistaken).   The text is accordingly as follows : πάντα δὲ τὰ παρηγγελμένα
τοῖς περὶ τὸν Πέτρον συντόμως ἐξήγγειλαν· μετὰ δὲ ταῦτα αὐτὸς ὁ (ὁ omitted
in Ψ) Ἰησοῦς (ἐφάνη+ΨT) ἀπὸ ἀνατολῆς (τοῦ ἡλίου+T) καὶ ἄρχι (μέχρι, Ψ)
δύσεως ἐξαπέστειλεν δι' αὐτῶν τὸ ἱερὸν καὶ ἄφθαρτον κήρυγμα τῆς αἰωνίου
σωτηρίας· ἀμήν (omitted in L).   In Ψ this portion is separated from xvi. 8
only by τέλος, which indicates the close of a Church lection, and is followed
by ἔστιν καὶ ταῦτα φερόμενα μετὰ τὸ " ἐφοβοῦντο γάρ". ἀναστὰς δὲ πρωὶ κτλ.
=xvi. 9–20.   Not until this point does the subscription εὐαγγέλιον κατὰ
Μᾶρκον (without ἀμήν) occur.   In L the shorter ending is introduced by
φέρεταί που καὶ ταῦτα, then follows the longer ending without an ἀμήν as
conclusion of what precedes, introduced by ἔστιν δὲ καί ταῦτα κτλ. (except for
the δὲ interpolated here as in Ψ, see above) and concluding with ἀμήν. εὐ.
κ. Μᾶρκον.   In Ol all intervening remarks are wanting.   So also in T¹,
where, however, the shorter ending is separated from xvi. 8 as from the
following longer ending by lines filled out with flourishes ; and at the beginning of the longer ending the words εἶχεν γὰρ—ἐφοβοῦντο γάρ of xvi. 8 are
repeated (cf. the Coptic MSS. concerning which, following Lightfoot, the
present writer has made some comments).   Only in the Latin Codex k
(Bobiensis, sæc. 5, *Old Latin Bibl. texts,* ii. 23) is B fully amalgamated with
the text of xvi. 8 ; but in such a way, that the text of xvi. 8 is violently
changed, in order to add the shorter ending without producing a contradiction (cf. *GK*, ii. 920).

7. (P. 471.)   Jerome, *contra Pelag.* ii. 15 (Vallarsi, ii. 758 ; cf. *GK*, ii. 919,
935) : "In quibusdam exemplaribus et maxime in græcis codicibus iuxta

Marcum in fine eius evangelii scribitur : ' Postea quum accubuissent undecim, apparuit eis Jesus et exprobravit incredulitatem et duritiam cordis eorum, quia his, qui viderant eum resurgentem, non crediderunt. Et illi satisfaciebant dicentes : Sæculum istud iniquitatis et incredulitatis sub satana (al. substantia) est, quæ (read qui) non sinit per immundos spiritus veram dei apprehendi virtutem : idcirco iam nunc revela iustitiam tuam."

8. (Pp. 473, 477, 478.) With regard to the Gospel of Etchmiadzin artistically considered, see Strzygowski, Byzantinische Denkmäler, i., Vienna, 1891. The statement "of Ariston the presbyter," which it contains, was first published and discussed by Conybeare in the Expos., Oct. 1893, pp. 241–254 ; again, Dec. 1895, pp. 401–421. Cf. the writer's discussion, ThLb, 1893, No. 51. Resch, Ausserkanon. Paralleltexte zu den Evv. ii. 450–456, on the basis of this phrase, argued the probability that Ariston of Pella (circa 135) was not only the author of the conclusion of Mark, but also the editor of the Gospel Canon. Rohrbach (see n. 5, above), who declares (26) the issue and circulation of an unfinished book to be "nonsense,"—in singular contradiction to the literary history of all ages,—and therefore treats the former existence of an original and genuine ending as a matter of course, holds the Gospel to have come to Asia Minor intact, and also to the place where the Gospel of Peter originated, which in all probability, however, is to be looked for elsewhere (p. 483, above). It was of this unmutilated book (C+X) that John the presbyter spoke with his pupils (Eus. H. E. iii. 39. 15). One of these pupils, Papias, wrote several decades later of a Gospel of Mark, which had meanwhile been deprived of its closing chapter (X) and furnished with a spurious addition, and wrote under the candid impression that he had in his hands the same book as that on which in his youth he had heard his teacher comment. So Papias did not notice that, in the meantime, the dissatisfaction with X in the circle of his fellow-students had led to its omission ; that the book thus mutilated had been widely circulated in Asia Minor, for example, in the places where Matt. and Luke originated ; and that in Asia Minor again, somewhere about 110–120, the spurious ending (A) had been attached, while at the same time X had been worked over into John xxi. And so we are not to be surprised that about 130 the genuine Mark (C+X) had completely disappeared wherever it had once existed, in Rome where it had originated, in Syria where the Gospel of Peter was probably written, in Palestine where Matt. was composed, in the unknown place of Luke's origin, also, and in Asia Minor itself, where so much had been done with X, and that it had given place partly to recension C, which presupposes B, and partly to recension A. The spurious ending (A) is said to be the concluding portion of a "kerugma" of the presbyter Aristion, that is, a sermon of his concerning the whole life of Jesus from the birth to the ascension. If the marginal gloss of the Oxford MS. of Rufinus on Eus. H. E. iii. 39. 9 is from a late hand (Expos., Dec. 1895, p. 415), it must nevertheless rest upon an older statement which could have come only from one who knew Papias' work. Rohrbach's assertion (17), that every reader of Eus. iii. 39 could have set the name Aristion in the margin of § 9, is more bold than obvious. If such a person was setting up conjectures as to the source of the story of Justus Barsabbas and the poisoned drink which proved harmless, he could only think of the daughters of Philip (there mentioned), or of Philip himself, as the authorities. The references to

Aristion in §§ 7 and 14 are apart from the question, and in the only passage where Eusebius mentions his communications more particularly it is not stories that he relates, but words of Jesus that he reports (§ 14). Mark xvi. 14–18 is such a διήγησις λόγων τοῦ κυρίου, but not xvi. 9–13 and 19, 20. What is made to show the original unity of A as a whole, namely, the preparation for the main section vv. 14–18 in ἠπίστησαν, ver. 11, and οὐδὲ ἐκείνοις ἐπίστευσαν, ver. 13, only shows that the writer of A proceeded with some reflection. Thus, also, he was led, in the same words which present themselves as a fitting introduction to ver. 14, to go beyond the authority from which vv. 9–11 are derived, namely, John xx. 1–18, where nothing is said of the disciples' unbelieving attitude toward the message of Mary Magdalene, and into inconsistency with the narrative in Luke xxiv. 13–35, from which he also makes excerpts, and especially with its close. That this modification of the materials found support in John xx. 8, Luke xxiv. 11, 22–24, Matt. xxviii. 17, is obvious. But that we have a compilation of excerpts in vv. 9–13 is unquestionably shown by the statement which is inserted from Luke viii. 2, and which is inappropriate in this connection. In opposition to the opinion of Westcott and Hort, *N.T. Appendix*, 51, that the opening words, ἀναστὰς δὲ πρωΐ without 'Ιησοῦς, indicate that the whole was borrowed from another connection, we may remark that the omission of the name is not rendered more intelligible by this hypothesis. In analogous cases, like John vii. 53, Luke xxi. 38, the interpolators have introduced the foreign material with a sentence of their own which simplifies the connection. In the present instance the compiler has followed the style of Mark. After the proper name has been given in xvi. 6, Jesus is indicated by αὐτόν, αὐτοῦ, and again αὐτόν, while between them stands a προάγει without noun or pronoun. One might just as well require 'Ιησοῦς, or a substitute for it, in xvi. 14, as in xvi. 9 ; but the modern ὁ κύριος does not appear till xvi. 19 (p. 476, above). Mark himself is very sparing in the use of the name Jesus and its equivalents. We miss it in i. 21b after 21a, and in i. 30–ii. 4 after i. 29, and in the entire section iii. 7–v. 21, with all its change of actors and speakers.

9. (P. 477.) Examples for the canon of textual criticism on p. 477 are : John vi. 47, πιστεύων—additions, εἰς ἐμέ and εἰς θεόν (Sc Ss) ; John vii. 39, πνεῦμα—additions, ἅγιον and δεδομένον, both, indeed, in B ; Jas. v. 7, πρόϊμον —additions, ὑετόν and καρπόν. It is without question that many readings which found considerable currency in the second and third centuries, among them some of no little extent and importance, from the fourth century on, were more and more supplanted, and have in part disappeared from the later tradition, and also that interpolations have become established which were not known in the second century. But even now we are always in a position to base our judgment, however it may incline in doubtful cases, on existing sources, *e.g.* John iv. 9b, v. 3b, 4, vii. 53–viii. 11 ; cf. vol. i. 535, above, 124, on Phil. i. 3 ; 1 Tim. iii. 1. Whoever considers "This day have I begotten thee" in Luke iii. 22 original, need not complain that the true reading has disappeared from the tradition after 300. Of peculiar readings which Marcion did not invent, but found existing in part, as in Luke xi. 2 f., Gal. iv. 26 (*GK*, ii. 471, 502, 1015 ; *ZKom. Gal.* 298), there are certainly but few, though various traces in the following centuries, and even on internal grounds their genuineness is to be doubted. The variant readings of Cod. D

and allied MSS. in Acts do not belong here, for they are part of a comprehensive recension standing over against another which is likewise original.
See § 59.

10. (P. 479.) The length of the historical books of the N.T. reckoned
according to the ancient stichoi (*GK*, i. 76, ii. 395) is : Matt., 2480 ; Mark,
1543 ; Luke, 2714 ; John, 1950 ; Acts, 2610. The difference, then, between
Mark and John, the next smallest, is 407 stichoi, about the length of 1 and
2 Pet. together (403), or 1 and 2 Tim. (420) ; between Mark and Luke, 1171
stichoi, which is considerably more tha Rom. (979).

11. (P. 480.) Tertullian, *contra Marc.* i. 1, relates that the original copy
of the second edition of his *Antimarcion* was borrowed by a friend, who
afterward fell away from the Church, transcribed inaccurately, and published
(*exhibuit frequentiæ*).   The subsequent lapse does not affect the matter.
Premature publication against the wish of the author was nothing infrequent
(Cicero, *ad Attic.* xiii. 21. 4).   Before all, however, one must keep in mind
that in ancient times the real *editio* by the booksellers, with which the
earliest Christians were hardly concerned, was often preceded by a private
circulation among friends, sometimes for examination and correction, and
sometimes by the way of gift, or to satisfy curiosity (cf. Haenny, *Schriftsteller
u. Buchhändler in Rom.* 1884, S. 9 ff., 17 ff.).   The history of *opera imperfecta*,
all of which were by no means *opera posthuma*, gives free play to the
imagination (cf. also *GK*, ii. 930 f.).

§ 53. COMPARISON OF MARK'S GOSPEL WITH THE TRADITION.

According to tradition, the Gospel was written in
Rome by the Mark mentioned in Acts xii. 12, 25, xiii.
5, 13, xv. 37–39 ; Col. iv. 10 ; Philem. 24 ; 2 Tim. iv. 11,
after he had been engaged for some twenty years in
missionary work outside of Palestine (§ 51).   His original
name, John, as well as that of his mother, Mary (Mariam),
and of his cousin, Joseph, who bore the Aramaic surname
Barnabas, make it extremely probable that the family,
which was settled in Jerusalem, belonged to the Hebrews,
not to the resident Hellenists (Acts vi. 1), although the
fact that Barnabas was a native of Cyprus (Acts iv. 36)
shows that it had relations to the Diaspora living in
regions where Greek predominated.   This is in keeping
with the fact that Mark reproduces in his Greek book
with apparent pleasure the Aramaic form of Jesus' words
and those of other persons, although it is always necessary

to append a Greek translation for the benefit of his readers.
This impression is strengthened by comparison with the
longer Gospels of Matthew and Luke, the first of which was
written by a Jew, if we may believe the tradition, but is
preserved to us only in a translation ; the second, however,
by a Greek (n. 1).   It is also to be noticed that Mark's
Greek shows Hebraic colouring more strongly than any
other of the Gospels and almost beyond that of any other
N.T. writing.   Although Mark does not exhibit as many
flagrant errors against grammar, conscious or unintentional,
as does the Book of Revelation, he has more genuine Semitic
idioms (n. 2).   Not only is he familiar with the geography
and customs of the Holy Land, but he endeavours also
to acquaint his readers with them.   He portrays, as
does no other evangelist, the shrill lamentations for the
dead (v. 38, where very probably reference is made
to instrumental music, cf. 1 Cor. xiii. 1).   He is familiar
with the fact that the Jewish fasts were no longer a
voluntary exercise of religious earnestness, but that
there were certain fast days which the zealous were required to observe, and explains in great detail that the
marriage festivities, which lasted for several days, and
which on that account could conflict with the two weekly
fast days of the Pharisees (Luke xviii. 12), relieved one
from every obligation to fast (ii. 18–20).   The Jewish
conception of "defiled hands" he explains clearly, and
makes use of the occasion to inform his readers in detail
how the Pharisees and the Jews generally laid weight
upon the washing of hands before meals, and upon similar
purification of all sorts of vessels, and how all this was
regulated by traditional Rabbinic rules (vii. 2–4).   Just
as he translates Aramaic words and phrases for his readers
(n. 1), so he explains Jewish ideas even when expressed
(παρασκευή, xv. 42) or transliterated (γέεννα, ix. 43, but
not in v. 45, 47) in Greek.   With Pilate and his office,
on the other hand, the readers appear to be entirely

familiar (xv. 1, n. 3), likewise with a certain bloody revolt
which took place during his term of office (xv. 7).

The fact that Mark uses more Latin technical terms
than the other evangelists has only comparative value,
since such words were in common use everywhere in the
provinces, even among the Jews in Palestine (n. 4).   The
use of such terms instead of the Greek expressions
indicates difference of taste, not the author's nationality.
Still it must have been very natural for an author writing
in Rome for Romans to employ Latin names for Latin
things.   It is also conceivable how a Jew, born in
Jerusalem, who was repeatedly in Rome, who lived there
for considerable periods of time, and wrote his book there,
could come to employ Latinisms in his Greek book
without necessarily being familiar with the Latin language.
The passages in which he explains Greek terms by Latin,
or, more accurately, Roman expressions (xii. 42, xv. 16,
n. 4), are decisive proof that the book was intended for
Western readers.   This is still more definitely indicated
by Mark xv. 21 (n. 5).   Mark agrees here with Matthew
(xxvii. 32) and Luke (xxiii. 26) in representing Simon of
Cyrene as an unknown person, accidentally met on the way
to the Cross ; but the phrase which he adds, that this man
was the father of Alexander and Rufus, makes it certain
(1) that the sons of Simon were known to the readers, just
as it renders it clear that the father was unknown ;
(2) that the only purpose which Mark had in view in this
addition peculiar to his account was to render the history
more interesting to his readers by connecting it with what
was familiar to them, since for the understanding of the
development of thought in the passage it is a matter of
no consequence whether Simon had sons or not, much less
what their names were.   Now, from Rom. xvi. 13 we
know that in the year 58 there was a Christian by the
name of Rufus living in Rome with his mother, both of
whom had migrated thither from the East not long before.

In brief, the situation is this : a Gospel which, according to the oldest tradition, was written for Roman readers, between 64 and 70, takes for granted, in a purely incidental way, personal acquaintance on the part of his readers with two brothers, Alexander and Rufus, formerly resident in Jerusalem ; and, according to a document of the year 58, there was in the Roman Church a Christian, Rufus by name, living there with his mother, both of whom had come thither from the East. With persons possessing so little judgment as to explain this coincidence as accidental, further discussion is useless. Granted that the tradition that Mark was written in Rome has strong and independent support in many passages of the book, it becomes probable that it was the tendency among the Roman Christians with which we became acquainted in Rom. xiv.—noticed also in Heb. xiii. 9 (above, pp. 332 f., 346 f.)—that influenced Mark to reproduce with such great detail the discourse concerning things clean and unclean (vii. 1–23), and generally to emphasise strongly Jesus' opposition to ceremonialism (above, p. 463).

The author of Mark nowhere speaks in the first person, nor does he make any reference to himself at once intelligible to every reader. It is very noticeable, however, that he calls the apostle John τὸν ἀδελφὸν τοῦ Ἰακώβου both in the list of apostles, iii. 17, and in v. 37, instead of designating him, as in other passages where he is mentioned with James, either as the brother of the preceding (αὐτοῦ, Mark i. 19 ; Matt. iv. 21, x. 2, xvii. 1), or without any definite characterisation (Mark i. 29, ix. 2, xiv. 33 ; Luke vi. 14, viii. 51), or both brothers as the sons of Zebedee (Mark x. 35 ; Luke v. 10 ; Matt. xx. 20 ; John xxi. 2). This characterisation does not occur elsewhere in the N.T., and is very noticeable in view of the much greater importance of the apostle John in comparison with his brother James, who died in 44 (n. 5a). It must have been employed by the author to distinguish one John

from another, just as the reverse form is used in Acts
xii. 2 to distinguish one James from another (Acts xii.
2, 17 ; cf. Jude 1). It would have been natural for an
author himself called John, and standing in close relation to the events which he recorded, occasionally thus
to distinguish the apostle of the same name. Though
it may be doubtful whether in this case the original
readers, when they read the words "John the brother of
James," perceived the feeling with which they were written
("John, but not the narrator surnamed Mark"), they were
undoubtedly in a better position than later readers to
understand that xiv. 51 f. recorded a personal experience
of the author (n. 6). After it is narrated that all those
who accompanied Jesus, i.e. according to the context (xiv.
17, 26, 32, 47) all the apostles, with the exception of the
traitor, forsook Him and fled, we are told the experience
of a certain youth who followed Him. The characterisation
νεανίσκος τις shows at once that he was not one of the
apostles named and partially described in iii. 16–19. It
is self-evident that no one of these could have partaken of
the Passover and have accompanied Jesus through the
city to Gethsemane clad as was this young man. Finally,
it could not here be said abruptly of an apostle that he
simply accompanied Jesus (συνηκολούθησεν) or followed Him
(συνηκολούθει) during the transactions previously described,
which, however, is the chief statement in xiv. 51 ; on the
contrary, in making any remark in this connection about
the clothing or fate of an apostle, it would have been
necessary to say that he was one of those who up to
this time had been in Jesus' company (cf. xiv. 37).
Whether the σινδών, which was the only clothing that
the youth had on, was a garment (Judg. xiv. 12 ; 1 Macc.
x. 64, variant reading) or a large cloth (Matt. xxvii. 59),
at all events it should not again be questioned, having
been proved. by Casaubon (above, p. 447, n. 6) that
the youth had got up suddenly out of bed, and, in his

curiosity or anxiety to find out whither Jesus would go and what might happen to Him, had not taken time to clothe himself again, but had stealthily followed Jesus and the apostles clad in his night garments or bed blanket. This confirms the ancient conjecture that he was a member of the household where Jesus celebrated the Passover, since in no other house in Jerusalem would it be possible for a person, who had already retired, to know the moment of Jesus' departure, and to be led suddenly to the decision by the breaking up of the Passover gathering to follow the group in his night garments. But why should this event be recorded by Mark, and by him only ? It does not add anything to the description of the peril of the situation or even to the fury and madness of those sent to make the arrest, since the picture of a strong and well-armed police force (xiv. 43, 48) getting only the garment of the man whom they design to arrest makes a ludicrous rather than a terrifying impression. The episode explains nothing that precedes or follows, and must have been narrated only because of its interest to the author, and, as he thought, to the readers. The same hesitancy which led him to withhold the youth's name, and his relation to Jesus and the apostles, also kept him from saying anything from which we can infer directly that the youth belonged to the household where Jesus spent His last night with His disciples. This reserve is to be explained only if the narrator was identical with the youth who fled. The house in question was his own home, whose guest-room the author describes with detail in xiv. 17—in striking contrast to Matt. xxvi. 18 f. ; John xiii. 1 ff.

That Luke, who practically repeats Mark's description (xxii. 12), here as in other passages, was not independent of our author, we shall show later (§ 61). Luke does not, however, repeat the sentence with which Mark begins the account of the last supper. "And when it was evening,

he cometh with the Twelve" (xiv. 17).   We have a sudden
transition to the present, and Mark describes the approach
and arrival of the announced guests as if he were in the
house in which the Passover was prepared (n. 7).   Involun-
tarily he reproduces the impression which he had received
at the time.   Here the opinion of the Muratorian Fragmentist, "aliquibus tamen inte fuit et ita posuit," is correct,
and the oldest tradition, when rightly understood, offers
no contradiction (above, pp. 428, 442 f.).   The correct interpretation of Mark xiv. 17, 51 f., finds independent support
in the narrative of Acts xii. 12–17.   The household in
which Mark grew up was well-to-do; it did not lack for servants, and the house had room for a considerable gathering
of Christians.   The fact that they assembled there for prayer
in the middle of the night could possibly be explained on
the ground that their solicitude for the imprisoned Peter
led them to engage in tireless, united petition on his behalf (xii. 5).   When, however, Peter, who knew nothing
of this fact, sought out the house of Mary instead of going
to his own dwelling,—which he must certainly have had,
and indeed, as the narrator clearly indicates (Acts xii. 12),
because he knew that there would be a large gathering
there on that night,—the most natural explanation is that
it was the Passover night (xii. 3 f.), and that the Jerusalem
Christians were fond of celebrating the Passover meal in
the house and room where Jesus had celebrated it with
the apostles just before His death.   The interpretation of
Acts xii. 12–17 leads to the same result as that of Mark
xiv. 17, 51 f.   Jesus celebrated His last Passover in the
home of Mark, and the son of this household is the author
of this Gospel.   In spite of the large number of spurious
titles of honour gathered about this house in the Church
legends (above, pp. 428, 447, n. 7), they must contain a
grain of genuine tradition, since it is not conceivable that
they should have grown up from exegetical combinations
such as those above.   The father (Mark xiv. 14; Matt.

xxvi. 18) must have been in sympathy with Jesus even
before His death.   He regarded Him as a rabbi, and gladly
showed Him a favour.   Jesus, in His turn, is confident of
not being betrayed before His time, either by him or any
member of his household.   The curiosity which led the
half-grown boy to follow the Passover guests of the house
is entirely conceivable, and we can also understand how in
riper years, when he wrote his Gospel, he should mention
briefly his own part in the great events which he narrates.
Instead of indicating the *ipse feci* with a monogram, as do
others, he paints a small picture of himself in the corner
of his work which contains so many figures.   What he
narrates of himself is no heroic deed, but only a thought-
less action of his youth.

In case we possessed no tradition regarding the person
and relations of the writer, xiv. 17, 51 f. would not be the
only passages from which the reader would receive the
impression that the narrative of the book is that of an eye-
witness.   This would be the most natural way in which to
explain the above-mentioned peculiarities of style in most of
the accounts (above, pp. 461 f., 481 f., n. 4).   There are other
observations, however, which are against this impression.
The barest comparison of Mark ix. 14 with Matt. xvii. 14,
Luke ix. 37, is sufficient to show that the former was
written not from the point of view of the historian, to
whom all the subjects in his narrative have the same
interest, nor from the point of view alone of the chief
person in the narrative, but according to the reading
($\dot{\epsilon}\lambda\theta\acute{o}\nu\tau\epsilon\varsigma$ . . . $\epsilon\tilde{\iota}\delta o\nu$, $\aleph$BL$\varDelta$KSs Armenian), which is undoubtedly correct, from the point of view of Jesus and
His three most trusted disciples.   As they come down
from the mountain and draw near to the place where the
other apostles are, the first thing which they notice
is a large crowd, in the midst of which the apostles are
standing engaged in discussion with the scribes.   As the
four approach they are noticed by several of the crowd

surrounding the persons engaged in discussion. The crowd then turns and leaves the scribes and the nine apostles standing, and (some of them) run to greet Jesus, among them the father of the possessed child, whom the disciples had been unable to heal. Before Jesus reaches the scribes and the disciples who had been left behind, He inquires of the crowd the occasion of the animated discussion. Then He suffers the father to tell his story, and as He goes on complains of the wearisomeness of His work in this faithless generation. He commands that the sick child be brought to Him, but does not perform the act of healing until the crowd begins to press about Him on all sides (ver. 25). The original narrator of this incident was evidently one of the three witnesses of the transfiguration upon the mountain, Peter, John, or James (Mark ix. 2 ; 2 Pet. i. 18). According to the tradition it was Peter, whose narratives Mark reproduced in several parts of his Gospel so accurately that it is possible to recognise his source from the style of his narrative. The attempt was repeatedly made in the common text tradition and also in the ancient versions, for palpable reasons, to eliminate this peculiar style of Mark both in xiii. 3 and ix. 14. If the singular ἐπηρώτα is to be retained in xiii. 3 with אBL, the most natural explanation is to suppose that, in the original account of Peter, the verse ran somewhat as follows : "Then I asked the Lord confidentially, and James, John, and Andrew joined me in the question." It may have been Peter also who earlier called the Lord's attention to the beauty of the temple buildings (xiii. 1, εἰς τῶν μαθητῶν αὐτοῦ ; cf. xiv. 47). At all events, we have features here not found in Matt. xxiv. 1–3, Luke xxi. 5–7, which are naturally explained by assuming that Mark is reproducing the account of one who took part in the scene. The same observation is forced upon us by xi. 12–14, 20–25 (cf. Matt. xxi. 18–22). The naïve detail of the narrative, the exact indication of the day and hour of the

various incidents in the story, and the rabbi with which
the master is addressed, have been mentioned above (p.
482). It is especially to be noticed that what is said in
xi. 14 appears to be a very independent remark, "His
disciples heard Him (make this remark);" but that is
followed in xi. 21 by the sent̓nce, "And Peter, calling to
remembrance (what was said on the morning of the preceding day), saith unto Him, 'Rabbi,'" etc.

A more remarkable account than that which we have
in i. 29 cannot be imagined, "And straightway, when
they were come out of the synagogue, they came into the
house of Simon and of Andrew, with James and John"
(n. 8). The subject is not specifically indicated, but from
i. 16–21 is without doubt Jesus, Peter, James, John, and
Andrew. But why are the four apostles mentioned again
by name, and two of them as accompanying the others, as
if they were not already included in the subject? Why
is the plural of the verb, so often employed elsewhere to
include Jesus and those with Him at the time, not
sufficient here (i. 21, vi. 53, ix. 14); or, if the author
desired to mention the presence of the disciples expressly
after i. 21b–28, where only Jesus is spoken of, why did
not an expression like that in ii. 15, iii. 7, viii. 27 suffice?
Peter's original account at the basis of the narrative
evidently ran somewhat thus : "We came direct from the
synagogue to our house, and James and John accompanied
us ; and my mother-in-law lay sick of a fever, and we
spoke with Him at once concerning her." Mark transfers
the narrative from Peter's lips into the language of another
not very skilfully, but faithfully. Peter must have said
"our house," not "my house," because it was the dwelling
of his brother and mother-in-law, and possibly belonged
to the latter originally; for Peter's own home was in
Bethsaida, not Capernaum. Mark translates ἡμῶν by
Σίμωνος καὶ 'Ανδρέου, and then returns to Peter's words,
and says that James and John accompanied the others,

with the resulting awkwardness that it remains unclear
who else came into the house, in particular, whether James
and John were accompanied by Andrew and Peter.   The
use of the expression Σίμων καὶ οἱ μετ' αὐτοῦ, i. 36, to
designate the disciples, is unparalleled in the other Gospel
accounts, and represents a "we" of Peter's discourses.
Just as the expression used in iii. 13 (n. 7) shows that
the choosing of the Twelve is viewed and narrated from
the standpoint of one of their number, so the exceedingly
awkward character of the narrative, iii. 16, is very much
easier to understand, if we suppose that it is based upon
some such words of Peter as follows : " He chose us twelve,
and gave me the name Peter" (cf. Klostermann, 72).
Otherwise it cannot be said that Peter is noticeably prominent.   He is one of the first four to be called to assist
Jesus in His work (i. 16–20, 29, xiii. 3), and one of the
three with whom He was most intimate (v. 37, ix. 2, xiv.
33).   The giving to him of the name Peter (Cephas) is dismissed with a word (iii. 16, cf. *per contra*, Matt. xvi. 18 ;
John i. 42).   His great confession, viii. 29, is reproduced
in the shortest possible form (cf. *per contra*, Matt. xvi.
16–19 ; John vi. 68 f. ; also Luke ix. 20).   At the beginning
of the resurrection history, xvi. 7, he is no more prominent
than in Luke xxiv. 34 ; John xx. 2–9.   His name does
not appear in vii. 17, though he is expressly mentioned
in Matt. xv. 15 ; nor is it to be found in xiv. 47 (cf. Matt.
xxvi. 51 ; Luke xxii. 50), in case Peter is here specifically
meant (John xviii. 10).   The narrative concerning him,
which we have in Matt. xiv. 28–31, is wanting in Mark
vi. 50.   In the account of his denial, however, the close
delineation of details reappears ; he *warms* himself by the
fire, the *reflexion* of which enables the maid who sees him
standing there, and who *looks upon him* scrutinisingly, to
recognise his features.   His asseveration that he does not
know Jesus, is reproduced with greater fulness than in the
other Gospels.   Corresponding to the more pointed way in

which Jesus' warning prophecy is given, the narrative
indicates that the cock crowed twice (xiv. 29–31, 54,
66, 72). It would not have been natural for Peter, in a
narrative concerning Jesus, to represent himself as the
chief of the apostles, as the rock upon which Jesus meant
to build His Church, as the chief steward in this house, and
as the leader who was to strengthen and encourage the
company of the brethren (Matt. x. 2, xvi. 16–19 ; Luke
xxii. 32 ; John i. 42, vi. 69 f., xxi. 15–22). On the other
hand, he could not narrate the Passion history without
giving strong expression to the inglorious part which he
had taken in the same, and which was so indelibly stamped
upon his memory. The lament of Jesus over the human
weakness of His most faithful disciples in the hour of
temptation has in Matt. xiv. 37 a pointed reference to
Peter which does not appear at all in Luke xxii. 46, and
which is much less direct in Matt. xxvi. 40. Only in
Mark's account does Jesus call Peter by name, and blame
him alone because he could not watch for a single hour
(n. 9).

According to the opinion of the disciple John, Mark
did not write a narrative which reproduced the order of
events (above, p. 439). This agrees with the fact that
frequently in Mark a new narrative is introduced by καί,
even in cases where the preceding context has no chronological connection. In i. 16, 40, iii. 13, the descriptions
which precede are general ; in iii. 20 we find ourselves in
Capernaum again without statement to this effect, though
just before we were upon the mountain (iii. 13), where it
is entirely possible that other things besides the choosing
of the disciples took place. In other passages the events
could not have taken place in the succession indicated,
e.g. in i. 21, notwithstanding the εὐθύς after the second
καί, since what is narrated in i. 16–20 could not have
taken place on a Sabbath. In iv. 26 the hearers are no
longer confined to the disciples as in iv. 11, 21, 24, but the

words are addressed to the multitude again as in iv. 1–9
(cf. iv. 33 f.) ; so that the account belongs after iv. 10.   In
the first half of the book especially, where the influence of
the governing idea is strongest (above, p. 462 f.), the content
of the separate narratives is throughout the connecting
bond among them, which does not prevent occasionally
the clear indication of the chronological order of events
(i. 29, 32, 35, or iv. 35, v. 1, 21, or xi. 12, 20, and xiv. 12–
xvi. 8).   When Papias reminds us, in his explanation of the
opinion of his teacher John concerning Mark's Gospel, that
Peter was under the necessity of arranging his accounts of
Jesus' sayings, upon which accounts Mark drew in many
passages of his book, in accordance with the practical
purpose of his discourses and the necessities of his hearers,
he implies that these sayings were reproduced with a
certain freedom.   Their use for edification and the effort
after clearness render impossible a scrupulously exact
reproduction of Jesus' words spoken years before under
entirely different conditions.   This is the case in Mark's
Gospel.   Comparison of Mark viii. 35, x. 29 with Matt.
xvi. 25, xix. 29, Luke ix. 24, xviii. 29, shows that the $\kappa \alpha \grave{\iota}$
$\check{\epsilon}\nu\epsilon\kappa\epsilon\nu$ $\tau o\hat{\upsilon}$ $\epsilon\grave{\upsilon}\alpha\gamma\gamma\epsilon\lambda\acute{\iota}o\upsilon$, which occurs in both passages, is only
an addition due to an intention to make what Jesus had
said in language appropriate to that situation ($\check{\epsilon}\nu\epsilon\kappa\epsilon\nu$ $\grave{\epsilon}\mu o\hat{\upsilon}$)
applicable to every Christian after Jesus' departure from
this world.   Likewise the mention of Jesus' words with
Jesus Himself in viii. 38 is without support in the nearest
parallels, Matt. x. 33 f. ; Luke xii. 9.   Further, the sharp
distinction between the rewards which one has in this
world and in the world to come,—which we notice in
x. 30 f. when compared with Matt. xix. 29,—suggests the
endeavouring of the preacher to guard himself against
possible misunderstanding.   The comparison of Mark ix. 1
with Matt. xvi. 28, Luke ix. 27, makes it clear that the
saying of Jesus about His return in the lifetime of some
of His contemporaries (cf. Matt. xxiv. 30 ; Mark xiii. 30 ;

Luke xxi. 32),—a saying which was regarded as an un-
solved problem in the apostolic age (John xxi. 22 f.),—is
reproduced with puzzling abruptness in Matthew, replaced
in Luke by a more general idea, but in Mark, on the other
hand, is given a definite didactic turn which modifies this
more general idea. Standing as it does in immediate
connection with a direct prophecy of the second coming of
Jesus as the judge of the world (viii. 38), the expression
about the coming of the kingdom of God with power
cannot have exactly the same meaning, but points to
events which, while proving the power of the kingdom
of God in the world for the believers who experience
them, are only a pledge of the fulfilment of the promise
of His personal return. If τὸ βδέλυγμα τῆς ἐρημώσεως ἑστη-
κότα ὅπου οὐ δεῖ is the correct reading in Mark xiii. 14,
then, in spite of grammar, the verse contains a definite
interpretation of a saying which in its original indefinite
form is found in Matt. xxiv. 15, and which was developed
in the apostolic age, principally in view of events which
took place in the reign of the emperor Caligula (vol. i.
pp. 228, 235 ff.). Mark ii. 27 gives a suitable reason for
the saying of Jesus which follows, a saying preserved
also in Matt. xii. 8; Luke vi. 5. The same general
thought we find in John vii. 22, 23; but as the verse
stands in Mark is it not the interpretation of a preacher in
his narrative? The distinction of the literal from the
spiritual temple in xiv. 58 (cf. *per contra*, Matt. xxvi. 61;
John ii. 19; Acts vi. 14) sounds exactly as if the interpretation of the preacher's narrative had been taken
over into the account. So far as we know, the expression ὅτι Χριστοῦ ἐστέ (ix. 41), added as an explanation of ἐν τῷ ὀνόματί μου (cf. Matt. x. 42), is not the
language of Jesus but of His Church (Rom. viii. 9; 1 Cor.
iii. 23; 2 Cor. x. 7). Of itself it is possible that Mark
arbitrarily introduced into the tradition which he received
all these additions, which in the usage of the Christian

Church and in the interpretations of the Church teachers were ascribed to Jesus Himself. But this is against the assumption of scrupulous exactness and conscientiousness in reproducing Peter's discourses, for which Mark is praised by his contemporaries, and of which we have gained an impression from numerous passages of his work. The assumption is also rendered improbable by the fact that other authors, like John and Matthew, who handle their material with perceptibly greater freedom than Mark, who was a disciple of one of the apostles, kept such historical inaccuracies out of the sayings of Jesus. Such free reproduction of Jesus' words is to be ascribed, first of all, to the missionary preacher and Church teacher, Peter, who was conscious of possessing faithful recollections, and who did not make a sharp distinction between the commands of Jesus and their proclamation in the apostolic teaching (2 Pet. iii. 2 ; cf. Matt. xxviii. 20). When John became acquainted with Mark's Gospel, it seemed to him as if Peter were again alive, and as if he were hearing, as in earlier years, his story about the words and deeds of Jesus ; and so he called the evangelist Mark, Peter's interpreter.

The testimony of the disciple John, as correctly interpreted by Papias and the tradition generally, when rightly understood and kept free from later exaggerations, does not exclude the possibility of Mark's having employed other sources and helps besides his recollection of Peter's narratives. He himself indicates here and there that what he gives is selected from a fuller narrative, cf. iv. 2, 33 f., xii. 1, 38. He seems to be excerpting from a longer discourse when, contrary to his habit, he reproduces the instructions to the disciples in vi. 8 f., in indirect discourse, and then in vi. 10 f. gives a single saying in direct form, as if beginning the narrative again. The brief account of the temptation, some of the details of which are unintelligible (i. 13), is not here given in a form in which accounts of such events are wont to pass from mouth to mouth, but is presented in a way that impresses one as being an excerpt taken from a written exemplar. Positive judgment on this point must be reserved, however, until after other accounts employing related material have been investigated.

1. (P. 488.) With regard to Hebrew and Aramaic words in the N.T., see vol. i. 15–22. Mark uses such words (1) in sections which are peculiar to him : Βοανηργες, iii. 17 ; εφφαθα, vii. 34 ; (2) in sections to which Matt. and Luke, or one of the two, offer parallels, corresponding more or less closely, but expressed in a purely Greek form : Καναναῖος, iii. 18 (so also Matt. x. 4, but ζηλωτής, Luke vi. 15); ταλιθα κουμ, v. 41; κορβαν, vii. 11 (δῶρον, Matt. xv. 5, but the Aramaic word in xxvii. 6) ; Βαρτιμαιος along with υἱὸς Τιμαίου, x. 46 ; ραββουνι, x. 51 (κύριε, Matt. xx. 33 ; Luke xviii. 41); ραββι, ix. 5 (κύριε, Matt. xvii. 4 ; ἐπιστάτα, Luke ix. 33), xi. 21 (not in Matt. xxi. 20) ; once in xiv. 45, where Matt. xxvi. 49 also has it ; twice in Matt. xxiii. 8, xxvi. 25, without parallels in Mark ; not at all in Luke, but eight times in John ; αββα, xiv. 36; αμην, iii. 28, viii. 12 (not in Matt. xii. 31, 39, xvi. 4), xii. 43 (ἀληθῶς, Luke xxi. 3), xiv. 25 (not in Matt. xxvi. 29 ; Luke xxii. 18) ; also (3) in sections where the parallels also give the Hebrew or Aramaic expression : αμην (see under No. 2) ; γεεννα, ix. 43–47 ; Βεελζεβουλ, iii. 22 ; σατανας, iii. 23, 26, viii. 33 ; ωσαννα, xi. 9, 10 (so Matt. xxi. 9, John xii. 13, but not Luke xix. 38); Γεθσημανει, xiv. 32 (Matt. xxvi. 36 ; avoided by Luke xxii. 39 ; John xviii. 1); Γολγοθα, xv. 22 (Matt. xxvii. 33, John xix. 17 ; only the translation Luke xxiii. 33) ; ελωϊ, etc., xv. 34 (Matt. xxvii. 46, vol. i. 15 ; without parallels in Luke or John). The passages in which Matthew gives Hebrew or Aramaic words or names which are lacking in Mark have no parallels at all in the latter Gospel (Matt. v. 22, xvi. 17). Χαναναία is hardly to be included here (Matt. xv. 22, cf. Mark vii. 26).

2. (P. 488.) Hitzig, *Ueber Johannes Marcus und seine Schriften, oder welcher Johannes hat die Offenbarung verfasst?* 1843, S. 29–37, 65 ff., has called attention to the Hebraising style of Mark with special emphasis. Elsewhere in the N.T. a double δύο is unheard of ; likewise συμπόσια and πρασιαί doubled in a distributive sense, vi. 7, 39, 40 (cf. the writer's *Hirt des Hermas*, 490) ; also the oath formula with εἰ, viii. 12 ; elsewhere only in O.T. quotations, as Heb. iii. 11, iv. 3, though perhaps also 1 Cor. xv. 32. Pleonastic use of αὐτοῦ, αὐτῆς κτλ. with the relative i. 7, vii. 25. The use of καί to carry on the narrative, instead of syntactical articulation, is not so noticeable in Mark as, say, in 1 Macc., but decidedly more frequent than in the other Gospels and Acts ; cf. for example, Mark iii. 13–19. In Bruder's *Konkordanz*, under "καί in oratione historica," p. 456 ff., Matt. occupies 4 columns, Luke 6½, John 1¾, Acts 2⅔, while the short Gospel of Mark occupies 6½. Even where the relation is adversative he is satisfied with καί, vi. 19, xii. 12 ; ἀλλά he hardly uses except after negative clauses.

3. (P. 489.) With the simple Πιλάτῳ, xv. 1, cf. Matt. xxvii. 2, Ποντίῳ Πιλάτῳ τῷ ἡγεμόνι. The equally simple form in Luke xxiii. 1 is prepared for in iii. 1 ; cf. xiii. 1. John, writing considerably later, everywhere assumes acquaintance with the main facts, and perhaps his readers already knew

Pilate (xviii. 29) from a baptismal confession (1 Tim. vi. 13, above, p. 131,
n. 20 ; cf. the writer's work, *Das Apost. Symbolum*, 39–44, 68 f.). On the
other hand, a title is given to Herod Antipas when he is first introduced,
vi. 14, to be sure not the exact title of tetrarch (Luke iii. 1, 19, ix. 7 ;
Matt. xiv. 1 ; Acts xiii. 1), but that of king. If one reflects, however, that
Matthew, in spite of his knowledge of the official title (xiv. 1), calls him
king in the narrative (xiv. 9 = Mark vi. 22 ; cf. ver. 23, βασιλεία ; John iv.
46, βασιλικός), and that Josephus also speaks occasionally of Archelaus,
who had likewise received and borne nc royal title, although he hoped
to receive one from Rome, as king, and of his rule as βασιλεύειν
(cf. Matt. ii. 22, and § 56, n. 6), it is evident that one has to do with a
usage current among the Palestinians, who, in the interval between the
death of Herod the Great (Matt. ii. 1 ; Luke i. 5) and the designation of
Herod Agrippa I. as king (Acts xii. 1), did not cease to speak of " king,
kingdom, royal officers," etc. So too Mark, although he knew that this
Herod had inherited only a part of the dominion of his father (vi. 21,
Γαλιλαίας), and of course, also, that he had not received his full title. On
the other hand, it is probable that in Mark vi. 17 there is real ignorance of
the complicated family relationships of the Herods ; see § 56, n. 6. Only
Mark xi. 13, and not Matt. (xxi. 19), who wrote for Palestinians, observes
that there are no fresh figs at the Passover time. In Rome they did not
know when figs ripened in Palestine.

4. (P. 489.) On the Latin see vol. i. pp. 41 f. 64 ff. ; κεντυρίων, Mark
xv. 39, 44, 45 ; in the parallel passages and everywhere else in the N.T.
only ἑκατόνταρχος or -χης (Matt. 4 times, Luke 3 times, Acts 14 times, but
Gospel of Peter κεντυρίων 4 times, so also the Syrian translators, where
the original has the Greek word, *e.g.* Sc. Matt. viii. 5–13, Luke xxiii. 47 ; and
Ss. Matt. xxvii. 54) ; σπεκουλάτωρ, vi. 27, not elsewhere in the N.T., but in
the Targum and Midrash ; similarly λεγιών, v. 9, 15 (also Luke viii. 30 ; Matt.
xxvi. 53, vol. i. 66) ; δηνάριον, vi. 37, xii. 15, xiv. 5 (also Matt. 6 times,
Luke 3 times, John twice, Rev. twice) ; ξέστης, vii. 4, 8, which is not, as
Epiphanius, *de Mens.* 55 (ed. Lagarde, 199 f.), thought, a Greek word adopted
by the Romans, but is deformed from the Latin *sextarius*, and was also current
among the Jews as כסטא and כסטוס ; cf. Krauss, *Lehnwörter*, ii. 293, 535, only
Mark in the N.T. ; also φραγελλοῦν, xv. 15 = *flagellare* (also Matt. xxvii. 26,
cf. John ii. 15) ; κῆνσος, xii. 14 (also Matt. xxii. 17, 19 ; vol. i. p. 66) ; and
κοδράντης, xii. 42 (Matt. v. 26) ; πραιτώριον, xv. 16 (Matt. xxvii. 27 ; John
xviii. 28, 33, xix. 9 ; Acts xxiii. 35 ; Phil. i. 13). On the other hand,
κράββατος (Mark 5 times, John 5 times, Acts 5 times) is not the Latin
grabatus, but *vice versa* a Macedonian word (Lobeck, *ad Phryn.* 62) used
in the common Greek speech, but despised by the Atticists, which was
adopted by the Latins as well as by the Jews, Krauss, ii. 570. The parallel
passages themselves show that, as has been said above, p. 489, the occurrence
of these Latin words cannot of itself prove that Mark was written in a Latin-
speaking region. They had all (even κεντυρίων, Krauss, ii. 529) gone over into
the current speech of Palestine. It might also be a mere matter of taste that
Luke preferred the Greek φόρος to the Latin *census* in xx. 22, and δύο λεπτά
to *quadrans* in xxi. 2. The decisive point is that Mark explains Greek by
Latin : xii. 42, λεπτὰ δύο, ὅ ἐστιν κοδράντης ; and xv. 16, ἔσω τῆς αὐλῆς, ὅ ἐστιν

πραιτώριον. As a counterpart to the former, Plutarch (*Vita Cic.* xxix.) says to his Greek readers, of the Romans, τὸ λεπτότατον (cf. τὸ λεπτόν) τοῦ χαλκοῦ νομίσματος κουαδράντην ἐκάλουν (*al.* καλοῦσιν, see Blass, *ET*, x. 186). If ἐκάλουν is the correct reading, the explanation of the imperfect is not, as Blass supposes, that the Quadrans was not minted after Trajan's time (which, more-over, is only Mommsen's conjecture), for Plutarch wrote under Trajan, and even twenty or thirty years after the introduction of the mark and pfennig coinage a German historian would make himself ridiculous by using the imperfect to introduce a bit of archæological instruction regarding the meaning of thaler and groschen, gulden and kreuzer. It is only because Plutarch's narrative deals with past time that he gives his information in the imperfect (see vol. iii. § 69, n. 6). The discussions between Blass and Ramsay (*ET*, x. 232, 287, 336) have only made it evident that it could not possibly occur to one who was writing for Greeks to explain the common expression δύο λεπτά by the word κοδράντης—a word to them at least much less familiar; cf. Ramsay, *ET*, x. 232. This is just the situation in Mark xv. 16. To support his assertion—which has no support whatever in the tradition—that Mark is a translation of an Aramaic book, Blass (*loc. cit.*) says that ὅ ἐστιν πραιτώριον is a mistranslation of αὐλή, which there denotes not palace, but courtyard. The word has the latter meaning only in xiv. 66 (" below in the court," in distinction from the transaction in the hall "above," the scene of the preceding narrative), but not in xiv. 54 (Matt. xxvi. 58). The Sanhedrin does not assemble in the "courtyard of the high priest" (Matt. xxvi. 3), which would be an extraordinary expression in any case, but in the residence of the high priest, consisting of various buildings, courtyards, and so forth. In contrast with Pilate's dealings with the Sanhedrin and people, which took place in the street *before* his residence (Mark xv. 1–15, cf. John xviii. 28 f.), it is said in xv. 16 that the soldiers led Jesus into the interior of the palace, without specifying whether the following scene took place in an enclosed building or in the courtyard of the palace. The use of ἡ αὐλή to denote the ruler's abode for the time being was common with all Greek writers (cf. *Forsch.* iv. 276; also, for example, *Epist. Aristeæ,* ed. Wendland, p. 48. 12, 21, 80. 15, but p. 50. 9, ἡ ἄκρα, royal residence. On πραιτώριον see vol. i. 551 f. It is difficult to decide whether the peculiar expressions, often altered by copyists, συμβούλιον διδόναι, iii. 6 (BL, etc.; Klostermann, 62 f. = *edere*); φαίνεται, xiv. 64 (for δοκεῖ = the ambiguous *videtur* ?); ῥαπίσμασιν αὐτὸν ἔλαβον, xiv. 65 (*verberibus eum acceperunt*); ἐπιβαλών, xiv. 72; ποιῆσαι τὸ ἱκανόν, xv. 15 (*satisfacere*), are to be considered Latinisms, and what value they have in determining the historical and local circumstances of Mark's Gospel.

5. (P. 489.) Concerning Rufus (Rom. xvi. 13) see vol. i. 392. There is no tradition about him and his brother Alexander, independent of the N.T. Alexander and Rufus are called companions of Andrew and Peter in the *Acts of Andrew and Peter* (*Acta Apocr.*, ed. Lipsius et Bonnet, ii. part 2. 117. 5, 118. 9, 119. 13; cf. Lipsius, *Apokr. A. G.* i. 553, 617, 621, ii. part 2. 77, 79, 83; Papadop. Kerameus, *Cat. Bibl. Hieros.* ii. 497, No. 8). Other fables in Forbes Robinson, *Copt. Apocr. Gospels,* p. 50. Epiph. *Hær.* lxxviii. 13, evidently confuses the nameless mother of Rufus (Rom. xvi. 13) with the Mary of Rom. xvi. 6 (vol. i. 430), where he probably read ἡμᾶς, and identified these with the women under the cross (John xix. 25). The old tradition

used by Epiphanius in his confused way, probably referred to that "other Mary," the mother of James "the less" and a Joseph (Matt. xxvii. 56, xxviii. 1 ; Mark xv. 40, 47, xvi. 1). The interest in this Mary and her sons, which Mark, in contrast to Matthew, mentions and presupposes on the part of his readers, and other traces of a (Joseph) Barsabbas Justus (Acts i. 23 ; Papias in Eus. *H. E.* iii. 39. 9) in the early Roman Church (*Acta Apocr.*, ed. Lipsius, i. 108. 13, 116. 12) in fact makes probable the identity of the Mary of Rom. xvi. 6 with the "other Mary" of Matthew (cf. *Forsch.* vi. 348–350). If this is so, we would have a companion-piece to "Simon of Cyrene, the father of Alexander and Rufus" (Mark xv. 21). This narrative presupposes that this Simon was known to the Jews as one who esteemed Jesus, and was therefore pointed out to the soldier who had charge of the execution (*ZKom. Matt.* 703). He was therefore not a festival pilgrim from abroad, but a Jew of Cyrene, dwelling in or near Jerusalem. The ἀγρός from which he was coming into Jerusalem (Mark xv. 21) must have been his country-place outside of the city, cf. Lightfoot's note to *Mart. Polyc.* chap. v. In any case he cannot be identified with the Simon Niger, Acts xiii. 1 (a conjecture made by Spitta, *Die Apostlegesch.* S. 134, and not yet abandoned (*Untersuch. über den Rm.* S. 73)) ; for, since the Lucius who is named with him is referred to as "of Cyrene," this designation is indirectly denied concerning Simon Niger.

5a. (P. 490.) Acts (iii. 1–iv. 31, viii. 14) gives evidence of the prominence of John, for it mentions James only in connection with his own execution, and, on the other hand, joins John with Peter ; cf. also Luke xxii. 8 ; John xiii. 23 f., xx. 3 ff., xxi. 20–22. Paul also in Gal. i. 18 f. does not name along with Peter, James the son of Zebedee, who was then living, but just as in Gal. ii. 9 in relation to a later incident, he mentions another James in connection with Peter and John.

6. (P. 491.) For the opinions of the ancients with regard to the fleeing youth see p. 446 f. above. Among modern writers the combination presented above was first brought forward as a conjecture by Olshausen, *Komm. zum NT³*, ii. 474, and then more carefully elaborated by Klostermann, 281 f., 337 f. The reading εἰς τις νεανίσκος (AE, etc., against אBCDL Ss S¹, the Egyptian and Latin versions, which have καὶ νεανίσκος [or νεανίσκος δέ] τις) is evidently conformed to ver. 47 with the mistaken idea that another of the apostles' circle is referred to here. The addition οἱ νεανίσκοι after αὐτόν, which has still less support, presupposes that the fleeing youth was not one of the disciples, but one of the δῆμος ; cf. Anonymus in *Catena in Marc.*, ed. Possimus, 327.

7. (P. 493.) To be sure, ἔρχεσθαι does not always mean to come, but sometimes also to go, Matt. xvi. 5 ; Mark xi. 13a (in distinction from 13b), John vi. 17, but also Matt. xix. 1 ; Mark x. 1 (cf. *ZKom. Matt.* 579, n. 48), a signification which appears particularly in ἀπέρχεσθαι, διέρχεσθαι, and sometimes also in ἐξέρχεσθαι, *e.g.* John iv. 30 ("they went out of the city and came to Him "). But it would be hard to point out an ἔρχεσθαι entirely undefined which describes the movement from the standpoint, not of the goal, but of the starting-point. After Mark xiv. 16, if the standpoint of the narrative thus far was to be preserved, Jesus' going to the house could be expressed only by ἀπῆλθεν, ἐπορεύθη, or similar terms It is instructive to

compare iii. 13, where it is not said, "Jesus called them and they came '
(cf. Luke vii. 8, for example), but "they went to Him," so that one sees that
the story is not told from the standpoint of the one who called and awaited
the result of his call, but from the standpoint of the disciples who were
summoned (cf. Klostermann, 70).

8. (P. 496.) The alterations of i. 29 (B ἐξελθὼν ἦλθεν, D b c e q S¹ practically the same) are not improvements, for by them the presence of Peter and
Andrew is actually excluded. Ss is peculiar : "And he went out of the
synagogue and came into the house of Simon Cephas—Andrew and James
and John were with him—and the mother-in-law," etc.

9. (P. 498.) Eusebius, *Demonstr.* iii. 5. 89–95, and more explicitly
Theoph. (Syriac trans.) v. 40, on the supposition that Peter spoke through
Mark, found the omission of the contents of Matt. xvi. 17–19 and Mark's
more detailed account of Peter's denial an indication of the apostle's freedom
from all self-sufficiency.

§ 54. THE TRADITION REGARDING MATTHEW AND HIS GOSPEL.

The Matthew who occupies the seventh or the eighth
place (n. 1) in all the lists of the apostles in the N.T. is
the only person who has ever been regarded as the writer
of the Gospel which bears this name. In only one passage
is he called a tax-gatherer (Matt. x. 3), and here with the
narrative of ix. 9–13 in view. We find exactly the same
account with all its details in Mark ii. 13–17 ; Luke v.
27–32 with reference to a tax-gatherer Levi. Since there
can be no doubt that the same incident is related in all
three cases, this Levi must be identified with the apostle
Matthew. This takes for granted, of course, that Matthew
is trustworthy, which, however, we have no reason to
question in this instance, because there is no conceivable
reason why a writer should identify the apostle Matthew,
in whom later he shows no particular interest, inasmuch as
he is not mentioned again anywhere in his book, with a
man of another name, the account of whose call in the
other two reports which have come down to us is in no
way connected with the apostles. The difference is to be
accounted for as follows :—In the account of his calling,
Mark and Luke employ the name by which he was

commonly known at the time; while in Matthew the name which, according to the four lists of the apostles, was regularly used to designate him as an apostle and member of the Christian community, is employed also in this passage of the history. Whether Jesus gave him a new name as He did other of His disciples, and if so, why the particular name Matthai ("Gift of Yahweh") was chosen, we do not know (n. 1). In view of the way in which the tax-gatherers were hated by the Jews, a person who had given up this calling must have been doubly glad to be known by another name. His father, Alphæus (Mark ii. 14), can hardly be identical with the Alphæus whose son James was also one of the Twelve; since, if Matthew and this James were brothers, it would be so indicated in the lists, as are the brothers Peter-Andrew and the sons of Zebedee, particularly in Matt. x. 3, Acts i. 13, where they are mentioned together.

As a tax-gatherer in Capernaum, in the territory of Herod Antipas, Matthew was not a Roman official, but stood either directly in the service of the reigning prince (cf. John iv. 46; Luke viii. 3), or under the person who had the taxes of the city or a larger district in tenure. In order to fill this office he must have had considerable readiness with the pen, and, in addition to the Aramaic dialect of the land, must without question have been able to use Greek. Judging from the fact that He interrupted him in the midst of his work and also from the result of the call, Jesus must have intended that Matthew, like the fishermen earlier, should give up his former vocation and attach himself to Him as a constant companion and future worker. Such a demand and Matthew's immediate compliance presuppose that he had been acquainted with Jesus for a long time, had been affected by His preaching, and felt the utmost confidence in Him. Consequently, for a considerable time he had been one of those publicans and sinners who more than others in Galilee felt drawn to

Jesus (Matt. xi. 19; Luke vii. 34, xv. 1). A large number of persons belonging to the same class as himself, and of like feeling, he invited to a feast in his house, in order to celebrate along with them and with Jesus the decisive change which had taken place in his life (n. 2). Exactly when Matthew became a constant companion of Jesus cannot be determined, at least not here in passing. So much, however, may be said, namely, that according to the accounts in the N.T. he had not been a companion and disciple of John prior to his association with Jesus, as was the case with the first six of the apostolic group; he had no part in the series of events which, according to John i. 19–iv. 54 (or v. 35), preceded the arrest of the Baptist; and after this event and the beginning of Jesus' extensive prophetic work in Galilee considerable time elapsed before the publican became a regular disciple. Others had been for some time constant companions of Jesus. Peter, James, and John are mentioned as already the most trusted of the disciples on the day in which Matthew received his call (Mark v. 37; for the order of events cf. Matt. ix. 11, 14, 18). The battle with the Pharisees was already in full progress. The choosing of the apostles and the Sermon on the Mount were almost at hand. That is all that the N.T. relates concerning the apostle Matthew. The meagreness of the record about him, with the corresponding implication that he was called late, and was one of the less important of the apostles, gives the tradition that he was the author of the first Gospel particular weight. If the name had been chosen arbitrarily, an Andrew or James the son of Zebedee, a Philip or a Thomas, would have been preferred to Matthew. The reports which we have outside the N.T. concerning Matthew are so late, so fantastic, and in part so confused on account of the interchange between the names Matthew and Matthias, that they possess no historical value (n. 3). This also shows that the name

Matthew was not one that would be naturally chosen for a Gospel in circulation in the Church, the origin of which Gospel was unknown, or whose real origin one would wish to conceal. That the author himself did not make it a point to be known as the apostle Matthew, or to pass for the same, is perfectly clear.

For the oldest and most important report concerning Matthew's literary activity we are indebted to Papias, just as we have to thank him for the oldest report regarding Mark as a writer of gospel history. What Eusebius preserves is not an opinion of the presbyter John, but what Papias says himself (n. 4). Papias' words read : "Matthew compiled the sayings, to be sure, in the Hebrew language, but everyone translated the same as best he could." The Greek expressions used by Papias show even more clearly than this English translation that the whole emphasis rests upon the contrast between the language in which Matthew wrote and the translation which this rendered necessary, but which not everyone who attempted it could make successfully. The emphasis does not, as has been so often assumed since Schleiermacher (above, p. 411), rest upon the result of Matthew's literary work. He does not begin by saying that among others the apostle Matthew also had written a book, but he speaks in exactly the same manner as does the Presbyter concerning Mark (above, p. 439 ff.), under the presupposition that the readers are aware that Matthew had written, and that they are familiar with his work. He states what possibly is not known to them all, namely, that Matthew did not write in the language of Papias and his readers, but in Hebrew, a language with which they were not familiar. For this reason Papias could use the extremely abbreviated expression τὰ λόγια to designate the subject of Matthew's work. There can be no acceptance of the view that τὰ λόγια was the title of a work known at the time. Hebrew book could not well have had a Greek

title ; but, apart from this, a title translated by the Greek
τὰ λόγια, or rather, if it were a title, by λόγια without
the article, would have been an incomprehensible puzzle.
" Oracles," or, according to the predominating usage,
" Divine Oracles," would have been an utterly senseless
title for a book which certainly was not a collection of all
the words of God's revelatio. or of single oracles, but
which dealt with Jesus. Moreover, if there was a work
with this title which at the time of Papias and in his
vicinity was assigned without contradiction to the apostle
Matthew, it would not have been so easy for every trace
of it to disappear from the remaining literature. Papias
does not say that the author of the known Logia was the
apostle Matthew, but he says that the distinguished
apostle Matthew, whom he had already mentioned in his
preface as a disciple of Jesus, wrote in Hebrew. Nor does
any author of the ancient Church, not even those who are
quite at home in the extra-canonical Gospels and kindred
literature, as Irenæus, Origen, Eusebius, Epiphanius, and
Jerome, ever say anything of a book of this title, much
less of such a book from Matthew's hand. This universal
silence is conclusive evidence that these persons had never
read or heard anything of such a work. Consequently it is
also very improbable that such a work existed in Papias'
time. On the other hand, the unemphatic position of the
τὰ λόγια and the lack of all explanatory definition of the
words exclude the possibility of Papias having meant that
Matthew, in distinction from other authors who narrated
also the deeds of Jesus, limited his account to the words.
The only possibility left is to suppose that Papias took it
for granted that the content of Matthew's writing was
known, and used an abbreviation of the same, which in
its connection could not be misunderstood. According to
the title, Papias' entire work was devoted to the interpretation of the λόγια κυριακά. He had always been a
searcher after " The commands that are given from the

Lord to our faith, and that come from the truth itself,"
as he says in the preface. That is, he was a searcher
after the words of Jesus, not His deeds. As to the books,
moreover, which dealt with Jesus, those parts which
contained the words interested him by far the most.
This is indicated by his comment upon John's judgment
concerning Mark. John mentions as the subjects which
Mark had handled, without giving the exact chronological
order, the "words or deeds of Christ"; Papias speaks
only of the "words of the Lord," which were without
ordered connection in the discourses of Peter, upon which
Mark drew. From this we may assume that here also,
where he uses the words τὰ λόγια to designate the subject
of Matthew's work, he mentions only that part of the book
to which his own special interest was directed, without
thereby implying that Matthew did not record also deeds
of Jesus and the historical occasions of all the words which
he preserved.

The idea of a collection of sayings by Matthew, or even
of a work bearing the remarkable title λόγια, has therefore no support from the words of Papias. It lacks also
internal probability; by far the greater number of Jesus'
words which have been preserved to us were spoken in
conversation with His disciples and in discussion with His
opponents. According to the tradition, upon which we
are in any case dependent, even the longer discourses had
definite occasion in outward events, without knowledge
of which they cannot be understood, and which must
have been communicated for their intelligent transmission.
They are pictures which could never have existed without
frames, in literature any more than in fact (n. 4). When,
now, Papias sets in contrast to the fact that Matthew compiled the Logia in Hebrew, the other fact that for this
reason a ἑρμηνεύειν was necessary, which everyone exercised
according to his ability, it is self-evident (1) that ἑρμηνεύειν
here can mean only translating; and (2) that this was a

translation into the Greek language, which did not need to
be mentioned expressly, because this was the language of
Papias and his readers. Those who knew Hebrew required
no translation of a Hebrew document, and the Phrygian
bishop knew nothing of hearers or readers unfamiliar with
both Hebrew and Greek. (3) The fact deserves more attention than has been paid to it heretofore, that Papias does
not speak of the translation of Matthew's writing, but of
the words of Jesus which it contained. The idea that the
words ἡρμήνευσε δ' αὐτὰ (sc. τὰ λόγια) ἕκαστος mean that a
number of written translations or revisions of Matthew's
Gospel were made, can be arrived at only under the presupposition already shown to be untenable, that τὰ λόγια
was the title of a book. Even if this presupposition were
as correct as it is palpably false, the construction would be
out of harmony with the words; the fact to which they are
supposed to attest Papias would have to express in some
such way as this: πολλοὶ δὲ τὴν τοῦ Ματθαίου συγγραφὴν
ἡρμήνευσαν or ἑρμηνεύειν ἐπεχείρησαν. Then we would have
the impossible puzzle to solve, how so many written translations, say five or six, of which Papias still had knowledge in 125, so suddenly disappeared from the life and
recollection of the Church, and were replaced by the sixth
or seventh translation, which is the only one preserved in
all the Greek MSS., and the only one which was made the
basis of all the ancient versions. We are freed from all
these historical, linguistic, or logical impossibilities as soon
as we realise that Papias is talking about *oral translation*,
and, indeed, oral translation such as was made in assemblies of Greek-speaking Churches or congregations whose
language was mixed. We cannot recall the fact too often
that the oral translation in the religious assembly of books
written in a foreign language played an important rôle not
only among the Jews, but also in the Christian Church of
antiquity (cf. vol. i. 11 f., 23; *GK*, i. 39–60). For the
benefit of Christians who did not know Greek, in Jerusalem

and Scythopolis all the Scripture readings, prayers, and discourses were translated orally into Aramaic in 300 as in 400,
and certainly very much earlier. Before the preparation of
the Latin Bible, such oral translation was the only means
employed by Occidental Christians, who were ignorant of
Greek, for the transference of the words of the Gospel and of
the apostolic letters from Greek into Latin. Among the
Africans who knew only Latin, this was the case until Tertullian's time; whereas among the Punic-speaking population of
the same province in the time of Augustine, and among the
Celts in Gaul, it was never otherwise. From this point of view
Papias' statement is very luminous. Then the ἕκαστος, which
is out of place when his words are interpreted to refer to a
number of Greek translations of Matthew's Gospel, is
limited in the nature of the case to Christians who had
some knowledge of Hebrew and Greek, and who attempted
to make the content of a Hebrew book intelligible to congregations with little or no knowledge of this language.
It was necessary for them to translate. There were persons, like the disciples John and Aristion, Philip and his
daughters,—to confine ourselves to Papias' vicinity,—who
certainly possessed considerable ability in this direction,
but not everyone requested to do the work was equally
skilled in translation, and it was possible to succeed once
and fail the next time. The work was burdensome, and
the method of discourse defective. We have a repetition
of conditions and occurrences such as are described in
1 Cor. xiv. 11–19, 26–28 in another connection. Now
we understand the distributive ἕκαστος (cf. 1 Cor. xiv. 26);
on each occasion—and this could recur hundreds of times
—the question arose as to how the acting interpreter
would succeed in edifying the congregation by his translation. It is also clear why Papias did not think of the
translation of the Book of Matthew, but of the sayings of
Jesus which it contained. Through Hebrew Christians
the existence of a great sermon which Jesus had preached

on the mountain became known, which was recorded in
the Hebrew Matthew but not in the Gospel of Mark, which
was in circulation in the province of Asia at the time (above,
pp. 444, 456 n., 16).   If this or some other discourse was
to be brought to the ears of the congregations in Ephesus or
Hierapolis, it must be through the translation of a Hebrew
Christian.   It was never the Book of Matthew which was
translated, but always and only single pericopes from the
same, and, what was the chief point for Papias, always
a portion of the λόγια κυριακά.   Papias' words give us a
glimpse into the history of the Christian worship at a time
when the Greek Gospel of Matthew did not yet exist in
Asia Minor, but while there were still numerous Hebrew
Christians who possessed a Hebrew Matthew.   Papias
does not describe Christian worship as conducted during
his younger years ; in this case he would have used the
imperfect (ἡρμήνευε) to express the fact that the reading
of sections of Scripture in Greek was exchanged for the
translation of Hebrew pericopes.   Neither does he describe
a condition of things in existence at the time when he
wrote (ἑρμηνεύει), but employs the aorist (ἡρμήνευσε) to
indicate that it was something belonging entirely to the
past.   It was so once ; when Papias wrote it was no
longer necessary.   This statement carries with it the
explanation why it was that the earlier state of things of
which Papias speaks was no longer in existence when he
wrote.   It is inconceivable that a Hebrew book made
familiar by reiterated translation and doubtless also highly
prized should have been forgotten, possibly because the
other Gospels were a sufficient substitute, or because the
interpreters who knew the language, the emigrants from
Palestine, had died out in Asia Minor.   In this case there
would have been no longer any Matthew, and Papias
would no longer have had any interest in speaking of
Matthew's literary work.   He did have such an interest,
however, because when he wrote there was a Greek Gospel

whose content purported to be the same as that of the
Hebrew Matthew. The same process must have taken
place here that we observe elsewhere under similar conditions. Just as the oral translation of the Hebrew Scriptures in the Palestinian and other Oriental synagogues was
finally crystallised in the written Targums, and just as
Cyprian's Latin Bible grew out of the translation of the
Greek Bible in the African Church into which Tertullian
gives us a glimpse, so the Greek Matthew is the final
outcome of the translation of the Hebrew Matthew, testified to by Papias, in the Greek congregations of Asia
Minor, and perhaps also in other regions.

We know also from other sources that when Papias
wrote, 125 A.D., or possibly somewhat later, that the Greek
Matthew was not only in existence, but already somewhat
widely circulated. To mention only the most striking
evidence, the *Epistle of Barnabas* (130 A.D.) cites as Holy
Scripture the saying which we find preserved in Matt. xxii.
14, and in the letters of Ignatius and Polycarp (110 A.D.),
a friend of Papias (Iren. v. 33. 4), also in the *Didache*
(probably written at the same time), we find several sentences peculiar to Matthew employed as if they were the
common property of the Christian Churches (n. 5). The
Greek Matthew, which is the only known source to which we
can refer these citations, was, however, universally accepted
as a work of Matthew (above, p. 386 ff. ; below, n. 5).
Consequently, the data for the history of Matthew derived
from other sources confirms the interpretation of Papias'
testimony given above. The latter remains, however, of
inestimable value, since Papias gives us no mere literary-
historical report of uncertain origin handed on by him,
but testifies to a condition which had existed for a long
time in his native Church, an unfortunate condition
burdening the Church's life, beyond one's imagination.
If, during Papias' earlier years, there was a Hebrew Gospel
purporting to be the apostle Matthew's, which persons in

the province of Asia had long been in the habit of translating into Greek, often orally in the manner which he
describes, it is (1) incontrovertible that the original language of the book in question was Hebrew (or Aramaic,
see below), and that at this time there was no Greek
translation or recasting of the same.   (2) The tradition
that Matthew wrote this Hebrew book was just as firmly
believed as that regarding Mark's authorship of the Gospel
bearing his name, since this Hebrew book was much read,
translated, and also highly esteemed as a work of the
apostle Matthew at a time when personal disciples of Jesus
and other "Hebrews" from Palestine were to be found in
the Churches of Asia Minor.   (3) This shows that the
book whose oral translation appeared to be rendered unnecessary by the existence of a Greek book bearing the
name of the same author was no unknown work.   The
transference of Matthew's name from the Hebrew to the
Greek Gospel, which took place under the eye of Papias
and of others who, like himself, were disciples of apostles,
presupposes that in this circle the Greek Gospel was
regarded as a complete substitute for the Hebrew book,
i.e. as a substantially correct translation of the same.

We are not informed in so many words as to the time
and place of this transition.   Inasmuch, however, as we
have no knowledge of another Greek-speaking province
outside of Asia where the Hebrew Matthew was in use,
and since we are informed by Papias that this Gospel had
been translated orally for a long time in the Churches of
Asia, the only natural inference is that the change from
the Hebrew to the Greek Matthew was made in this
region.   In view of the practical advantage to be derived
from such a work, it is not likely that it was left until
only one or two interpreters were to be found capable of
executing the translation.   It may, therefore, be considered very probable that the Greek Matthew originated
before the close of the first century in the province of

Asia, whence it was circulated, and, in view of the witnesses cited, more probably before 90 than after 100.
The fact that the name of the translator of this book, like
those of all the ancient Bible translators, has disappeared,
requires no explanation (n. 6). There are two things,
however, that must not be forgotten, first, that Papias'
statement to the effect that the oral translation of the
Hebrew Matthew was not always made in a manner
entirely satisfactory, will hold good also of one of these
oral translators who wrote out the Greek Matthew. Then,
secondly, we must bear in mind that at least *one* Greek
Gospel, that of Mark, was already in circulation in his
vicinity (above, p. 444 f.) when the Greek text of Matthew
was prepared.

The report that Matthew wrote his Gospel in Hebrew
was often recalled in the ancient Church and never contradicted (n. 7). Undoubtedly, Papias' work and, after
325, the Church History of Eusebius, which was widely
read, contributed much to the circulation of this tradition.
This is not enough, however, to render Papias entirely
responsible for the same. Origen, whose writings betray
not the slightest trace of acquaintance with Papias' work,
speaks of the original language of Matthew with as much
confidence as does Irenæus, who had read Papias' book.
The Alexandrians received the information from another,
or indeed an additional source. The Alexandrian teacher
Pantænus is reported to have found on the occasion of
his journey to India, *i.e.* probably to South Arabia
(before 180), a Gospel, written in Hebrew characters and
the Hebrew language, in use among the Christians in this
region. These Christians, who for this reason are called
Hebrews, are reported to have held this Gospel to be a
work of Matthew, which they claimed to have received
through the apostle Bartholomew, to whose preaching they
were said to owe their Christianity (n. 7). Regardless of
the correctness or incorrectness of the statements and

opinions of these Jewish Christians, they had a tradition
that Matthew wrote a Hebrew Gospel, which, in any case,
was not derived from the Greek work of the Phrygian
bishop.   It was at that time at the latest, however, that
Pantænus learned this same tradition and brought it to
Alexandria.   The opinion that the entire tradition of the
Hebrew Gospel of Matthew is due to an error of Papias,
who had heard of the Aramaic Gospel in use among Jewish
Christians in Syria and Palestine, is not only inconsistent
with the proper understanding of Papias' testimony concerning the Hebrew Matthew, and unsuited to explain the
circulation of the tradition regarding the same, but is in
itself also historically improbable.   For, to our knowledge,
the Jewish Christians in question, the Nazarenes, never
called their only Gospel (the so-called *Gospel of the
Hebrews*) after Matthew (*GK*, ii. 723); and the older
scholars who deal with the *Gospel of the Hebrews*,
Clement, Origen, and Eusebius, do not say anything
which indicates that it was closely related to Matthew.
Only those who, like Irenæus (n. 7), were unacquainted
with the conditions and Scriptures of Jewish Christians
in the far East were liable to be led into the error of
supposing that the Ebionites, as these Jewish Christians
were indiscriminately called, used only the Hebrew
Matthew.   The tradition that Matthew wrote in Hebrew
for the Hebrews, together with the reported existence of
a Hebrew Gospel in use among Jewish Christians, and
uncertain reports of correspondence between the Greek
Matthew and the *Gospel of the Hebrews*, gave rise to
the opinion that the latter was the original upon which
the Greek Matthew was based.   Jerome, who was exactly
informed as to the facts, gave occasional support to the
view in order to establish a reputation for being also a
N.T. scholar by rediscovering the *veritas hebraica*.   These
obscure statements and errors are not the source of
the tradition regarding the Hebrew Matthew, but pre-

suppose its existence. In reality the relation between the Aramaic *Gospel of the Nazarenes* and the Greek Matthew is very close. If, on the other hand, it be accepted as proved that no relation of dependence of the *Gospel of the Hebrews* on the Greek Matthew exists, or *vice versa* (*GK*, ii. 704–723), we have a new proof, entirely independent of the witness of Papias, that the Greek Matthew goes back to a Hebrew original which is also the basis of the *Gospel of the Hebrews.* In every case where Jerome speaks of the Hebrew original of Matthew as a book in his possession, he means this Aramaic *Gospel of the Nazarenes* (*GK*, ii. 648 ff., 681 f.). It is not impossible that the book shown to Pantænus by Jewish Christians in South Arabia was likewise a copy of the *Gospel of the Hebrews.* But it is just as possible that at that time copies of the original Matthew were really preserved in this far-off corner of the Christian world. In his account of the incident, Eusebius expresses surprise (n. 7) that the Hebrew Matthew should be still in existence in Pantænus' time (180), as he concluded from the incident which he narrates. This fact shows us that the learned bishop of Cæsarea, who had the largest Christian library of the fourth century at his disposal, would have sought in vain for the Hebrew Matthew in his age and vicinity. When Epiphanius repeats what he had heard from eye-witnesses about a Hebrew Matthew and also a translation of John's Gospel and of the Acts in the possession of the Jews in Tiberias in 330 (n. 7), and states, further, that this Hebrew Matthew was not a translation but the original, the latter is an incorrect addition of his to the otherwise credible narrative which he had heard. It is possible that here also, as so often by Jerome, the *Gospel of the Hebrews* was taken to be the original Matthew. It is improbable, however ; since, in the first place, as already remarked, the single Gospel used by the Nazarenes was not called by Matthew's name, and, in the

second place, the contemporaneous existence of a Hebrew
John and Acts indicates rather that the Hebrew Matthew,
like the other two books, was a translation from the Greek.
These Aramaic translations originated from the oral translation of the Greek N.T. which, according to traditions which
come down to us from the time, was still customary in the
Churches of these regions in 300. Large portions of the
same are preserved for us in the *Evangeliarium Hieroso-
lymitanum* and the accompanying fragments of other N.T.
books. This explanation of the origin of the translation
is not weakened by the fact that several parts of the same,
including the three books mentioned, were in existence as
early as 330. There is no doubt that the translation of
Matthew, as of the other N.T. writings, goes back to a
Greek original. Here we have a new proof that at the
beginning of the fourth century the original Hebrew
Matthew no longer existed in Palestine. No one would
translate Matthew's Gospel from the Greek into the vernacular if the original Gospel written in this language
were still in existence. The same is true of the oldest
Gospel translations of the East Syrians (Sc, Ss), in which
Matthew is also dependent upon the Greek. The Hebrew
Matthew has disappeared. And why not ? The Nazarenes
who retained their native language had their *Gospel of
the Hebrews* not later than 150. Other Jewish Christians
in Palestine and Syria had a Greek translation of their own
apparently from 170 onwards (*GK*, ii. 724–742). By 100
at the latest, the Gentile Christian Churches of Asia Minor,
perhaps also of other regions, where once the Hebrew
Matthew was orally translated with great effort, were in
possession of a Greek translation which was considered in
every sense a substitute for the original. After the middle
of the second century, none of the Churches that we know
anything about had any interest in retaining the Hebrew
Matthew. The disappearance of the book in no way obscures the clear traces of its earlier existence. Scholars who

regard our Matthew as an original Greek work (n. 8) have
not succeeded in showing the unanimous tradition against
them, which goes back into the first century, to be in error,
and therefore have not succeeded in setting it aside.
Further, the assumption that Matthew himself wrote his
Gospel both in Greek and in Hebrew stands in irreconcilable contradiction with the testimony of Papias, when
rightly understood, which rests upon the experience of a
large section of the Church, and it finds no support in the
tradition.   How the theory goes to pieces when the
attempt is made to reconcile it with the text itself, we
shall show later (§ 56).

The evidence derived from its original language showing
that Matthew was written for Hebrews, *i.e.* for non-
Hellenised Jews in Palestine, is frequently stated by the
Fathers.   No more definite tradition than this appears to
be at the basis of the statement occasionally made that
the original readers were Jews who had been already converted to Christianity (n. 7).   The objection can be made
at once on purely external grounds, that James and Judas,
as well as Peter in 2 Peter, wrote in Greek to the Jewish
Christians of Palestine and the neighbouring regions.   If
the readers whom Matthew had in mind were of exactly
the same character, in using Hebrew he would be departing from the rule which we find otherwise to be observed.
Matthew's use of the ἑβραὶς διάλεκτος, like Paul's (Acts
xxii. 2), indicates that he has in view compatriots and
countrymen in general, and wrote the book in the vernacular
because he desired to show also in this outward manner his
geniune Israelitish feeling, and to bring its contents as close
to their hearts as possible.   The choice of the language was
one of the means by which he sought to accomplish his
apologetic purpose,—a means which, to say the least, would
have been unfortunately chosen if it was Hebrew in the
strict sense, *i.e.* the sacred language of the O.T., or the
modernised Hebrew of the rabbis.   In this case he would

have transferred the discourses of Jesus and His conversa
tions with friend and foe out of the language of the
common people (Aramaic) into a learned language little
understood by the majority, especially the poor, to whom
first of all the gospel was to be brought. The assumption
may be rejected at once as historically impossible. The
language in which Matthew wrote could have been no
other than the language of Jesus, "the original language
of the gospel" (§ 1), the Aramaic vernacular of Palestine
(n. 9).

The only tradition regarding the time of composition which is of sufficient age and definiteness to be of
value has been already discussed (above, p. 392 ff.). It is
limited to the two points : that (1) of the four evangelists
Matthew wrote first, and (2) his gospel was written be
tween 61 and 66. For the latter, Irenæus is, to be sure,
the only witness ; but he speaks with a definiteness and
certainty which indicates dependence upon older sources
(n. 10).

1. (Pp. 506, 507.) The position of Matthew in the lists is not always the
same ; in Mark iii. 18 and Luke vi. 15 : 6th Bartholomew, 7th Matthew,
8th Thomas ; in Matt. x. 3 : 6th Bartholomew, 7th Thomas, 8th Matthew ;
in Acts i. 13 : 6th Thomas, 7th Bartholomew, 8th Matthew. In the fact
that Matthew alone in his list calls himself the publican, and puts his
name after that of his σύζυγος Thomas, Eus. *Demonstr.* iii. 5. 81–86
Theophan. v. 38, saw a proof of his humility. Cf. Orig. *Schol. in Prov.*
(Tischendorf, *Not. Cod. Sin.* pp. 78, 119) ; *Didascalia*, ed. Lagarde, p. 44. 9 ff.;
Epiph. *Hær.* li. 6 ; also Barnabas v. 9. In the *Diatessaron*, according to the
testimony of the Syrian Ischodad of the ninth century (given by Goussen, *Stud.
Bibl.* i. 66, cf. Harris, *Fragments of the Comm. of Ephrem on the Diatessaron,*
p. 101 ; *ThLb*, 1895, p. 499), the five apostles invariably placed first were
followed by : 6th Bartholomew, 7th Thomas, 8th Matthew the publican,
9th James Lebbæus, son of Alphæus, 10th Simon Cananæus, 11th Judas, son
of James, 12th Judas the traitor. So Ss in Matt. x. 3 f., except that James
the son of Alphæus has not the added name Lebbæus. Tatian seems to have
found a ὁ before καὶ Λεββαῖος in Matt. x. 3 (or Mark iii. 18), or to have
invented it in the effort to harmonise the lists. This combination presupposes
the reading Ἰάκωβον instead of Λευίν, Mark ii. 14, which Tatian shared with
D and the old Latins according to Ephrem, *Exposit.* p. 58, and which was
also known to many Greeks, and probably was before Origen as well (cf.
Forsch. i. 130 ; Tischend. and Matthäi on Mark ii. 14, iii. 18; Matt. x. 3 ;
Sc, Ss on Mark ii. 14 are unfortunately lacking). Λευίς, which is written

Λεβῆς in Orig. *c. Cels.* i. 62, was mistakenly identified with Λεββαῖος. Since the same publican who in Luke v. 27 was called Levi, with the addition τὸν τοῦ Ἀλφαίου, according to Cod. D, was called James the son of Alphæus in Mark ii. 14, according to the same text, it followed that the apostle James the son of Aiphæus was also a publican. Tatian, therefore, found it appropriate to put the two publicans together among the apostles. It cannot be doubted that in Luke v. 27, 29 Levi without addition, in Mark ii. 14 Levi, son of Alphæus (so also *Gospel of Peter*, xiv. 60 from Mark), is the original text; and also that in Mark ii. 13-17, Luke v. 27-32 the same event is recorded as in Matt. ix. 9-13. Now, as this publican bears the name Matthew in Matt., and in Matt. **x.** 3 the apostle is expressly characterised as the publican mentioned shortly before, the identity of Levi and Matthew really followed of necessity in the interpretation of the Church. Nevertheless the distinction between the two publicans, called by Jesus in very similar circumstances, is found not only in the Valentinian Heracleon, which is passed over without criticism by Clement in his report of it (*Strom.* iv. 73), but also in Orig. *c. Cels.* i. 62, who says expressly that this Levi did not belong to the number of the apostles, in contradiction to which the preface of his *in Epist. ad Rom.* (Delarue, iv. 460) is of no consequence, since the whole discussion about the names of the apostles comes from the translator Rufinus. Cf. also Ephrem, *Exposit. Ev. Conc.* 287; *Forsch.* i. 130. This distinction was at least more reasonable than that, say, between Peter and Cephas, in so far as Mark iii. 18, Luke vi. 15, Acts i. 13 do not indicate the identity of Levi with an apostle. This follows only from the comparison with Matt. ix. 9, but should not have been overlooked by those who, like Origen, acknowledge the credibility of Matt. The cases where to a Hebrew name is added a Latin one (John —Mark, Saul—Paul, Jesus—Justus) or a Greek one (Judas—Aristobulus, Jonathan—Jannai—Alexander, vol. i. 37) are not wholly analogous to the combination of Levi and Matthew in one person. Nor is the union of the father's name with one's own exactly similar (Joseph Bar-Sabu, Acts i. 23; Simon Bar-Jochanan, John i. 42, xxi. 15-17; probably also Nathanael Bar-Tholmai, vol. i. 31). Yet we do also find two independent Hebrew names applied to one person, as Ἰωσὴφ ὁ καὶ Καϊάφας, Jos. *Ant.* xviii. 2. 2. As a rule, one is probably a by-name received later, as Joseph Kabi (Jos. *Ant.* xx. 8. 11), Simon Kepha, Joseph Barnaba. Just this is to be presumed in the case of Levi—Matthew, and from the analogy of Simon—Kepha (Peter), Joseph—Barnaba, it is probable that the name by which the man was famed among Christians, and by which in his own lifetime he was regularly called, was the later of the two. With historical precision Mark ii. 14, and Luke v. 27, 29 following him, have stated that the publican at the time of his call was known as Levi, while in Matt. ix. 9 the name which he uniformly bore as apostle and in the Church is carried back into the story of the call. This corresponds with the fact that until he has related Peter's change of name (iii. 16) Mark speaks of him only as Simon (i. 16, 29, 36), whereas the second name is introduced at once in Matt. iv. 18, and, except for the solemn moments, x. 2, xvi. 16 f., is used exclusively. That tradition tells us nothing of Levi's renaming, and its occasion follows from the fact that tradition leaves him personally altogether in the background. It is only Mark iii. 17 that tells us even of John and James, that Jesus gave them the surname of Boanerges, and then it is simply the fact we learn and not the circumstances and occasion. The same is true of Nathanael as regards double naming. According to John i. 46–51, he was one of the first disciples, and according to John xxi. 2 a permanent member of the most intimate circle, and so certainly one of the apostles (cf. John vi. 66 ff.). And yet he is missing from all the lists of apostles, unless he is identical with Bartholomew, who is the sixth in order in Matt., Mark, and Luke, as Nathanael is the sixth disciple of Jesus according to the correct understanding of John i. 35–51. The formation and meaning of the name Ματθαῖος (so in the oldest MSS. אB, and also D, instead of Ματθαῖος of the later MSS. corresponding to the Greek rule) are much debated, but in any case it is to be written מתּי or מתּאי. In B. Sanhedr. 43a (omitted in the expurgated editions, printed in Laible-Dalman, *Jesus Christus im Talmud*, S. 15,* translation, S. 66 ; Eng. trans. by Streane, text, p. 15,* translation, p. 71 f.) we read : "Jesus had five disciples, Matthai (מתאי), Naḳai (נקאי), Nezer (נצר), Bunai (בוני), Thoda (תודה). They took Matthai before the court. He said to the judge : Shall Matthai be put to death ? It stands written : When (מתי) shall I come and appear before God ? (Ps. xlii. 3). They said to him : By all means Matthai shall be put to death, for it is written : When (מתי) will he die, and his name perish ? (Ps. xli. 5)." According to frequent analogies (e.g. Ζακχαῖος = וכאי, abbreviation of וכריה, מתאי is probably an abbreviation of מתּניה (2 Kings xxiv. 17 ; Neh. xi. 17, 22, Ματθανίας, gift of Yahweh). Just as the name מתּתיה of similar meaning (Neh. viii. 4 ; 1 Chron. ix. 31, Ματθαθίας) was customary as a special name, in addition to the other, so we find the abbreviation of the one name (Ματθαῖος) along with the abbreviation of the other (Ματθίας, Acts i. 23 ; מתּיה, Jastrow, 861). *Onom.*, ed. Lagarde, 174. 79, Ματθαῖος δεδωρημένος, Ματθίας δόμα θεοῦ. Cf. Dalman, *Gram. des jüd. Aramäisch.*[2] 178. A discussion of various derivations and explanations by Grimm (*ThStKr*, 1870, S. 723–729), who for his part would derive מתאי from the unused singular מת (man). Still other views in Schanz, *Komm. zu Mt.* 1 f. Like Ewald and Hitzig, Nöldeke also, *GGA*, 1884, S. 1023, takes the name to be an abbreviation of אמתּי or אמתּה.

2. (P. 508.) What Luke v. 29 says more expressly, that the publican gave a feast in his house in honour of Jesus, and to celebrate the day (cf. Luke xiv. 13, 16 ; John xii. 2), is also the meaning of Matt. ix. 10 ; Mark ii. 15 ; for, aside from the improbability that Jesus was able to entertain a large company in His own lodging, τῷ Ἰησοῦ makes it certain that the αὐτοῦ which Matt. puts forward with strong emphasis, and the αὐτόν of Mark, do not refer to Jesus, but to the publican, the principal person in the preceding sentence. The account in Matt. as in Mark is brief but perfectly clear. First the publican is sitting at his place of business ; at the call of Jesus he leaves it and attaches himself to Him ; finally, he sits at table in his own house. Matt. expresses only the difference in the localities, while Mark with αὐτοῦ after ἐν τῇ οἰκίᾳ expressly indicates that which is of itself obvious. Matt. gives the most unassuming form of the story ; cf. *ZKom. Matt.* 370 f.

3. (P. 508.) Aside from the accounts which refer to the Gospel, the only statement which can be called traditional is that of Clement, *Pæd.* ii. 16 : Ματθαῖος μὲν οὖν ὁ ἀπόστολος σπερμάτων καὶ ἀκροδρύων καὶ λαχάνων ἄνευ κρεῶν μετελάμβανεν. But there is a suspicion that Clement drew here from the *Paradoses of Matthias* or the *Gospel of Matthias*, and so that Ματθαῖος is to

be emended to Ματθίας; cf. *GK*, ii. 751-761.   The suggestion concerning
Matthew's ascetic manner of life in *Martyr. Matthæi (Acta Apocr.*, ed. Lipsius
et Bonnet, ii. part 1. 218) is not contrary to this view : for in this as in other
legends (*op. cit.* pp. 65 ff., xxi, xxxiv) the interchange of the name Matthew
and Matthias is so confused, that it is difficult to determine which name is
original.   The confusion of these two names is in many instances an unintentional error, *e.g.* in the list of "the ·ːxty books," *GK*, ii. 292, A. 7, cf. 753,
A. 1, 759, A. 2.   But it took place designedly when, in an apocryphal variation of the story, Luke xix. 1-10, the name of the chief publican *Matthias* was
substituted for that of Zacchæus, Clem. *Strom.* iv. 35 ; cf. *Quis Div.* xiii. ; *GK*,
ii. 752 ; as it was conscious trifling, also, when a Gospel was· ascribed to the
last chosen apostle Matthias, whose name was enough like that of the evangelist Matthew in derivation, meaning, and sound to be exchanged with it.
In the region of the· apocryphal Gospels of the childhood the unaltered
name of Matthew had yet once more to suffer, *Ev. Apocr.*[2] Tischend. 51-112.
With regard to the legends concerning him, see Lipsius, *Apokr. Apostelgesch.*
ii. 2. 109-141 *et passim.*   With regard to a copy of Matt., ostensibly from the
hand of Barnabas, of which much was said in the sixth century, see *ibid.* 291 ff.

4. (Pp. 509, 511.)   After the quotations from Papias concerning Mark, Eus.
H. E. iii. 39. 16 continues : περὶ δὲ τοῦ Ματθαίου ταῦτ᾽ εἴρηται (*sc.* τῷ Παπίᾳ).
"Ματθαῖος μὲν οὖν ἑβραΐδι διαλέκτῳ τὰ λόγια συνεγράψατο (*al.* συνετάξατο),
ἡρμήνευσε δ᾽ αὐτὰ ὡς ἦν δυνατὸς (*al.* ἠδύνατο), ἕκαστος."   For the expression
cf. *Berl. ägypt. Urk.* No. 1002 of 55 A.D. ἀντίγραφον συγγραφῆς πράσεως
Αἰγυπτίας, μεθερμηνευομένης κατὰ τὸ δυνατόν.   The Syrian translates : "But
of Matthew he says this : Matthew wrote a Gospel in the Hebrew language,
but everyone (literally "man for man") translated it as well as he could."
Rufinus : "Matthæus quidem scripsit hebræo sermone ; interpretatus est
autem ea, quæ scripsit, unusquisque sicut potuit."   The fact that Rufinus
leaves τὰ λόγια untranslated, confirms what was said above (p. 509 f.) as to the
unemphatic nature of the object of the verb.   The Syrian, on the other hand,
corroborates the view that Papias was speaking of nothing else than the
Gospel of Matt. already current in his time.   Irenæus understood him so
when he made acknowledgment to Papias for his information concerning
the original language of Matt. (see p. 393 f. above, and note 7 below) ; and so did
Eusebius himself when he added this testimony regarding Matt. to that concerning "the Mark who wrote the Gospel," without finding any further
explanation needful.   The authorities on biblical introduction, too, long
assumed it as a matter of course that Papias was speaking of the Gospel of
Matt.   Michaelis, *Einl.* 951, translated, as Rufinus did, Eichhorn, *Einl.*[2] i. 200,
458, like the old Syrian, Hug, *Einl.*[3] ii. 16 : "Matthew wrote his history in the
Hebrew language."   Schleiermacher (see p. 441 above), in 1832, was the first
to emphasise τὰ λόγια, and to infer that Papias was discussing a Hebrew book
very different in its content from our Matt.   Since then the Λόγια of Matthew
have been constantly spoken of as a lost source of our Gospels.   For the idea
of λόγια see *GK*, i. 857 ff., ii. 790 ff.   It is, of course, granted that λόγια κυριακά
or λόγοι Ἰησοῦ (cf. Amos i. 1) might have been the title of a book containing
a collection of extended discourses and short sayings of Jesus.   But if one
recalls what was said (above, p. 511) with regard to the historical framework
of Jesus' discourses, this is most improbable.   The Greeks had collections of

anecdotes whose real content lay in some brilliant saying, called ἀποφθέγματι a *potiori*, *e.g.* Plutarch's various collections (*Moralia*, pp. 172-236, 240-242). The Jews called an anecdote of this sort rather מעשה = πρᾶξις. Of the innumerable discussions of Papias' testimony regarding Matt. (and Mark), besides Schleiermacher's famous treatise (see above, p. 425, note 12) and the writer's discussion (*GK*, i. 889-897), let us mention, further, only Weiffenbach, *Das Papiasfragment über Marcus und Matthæus*, 1878, and Lipsius, *JbfPTh*, 1885, S. 174-176, claiming the reference of Papias' evidence to our Gospels of Mark and Matt. Among the unfounded prejudices from which the correct understanding of the few words of Papias has suffered, there is the idea that he was a Jewish Christian. So even Hofmann, ix. 270. The name of a Papias of Scythopolis, but also the name of an Ammia of the same city, which is likewise a Phrygian name (*Forsch.* v. 94, vi. 364) are found on Sarcophagi, which were recently brought to light in Jerusalem (known to the present writer from the *Quartalschrift des Syrischen Waisenhauses* of May 1905, and from photographs). Papias is a genuine Phrygian and Gentile name. *Forsch.* v. 94, vi. 109. One should not infer that he had the *Gospel of the Hebrews* in his hands from the fact that, according to Eus. *H. E.* iii. 39. 16, he embodied in his work the account of the sinful woman accused before Jesus, which was included in the *Gospel of the Hebrews* also, and which was probably the same as was inserted later in John viii. 1-11. As Eusebius says, just before, that Papias cited passages from 1 John and 1 Pet. (κέχρηται μαρτυρίαις ἀπὸ κτλ.), it follows rather from the form of his statement regarding Papias and the *Gospel of the Hebrews* that Papias did not name this book, but merely presented matter which Eusebius, who had himself studied the *Gospel of the Hebrews*, knew to be contained in it as well. For Papias, as for all Asiatic Christians, a Hebrew book was a closed book, unless a Jew was at hand who could translate it for him. The only Hebrew book of which, according to the extant fragments and statements, he made any mention was the Book of Matt. When, in describing the studies on which his work rested, he names Matthew among the other disciples of Jesus from whose oral statement he used to seek information, and when he explains this diligent inquiry by saying that he proceeded on the assumption that he could not derive so much benefit from books as from the spoken words of living witnesses, he does not express any indifference toward books in general which would be inconsistent with his remarks on Mark, Matt., 1 John, 1 Pet., and Rev., nor does he say what was his own opinion of the value of books now that he himself had become an author (he writes ὑπελάμβανον not ὑπέλαβον or ὑπολαμβάνω), but what he thought in earlier years, at the time of this investigation. Mark was not sufficient. The Book of Matt. he could not understand. Interpreters were not always at hand, and did not always understand their business as well as they might have done.

5. (P. 515.) Barn. iv. 14: προσέχωμεν, μήποτε ὡς γέγραπται "πολλοὶ κλητοὶ, ὀλίγοι δὲ ἐκλεκτοὶ" εὑρεθῶμεν, Matt. xxii. 14; cf. *GK*, i. 848, 924. From Barn. v. 9 one must conclude that he always knew the Gospel of Matt. by this name. When he there asserts that, in confirmation of Matt. ix. 13, Christ chose the most sinful men to be His apostles, he has in view primarily the narrative in Matt. ix. 9 (cf. x. 3), the only passage where the publican is designated as the *apostle* Matthew. The generalisation of this fact and the

characterisation of the apostles at the same time as those who were afterward
to preach the gospel of Christ, would be unintelligible, if Matthew were not
known to the author as one who had a peculiar share in this work, and in
general as a prominent apostle fitted to serve as the type of the whole
company. But both these statements are true of Matthew only in so far as he
was author of a Gospel. With regard to the time of Barnabas, cf. Funk,
ThQSc, 1897, S. 617 ff., who assigns him once more to the time of Nerva, or
the end of the first century ; and A. Schlatter, *Die Tage Trajans und Hadrians*,
1897, S. 1, 61–67, who comes forward with new arguments for the date
which is probably correct, 130–131. With regard to Ignatius, Polycarp,
Didache, etc., cf. *GK*, i. 922–932, 840–848. Nestle, *Marginalien und
Materialien*, ii. 72, calls attention to a passage in the writing of the pseudo-
Eusebius on the star of the Magi (preserved in the Syriac), which reads :
" In the second year of the coming of our Lord, in the consulate of Cæsar
and Capito (? 5 A.D., Klein, *Fasti Cons.* 17), in the month of Kanun II.
(=January), these Magi came from the East and worshipped our Lord. And
in the year 430 (Oct. 1, 118–119), in the reign of Hadrian (117–139), in the
consulate of Severus and Fulgus (read Fulvus = 120), and the episcopate of
Xystus, bishop of the city of Rome (*circa* 115-125), this question was raised
among the people who were acquainted with the Holy Scriptures, and
through the efforts of great men in various places this history was sought
out and found, and written in the language of those who attended to the
matter." The exactness of the fourfold dating is surprising. If we change
the first figure 430 to 431 (Oct. 1, 119–120 A.D.), all four dates agree, a great
rarity in chronological notices of this sort. In the year 120, then, and
primarily in Rome, as the manner of dating shows, the question in what
year the Magi had come to Bethlehem was actively discussed. We are reminded of discussions like those concerning the census of Quirinius and of
the fictitious *Acts of Pilate* (Justin, *Apol.* i. 34, 35). If there is anything
in this remarkable statement, then in 120, in Rome and " in various places,"
men were occupied in a scholarly fashion with Matt. ii., that is, of course,
with the Greek text of this chapter of our Matt. This agrees with the
citations previously mentioned.

6. (P. 517.) The Greek translator of Matt. was a someone, nameless
and unknown to Eusebius (see the following note). We cannot conclude
with certainty from Jerome, *Vir. Ill.* iii., that at this time conjectures on the
subject had already been advanced. In Greek minuscules (Tischendorf, i.
212) the translator is identified with John (which has a certain justification
in older legends, such as may be read in the *Acts of Timothy*, ed. Usener, p.
9, cf. *GK*, i. 943), with Bartholomew (which has some connection with the
account of the journey of Pantænus to India, Eus. v. 10. 3), and, finally, with
James the brother of the Lord. This is also the view of the *Synopsis*
which goes under the name of Athanasius (ed. Montfaucon, ii. 202). According to Epiphanius, *Mon.*, ed. Dressel, p. 44, who finds evidence in Matt.
x. 23 that no apostle had travelled far from Palestine before the destruction
of Jerusalem, and who in the same passage advances the pseudo-Clementine
idea that James was the overseer of the apostles, Matt. would have written
his Gospel thirty years after the Ascension at the direction (κατ᾽ ἐπιτροπήν)
of this James, who died two years before.

7. (Pp. 517, 518, 519, 521.) That Matt. was written in Hebrew and intended for Hebrews, cf. Iren. iii. 1. 1 (p. 398, above). Also a fragment of a catena in Stieren, p. 842 : τὸ κατὰ Ματθαῖον εὐαγγέλιον πρὸς Ἰουδαίους ἐγράφη· οὗτοι γὰρ ἐπεθύμουν πάνυ σφόδρα ἐκ σπέρματος Δαβὶδ Χριστόν, ὁ δὲ Ματθαῖος ἔτι μᾶλλον σφοδροτέραν ἔχων τὴν τοιαύτην ἐπιθυμίαν, παντοίως ἔσπευδε πληροφορίαν παρέχειν αὐτοῖς, ὡς εἴη ἐκ σπέρματος Δαβὶδ ὁ Χριστός· διὸ καὶ ἀπὸ τῆς γενέσεως αὐτοῦ ἤρξατο. Cf. the excerpts from Matt. in I. 'n. iii. 9 : iii. 11. 8 on the beginning of the book ; iii. 11. 7 : " Ebionæi etenim eo quod est secundum Matthæum solo utentes, ex illo ipso convincuntur, non recte præsumentes de domino." This statement regarding the Gospel of the Ebionites, to which is added i. 26. 2, *et apostolum Paulum recusant*, rests on Irenæus' inexact knowledge of the circumstances of the Jewish Christians ; cf. *GK*, ii. 664. Eus. *H. E.* v. 10. 3 : ὁ Πάνταινος καὶ εἰς Ἰνδοὺς ἐλθεῖν λέγεται, ἔνθα λόγος εὑρεῖν αὐτὸν προφθάσαν τὴν αὐτοῦ παρουσίαν τὸ κατὰ Ματθαῖον εὐαγγέλιον παρά τισιν αὐτόθι τὸν Χριστὸν ἐπεγνωκόσιν, οἷς Βαρθολομαῖον τῶν ἀποστόλων ἕνα κηρῦξαι αὐτοῖς τὲ Ἑβραίων γράμμασι τὴν τοῦ Ματθαίου καταλεῖψαι γραφήν, ἣν καὶ σώζεσθαι εἰς τὸν δηλούμενον χρόνον. Cf. *Forsch.* iii. 168–170 ; *GK*, ii. 666, 680. While Irenæus supposes Matt. to be written for the Jews, and, according to the fragment at least, primarily for the Jews not yet converted to Christianity, Origen (in Eus. *H. E.* vi. 25. 3, and tom. vi. 17 *in Jo.*, see above, p. 397) says it was meant "for those converted from Judaism" and "for the believing from the circumcision." Elsewhere, however, he too says (tom. i. 6 *in Jo.*) : τοῖς προσδοκῶσι τὸν ἐξ Ἀβραὰμ καὶ Δαβὶδ Ἑβραίοις. Eus. himself says, *H. E.* iii. 24. 6 : Ματθαῖος μὲν γὰρ πρότερον Ἑβραίοις κηρύξας, ὡς ἤμελλε καὶ ἐφ᾽ ἑτέρους ἰέναι, πατρίῳ γλώττῃ γραφῇ παραδοὺς τὸ κατ᾽ αὐτὸν εὐαγγέλιον, τὸ λεῖπον τῇ αὐτοῦ παρουσίᾳ τούτοις, ἀφ᾽ ὧν ἐστέλλετο, διὰ τῆς γραφῆς ἀπεπλήρου. On what grounds Eusebius claims to know this no one can say. It goes beyond Iren. iii. 1. 1 (see above, p. 397), where it is said, to be sure, that Matthew "preached among the Hebrews" and wrote his Gospel, but where it is in no way implied that he ever left Palestine. Of this, too, there is no ancient and credible tradition. The Jewish Christians in "India" (see above) believed that they had received the Gospel not from Matthew himself, but from Bartholomew. Eus. *Quæst. ad Marinum* (Mai, *N. Patr. Bibl.* iv. 1. 257 ; cf. Jerome, *ad Hedibiam Epist.* cxx. 4 on Matt. xxviii. 1) : λέλεκται δὲ "ὀψὲ τοῦ σαββάτου" παρὰ τοῦ ἑρμηνεύσαντος τὴν γραφήν· ὁ μὲν γὰρ εὐαγγελιστὴς Ματθαῖος ἑβραΐδι γλώττῃ παρέδωκε τὸ εὐαγγέλιον, ὁ δὲ ἐπὶ τὴν Ἑλλήνων φωνὴν μεταβαλὼν αὐτὸ τὴν ἐπιφώσκουσαν ὥραν εἰς τὴν κυριακὴν ἡμέραν "ὀψὲ σαββάτων" προσεῖπεν. Directly afterward he calls not the Greek translator who is here held responsible for the obscure expression, but the apostle John, ὁ διερμηνεύων, referring to John xx. 1 in comparison with Matt. xxviii. 1 ; as immediately before he writes : ὥσπερ διερμηνεύων αὐτὸς ἑαυτὸν ὁ Ματθαῖος. Eus. *in Ps.* lxxviii. (Montfaucon, *Coll. Nova Patr.* i. 463) : ἀντὶ γὰρ τοῦ "φθέγξομαι προβλήματα ἀπ᾽ ἀρχῆς" Ἑβραῖος ὢν ὁ Ματθαῖος οἰκείᾳ ἐκδόσει κέχρηται εἰπών· "ἐρεύξομαι κεκρυμμένα ἀπὸ καταβολῆς" (Matt. xiii. 35). Here οἰκεία ἔκδοσις, of course, does not mean a particular Greek translation distinguished from the LXX, like those of Aquila and Symmachus which are cited immediately after, but the native, *i.e.* the Hebrew, text which belonged to Matthew as a Jew. The statement (Eus. *H. E.* vi. 17, cf. *GK*, ii. 740 f.) regarding the polemic of Symmachus the Ebionite against the Gospel of

Matt. has no importance in this connection. What is handed down (Mai, *op. cit.* 270) as a declaration of Eusebius (καὶ δὴ συνόρα ἐν τούτοις ὕφος καὶ ἀπολουθίαν ἱστορικῆς διηγήσεως, ἣν ὁ Ματθαῖος ἐκτίθεται, Σύρος ἀνήρ, τελώνης τὸν βίον, τὴν φωνὴν Ἑβραῖος), but should probably be assigned to Julius Africanus (cf. Spitta, *Brief des Africanus an Aristides*, 70 ff., 111), presupposes the composition of Matt. in Hebrew. This tradition is repeated by Cyril, *Hieros. Cat.* xiv. 15 ; Epiphanius, *Hær.* xxx. 3 (ἐβραϊστὶ καὶ ἐβραϊκοῖς γράμμασιν), xxx. 6 (τὸ κατὰ Ματθαῖον εὐαγγέλιον ἐβραϊκὸν φύσει ὄν, a gospel said to have been extant as late as 330 along with a Hebrew translation of John and Acts in the possession of Jews in Tiberias ; cf. *Forsch.* i. 345 ff. ; *GK*, i. 411, A. 1, ii. 672) ; *Hær.* li. 5 (ἐβραϊκοῖς γράμμασι) ; Chrysost. *Hom.* i. 3 *in Matt.* ; Jerome, *Vir. Ill.* iii. ("evangelium Christi Hebræis litteris verbisque composuit, quod quis postea in Græcum transtulerit, non satis certum est") ; Præf. *Comm. in Mt.* ("qui evangelium in Judæa Hebræo sermone edidit") ; *Comm. in Oseam* (Vall. vi. 123 : "Matthæum evangelium Hebræis litteris edidisse, quod non poterant legere, nisi hi qui ex Hebræis erant"). What Jerome meant here and in many other passages by the *Hebrew* language of the Gospel of Matt. is most plainly shown by the fact that the Aramaic *Gospel of the Nazarenes*, which he studied with care, copied, and translated into both Latin and Greek, was sometimes considered by him to be the original of Matt. ; cf. moreover, vol. i. 23 f., 27. Nothing but absolute ignorance could find in the frequent mention of the Hebrew characters in which Matt. wrote a proof that the Gospel was composed in the ancient Hebrew language. The same statement is made by Jerome regarding the Aramaic sections in Daniel and Ezra, and by him and others as well regarding the *Gospel of the Hebrews*, the language of which has never been a matter of doubt ; cf. *GK*, ii. 661, 667, 718. The tradition of the Hebrew Matt. came to the Syrians chiefly, if not exclusively, through the Syriac translation of Eusebius' Church History. Ephrem shows his dependence on Eusebius in this as in many matters (*Ev. Concord. Exposit.* 286). An anonymous Syriac fragment also, which from the excerpt in Wright, *Catalogue of Syr. MSS.* p. 1016, the present writer took to refer to the *Gospel of the Hebrews* (*GK*, ii. 681), is shown by the fuller account given by Barnes in the *Academy*, 1893, p. 344, to refer to Matt., and repeats only the ἐν τοῖς Ἑβραίοις of Irenæus (see p. 398 above). The Syrian Ischodad in the ninth century (Harris, *Fragments of the Comm. of Ephr. Syr.* p. 16, cf. *ThLB*, 1896, col. 2) remarks on Matt. i. 20 : "Others (say) that he who translated (this) out of Hebrew into Syriac altered (the expression), and for (the words) *is conceived in her* substituted *is born.* But the *Diatessaron* says, 'The one who is born in her is of the Holy Spirit.'" These exegetes went on the supposition that the Syriac version of Matt. was taken directly from the Hebrew original and not from a Greek translation, a view which in modern times has been revived by W. Cureton for the Sc discovered by him (Preface, p. 76 ff.), and by Minischalchi Erizzo for the Sh (*Evang. Hieros.* Præf. p. 45) which he published. On the other hand, the Arabian bishop George in the seventh century still knew that the Hebrew Matt. was first translated into Greek, and that errors crept in at this point which the Syriac text shares with the Greek ; cf. Georg, *Gedichte und Briefe*, translated by Ryssel, S. 140.

8. (P. 521.) Erasmus is said to have been the first to dispute the tradition of the composition of Matt. in Hebrew. Several Catholics, like cardinal Cajetan, and the representatives of both Reformed and Lutheran orthodoxy followed him; cf. the counter-argument of R. Simon, *Hist. Crit. du Texte du NT*, 1689, p. 47 ff., and the excerpts in Credner, *Einl.* i. 78 ff. It is significant of Luther's historical insight and freedom that he held to Hebrew as the original language of Matt. In the discussions concerning the institution of the Lord's Supper, according to the report of Gregor Casel in 1525 (Kolde, *Anal. Lutherana*, 72), he said what still holds true for a hundred other problems, "Si haberemus Hebræum Matthæum, facile expediremus!" Following in Simon's steps, Michaelis, *Einl.* 946 ff., defended the older tradition with great thoroughness. Yet theologians of the most various schools have again and again set it aside, e.g. Hug, *Einl.*[2] ii. 16–63; Fritzsche, *Comm. in Ev. Matthæi*, 1826, p. xvii ff.; Harless, *Fabula de Matthæo Syrochaldaice Conscripto* (Erlanger Programm, 1841). That our Matt. is not a translation, but written in Greek at the beginning, is the prevailing opinion to-day. Bengel's suggestion in the *Gnomon* (*Vorbemerkung zu Mt.*, ed. Stuttg. 1860, S. 2), that Matt. himself published his Gospel in both Hebrew and Greek, has been seriously adopted by a few, among them men like Thiersch, *Versuch*, 192 ff., and Hofmann, ix. 326. The self-contradiction in which Thiersch becomes involved is very remarkable. On p. 103, in an explanation of Papias' statement which is otherwise essentially correct (cf. S. 222 f.), he amplifies it to mean that the oral interpretation of the Hebrew Matt. continued "until he (Matt.) himself published the Greek writing which is read in the whole Church as his Gospel"; while, according to p. 197, Matt. gave his two versions to the Churches of Palestine, the Greek to the Hellenistic and the Hebrew to the Hebrew congregations, "at the same time or nearly so." In that case the translating of Matt. would have been superfluous everywhere, and the Hebrew Matt. could not have been brought to Asia Minor in place of the Greek except by an extraordinary confusion.

9. (P. 522.) The only scholar familiar with linguistic conditions in the time of Jesus and the apostles who has declared in favour of Hebrew in the stricter sense as the original language of Matt. is Franz Delitzsch (*The Hebrew NT*, Leipzig, 1883, p. 30), and he himself previously held that it was Aramaic (*Neue Untersuchungen über Entstehung und Anlage der kanon. Evv.* 1853, S. i. 7, 45, 49, 50). The long-continued and valuable labour which this distinguished Hebraist devoted to the restoration of a Hebrew version of the N.T. seems to have been the chief influence which led him thus to change his view. In his *Brief an die Römer, in das Hebr. übersetzt und aus Talmud und Midrasch erläutert*, 1870, S. 16 f., he already showed some uncertainty with regard to the language even of the *Gospel of the Hebrews*. On other representatives of this view see *GK*, ii. 718 f.

10. (P. 522.) The statement made by Gla, *Die Originalsprache des Mtev.* 1887, S. 177, that Eusebius in his *Chron. ad Ann.* 41 assigned the composition of Matt. to the eighth year after the Ascension, is false in every particular. In *anno Abrah.* 2057 = 41 A.D., or according to Jerome's revision *anno Abrah.* 2058, Eusebius says nothing of Matt., and of Mark only that he went to Egypt to preach (ed. Schoene, pp. 152, 153). The *Chronicle* has nothing whatever to say about the composition of any Gospel.

§ 55. CONTENTS, PLAN AND PURPOSE OF MATTHEW'S GOSPEL.

The words which stand at the beginning of the book form an introductory title. It would seem as if the fact that these words stand at the beginning of a book in the further course of which there are no other titles were sufficient to make it clear beyond all doubt that βίβλος γενέσεως Ἰησοῦ Χριστοῦ κτλ. is the title of the entire book, just as we have seen that ἀρχὴ τοῦ εὐαγγελίου κτλ. is the title of Mark's Gospel. On the supposition that it is applicable to only a part of the same, we have great difference of opinion as to how much shall be included in the section. The title has been variously referred—(a) to i. 1–17; (b) to i. 1–25; (c) to i. 1–2, 15; (d) to i. 1–2, 23, the number of which divisions shows that the author never thought of the possibility of so many interpretations. If he had, how could he have omitted to make clear by a new title or in some other way where the first division ended and the second began? The words themselves will bear the translation, "Book of the origin of Jesus Christ," with corresponding reference to i. 18–25 where the γένεσις or γέννησις τοῦ Χριστοῦ, to follow what is probably the original reading, is described (n. 1). But this applies only to this second paragraph of the book, not to the entire chapter. In the first place, in i. 18α, which reads almost like a title, it is very clearly implied that the discussion of the generation and birth of Jesus begins with this passage, and therefore that it was not the subject of what precedes, i. 2–17. In the second place, it is perfectly self-evident that no informed person could have called the enumeration of a man's ancestors an account of his γέννησις, or even his γένεσις (cf. Luke i. 17). A title with this meaning would not have been in place until after i. 17; and there even it would have been as strange as it was superfluous, since what follows is not

properly an account of the beginning of Jesus' life.
Neither the time nor the place of the events related is
indicated, and the birth is mentioned only in a subordinate
sentence, i. 25, as was the case also in i. 16.　Not until
ii. 1 do we have the statement of the time and place of
the birth, and there because both are significant for the
narrative which begins with this verse.　Reference of the
title to i. 2–17 is to be rejected as impossible linguistically
until a case is cited where a Greek or Hellenist calls a
genealogical table βίβλος γενέσεως (n. 2).　On the other
hand, the expression was familiar to the Greek Christians,
for whom the Greek Matthew was written, from their
O.T., and it was certainly not in keeping with the intention of the author, or rather of the translator, that,
perhaps at a very early date, in spite of the clear dependence of the words upon very familiar passages in the
Greek O.T., the first clause of the book was mistaken
for a title of the genealogy of Jesus or of the history
of His birth.　It was certainly a misunderstanding if
the expression was borrowed from the Greek O.T., since
in no O.T. passage where this or a similar expression
occurs is it employed to introduce a list of the ancestors
of the person with whose name it is used, or a narrative
of his birth.　Where genealogies follow they are those of
descendants, not of *progenitors*.　From other passages we
see that the etymological meaning of the Hebrew word,
"a man's generations," has been widened in usage to the
more general conception of the family history beginning
with the person mentioned, or of history in general (n. 2).
Since descendants of Jesus were out of the question, the
translator could take it for granted that this O.T. expression would be understood in the sense in which it was
used in the O.T.　He gave his writing the title "Book of
the History of Jesus."　When, however, he adds immediately to the name Jesus the title of His office, Christ,
which had come to be used in the Church as a second

proper name, and then goes on to indicate that the bearer
of the same is a son of David, a son of Abraham, it is
clear that he intends to set forth the history of Jesus in
such a way that He shall be recognised from the history
as the Messiah, and as the fulfilment of the promise made
to the house of David and the seed of Abraham.   The
appositives attached to Χριστοῦ show that here it is not
used as in Mark i. 1 and frequently elsewhere as a common
expression of the author for his Christian faith, but indicates the point of view from which the author intends to
set forth the history of Jesus; and this is confirmed by his
usage of ὁ Χριστός, which varies from that of the other
Gospels (i. 17, 18 [n. 1], xi. 2).   The more exact meaning
of the thought expressed in the title of the book is to be
derived from the investigation of the fulfilment which
he found disclosed in the history.

The *first section*, i. 2–ii. 23, is not only without parallel in
the other Gospels, but is distinguished also for other reasons.
The genealogical table at its beginning could hardly be
more grossly misunderstood than to construe it as a proof of
the Davidic descent of Jesus, and His accompanying natural
right to the throne of David.   That David was an Israelite
and therefore a descendant of Abraham, and that Zerub-
babel was the offspring of the Davidic house, required no
proof.   For this supposed purpose two-thirds of the table
is superfluous; and in view of the long period which it is
made to cover, and the much longer list of names in Luke
iii. 23–27, the remaining third is clearly so short that it
would have been very poorly adapted for such an alleged
purpose.   In general, it would have been difficult for
anyone to conceive such a purpose.   That the carpenter
Joseph, who was known to all as Jesus' father (Matt. xiii.
55; Luke iii. 23, iv. 22; John i. 46, vi. 42), and whose
line of descent Matthew represents to be that of Jesus,
was a "son of David," was not the peculiar belief of the
Christian Church, which could have originated from the

confession of Jesus as the Messiah (Matt. i. 16, 20 ; Luke i. 27), but was universally known and acknowledged by his countrymen and contemporaries. When all the people called Jesus the son of Joseph, the son of David, and showed themselves inclined to affirm that He was the one expected son of David (Matt. ix. 27, xv. 22, xx. 30, 31, xii. 23, xxi. 9, 15), His opponents, to be sure, denied the latter, but without contesting the presupposition. According to the testimony of the Gospels, which bring before us the greatest variety of objections which the opponents of Jesus raised against Him, they never attempted, not even in their bitterest attacks, to deny Jesus' Davidic descent, *i.e.* Joseph's, and thereby to remove the entire basis of His claims. The bitterest insults of the Talmud are accompanied by the recognition that Jesus was closely related to the royal house (n. 3). To be sure, His descent was suspected, but not in the direction of the descent of Joseph from David as set forth by Matthew. The legitimacy of His birth was denied. It was claimed that He was a bastard, whom the unfaithful Mary had borne to another man and then passed off as the son of Joseph, and thus as the son of David. It is, therefore, historically impossible that Matt. i. 2--17 should have been intended to prove the descent of Jesus from David and especially from Abraham.

Matthew's object is not *proof* of any kind, but to bring before his readers in the shortest possible form—in the form of a genealogical table—the whole history of Israel from the founder of the race to the Messiah, in order to express the thought, already hinted at in the title of the book, that the Jesus who received the name Messiah (i. 16) was the goal of the entire history of His people. For this purpose he not only employs a list of names which is incomplete, a fact to which he betrays striking indifference (n. 4), but also gives it an artificial arrangement to which he directs our attention in i. 17 more expressly than in the genealogy itself. He divides the

latter into three groups of fourteen members, each indi
cating the division between the groups within the list
itself.   In i. 6 he mentions David the king, which marks
the end of the first group, and in i. 11, 12 the deportation
to Babylon is twice mentioned as the event which separated
the line of ruling Davidic kings from the line of dethroned
successors of David.   The first indicates the highest, the
second the lowest point in the historical development from
Abraham to Christ.   That the names meant to him an
outline of the history, is also indicated by the fact that in
two cases the brothers are mentioned along with the representative of the line.   By this means he indicates in
i. 2 the transition from family to national history, and in
i. 11 the change brought about in the Davidic house when
the unity of the family and the inheritance of the promise
was no longer represented in one person who occupied the
throne, but when what was once the royal seed continued
to exist only as a number of families, with uncertainty as
to which one would enter upon the inheritance.   In order
to express this thought and in this outward way to represent the symmetry of the history in which he believed,
Matthew's arrangement of fourteen members in each group
of the genealogical table is evidently intentional (n. 4).
It is inconceivable that an author who intentionally invited
his readers to recount the list of names should have left
out from pure carelessness the three kings, Ahaziah, Joash,
Amaziah, whose names are wanting in ver. 8 after Joram.
It is inconceivable also that he should have made a mistake of one figure when he reckoned the whole as 42, *i.e.*
3 × 14, instead of 41, the number actually found (i. 17).
Inasmuch as the O.T. gave him fourteen members for the
period from Abraham to and including David, he assigned
the same number to the two groups that followed.   In
order to do this he threw out the names of the three kings
from the second group, and, as we have seen, made the
third list short in proportion to the period which it

covered. We get a further insight into the author's purpose from his remarks regarding Tamar, Rahab, Ruth, and Bathsheba which would have been out of place in a simple genealogical table (i. 3, 5, 6). These four names are not used to adorn the genealogical table in some such way as those of the distinguished ancestresses, Sarah and Rebecca, are employed in the Old and New Testament (cf. 1 Pet. iii. 6 ; Gal. iv. 23 ; Rom. ix. 9 ; Heb. xi. 11 ; for Rebecca, Rom. ix. 10), but their sole purpose is to point to dark blots in the history. That the first heir of David's throne was the offspring of an unlawful marriage is expressed delicately but clearly when his mother is called not Bathsheba, but the wife of Uriah. Ruth was a Moabitess and therefore a heathen, as was also Rahab, who according to a legend which has no basis in the O.T. was the mother of Boaz, and from Josh. ii. 1 (cf. Jas. ii. 25 Heb. xi. 31) was known as a harlot. The names of Tamar and her twin sons must have recalled to every reader for whom the passage had any meaning at all the incestuous intercourse between her and her father-in-law (Gen. xxxviii. 13–30). Since it is self-evident that the author could not have designed to cast reflections upon the ancestry of the Messiah and so upon Him, his purpose in these references can be only apologetic. In answer to the Jewish slander concerning Mary's adultery (n. 3), Matthew points out the fact that the things which are slanderously charged against the last son of David are actually to be found in the early history of the Davidic house, and, above all, in the history of the birth of David's first son. If these blots on the history of his people and of the royal house do not hinder the Jew from recognising in the same a sacred account of the divine revelation, certainly the evil suspicion cast upon the birth of Jesus by malicious enmity should not prevent him from investigating the facts and from hearing patiently the exposition of the same. Jesus is not a bastard, but a true son of David,

inasmuch as He was born of the legitimate wife of a
descendant of David, Joseph. That Joseph's paternity
was the particular point from which the suspicion of the
Jews could originate is suggested already in i. 16 (n. 5),
and the explanation which this demands follows in i.
18–25. As a history of the birth these verses would be
entirely incomplete (see above, p. 531 f.), but they are perfectly adapted for the purpose indicated in i. 18a, namely,
to show how the conception and the birth of the Messiah
had taken place. He was conceived before Mary was
married, but not born until she was the wife of a son of
David, Joseph. The condition which appeared to him
even to be due to sin on the part of his bride, and which
he was justified in not enduring until informed of its cause
by divine revelation, was a miracle of the Holy Spirit.
The very thing which was an offence to the Jewish people
because not in accordance with their expectations, corresponded so literally in all its details, notwithstanding, to
the prophecy regarding the Immanuel (Isa. vii. 14), that
Matthew does not hesitate to say at this point what is
often repeated later, namely, that the history of Jesus
took place as it did by divine arrangement even in
those details which were most objectionable to the Jews,
because God designed thereby the fulfilment of the prophecy in which long before His decree was declared.
From this agreement between the history of Jesus and
the O.T. prophecy it should be recognised that He was
the Christ in spite of all appearance to the contrary
(i. 22, n. 6).

In significant contrast to this passage, which bears a
genuine Israelitish stamp, particularly in the description
of Jesus' future vocation as the Saviour of His own
people (i. 21), we have the narrative concerning the Magi
(ii. 1–12), in the course of which account itself the same
contrast comes strongly to the front. Whereas heathen
astrologers, incited by an observation in the field of their

occult science, and animated with a religious interest,
make the long journey to Palestine to pay homage to the
newborn King of the Jews, and do not rest until they
find Him; the high priests and scribes are satisfied with
giving the correct answer to the scholastic question about
the place where the Messiah was to be born. The reigning
king of the Jews, however, alarmed by the news brought
by the strangers and the definite answer of the Sanhedrin
to the question which he had put to this body, allows
himself to be moved to nothing less than a plan to murder
the true King of the Jews, born in Bethlehem in accordance with the prophecy. The wickedness of Herod and
the indifference of the guardians of Israel's holy things
make it appear as if the King and Saviour of Israel,
hailed with joy by the heathen, had been born in vain in
so far as His own people were concerned. For this reason
He does not grow up in the place out of which, according
to prophecy, He was to come forth (ii. 6), but at first found
refuge outside the "land of Israel" (ii. 20, 21; vol. i.
24, n. 7) among the Gentiles in Egypt (ii. 15). In this
also He appears to be estranged from His people; and
this must have been a further occasion for Jewish
suspicion (n. 3). Although the flight into Egypt was
caused by Jewish wrong-doing, it was none the less of
God's ordering. By this also a word of prophecy found
fulfilment, not a prophecy with regard to the coming
Messiah, but a passage in which Hosea recalls historically
Israel's departure from Egypt (ii. 15). The fact that the
child Jesus fled to Egypt and not to Damascus, for
example, the author regards as a significant ordering of
events on the part of God from which we should recognise
the repetition of the history of Israel in the history of
Jesus; He was no more unfitted for the fulfilment of His
vocation by His residence in Egypt than was Israel by
theirs. The slaughter of the innocents in Bethlehem,
viewed from one side, was a lamentable misfortune which

overtook the innocent; from another point of view it
was gruesome folly. For this reason Matthew could not
say that the horror was ordered of God for the fulfilment of His word. Nevertheless it did fulfil a part of
Israel's history experienced by Jeremiah, and expressed
by him in impressive words (ii. 17 f.). After Herod's
death the child Jesus was able to return to the "land of
Israel," but not to Judea and Bethlehem, out of which,
according to prophecy (ii. 6) and the popular expectation,
the Messiah was to come (John vii. 42). On the contrary,
he came to the half-Gentile Galilee, out of which no
prophet ariseth (John vii. 52), and to the village of
Nazareth, which is not once mentioned in the O.T., and
which appears to have been despised by its neighbours
(John i. 47). This, in turn, was another consequence of
the wickedness which had become hereditary in the Jewish
kings. This, however, was so ordered by God that thereby
not merely a single word of an individual prophet, but
the prophetic word in general should be fulfilled in Jesus,
inasmuch as He was to be called the Nazarene, from
Nazareth, where He grew up and whence He made His
appearance among the people. This name was employed
to express the complete repugnance felt by the Jewish
people toward Him and His Church (ii. 23, cf. xxvi. 71 ;
John i. 46 f. ; Acts vi. 14, xxiv. 5, xxvi. 9, and n. 7).
This points at the same time to the history of the man
Jesus among His people, which we expect to find set
forth from the same apologetic point of view evidenced
by every line of the first section.

Before this, however, we have a *second section* (iii.
1–iv. 11) devoted to the account of preparatory events.
Just as in Ex. ii. 11, whole decades are passed by with
an "in those days," and the figure of the Baptist and the
preacher, John, is introduced as the prophesied forerunner
of the Lord. It is especially noticeable that the kingdom
of God, whose coming John announced, is characterised

as the kingdom of heaven in the short summary of the
Baptist's preaching (iii. 2), as generally in Matthew (n. 8).
Without the earth's ceasing to be the scene of the action
(cf. v. 4 *al.* 5, vi. 10, xiii. 24, 38, 41), the expression
indicates that it is a rule of God over the world which
comes down from heaven, *i.e.* by God's act.   This conception of the Baptist stands in contrast to the expectation
of a Messianic kingdom which is a purely earthly product.
The masses accepted John's testimony ; also representatives
of the two parties, the Pharisees and the Sadducees, who
in general stood for the two classes, the scribes and the
high priests, in the Sanhedrin (ii. 4), visited the place where
he baptised.   It was just this appearance of the leaders
of the people, however, that furnished the Baptist with an
occasion to deliver a scathing denunciation, in which the
work of the coming founder of the kingdom is described
as predominantly that of the judge of His own people and
in which God's freedom to receive the Gentiles into His
Church in place of the unworthy Israelites is maintained.   Jesus also visits the scene of baptism in order
Himself to be baptised.   In the case of all others it is a
confession of sin (iii. 6) ; with Him, however, it is only an
exemplification of the principle that it was fitting for
Him to fulfil the entire legal economy of God (iii. 15).
This self-humiliation on the part of Jesus, God answered
from heaven by the impartation of His Spirit, an inner
experience, which was externalised for Jesus Himself in
a visible form as well as in the audible message that
Jesus was the beloved or the only Son of God whom He
had chosen as the instrument for His approaching work
(iii. 17, cf. xxi. 37).   In what spirit Jesus would carry
out the commission thus entrusted to Him is indicated
in the Temptation history (iv. 1–11).   As a humble, pious
man, and an Israelite who believed in the Scriptures, He
overcomes every temptation to win the world-rule which
belonged to Him by any means other than that which

God had apppointed,—the way of patient faith and self-denying obedience.

The *third section* (iv. 12–xi. 1) sets forth by general descriptions and selected examples Jesus' public work in Galilee which followed the arrest of the Baptist. All that follows the second section is appended to the announcement made to Jesus of John's arrest, without bringing this event into any chronological connection with the narratives that precede, and without narrating the story, well known to the author, of the way in which he came to be cast into prison (xiv. 3–5). The return of Jesus (John v. 35) to Galilee from Judea, where at the time He seems to have been residing, is a second retreat (iv. 12, ἀνεχώρησεν, cf. ii. 22), naturally not in the sense that He sought thereby to escape the danger of a fate like John's, for Herod Antipas, who had put an end to the Baptist's work, was also the ruler of Galilee. But Judea and the Holy City (iv. 5, xxvii. 53), "the city of the great King" (v. 35), seemed the appropriate place for the public appearance (John vii. 3 f.) of the anointed King who was born in Bethlehem. It denoted self-denial on Jesus' part when He withdrew to the despised Galilee. In keeping with this is the fact that He began His preaching there (iv. 17) with exactly the same sentence that the Baptist employed (iii. 2). He does not appear as the King whom the Baptist had announced, but as the prophet continuing the Baptist's work, and, indeed, in Galilee, where the latter had never worked. The fact, however, that He did not make Nazareth, where He grew up, His headquarters, but Capernaum, where He settled later, and whence He planned to make tours in all directions in Galilee, appeared to Matthew to be a remarkably literal fulfilment of the prophecy to be found in Isa. viii. 23–ix. 1. He quotes it not as Jesus' motive, but in order to justify this feature in the history of Jesus which was offensive to orthodox Jews (iv. 14–16). The lack of

connection between the account of the call of the fishermen to become fishers of men and what precedes and
follows, only shows more clearly that it is merely a part of
the introductory portion of this section (iv. 18–22). The
Prophet of Galilee was accompanied from the beginning
by countrymen who were to share His work. In
iv. 23–25 we have a general description of this period
of Jesus' work in Galilee, ending with the climax where
Jesus is represented as surrounded by persons seeking
His help, who come from all parts of Palestine and even
from the neighbouring Gentile regions. Three additional
points are brought out : (1) The constant moving from
place to place throughout Galilee ; (2) the teaching and
preaching ; and (3) the healing of all sorts of diseases.
Thus we have in iv. 12–25 a sketch of Jesus' entire work
in Galilee, which, according to ver. 24 f., must have
occupied at least several months. The elaboration of this
sketch proposed in the plan begins with an *example of
His teaching* (chaps. v.–vii.). This great discourse is not,
however, what we should expect from iv. 17, 23. It was
not delivered in a synagogue (iv. 23), but under the open
sky ; nor was it a sermon directed to the people sitting
in darkness in Galilee, but instruction (v. 1 f.) intended
for the disciples, who are the light of the world (v. 14).
Not until toward the close of the discourse does Jesus
direct His attention to the crowd (vii. 24, 28 f.), in the
presence of whom the disciples had received the preceding
instruction, with its constant reference to their particular
religious condition, their deeper relation to Him, and
their special vocation in the world. The Sermon on the
Mount in Matthew is not the preaching of repentance
(iv. 17) nor the gospel of the kingdom (iv. 23), but a
setting forth of the moral conduct which the disciples of
Jesus are to exhibit before the world as His disciples and
as children of God (v. 16 ; n. 9).

Why Matthew chose as an example of Jesus' teaching

this instruction of His disciples, which presupposes
throughout faith in Himself and His gospel, we must
learn from the elaboration of the theme (v. 16). First
of all, He warns them against the folly of supposing that
it was their Master's mission to set aside the O.T., and,
as the further context shows, its authoritative content.
It is not His mission to destroy anything whatever
that is divine in its origin, and that exists for the
sake of what is right, but rather to fulfil the sacred
forms which He found existing, to put into them the
content which they themselves demanded (v. 17, cf.
iii. 15). As long as this world stands, not even the
smallest portion of the O.T. law can pass away unfulfilled
(18). The same reverence for the law in word and deed,
which He here confesses and Himself always exhibited,
He demands in His disciples (19). Far from allowing
the exact interpretation and fulfilment of the law to
remain solely the distinction of the rabbinic guild and
the party of the Pharisees, He makes actual righteousness,
which exceeds by far that of the scribes and Pharisees, a
condition of blessedness on the part of His disciples (20).
Thus by the standard of Jesus' favourable attitude toward
the O.T. law, and His condemnation of the rabbinic
interpretation and Pharisaic observance of it, shall the
good works be measured by which His disciples are
to demonstrate that they are children of God. The
theme thus more closely defined is now elaborated in such
a way as to show first of all (v. 21–48) by a series of
examples, and in contrast to the superficial and, in part,
even foolish *rabbinic interpretation of the law*, how the
Israelitish laws, written and unwritten, are to be treated
in order to discover in them the will of the divine Lawgiver concerning the moral conduct of the individual. In
the light of this exposition, in vi. 1–18, He sets forth
the kind of alms, prayer, and fasting which becomes the
children of God, in contrast to the *Pharisaic* externalisa-

tion of the principal acts in which *piety* finds expression. Rabbinic interpretation of the law and Pharisaic piety do not take us beyond the standard of heathen morality and piety (v. 46 f., vi. 7). In relation to the things of this world also, children of the heavenly Father may not, as do many of the Pharisees, sink to the level of the Gentiles (vi. 32), but, free from inordinate covetousness and unbelieving anxiety, the two principal forms in which slavery to mammon exhibits itself, they are to make the kingdom and the righteousness of God first and last the only goal of their life (vi. 19–34). Opposition to the Pharisees, which is already less prominent in this part of the discourse, recurs only once in what follows (vii. 5). For our purpose we do not need to investigate the last part of the discourse (chap. vii.). It is clear that the choice of the Sermon on the Mount as an illustration of Jesus' teaching was due to Matthew's apologetic, and at the same time polemic, purpose, and that, in so far as this discourse is his composition, its form is the result of his work.

Three *examples of healing* follow. That viii. 1–17 is to be taken as an independent unit, is shown not only by the fact that we have, beginning with viii. 18, a series of narratives which cannot be included under this title, but also by the citation with which the whole is solemnly concluded by the author in viii. 17. The first example is that of a leprous Jew whom Jesus enjoins to observe the prescriptions of the law. Here we have actual evidence that Jesus was not a revolter against the Mosaic law (viii. 1–4, cf. v. 17–20). The second example is that of a Gentile whose importunate faith puts the Jews to shame and opens a vista into the future, when in the place of the unworthy Jews the Gentiles of the entire world shall have part in the blessings of the kingdom of God (viii. 5–13). These two narratives bear the same relation to each other as i. 21*b* to ii. 1–12, or iv. 23 (ἐν τῷ λαῷ) to iv. 24 (ὅλην

τὴν Συρίαν). The third example forms the introduction to
a scene in which Jesus is pictured as engaged with multitudes of the sick until the day begins to fade. Such work
as this shows Him to be the Servant of God who bore as
His own all the infirmities of His people, even in the form
of physical disease (viii. 14–17). The series of narratives
which follows, viii. 18–ix. 34, is made up of a variety of
very different incidents which, taken together, serve to
expand a third feature of the programme laid down
in iv. 12–25 (above, p. 541 f). It is the *restless wandering
life* of the teacher and physician which is here pictured
in a long series of very brief but chronologically inseparable narratives. The saying of Jesus in viii. 20 serves as
an introduction for the whole. At first glance it might
seem as if iv. 23 and ix. 35, which contain practically the
same words, formed a sort of frame for what stands
between ; but closer observation shows at once that in the
latter case the tireless journeying through all the cities
and villages is recalled primarily for the sake of what
follows in ix. 36 f., which seems to give the motive for the
sending out of the apostles (x. 1 ff.). Jesus' own work
is not sufficient ; the harvest requires many labourers.
Moved by sympathy for the neglected multitudes, He
sends out His apostles to do a work of preaching and
healing similar to His own. Not until now does the
reader learn that twelve disciples had been chosen earlier
for this purpose, and what their names are. The special
injunction to confine the work of their preaching journeys
to the Jews (x. 5 f., 23) is in accord with Jesus' sympathy
for His people (ix. 36) and Matthew's apologetic purpose
(cf. i. 21, iv. 23, ἐν τῷ λαῷ ; also xv. 31 end) ; what
follows, namely, ix. 36–x. 42, is an elaboration of the
fourth point of the introductory programme. Jesus designed to carry on His prophetic work in Galilee supported
by regular helpers (iv. 18–22). The third section is concluded by the notice that Jesus did not on this account

cease His own work of preaching in different places (xi. 1).

The *fourth section*, xi. 2–xx. 34, brings before us the different impressions which the work of Jesus previously described made upon the different individuals and classes who were affected by it. This is done in such a way, however, as to bring out at the same time the particular actions and discourses of Jesus occasioned by it. The words which we find in xi. 6 may serve as a title for the whole section. It is conceivable that men should be offended in Jesus, but deeper reflection as to what creates objection to Him helps to remove the offence. Happy the man for whom this is true! Even the great prophet in imprisonment, the prophet who surpasses all others, who in his original greatness is inferior to no man, since he ushered in the great epoch of the approaching kingdom of God steadfastly and without fear,—even he cannot understand the work of Jesus of which he hears. The works which Matthew describes as the works of the Messiah, because they distinguish Jesus as the Messiah (xi. 2), the Baptist cannot understand as the fulfilment of his own proclamation. By means of the fresh impression which the Baptist's messengers carried back, and the warning with which this answer was concluded, Jesus hopes to save His impatient friend from a fall. He strives also to ward off the possible injurious effect of John's inquiries upon the crowd (xi. 2–15). The frivolous multitude is totally incapable of comprehending the significance of the times. Like whimsical children, they find fault with the Divine wisdom manifested differently in its different personal agents, in one way in John, in another way in Jesus (16–19). The cities of Galilee, distinguished above measure by the works of Jesus, exhibit a worse blindness than the heathen cities whose sins and destruction made them a proverb (20–24). But Jesus does not allow Himself to be disturbed by such experiences. In that hour He praises

His Father, the God who rules the world, that He has so determined the revelation of the Divine counsel of salvation through Him, the Son, that it is intelligible to babes, but misunderstood by the wise and understanding. He is not weary of calling to Himself those who are burdened with a heavy yoke (25–30). The wise ones and those who lay the yoke of their precepts upon others are the Pharisees and scribes (cf. xxiii. 4). When Jesus is attacked by these on the ground of supposed profanation of the Sabbath, He proves to them from the sacred history, the temple worship prescribed by the Torah, and their own daily practice, that He is not a transgressor of the Law, but that they accuse Him without justification on the ground of a Law which they themselves have misunderstood (xii. 1–13). Jesus retires before the hostile attempts which are thereupon planned (14), but continues to minister to the suffering. The absence of all display which characterised this work, as well as the fact that Jesus refrained from all violence in the conflict with His enemies, led Matthew to bring forward again from Second Isaiah, as he had done in viii. 17, the picture of the Servant of Yahweh, who works with perfect quietness, and yet through the power of the Spirit wins victory for all peoples, as a prophecy fulfilled and to be fulfilled in Jesus (15–21). When, however, the Pharisees blaspheme the Spirit by whose power He worked His deeds of healing, calling the same a satanic power, He does not remain silent, but shows them the self-contradiction in their charge, and, more than this, warns them against committing the unpardonable sin (22–37). When, thereupon, they seek a sign from Him which will render it unnecessary for them to exercise faith, He gives them the sign of His resurrection, represented by the sign of Jonah, which, in turn, will be of use only to the believing. In spite of temporary improvements in their condition, He sees the multitude of His compatriots and contemporaries facing

an incurable state (38–45). From this generation, however, involved as it is in destruction, is gathered the
company of Jesus' followers; these are not His kinsmen,
but those who hear and do His words (46–50). The
same distinction appears also in the fact that, in order to
punish the multitude for their indifference to the truth,
Jesus conceals it from them entirely by the use of
parables, while He interprets these to His disciples, and
teaches them to grasp the truth even in this form (xiii.
1–52). The account of the impression which Jesus made in
His native city,—characterised by the word ἐσκανδαλίζοντο,
xiii. 57, cf. xi. 6,—and of the superstitious utterances of
the ruling prince when he heard of the miracles of Jesus
(xiv. 1–2), serve also to complete further the series of
incidents begun in xi. 2. In order to explain the latter,
he formally narrates the account of the Baptist's execution
and the cause of his arrest, already presupposed in iv. 12,
xi. 2. Although this is only an episode, it determines
the further trend of the narrative, which from xiv. 13 to
xvii. 21 appears to retain a chronological order, as in
viii. 18–ix. 34. Constant change of residence is noted
(cf. ἀναχωρεῖν, xiv. 13, xv. 21; also other passages where
Matthew does not use just this word). Jesus constantly
avoids contact with the crowds and with His opponents,
and devotes Himself to the training of His disciples, as
we have seen already in the corresponding part of Mark
(vi. 14–ix. 32; cf. above, p. 465 f.). This suits Matthew's
plan also, only he makes the separation between the
disciples and the multitude with their religious leaders
much sharper. It does not appear for the first time
in this section of the Gospel, but the way is prepared for
these statements by what is said earlier in v. 10–12,
x. 16–39. From chap. xiii. onwards, Matthew does not say
anything more about the preaching of Jesus to the people
of Galilee (cf. Matt. xiv. 14 with Mark vi. 34). Matthew
alone (xv. 12–14, not in Mark vii. 17 f.) narrates how

the disciples called Jesus' attention to the fact that His severe condemnation of the Pharisaic overvaluation of the rabbinic statutes was offensive to the Pharisees. Likewise peculiar to him is the severe judgment with which Jesus replies : they are a foreign growth which God has not planted in His garden, and which deserves no care ; as is also the injunction of Jesus to His disciples to leave these blind leaders of the blind multitude to their inevitable fate. Only in Matt. xvi. 6, 11, 12 (not in Luke xii. 1 ; cf. Mark viii. 15), are the Sadducees included also in the warning against the leaven of the Pharisees ; and this warning itself repeated three times, and its meaning expressly stated. No concealment is made of the incurable divisions which Jesus made among His people by His testimony concerning the true law of God (xv. 3, 6, 9 ; cf. xxiii. 2 ff., 23, v. 17–48, xii. 1–11, xix. 3–9). On the other hand, the same section discloses clearly the author's apologetic purpose. The agonising struggle of the Gentile woman with Jesus, who disregarded her cries and went on His way in silence, is impressively described (xv. 22 ff., cf. *per contra*, Mark vii. 25 ff.). The sympathetic Jesus appears to be severer than His disciples, who, for the sake of being rid of her cries, are willing to be a little inconsistent. Only in Matthew does Jesus state the principle that His lifework is limited to Israel (xv. 24, cf. i. 21, x. 5 f.). To this principle He remains true even to the extent of harshness toward the Gentile woman. Not until she recognises to the full Israel's prior rights does He give her help. When in another region—from Mark vii. 31 we know that it was the half-Gentile Decapolis— we find Him scattering the gifts of His mercy with free hand, the gratitude of all the people finds expression in praise of the " God of Israel " (xv. 31). Those, therefore, who say that Jesus is disloyal, an enemy and a disgrace to His people, and a blasphemer of the God of Israel, are condemned as liars.

In the description of the intercourse between Jesus and His disciples there is less emphasis than in Mark upon the slowness with which they progressed in knowledge. Severe judgments concerning them, such as we have in Mark vi. 52, viii. 17 f., are either wanting altogether or less bluntly expressed (Matt. xvi. 9). On the other hand, the way for Peter's great confession (xvi. 16) is prepared by the account of his experience on the sea with the confession which it called out (xiv. 28–33). His later confession is more fully reproduced than in Mark, and is solemnly acknowledged by Jesus; it is declared to be due to God's revelation (xvi. 17, cf. xi. 25), and rewarded by a great promise. The separation between the disciples and the Jewish people had been mentioned before; now we hear that the company of disciples, who hitherto had been gathered about Jesus like a *family* (x. 25, xii. 49 f., cf. ix. 15),—one of a number of groups within the same national bounds,—is to become a Church which is to exist alongside of the Israelitish Church and outlast all hostile attacks. The ἐκκλησία is not yet in existence; Jesus will build it in the future, and He will rear it upon the man of rock-like character, who in the name of the other disciples has given utterance to the true confession, and who is to exercise the office of a steward in the house of this Church, with the power accompanying this office to institute rules for the ordering of the house (n. 10). What is said primarily to Peter as the first confessor is on that account none the less applicable to the companions of his calling, who have received a similar office not from him, but like him and with him from Jesus (xix. 28, x. 1–5). As to the right to establish ordinances in this future household of Christ upon earth, to enforce their observance, and to punish their transgression, that belongs to the whole Church (xviii. 15–20), *i.e.* the Church separated from the Jewish people by their confession of Jesus as the Christ. It is this idea of the Christian Church which distinguishes the entire fourth section of Matthew's Gospel from the parallel sections in Mark, which in other respects are so similar. By the latter the disciples are represented as preachers of the gospel in course of training for their future calling. In Matthew, on the other hand, we are taught to look upon them as the foundation and leaders of the Church of Jesus in process of formation. When, however, this confession of Peter and Jesus' answer is followed by the first express *announcement of the sufferings and death* in Jerusalem (xvi. 21); and when, further, the instruction of the disciples with reference to the future conditions of the Church is interrupted repeatedly by the announcement of His sufferings (xvii. 12, 22 f., xx. 17, 22, 28), we infer that the two conceptions are intimately connected. It is because Jesus is condemned to death by the heads of the people and delivered over to the Gentiles for the carrying out of their sentence (xvi. 21, xx. 18 f.) that the kingdom of God is to be stayed in its sweeping onward progress (cf. xi. 12), and a period intervene between its beginning through the word of Jesus and its completion with His parousia, during which the kingdom of heaven shall have its preliminary realisation in a Church of the Christian confession by no means free from foreign elements, in which even the best members are still tainted with sin (xiii. 36–43, 48, xviii. 7–35, xxii. 11, xxiv. 12). This Christian Church and the Jewish people are represented as two sharply distinguished bodies. The teaching concerning discipline within the Church (xviii. 15–35), marriage (xix. 3–12), the relation of children to Jesus and so to His Church (xix. 13, 14), the attitude toward earthly possessions (xix. 16–26), the Divine reward in relation to human labour (xix. 27–xx. 16), ruling and serving (xx. 20–28, cf. xxiii. 8–12, xxiv. 45–51),—all these presuppose a Church of Jesus, which, whatever its organisation, was certainly separate from the Jewish people, and regulated

by a different law from that which prevailed among the
Jews. Still, these two groups are not without relation to
each other. The twelve apostles are never to forget their
relation to the people of the twelve tribes (xix. 28, cf. x.
23), and the disciples in general are to follow Jesus' example, and from pure love are to cherish their relation to
Israel. This we learn from the profound narrative preserved
in xvii. 24–27 (peculiar to Matthew). Though fundamentally separated from the Jewish cultus, and though
freed by sonship of the "great King," whose dwelling is
not in Jerusalem but in heaven (cf. v. 34 f.), from every
obligation to observe the ceremonial law, as long as the
temple stands they are still to pay the temple tax, *i.e.* to
fulfil the cultus duties incumbent upon an Israelite, as
Jesus had done (iii. 15, v. 17–20, 23 f., xxiii. 3, 23). The
words, "in order that we may not offend them," contain
the entire programme of the politics of the Israelitish
Church of Jesus before the year 70. Jesus intended to
make the distinction between the Jewish people as represented officially in the high priests and rabbis, further in
the Pharisees who were beyond all hope of improvement,
and the blind multitude that followed them, on the one
hand (xv. 12–14), and the house of Israel, the people of
the twelve tribes, on the other, many of whom had erred
but could yet be brought back to the fold (x. 6, xv. 24).
The former may be offended if they will (xv. 12); no one
is to place a stumbling-block in the way of the others
which can keep them from the truth (xvii. 27, cf. xi. 6).
The last narrative of the fourth section (xx. 29–34) has
the appearance of an allegory, because it stands without
any practical connection with what precedes and what
follows. Besides the blind who fall into the ditch (xv. 14,
xxiii. 16), there are also those blind persons in Israel who
appeal to the mercy of the Son of David, and who become
His followers after He has healed them. The localities of
the single narratives in this section are for the most part

very indefinitely indicated (xiv. 13, 22, xv. 29, xvi. 5,
xvii. 1, 22, xx. 17). The reader is able to form no idea
of the journey to Jerusalem. Similarly, the change from
Galilee to Perea in xix. 1 is marked by no break in the
narrative, since the arrangement of the material is determined by the contents.

In the *fifth section* we have the description of Jesus'
work in Jerusalem (xxi. 1–xxv. 46), where the same material
is employed throughout that we find in Mark. Still even
here the features that distinguish Matthew are not wanting. It is the prophet of Galilee (xxi. 11) who as King
enters the royal city, and it is prophecy which He fulfils
in the choice of the method of entrance (xxi. 5), designing
thereby to show that while He gives up none of the claims
which belong to Him, He will not make use of force.
The enthusiasm of the people, which is caught up even
by the children, is more offensive to the members of the
Sanhedrin than the cleansing of the temple and the
severe condemnation, that its guardians who are responsible for its sacredness, have allowed it to become a
den of thieves (xxi. 15 f.). The parable in xxi. 28–32
brings the resistance of the ruling classes to the testimony
of Jesus into stronger relief than the discussion (recorded
also by Mark and Luke) which precedes. Only in Matthew
is the parable of the husbandmen followed immediately
by the unmistakable declaration that the kingdom of God
shall be taken from the Jewish people as a nation and
given to another people, *i.e.* to a people independent of
every nationality (xxi. 43). In the parable which follows
(xxii. 1–14, Luke xiv. 16–24 is only remotely parallel)
we have a sentence, not an essential part of the picture,
pointing clearly to the destruction of Jerusalem as the
punishment of the Jewish people for their refusal to
accept the invitation to enter the kingdom of God (xxii. 7).
The teaching discourses, which arouse the astonishment
of the crowd here as in Galilee (xxi. 46, xxii. 33), and

the discussions in which Jesus overcomes the Pharisees and Sadducees are followed (chap. xxiii.) by a comprehensive discourse addressed alike to the undecided multitude and the disciples, in which He condemns the scribes and Pharisees occupying Moses' seat, who will not be satisfied until they have made full the sin of Israel and of Jerusalem against the bearers of all God's revelation. The rejection of Jesus' witness is not the last step in this direction. There remains still the persecution of the prophets, the wise men, and the scribes whom Jesus will send to His people (xxiii. 34). The present generation, however, shall live to see the judgment upon Jerusalem. The decisive cause of the catastrophe lies in the rejection of the repeated efforts of Jesus to shelter the inhabitants from the coming storm. This condemnation, and at the same time the public testimony of Jesus, are brought to a close with an outlook toward the day when this unfortunate people shall hail Jesus as their Messiah with more sincerity than they had shown on the preceding Sabbath. Connecting itself directly with the words concerning the destruction of Jerusalem, we have in what follows Jesus' instruction of His disciples with regard to the end of the world (chaps. xxiv., xxv.).

The *sixth section* (chaps. xxvi.–xxviii.) covers the history of the Passion and the Resurrection. The following features are peculiar to Matthew :—(1) A sharp portrayal of the betrayer and his history. Only Matthew records the bargain with the high priest about the price of the betrayal and the sum agreed upon (xxvi. 15), the conversation between him and Jesus while they were still at table (xxvi. 25), the remark which Jesus made to him at the arrest (xxvi. 50), and the account of his end (xxvii. 3–10). (2) Only Matthew emphasises the way in which Jesus, in obedience to the will of God as He found it indicated in the Scriptures, refused to call the Divine help to His aid in order to deliver Himself from His enemies (xxvi. 52–54, cf. xxi. 5).

The evidence for Jesus' innocence, to which, according to all the records, Pilate testified several times, is rendered still stronger in Matt. xxvii. 19, 24 by the accounts of his wife's dream and of the washing of his hands. Responsibility for the blood of this man, whom the Gentile judge more than once declared to be innocent, is assumed by the whole people, in so far as they have a part in the transactions (xxvii. 25). If Barabbas was also called Jesus, as possibly may have been the case in the original text of Matthew (n. 11), the narrative of the choice between Barabbas and Jesus would be more pointed than anywhere else. In any case, it is made clear that the people delivered up their Messiah (xxvii. 22), and that it was the king of the Jews upon whom the Roman soldiers heaped every mockery (xxvii. 27–30, simpler in Mark xv. 16–19). To the account of the rending of the veil of the temple, found also in Mark xv. 38, Matthew (xxvii. 51–53) adds notice of the earthquake and of the opening of the graves of departed saints, who after the resurrection of Jesus appeared to many in the "Holy City." This is also witness against the Jewish people, but they will not be convinced. The sealing and guarding of the tomb, arranged between the Sanhedrin and Pilate (xxvii. 62–66), was due to a sincere disbelief in Jesus' prophecy of His resurrection. When, however, unsuspected witnesses informed the Sanhedrin that the grave had been opened by other than human hands, the highest officials took refuge in intentional falsehood, and circulated the report which still existed "among the Jews" at the time when Matthew was written, that Jesus' friends had stolen His body (xxviii. 11–15). But the one thus declared to be dead appears alive to His friends in Jerusalem as well as in Galilee (xxviii. 9, 17). The same person who refused to call either the power of God or that of the devil to His aid in order to disarm His foes and to gain dominion over the world (iv. 8, xxvi. 53), speaks as a Lord of heaven

and earth.   The Messiah of Israel who longed to save His
people from sin, and who remained loyal to this His first
duty, even unto death (i. 21, x. 5 f., 23, xv. 24), commissions the Eleven to make all peoples without distinction
His disciples through baptism and teaching.   With this
Church, which shall increase constantly as the majestic
command is carried out, His invisible presence shall abide
until the end of the world, *i.e.* until His visible return
(xxviii. 18–20, xxiv. 3, 14).   Thus ends "The Book of
the History of Jesus Christ, the Son of David, the Son
of Abraham."

If the preceding summary of the principal thoughts
of the book is in the main correct, we must admit that
the work is exceedingly rich in its content, that it is
constructed according to a plan, and that this plan is
carried out to the smallest detail.   In greatness of conception, and in the power with which a mass of material is
subordinated to great ideas, no writing in either Testament,
dealing with a historical theme, is to be compared with
Matthew.   In this respect the present writer would be
at a loss to find its equal also in the other literature of
antiquity.   On the presupposition—which is justified—
that the author believed the incidents which he recorded
to be real facts, and sharing with him the conviction that
history is governed by God and not by blind chance, we
need only a little historical imagination to discover in
Matthew a genuine Jewish book, that is, in so far as the
method of exposition is concerned.   It would not pass
for history in the Greek sense.   Matthew makes little
effort to give us what is called historical narrative.
What he gives as a history of Jesus' birth is in no sense
narrative (above, pp. 531 f., 537).   He records the sending
out of the apostles, and indicates by an introduction (ix.
35–38) and the communication of a long preparatory discourse that it is an event of great importance.   But he
says nothing whatever as to how the apostles fulfilled the

commission, and whether they returned to Jesus. When
and from what quarter Jesus came to His native city, and
whither He went upon leaving (xiii. 54), are questions to
which he seems entirely indifferent. Evidently he finds
no difficulty in giving us Jesus' words in which Chorazin
and Bethsaida are said to be the chief scenes of His
miraculous work (xi. 21), without himself mentioning the
two cities in any passage of his history of Jesus. The
book is concluded, not with words appropriate for a work
which began as a narrative, but with a saying of Jesus.
Even in the case of those actions and discourses which
have great weight for him, the outward circumstances are
treated with great carelessness. Without the help of
other accounts, no reader could form a picture of the
situation in v. 1, vii. 28, or ix. 10–14, or explain wherein
Jesus "saw" the faith of the bearers in ix. 2, or whether
Jesus entered Jerusalem riding upon the ass, or the foal,
or upon each alternately, xxi. 7, or why the sick did
not besiege the house of Peter until after sundown (viii.
16, cf. Mark i. 32 with i. 21). Matthew disdains all external pragmatism. In a passage where he gives us a
series of closely connected events (viii. 18–ix. 34, xiv.
13–xvii. 21), the reasons for this arrangement have nothing
to do with the chronology. The charge that Matthew
transferred the Sermon on the Mount to the beginning
of the Galilean ministry, and the choice of the apostles
to a later time, was a misunderstanding for which the
author is not responsible, since he does not narrate the
latter incident at all (x. 1 ff.), and, moreover, the Sermon
on the Mount is introduced without connection with any
other single event, after he had brought the readers to
the climax of Jesus' work in Galilee.

Far greater weight is laid upon the discourses of Jesus
than upon the clearness of the narratives and the external
connection of events. Matthew closes his book with words
of Jesus (xxviii. 18–20), and often represents Him as speak-

ing at length. Five times discourses of considerable length
or series of discourses are concluded with the formula, καὶ
ἐγένετο ὅτε ἐτέλεσεν ὁ Ἰησοῦς τοὺς λόγους τούτους (vii. 28,
xi. 1, xiii. 53, xix. 1, xxvi. 1). That he used a large
amount of freedom in the composition of these discourses
is clear even without comparison with the parallels in
Mark and Luke. The connected and well-arranged discourse of chap. x., which is associated with a definite
occasion, could not have been spoken on the occasion
there indicated. While the ἰδοὺ ἀποστέλλω (not ἀποστελῶ)
ὑμᾶς (x. 16) cannot be referred to any other sending out
of the apostles than that which is narrated in x. 5, every
intelligent reader says to himself that on this preaching
tour the apostles could not possibly have been in a position
where they would be brought before kings and rulers, and
where they would flee from city to city in expectation of
Jesus' return (x. 16–23). In x. 38 it is taken for granted
that Jesus has already spoken of His death as a death
on the cross. Comparison with Matt. xvi. 21–27, John
xvi. 4, and the parallels, Mark xiii. 8–13, Luke xii. 2–9,
51–53, xxi. 12–17, shows beyond doubt that Matthew
connected the commission which Jesus gave His disciples
when He sent them out for the first time with other sayings relative to their later work, weaving the whole into
an ordered discourse. The same is true of the Sermon on
the Mount (chaps. v.–vii.). Comparison with the discourse
in Luke vi. 12–49 proves that in both the same historical
fact is related. Luke's account has the same beginning
and conclusion as that of Matthew ; all the parts of the
discourse are to be found in Matthew, and with the single
exception of Luke vi. 31 (=Matt. vii. 12) in the same
order. There is no reason to doubt that v. 16–48, vi.
1–6, 16–18, which are essential for Matthew's extended
plan of the Sermon on the Mount, and of importance for
the apologetic purpose of his Gospel, were in their essentials a part of the original discourse, and that Luke

omitted these sentences which related to the O.T. and
Judaism, retaining only the main principles of Christian
morality (vi. 27–36). Still even here the work of
Matthew's free hand is undeniable. The Lord's Prayer,
with its introduction and the application at the end (vi.
7–15), spoils the perfect symmetry of the three parts of
the discourse concerning alms, prayer, and fasting. To
this must be added the fact that the historical occasion
for the Lord's Prayer, given in Luke xi. 1–4, has every
appearance of genuineness, and that a second impartation
of the same prayer, without any reference to a previous
giving of the same, is extremely improbable. Matthew
must therefore have taken it out of its historical connection and incorporated it in the Sermon on the Mount,
with the fundamental thought of which it thoroughly
agrees. This prayer, which every Jew could use, and
which even in Luke is given in answer to the request
for a specific formula for Christian prayer, shows, on the
one hand, that Jesus did not desire to replace Jewish
forms by new forms, but to fill the same with genuine
content. On the other hand, it serves to throw a glaring
light upon prayer as practised by the Pharisees, which
had sunk to the level of the heathen abuse of this
office. The same is possible and probable with reference
to other parts of the Sermon on the Mount. In chap. x.
the historical foundation of a great discourse is reproduced
along with a disproportionate amount of material borrowed
from elsewhere, but the reverse is true in the case of the
Sermon on the Mount, chaps. v.–vii. ; the parable discourses, chap. xiii. ; the great sermon against the scribes,
chap. xxiii. ; and the eschatological discourses, chaps.
xxiv.–xxv. That, however, in the last three groups of
discourses also the author has handled the historical
material with freedom, is not only rendered probable from
the analogy of the discourses in chaps. v.–vii. and chap. x.,
but is proved by comparison with the parallels ; cf. *e.g.*

Luke xi. 37–53, xiii. 31–35 with Matt. xxiii. 23–39, or Luke xvii. 20–37 with Matt. xxiv. 26–28, 38–41.

When we survey the entire book, its material and method of exposition, its aim and the means by which its aim was accomplished, the purpose of the whole is no longer obscure. It is an *historical apology of the Nazarene and His Church over against Judaism.* The book takes for granted that the Jewish people to whom Jesus was sent as a Saviour from sin had rejected Him, had been offended in Him, and had crucified Him as a revolter against the Law and its authentic interpretation, as a false Messiah and a blasphemer against God, by which act they had made Him all the more a σκάνδαλον to themselves (cf. 1 Cor. i. 23 f. ; 1 Pet. ii. 7). It is further presupposed that the spiteful slanders of this people, whom Jesus had loved so deeply and so faithfully, followed Him after His death (pp. 536 f., 555), and that up to the time when the Gospel was written false aspersions rendered faith in Him difficult for the "Jews" (xxviii. 15), also that now a Church bound together by Christian confession exists as an independent body alongside of the Jewish people, identifying themselves with their rulers (xvi. 18, xvii. 24–27, xviii. 17, xxi. 41–43), and that this Church, whose nucleus was gathered from the lost sheep of Israel (x. 6, xv. 24, xix. 28), was nevertheless hated and persecuted by the Jews (v. 10–12, x. 17–26, xxiii. 34–36), whereas it opened its doors more and more to the Gentiles (viii. 10–12, xxi. 43, xxii. 8–10, xxiv. 14, xxv. 32, xxvi. 13, xxviii. 19, 20, cf. ii. 1–12, iii. 9, v. 13, 14, xiii. 38). None of these facts are concealed or apologised for, but all are clearly brought out and defended. It is admitted that Jesus and His Church have appearances strongly against them. Joseph, a son of David, was offended at the son of David yet to be born, the greatest of the prophets at the prophet Jesus, and the chief of the apostles at the Messiah who chose the cross (i. 19, xi. 6,

xvi. 22 f., xxvi. 31–35). Still the true Israelite does
not need to be offended in Jesus, and for those who
have been thus offended there remains always only one
choice, that between the fate of a Judas (above, p. 554 f.)
and the blessedness of a Peter, since in spite of all
Jesus is the Messiah. Those very features in His history
which appear to be against His Messianic claims when
rightly understood, will be found to be in harmony with
prophecy; all charges of infraction of the law are set
aside by Jesus' words and deeds, and what is really
strange and objectionable to the Jew who judges the
matter superficially, the flight into Egypt, His bringing
up in Nazareth, the choice of Galilee as the scene of His
labours, and His crucifixion,—all were brought about by
the sin of the Jewish people which will not remain unpunished. His blood is upon this entire "people and
their children" (xxvii. 25), and indeed upon the same
generation that would not believe His testimony (xii.
38–45, xxiii. 36–38, xxiv. 34).

*A book of this character must have been written by
a Jew for Jewish readers.* In keeping with the usage of
the Hebrew Paul (1 Thess. ii. 14; 2 Cor. xi. 24; Rom. ii.
17, cf. Gal. i. 13 f.) is the author's employment in one
instance of the name Ἰουδαῖοι to designate those of his
contemporaries who had not become disciples of Jesus
(xxviii. 15), whereas in Mark vii. 3 the name is used only
to describe the Jewish nationality in contrast to those who
are not Jews. Matthew's language is in general that of
a Jewish Christian. On the one hand, he makes use of
conceptions which of themselves could not be understood
by a Gentile (*e.g.* v. 22, xvi. 19, xviii. 18). He takes for
granted that his readers understand the difference between
the Galilean and Judæan dialects (xxvi. 73), as is not the
case in Mark xiv. 70 in the genuine text. Matthew never
explains Jewish words and customs as something strange
to his readers (n. 12), as is the case with Mark (above, p.

488 f.).   On the other hand, from the title onwards, he does
not hesitate to avow his Christian confession.   For this
reason the book could have been written for the Jewish-
Christian Churches of Palestine ; it was adopted by them,
and afterward recast in the *Gospel of the Hebrews.*   But
the prominent apologetic and polemic character of the
book as well as the choice of the language (above, p.
521) makes it extremely probable that Matthew desired to
see his book read primarily by Jews who were not yet
Christians.   It was always possible to find in the Jewish-
Christian Church persons enough who were almost more
Jewish than Christian (Acts xv. 5), and others who were
open to the influence of Jewish insinuations ; but the
Churches of Palestine as a whole as they are known to us
from the Greek Epistles directed to them, the hints of the
Acts, and the occasional remarks of Paul, were not in need
of such an apology for Christ and of such a defence of the
right of His Church to exist, nor of such a sharp attack
upon Judaism as governed and misled by Sadducaic high
priests and Pharisaic rabbis.   The book was suited for
Jewish Christians who were still open to Jewish influences,
or who had again become so after conversion, also for Jews
who still resisted the Gospel.   And for such readers it was
probably intended (n. 13).

1. (Pp. 531, 533.)   More detailed proof of many points can be found in the
writer's commentary on Matthew (*Komm. zum NT* unter Mitwirkung
anderer herausgeg. von Th. Zahn, Bd. i. 2te Aufl. 1905), cited in this work
as *ZKom. Matt.*   With regard to the text of i. 18, observe first of all that
Origen (Scholion in Migne, xvii. col. 289, cf. Delarue, iii. 965) knew no other
reading than γέννησις, and on that basis discussed the difference between it
and γένεσις, i. 1 ; also that Ss Sc S¹ use different words in i. 1 and i. 18 ; and,
finally, that the important D is defective at this point.   Furthermore, with
Iren. iii. 11. 8, Sc Ss, etc., we are probably to read τοῦ δὲ Χριστοῦ without
Ἰησοῦ.

2. (P. 532.)   We find the usual designation of a genealogy, γενεαλογία, in
1 Tim. i. 4 ; Tit. iii. 9 ; cf. γενεαλογεῖσθαι, Heb. vii. 6, cf. ver. 3 ; 1 Chron
v. 1.   No Hellenist would have translated the Jewish words סֵפֶר חֹלֵדֹת אָדָם,
with or without סֵפֶר (Jerusalem Targum, Gen. v. 1 ; 1 Chron. v. 1 ;
2 Chron. xii. 15) or מְגִלָּה (Jerusalem Targum, Taanith, 68a ; Bab. Jebam. 49b)
otherwise than by γενεαλογία.   The earlier Syriac translators, Ss Sc, have in

Matt. i. 1 כתבא דחלולדתא, like the O.T. Peshito, Gen. v. 1 (except ספר for כתבא);
only S¹ ventured to reproduce γενέσεως Ἰησοῦ more exactly by דיליתה דישוע
The LXX has αὕτη ἡ βίβλος γενέσεως not only for ספר תולדת, Gen. v. 1, but
for אלה תולדות, Gen. ii. 4, while in Gen. vi. 9, x. 1 the latter phrase is more
accurately represented by αὕται αἱ γενέσεις, which is the rendering of Aquila
and Symmachus in Gen. ii. 4 also.   On the ground both of content and of
form, Gen. v. 1 must be regarded as the basis of Matt. i. 1, for here the Hebrew
text, both Targums, the LXX, and Aquila (βιβλίον γεννημάτων) all agree.
There the creation of the first man is briefly recalled, and then the successive
generations from Adam to Noah are enumerated.   Gen. xxv. 12, 19 are the
only other instances in which the birth of the person named in the heading
is so much as mentioned ; everywhere else either the history of the man in
question, without reference to his own birth, or else the history of his
descendants is entitled his "Toledoth," Gen. vi. 9, x. 1 (32), xi. 10, 27, xxxvi.
1, 9, xxxvii. 2—nowhere an enumeration of his ancestors.   According to O.T.
usage, therefore (and we can refer to no other for βίβλος γενέσεως), Matt. i. 1
could not in any case be the heading of a genealogy, but rather that of
an account of Jesus which, like Mark and John, made no mention of His
parentage and birth.   It is possible that this phrase, borrowed from the
LXX, seemed to the translator less unsuitable for Greek readers than it does
to us, because he had also in mind the wider sense of γένεσις, "being in its
activity—life" (cf. Jas. i. 23, iii. 6).

3. (Pp. 534, 536, 538.) Sanhedr. 43a, דקרוב למלכות הוא הוא (Cod. Mon. add הנוצרי)
ישו "Jesus (the Nazarene), who was connected or related with the royal house";
cf. Laible-Dalman, Jesus im Talmud, S. 79 and 15* ; Delitzsch, Jesus und
Hillel, 2te Aufl. S. 13 ; Dérenbourg, Hist. et géogr. de la Pal. p. 349 ; ZKom.
Matt. 43 f. A. 6. As long as the temple stood the Davidic family claimed
to be able to prove their descent, as appears from the table of the days on
which the different families were to provide wood for the altar of burnt-
offering. Mishnah, Taanith iv. 5 (cf. Schürer, ii. 260 [Eng. trans. II. i. p.
252]) ; on the 20th of Thammuz the house of David. In the N.T. cf. Luke
i. 5, ii. 36 ; Rom. xi. 1 ; Phil. iii. 5. The great concern which the Jews, and
the priests in particular, felt in establishing their descent (Jos. c. Ap. i. 7 ;
Vita, i. ; Jul. Afric. in Eus. H. E. i. 7) was invariably satisfied by proving
the links between the latest admittedly legitimate member of the family and
the one whose legitimacy was in question ; cf. Schürer, ii. 229 [Eng. trans. II.
i. 210].   The accusation that Jesus was born out of wedlock, through an
adulterous relation between His mother Mary, the wife of Joseph, and a
soldier named Panthera or Pandera, is brought forward by the Jew whom
the pagan Celsus introduces into his polemic against Christianity, circa 170
(Orig. c. Celsum, i. 28, 32 ; cf. Eus. Eccl. Proph. iii. 10, ed. Gaisford, p. 111).
But the ramifications of this fable in the Talmudic literature show that its
kernel is still older ; cf. Laible-Dalman, S. 9–39, 5*–8* ; Dérenbourg, pp.
203 f., 468 ff. Justin also seems to have it in mind, Dial. xxiii. (δίχα ἁμαρτίας), lxxviii. (Joseph's suspicion, ἐγκυμονεῖν αὐτὴν ἀπὸ συνουσίας ἀνδρός, του-
τέστιν ἀπὸ πορνείας, cf. xxxv. cxvii.) ; cf. Forsch. vi. 266–269. Nor did Celsus
invent for his Jew the story that Jesus spent part of His youth in Egypt,
and there learned magic arts by means of which He imposed on the people
when He returned to His own land (Orig. c. Celsum, i. 28, 38, 46). It is

a much older Jewish fable; cf. Laible-Dalman, S. 40–48, 8*ff.; Dérenbourg, 203, note 2; 361, note 1; 471.

4. (Pp. 534, 535.) Except for insignificant variations in the spelling of individual names, the text of Matt. i. 1–15 is certain. When Sc—but not Se Sh S¹ S³—inserts the three missing kings in ver. 8 (as does D in the arbitrarily arranged genealogy which it inserts at Luke iii. 23) without altering the figures in ver. 17, the interpolation is self-evident. If the genealogy in Matt. were Greek to begin with, and constructed on the basis of the LXX, the omission of the three kings might be explained, perhaps, as an error due to the similarity of Ὀχοζίας (2 Kings viii. 24–29; 2 Chron. xxii. 1) and Ὀζίας (Isa. i. 1; 2 Chron. xxvi. 2), especially in view of the mistakes which this similarity had already occasioned in the LXX itself (1 Chron. iii. 11, Ὀζίας wrongly for Ahaziah; 2 Chron. xxvi. 1, Ὀχοζίας wrongly for Uzziah). But the premise does not hold; see § 56, n. 11. If it is probable, further, that the author took the names of the kings from the list in 1 Chron. iii. 10 ff., instead of collecting them laboriously from the narrative (cf. what Africanus says of the genealogical inquiries of Jesus' relatives, Eus. H. E. i. 7. 14; Spitta, Brief des Africanus, 102), the text there gave no occasion for confusion. In that passage Uzziah bears the name עזריה, LXX Ἀζαρίας, which bears no marked resemblance to אחזיהו, LXX Ὀζίας (wrongly for Ὀχοζίας). Matthew, then, must have excluded the three kings intentionally, among them Joash, who reigned forty years, and Amaziah, who reigned twenty-nine. Any particular reason for omitting just these names is not to be sought or found; but, on the other hand, it is quite conceivable that Matthew did not care to dispense with the names from Uzziah onwards, made famous by Isa. i. 1, vi. 1, vii. 1, xxxvi.-xxxix.; Hos. i. 1; Amos i. 1. The fact that Jehoiakim is also lacking before Jeconiah in Matt. i. 11 cannot be independent of the further fact that one of the 42 (3 × 14) vouched for by ver. 17 is missing. We cannot here appraise the various attempts (ingenious attempts in part) to show that this defect is only apparent (Hilarius (?) in Florileg. Biblioth. Casin. ii. 66; Hofmann, Weissag. u. Erf. ii. 42). It is clear that the insertion of the name Jehoiakim in ver. 11 (so as early as Iren. iii. 21. 9, which, according to ZKom. Matt.² 58, A. 18 is rather to be denied) does not relieve the difficulty. By that means the second section is made to contain fifteen names; for, according to the analogy of the first section, Jeconiah is the concluding member of the second, and the third section still lacks one. If one recognises the mistake, and holds it inconceivable that the writer of the table and of ver. 17 should have miscounted, the most natural supposition is that which Jerome was the first to put forward, distinctly, at least (on Matt. i. 11, Vallarsi, vii. 11; cf. Eus. Quæst. ad. Steph., in Mai, Nova P. Bibl. iv. 1. 243), namely, that Ἰεχονίας in ver. 11 is an erroneous rendering of יהויקים, while in ver. 12 the same form stands for יהויכין. If the LXX represents both these names by Ἰωακείμ in a single sentence (2 Kings xxiv. 6; cf. xxiii. 36, xxiv. 1, 5 = Jehoiakim; xxiv. 8, 12, 15, Jehoiachin—which led Eusebius, loc. cit., into very inapt comments), the Greek translator of Matthew may equally well have obliterated the distinction made in the original. In that case Matthew himself meant Jehoiakim, son of Josiah, eleven years on the throne, and in καὶ τοὺς ἀδελφοὺς αὐτοῦ grouped the other princes with him, his brother Jehoahaz who reigned

for three months before him, his brother Zedekiah who came to the throne later, and also his son Jehoiachin or Jeconiah who was king only three months. He does not refer to the latter by name till ver. 12, but he mentions him as the one who maintained the succession (1 Chron. iii. 17).

5. (P. 537.) The text of Matt. i. 16 has been handed down in the three forms which follow, designated by the present writer as A, B, C. (A) Ἰακὼβ δὲ ἐγέννησεν τὸν Ἰωσὴφ τὸν ἄνδρα Μαρίας, ἐξ ἧς ἐγεννήθη Ἰησοῦς ὁ λεγόμενος Χριστός. So all Greek uncials, and all MSS. and versions except those named under B and C. (B) Ἰακὼβ δὲ ἐγέννησεν τὸν Ἰωσήφ, ᾧ μνηστευθεῖσα παρθένος Μαριὰμ ἐγέννησεν Ἰησοῦν τὸν λεγόμενον Χριστόν. So (1) the minuscles 346, 543 (Scrivener's, 556), 826, 828 (cf. Ferrar, *Collation of four MSS.* 1877, p. 2 ; Scrivener, *Adversaria Critica Sacra*, 1893, p. 1 ; Lake, *JThS*, i. (1899) p. 119 ; Harris, *Further Researches in the History of the Ferrargroup*, 1900, p. 7). (2) This text forms the basis of the old Latin version. The Codex k, which is considered the truest witness for its oldest form, gives : "Et Jacob genuit Joseph, cui desponsata virgo Maria genuit Jesum Christum" (*Old Latin Bibl. Texts*, ed. Wordsworth, ii. 24). Essentially the same is found in other old Latin MSS. (*op. cit.* i. 5, iii. 1 ; Bianchini, *Ev. Quadruplex*, i. 4, 5 ; also in d [D is defective]) and in Latin writers, cf. for example, *Chron. Min.*, ed. Frick, i. 60. 24, 100. 7, 102. 1. This text also underlies (3) Sc : "Jacob begat Joseph, to whom was betrothed Mary the virgin, who bare Jesus Christ." (4) The Armenian version presents a conflation of texts A and B (according to Robinson, *Euthaliana*, p. 82) : "Jacob begat Joseph, the husband of Mary, *to whom being betrothed Mary the virgin*, from whom was born Jesus, who was named Christ." The words in italics have been introduced very awkwardly from B into A. In the same way, moreover, only without παρθένος, the citation of the Christian, Timothy, is given in his dialogue with the Jew Aquila, concerning the Christ (ed. Fr. Conybeare, *Anecd. Oxon.*, Class. Ser. viii. 76) : Ἰακὼβ δὲ (*sc.* ἐγέννησεν) τὸν Ἰωσήφ, ᾧ μνηστευθεῖσα Μαρία, ἐξ ἧς ἐγεννήθη Ἰησοῦς ὁ λεγόμενος Χριστός. Similarly, but still more freely, on p. 88 [C] Ss : "Jacob begat Joseph ; Joseph, to whom Mary the virgin was betrothed, begat Jesus, who is called Christ." A trace of this text appears, as it seems, in a sentence of Dionysius Barsalibi on Matt. i. 18, perhaps copied from an older source, which Burkitt, *Evangelion da-Mepharreshe*, ii. 266, gives, following the MSS. : " And when he (the Evangelist in his genealogy) comes to Joseph, he says, ' Who begat the Messiah,' and for that reason afterwards he says, ' The birth of Jesus the Messiah was thus,' etc." On the other hand, as Burkitt shows on p. 265, one has no right to discover in a passage of the dialogue of Timothy with Aquila (viii. 76, line 11 f.) a Greek witness for the text C. The Jew cites from the Gospel of Matt. (κατὰ Ματθαία !) exactly the text A, and adds to it : καὶ Ἰωσὴφ ἐγέννησεν τὸν Ἰησοῦν τὸν λεγόμενον Χριστόν, περὶ οὗ νῦν ὁ λόγος, φησίν, ἐγέννησεν ἐκ τῆς Μαρίας. Although the text does not appear to be entirely in order, still it is clear that these words are not a second citation added to the first, but a Jewish interpretation of the A text. It is easy to understand that before the discovery of Ss no especial attention was paid to the variant readings of Matt. i. 16 (see Tischendorf and Westcott-Hort, 1881, i. 4 ; *Appendix*, p. 7) ; for it was and is evident

that A did not arise from B, but B from A, and from the necessity to obtain
a text which corresponded better with the belief of the Church. That the
designation of Joseph as the husband of Mary (A) was found objectionable,
is proved also by the fact that Sc, which is also a principal witness for B,
i. 19, has omitted τὸν ἄνδρα, and in i. 20 has translated τὴν ἐμνηστευμένην
σου instead of τὴν γυναῖκά σου. Even more necessary appeared a change of
i. 16, since the relative sentence in that verse hints at the condition of
affairs presented in i. 18 ff., but in no way clearly expresses it. Accordingly
the meaning of Matthew would be made sure against any danger of misunderstanding by μνηστευθεῖσα and παρθένος, and at the same time, through
a change of construction, an ἐγέννησεν substituted for ἐγεννήθη, and thereby
an external harmony would be obtained with the form of the preceding
sentences, which occurs thirty-nine times. In this last instance, however,
ἐγέννησεν does not mean "begat" but "bare." Moreover, τὸν λεγόμενον
was in all probability struck out by the originator of the B text; for the
agreement of the old Latin witnesses (and, judging by d, also D) with Sc
outweighs the evidence of the Greek min., which in this passage have
accommodated themselves to the reading of the A text. τὸν λεγόμενον
corresponds to the style of Matt. (iv. 18, ix. 9, xxvi. 3, 14, xxvii. 16, 17, 22),
and is therefore surely genuine; however, not original to B, but omitted
because of its indifferent tone. Consequently the B text in comparison
with A is proved to be a secondary transformation, and the peculiar C text,
which is found only on Syrian soil, a tertiary form. C shares with B, the
μνηστευθεῖσα and παρθένος, changes of the A text, prompted by dogmatic
caution, and only in respect of the unimportant ὁ λεγόμενος does it show
dependence on the A text, as do the Greek MSS. mentioned above under
B, No. 1, and the mixed texts under B, No. 4. These last disprove the
assumption of Burkitt (p. 263), that on Syrian soil Ss represents the original
(appearing essentially in the B text), and Sc an emended form of the first
Syriac translation. To be sure, Sc with its double relative sentence is an
awkward rendering of the B text, but yet inexact only in so far as B,
accurately translated, would read: "to whom being betrothed, a virgin
(named) Mary," etc., and Sc translates as though it had found ἡ παρθένος
before or after Μαριάμ. This inexactness is also found in Ss; and even if
Burkitt were correct in his opinion that Ss connected the ᾧ found in B,
both with ἐγέννησε and μνηστευθείσῃ (i.e. would perhaps read: "to whom
the Virgin Mary, betrothed to him, bare Jesus, who is called the Christ"),
would not this have been a very awkward and in the highest degree
erroneous translation? And how then could the second Joseph peculiar to
Ss be explained? For every uncritical reader would have understood it to
be the subject of ἐγέννησεν. Why did Ss not write like Sc a ⁊, instead of
repeating the name, in order to have the relative sentence depend upon it?
The emendation of the reading of the B text, supported by a prevalent
tradition, which was in essentials correctly rendered by the first Syriac
translation, lacks support from any other tradition. The reason for the
change is that he made Joseph the subject of ἐγέννησεν. His intention
cannot have been to represent Joseph as the physical father of Jesus, for it
is impossible that one who had this purpose should at the same time and in
the same sentence speak even more clearly then the A text of Mary's vir-

ginity ; exclude the existence of marital relations between her and Joseph ; and in i. 18–25 emphasise as strongly as does the catholic text that Jesus was begotten through the agency of the Holy Spirit. Moreover, Ss does not show elsewhere either in respect of this or any other writer an especially dogmatic bias. Presumably the translator stumbled unawares into his strangely self-contradictory reading through the comparison of a Greek text with the form of the Syriac version which lay before him. As he took from this τὸν λεγόμενον, so also the ἐγέννησεν. The Greek MS. compared by him was similar to those mentioned under B, No. 1. Of this ἐγέννησεν, which, just as in the thirty-nine preceding instances, he thought, must be understood to designate the connection between father and son, only Joseph could be the subject. He must therefore repeat his name as subject of a new sentence. He could do this unhesitatingly, since also in many of the preceding sentences (e.g. ver. 8) the same word in no sense expresses physical fatherhood. He wished by this to designate Jesus as Joseph's son only in the same way as in i. 1 He was called David's son. The zeal with which many have seized upon the reading of Ss as a bit of the primitive Gospel, without looking to right or left, is explained by the old prejudgment that the genealogy of Jesus, leading as it does to Joseph, could have been prepared only by one who took him to be the actual father of Jesus. But the alleged contradiction between the genealogy and the following narrative is found equally in Luke—and so in both of the only old Christian writings extant which trace the Davidic descent of Jesus in a genealogy. That His Davidic descent was ever understood in the Christian community in any other sense is an hypothesis without support in the existing literature ; cf. with regard to the Gospel of the Hebrews, GK, ii. 670 f., 686 f., 690 ; and on the whole question, the writer's Das apos. Symbol., 2te Aufl. S. 54–68. The hope of finding indications in old MSS. and versions that the authors of lost Gospels or brief writings which may have been worked over in our Matt. and Luke regarded Joseph as the physical father of Jesus, should at last be dismissed. An author who knew how to make even the dry material of a genealogy to its least detail contribute to the purpose of his thought regarding the slandered miracle of the Messiah's birth (see p. 534 ff. above), cannot at the same time have taken over statements from a genealogy of Joseph or Jesus used by him which directly contradicted his conception of this fact. Any text of Matthew which contained such statements would be condemned in advance as one altered against the author's intent.

6. (P. 537.) The formula used nine times by Matthew, ἵνα or ὅπως πληρωθῇ κτλ. (to which the similar expressions in ii. 17, xxvi. 54, xxvii. 9 should be added), appears elsewhere only in Mark xiv. 49 (a parallel to Matt. xxvi. 54), and seven times in John, referring to O.T. predictions and prophetic words of Jesus ; it does not occur in Paul or in either of Luke's books, and Jas. ii. 23 is the only further passage to be brought into comparison. This is not the place to defend against unintelligent fault-finding the thoughtful conception of history which is set forth in these words. For a proper appreciation of the Gospel of Matthew in this regard, the point which is before all else decisive is the fact that the author, who in i. 23, ii. 6, xii. 18–21, xv. 8 f., xxvii. 9 (also probably xiii. 13–15, see ZKom. Matt. 474) shaped the O.T. texts to his purpose with entire freedom, makes not the

slightest attempt to transform historical statements, like those cited in ii 15, 18, viii. 17, into predictions of future events.

7. (P. 539.) We must reject every interpretation of Matt. ii. 23 which disregards the fact that the passage differs from i. 22 f. (ii. 5), ii. 15, 17, iii. 3, iv. 14, viii. 17, xii. 17, xiii. 35 (xv. 7), xxi. 4 (xxii. 31, 43), xxvii. 9, first, in that it mentions not an individual prophet, but the prophets in general ; and, secondly, in the omission of the λέγοντος or λεγόντων of citation. These facts make it impossible to look here for a quotation from either a canonical or an apocryphal book. Moreover, ὅτι cannot introduce, in indirect quotation, a summary of the whole prophetic teaching with regard to the lowliness of the Messiah and the possibility of misjudging Him (so practically Hofmann, Weiss. u. Erf. ii. 63–66, in an otherwise admirable discussion), nor yet a composite of passages like Isa. xi. 1 ; Jer. xxiii. 5, xxxiii. 15 ; Zech. iii. 8, vi. 12 ; for it is not said in any of these passages that the Messiah is to bear any name approaching that of Ναζωραῖος, but He is spoken of figuratively by the prophets themselves as a נצר or צמח. The appeal to the prophets collectively is not followed by any sort of citation, exact or inexact, any more than in xxvi. 56 or the other passages that might be compared (Mark xiv. 49 ; John xvii. 12). ὅτι, then, instead of which γάρ would be plainer and better Greek, is to be understood causally, as in Matt. xxvi. 54 ; Acts i. 17. In justification of his view that the settlement of the Holy Family in Nazareth, a city unnamed in promise, was not a mere accident, but a fulfilment of the whole tenor of prophecy, Matt. recalls that the Child who there grew to manhood was one day to receive from His people the opprobrious title of the Nazarene. The Promised One was to enter upon His mission misunderstood and misjudged. The harshness of the construction, which lies in the fact that κληθήσεται must be understood from the standpoint of a moment already past at the author's time (= ἤμελλε γὰρ Ναζωραῖος κληθῆναι), is paralleled in Rom. iv. 24, and for that matter also in Matt. xvii. 11, cf. 12, and is not without support in the best Greek ; cf. Kühner-Gerth, i. 173 f. The translation is obscure and liable to misunderstanding, perhaps in consequence of a too anxiously exact fidelity to the Aramaic original. It might also be doubted whether the translator himself understood the original correctly.

8. (P. 540.) In Matt. ἡ βασιλεία τῶν οὐρανῶν occurs thirty-three or thirty-four times ; elsewhere in the N.T. only once (namely, John iii. 5), according to the correct text. The conception is thoroughly Jewish, and very common in the Mishnah and allied literature (cf. Schürer, JbfPTh, 1876, S. 166 ff.); but it is there quite colourless and divested of its eschatological character. The root of the idea, to speak briefly, lies in Dan. ii. 34 f., 44 f., and its authentic interpretation in John xviii. 36 ; cf. ZKom. Matt. 124 ff.

9. (P. 542.) On the 25th of April 1868, in Göttingen, the present writer publicly defended this thesis among others : " Orationis montanæ a Matthæo evangelista traditæ summa in cap. v. 16 proposita est," i.e. not in v. 17 ; for the latter statement covers only the discussion through v. 48 ; and even if one takes v. 17–20 as the theme, it is impossible to bring the whole content of the discourse within it. Moreover, while vii. 12 may appear to be a summing up of the whole with v. 17 in mind, it is only apparently so. Concern lest the accentuation of v. 16 should result in a contradiction of vi. 1 is needless, for the discrepancy is not increased by taking v. 16 as the fundamental thought

of the discourse. As a matter of fact, there is no contradiction. The only possible query is whether opposition to the Pharisees still exists in vi. 19-vii. 5 ; cf. xxiii. (14 ?) 25 ; Mark xii. 40 ; Luke xii. (1) 22–31, 34, xvi. 13–31. ὑποκριτά, vii. 5, would indicate that the contrast was still in mind.

10. (P. 550.) We cannot introduce here an exposition of the passage xvi. 16–20, which, on account of the practical ecclesiastical interest which attaches to it, has been so variously misinterpreted. The present writer confines himself to the following suggestions : (1) The attempt to show from Tatian's *Diatessaron* that even past the middle of the second century xvi. 18 f. was lacking in many or all manuscripts of Matt., and so that what we have before us is a later catholic interpolation, has been futile (*Forsch.* i. 163 f., 243 f., 290 f. ; *GK*, ii. 546). How essential the statements about the Church are in the construction of Matthew's Gospel appears above. (2) ἡ βασιλεία τῶν οὐρανῶν does not signify here, any more than elsewhere, the kingdom of God to be found in heaven, the other-world abode of the exalted Christ and the blessed who wait for the resurrection (2 Tim. iv. 18 ; John xiv. 2), but the kingdom of God from heaven set up on earth. Between Hades below and heaven above is the kingdom of God on earth. This kingdom is not represented here, however, in its future completion after the parousia (xvi. 28), but in its preparatory, still imperfect form. Such a form the kingdom—in its essence invisible, and established in men's hearts through God's Word (xiii. 18 ff., 37) and His Spirit (iii. 11)—already before its completion possesses in the Church of Jesus. This conception, so clear in xiii. 41, is demanded by the connection of thought in the present passage. The keys, ver. 19, belong to the house, ver. 18 ; the house, therefore, is identical with the kingdom, cf. xxi. 42, 43 and also xii. 25–29. (3) The key or keys are the symbol of the steward's office, cf. Isa. xxii. 22 (in Rev. iii. 7 the master of the house himself carries them). Peter is the (chief) οἰκονόμος in the administration of the Church ; cf. Matt. xxiv. 45–51 ; Luke xii. 42–48 ; 1 Cor. iv. 1, ix. 17 ; and, to the point, John xxi. 15–17. (4) To the administrative authority thus announced ver. 19b adds legislative power ; for δέειν and λύειν correspond to the Rabbinic אָסַר " declare forbidden," and הִתִּיר " declare permitted." The reference, as a rule, is to courses with regard to whose permissibility different opinions might be entertained, but never to past actions, sins committed. Matt. xvi. 19 has absolutely no connection with John xx. 23.

11. (P. 555.) Origen (Gallandi, xiv., Appendix, p. 81 ; *Comm. in Matt.*, Delarue, iii. 642, 918) found Jesus as the real name of Barabbas, Matt. xxvii. 16 ff., " in very old manuscripts." So also Ss (Sc is defective), Arm., Sh (which is entirely independent of the other Syriac versions), and also a few Greek minuscules and scholia. Tatian probably did not have it, for Bar-Bahlul refers to it expressly as a reading of the *Gospel of the Separated* (*Forsch.* i. 105 ; cf. 108, 211). Nor can it be established in the *Gospel of the Hebrews* ; *GK*, ii. 697–700. Still, the reading, which could easily give offence, and may for that very reason have been set aside by the redactor of the *Gospel of the Hebrews* also, is early and well enough attested to permit the conjecture stated on p. 555 above ; cf. *ZKom. Matt.* 702 ; Burkitt, *Evangelion da-Mepharreshe*, ii. 178, 277.

12. (P. 561.) If the reading of the later MSS., οἱ λέγοντες, were authentic,

Matt. xxii. 23, like Mark xii. 18, Luke xx. 27, Acts xxiii. 8, it would be at instance of information to the readers with regard to the doctrines of the Sadducees. According to the original text without οἱ, the meaning is rather that the Sadducees disputed with Jesus concerning the Resurrection, which they denied, and in the course of a discussion of this sort laid before Him the captious question about the woman seven times married.

13. (P. 562.) Among the many characterisations of the Gospel of Matt., the following are worthy of special attention :—Hofmann, *Vermischte Aufsätze* (1878, written in 1856), S. 15–33 (cf. also his *N.T.* ix. 297–317), and Aberle, *ThQSc*, 1859, S. 567–588 (cf. his *Einl. ins N.T.*, published by Schanz, 1877, S. 20–32). Aberle brought out the apologetic and polemic aim of the Gospel more clearly than others have done ; but his idea that it was written as a reply to a document traducing Christ and His Church, circulated by the Sanhedrin and known to Justin (*Dial.* xvii. 108, 117) and even to Origen (*c. Cels.* i. 38, vi. 27), has met with little acceptance. Neither Matt. (xxviii. 15, ἐφημίσθη ὁ λόγος οὗτος) nor Justin nor Origen refers to such a document. Eusebius (on Isa. xviii. 1 f. ; Montfaucon, *Coll. Nova Patr.* ii. 424 f.) was the first to conceive of these Jewish slanders as taking the form of official communications from the Sanhedrin at Jerusalem to the Jews of all the world ; and, while Eusebius appealed to older authorities, he wrote under the influence of the text upon which he was commenting, and for the purpose of contrasting the apostles of Christ, who were also letter-writers, with the "apostles" of the Jewish "patriarch." This, then, is not old tradition, but learned invention. The passages in the N.T. which refer to Jewish calumnies and Jewish opposition to Christianity outside of Palestine (Rom. iii. 8, cf. Rom. as a whole, and vol. i. 424 ; 1 Thess. ii. 15 f. ; Gal. iv. 29; Rev. ii. 9, iii. 9 ; and the narratives in Acts, perhaps with the exception of ix. 2), convey no hint of any action of the Sanhedrin to that end, and Acts xxviii. 21 f. is evidence to the contrary. It is true that the Jewish slanders, in oral circulation, to which Matt. has reference, were still current to some extent in Justin's time ; but the very ones which are most clearly indicated by the apologetic attitude of Matt. i. and ii. are hardly hinted at in Justin (see p. 563, n. 3). The alleged theft of Christ's body by the disciples is known to Justin (*Dial.* cviii) from Matt. xxviii. 13.

§ 56. COMPARISON OF THE GOSPEL OF MATTHEW WITH THE TRADITION REGARDING IT.

It has been established by the preceding investigation that Matthew was written for Jews and Jewish Christians in Palestine, as the tradition reports (above, pp. 521, 560 f.). The fact that in spite of this it was circulated as early as the first century even in Churches predominantly Gentile, was orally translated, and then finally translated into Greek (above, p. 513 ff.), is easily explained by the

richness of its contents, and by the absence of all such
Jewish ideas as were out of harmony with the Christian
confession in general, or with the views which prevailed
in the Gentile Christian Churches at the beginning. Paul
would have no objection to this Gospel, which represented
Jesus as " a servant of the circumcision " under the law,
and yet at the same time the King of heaven and earth,
who bestows the gospel upon all peoples (Gal. iv. 4 ; Rom.
xv. 8). Not until the true historical picture of Jesus and
of the situation of His first Church had faded out, did
critical questionings arise among Gentile Christians as
to the truth of Matthew's peculiar setting forth of the
history and his new uncritical interpretations of it (n. 1).

There is nothing in the Gospel which contradicts the
tradition that it was written between 61 and 66. If the
" to this day " (xxvii. 8, xxviii. 15) were after the destruction of Jerusalem and the temple, we would expect that
an author who values so highly as does Matthew proof
based upon the concurrence of prophecy and its fulfilment
for the justification of Christ over against Judaism, would
indicate somewhere and in some manner that the prophecy
of Jesus had been fulfilled in this judgment (xxii. 7, xxiii.
35–xxiv. 2, xxvi. 61, xxvii. 40). Matthew makes no
attempt whatever to separate the prophecy concerning the
parousia from the prophecy concerning the judgment upon
Jerusalem and the Jewish contemporaries of Christ (xvi.
28, xxiv. 3, 34, xxvi. 64 ; see above, p. 449 f.). There are
sayings which make it appear as if the apostolic preaching
was to continue in Israel until the parousia of Christ, and
as if the spread of the gospel among the Gentiles was not
to begin until after the destruction of Jerusalem (x. 23,
xxii. 7–10, xxiii. 34–36), standing alongside of other sayings in which the completion of the preaching among all
peoples is made the condition of the parousia (xxiv. 14, cf.
v. 14, viii. 11, xii. 18–21, xiii. 38, xxiv. 31, xxv. 32, xxvi. 13,
xxviii. 19). The author makes no attempt to harmonise

these differences. Because when Matthew was written there was as yet no sign of fulfilment, the relation in which the predicted setting up of the idolatrous abomination in the temple, with the accompanying desolation, *i.e.* desecration of the temple (xxiv. 15), stood to the other event prophesied at the same time, namely, the destruction of the temple and of the city (xxii. 7, xxiii. 38–xxiv. 4), is left obscure. It is evidence of the faithfulness with which this particular prophecy is recorded in Matthew, that the author, unlike Mark (xiii. 14 ; above, p. 500 f.), does not employ the language in keeping with the later understanding of apostolic Christianity which was the result of actual experience (n. 2). In the prophecy of the fall of Jerusalem itself we do not find such features in Matthew as appear in Luke's account (xix. 41–44, xxi. 20, xxiii. 28–30), which could be judged a reflection of the event after its fulfilment. The attempt has been made to derive from Matt. xix. 1 the idea that, from the point of view of the author, Judæa lay on the other side of the Jordan, and that accordingly the book, or this portion of it, was written on the east side of the Jordan, about the time when the Christian refugees from Jerusalem found a place of safety in Pella. This would bring us down a little beyond the time limits drawn by Irenæus, since the departure from Jerusalem certainly did not take place before the year 66 (n. 3). It is, however, inconceivable that merely in consequence of a change of residence to the other side of the river, which had taken place shortly before, and against the regular Jewish usage and the usage which he himself follows in other passages of his book, a Jew, who up to this time had lived west of the Jordan, should have characterised the latter region πέραν τοῦ 'Ιορδάνου in a narrative the scene of which up to this point had been Galilee. The words themselves do not forbid, but favour the interpretation that on this occasion Jesus made the journey from Galilee to Judæa through

Perea instead of Samaria (n. 4). Equally erroneous is the
opinion that in Matt. xxiii. 35 Jesus is made to refer to
an event which took place in the year 67 or 68, not
prophetically, but in historical reminiscence (n. 5). If this
were an unintentional error, the composition of Matthew
would have to be brought down at least to the year 100,
a date which, as has been shown, does not agree with the
other contents of the book. If, on the other hand, it were
an intentional modification of a word of Jesus in the
tradition (Luke xi. 51), it would represent an inconceivable
mixture of thoughtlessness and perverseness. In reality
the occurrence of the name Barachiah instead of Jehoiada
is only one of those oversights on the part of Matthew
which the learned redactor of the *Gospel of the Hebrews*
saw fit to correct (n. 5). There are no critical reasons
why we should not accept the tradition according to which
Matthew wrote his Gospel in Palestine between the years
61 and 66 (n. 6).

Likewise the supposition that he wrote in the common
language of Palestine, and that our Greek Matthew is a
translation from the Hebrew, *i.e.* Aramaic, made considerably later (above, pp. 506–522), finds support in the
text. In the discussion of this question it is first of all
to be kept in mind that Jesus made use of Aramaic (§ 1)
in His preaching to the people and in instructing His
disciples, as well as in all His intercourse with His contemporaries, so that *all* the discourses of Jesus and the words
spoken by Him to the Jews, who had intercourse with
Him, preserved to us in Greek books, are only translations.
And we are not the first to be dependent on such translations; but this was likewise true for the Christians in
Antioch, Ephesus, Corinth, and Rome in the days of the
unwritten Gospel (§ 48). The possibility or the necessity
of referring one of Jesus' words to an Aramaic original in
order to understand it fully or to explain the different
forms in which it occurs in the tradition, proves nothing

as to whether the writings in which it is found were originally Greek or translations from the Aramaic. The material which an evangelist like Luke, who knew little or no Aramaic, took from the oral or written tradition must have been already in Greek, and the Hebrew or Aramaic idioms which are observable in his accounts may be regarded as in so far proof of the faithfulness with which he reproduces what he received from the tradition. It does not, however, establish anything with reference to his linguistic ability, nor prove that one of his sources was in Aramaic, since the oral account or writing at the basis of his narrative can go back either directly or indirectly to a Jewish Christian who knew Greek enough to be able to give an oral or written account of Jesus in this language, and who at the same time was still "Hebrew" enough to betray himself in his language either intentionally or unintentionally. Even an evangelist like Mark, whose native language was Aramaic, but who for decades had been in the service of missionary work outside of his native land, and had finally come to know Greek well enough to undertake composition in this language, did not have to construct the Greek form of his Gospel entirely new. He was influenced by the manner in which the words and deeds of Jesus were customarily related in Greek in connection with the missionary work. This would be even more true in the case of a translator who put the Aramaic Matthew into Greek after it had been translated orally for a number of years, especially if the work was done at a time when Greek Gospels were already in existence and circulated in the circle to which the translator belonged. In the case before us, however, this is at least very probable. Besides Mark (above, pp. 444, 516 f.), still other Greek Gospel writings could have been in existence in the vicinity of the Greek translator of Matthew, as the Gospel of Luke or one of the writings mentioned in Luke i. 1 which have not come down to us. Besides being

influenced by the ecclesiastical language of the Greek
Churches, it was unavoidable that the author should be
affected also by the oral translation of the Aramaic
Matthew, which had been practised for years, and from
which, finally, the written translation originated, as well
as by Greek Gospels like that of Mark.   We must also
remember that translations made in ancient times varied
greatly in character.   We find a disposition to translate
a text which was already regarded as Holy Scripture with
slavish literalness.   For this reason the LXX is on the
whole a very literal translation which everywhere does
violence to the genius of the Greek language, a particular
in which Aquila's translation is even a greater offender
(vol. i. p. 56).   The Old Latin translation, particularly
that of the N.T., which was not made until the N.T. had
long been accepted as Holy Scripture by the Church,
was designed to be literal.   In this point the revisers
had few changes to make ; they simply freed it from its
slavish dependence upon the original, and made the Latin
smoother.   The translation of the Gospels among the
Syrians exhibits the reverse process.   From the *Diatessaron* or Syrus Sinaiticus to the work of Thomas of
Heraclea we notice a constant development away from
great freedom to slavish literalness ; a tolerably good
manipulation of the native language gives place to a
handling of the same which grows constantly worse and
worse as the attempt is made to render the original
more and more faithfully.   When the Greek Matthew was
produced (above, p. 516), the development in the direction
of treating the original upon which it is based as Holy
Scripture could not yet have gone very far.   The translator could not have been a pure Hellenist, since as such
he would not have understood the original, but was
simply one of those " Hebrews " who, like Paul, was not
only proficient in his own language, but master also of
Greek (vol. i. p. 48 ff.).   He must have been born or have

grown up among the Hebrews, and therefore have been accustomed to the oral translation of the Hebrew original into Aramaic as it was practised in the synagogues of the Hebrews. Here literal exactness was not regarded as essential even in relation to the O.T. Much less, then, could it have appeared to the translator to be his first and only duty with reference to Matthew,—a writing not yet old enough to be regarded as sacred. Finally, it is to be remembered that the language of a translator does not always show stronger traces of dependence upon the original language than that of an independent author who is under the necessity of using a language other than his own. A German writing in English and for English readers about conditions in his native land would be far less careful to avoid Germanisms than a German translating a work of Goethe or Ranke into English.

The style of Matthew shows throughout fewer Hebraisms than that of Mark and Revelation. Constructions entirely foreign to Greek idiom do not occur, and the use of καί in the narrative is much less frequent (n. 7, and above, p. 502, n. 2). Indeed, the question arises whether the painful frequency of certain formulæ and constructions which take the place of the Semitic form of narrative are not due to the translator's effort to avoid the latter (n. 7). That Matthew is a translation from a Semitic original is proved primarily on other grounds. An author writing originally in Greek could not have written i. 21. A Greek reader unfamiliar with the etymological meaning of ישוע could not see the logical force of the explanation of the choice of the name here given, and, therefore, for such the sentence is simply unintelligible. The Aramaic-speaking Jews, among whom the Hebrew proper name Jesus was very common, and to whom the meaning of the stem must have been generally familiar from the liturgical use of hosanna, understood the sentence at once even if the σώζειν of the Greek Matthew did not represent

the corresponding Hebrew verb, but the purely Aramaic
פרק (n. 8). The Greek translator could or should have
helped his reader out of the difficulty by a ὅ ἐστιν
μεθερμηνευόμενον σωτήρ or σωτηρία κυρίου, which would have
rendered the following αὐτὸς γὰρ σώσει intelligible. Justin
(*Apol.* i. 33) did so. That the author of the Greek
Matthew omits this explanation, is proof of the exactness
of his translation, but not of his skill as a translator. The
case is similar in Matt. x. 25, where the connection between
the literal meaning of the name Beelzebub and the figure
of the οἰκοδεσπότης and the οἰκιακοί (vol. i. p. 20) is lost to
the Greek reader, and therewith the point of the discourse.
If they had recorded this saying at all, Mark, and certainly
Luke, would not have omitted an explanation of the word.
A simple explanation of the content such as we have in
Matt. xii. 24 (cf. Mark iii. 22 ; Luke xi. 15), would not
have been sufficient. The absence of an explanation of
the word κορβανᾶς, xxvii. 6, is all the more striking, because
in xv. 5 the Hebrew and Aramaic word, which was unintelligible to Greek readers, is replaced by the Greek
translation which Mark found it necessary to add in
vii. 11. Here and in other places the Greek Matthew
not only makes less effort than does Mark to retain the
form of the original language, but rather betrays a purpose
to furnish his Greek readers with a text at once intelligible, with the fewest possible foreign expressions (n. 9).
This fact makes the other cases where Hebrew and Aramaic
words and names are left unexplained, as in Ἰησοῦς, i. 21 ;
Βεελζεβούλ, x. 26 ; ῥαχά, v. 22 ; κορβανᾶς, xxvii. 6, seem
to be due to dependence upon the Aramaic original, and
to a lack of courage on the translator's part to render
this freely. In the same way is to be explained the
obscurity of the expression in ii. 23 (above, p. 568, n. 7) ;
further, the use of πέραν τοῦ Ἰορδάνου as a substantive
without the article in iv. 25, which is contrary to Greek
idiom, and also the occurrence of genitives like Γαλιλαίας

and 'Ιουδαίας governed by ἀπό (iv. 25, cf. iv. 15), likewise
the translation of Jewish scholastic terms by δέειν and
λύειν (xvi. 19, xviii. 18 ; above, p. 569, n. 10), which is
literal but unintelligible to Greek readers. If, according
to John i. 42, xxi. 15–17, and the *Gospel of the Hebrews*,
Peter's father was called Jochanan, the Bar-Jonah of
Matt. xvi. 17 is a mistake more likely to have been made
by a translator than by the author (vol. i. 17). The
retention of the Aramaic *bar* without an added translation
seems to be without purpose, and its employment along
with the Greek form Πέτρος (cf. *per contra*, John i. 42)
is inconsistent, and exhibits poor style. Κανavαῖος (x. 4),
which an ignorant scribe changed to Κανavίτης, and
Χαναvαία (xv. 22), are correct transcriptions of קַנְאָנָא (Dalman, *Gr.*¹ 138, better than 2te Aufl. 174) and כנעניתא ; but
it would have been better for his Greek readers if the
author of the Greek Matthew had given the translation
of the first, which is customary in Luke and Josephus,
ζηλωτής, and if he had substituted for the latter the
specification which we find in Mark vii. 26. Perhaps if
we could compare the original with the translation, we
should be able to make the same definite claim with
regard to other passages where now we must be content
with modest conjectures (n. 10). The omissions of things
it was incumbent upon a translator to say, which are noted
above, lose none of their force as proof because in other
places the translator is more careful to make himself intelligible to his readers. In xxvii. 46 he himself must
have felt that a translation of the Aramaic words was
quite as indispensable as the translation of the Hebrew
name Immanuel in i. 23 (n. 9). Familiarity of his readers
with Mark xv. 22, 34 (cf. John xix. 17) may have induced
him to retain the original in xxvii. 46, and to add the
translation of the Hebrew name in xxvii. 33, which was
not absolutely necessary.

Stronger proof that Matthew is a translation is to be

derived from a consideration of the form of its citations
from the O.T.   When a Hebrew like Paul makes only
very moderate use of his knowledge of the Hebrew O.T.,
and when the author of the Epistle to the Hebrews, who
was likewise learned in the Scriptures, takes his citations
wholly from the LXX, it is inconceivable that an evangelist writing originally in Greek for Greek or Hellenistic
readers, whose knowledge of the Scripture was inferior
to that of the persons mentioned (n. 11), should, while
following the LXX in many instances, still, wherever
he felt it necessary, give a translation of the Hebrew
text entirely independent of the LXX.   On the basis of
the differences observable in Matthew in this respect, the
attempt has been made to distinguish two elements in
our Gospel, and to prove, on this ground, that it is a
compilation.   Where the redactor cites the O.T. on his
own responsibility, he takes his quotations direct from the
Hebrew original, without paying much regard to the
LXX, and reproduces them in free translation.   On
the other hand, citations which occur in the discourses of
Jesus, and such as are made by other persons represented
in the narrative as speaking, he takes from a Greek book
before him in which all the citations were quoted from
the LXX (n. 12).   The rôles here assigned are impossible.
Since Jesus spoke Aramaic, it is extremely improbable
that His own quotations from the O.T. were influenced
by the LXX.   The same must have been true of the oral
tradition of the discourses among the Hebrews in Palestine, and of the supposed record of these discourses by
Matthew.   Therefore the person who translated into
Greek the Hebrew or Aramaic Λόγια, discovered by
Schleiermacher, must have obliterated all traces of his
original's independence of the LXX, looked up all the
passages cited in the LXX, and have copied them
from this source ; while, on the contrary, the author of
Matthew, who wrote in Greek, to begin with, for Greek

readers, ignored the existence of an O.T. in Greek, and everywhere paraded his Hebrew learning. The real state of the case was different, and is very easily explained if we recognise what is not only handed down by the tradition, but also sufficiently proved from what precedes, namely, that our Greek Matthew is the result of an effort to give a literal translation of a uniformly Aramaic original document. Since the translator was proficient in Greek, he must have been familiar also with the LXX, which was industriously read by those about him. In the translation of an Aramaic book he used the LXX as one of his models. He made use of its expressions where it was not easy to produce better ones of his own (i. 1 ; above, p. 532). Sayings such as must have been often employed in preaching the gospel in Greek, and in instruction within the Church, in part also to be found in the Greek Gospels which existed in his vicinity (*e.g.* iii. 3), he reproduced as he found them in the LXX, especially if no violence was done to the sense of his original. In other passages it must have seemed to him that the substitution of the text of the LXX would obscure the sense of his original and the purpose of the citation. In such cases he translated the O.T. quotations of his original in exactly the same way that he did the rest of the Aramaic book. Familiarity with the LXX, and with the language employed in the Church in his vicinity, made it inevitable that expressions which we find in the LXX should flow from his pen, especially in such passages as were often read in Christian circles. That he looked up the quotations and allusions regularly in the LXX, and translated them with this before him, is extremely improbable, otherwise he would have corrected a number of mistakes in his original, as the learned redactor of the *Gospel of the Hebrews* did in at least one case (n. 11).

The question remains still as to whether or not the

unanimous tradition which assigns the authorship of our
Gospel to the apostle Matthew is borne out by the book
itself. Scholars who deny this claim base their opinion
partly upon the content,—which, it is claimed, is inconsistent with authorship by one of the twelve apostles,—
partly upon the dependence of the account upon older
documents of similar content, either still extant or to be
assumed. With regard to the latter point, the real relation that exists between Matthew and Mark deserves
special investigation (§ 57). Particularly, certain repeti-
tions of the same or similar words and actions—the so-
called doublets—have played an important rôle in proving
Matthew's dependence upon various written sources.
Evidence, convincing to one who does not already believe
the point to be proved, has not been produced (n. 13).
Granted, however, that it is possible to prove—a possibility which is here contested—that the original Matthew
is dependent upon our Mark or a similar document, it
would not follow that it was not written by an apostle.
It must always be borne in mind that Matthew became a
disciple and companion of Jesus comparatively late. It
cannot be proved at this point, but simply claimed on
the assumption that the order of events accepted as
correct by the present writer is, that Matthew was no
more an eye-witness of what is recorded in Mark i. 4–39,
ii. 1–12, iii. 20–v. 20 (Matt. iii. 1–iv. 25, viii. 14–ix. 8,
xii. 22–xiii. 52, possibly xiii. 58) than he was of the events
narrated in Matt. i.–ii. or John i. 19–v. 47. With reference to such portions of the history, Matthew was less
favoured than Mark, if the latter was able to draw upon
the narratives of Peter, who became a disciple of Jesus
so much earlier. Further, it is hard to understand why
an apostle should have hesitated to make use of the record
by a disciple of one of the apostles for such parts of his
book. But even in connection with the narration of such
events as he may have witnessed, an intelligent author

is always glad to make use of existing records in prepara
tion for his own work, no matter from whom they may
have originated. In his own recollection he has a certain
standard by which to estimate its worth and to correct its
errors.

With reference to the content of the book and
Matthew's method of exposition, apart from the question
of its dependence upon older written sources which cannot
be demonstrated, it cannot be considered the task of a
text-book like this to combat the dogmatic prejudices of
those who conclude, from the miraculous character of the
events recorded in Matthew, as in all the Gospels, that
none of these books could have been written by a companion of Jesus and an eye-witness of even a part of the
history here recorded. It was necessary to touch upon
this question earlier in connection with 2 Pet. i. 16–18,
and it will recur again more pointedly in the consideration
of the Fourth Gospel. Whoever finds *one* miracle of
feeding a difficulty to begin with, will be under the
necessity of regarding the feeding of the 4000 (Matt.
xv. 32 ; Mark viii. 1), and that of the 5000 (Matt. xiv.
15–21 ; Mark vi. 34 ; Luke ix. 12 ; John vi. 5), as a
double form of one and the same fact, exaggerated by
legend. In the same way he must regard the conversation connected with the two events (Matt. xvi. 5–11 ;
Mark viii. 14–21) as the patchwork of a compiler whose
attitude toward the traditions, already varying widely
from the truth, was uncritical and generally helpless.
This judgment would apply in the same way to Mark,
and finally to all Gospel tradition. Hypothetical reference of the existing Gospels to written sources which are
now lost, the content and form of which each constructs
according to his own liking, puts us in a position where
we can neither answer nor escape the great dilemma
whether the Gospel history is unconscious and conscious
mythologising, or whether it goes back to actual facts.

Criticism of the Gospel literature, and the counter criticisms, can render at best only preliminary service. For
this end it is, to be sure, important to observe that
Matthew's narrative lacks the clearness which characterises that of the eye-witness. It must be admitted that
we cannot make such observations in connection with this
Gospel as led us to refer Mark's account to an eye-witness
(above, p. 491 ff.). The theological thought which domi-
nates Matthew, determining the choice as well as the
form of the subject-matter, does not admit ample breadth
of narrative, depiction of the scene, and delineation of the
characters. But we must remember, *in the first place*,
that the purpose of the writing, as developed in § 55,
gave little occasion for the features which we miss in
Matthew. The Roman Christians for whom Mark wrote
desired a *narrative* concerning Jesus, whom they had not
seen, but whom they nevertheless loved (1 Pet. i. 8). To
the Jews and Jewish Christians for whom Matthew wrote,
it needed to be *proved* that, in spite of all Jewish prejudices to the contrary, Jesus was the promised Messiah.
For this purpose the appropriate material was a few
characteristic actions and detailed discourses. *In the
second place*, it betrays ignorance of real life to decide
a question of this character by reference to a common
standard, instead of by the actual diversity of individual
inclination and capacity. It is possible for everyone to
find, in his daily experience, examples of such difference
between a fact and the same as reported by two different
persons, when exactly similar conditions had existed for
both. *In the third place*, in the criticism of Matthew we
must take into consideration also the fact that narratives
which, in comparison with those of Mark, make the
impression of unelaborated sketches, *e.g.* Matt. viii. 18–
ix. 8, could have been reproduced by Matthew in part
only from extraneous accounts. Further, he purposed in
this whole section,—viii. 18–ix. 34,—by a rapid succession

of chronologically connected events, and by constant change of scene, to give us a picture of the restless activity with which Jesus performed His lifework (n. 14). Is it to be considered a coincidence that Matthew, who follows the Jewish method and reckons the day from evening to evening, chooses for this purpose the particular day in the middle of which his own call took place, and that an apostle selects, as an example of Jesus' teaching, the great discourse which followed directly upon the choosing of the apostles, perhaps the first longer discourse which Matthew, who had been called shortly before from the stall of the tax-gatherer to be a disciple, had heard from Jesus' lips? Most of the objections to the apostolic authorship of Matthew are due either to a failure to recognise its plan and method of exposition, or to opinions about the history, which, in their turn, lack sufficient basis ; or, finally, to preconceived opinions with reference to the uncertain beginnings of literary activity in connection with the Gospel. If the outline of the plan and character of the book given above, pp. 531–562, is relatively correct, the complaints about the lack of chronological order in Matt. iii. 1–xiv. 12, and the contradictions between the arrangement of material in this part of the book and the more trustworthy accounts in Mark and Luke, are without purpose. The requirement that a historian, in close touch with the events which he narrates, must maintain a chronological order in all details, is not met even by Luke in either his Gospel or in Acts, though in the former this appears to be promised, i. 3 ($\kappa\alpha\theta\epsilon\xi\hat{\eta}\varsigma$). It is entirely inapplicable to Matthew, who is in no sense primarily a historian, but an apologetic preacher in Israel of the Nazarene denied by His own people. The freedom with which Matthew handles the form of the great discourses (above, p. 558 f.) is much more conceivable in case of an apostle, who is not called to write history, but to publish the commandments of Jesus to others (Matt.

xxviii. 20 ; cf. 2 Pet. iii. 2),—and who, moreover, felt confidence on account of his own recollection,—than in that
of a younger contemporary who constructed his work from
the narratives of those who heard the discourses, or from
documents in which the same could have been recorded,
part of them not without historical setting. The idea
that the first records of the words and deeds of Jesus
must have been simply collections of material, with no
other purpose than to preserve the memory of them, and
that for this reason a book so thoroughly planned as is
Matthew, so rich in thought, and written with such a
clear purpose, could not have originated except upon the
basis of such purposeless collections of material, is a prejudgment. Of course, lack of knowledge on the author's
part with regard to important facts in the Gospel history,
especially with regard to events which took place when
the apostles were present, would be proof that the book
was not written by an apostle. Apart, however, from the
consideration that, as far as this point is concerned, it
does not make any essential difference whether the book
was written by an apostle or some other Palestinian
Christian in the year 65, or even 75, such ignorance on
Matthew's part remains to be demonstrated (n. 15). The
older criticism of Matthew, which in many instances proceeded upon the presupposition of the apostolic origin and
essential trustworthiness of the Fourth Gospel, is inconsistent, to the extent that objections to the apostolic
origin and historicity of this Gospel are as strong as those
against Matthew. The more important points of difference
will not be considered until we discuss the Fourth Gospel.
Also the question as to why Matthew and Mark begin the
account of Jesus' public work with the arrest of the Baptist,
thereby limiting their narrative practically to Galilee, must
be postponed, in order to avoid repetition (§ 63).

1. (P. 571.) Marcion contended that Matt. v. 17 was not spoken by
Jesus (Tert. *c. Marc.* iv. 7, 9, 12, 36, v. 14), that either He Himself spoke its

direct opposite or His disciples after Him (and before the fourth century)
substituted it for this saying, which was alleged to have been smuggled into
the Gospel by the Judaists (*GK*, i. 609, 666–669). Holsten (*Die drei ursprüngl.
Evv.* 61 ff.) and Holtzmann (*HK²*, i. 5) still take practically the same position
with regard to Matt. v. 17–19, and the latter with regard to xxiii. 3, xxiv. 20
also. According to Weizsäcker, also (*Unters. über d. ev. Gesch.* 125), xxiv. 20
contradicts "the whole gospel tradition concerning Jesus' attitude in regard
to this day." But the fundamental principle on which all depends is preserved
besides in Luke xvi. 17, and also in Matt. iii. 15, only in a still more general
form. Nothing is gained by the excision of xxiii. 3 as long as xxiii. 23 (ταῦτα
ἔδει ποιῆσαι) remains. That Jesus assumed and required the observance of
the ceremonial law by His disciples, and consequently also that xxiv. 20 is in
entire accord with the historical conditions in which Jesus and His disciples
moved, is one of those facts which can be disputed only by a dogmatism,
whether orthodox or heterodox, which is absolutely devoid of historical insight.
According to John, as well as according to Matthew and the other Synoptists,
Jesus never conceded to His accusers that He had annulled one jot or tittle
of the law, and never claimed for Himself a peculiar position either above
or outside the law. On the contrary, He repeatedly proved from the law and
the prophets, from the recognised requirements of the temple service, and from
His opponents' own practice, that His attitude toward ceremonial regulations
—so much freer, as compared with Pharisaism—was the only fulfilment of
the law which answered to the will of the divine lawgiver, the idea of the
regulations themselves, and the patterns of O.T. history. It was rather His
opponents who made empty the law, who nullified and evaded it (Matt. v.
20–48, xii. 1–13, xv. 1–20, xix. 3–12, xxi. 30, xxiii. 1–33 ; John v. 16–18, 42,
45, vii. 19–24). Matt. ix. 14–17 (cf. xv. 2, 7–20) has nothing to do with the
law, which prescribed fasting only on the Day of Atonement, and neither
there (ix. 15) nor elsewhere (vi. 16–18, xvii. 21) does Jesus belittle the pious
observance of voluntary fasting. On the other hand, also, Jesus never taught
that the law given to the people of Israel (Mark xii. 29), to His own and His
disciples' forefathers (Matt. v. 21, τοῖς ἀρχαίοις), was to be extended to all
nations. Yet His Jewish disciples were not to imagine that the nearness of
the kingdom of heaven and of the accompanying collapse of the hitherto existing order, released them from their duty toward the God-given though nationally limited appointments of the O.T. Jesus did not touch upon the question of
the Gentile Christians' position with regard to the law. Only in regard to His
own commands is it His will that they be communicated to all peoples (xxviii.
20). Even according to Matthew no details of the future form of life in His
Church, composed as it was of Jews and Gentiles together, were legally
prescribed by Jesus. Rather was it left to the Church and its leaders to
institute such rules of administration as might be required (xvi. 19, xviii.
18 ; above, p. 550 f.). Intimations are not lacking that in the course of the
historical development even essential portions of the law would be set aside
(xvii. 24–27 ; cf. John iv. 21 ; above, p. 552). In the two ideas, namely,
that Jesus Himself recognised it as His calling to bring the law to its fulfilment, and that so long as the world stands no element of the law can perish
unfulfilled, lie the fruitful germs of thought which were to be developed
later. Hilgenfeld attempted (above, p. 414) to distinguish in Matt. be-

tween a Jewish particularistic tendency derived from the primitive Matt. ir
Aramaic or from the *Gospel of the Hebrews*, and a universalistic tendency
attributable to the Greek redactor, and to sort out the inserted sections. In
this he could not possibly succeed ; for, as (pp. 531–556) has been shown, the
whole book is built up upon the antithesis which he would thus explain.
The supposed redactor speaks of Jesus' redemptive mission in i. 21 as if it
were confined to Israel, while the supposedly Jewish writer of the Sermon
on the Mount points (v. 13–16) to the whole world as the sphere of the disciples' labour and the field of the Gospel, as clearly as does the universalistic
editor in xiii. 38, xxiv. 14, xxvi. 13, xxviii. 19. If vii. 6 were a prohibition
of preaching among the Gentiles, Matthew would reduce Jesus to a standpoint
lower not only than that of the O.T., but lower than that of the Pharisees
(Matt. xxiii. 15) and the narrow-minded Jewish Christians, who never
doubted that the Gospel was intended for all mankind, but simply disagreed
with Paul and others as to the conditions upon which this was to be realised.
Indeed, that group of Jewish Christians which made use of the *Gospel of the
Hebrews*, alleged to be the primitive Matt., fully recognised Paul's Gentile
mission (*GK*, ii. 669). But Matthew has nothing to say about these conditions
for the reception of the Gentiles ; there is simply a certain obscurity as to
when and how the Gospel is to pass from Israel to them, which, however, is
only a proof that Matthew has preserved the words of Jesus with remarkable
fidelity uncoloured by later conceptions (above, p. 571). Jesus Himself knew
that for the period of His earthly life He was confined to Israel (xv. 24) ; it
would have been unfair to the privilege which rightly belonged to that
nation if He had withdrawn from it and turned at once to the Gentiles
(xv. 26). This is quite in accord with Rom. xv. 8 and with the Fourth Gospel,
which represents Jesus' death and exaltation as the indispensable precon-
dition of the extension of His work to the Gentiles (iii. 14–16, x. 16–18, xi.
51 f., xii. 20, 23, 32 ; cf. *per contra*, vii. 35). From this followed naturally
the similar restriction of the apostles ; primarily for the like period (Matt.
x. 5 f.). But in accord also with the actual situation until after 60 A.D.,
which Paul himself acknowledged to be justified (Gal. ii. 7–10), and with
another report of Jesus' words (Luke xi. 49, xxiv. 47 ; Acts i. 8), it is intimated that even after His departure the disciples were to preach first in Israel
(Matt. xxiii. 34, xxii. 4). Neither the promise of x. 23, nor the expectation it
presupposed, namely, that the Twelve would preach in Israel until the time
referred to (the destruction of Jerusalem), failed of fulfilment. It was only
when the signs of the approaching end were multiplying that Peter went to
Rome. The other apostles remained still longer at their posts, and not till
about 70 and from then onwards do we find John and others of the early
apostolic circle, like Philip and Aristion, at work among the Gentile Churches
of Asia Minor. With this corresponds the representation of Matt. xxii. 7–9,
that the Gospel is to turn from Israel to the Gentiles only after the destruction of Jerusalem, and it is not at variance with the missionary command,
xxviii. 19 ; cf. Luke xxiv. 47, and all the similar sayings recorded in Matthew.
For (1) Israel also belongs among "all the nations" (vol. i. 370, n. 2).
(2) The allegorical language of the parable, xxii. 1–14, makes it necessary to
represent the call of Israel and the call of the Gentiles as two absolutely
distinct acts, the latter taking the place of the first. (3) According to

Matthew, Jesus represents His future Church as a community separated from the Jewish nation and open to non-Israelites, which comes into independent existence immediately after His rejection by the Jewish authorities (xxi. 40–43; above, p. 550 ff.). (4) Only a part of this Church is to be found in Judea at the time of the parousia (xxiv. 16); others are scattered among the Gentile nations of the world (xxiv. 9, 31). One who, with the fullest recognition of Israel's prior claim upon its Messiah, repeatedly noticed the call of the Gentiles to salvation and the universal significance of Christ and His Church (ii. 1–12, iii. 9, iv. 24, v. 13–16, viii. 11, 12, x. 18, xii. 18–21, xiii. 31–33, 38, xxii. 7–14, xxiv. 14, 31, xxv. 32, xxvi. 13, xxviii. 19), certainly did not look askance at the mission to the Gentiles which was undertaken before the fall of Jerusalem and independently of the twelve apostles of the twelve tribes of Israel. He found in it no violation of a single command or prohibition of Christ's which he reported, and no unfaithfulness, furthermore, to Jesus' example. For Jesus marvelled at the faith of a Gentile man and a Gentile woman (viii. 10, xv. 28), granted His assistance to them both ; and though He in neither case permitted the great faith which He found among Gentiles to draw Him away from Israel and His primary calling, He did not conceal from the Canaanitish woman that after the children were satisfied the dogs should have their turn. It is the more impossible to find a contradiction between the two narratives if one recognises what Fritzsche pointed out as long ago as 1826 (*Comm. in Mt.* p. 311), that ἐγὼ ἐλθὼν θεραπεύσω αὐτόν, viii. 7, is to be taken interrogatively (cf. *ZKom. Matt.* 335). Astonished at the implied request of the centurion, and hesitating to comply with it, Jesus asks, "I am to come and heal him ?" Only so can we understand the emphatic ἐγώ and the centurion's second remark. He divined the Jew's hesitation to enter a Gentile house (cf. Luke vii. 3 ff.), and, by the opposition it at first met from Jesus, his faith was roused to unexpected earnestness, to which Jesus yielded in this instance as in xv. 28.

2. (P. 572.) Whereas Colani, *Jésus-Christ et les Croyances Messianiques de son Temps*, 1864, p. 201 ff., explained the whole eschatological discourse (Matt. xxiv., Mark xiii.) as an apocalypse from the later apostolic period, Weizsäcker, *Unters. d. ev. Gesch.* 124 ff., would find in Matt. xxiv. 6 ff. and Mark xiii. 7 ff. a Jewish apocalypse under the name of Enoch, referred to also in *Barn.* iv., and dating from the time immediately before the destruction of Jerusalem, just as he considers also that Luke xi. 49 (= Matt. xxiii. 34) points to the use of a Jewish writing. It follows next from this that there is nothing to be said for the Petrine origin of Mark (127), and—though not on this account alone, to be sure—that Matt. was not written till soon after 70 (201 ff.). Similar conjectures, which cannot be supported at any point by valid proofs, were put forward by Renan, *L'Antéchrist*, 3me ed. pp. 289–300.

3. (P. 572.) Eus. *H. E.* iii. 5. 3. After the death of the bishop, James, and the expulsion of the apostles from Judea, and before the outbreak of the Jewish war, the Jerusalem Church removed to Pella in Perea, in accordance with the revelation made to its leading members (κατά τινα χρησμὸν τοῖς αὐτόθι δοκίμοις δι' ἀποκαλύψεως ἐκδοθέντα). Epiphan. *de Mens.* xv : ἡνίκα γὰρ ἔμελλεν ἡ πόλις ἁλίσκεσθαι ὑπὸ τῶν Ῥωμαίων καὶ ἐρημοῦσθαι, προεχρηματίσθησαν ὑπὸ ἀγγέλου πάντες οἱ μαθηταὶ μεταστῆναι ἀπὸ τῆς πόλεως, μελλούσης ἄρδην ἀπόλλυσθαι· οἵτινες μετανάσται γενόμενοι ᾤκησαν ἐν Πέλλῃ κτλ. (cf. *Hær.*

xxix. 7, xxx. 2). These accounts probably go back to Hegesippus, cf. *Forsch*, vi. 269 f. The time was the year 66 at the earliest, 69 at the latest. Josephus (*Bell.* ii. 20. 1, iv. 6. 3 ; *Ant.* xx. 11. 1) also says that many Jews fled from Jerusalem for fear of Zealot rule and of siege ; and in *Bell.* iv. 6. 3 end, vi. 5. 3, tells of prophecies old and new announcing the city's fall.

4. (P. 573.) It is needless to say that under certain circumstances πέραν τοῦ Ἰορδάνου = עבר הירדן can denote the west side of the Jordan, namely, when it is clear from the connection of a narrative, or from an express statement, that the speaker's standpoint is east of the Jordan (Deut. iii. 25). But it is just this condition which Matt. xix. 1 does not present. The term can be understood, therefore, only in its invariable, technically geographical sense, a fully established usage in the N.T. period, especially where two other sections of the Holy Land are mentioned at the same time ; cf. Mishnah, Baba Bathra iii. 2 ; Shebiith ix. 2, יְהוּדָה וְעֵבֶר הַיַּרְדֵּן וְהַגָּלִיל. So Pliny, *H. N.* v. 14. 70, *Peræa* along with *Galilæa* and *reliqua Judæa*, from which Perea is separated by the Jordan. In Josephus, regularly ἡ Περαία, *Bell.* i. 30. 3, iii. 3. 3, and less frequently ἡ πέραν τοῦ Ἰορδάνου, *Ant.* xii. 4. 9 end. So, also, unquestionably the substantive adverbial phrase Matt. iv. 25 (iv. 15) and the simple adverbial phrase everywhere in those Gospels which were written neither east nor west of the Jordan (Mark iii. 8, x. 1 ; John i. 28, iii. 26, x. 40). The idea that Matt. departed here from his own usage and set πέραν τοῦ Ἰορδάνου as an attribute to τὰ ὅρια τῆς Ἰουδαίας, thereby indicating his east-of-the-Jordan standpoint, is to be dismissed for this further reason also, that he nowhere else found it necessary to give his Palestinian readers such information with regard to the divisions of the country. Again, it would be impossible to speak of a part of Judea as situated across the Jordan, for this would require the article before πέραν, and would be an incomprehensible error, not to be explained by Ptolem. *Geogr.* v. 16. 9. Ptolemy did not know the term Perea at all, but divided Palestine, or Judea in the wider sense (v. 9. 1), exclusive of the coast towns (§ 2), into the districts of Galilee, Samaria, Judea (including Perea), and Idumea. Everyone knows that designations of locality with εἰς by no means denote invariably the place into which, but very often the point toward which the motion is directed (Matt. xvi. 21, xvii. 27, xx. 17, xxi. 1), and everyone might know that in such connections ἔρχεσθαι means "go" as well as "come" (cf. Matt. xvi. 5, and above, p. 505, n. 7). What Matthew says, then, is this : Jesus left Galilee and journeyed to Judea (choosing of the two possible routes the one) east of the Jordan. Mark x. 1 means the same thing, but expresses it still more clumsily, mentioning first the main goal of the journey, and then connecting the nearer and less important objective with the other by means of καί ("and, indeed, first of all").

5. (P. 573.) Acting upon a suggestion of Grotius (i. 454) with regard to Matt. xxiii. 35 (already Lightfoot, *Opp.*, ed. Rotterdam, 1686, ii. 361, had rejected this view which had been widely accepted), many even down to the present time have ventured the assertion that the author or redactor or translator of Matt. made the Zachariah here intended—the son of Jehoiada (2 Chron. xxiv. 20–22), as he is correctly called in the corresponding passage in the *Gospel of the Hebrews* (Jerome *in Matt.* xxiii. 35, Vall. vii. 190 ; cf. *GK*, ii. 695)—into a son of Barachiah, in order to identify him with the Zachariah

who, according to Jos. *Bell.* iv. 5. 4, was murdered by the Zealots. This is attributing a senseless piece of folly to the editor, who must have said to himself that at most Jesus might have foretold this deed. The name of the father of that Zachariah, mentioned by Josephus, is very uncertainly reported. Niese writes it Βάρεις, and we find besides, Βαρισκαίου and Βαρούχου, but not Βαραχίου. The scene of the event is given merely as ἐν μέσῳ τοῦ ἱεροῦ. The designation of the place in Matt. xxiii. 35 points to 2 Chron. xxiv. 21 (LXX, ἐν αὐλῇ οἴκου κυρίου). The martyr death of a righteous man and a prophet, recorded in the last historical book of the O.T., corresponds with the murder of Abel reported in its first book ; cf. Gen. iv. 10 with 2 Chron. xxiv. 22. The mistake of our Matt. in calling him the son of Barachiah is due to a confusion of the martyr of 2 Chron. xxiv. 20 ff. with the prophet Zechariah, i. 1 (cf. Isa. viii. 2 ?; 2 Chron. xxvi. 5 ?) as it also appears in the Targum to Lam. ii. 20 ; cf. *ZKom. Matt.* 649 ; Lightfoot, ii. 362 ; and concerning other instances of confusion in respect of these persons, Fürst, *Kanon des AT's*, S. 44 ; Hamburger, *RE*, i. 887. For the fable identifying the Zachariah of Matt. xxiii. 35 with that of Luke i. 5 ff. (*Protev. of James*, xxiii. xxiv.), cf. *GK*, ii. 695, 711 f., 776 f. Berendts, *Studien über Zacharias-apokryphen u. Zachariaslegenden*, 1895, gives a more detailed account, not all of which, however, is beyond dispute.

6. (P. 573.) F. L. Sieffert, *Ueber den Ursprung des ersten kanon. Ev.* 1832, and M. Schneckenburger under the same title, 1834, have already stated with measurable fulness what seems to weigh against the apostolic authorship of Matt. Mistakes with regard to the political history, at points where it comes in contact with the Gospel story, would not furnish sufficient ground for assuming that the author must have been somewhat widely removed in time or place from the events recorded. The historical trustworthiness of the narratives in Matt. ii. 1–18, xvii. 1–13 (cf. Mark ix. 2–10 ; 2 Pet. i. 16–18), xvii. 24–27, xxvii. 51–53, xxviii. 11–15, cannot be investigated here. It is unthinkable that a Christian in Palestine should have invented the Jewish explanation of Jesus' resurrection (xxviii. 15) and the Jewish insinuations to which he replies in chaps. i. ii. ; and it will be impossible also to discover any middle ground between the Jewish and the Christian estimate of the beginning and the close of Jesus' life. If the word βασιλεύει is used of Archelaus in ii. 22, although he had simply the rank of ethnarch and the royal title in expectation only (Jos. *Ant.* xvii. 11. 4 ; *Bell.* ii. 6. 3), Josephus himself, notwithstanding that he is the source of this very information, does the same thing (*Vita*, 1) ; in fact, he calls him βασιλεύς outright, *Ant.* xviii. 4. 3 ; cf. above, p. 503, n. 3. If the name Philip were authentic in Matt. xiv. 3, we should have there the same confusion with another brother of Herod Antipas named Herod that actually occurs in Mark vi. 17 (cf. Schürer, i. 435 [Eng. trans. I. i. 401 f.]) ; but it is most improbable that the MSS. (D and important Latin witnesses) which left the name unquestioned in Mark vi. 17 should have erased it in Matt. xiv. 3 for reasons of historical erudition. Rather have they preserved the original, while the great body of MSS. and versions (also Ss) have interpolated the mistaken name here (and many of them in Luke iii. 19 also) from Mark vi. 17. Mark alone is open to the charge of being somewhat less familiar than Josephus with the complicated elationships and scandals of the Herodian family.   Matt. xvii. 24–27 is

intelligible only in a work written before the year 70, see above, p. 552 f. The gist of the narrative in xxvii. 51–53 is confirmed by the statements of two Jewish contemporaries of Matthew, independent of each other and of him ; cf. the writer's article, "Der zerrissene Tempelvorhang," *NKZ*, 1902, S. 729–756. It has been argued against the authenticity of Matt. xxviii. 19 and against the apostolic authorship of the first Gospel, that according to Acts ii. 38, viii. 16, x. 48, xix. 5, cf. 1 Cor. i. 13–15, vi. 11, believers in the early apostolic times were baptized into or in the name of Christ, not into the name of the Father, Son, and Spirit. But these passages do not give a formula used in Church baptism any more than Gal. iii. 27 or Rom. vi 3 (cf. 1 Cor. x. 2, xii. 13), and, on the other hand, in Matt. xxviii. 19 the use of the threefold name in administering baptism is not commanded. In the *Didache* we find a reference to Christians as οἱ βαπτισθέντες εἰς ὄνομα κυρίου (ix. 5) along with the trinitarian formula (vii. 1, 3). Why should the occurrence of this phrase of the *Didache* in the time of Paul or Acts disprove the use of the trinitarian formula, or its origin from a saying of Jesus in reference to baptism ? That arbitrary assumption deprives us of an explanation for the other trinitarian formulas in the N.T. (2 Cor. xiii. 13 [Eng. 14] ; Rev. i. 4 f.). Nor is it strange (cf. John xvii. 3) that precisely in such a formula as this Jesus should have spoken of Himself thus objectively as the Son without qualification (cf. Matt. xi. 27). Against the attempt of Conybeare, *ZfNTTh*, S. 275 ff., to prove that the trinitarian formula is a late interpolation in the text of Matt. xxviii. 19, cf. *ZKom. Matt.* 713.

7. (P. 576.) Such sentences as xix. 1–3, καὶ ἐγένετο, ὅτε . . . μετῆρεν . . . καὶ ἦλθεν . . . καὶ ἠκολούθησαν . . . καὶ ἐθεράπευσεν . . . καὶ προσῆλθον, are not common in Matt. According to the Concordance, the use of δέ is about as frequent as in Luke, and twice as frequent as in Mark, and μέν—δέ considerably more common than in Luke, and decidedly more so than in Mark. It is quite noteworthy that the asyndetic use of λέγει, λέγουσιν, so frequent all through John, does not occur at all in Matt. i.–xviii. (for in viii. 7, as also in viii. 4, 20, 26, ix. 9, καὶ λέγει has quite the preponderance of evidence), whereas it is found in rapid succession in xix. 7, 8, 10, 20, 21 (ἔφη), xx. 7 (twice), 23, 33, xxi. 31 (twice), 41, xxii. 21, 43 ; also in xxvi. 25, 64, xxvii. 22. The construction and order, ἐγερθεὶς δὲ Ἰωσήφ . . . ἐποίησεν, occurs repeatedly, i. 24, ii. 3, viii. 8, 10, 14, 18, etc. (cf. Gersdorf, *Beiträge zur Sprachcharacteristik*, 90 f.) ; also without mentioning the subject by name, ii. 10–12, 22, iv. 12, 18, v. 1, and in other cases than the nominative, καταβάντι δὲ αὐτῷ . . . ἠκολούθησαν αὐτῷ, viii. 1, 23 ; εἰσελθόντος δὲ αὐτοῦ . . . προσῆλθεν αὐτῷ, viii. 5, 28. Cases of the genitives absolute followed by ἰδού are not infrequent, i. 20, ii. 1, 13, 19, ix. 10, 18, 32, xii. 46, xvii. 5, xxviii. 11, and it is noticeable that the formula occurs repeatedly in some passages and then again is quite absent. The commonest formula for the continuation of the narrative is τότε, which is used in Matt. some ninety times in all. This usage is quite unknown to Mark, nor is it exactly paralleled in Luke and John, for in Luke xi. 26, xiv. 21, xxi. 10, xxiv. 15, τότε signifies "at that moment," immediately after the occurrence of what has just been related, *i.e.* in reality, "thereupon" ; so also τότε οὖν in John xix. 1, 16, xx. 8. Matt. also, to be sure, uses the word sometimes to denote immediate sequence, ii. 7, 16, iii. 15, iv. 1, 5, 10, 11, ix. 6, 14, but very often, also, as an indefinite term

for approximate correspondence in time, where there is no single preceding incident which leads up to the account that follows, iii. 5, 13, xii. 22, xv. 1, xx. 20, xxiii. 1, xxvi. 3, 14, so that the phrase does not differ appreciably from ἐν ἐκείνῳ τῷ καιρῷ, xi. 25, xii. 1, xiv. 1. This latter expression, which is not found elsewhere in the N.T. (cf., however, Acts xii. 1), is confined in Matt. itself within narrow limits. Semitic scholars may decide whether the Aramaic אֱדַיִן, with and without מִן or בְּ, does not after all underlie τότε and ἀπὸ τότε (iv. 17, xvi. 21, xxvi. 16; elsewhere in the N.T. only Luke xvi. 16), as in the LXX, for example, Ezra v. 16; cf. Dalman, Gr.² S. 213 (different from 1te Aufl. S. 169) and the lexicons under אֱדַיִן, עֲדַיִן. The participial constructions just mentioned give the style a more pleasing effect as compared with that of Mark, but may also create the impression of a closer connection in time and occurrence than was intended by the original. If in viii. 5, 14, xii. 9, for example, the narrative were carried forward simply in independent clauses connected by καί, as in xix. 1–3, it would not seem that the last incident related was immediately connected with that mentioned just before, or even fell on the same day.

8. (P. 577.) With regard to Hosanna and the root ישׁע see vol. i. 21. Delitzsch translates Matt. i. 21, כִּי הוּא יוֹשִׁיעַ. Cf. the explanation of the change of name Hoshea-Joshua, Num. xiii. 16, in Sota, 34b (יהּ יוֹשִׁיעֲךָ), and also in the Midrash on the passage (translated by Wünsche, S. 418). Cf. still other passages in Jastrow, 601b, 751b. The fact that in the Talmud the name of Jesus of Nazareth is constantly given in the mutilated form ישׁוּ, while others of the same name are always written ישׁוּע, serves to mar that καλὸν ὄνομα (Jas. ii. 7) whose literal meaning was understood by every Jew; cf. ZKom. Matt. 76, A. 48, 49.

9. (Pp. 577, 578.) Matthew contents himself with the Greek term where Mark has attached it as a translation to the Aramaic original; Matt. xv. 5, cf. Mark vii. 11; Matt. xxvi. 39, cf. Mark xiv. 36. Mark vii. 34 has no parallel in Matt., and Matt. ix. 25 corresponds but partially to Mark v. 41. Here, too, we note that Matt. uses ὁ διάβολος, iv. 1, 5, 8, 11, xiii. 39, xxv. 41; ὁ πειράζων, iv. 3; ὁ πονηρός, xiii. 19, 38, where Mark in the parallel passages, so far as there are such, has σατανᾶς, i. 13, iv. 15. Inconsistently, the latter appears also in Matt. xii. 26, xvi. 23. In this case the Greek translation was not needed. On the other hand, the necessary Greek interpretations, which cannot have been found in the original, are introduced in Matt. xxvii. 46 just as in Mark xv. 34. Perhaps also xxvii. 33 = Mark xv. 22. The explanation in i. 23 might also be an addition by the Greek translator, although the corresponding statement may equally well have stood in the Aramaic original, since Immanuel was a Hebrew name whose Aramaic interpretation would not sound absolutely tautological. The name of the city Jerusalem must also be mentioned here. Like Strabo, pp. 759–762; Ptolem. v. 16. 8, viii. 20. 18; Josephus, Tacitus, and others, Mark (ten times—also xi. 1) and John (twelve times) use only (τὰ) Ἱεροσόλυμα, and never Ἱερουσαλήμ. The latter genuinely national form, which seemed to Aristotle (in Jos. c. Apion. i. 22. 7) an ὄνομα πάνυ σκολιόν, is used by Paul, Gal. iv. 25, 26, in elevated theological discourse, alongside of the Hellenised form in the simple narrative, Gal. i. 17, 18, ii. 1. Similar is the use of -λημ in Rev. along with -λυμα in John. In the discourses of Jesus and others, Luke writes always

-λημ (xiii. **33, 34**, xxiii. **28**, xxiv. **18, 47**; also certainly xviii. **31**), and
so also in Acts, with the exception of Paul's addresses before a Gentile
audience in Cæsarea, xxv. **15, 24**, xxvi. **4, 10, 20**. It should be noted in this
connection that in Mark the name does not occur in a discourse of Jesus
and in John only once (iv. 21), and that with Luke, as with Paul, -λημ is
much commoner than -λυμα, the latter occurring in Luke only four times,
and -λημ twenty-six or twenty-seven times, and irregularly interchanged
(cf. Luke ii. **22, 43**, xix. **11, 28**). Matt., on the other hand, has Ἱεροσόλυμα
throughout (eleven times, including words of Jesus, v. 35, xx. 18), except in
xxiii. 37 = Luke xiii. 34, Ἱερουσαλήμ. Whoever traces this exception to a
source used by Matthew here, but not in v. 35, xx. 18, ought also to divide
Gal. between two writers, and would have to refer the alternation of terms
in Luke's two books to similar causes. The real reason, however, for the
change is easy to understand ; even in Matt. -λημ was better suited to the
solemn declaration of xxiii. 37 ; and, besides, in this address to a personified
Jerusalem (ἡ ἀποκτείνουσα . . . τὰ τέκνα σου), the form (τὰ) Ἱεροσόλυμα would
have been very inconvenient rhetorically ; likewise for Paul, where he
represents Jerusalem as mother. The translator would not care needlessly
to repeat the awkward treatment of the Greek form as a feminine singular,
ii. 3 (along with neuter plural, ii. 1) and perhaps iii. 5 (where, however,
πᾶσα is a spurious addition). He might have used -λημ everywhere in Jesus'
discourses, as Luke did. But the Greek form is more easily declined (v. 35),
and directly after xx. 17 -λημ in xx. 18 would have been forced. And, finally,
what translator is ever consistent in such matters ?

10. (P. 578.) The traces of Hebrew or Aramaic originals in Matt. and
in the Gospels generally were investigated as early as Michaelis, *Einl.* 982–
1003, and Eichhorn, *Einl.*[2] i. 510–530. Cf. the bibliography, vol. i. 14 f.
It requires a better knowledge of the Aramaic dialect than the present writer
possesses, and more caution than others have shown, to arrive at trustworthy
conclusions in this matter. Merely by way of example, and without claiming
originality for the observations, the following illustrations are adduced in
addition to the remarks above, p. 577 ff., and in nn. 7–9, 12 : (1) iii. 15,
πᾶσαν δικαιοσύνην, can mean nothing else than πᾶν δικαίωμα = every legal
requirement or ordinance. Now, as the LXX translates צדקה and משפט
without fixed distinction by δικαιοσύνη (which stands, besides, also for צרק,
אמת, Aram. זכו, Dan. vi. 23, etc.), as well as by δικαίωμα (which also represents
חק, מצוה, etc.), it would seem that משפט, or rather one of its Aramaic equivalents,
underlay Matt. iii. 15. As such equivalents we may mention דינא, Targ. Onk.
Ex. xxi. 1, 31 ; *Num.* xv. 16 ; *Deut.* vii. 11, 12 ; also Targ. *1 Sam.* viii. 3 ;
Isa. xlii. 1, 2 (LXX and Matt. xii. 18, 20, κρίσις), נימוסא or נמוסא (νόμος),
1 Sam. ii. 13, viii. 9, 11 ; *Ezek.* xx. 25 ; especially, however, הלכתא, Onk. *Ex.*
xxi. 9. (2) Since δικαιοσύνη in the LXX not infrequently stands for אמת
(Redpath's Concordance gives seven instances), to which קשוט, קושטא corresponds in Aramaic, the phrase ἐν ὁδῷ δικαιοσύνης, xxi. 32, which is unnatural
as Greek, and unusual in conception as well, is to be explained as a literal
translation of קשוט באורח, Onk. *Gen.* xxiv. 48 (LXX, ἐν ὁδῷ ἀληθείας) ; cf.
Matt. xxi. 16 ; but cf. also Prov. viii. 20 in original, Targ., and LXX.
(3) Since צדקה and צדקתא, like the Syr. זדקתא also, acquired the meaning of
charity, alms, which led even the LXX to translate the first-named nine or

ten times by ἐλεημοσύνη (cf. also Clem. *Strom.* vii. 69, ἡ ἕξις ἡ παρ᾽ ἡμῖν μεταδοτικὴ δικαιοσύνη λέγεται, and Acts x. 2 with x. 35), we have constantly to consider whether δικαιοσύνην (vi. 1), if it is the true reading, may not represent this Aramaic word in the sense of ἐλεημοσύνην, and whether the very early variants of this saying do not finally go back to the time when the Aramaic Matt. was still translated orally in these various ways : ℵ*BD Sa (this latter, also, distinguishing clearly between vi. 1 and vi. 2), τὴν δικαιοσύνην ὑμῶν. Sc "your gifts," cf. Ephr. *in Epist. Pauli*, p. 74, *dona vestra* ; ℵ^a τὴν δόσιν ὑμῶν, S¹ and the later Greek authorities, τὴν ἐλεημοσύνην ὑμῶν. (4) In Aramaic, עֲבִדָא means servant ; עַבְדָּא, עָבִידְתָּא (עֲבִידְתָּא, עָבִידָא fem.), work, act. Consequently the Syriac translator of Clem. 1 *Cor.* xxxix., or one of his copyists, has rendered עבד by ἔργων instead of παίδων (Lightfoot, *St. Clement*, i. 138, ii. 119). Lagarde, in his *Agathangelos* (*Abh. der gött. Ak.* 1889, xxxv. 128), commenting upon the variants, Matt. xi. 19, ἔργων ; Luke vii. 35, τέκνων, recalls Orig. *Hom.* xiv. 5 *in Jerem.* (Delarue, iii. 211 ; an earlier commentator, he says, understood by the "mother" in Jer. xv. 10, Wisdom, τὰ δὲ τέκνα τῆς σοφίας καὶ ἐν τῷ εὐαγγελίῳ ἀναγέγραπται "καὶ ἀποστέλλει ἡ σοφία τὰ τέκνα αὐτῆς," cf. Luke xi. 49). If ἔργων is the original reading in Matt. xi. 19, it is then the correct rendering of the Aramaic word spoken by Jesus (see *ZKom. Matt.* 431 f. in contradiction of the 1st and 2nd editions of the *Einleitung*). Luke, or rather the earliest authority for the tradition, which Luke followed, heard and spoke *abdeh* (your servants), instead of *abadeh* (your works). He thought of wisdom as a person ; cf. Luke xi. 49, and found in this passage the children of the divine wisdom contrasted with the capricious children of that generation. Instead of the more exact παῖδες (servants, cf. Matt. xiv. 2 ; Luke i. 54, xii. 45), he chose τέκνα, having in mind, doubtless, such Wisdom passages as Prov. i. 8, ii. 1, xxxi. 2 ; Sir. ii. 1. He might equally well have said υἱοί (cf. John xii. 36 with Eph. v. 8). (5) If the *Gospel of the Hebrews* has preserved the original form of the fourth petition of the Lord's Prayer as it was offered from the beginning by Aramaic-speaking Christians (Lat. "panem nostrum crastinum da nobis hodie," *GK*, ii. 693, 709 f., recently confirmed anew, *Anecd. Maredsol.* iii. 2. 262), we have a substantially correct translation of it in Matt. vi. 11 ; ἐπιούσιος is derived from ἡ ἐπιοῦσα, *sc.* ἡμέρα. But Matthew's phrase is not a natural one, for the proper antithesis to σήμερον is αὔριον, not ἡ ἐπιοῦσα. The latter denotes the day next following, as reckoned from whatever day may have been previously mentioned (Acts xvi. 11, xx. 15, xxi. 18 ; cf. vii. 26, xxiii. 11). Hence it is approximately used in Luke xi. 3 in contrast with τὸ καθ᾽ ἡμέραν, but inappropriately by Matthew, who might more properly have written τὸν τῆς αὔριον or εἰς τὴν αὔριον instead of τὸν ἐπιούσιον. Observe that Greek, like German (and English), has no proper equivalent for *crastinus* (but cf. Pape under αὔριος, and Heyne, *Deutsche Wörterbuch*, ii. 867, under "morgend"). Cf. *ZKom. Matt.* 275 ff. The wording of the Greek Matt. can be explained only on the supposition that the translation was influenced, not directly by the Gospel of Luke, but by the Church usage of those regions where the Lord's Prayer was customarily spoken in the form which Luke has preserved. Here, then, we have strong evidence that our Greek Matt. is (*a*) a translation ; (*b*) a translation made in the Greek Gentile Church ; (*c*) a translation not always felicitous, but in its intent exceedingly faithful. It has not substituted traditions of a later time or other localities for the original, but has translated the Lord's Prayer just as the Jewish Christians said it in Jerusalem, Kokaba, or Berœa about 60–70 A.D., and even down to about 400. (6) The saying, Matt. v. 34–37, yields no other meaning than : " Instead of using all manner of oaths, let your speech be confined to a double Yea or Nay." One might compare the reduplicated ἀμήν of Jesus Himself in the Fourth Gospel, and the ναί, ἀμήν of Rev. i. 7, cf. xxii. 20. It would be less strange that Christians should thus emphasise their affirmations and denials than that, in spite of the Sermon on the Mount, they should take oaths and, as in Paul's case, use other strong forms of assertion as well ; yet it is hardly thinkable that, in the very connection where he declared all περισσόν in the attestation of truth to be a consequence of evil, and therefore unworthy of the sons of God, Jesus should have recommended a reduplication of the Yea and Nay which in itself is needless. If we compare the saying in Jas. v. 12 (which can hardly be independent of Matt. v. 37, if the latter really originated with Jesus) and other citations of Jesus' words which correspond with Jas. v. 12 (Just. Apol. i. 16 ; Clem. Strom. v. 99 [al. 100], vii. 67 ; Clem. Hom. xix. 2 ; Epiph. Hær. xix. 6), we must give the preference to the form ἔστω ὑμῶν τὸ ναὶ ναί, καὶ τὸ οὒ οὔ. This seems the more certain, since it accords with an actual Jewish idiom. Jesus had cited Lev. xix. 12 ; on Lev. xix. 36 the Talmud (Baba Mezia, 49a) makes the exegetically impossible comment, "That thy yea may be a true (yea) and thy nay a true (nay)." Cf. Midrash on Ruth iii. 18 (Wünsche's trans. S. 53), and several similar passages in Levy, i. 465 ; Jastrow, 348, 365, under נין, הן=yes. Jesus doubtless said נא, cf. Levy i. 67 ; Dalman, Gr.² 223 ; also Paul, the Pharisee, assumes in 2 Cor. i. 17–20 that the yea must be a real yea, and not nay at the same time. The original of Matt. v. 37 need not have been absolutely identical with the original of Jas. v. 12 ; ὁ λόγος ὑμῶν suggests some such form as "let your yea-saying be a yea," etc. Jas. v. 12 may have had an influence in spreading the uncanonical form of the saying (GK, i. 323, A. 2). But we must reckon also here with the possibility that forms of much-quoted sayings which date from the time of the oral translation of Matt. were preserved in Church use till Justin's time or beyond it. (7) With regard to the use of participles in the N.T., it must always be remembered that in Aramaic, as in Hebrew, these forms are entirely timeless. A noteworthy example is Matt. v. 10, where the context makes it impossible that those should be called blessed who have survived a persecution, so that δεδιωγμένοι stands for διωκόμενοι. Polycarp (baptized in 69), who writes the latter form (ad Phil. ii.), might have heard in his youth some interpreter who did his work better than the Greek Matt. Perhaps a participle underlies the ἄρτι ἐτελεύτησεν of ix. 18, which Luke's authority rendered more satisfactorily by the imperfect ἀπέθνησκεν (viii. 42) ; cf. Matt. v. 23. We might point also to ζητοῦντες for ζητήσαντες, ii. 20, and the uncertain interchange of παραδούς and παραδιδούς, x. 4, xxvi. 25, 46, xxvii. 3, 4. If the very common use of the participial constructions (see above, n. 7) seems on superficial observation to give to the style of Matthew a more distinctively Greek impress, in comparison with the stronger Hebraistic character of Mark and also John, then the hand of a translator, who seeks to avoid the monotony of the Semitic narrative style by employing the correct Greek expression, is betrayed in the immoderate use of this construction in

the resultant awkwardness of expression (concerning xiv. 6, see *ZKom. Matt*
504, A. 79), and in the consequent obscuring of the facts.   In ὀψὲ σαββάτων,
xxviii. 1, which appears strange to us, Eus. *Quæst. ad Marin* (Mai, *Nova Patr.
Bibl.* iv. 1. 255 ff.), and Jerome, *Epist.* cxx. 4 *ad Hedib.*, think they have discovered a mistake of the translator ; but it corresponds to later Greek usage
(cf. *ZKom. Matt.* 710, A. 1).   For possible Hebrew or Aramaic equivalents,
cf. Lightfoot, *Opp.* ii. 389 ; on the other hand, however, Dalman, *Gr.*[1] 197,
and positively *Gr.*[2] 247.

11. (Pp. 579, 580.)   As to the pardonable error in xxiii. 35, see above,
p. 589, n. 5.   Matt. ii. 23 is not an error on the part of the evangelist (see
above, p. 568, n. 7).   The *Gospel of the Hebrews*, or, as Jerome calls it in
Vir. Ill. iii. and elsewhere, the *ipsum Hebraicum* of Matt., also contained the
words *quoniam Nazaræus vocabitur*, and, as one must infer from Jerome's
silence in the passage where this is mentioned, introduced the alleged citation
with no different formula.   The learned but mistaken conjecture of certain
Hebrew Christians, whose guidance Jerome followed (*Comm. in Jes.* xi. 1,
Vallarsi, iv. 155 ; cf. *Comm. in Mt.* ii. 23, Vall. vii. 17), that the passage
presents a citation from Isa. xi. 1, is not to be imputed to the redactor of the
Gospel of the Hebrews some 250 years earlier.   There is a mistake in Matt.
xiii. 35, in that Ps. lxxviii. 2 (entitled a psalm of Asaph) is cited as τὸ ῥηθὲν
διὰ 'Ησαΐου τοῦ προφήτου.   The genuineness of 'Ησαΐου (wrongly placed in
Tisch. ed. 8) is attested by א* min. 1, 13, 124 (these two belonging to the
Ferrar group), 33, 253 ; and, further, many MSS. seen by Eusebius (Montf.
Coll. nova, i. 462) and Jerome (*in Mt.* xiii. 35, Vall. vii. 94), and especially by
its offensiveness, which would be the more keenly felt because Porphyry had
made use of it to prove Matthew's ignorance (as shown by the *Breviar. in
Psalmos* under Jerome's name, which is now proved to be genuine in this
portion ; see *Anecd. Maredsol.* iii. 2. 60).   When Eus. *loc. cit.* maintains that
in the accurate MSS., and Jerome *in Mt.* that in the *vulgata editio,* the
name Isaiah is wanting, it only indicates the early date of the emendation,
which is apparent also from its wide attestation (add Ss, Sc, and Clem. *Hom.*
xviii. 15).   Jerome conjectured (*Comm. in Mt.*) that "Asaph" was originally
written, then exchanged by an early copyist for the better known name of
the prophet Isaiah, and finally that the mistaken emendation was set aside
again by the deletion of the name.   This supposition is valueless, but still
it is better than the bold assertion in *Breviar.* p. 59 f., that all the old MSS.
of Matt. read *in Asaph propheta*, which was altered by stupid persons.   Since
Jerome nowhere appeals to the *Gospel of the Hebrews* to establish the original
text of Matt. xiii. 35, we must infer that the error was found there also, and,
furthermore, that the reading which in substance is incorrect was the original
one.   The same is true of Matt. xxvii. 9, where one would look for a reference to Zechariah rather than to Jeremiah.   If the former had appeared in the
Gospel of the Hebrews, it would be hard to explain not only the silence of those
familiar with that book, who discussed the problem of Matt. xxvii. 9, namely,
Orig. *Comm. in Mt.* (Lat.), Delarue, iii. 916 ; Eus. *Demonstr.* x. 4. 13 ;
Jerome *in Mt.* p. 228 ; *Breviar.* p. 60 f., but especially the appearance of
an apocryphal Hebrew or Aramaic Book of Jeremiah, containing word for
word the quotation which is not to be found in the canonical Jer.   Because
the *Gospel of the Hebrews* also assigned the words in Matt. xxvii. 9 to Jeremiah,

the Nazarenes fabricated the apocryphal book, or booklet, which they showed
to Jerome ; cf. his *Comm. in Mt.* xxvii. 9, and *GK*, ii. 696 f. The only
instance in which the *Gospel of the Hebrews* evidently corrects a mistake due
to imperfect knowledge of the O.T. is Matt. xxiii. 35 ; see above, p. 589,
n. 5 ; *GK*, ii. 711 f. The incorrect forms of the names in i. 5, 7, 8 (see following note) are due probably to the translator, not to the author.

12. (P. 579.) Eusebius (on Ps. lxxviii.—cf. above, p. 528) explained the
variation of citations in Matt. from the text of the LXX on the ground that
the Hebrew Matthew made use of the Hebrew O.T. Jerome's opinion was
that both Matthew and John in their Gospels quoted directly from the
Hebrew original without reference to the LXX (*Comm. in Osee* xi. 1 ; *in
Isaiam* vi. 9, ix. 1 ; Prol. *in Pentat.*, Vall. iv. 97, 128, vi. 123, ix. 3), and he
appealed in proof of his opinion to the supposed Hebrew original of Matt.
in the library at Cæsarea, *i.e.* to the *Gospel of the Hebrews* (*Vir. Ill.* iii. ; cf.
GK, ii. 697 f.). The view to which exception is taken on p. 579 was first
developed by Bleek, *Beiträge zur Evangelienkritik*, 1846, S. 57 f. Since
then the matter has been repeatedly discussed without convincing results.
Anger, "Ratio qua loci VTi in ev. Matt. laudantur, quid valeat ad illus-
trandam huius ev. originem," parts i.–iii., *Leipzige Programme* of 1861 and
1862, collated the material most thoroughly. The hypothesis defended by
Böhl (*Forschungen nach einer Volksbibel zur Zeit Jesu*, 1873 ; cf. his *Alt Citate
im NT*, 1878), that in Jesus' time there was an Aramaic translation of the
O.T. dependent on the Greek LXX, and that this was used by Jesus and the
apostles (by the latter in conjunction with the LXX), would have thrown
everything into confusion, if anyone had accepted it. The comparison of
Matthew's quotations with the LXX is made more difficult by the fact that
in those MSS. of the latter which were transcribed by Christian hands,
especially the Cod. Alex., the O.T. text has frequently been altered to correspond with the wording of the citation in the N.T. Moreover, also, the
text of the citations in Matt. is in many passages by no means certain. It
remains to be proved whether it be allowed, as the present writer has sought
to prove in detail (*ZKom. Matt.* 474 ff.), that the citation in xiii. 14b–15
originally consisted only of the words : πάχυνε τὴν καρδίαν τοῦ λαοῦ τούτου
καὶ τὰ ὦτα αὐτῶν βάρυνε καὶ τοὺς ὀφθαλμοὺς αὐτῶν κάμμυε, or that the incorrect forms of the names Ιωβηδ (for Ωβηδ), i. 5, Αβιουδ (Αβια), i. 7, Ασαφ (Ασα),
i. 7 f., Αμως (Αμων), i. 10, were original in the Greek Matt. (see *ZKom. Matt.*
57–61). The familiarity of the one, who gave Matt. its present Greek form,
with the LXX is very evident. Just as clear, however, is his relation to the
Hebrew text of the O.T.—a relation which was not brought about by the
LXX or by any other known Greek translation whatsoever. This double
relation, which can be accurately determined in a single instance, is also on
that account an extremely complicated task, since Matthew gives many and
especially the more extended citations with great freedom, in order to make
the text serve the purpose of its use, for example, ii. 6, iv. 15 f., xi. 10, xii.
18–21, xiii. 14–15 (see above), xxii. 24, xxvi. 31, xxvii. 9. The erroneous
reference of the citation in xiii. 35 to Isaiah instead of to Asaph—the
composer of Ps. lxxviii.—as of that in xxvii. 9 to Jeremiah instead of to
Zechariah (see above, No. 11), proves that the author, at least in these
cases, had consulted neither a Greek nor a Hebrew Bible, but had trusted his

memory. Accordingly, it is probable that in many other, if not in all instances, the author's memory of Bible passages, frequently heard or read, was the source of his citations. The present writer feels that he must here forego a complete presentation of the list of citations, and a comparison of them with the Hebrew text, the LXX, and the Targum, as he gave in the first and second editions of his *Einleitung*. A specific difference in respect of their relation to the original text and to the LXX cannot be shown between those citations through which the author desires to prove the agreement of prophecy with fulfilment (Class A), and the citations given in the sayings of Jesus and other persons (Class B). To Class A belong, in their contents, i. 23 and ii. 5, although, according to their form, an angel speaks in i. 23, and the Sanhedrin in ii. 5. Translations, made independently of the LXX from the Hebrew, or an Aramaic original, are found not only in Class A (ii. 15, viii. 17, xxvii. 9), but also in Class B (xi. 10, xxvi. 31; cf. also x. 36 = Mic. vii. 6); furthermore, clear traces of a consideration of a Hebrew or Aramaic text appear in Class A (ii. 5, 18, xii. 18–20, xiii. 35); but also in Class B (xi. 29 = Jer. vi. 16; and in the order of the Decalogue, xix. 18, cf. v. 21, 27; *ZKom. Matt.* 590, A. 65). Likewise, essential dependence upon the LXX is shown in Class B (*e.g.* iv. 6, 7, 10), but also in Class A (i. 23, iii. 2). As translator of a Hebrew or Aramaic original, Matt. is characterised by several transcriptions of Hebrew personal names at variance with the Greek tradition; for example, Ραχαβ, i. 5 (רחב = Ρααβ in LXX, everywhere, and without variants, Jas. ii. 25; Heb. xi. 31; Clem. *1 Cor.* xii.; in Jos. *Ant.* v. 1, 2, 5, 7, Ρααβη, here, to be sure, with the variant reading Ραχαβη). Further discussion of this subject, and consideration of the absolutely incorrect forms of names, which are possible only on the part of a translator, are to be found *ZKom. Matt.* 57–61. All the facts in the case are most easily explained by the presupposition, which is offered by the tradition and confirmed by a series of observations independent of it (above, pp. 573 f., 593), that our Matt. is a translation of an Aramaic writing, in which latter the O.T. citations and allusions were often given in a very free Aramaic form; and that the Greek translator was guided partly by an effort to give a true rendering of his text, and partly by his memory of the LXX, especially of the sayings most frequently used by the Christians about him, or already introduced into Greek Gospels which were known to him. He freed himself more or less from the influence of the LXX familiar to him : (1) in passages where, through dependence on it, the thought of the Aram. Matt., expressed in a free form of the citation, would be obliterated, or the purpose of the citation made of none effect; (2) where, on account of a lacking, or unclear, or incorrect statement of the source, the passage cited could not easily have been found, even if he had looked for it.

13. (P. 581.) With regard to doublets, we have first to notice that Matthew is fond of repeating the same formula like a refrain : five times, καὶ ἐγένετο ὅτε ἐτέλεσεν ὁ Ἰησοῦς τοὺς λόγους τούτους, vii. 28, xi. 1, xiii. 53, xix. 1, xxvi. 1; five or six times, ἠκούσατε ὅτι ἐρρέθη τοῖς ἀρχαίοις, v. 21, 27, (31), 33, 38, 43; the opening and conclusion of the Beatitudes with the same phrase, "for theirs is the kingdom of heaven," v. 3, 10; the repetition of the words xix. 30 and xx. 16 at the beginning and end of the parables (Mark x. 31; Luke xiii. 30—once each, but in an entirely different connection in Luke);

also xxiv. 42, xxv. 13; cf., further, above, p. 567, note 6. Moreover, the repetition of a maxim, whether it be original or derived from the O.T. or from the popular proverbial philosophy, is not of itself a sign that discourses are not trustworthily recorded. As Paul repeatedly made use of such sayings in letters separated by some interval of time (Gal. v. 9=1 Cor. v. 6; 1 Cor. i. 31=2 Cor. x. 17; 1 Cor. ix. 9, 14=1 Tim. v. 18; 1 Cor. vi. 9 f.=Gal. v. 19–21), so, too, Jesus may have used quotations like that in Matt. ix. 13 arid xii. 7 (without parallels), or sayings like Luke xiv. 11, xviii. 14, and in another connection, Matt. xxiii. 12, not only three but twenty times. The same applies to Matt. xiii. 12 (=Mark iv. 25) and xxv. 29, to Matt. xvii. 20 and xxi. 21 (=Mark xi. 23—Luke xvii. 6 is only related), and would apply to Matt. xx. 16b and xxii. 14 if xx. 16b were not to be omitted, with אBLZ, Orig. and the Egyptian versions; cf. ZKom. Matt. 600. As for the narrative sections, it is not in the least improbable that Matt. xii. 38–40 (=Luke xi. 29–30) and xvi. 1–4 (=Mark viii. 11–12) are different occurrences; the request for a sign came up more than once, according to other reports as well (John ii. 18, vi. 30, cf. vii. 3 f.; Mark xv. 29 f.; Matt. xxvii. 42 f.; 1 Cor. i. 22). According to Matt., the request is made by different persons in the two instances, and in the second it is more precisely defined by ἐκ τοῦ οὐρανοῦ. Only the answer is in both instances the same, if the sentences of vv. 2b–3, which are connected with the word "heaven," but are otherwise most original, are accepted. They are, to be sure, not to be considered as an interpolation from Luke xii. 54–56 because of a merely remote similarity to that passage, but rather as an early gloss, taken from a good source. Accordingly, if the narrative Mark vii. 11 ff. is to be considered more historically exact than Matt. xvi. 1–4, then the complete similarity of Matt. xii. 39 and xvi. 4 is not only a new proof of the great freedom with which Matthew shapes the discourses of Jesus, but especially also an example of his preference for the refrain (see beginning of this note). Also in content the answer of Jesus to the similar demand (John ii. 19) is related to Matt. xvi. 1–4, and in form also in so far as Jesus uses in both the enigmatic saying (Mashal). With Matt. ix. 33 f.=xii. 22 f. the case is not quite the same. Since there is no chronological connection between chap. ix. and chap. x., and between chap. xi. and chap. xii., it would not be inconceivable (so the present writer judged in the first and second edition) that Matthew should, in passing, touch upon a single event as a conclusion of the sketches, viii. 18–ix. 34 (see n. 14), which are in time very closely connected, and then, moreover, should once again narrate the same event with more precision and detail (xii. 22 f.) in a connection where it was of importance for describing the conflict with the Pharisees. The fact that in ix. 32 f. the author tells about a dumb man, and in xii. 22 about a blind man who is also dumb, gives no warrant for distinguishing the narratives; but just as little also for identifying them. If ix. 34 is to be omitted with D a k Ss, every reason for this disappears; for the words of the people, ix. 33, have nothing in common with xii. 23, and do not refer to the one deed of healing last mentioned, but to the entire chain of varied deeds and words in viii. 18–ix. 32; cf. ZKom. Matt. 385, 451 f. If the discourses Matt. v.–vii. and x. are in part free compositions of the author (above, p. 558 f., then v. 29 f. can be historically identical with xviii. 8 f., v. 32 with xix. 9, x. 38 f. with xvi. 24 f. If, furthermore, one compares the sentences x. 17–22, which do not suit the historical situation described in x. 5 (above, p. 558), with Mark xiii. 9–13 and Luke xxi. 12–19, where they are found in an historically probable connection, it can hardly be doubted that, when Matthew came to the passage (xxiv. 9–13) where these sentences historically belonged, he deliberately abbreviated them, in order not to repeat too much.   There is no trace anywhere of an unconscious procedure based upon mechanical use of sources ; such a procedure, also, would be inconsistent with the thoughtful care to be observed in all parts of the book and the unity of just this Gospel.   The remaining instance in which it might at first be suspected that a single incident had been doubled through ignorance of the facts and dependence on two varying narratives—the feeding of the five thousand and the feeding of the four thousand—is safeguarded against such suspicion by the occurrence of the same phenomenon in Mark, and by those discourses of Jesus, reported by Matthew and Mark, which refer to both occasions (see above, p. 582).

14. (P. 584.) On the place of viii. 18–ix. 34 in the plan of the Gospel, see above, p. 545. Cf. Hofmann, "Zwei Tage des Menschensohnes," *ZfPuK*, xxii. (1851), S. 331 ff. Assuming the credibility of the express and careful statements of time and place in this section of Matt., the events make up a definitely ordered series, which may be extended from the accounts of Mark and Luke, but not corrected. According to Matt. xiii. 1, Jesus spoke the succeeding parables on the same day upon which the discourses and conversations of xii. 23–50 fall. The change of place, xiii. 53, with which xiii. 54 is but loosely connected, is, according to Mark iv. 35, the same crossing of the Sea of Galilee at evening with which Matt. viii. 18 opens a new section. In Luke viii. 22, also, it has no immediate connection with anything that precedes. Further, the connection of Mark ii. 1–22, Luke v. 17–39 (=Matt. ix. 1–17), with the preceding and following context, is so entirely free that it argues nothing against the concatenation of the incidents in Matt. The passage viii. 18–ix. 34, then, is an account of a single day from one evening to the next, which followed immediately the day of the events and addresses in xii. 23–xiii. 53 ; cf. *ZKom. Matt.* 344, A. 3.

15. (P. 585.) Mention has already been made (above, p. 590, n. 6) of individual instances of alleged lack of knowledge on Matthew's part. Other criticisms have been based on a misunderstanding of his presentation of the subject. It is said that Matthew did not know what we learn, indeed only from Luke i. 26, ii. 4 (cf. John i. 45), that Joseph and Mary lived in Nazareth before Jesus' birth. But . . . .e is no mention in i. 18–24 of the place of any of the events there recorded ; and even the place of Christ's birth (first referred to in i. 25) is not given there, but in ii. 1, where it leads up to the questions and answers ii. 2, 4–5. It is true no narrator proceeds in this fashion, whether the clumsy compiler of a " curriculum vitæ " which is to be presented to the examiners or read at a memorial service, or a master of the biographic art. But what this proves is only that Matthew had no intention of writing either a good or a poor account of Jesus' life for those who were not acquainted with it. The reader unfamiliar with the facts first discovers from ii. 23 that the Holy Family had close relations with Nazareth even before Jesus' birth. This is presupposed by the choice of Nazareth as a residence from among the many villages of Galilee ; for the angels com-

manded only the return from Egypt to the "land of Israel." Joseph's
reflection on the political situation prompted the choice of Galilee rather
than Judæa, and the reason for the choice of Nazareth remains unstated.
The reference to a fulfilment of prophecy is no substitute for it, for the
divine counsel which is realised by the settlement in Nazareth is not
announced to Joseph by man or by angel, but only by Matthew to his
readers.

§ 57. THE RELATION OF MARK'S GOSPEL TO THE GOSPEL OF MATTHEW.

The oldest tradition concerning the origin of the
Gospels which we have found heretofore to be a trustworthy guide shall be considered first, with reference also
to the question of their relation to each other.   According
to the tradition, Matthew wrote before Mark, but there
was no great interval intervening (above, p. 392 ff.).   In
this case, if one used the work of the other, it must have
been Mark who employed Matthew, not, however, the Greek
translation, which was made considerably later than the
time when Mark composed his Gospel (above, p. 516 f.),
but the Aramaic original.   Of all the conjectures with
regard to the relation between Mark and Matthew, only
those of H. Grotius agree with the tradition (above,
p. 422, n. 4).   If it was possible for it to come into his
possession, the Gospel of Matthew, written in his mother
tongue, must have had the greatest interest for Mark,
who was a native of Jerusalem.   And it is inconceivable
that he should have left it unread and made no use of it,
if he had become acquainted with it before he had begun
the composition of his own book.   If the journey to Asia
Minor, which Mark had in view at the time of Col. iv.
10, was made in the interval between his first residence
in Rome, of which we learn in this passage and in Philem.
24, and the second sojourn there, witnessed to by 1 Pet.
v. 13 and the traditions as to the origin of his Gospel
(above, p. 427 f.), there is nothing in the way of supposing that this journey to the East was extended to include

a visit to his native city, and it is very probable that he returned from Jerusalem, or some other point in Palestine, to Rome in company with Peter in the autumn of 63 or the spring of 64.   Since the tradition gives us nothing further with reference to the date of Matthew's Gospel than that it was written earlier than Mark—which was begun at the earliest in the year 64—and that Matthew wrote his Gospel between 61 and 66 ; and since, moreover, nothing has appeared in either of the Gospels which proves that Matthew was composed after 61–63, or Mark before 64–70, there is no reason why Mark, on the occasion of his eastern journey in 62–63, should not have learned in Palestine of Matthew's Gospel, which had been written shortly before.   He might, therefore, have brought it back with him to Rome, and have used it shortly afterwards in the composition of his own Gospel.   This conjecture would be raised to probability bordering on certainty, if it should appear that Mark is dependent upon an older document, which only resembles our Matthew.   But it is at least equally probable that the Greek translator of Matthew was acquainted with Mark, which had appeared in the meantime, and used it, along with other helps, in the execution of his difficult task (above, p. 575 f,). Following the tradition, it is possible and probable, from the order in which the books in question originated (Aram. Matthew, Mark, Greek Matthew), that a relation of mutual dependence exists between our Matthew and our Mark.   Mark could have used the Aramaic Matthew, and the person who translated Matthew into Greek could have used Mark.   The first would necessarily show itself chiefly in traces of dependence in content, the second in traces of dependence in form.

Before entering upon the discussion of details, with regard to which there has been so much dispute, and with reference to which endless strife is possible, it may be advantageous to make several general statements some of which have been proved already, others of which are self-evident. (1) The employment of an older writing by Mark is not excluded either by the tradition concerning the relation of Mark to Peter or the special occasion and purpose of his Gospel (above, pp. 440 f., 501 f.). (2) Entire ignorance on the part of a later author regarding earlier writings dealing with the same theme is rendered improbable by the constant intercourse which, in the apostolic age, bound all parts of the Church together, and by the difficulty of constructing a history of Jesus from the oral tradition alone, which would be in any degree systematic and free from contradiction. This would have been, of course, unlikely in the case of a disciple of one of the apostles like Mark, and entirely so, if a rumour had reached him that shortly before an apostle had written a comprehensive book concerning the deeds and sayings of Jesus. (3) The number of those who believe that the extensive agreement between Matthew and Mark in single narratives and in whole series of narratives (n. 1) can be explained by the uniformity of the oral tradition, upon which both are dependent, will always be small. Comparison of Matthew with Luke proves that widely differing traditions existed together in the apostolic Church regarding the most important parts of the Gospel history. Notwithstanding the fact that the Lord's Prayer was employed in the second century in parts of the Church most widely separated—by the Aramaic-speaking Jewish Christians as well as by Marcionitic congregations and the catholic Church—certainly also frequently used as early as the apostolic age, it is reproduced in Matt. vi. 9 ff. and Luke xi. 2 ff. in two widely variant forms. The account of the institution of the Lord's Supper which was recalled to the Church by every celebration, is given very differently in Matt. xxvi. 26 ff., 1 Cor. xi. 23 ff., and in the corrected text of Luke xxii. 17–20. Further, a comparison of Matt. i. 1–17 with Luke iii. 23–38, or of Matt. v.–

vii. with Luke vi. 20–49, or Matt. xxvi. 57–68 with Luke
xxii. 54, 63–71, will show the impossibility of the existence of a stereotyped tradition circulated throughout the
entire apostolic Church, even regarding the most important facts of the Gospel history.   The assumption of
literary dependence in order to explain the agreement
between Matthew and Mark is rendered all the more
necessary by the fact that the two books were written
under entirely different conditions and for entirely different readers.   In this respect the disparity between
Matthew and Mark is incalculably greater than that
between Mark and Luke, and scarcely less than that
between Matthew and Luke.   (4) So long as the impossibility of a relation of direct dependence between two
extant documents remains undemonstrated, it is arbitrary
or unscientific to explain the agreements between them by
supposing that both are dependent upon documents no
longer extant and without witnesses.   But if one of these
Gospels is dependent upon the other, an historical consideration of the relation existing between them will be enough
to render impossible the belief that a Gospel written for
Jews and Jewish Christians in Palestine, the form and
content of which is determined in detail by this purpose,
is dependent upon a Gospel written for Christians outside
of Palestine.   (5) It does not follow because important
parts are wanting in one Gospel that the author did not
have before him another Gospel containing these portions ;
since neither of these books supplies a basis for presupposing that their authors intended to record all that was in
itself commemorable, or all that they themselves regarded
as trustworthy.   Mark, as well as Matthew, exhibits proof
to the contrary.   We have already seen, in considering
the title of the book, that Mark's plan permitted only a
sketch of the work of the Baptist, and of the baptism
and temptation of Jesus, which could not have been the
original form of the oral or written tradition concerning

these facts (above, p. 460). The same reason accounts
also for the absence of a narrative regarding the origin,
birth, and childhood of Jesus. To conclude that Mark
had not read the narrative in Matt. i.–ii. is quite as inadmissible as to assume that it was known to him but
rejected as untrustworthy, or, moreover, to suppose that
all the traditions or fictions preserved in Matt. i.–ii. and
Luke i.–ii. originated later than the time when Mark wrote.
It is absurd to imagine that more than thirty years elapsed
after the death of Jesus before the Christians began to
make inquiries and to construct narratives about His
origin, birth, and childhood. If Mark could leave un-
noticed these narratives, which he certainly must have
known, he could have done so notwithstanding his knowledge of Matt. i.–ii. The Sermon on the Mount, which
is found in Matt. v.–vii. and Luke vi. 20–49 in two very
different recensions, must, for this reason, as well as on
account of its significance in each of the recensions, be
regarded as an important part of the Gospel tradition.
Mark, however, could not use it as an example of Jesus'
preaching characterised in i. 14 f., since it does not come
under this head. The Sermon on the Mount is not the
Gospel (above, p. 542 f.). In the form in which it occurs
in Matthew, he could not have used it at all. Sentences
like those in Matt. v. 17–20, which have a very important
place there, could have produced only confusion among
the Roman Christians as we know them from the Epistle
to the Romans (vol. i. 421 ff.). To say the least, a commentary would have been necessary—a commentary of
an entirely different character from that which we find in
Jesus' discourse itself (Matt. v. 21–48)—in order to render
the words intelligible and profitable to the Roman Christians for whom Mark wrote. So Mark himself must have
thought, provided that Paul's judgment regarding his work
as a missionary in Rome was at all just (Col. iv. 11 ; vol.
i. 450, n. 4). The omission of the Sermon on the Mount

in Mark is no proof that the author had not read Matthew.
(6) Nor does the lack of τάξις in Mark, of which notice
had been taken already by those in the neighbourhood
of John in Ephesus, argue against Mark's dependence on
Matthew. We were under necessity of admitting earlier
that Matthew made no attempt in most parts of his book
to reproduce the events in chronological order. This must
have been especially evident to a person like Mark, who
knew from the narratives of an eye-witness the historical
place of many incidents which Matthew took out of their
historical connection and arranged again after the order
of content (above, p. 556 ff.). Matthew was not suited to
serve as a guide for the arrangement of the historical
material in Mark. If Mark had followed Matthew entirely, the result could have been what John sums up in
the words—οὐ μέντοι τάξει.

With these prefatory remarks we pass to the comparison of the two Gospels. Here weight is to be given, first of
all, to the total impression which they produce. Matthew
appears as a work of large proportion, cast in one mould ;
Mark is a mosaic, carefully constructed out of numerous
pieces. In Matthew we notice the freedom with which
the author handles a mass of material, the arrangement of
which, from beginning to end, is determined by his theological conception and apologetic purpose, and at the same
time his frequent carelessness with regard to the narrator's
literary task, and the lack of all effort to fulfil the duties
which to us seem incumbent upon the accurate historian.
While Mark made a similar effort to follow a leading
thought, we notice that this is much less definite and more
neutral than the controlling idea in Matthew ; and more
than this, that he is unable to carry the idea through.
The material stifles the thought. On the other hand, in
spite of numerous infelicities of expression, Mark shows
himself a master in clear narrative, in his ability to portray a situation and to reproduce with exactness trivial

details, which, in the memory of an eye-witness, are in-
separably connected with the kernel of the event.   If this
is true, it follows that Matthew is more original.   That
Matthew should show deficiency as a narrator is in keeping
with the peculiarity of the author, which appears uniformly in every part of his book.   It would, however, be
inconceivable that with the narratives of Mark before him,
which for the most part are very clearly drawn and accurate
in details, he should have obliterated or otherwise destroyed
these characteristics without intending either to correct
errors or to make considerable abridgement.   Matthew
could not have been influenced by the effort to secure
convenient brevity of narrative, in case the short Gospel of
Mark was before him when he wrote, since his own Gospel
is much more elaborate.   Matthew's narratives do not
exhibit the character of excerpts, as do sentences like
Mark xvi. 9–13, but give the impression of unfinished
sketches.   Moreover, the universal rule will apply here,
that the unfinished sketch precedes the completed drawing
and the highly coloured painting.   Nothing was more
natural than for Mark, in the narratives which he both
found in Matthew, and also had often heard from Peter,
to pick out such touches as would render the pictures
more accurate, richer in colour, and clearer.   A writing
constructed as was Matthew (above, p. 556 f.) must have
made every later narrator who had it in his hand desire
to add explanatory additions.   That such a document
was before Mark, and that he followed it, has been
proved beyond all question, particularly by Klostermann.
The entire Gospel of Mark furnishes evidence that, with
all his independent knowledge of details, resting as it
did upon the eye-witness of Peter, Mark had a written
exemplar from which he sometimes made excerpts and to
which he sometimes added glosses (n. 2).   In some passages this is evident at once from the expressions used,
which can be explained only under this presupposition.

Although designing to record only a single parable in
xii. 1, Mark writes, " He began to speak to them in
parables," because an account lay before him according to
which Jesus spoke three parables in succession on the
same day in the temple (Matt. xxi. 28–31, 33–41,
xxii. 1–14). In the parallel narrative of Matthew (xxi.
33), the words, "Hear another parable," indicate to the
reader expressly that this parable is only one in a series
of such discourses (cf. xxi. 45, xxii. 1). Further, this
occurs in a passage having an extended context (Mark xi.
27–xii. 37 = Matt. xxi. 23–xxii. 46, n. 1), which, with the
exception of the two parables that are intentionally cut
out by Mark, is practically without variation in both
Matthew and Mark. Therefore the book employed by
Mark was not some work which simply resembled our
Matthew, but, as far as content and arrangement go, our
Matthew itself. The fact that here, as in most other
cases, the expression is more awkward in Mark than in
Matthew, is accounted for when we remember that it
was the Aramaic Matthew which Mark had before him.
On the other hand, the numerous agreements between
Matthew and Mark in the choice of words is explained,
if the person who translated Matthew into Greek was
familiar with Mark, and if he followed this in cases where
he found an expression that suited him, without, however,
abating his effort to find expressions that were more
pleasing (n. 3). It is entirely contrary to Mark's habit
to reproduce the discourses of Jesus and of other persons
in indirect discourse. Even discourses which are really
summaries of repeated and much more elaborate utterances are thrown into direct form (Mark i. 15, vi. 14–16,
x. 33 f.). When he departs from this rule in vi. 7–8, then
passes to the direct form in ver. 9 without notice, and,
finally, in vv. 10–11 introduces a single independent
saying with a special introduction (καὶ ἔλεγεν αὐτοῖς), the
inconsistency is explained if, in the first place, he made

a summary of the elaborate discourse in Matt. x. 5 ff.,
which was before him, but afterwards saw fit to excerpt
parts with greater accuracy. The same is true of Mark i.
4, 7–8 in relation to Matt. iii. 2, 7–12, and of several other
passages in which the discourse of Jesus is interrupted
by a καὶ ἔλεγεν αὐτοῖς, not called for by the context of the
discourse in Mark (ii. 27, vii. 9 ; cf. i. 7, n. 2).

The use of the O.T. in the two cases deserves special
notice. No great weight can be laid upon the fact that
at least in one instance (xiv. 49) Mark reproduces the
ἵνα πληρωθῶσιν αἱ γραφαί, which occurs so frequently in
Matthew, and is of so much importance for his purpose ;
since it is not used to express his own thought, but is
put into the mouth of Jesus, who is represented in Matt.
xxvi. 56, cf. 54, as speaking similar words on the same
occasion. Moreover, the words are in keeping with Jesus'
attitude to O.T. prophecy. It is, however, significant
that Mark quotes no O.T. passages not also cited by
Matthew (n. 4). Only in one instance does Mark cite
the O.T. on his own responsibility (i. 2 f.). All other
citations from the O.T. are put into the mouth of the
speakers in the narrative, particularly the Lord, and,
what is more striking, always in the same connection in
which the same O.T. words are employed by Matthew,
whose book is so much richer in quotations, both direct
and indirect. This not only furnishes new evidence that
Mark and Matthew are very intimately related, in a way
that cannot be explained except by the assumption that
one is dependent upon the other, but it also shows that it
is Mark which is dependent upon Matthew. The poor
borrows from the rich, not the reverse. In the case before
us this would necessarily appear doubtful, if it were the
Greek Matthew upon which Mark drew ; for then the
numerous variations from Matthew shown by Mark in the
citations, which for the most part affect the sense very
little, and which are by no means always improvements,

must be regarded as particular caprices of the author. In this connection, also, the tradition, according to which Mark could have had only the Aramaic Matthew before him, proves to be the thread of Ariadne. In Mark's exemplar, also, the words taken from the O.T. were in Aramaic; that is, his native language. It was just as easy for him to translate these citations into Greek as words like *Abba*, *Rabboni*, *Talitha kumi*, etc. (n. 5). On the other hand, it is conceivable and self-evident that after twenty years of intercourse with the Greek Churches, where it was customary to study the LXX to determine "whether these things were so" (Acts xvii. 11), Mark was very familiar with this text, particularly in passages that were often quoted in Christian circles, and that in his book intended for Greek-speaking Christians he would make use of the LXX where it was convenient. Whether for this purpose he ever found it necessary to unrol the LXX may be considered doubtful. Mark was in the same position in relation to the Aramaic Matthew as was the person who translated the whole of Matthew into Greek some fifteen or twenty-five years later (above, p. 579 f.). The fact that in many instances the text is the same, or practically the same, in both, is satisfactorily explained by the assumption of the dependence of both Mark and the Greek Matthew upon the same Aramaic original, the LXX, and the language current in the Church of their time. The fact, however, that they vary in numerous details, which for the most part do not affect the sense, is just as simply accounted for by the supposition that Mark was not as yet acquainted with the Greek Matthew, and that the translator of Matthew into Greek was bound, first of all, to follow his original, and in other respects was under even less obligation to take into consideration the form of the citations in Mark than he was to pay attention to the LXX and the language of the Church (n. 6). The dependence of Mark upon the

Aramaic Matthew is shown also by the relation of the citations in both to the Hebrew text.   While we are able to recognise, even in the Greek form in which we possess his work, that the author of Matthew used the Hebrew text of the O.T., though the citations which he took from this source are freely handled, and while we observe that the Greek translator retained this relation to the Hebrew text in many decisive passages in spite of his frequent dependence upon the LXX, Mark is much more strongly under the influence of the LXX, and gives us a translation which is independent of the LXX only where Matthew does the same.   This he was able to do, not by reason of his independent knowledge of the Hebrew text, of which he nowhere shows a clear example, but from his acquaintance with Matthew in its original Aramaic form.   We have decisive proof of this in the citations in Mark i. 2 f. and xiv. 27 (n. 6). In the first passage, Mark quotes a combination of Mal. iii. 1 and Isa. xl. 3 as a single connected saying of Isaiah. All the efforts made by the early Church to defend the evangelist against the censures of the Neoplatonist Porphyry, by means of emendations of the text and apologetic interpretations of the only trustworthy text, were not enough to explain away the fact that at the very beginning of his book, and in the single passage where he quotes an author by name, Mark makes a mistake in citing his source.   This would have been avoidable, if he had drawn upon the O.T. directly.   If he had cited the passage freely from memory, it could be explained as a mere slip ; but since both fragments of which the quotation is made up show clear traces of Mark's dependence upon Matthew (n. 6), the incorrect reference of the combined passages to Isaiah is to be explained as due to the same cause.   Mark found both passages used in Matthew in connection with the Baptist, the one correctly referred to Isaiah (Matt. iii. 3), the other, however, quoted as

Scripture without the name of a prophet (Matt. xi. 10). More than this, the latter was produced in Matthew freely, and for this reason, possibly, was not to be found at once in the Hebrew or Greek Bible. Accordingly, Mark, who wished to connect these words with those of Isaiah, took them also as the words of the prophet.

1. (P. 603.) In the first part of both Gospels the similarity of substance and form appears chiefly in single sentences (Mark i. 3, 5 = Matt. iii. 3, 5) and short narratives (Mark i. 16–20 = Matt. iv. 18–22 ; Mark i. 40–44 = Matt. viii. 1–4) ; farther on it is rather in whole series of sections (Mark x. 1–xi. 17 = Matt. xix. 1–xxi. 13, interrupted only by the parable in xx. 1–16 ; Mark xi. 27–xii. 37 = Matt. xxi. 23–xxii. 46, interrupted only by the parables xxi. 28–32, xxii. 1–13 ; Mark xiv. 1–xv. 47 = Matt. xxvi. 1–xxvii. 61, interrupted only by xxvi. 52–54, xxvii. 3–10, 51*b*–53). Single rare words or forms deserve less stress than is sometimes laid upon them. In the first place, every argument for literary dependence, based upon such resemblances, is confronted by the fact that no form of textual corruption is more frequent in the Gospels than the assimilation of one Gospel with another. Thus, for example, in Luke v. 20, 23, ἀφέωνται is undoubtedly the correct reading, whereas, taking the parallels in Matt. ix. 2, 5, the weight of evidence is for ἀφίονται or ἀφίενται, and in Mark ii. 5, 9 the external evidence leaves us undecided. This Doric form of the perf. ind. (Kühner-Blass, *Gram.* i. 2. 201) is clearly supported in Luke vii. 47. 48 ; John xx. 23 ; 1 John ii. 12, which shows its general currency. The form ἀφίονται also meets the case in Matt. ix. 2, 5 and parallels (against Winer-Schmiedel, § 14. 6), though not in these other passages. In the second place, much that has been represented as remarkable is not so to a connoisseur, as ἀπεκατεστάθη, Matt. xii. 13 ; Luke vi. 10 ; Mark iii. 5 ; cf. ἀπεκατέστη, Mark viii. 25. Besides the instances in Winer-Schmiedel, § 12. 7, note 12, cf. Ign. *Smyrn.* xi. 2. It is entirely out of place to adduce in evidence ἀπεκρίνατο (for ἀπεκρίθη) in Matt. xxvii. 12 ; Mark xiv. 61 ; Luke xxiii. 9 ; for these three passages deal with three different occurrences, while in the actual parallels, Matt. xxvi. 63 ; Mark xiv. 61 ; Luke xxii. 66, or Matt. xxvii. 12 ; Mark xv. 5 ; Luke xxiii. 3, both content and form are very different ; cf. Veit, ii. 125. Moreover, in Matt. xxvii. 12 we are probably to read ἀπεκρίνετο alongside of ἀπεκρίθη, xxvii. 14 (= Mark xv. 5). The Attic ἀπεκρίνατο is attested beyond question only in Luke iii. 16 ; Acts iii. 12 ; *per contra*, Mark xiv. 61 ; Luke xxiii. 9 (only L, to be sure, has -νετο, but correctly ; cf. Blass, *Ntl. Gram.*[2] § 20. 1 [Eng. trans. p. 44] ; John v. 17, 19, it is uncertain, and in John xii. 23, decidedly so. In the third place, every proof of the dependence of one author upon the other, based upon such phenomena, comes to nothing in the case of Matt. and Mark, if Mark was familiar with the Aramaic Matt., and the Greek translator of Matt. was familiar with Mark.

2. (Pp. 607, 609.) Mark i. 2–13 makes the impression not of a freely drawn sketch, but of an excerpt. Now excerpts are commonly made from books, not from oral traditions. Mark found the materials in Matt. iii. 1–6,

iii. 13–iv. 11, and also Matt. xi. 10 (see note 6 below). The only traces that Mark shows of an individual conception or tradition are that he represents Jesus alone as the recipient of the divine witness at the baptism (ver. 10 f.), and that he mentions the beasts (ver. 13). But that the narrative from which he made his extracts was wholly or substantially identical with Matt. iv. 1–11, must be inferred from the fact that Mark concludes his account with the ministry of the angels. This is intelligible only in Matt., where this διακονεῖν (serving at table, care for all physical needs, cf. viii. 15, xxv. 45, xxvii. 55) corresponds with the opening of the narrative iv. 2–4. Mark i. 16–20 = Matt. iv. 18–22. Matthew omits ὀλίγον, which in Mark i. 19 presents the situation more vividly, and μετὰ τῶν μισθωτῶν, which in Mark i. 20 renders the brothers' immediate decision more comprehensible, and saves it to some extent from the appearance of being unfilial. These omissions certainly could not be explained in Matt. on the ground of an effort to secure brevity, for Matthew's account is on the whole a trifle more extended than Mark's (89 words against 82), nor yet in any other way. It is Mark that contributed these illuminating details. Mark i. 40–45 = Matt. viii. 1–4. The principal difference lies in Mark's representation of the charge to the lepers as a very emphatic one, for the sake of contrasting with it the uninterrupted spread of the report of Jesus' mighty deeds (vv. 43, 45). This idea would have been entirely to Matthew's purpose, and very suitable as an example in connection with xii. 15–21. By the place to which he assigned the narrative, he gave it quite another significance (see p. 544 f.), and in the phrase εἰς μαρτύριον αὐτοῖς gave characteristic expression to his conception. As Mark, who shows no anxiety here, or elsewhere, to defend Jesus from the charge of annulling the law, preserves this detail, he is seen to be the dependent author. Mark ii. 1–12 = Matt. ix. 1–8. Mark's additions throughout serve to illuminate Matthew's less perspicuous account. The unintelligible ἰδών, Matt. ix. 2, is made clear by the account in Mark ii. 4, and with this in view the situation is already carefully described in vv. 1, 2. It would have been better to mention the presence of the scribes at this point, also, as Luke does in introducing the story, v. 17. But as Mark has Matthew's account before him, he first alludes to their presence at that point in the narrative (ver. 6) where Matthew assumes but does not expressly state it. The complaint οὗτος βλασφημεῖ, Matt. ix. 3, which would be obscure to readers unfamiliar with Jewish modes of thought, is explained in detail in Mark ii. 6–8, as is the way that Jesus "saw" the thoughts of the fault-finders. In Mark ii. 27 the separation by καὶ ἔλεγεν αὐτοῖς of two sayings of Jesus occasioned by similar circumstances, shows that Mark had before him a narrative in which the two were either separated by other matter or at least differently arranged. That is, Mark excerpts from Matt. xii. 1–8, passing over the sentences, xii. 5–7, between those two sayings. Of itself, it would be conceivable that Matthew, who, in accordance with his plan, sought in viii. 18–ix. 34 to present as rapid a succession as possible of changing scenes (above, pp. 544, 583 f.), was thus led to condense extended accounts from Mark, if he had them before him, by the omission of unessential details. For example, Mark iv. 36–41 (108 words) = Matt. viii. 23–27 (76 words), where Luke viii. 23–25, also (69 words from καὶ ἀνήχθησαν, ver. 22), has abridged decidedly. But this is incapable of proof. In any case, the striking οἱ ἄνθρωποι, Matt. viii. 27, cannot be derived from

Mark iv. 41, where the reference is plainly to the disciples, whom Matthew everywhere designates as μαθηταί, never ἄνθροποι (x. 35, 36 cannot be used in evidence, nor can xiv. 33 also be compared with it, where the disciples who remain in the ship, in distinction from Peter and Jesus, are called οἱ ἐν τῷ πλοίῳ). Also the people in general cannot be intended, who later heard of the act of Jesus, for whom Matthew commonly uses a different form of expression (ix. 8, 33, xii. 23, xiv. 13, xv. 37, xxii. 33). Finally, Matthew did not refer to other persons who were with Jesus and the disciples in the same boat, for the practised fishermen did not need the help of sailors, and the company of strangers was not in place when Jesus desired to withdraw from the people, and had dismissed all who were not entirely suited to accompany Him (viii. 20) in order to cross the lake alone with the disciples (ver. 23). A solution of this difficulty, as well as of the use of ἰδών in Matt. ix. 2, cannot be found in Matt., but, on the other hand, is found in Mark, in the statement iv. 36, that yet other ships alongside of or following the boat which held Jesus and His disciples, crossed the sea with them. This is one of the fine strokes of the brush which correctly reproduces the recollection of Mark's authority, Peter, and, without any intention on the part of Mark, it serves us as an historical explanation of the enigmatical ἄνθρωποι in Matt. It would be entirely incomprehensible, however, that Matthew, when Mark's Gospel was before him, should have omitted this remark, which was essential for the understanding of his narrative ; and also why he placed the exclamation of astonishment in the mouths of the puzzling "men," instead of the disciples, as is the case in Mark.   Mark vi. 14–32 = Matt. xiv. 1–13.   It is self-evident that Mark vi. 14–16 is not spontaneous narration, but an explanation of a received account by means of glosses (by φανερὸν—αὐτοῦ in ver. 14, and then by ver. 15 ; cf. viii. 28), and that in consequence of these glosses the author is obliged to return to the beginning of the story as he had received it, in altered form, with ver. 16.   Even those who are not sensitive to stylistic impressions must recognise this on comparing the passage with Luke ix. 7–9. It is equally clear, however, that Luke's smooth account is not the basis of the awkward narrative in Mark, especially as everything added in Mark vi. 17 ff. is found in Luke, not in this connection, but in a partial and most condensed form at iii. 18–20. On the other hand, Matt. xiv. 1 ff. presents the original text which Mark glosses. If Mark did not find Herod's brother designated by name in Matt. xiv. 3, the mistaken Φιλίππου of Mark vi. 17 is his addition (above, pp. 503, note 3, and 590). The omission of the name cannot be viewed reversely as a correction made by Matthew in material drawn from Mark, for a critical reader working upon Mark and, with more exact historical knowledge, noticing the error, would not simply have deleted the mistaken name, but have put the right one in its place, as the redactor of the *Gospel of the Hebrews* did in Matt. xxiii. 35 (above, p. 589, n. 5). But here, also, Mark is not simply a compiler of extracts. The lively and graphic treatment, richer in every way as compared with Matthew, cannot be the product of the free artistic fancy of this Mark, who yet showed himself so painfully bound to the written source before him. It can only have come from the accounts of those who stood nearer the events themselves, and in this connection—besides Peter—we are to bear in mind Luke viii. 3 ; John iv. 46 ; Acts xiii. 1. From Peter, too, he would have known, what did not appear from Matt., that the feeding of the five thousand was connected with the return of the apostles from their preaching tour. The champions of Mark's priority over Matthew have with singular unanimity found a leading proof of Matthew's dependence in the comparison of Matt. xiv. 12–13 and Mark vi. 30–33. Matthew, they say, thoughtlessly failed to observe that xiv. 3–11 was an episode growing out of what preceded xiv. 1 f., and connects the continuing narrative immediately with the close of the episode, and he transformed the returning apostles (Mark vi. 30 ; Luke ix. 10) into John's disciples informing Jesus of their master's death, because in his story the apostles had long since returned from their wanderings, being present with Jesus as early as xii. 1. In reply, let us note—(1) That Mark could not have betrayed Matthew into confusing Jesus' disciples with the Baptist's, for in Mark vi. 29 the disciples of the Baptist are plainly distinguished, even to the dullest comprehension, from the disciples of Jesus, who are spoken of as apostles, vi. 30. So if Matthew made the ἀπήγγειλαν of Mark vi. 30 the predicate of μαθηταί in vi. 29, it was not a case of confusion, but of wanton change. (2) There could be no occasion for Matthew to do this, in the fact that he had already recorded the sending out of the apostles in chap. x., for he had said nothing of their return, and he might mention that incidentally here as an introduction to something further. For by the whole arrangement of v. 1–xiv. 12 (above, pp. 542 ff., 558) he had precluded the readers' finding in the succession of the narratives any reflection of the chronological order of the events. Therefore xii. 22–24 may be identical with ix. 32–34 (above, p. 599), and xiii. 54–58 may precede 5–7. If a mere repetition of Mark vi. 30–33 had still seemed to him inconvenient, he could have omitted these statements and substituted a general note of time like iii. 1, xii. 1, xiv. 1. (3) If Matt. v. 1–xiv. 12 is not continuous narrative at all, but a series of narrative fragments, connected chronologically only here and there (viii. 1, viii. 18–ix. 34, xii. 46, xiii. 1—above, pp. 557 f., 584 f.), it must be considered a misunderstanding of the peculiarity of the Gospel to infer from the connection of xiv. 12 that what is related in xiv. 12 ff. followed the remarks of Herod in xiv. 2, which would then be incompatible with the immediate connection of these same events with the Baptist's execution. (4) As a matter of fact, there is nothing more likely than that Herod should have been visited by these superstitious fancies directly after the commission of his miserable deed. All that is related in Matt. xiv. 1–36, and also, with some additions, in Mark vi. 14–56, may easily have occurred in the space of a few weeks. Mark vii. 1–23 = Matt. xv. 1–20. Matthew's smoothly flowing account, which assumes acquaintance with Jewish customs, cannot be dependent on Mark's, which is broken by glosses intended to explain these customs to extra-Palestinian and non-Jewish readers, and so made very awkward at the very beginning. Here again, too, as in ii. 27, vi. 10, cf. i. 7, the interruption of the discourse by καὶ ἔλεγεν αὐτοῖς, vii. 9, shows that Mark was drawing upon a book in which the several parts of the discourse in question were differently arranged, or given in a more extended form. The former is the case in Matt. xv. 3–9. Mark found it more satisfactory to put first Isaiah's condemnation of externalism in worship, which had an immediate relation to the question in dispute, and then follow with the proof, which in Matt. precedes, that the Pharisees in other matters also over-esteemed the Rabbinic precepts, in that they even set them above the explicit law of God.

3. (P. 608.) The correctness of the above remarks on Matt. xxi. 23–
xxii. 46=Mark xi. 27–xii. 37 will appear to everyone from any sort of a
synopsis. Notice how Matthew reduces to bearable proportions the constant
repetition of καί in Mark xi. 27, 28, 31, 33, xii. 2, 12, 13, 23, 28, 35, 38, cf.
above, pp. 502, n. 2, 591, n. 7 ; also the smoother sentence-structure, Matt.
xxi. 26, as compared with Mark xi. 32, and the apt παγιδεύειν, Matt. xxii. 15,
instead of ἀγρεύειν, Mark xii. 13. The same consideration which led Mark
to cut down the series of parables directed against the Pharisees moved him
also to abridge Matt. xxi. 40–44, although Mark xii. 10 is thereby deprived of
its natural nnection.

4. (P. 609.) Mark xv. 28 is recognised to be an interpolation ; cf. Luke
xxii. 37. Mark ix. 48 (and, according to the later authorities, ix. 44 also) is
not so much a quotation as a free adaptation of Isa. lxvi. 24, only with such
divergences from the LXX as its introduction into Jesus' discourse required.
Mark xii. 29, where Deut. vi. 4 (exactly after the LXX) is prefixed to the
words from Deut. vi. 5, which Matthew also quotes (chap. xxii. 37), is not
to be regarded as a citation of Mark's own ; nor yet Mark xi. 17, where the
quotation from Isa. lvi. 7, abridged in Matt. xxi. 13, is filled out in harmony
with the LXX.

5. (P. 610.) On the Aramaic words in Mark see above, p. 502, n. 1.
On Mark xv. 34=Matt. xxvii. 46=Ps. xxii. 2, cf. vol. i. 15 f. This short
ejaculation of the crucified Christ, as well as the other words of Jesus which
Mark gives in Aramaic, might have been known to him from oral narratives
before he read Matt. xxvii. 46. In the translation his ὁ θεός μου approaches
the LXX more nearly than Matthew's θεέ μου, but εἰς τί departs from the
LXX and from the Greek Matt. (ἱνατί).

6. (Pp. 610, 611.) Certain citations call for more particular discussion.
(1) Mark iv. 27=Matt. xxvi. 31=Zech. xiii. 7. Mark's independence of the
LXX here is beyond doubt, and on the other hand, also, he gives a far from
exact translation of the Hebrew. He is, therefore, following a document in
which the Hebrew text was indeed the basis, but was very freely handled,
that is to say, Matt., which like Mark gives πατάξω instead of πάταξον
against the original text and LXX. But even here we see that it was not
the Greek Matt. that Mark had before him ; for what should have prompted
him to turn about καὶ διασκορπισθήσονται τὰ πρόβατα (τῆς ποίμνης) into τὰ
πρόβατα διασκορπισθήσονται ! Elsewhere Mark shows no aversion to a Semitic
word-order ; in comparison with the Greek Matt., he is throughout the less
elegant stylist. This is a mere chance, then, explained only by the supposition that the same Aramaic original was before them both ; whereas
Mark chose the order natural in Greek, the translator of Matt. preserved
the order of the original. For the rest, there is no such agreement as would
compel us to assume that Mark had the Greek Matt. before him, or that
Matthew was influenced by Mark. The word πατάσσω is usual, and offered
by the LXX ; besides, ποιμήν and πρόβατα were inevitable, and διασκορπισθήσονται was in use in similar connections ; cf. Jer. xxiii. 1, 2 ; John xi. 52 ;
Acts v. 37. It may still be a matter of discussion whether the addition of
τῆς ποίμνης (cf. Ps. lxxiv. 1, c. 3 ; Ex. xxxiv. 31), by means of which the contrast of shepherd and flock is made more noticeable to the ear, was already
contained in the Aram. Matt., and was omitted by Mark, or whether it is an

addition of the Greek Matt. (2) Mark i. 2 = Matt. xi. 10 = Luke vii. 27 = Mal. iii. 1. It cannot be doubted that the bold alteration of this verse independently of the LXX goes back to someone acquainted with the Hebrew. But if in Mark i. 2 ἐγώ is to be omitted, with BD, etc., and ἔμπροσθέν σου according to all good authorities, Mark cannot have been the model for Matthew, who took this ἐγώ from Ex. xxiii. 20, and through conflation with this passage came to his twofold " before thee." But neither can Mark's reading be based on the Greek Matt., for why should he drop the ἐγώ ? If, on the other hand, he had in the Aramaic Matt. some such phrase as we find in the Targum Mal. iii. 1, הא אנא שלח, he might take the pronoun to be unemphatic (as it is in the Targum = Hebrew, הנני), and unnecessary to be expressed in Greek. If, furthermore, he found without doubt in both parts of the clauses, supposing that his original was an Aramaic book, a קרמך with or without ל prefixed (= Hebrew לפניך), it was very natural to omit the second. On the other hand, the writer of the Greek Matt. appears here, too, as a translator intent at once upon exactness and upon a certain elegance. He does not leave the אנא (Hebrew אנכי in the underlying passage, Ex. xxiii. 20) untranslated, but renders the double לקרמך first by πρὸ προσώπου σου and then by the synonymous ἔμπροσθέν σου, to avoid monotony. (3) Mark i. 3 = Isa. xl. 3 = Matt. iii. 3 ; Luke iii. 4. As all three Synoptists, unlike John i. 23 (abridged form of the quotation), have no word that does not appear in the LXX, anyone might equally well pass as the exemplar of the other two. Luke, indeed, might seem to be entitled to this precedence, as it is evident from iii. 5–6 that he consulted the LXX, and from it extended the quotation. But if for other reasons Luke's priority is not to be thought of, Mark, too, can lay no claim to it ; for, first, by the mistaken combination of Mal. iii. 1 and Isa. xl. 3 he shows here his dependence on Matt. (above, 611) ; and, secondly, it is unlikely that he was affected by those apologetic considerations which prompted Matthew—who aimed to present Jesus primarily as the king veiled in the form of the lowly servant of God, and the guise of a prophet—not to set Him forth to begin with as the God of Israel, and led him accordingly to reduce the concluding τοῦ θεοῦ ἡμῶν to αὐτοῦ.

ADDENDUM.

VOL. II., PAGE 185, LINE 10.

Concerning *Christianos* or *Chrestianos*, it should be said that, according to Andresen, *Wochenschrift f. Klass. Philol.*, 1902, S. 780 f. (cf. *Codd. græci èt lat. photogr. depicti*, tom. vii., pars. post. fol. 38r ; also Harnack, *Mission des Christentums²*, i. 348), in the only MS. of this portion of the *Annals* of Tacitus, *Chrestianos* was written by the first copyist, and subsequently was corrected into *Christianos*, whereas the *Christus* which follows was written in this form by the first hand.